Shostakovich: A Life

Dmitriy Shostakovich

Shostakovich

 A Life

Laurel E. Fay

OXFORD
UNIVERSITY PRESS
2000

#40954268

OXFORD
UNIVERSITY PRESS

Oxford   New York
Athens   Auckland   Bangkok   Bogotá   Buenos Aires
Calcutta   Cape Town   Chennai   Dar es Salaam
Delhi   Florence   Hong Kong   Istanbul   Karachi
Kuala Lumpur   Madrid   Melbourne   Mexico City
Mumbai   Nairobi   Paris   São Paulo   Singapore
Taipei   Tokyo   Toronto   Warsaw
and associated companies in
Berlin   Ibadan

Copyright © 2000 by Oxford University Press, Inc.

Published by Oxford University Press
198 Madison Avenue, New York, New York 10016

Oxford is a registered trademark of Oxford University Press

Library of Congress Cataloging-in-Publication Data
Fay, Laurel E.
Shostakovich: A Life / Laurel E. Fay.
p.   cm.   Includes bibliographical references and index.
ISBN 0–19–513438–9
1. Shostakovich, Dmitriĭ Dmitrievich. 1906–1975.
2. Composers—Soviet Union Biography.
I. Title.
ML410.S53F39   1999   780'.92—dc21 [B]   99–25255

Book design and typesetting by
Glen R.J. Mules, New Rochelle, NY

1 3 5 7 9 8 6 4 2
Printed in the United States of America
on acid-free paper

To the Memory of My Father

Contents

List of Illustrations   ix
Abbreviations   xi
Note on Transliteration   xiii
Acknowledgments   xv

Introduction   1

1   Childhood (1906–1919)   7

2   Conservatory (1919–1926)   17

3   Spreading Wings (1926–1928)   33

4   Pioneer (1929–1932)   49

5   Tragedy-Satire (1932–1936)   67

6   Crisis (1936–1937)   87

7   Reprieve (1938–1941)   107

8   The War Years (1941–1944)   123

9   "Victory" (1945–1948)   145

10 Public and Private (1948–1953)   167

11 The Thaw (1953–1958)   185

12 Consolidation (1958–1961)   207

13 Renewal (1961–1966)   225

14 Jubilees (1966–1969)   247

15 Immortality (1970–1975)   265

Notes   289
List of Works   347
Glossary of Names   363
Select Bibliiography   387
Index   423

List of Illustrations

1. Dmitriy Shostakovich [*Musical America Archive*], *frontispiece*

2. Map: Union of Soviet Socialist Republics, *page xvii*

3. Map: Leningrad and Environs, *page xix*

4. Cartoon: "Pedagogical humor" by A. Kostomolotsky from *Sovetskaya muzïka* 4 (1948), *page 163*

Illustrations following page 234:

5. Portrait of thirteen-year-old Mitya Shostakovich by Boris Kustodiyev (1919) [*Novosti, London*]

6. DS, Nina Varzar, and Ivan Sollertinsky (1932) [*Novosti, London*]

7. Dmitriy Shostakovich (1935) [*New York Public Library*]

8. DS with his son Maxim at Ivanovo (summer 1943) [*New York Public Library*]

9. DS with his daughter Galina at Ivanovo (summer 1943) [*New York Public Library*]

10. DS attending a soccer match [*Musical America Archives*]

11. Shostakovich at work (1940s) [*Library of Congress, Washington, D.C.*]

12. DS presiding over the drawing of lots for violinists at the first Chaikovsky competition in Moscow (1958). Seated from left to right: jury members Galina Barinova, Dmitriy Tsiganov, David Oistrakh [*Musical America Archives*]

13. DS consulting with Tikhon Khrennikov [*Musikverlag Hans Sikorski, Hamburg*]

14. Shostakovich in rehearsal [*Musikverlag Hans Sikorski, Hamburg*]

15. DS with Mstislav Rostropovich and Yevgeniy Mravinsky after a performance of the First Cello Concerto in Leningrad (1959) [*Musikverlag Hans Sikorski, Hamburg*]

16. DS with his second wife Margarita in Paris (1958) [*Archive Photo*]

17. DS with the Beethoven Quartet. From left to right: Dmitriy Tsiganov, DS, Sergey Shirinsky, Vasiliy Shirinsky, Vadim Borisovsky [*Musikverlag Hans Sikorski, Hamburg*]

18. DS with his son Maxim on arrival at London airport en route to the 1962 Edinburgh Festival [*Archive Photo*]

19. DS with his third wife Irina [*Musikverlag Hans Sikorski, Hamburg*]

Abbreviations

ASM	Assotsiatsiya sovremennoy muzïki [Association of Contemporary Music], Moscow
f.	fond [collection]
FEKS	Fabrika ekstsentricheskogo aktyora [Factory of the Eccentric Actor]
GATOB	Gosudarstvennïy akademicheskiy teatr operï i baleta [State Academic Theater of Opera and Ballet], Leningrad
GITIS	Gosudarstvennïy institut teatral'nogo iskusstva [State Institute of Theatrical Art], Moscow
Glavrepertkom	Glavnïy komitet po kontrolyu za zrelishchami i repertuarom [Chief Committee for the Inspection of Entertainments and Repertory]
GTsMMK	Gosudarstvennïy tsentral'nïy muzey muzïkal'noy kul'turï imeni M. I. Glinki [Glinka Museum of Musical Culture], Moscow
kn.	kniga [book]
LASM	Leningradskaya assotsiatsiya sovremennoy muzïki [Leningrad Association of Contemporary Music]
LGK	Leningradskaya ordena Lenina gosudarstvennaya konservatoriya imeni N. A. Rimskogo-Korsakova [Leningrad Conservatory]
Narkompros	Narodnïy kommissariat prosveshcheniya [People's Commissariat of Enlightenment]
NKVD	Narodnïy kommissariat vnutrennikh del [People's Commissariat of Internal Affairs]
op.	opis' [inventory]
RAPM	Rossiyskaya assotsiatsiya proletarskikh muzïkantov [Russian Association of Proletarian Musicians]
RGALI	Rossiyskiy gosudarstvennïy arkhiv literaturï i iskusstva [Russian State Archive of Literature and Art], Moscow
RGALI (SPb)	Rossiyskiy gosudarstvennïy arkhiv literaturï i iskusstva (Sankt-Peterburg) [Russian State Archive of Literature and Art (St. Petersburg)]

RO RIII	Rossiyskiy institut istorii iskusstv, rukopisnïy otdel [Russian Institute of the History of Arts, Manuscript Department], St. Petersburg
SPgGMTMI	Sankt-Peterburgskiy gosudarstvennïy muzey teatral'nogo i muzïkal'nogo iskusstva [St. Petersburg State Museum of Theater and Music]
TRAM	Teatr rabochey molodyozhi [Theater of Working-Class Youth], Leningrad
VOKS	Vsyesoyuznoye obshchestvo kul'turnoy svyazi s zagranitsey [All-Union Society for Cultural Contact with Foreign Countries]
yed. khr.	yedinitsa khraneniya [storage unit]

Note on Transliteration

The system of transliteration I have adopted is a version of the system used by the *New Grove Dictionary of Music and Musicians* (London, 1980), as modified and explicated by Richard Taruskin in his *Musorgsky: Eight Essays and an Epilogue* (Princeton, 1993), pp. xix–xx.

The modifications are designed to ensure maximum consistency with minimum distraction and as an aid to English pronunciation. Soft and hard signs are eliminated in the text. The Cyrillic letter ы is represented by *ï* (pronounced as a thick, short *i*).

Exceptions have been made when standard English-language renderings of names have become commonly accepted (Glière, Neuhaus, Prokofiev, Richter). The familiar adjectival "-sky" ending in surnames (Musorgsky, Stravinsky) is also retained. Following Taruskin's example, I also adopt the more literal Chaikovsky instead of Tchaikovsky.

Where fidelity to Cyrillic characters is most important, in bibliographic citations the transliteration of authors and titles in the Russian language is strict, without concessions to common use. Hard and soft signs are retained. Names encountered in the text such as Alexander, Asafyev, Khaikin, and Oistrakh, are rendered as Aleksandr, Asaf'yev, Khaykin, and Oystrakh in bibliographic contexts, and the adjectival endings for surnames are rendered in full.

Acknowledgments

Among the many libraries and archives in which I spent untold hours while researching this book, I must single out the Glinka Museum of Musical Culture and the Russian State Archive of Literature and the Arts, both in Moscow, repositories of the two largest collections of Shostakovich's papers; the staffs at both institutions were unfailingly courteous and helpful. Support for research in Russia in 1991 was provided by the International Research Exchanges Board (IREX). I also want to acknowledge the staff of the New York Public Library, its Slavic and Music Divisions in particular. I could not wish for a better research base.

I am grateful to Irina Antonovna Shostakovich, the composer's widow, for her interest and ever gracious assistance. I owe a special debt of gratitude to two friends. Well before publication of her own book on Shostakovich, Elizabeth Wilson generously shared with me her edited translations of many of the most informative interviews and reminiscences she had gathered. Lyudmila Kovnatskaya provided research assistance, moral support, and the reserves of strength that enabled me to complete the book without sacrificing my sanity.

For their long-standing support and encouragement, I am profoundly grateful to Charlotte Douglas, Svetlana Golïbina, and Elizabeth Keitel. I am also indebted, in diverse ways, to Richard Brundage, Nina Drozdetskaya, Hans-Ulrich Duffek, Susan Feder, the late Oleg Felzer, Sofia Gubaidulina, Olga Manulkina, Gerard McBurney, Iosif Raiskin, Neva Smith, Ago Sommer, Richard Sylvester, and Manashir Yakubov. Malcolm Brown, Claude Palisca, and Richard Taruskin read the manuscript; their comments and advice were indispensable. I thank Stanley Sadie for recruiting me to the task, Bruce Phillips for his patience, and Maribeth Payne, Jonathan Wiener, and Helen Mules for shepherding the book through to publication. My sincere thanks to all.

New York City, March 1999   L.E.F

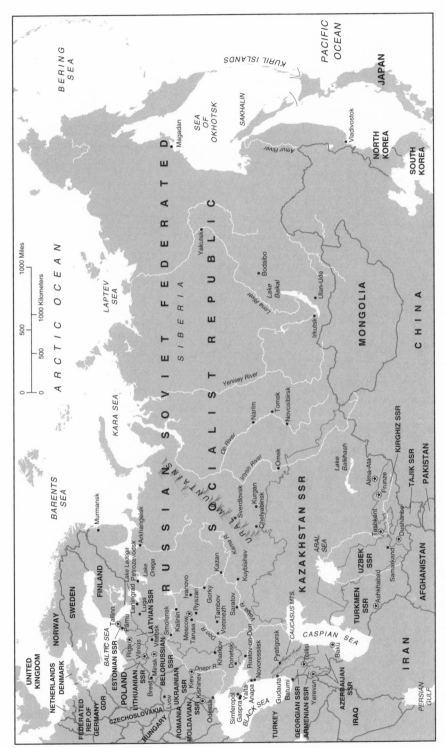

Union of Soviet Socialist Republics

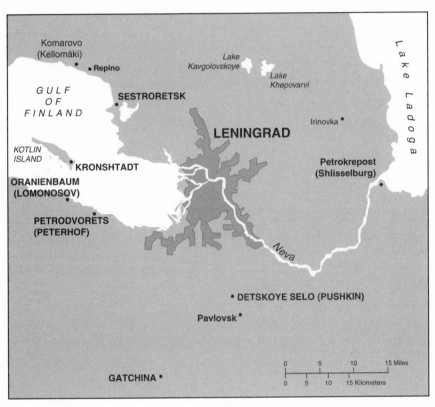

Leningrad and environs

Shostakovich: A Life

Introduction

The years since his death in 1975 have witnessed a surge of interest in the music and the person of Dmitriy Shostakovich. A broad legacy of inspired, arresting, often anguished musical scores—symphonic, dramatic, and chamber—has attracted legions of new listeners and piqued curiosity about the man who created it. To an extent unique among his artistic peers, Shostakovich managed to survive successive Stalinist cultural purges to rise again to unparalleled heights of national and international acclaim matched by genuine professional esteem and popularity. To many of his contemporaries his music extended a vital cultural lifeline, a latent "chronicle" in sounds of the harsh emotional realities of their times. To successive Soviet regimes, it supplied proof of the superior virtues of the socialist world-view, chronicling in sounds "the great struggle of the Soviet people to build communism." Shostakovich spent most of his life in the public eye. He was larger than life, a cultural icon, a legend. His career offered a paradigm for the evils or—depending upon one's perception—the benefits of totalitarian control over the arts.

What do we know of his life? Shostakovich made a point of speaking through his music, not about it. He was an intensely private person who guarded his personal life and feelings jealously. What all but a very few close friends and family members were permitted to experience of the man was the stiff façade of a civic-minded public servant and consummate music professional. This façade began to crack after his death as memoirs, diaries, and letters began to be published, a process that has escalated rapidly in the post-Soviet period. It is an exciting development that promises to contribute to a post-cold-war reassessment of Shostakovich and the whole phenomenon of Soviet culture.

Hasty attempts to assimilate the new revelations—some of them controversial, some contradictory—into revisionist interpretations of Shostakovich and his music have until now outstripped the basic research and fact-finding necessary to back up any sweeping pronouncements. Writing about Shostakovich remains laced with political and moral subtexts. At its most extreme, it simply replaces one orthodoxy with another, reversing the polarities of the old, shopworn Soviet clichés: the true-believing Communist citizen-composer is inverted into an equally unconvincing caricature of a lifelong closet dissident. The challenges Shostakovich confronted as a creative artist, a Soviet citizen, a family man, and an individual were a great deal more complicated, likewise his strategies for dealing with them. There is pressing need to sort fact from fiction, substance from speculation, the man from the myths.

As private a person as he was, Shostakovich was an indefatigable letter-writer. (Legend has it that he answered every letter sent to him.) For him it was an ephemeral form of communication; he destroyed the letters he received and counseled his correspondents to do the same. It is a testament to the early recognition of his artistic genius and probable historic stature that very few of them elected to heed his advice. A substantial reserve of Shostakovich's letters, dating from his Conservatory years on, has survived. Some collections remain in private hands, but many important ones are now becoming accessible.[1] While one must exercise due caution—the possibility of self-censorship must be considered and the perspective remains one-sided—these are a remarkably valuable resource, and not just for the factual information they supply. Shostakovich changed a great deal over the years. At all periods, he revealed different facets of himself to different people.

Memoirs and interviews have loomed large among the fresh evidence gathered. Glasnost untied the tongues of millions who had been intimidated, or censored, into silence during the Soviet era. Since Shostakovich symbolized something very important in their lives, and since his presumption to "greatness" seems unassailable, it is not surprising that many have hastened to set down their personal reminiscences of the man.[2] As fascinating and useful as these can be, memoirs furnish a treacherous resource to the historian. Reminiscences can be self-serving, vengeful, and distorted by faulty memory, selective amnesia, wishful thinking, and exaggeration. They can be rife with gossip and rumor. The temptation to recast the past to suit the present—especially now, when the victims and survivors of the Soviet "experiment" are grappling with discomfiting issues of complicity and culpability with a shameful past—can be hard to resist. In any case, factual accuracy is not generally one of their most salient features. Memoirs need to be treated with extreme care, evaluated critically, and corroborated by reference to established facts.

Unfortunately, there is not a single even remotely reliable resource in Russian, English, or any other language for the basic facts about Shostakovich's life and work. For all intents and purposes, there are two sources scholars turn to and depend on to provide reasonably "authoritative" information. The first is the introductory essays—widely varied in depth and quality—to the forty-two-volume collected edition of Shostakovich's music that appeared between 1979 and 1987.[3] The second is the two-volume biography of the composer by Sofya Khentova, the composer's official Soviet biographer.[4] Both of these sources are quintessential products of the late Soviet period. Both, for instance, were obliged by Soviet censorship to excise the names and roles played by important figures in the composer's life—including his own son, Maxim—because they had emigrated or defected from the Soviet Union.[5]

Such glaring omissions, and the stilted value judgments and interpretive biases of Soviet-style hagiographies, can be easily penetrated, even by amateur Sovietologists. It is so easy, in fact, that almost everyone has been lured into a false sense of security about the ability to distinguish between truth and hyperbole, fact and fancy. On the surface, and notwithstanding its ideological slant, Khentova's study seems an absolute gold mine of dates, names, and detail unavailable anywhere else. In fact, it is a minefield of misinformation and misrepresentation, incorrect dates and facts, errors of every stripe. To be fair, some of this was inherited inadvertently from earlier Soviet reference works. Nevertheless, the errors continue to proliferate in the rapidly expanding literature about Shostakovich.

I have tried in the following pages to correct as much of the factual record as I can within the framework of a straightforward, basic biography of the composer. Instead of relying on the accuracy of secondary sources for documentation, I have gone back to period newspapers, concert programs and reviews, personnel files, transcripts, letters, and diaries to reconstruct as precise a chronology of Shostakovich's life and works as the available evidence will permit. I have cross-checked facts to ensure their accuracy. I have not excluded the evidence of memoirs—Soviet, ex-Soviet and post-Soviet—but I have treated it with utmost caution, filtering out false or improbable allegations and screening for bias and hidden agendas. Where necessary and feasible, I have tried to mediate conflicting claims. I have also included representative extracts from Shostakovich's "public" pronouncements from different periods in full knowledge that they may not always have coincided with his private views. For millions of his contemporaries, Soviet and non-Soviet, of whom only a small percentage were sophisticated music lovers and even fewer were personally acquainted with the composer and in a position to gauge the sincerity of his statements with reasonable reliability, these offered the only insights into the "persona" of the famous composer they were ever permitted to encounter. To allow the book to function as a resource, I have endeavored to lay out the circumstances of Shostakovich's life in as balanced and objective a manner as possible.

Shostakovich's own reminiscences require special mention. When *Testimony*, a manuscript purporting to be the composer's authorized memoirs—"as told to and edited by Solomon Volkov"—was smuggled out of the Soviet Union posthumously and published in the West,6 the furor it ignited was understandable. A searing political document, a classic cold-war exposé, it makes riveting reading as a generic antidote to the Soviet gospel of a composer dedicating his art to the glory of communism. There can be little doubt that it was a major factor in "cracking the façade" of Shostakovich's public image and that it helped to reinvigorate interest in Shostakovich's music. Unfortunately, Volkov was not forthright about the nature of the manuscript and its authenticity was never properly vetted. Whether *Testimony* faithfully reproduces Shostakovich's confidences, and his alone, in a form and context he would have recognized and approved for publication, remains doubtful.[7]

Yet even were its claim to authenticity not in doubt, *Testimony* would still furnish a poor source for the serious biographer. The embittered, "deathbed" disclosures of someone ravaged by illness, with festering psychological wounds and scores to settle, are not to be relied upon for accuracy, fairness, or balance when recreating the impact of the events of a lifetime as they actually occurred. Such reflections may even willfully mislead. They cannot be taken at face value and must be scrupulously verified. Since *Testimony* is highly anecdotal anyhow, offering little specificity about the composer's activities or music, I have found it of little use. Its controversial disclosures must, in any case, be confirmed or rebutted by reference to verifiable evidence.

During the course of my research, I was fortunate to be able to consult some of the major archival holdings of Shostakovich material in Moscow and St. Petersburg. In the limited time I had available, I focused primarily on the study of letters and written texts; I have been able to incorporate here information from important letters and other documents, as yet unpublished. Nevertheless, this is not a study based principally on archival materials. Shostakovich scholarship is in its infancy. Much of the composer's personal legacy remains in private hands. His own archival repositories contain but a small fraction of the evidence that will eventually contribute to a fully nuanced assessment of the man and his career. Most of the letters he wrote were retained by their recipients. In the public arena, Shostakovich cut a wide swath across Soviet artistic and political life over a span of fifty years. Traces will be discovered in the archives of virtually every Soviet cultural and political institution. The process of uncovering them has barely begun.

Unless otherwise indicated, I have referred to and cited from original publications rather than from later compilations or translations, excepting those instances when a later publication offers a more complete text. Soviet history was always a work-in-progress; people, ideas, and facts that became unpalatable were routinely "airbrushed" out of existence in later Soviet sources. Only rarely was anything so erased later on restored. Shostakovich himself was obliged to reinvent his past on occasion. By the time successive generations encountered the "expurgated" pages of their history, they often had lost track of what had been excised, and why.

I have shadowed my subject as closely as possible, allowing the narrative of his life to unfold as he experienced it. Obviously, Shostakovich did not have the luxury of hindsight to guide him in his life's choices. He coped with the changing realities of Soviet life and his own personal circumstances from day to day. I have tried to record how he lived and composed in the context of his own times.

Music was what motivated him. This alone remained constant throughout a turbulent, often tortured life.

1906–1919

Childhood

Though the Shostakovich family was of Polish-Lithuanian extraction, the composer's immediate forebears came from Siberia. His paternal grandfather, Boleslav Petrovich Shostakovich, had been exiled there in 1866 in the crackdown that followed Dmitriy Karakozov's assassination attempt on Tsar Alexander II. After the expiration of his term of exile Boleslav Shostakovich decided to remain in Siberia. He eventually became a successful banker in Irkutsk and raised a large family. His son, Dmitriy Boleslavovich Shostakovich, the composer's father, was born in exile in Narïm in 1875 and attended St. Petersburg University, graduating in 1899 from the faculty of physics and mathematics. After graduation, he went to work as an engineer under Dmitriy Mendeleyev at the Bureau of Weights and Measures in St. Petersburg. In 1903, he married Sofya Vasilyevna Kokoúlina, another Siberian transplant to the capital.

Sofya's father, Vasiliy Yakovlevich Kokoúlin, a Siberian native, started as a modest clerk and worked his way up in the administration of the Lena goldfields in Bodaibo to become manager of the mine office. Born in 1878, Sofya was the third of his six children. She excelled as a student at the exclusive Irkutsk Institute for Noblewomen and was musically inclined; after her father decided to resign his position and move to the Crimea, she and a sister went to St. Petersburg, where an older brother already resided, to further their education. Sofya enrolled as a piano student at the Conservatory, where her principal teacher became Alexandra Rozanova. When she married Dmitriy Boleslavovich Shostakovich three years later, she abandoned her studies to devote herself full time to her husband and raising a family. Their Siberian roots remained a source of pride and cultural identity for both parents.

Dmitriy Dmitriyevich was the second of their three children; Mariya, his older sister, who also became a professional musician, a pianist and teacher, was born in 1903 and his younger sister Zoya, who became a veterinarian, was born in 1908. The future composer was born in St. Petersburg on 25 September 1906. His destiny as "Dmitriy" was not foreordained; his older sister recalled that the housekeeper ran into the sitting room shouting "Dmitriy Dmitriyevich has been born!" Being superstitious, a trait she bequeathed to her son, his mother thought it would be bad luck to have two people in one family—father and son—with the same surname and wanted to call the baby "Yaroslav."[1] Shostakovich's aunt, Nadezhda, informed the composer's first biographer that his parents had settled on the name "Yaroslav," but the priest who presided at the christening objected—the suspicion was that he did not know St. Yaroslav's name day—and persuaded them instead to accept his father's name, "Dmitriy."[2]

By all accounts, young Mitya, as he was nicknamed, grew up in a loving, nurturing home. His father was down-to-earth, with a genial disposition, a devoted family man. After the death of Mendeleyev in 1907, he was obliged to supplement the salary he earned at the Bureau of Weights and Measures and soon resigned to take on the well-paying post of general manager of the Rennenkampf estate, overseeing its peat extraction industry. One of the fringe benefits was that the family was able to spend the summers outside the city vacationing on the estate at Irinovka, near Lake Ladoga. After the outbreak of World War I, Dmitriy Boleslavovich took a management job in a joint-stock company which invested in the munitions business and, when industries were nationalized after the October Revolution, found employment in state industrial enterprises before returning to the Bureau of Weights and Measures as a deputy director.[3]

Music-making assumed an important place in the Shostakovich household. It was music—above and beyond their common Siberian heritage—that had brought Shostakovich's parents together in the first place. Dmitriy Boleslavovich had a pleasant tenor voice and enjoyed singing popular romances and opera arias to his wife's accompaniment. His renditions of gypsy romances made an indelible impression on his son, who cherished a special fondness for gypsy music the rest of his life. Sofya was regularly joined by colleagues from her Conservatory days for informal musicales. Chaikovsky, Beethoven, and Rachmaninoff numbered among their favorite composers.[4]

Despite the conducive environment, Shostakovich's musical gift did not manifest itself early. Years later he reminisced: "I didn't sneak to the door at the age of three in order to listen to music, and when I did listen to it, I slept afterward just as soundly as the night before." [5] His was a normal childhood. Sofya recalled that her son's special passion was for building blocks; he could spend hours on end engrossed in construction. The young boy demonstrated no great hankering to study music. He later rationalized this reluctance as the outgrowth of a fear of notation and the observation that her own music lessons reduced his older sister to tears.[6] But others recalled that he seemed to love listening to music. His mother preserved the program from a domestic concert that took place in September 1913, where, among the performers, seven-year-old Mitya was inscribed in jest as "under the piano," that is, he had concealed himself in a dark corner so as to remain past his bedtime and hear the music. Getting him to bed on a night when their musician friends were visiting amounted to high drama in itself.[7] When reminiscing about the formative musical experiences of his youth, Shostakovich would often recall the chamber music soirees organized in the next-door apartment by engineer and ardent cellist Boris Sass-Tisovsky, son-in-law of Mitya's godmother and close family friend, the popular children's writer Klavdiya Lukashevich. Through the wall, Mitya would listen for hours to the trios and quartets of Mozart, Haydn, Beethoven, Borodin, and Chaikovsky.[8]

In the spring of 1915, Mitya was taken to the musical theater for the first time, to see Rimsky-Korsakov's *Tale of Tsar Saltan*.[9] As much as he enjoyed the opera, it did not budge him from his indisposition to study music. He later confessed that what finally piqued his interest was a "Galop" for piano six-hands by Streabogg (pseudonym for Jean-Louis Goebbaerts, a prolific nineteenth-century Belgian composer of light piano pieces) that he heard his sister play with her girlfriends. He asked his mother to help him pick out two of the parts on the keyboard.[10] In the summer of 1915, just as she had done at the same age with his sister Mariya, his mother sat her eight-year-old son down at the piano for his first lesson.[11] Within minutes, she recognized that she was dealing with a youngster of precocious musical ability, possessing perfect pitch and a phenomenal memory. He demanded from the outset to be given a piece to play, so his mother placed the piano arrangement of an andante from a Haydn symphony in front of him. After asking her to explain the meaning of the various accidentals, he proceeded to play the andante slowly, but with perfect accuracy.[12] Shostakovich later recalled that his uncommon musical memory encouraged him to engage in deception, at least until he was caught in the act. His mother would play him a piece. At his next lesson, he would perform it, pretending to play it from score when, in actual fact, he was reproducing it from memory.[13] In any event, mastery of notation came quickly and he was soon effortlessly playing the Haydn andante, a Mozart minuet, Chaikovsky's *Children's Album*, and more. He also exhibited an exceptional facility for sight-reading. In retrospect, he would commend his mother as a fantastic teacher for beginners: "She managed to convey her love of music. She didn't pester one with exercises, didn't exact hours of practice. She simply wanted us to receive a good musical education." [14]

In mid-August 1915, a month after the lessons had commenced, Shostakovich's mother took him to play for the leading teacher in Petrograd, Ignatiy Glyasser. Glyasser was accustomed to the wunderkind delusions of doting mothers, but after he heard Mitya play, he was obliged to agree with Sofya that she had a remarkable boy. That autumn, Shostakovich enrolled in Glyasser's music school, studying initially with his wife, Olga. At one of his first school concerts, less than six months after he had begun his piano lessons, he performed from memory nearly half of Chaikovsky's *Children's Album*. His father was amazed that such musical talent had been revealed in his son. Mitya made rapid progress, transferring in 1916 to Glyasser's own class, where he studied sonatas of Haydn and Mozart and, later, Bach fugues. At the school concert on 26 April 1918, he performed Beethoven's Sonata no. 5 in C Minor.

Also in the autumn of 1915, Shostakovich began attending the Shidlovskaya Commercial School, a recently founded coeducational gymnasium attended by children of the well-to-do liberal intelligentsia. The sons of Lev Kamenev and Trotsky numbered among his classmates, and the sons of Alexander Kerensky studied in the classes above and below him. After the nationalization of schools by the Bolshevik government in 1918, Mitya continued to attend this school—now renamed "108th Soviet School" [15]—until its closing in 1919, at which point he transferred to the school attended by both his sisters, formerly known as the Stoyunina School, where he had often given piano performances in the past. If he was an able student, his academic attainments registered less indelibly in the memories of his contemporaries than his musical ones. His father possessed a good library, and Mitya did become an avid, lifelong reader (he was weaned on his godmother's stories and penned poetry as a youngster). By the age of twelve Mitya Shostakovich had resolved, in any case, to devote his life to music. Although he continued his secondary schooling after he enrolled in the Petrograd Conservatory and received private tutoring in mathematics, literature, and history, academic pursuits engaged less and less of his attention. By 1921, his poor attendance and insufficient application to the school courses paralleling his arduous schedule at the Conservatory became a bone of contention and Shostakovich abandoned them. Although there is some disagreement about exactly what transpired, the most persuasive account suggests that as a special dispensation the fourteen-year-old student was given an exam to allow him to leave school with some sort of credential. His failure to satisfy the inflexible requirements of his mathematics instructor, however, meant that he was obliged to leave empty-handed.[16]

Shostakovich's desire to compose was kindled as soon as he started to play the piano. Although most of his juvenilia was eventually either lost or destroyed, he was composing steadily from the age of nine. Family and friends were impressed not only by his pianistic facility but also by his imagination and improvisatory originality. Naturally, many of his compositions were for piano, including some inspired by extramusical stimuli, like "Soldier" or the trilogy, "In the Forest." Among other works was an opera on Pushkin's *Gypsies* (three excerpts from this setting have survived). In April 1918, he wrote that he was currently composing music to Gogol's *Terrible Vengeance*, was planning to set Lermontov's poem, "A Song about Tsar Ivan Vasilyevich, the Merchant Kalashnikov and the Soldier Kiribeyevich," and had already notched up a symphony.[17] His mother estimated that he had a portfolio of thirty pieces or so by the age of twelve or thirteen.

Unfortunately, Glyasser was a strict disciplinarian and offered no encouragement to the compositional endeavors of his young charge. According to Shostakovich, this was a major factor behind his mother's decision, most likely in the autumn of 1918, to abandon Glyasser's school and entrust both his and his sister's music instruction to Alexandra Rozanova, Sofya's own former teacher at the Conservatory.[18] Shortly before effecting the transfer, Mitya participated in a Glyasser class outing to hear Serge Koussevitzky conduct the State Symphony Orchestra (the former court orchestra) in performances of Beethoven's Eighth and Ninth Symphonies. The twelve year old followed the score keenly and during intermission went onstage with a classmate to inspect the instruments.[19]

The young Shostakovich's grasp of the import, and his conscious embrace, of the revolutionary milestones of 1917 were almost certainly exaggerated both by his Soviet biographers and, when expedient, by himself. Involvement in radical politics, it is true, was to be found on both sides of Shostakovich's family tree. His paternal grandfather had been a political exile. More recently, in 1907 one of his maternal aunts had married a member of the Social Revolutionary Party in prison as he awaited trial for the murder of a policeman during a police raid. (Sofya helped to galvanize support for his defense, and in the end he was acquitted.) Another aunt joined the Social-Democratic (Bolshevik) Party in the wake of the bloody events of 1905 and for a time duplicated illicit literature while living on the Shostakovich premises, placing them all in peril. Dmitriy and Sofya Shostakovich welcomed guests with a broad spectrum of beliefs—political, religious, and otherwise—into their home, without themselves engaging in extremist politics. There is little question that the Shostakovich children were exposed to a diversity of backgrounds and opinions. Nonetheless, like the majority of the liberal intelligentsia, the Shostakovich family was in fundamental sympathy with the February Revolution of 1917; Zoya recalled her father coming home at the time shouting, "Children, Freedom!"[20]

One image that was vividly etched in the memories of both Shostakovich's mother and his aunt Nadezhda was the solemn funeral procession through the streets of Petrograd, on 23 March (5 April) 1917, to lay 184 victims of the February Revolution to rest in a common grave. The Shostakovich family was among the nearly 1 million mourners who made their way to the Field of Mars, singing the revolutionary funeral march, "You Fell a Victim." When they returned home that evening, young Mitya played "You Fell a Victim" on the piano (in later years he would utilize this classic revolutionary tune in film scores and, most conspicuously, in the third movement of his Eleventh Symphony, *The Year 1905*, op. 103). Under its influence, he composed his own "Funeral March in Memory of the Victims of the Revolution."[21] The "Funeral March" and his "Hymn to Liberty," also for piano, were the two works he was invariably asked to play when anyone came to the house.[22] A contemporary recalled hearing the young Shostakovich perform his "Funeral March in Memory of the Victims of the Revolution" at a memorial service held at the Stoyunina School ten months later, in January 1918, this time commemorating casualties at the opposite point of the political compass, victims of the Bolsheviks' bloody dispersal of the duly elected Constituent Assembly.[23] (Petrograd's intelligentsia was especially horrified by the brutal murders by pro-Bolshevik sailors of two incarcerated leaders of the recently outlawed Constitutional-Democratic (Kadet) Party, Andrey Shingaryov and Fyodor Kokoshkin, in their prison hospital.) In a letter written to his Aunt Nadezhda early in April 1918, the young composer lists a funeral march "in memory of Shingaryov and Kokoshkin" among his recent works.[24]

The story that he went to meet Vladimir Ilyich Lenin's train when it arrived at the Finland Station on 3/16 April 1917 and heard the remarks Lenin delivered from the roof of the armored car is almost certainly one of the apocryphal episodes in Shostakovich's biography. The composer himself promoted this legend while at work on the Twelfth Symphony, saying that Lenin's words on that occasion had imprinted themselves on his memory.[25] His younger sister recalled that he rushed off with a group of boys from the Shidlovskaya School and returned "in raptures," saying he had seen Lenin.[26] In comments attributed to him in *Testimony*, Shostakovich claimed that although the incident did take place (presumably reconstructing this from what he had been told), he did not remember a thing about it.[27] However, as

Boris Losskiy, a slightly older schoolmate and a friend of the family, has pointed out, the story is utterly implausible.[28] Lenin's train did not arrive at the Finland Station until after 11 PM, and it was close to midnight before he made his historic appearance on top of the armored car. Shostakovich was ten years old. It is hardly conceivable that his parents would have permitted him out that late at night, let alone during such unstable times.

Evidently cultivated by the composer himself, the notion that Shostakovich met the Russian revolutions of 1917 "on the streets" gained currency quickly. It was invoked in 1927 in validation of his commissioned tribute for the tenth anniversary of the October Revolution, his symphonic *Dedication to October*, as was the story about having witnessed the brutal killing of a young boy by a policeman and having transmuted the image into his music.[29] Whether the ten year old actually witnessed such a slaying is open to question.[30]

Shostakovich's musical gift commanded notice. One of his classmates, Irina Kustodiyeva, daughter of the famous artist Boris Kustodiyev, told her family about her talented young friend who played Grieg and Chopin so well. Shostakovich was duly invited over to play for her father, a keen music-lover who was confined to a wheelchair and missed attending concerts. He liked to paint while listening to music. The mature artist and the adolescent musician developed a special, warm relationship, and Shostakovich and his older sister became frequent visitors to the Kustodiyev home. (Mariya even served as a model for some of the artist's paintings.) Kustodiyev was solicitous of his young friend's aspirations as composer; on one occasion, when the other children were complaining that Mitya's improvisations were too difficult for them to dance to, and even his rendition of a foxtrot came out spiked with unexpected rhythms and intonations, Boris counseled, "Don't pay any attention to them, Mitya, just play your own thing."[31] Shostakovich was invited to play at an exhibition of Kustodiyev's paintings on 8 May 1920, where he performed his music in public for the first time.[32]

Shostakovich dedicated one of the works he performed often in those days, a Prelude for Piano in G Minor (later catalogued as No. 1 of his Eight Preludes, op. 2), to Kustodiyev. The artist, in turn, made numerous drawings of Mitya, including a famous portrait—inscribed as a present to his young friend in September 1919—of the fresh-faced thirteen year old in striped shirt and sailor's middy, delicate hands resting on a dog-eared score of Chopin. Shostakovich was a thin, fine-featured boy, sensitive and quiet, to outward appearances an ordinary child. His hair was unruly, typically tousled, and he wore wire-rimmed glasses. To some, he conveyed an impression of nervous tension and kinetic energy. At the same time, he possessed a serious, introspective streak, and many describe seeing on his face an expression of rapt inner concentration. The appearance of fragility was deceiving; when he put fingers to keyboard he was transformed almost miraculously into a dynamic, arresting presence.

Mitya also had his fun-loving side. He was quick-witted and enjoyed wordplay. He participated willingly in school entertainments and at children's parties, and birthday and holiday festivities. His ability to furnish the latest dance music accentuated his popularity. During the lean Civil War summer of 1919, Sofya arranged to take Mitya to a boarding house in the country for a few weeks, the better to feed him. Shostakovich was busy preparing for the entrance exams at the Petrograd Conservatory, and he had little time for games, but periodically his mother forced him outside into the fresh air. With other vacationing children, he took part in play-acting the fables of Krïlov, evidently including two—"The Dragonfly and the Ant" and "The Ass and the Nightingale"—that he would soon set to music in his *Two Fables of Krïlov*, op. 4. Natalya Kube, a ten-year-old girl also staying there that summer, became the innocent and unsuspecting object of Shostakovich's interest; he dedicated "To N.K." three more (nos. 6–8) of his *Eight Preludes* for piano, op. 2.[33]

Rozanova was much more interested in cultivating Shostakovich's compositional potential than Glyasser had been. (Neatly copied autographs of three of Shostakovich's early piano miniatures, a minuet, prelude, and intermezzo, were found preserved among her papers.) To further his ambition, she recommended that he receive special instruction, so in the spring and summer of 1919 he took lessons from Georgiy Bruni,[34] who promoted improvisation as a means of stimulating the creative imagination. Also during the summer of 1919, in preparation for the Conservatory entrance exams, Shostakovich studied elementary theory and solfeggio.

There was some question in the minds of Shostakovich's parents whether it would be wise for the thirteen year old to pursue concurrently two courses of study—piano and composition—at the Conservatory. In one of his published memoirs, Shostakovich recalled that at his father's request, the famous pianist and conductor Alexander Siloti agreed to listen to him play. After the audition, Siloti was said to have confided to Sofya: "The youngster won't make himself a career. He has no musical abilities. But of course, if he's got the desire, why ... no harm in letting him study." After this, so Shostakovich claimed, he had cried all night and it was out of compassion that his parents had decided to present him to the patriarch of Russian composers and director of the Petrograd Conservatory, Alexander Glazunov, to receive his authoritative assessment.[35] The appointment with Glazunov would mark a pivotal moment in his life.

Glazunov had already had the opportunity, in social surroundings, to hear Shostakovich play the piano. On this occasion, Shostakovich played his own compositions, including some of the op. 2 preludes for piano.

Glazunov delivered the considered opinion that Mitya must, indeed, study composition as well as piano. Sofya noted down the words Glazunov uttered after having tested her son's musical knowledge and abilities, on the basis of which he had determined that Shostakovich might enroll in the Petrograd Conservatory's composition program immediately, bypassing any preparatory theoretical courses: "I cannot remember ever having had such gifted children as your son within the walls of the Conservatory." [36] Valerian Bogdanov-Berezovsky, who took entrance exams the same year and became Mitya's boon companion of their Conservatory years, recalled that Glazunov's extraordinary evaluation of Shostakovich as someone "possessing a gift comparable to that of Mozart" raced along the Conservatory grapevine.[37]

The focus of great expectations, Dmitriy Shostakovich was duly enrolled as a student of both piano and composition at the Petrograd Conservatory in the autumn of 1919.

1919–1926
Conservatory **2**

In the immediate postrevolutionary period, the Petrograd Conservatory changed little from prerevolutionary days. At the helm of the institution, Alexander Glazunov, prodigious late-nineteenth-century composer turned respected administrator, was a living link to the venerable traditions of Rimsky-Korsakov and the golden age of Russian music. He provided a source of continuity and stability for the institution through uncertain times. Glazunov's tireless devotion to the cause of professional music, his active involvement in all aspects of Conservatory life, and his magnanimous disregard for his personal tastes in the identification and advancement of gifted youth earned him the universal respect and affection of students and colleagues.

Shostakovich was a needy and grateful beneficiary of Glazunov's protection. At a time of civil unrest and widespread starvation, Glazunov traded on his considerable prestige to promote the budding young musician. He monitored the progress of his protégé closely. Dmitriy's first year at the Conservatory, 1919–1920, was an especially difficult one. Throughout the winter, the lack of heat in the Conservatory building forced students to attend classes and concerts bundled in overcoats and hats, taking off their gloves only to write exercises. With public transport unreliable or inaccessible, Dmitriy was obliged each day to cover on foot the considerable distance between his home (on Marat Street) and the Conservatory. While the temptation to skip lessons proved irresistible to many students and even to some of the teachers, Dmitriy stood out by his scrupulous attendance, his discipline and diligence in his studies. Nikolai Sokolov, with whom Dmitriy studied counterpoint and fugue, was not one of the most conscientious of professors. To reap the benefits of his expertise, Shostakovich was obliged to seek him out at home and secure his instruction there. Hardships notwithstanding, he looked back on the period with nostalgia: "Despite all the difficulties, I remember that time with a warm feeling. We listened to a great deal of fine music and played much of it ourselves. My Conservatory companions loved to make music. In order to hear or to play an unknown composition, we were ready to cover at least ten kilometers on foot, at times even to skip supper." [1]

After spending his first year at the Conservatory in the piano class of Rozanova, in the autumn of 1920 Shostakovich transferred to the class of Leonid Vladimirovich Nikolayev, whose prize pupils at the time were two stunningly gifted pianists, Vladimir Sofronitsky and Mariya Yudina. Nikolayev was a sometime composer himself and earned a reputation as a pianist and musician of refined intellect who brought a composer's perspective to his interpretative skills: "He trained not simply pianists, but in the first place thinking musicians. He didn't create a school in the specific sense of some single narrow professional direction. He shaped and nurtured a broad aesthetic trend in the sphere of pianistic art." [2] This was an approach bound to appeal to Shostakovich, who found in his teacher as sympathetic and astute a critic of his compositional experiments as of his pianistic progress.

As a developing performer, Shostakovich stood out not so much for technical virtuosity as for the memorable individuality of his interpretative approach, which did not always win the enthusiastic support of stylistic traditionalists. His distinctive interpretations were colored by an innate emotional restraint, but also by his commanding touch and riveting rhythmic drive. His favored concert repertory of his student years included works by Schumann and especially those of Liszt. Even in his earliest public performances, he regularly played his own compositions, most notably the op. 2 *Preludes* (1919–1920) and the *Three Fantastic Dances*, op. 5 (1920–1922), works in which the personality of the creator merged seamlessly with that of the interpreter.

Mariya Yudina, whose artistry and polyphonic mastery Shostakovich esteemed highly, goaded him to evade the standard repertory dependence on the *Moonlight* and *Appassionata* Sonatas and to tackle, instead, Beethoven's op. 106, the *Hammerklavier* Sonata. With his performance of the *Hammerklavier* Sonata at a concert of Nikolayev's class in the spring of 1922, when he was still fifteen, Shostakovich amazed listeners by his mature grasp of the conception, steel rhythmic strength, and lyrical penetration.[3] The artistry of his playing, rather than its technique, is what impressed critics most: "What an artist sees when he paints a picture, Shostakovich hears when he performs a piece. In both cases the work of art precedes its realization in the mind of its creator.... With most pianists, it works just the opposite—they learn the piece technically, and then sometimes manage to create its musical image in the soul. This is why when you listen to pianists like Shostakovich, you forget about technique and you enter into the spiritual content of the music." [4]

In retrospect, Shostakovich was to credit his composition teacher, Maximilian Steinberg, with having provided a thorough academic grounding, especially in harmony, and for having cultivated in him a love for the classics and an unerring sense of aesthetic taste. Son-in-law of Nikolai Rimsky-Korsakov and conservator of the proud musical lineage of nineteenth-century St. Petersburg, Steinberg was not noted for his progressive attitude to new directions in music. Shostakovich dedicated his first orchestral piece, the Scherzo in F-sharp Minor, op. 1, written in 1919 during his first months of study with Steinberg, to his teacher. Like a subsequent student exercise, Theme and Variations in B-flat Major, op. 3—composed during 1921–1922 and dedicated to the memory of Nikolai Sokolov—its deference to the stylistic and formal legacy of the Rimsky-Korsakov school made it a fitting offering to the dedicatee. Shostakovich, however, quickly mastered and outgrew his academic models.

As Shostakovich matured, his musical horizons expanded, and he gained self-confidence, the challenges of Steinberg's instruction—and the Conservatory curriculum as a whole—became increasingly stifling rather than liberating. The fossilized curriculum for composers at the Petrograd Conservatory in the early 1920s—almost completely lacking in an outlet for practical composition—had undergone no reform or modernization since the days when Sergey Prokofiev had chafed within its confines. It was hardly calculated to inspire an ambitious and gifted young composer to discover his own voice. Necessary reforms would begin only at the end of Shostakovich's student tenure. But Shostakovich was no *enfant terrible*. He did not vent his frustrations in defiant rebellion. His respect for craftsmanship and professionalism was deeply ingrained. Dutifully fulfilling his classroom assignments and maintaining cordial relations with his professors, he sought the extra stimulation he needed outside the classroom.

Shostakovich devoured new music and musical impressions voraciously. He became an active participant in an informal circle of student composers who met in the Conservatory cafeteria to play music, try out their new compositions, and share impressions. He was a regular at the gatherings of another circle, organized by fellow student Georgiy Rimsky-Korsakov, of devotees of quarter-tone music. Although he played one of the two pianos (tuned a quarter-tone apart) in their ensemble, he never delivered on his pledge to write something specifically for the group.[5] A remarkably gifted sight-reader, Shostakovich rarely turned down a request to explore four- and eight-hand arrangements of symphonic classics or the latest scores; in later years he would foster strong sight-reading and keyboard harmony skills in his own students. In collaboration with two other schoolmates, Pavel Feldt and Georgiy Klements, Shostakovich set out to compose a cycle of twenty-four preludes for piano, one in every major and minor key; five of Shostakovich's contributions to the collective effort are preserved.[6]

When it came to the pursuit of music, his friends knew him to be insatiable. With a violinist and cellist from the conservatory he went out to perform for Red Army soldiers, at local factories, and at Palaces of Culture.[7] He was a regular fixture at Philharmonic and Conservatory concerts and never missed an opportunity to expand his repertory or hear touring performers. Music-making inevitably occupied a central role in the social life of the Shostakovich household as well, although charades was a popular family pastime and—having inherited a superstitious streak from his mother—at this stage Mitya also indulged his fascination with chiromancy.

Shostakovich frequented the biweekly Monday gatherings at the home of Anna Fogt, where established professionals—Boris Asafyev, Vladimir Shcherbachov, and Nikolai Malko, for instance, as well as occasional visitors from Moscow—played and discussed music on an equal footing with members of the younger generation. New works by Stravinsky, Hindemith, Schoenberg, *Les Six* were unveiled and hotly debated here, and, in an atmosphere that was open-minded and constructive, the aspiring young composer was able to test and refine his musical ideas. Participants recalled the introduction of his new compositions, among them *Two Fables of Krïlov,* op. 4 (1921–1922) and the *Three Fantastic Dances.* "From the very beginning it was clear to everyone: a most talented, exceptional composer, for whom fate had ordained an extraordinary path, was emerging."[8]

In mid-February 1922, Shostakovich's father Dmitriy Boleslavovich suddenly fell ill; his death from pneumonia on 24 February was a devastating blow to the family. Left without income or resources and with no prior work experience, Sofya was obliged to find whatever employment was available, initially working as a cashier and later as a typist, to provide for her three children and keep them in school. Her eldest daughter Mariya took private piano pupils to supplement the family finances. Utterly sure of her son's musical genius, Sofya was determined to make the sacrifices necessary to provide a stable, nourishing home environment to allow his talent to blossom. She firmly rejected Dmitriy's own attempts to assume responsibility as a provider.

Fifteen-year-old Dmitriy bore his grief stoically. An observer at the funeral in the Alexander Nevsky Monastery recalled that "Zoya's distraught little face was wet with tears and her coat was unfastened. Dmitriy stood, his cap crushed under his arm, slowly wiping his spectacles. His eyes looked especially defenseless without them, but his entire face was filled with inward concentration and composure. No need to go to him with condolences!"[9] Dmitriy's mourning was expressed in music. In March, he completed a Suite for Two Pianos, op. 6, which he dedicated to the memory of his father. The four-movement work, a memorial of affecting dignity and solemnity, was designed to be performed with his sister Mariya. They played the work together at private soirées in Petrograd's musical circles[10] and later at Dmitriy's debut at the Circle of Friends of Chamber Music, on 22 June 1923.

The family's misfortunes did not end with the death of Dmitriy Boleslavovich. Early in 1923 Shostakovich began to complain of pains in the neck area; the doctors diagnosed tuberculosis of the bronchial and lymph glands. Loath to postpone his graduation from the piano faculty, Shostakovich took his public exam in late June shortly after his operation, his neck still swathed in bandages. He played impressively in his solo recital, where his program was exceptionally taxing: F-sharp Minor Prelude and Fugue from Bach's *Das wohltemperirte Clavier,* book 1; Beethoven Sonata no. 21 in C Major (*Waldstein*); Mozart C Major Variations; Chopin Ballade no. 3; Schumann *Humoresque*; and Liszt "Venice and Naples" from *Années de pèlerinage.* His performance of the Schumann Piano Concerto the next day, however, was less successful. Despite all expectations, he failed to garner a prize, a fact that did not escape caustic comment in the press. Nonetheless, Glazunov, who had admitted the sixteen year old to the final exam with the evaluation, "Despite his youth, he is already a fully mature musician," gave Shostakovich highest marks, grading his performance as "polished and distinguished by its simplicity and sincerity."[11]

The piano course completed, all the family's energies went into scraping together enough money to send Dmitriy south for the summer to continue the tuberculosis cure. Even while Dmitriy Boleslavovich had been alive, it had proved a struggle to feed the family during the lean years that followed the revolutions of 1917. To procure special rations for the sickly, anemic Mitya Shostakovich, Glazunov and Mitya's godmother, Klavdiya Lukashevich, had sent impassioned petitions to Soviet cultural commissar Anatoliy Lunacharsky, in the summer of 1921. That appeal had met with success.[12] Sofya was now obliged to sell personal possessions, including the family's piano. Glazunov sent another urgent appeal for help to the People's Commissariat of Enlightenment (Narkompros), warning that the "death of such a person would be an irreparable loss for the world of art."[13]

Accompanied by his sister Mariya, who had graduated together with her younger brother from the Conservatory the previous month, Dmitriy arrived in Gaspra on the Crimean peninsula on 20 July 1923. In what was the first lengthy separation from an obsessively protective mother, the teenagers were taken under the wing of Boris Kustodiyev, in residence at the sanatorium of the "House of Scientists," where he arranged for them to take their meals. For Shostakovich, the holiday yielded an unexpected dividend. As Mariya wrote home: "[Mitya] has grown, got a suntan, is cheerful and has fallen in love." [14] The object of Shostakovich's affections was Tatyana Glivenko, two weeks his junior, the daughter of an eminent Moscow philology professor.

In response to his mother's warnings about the pitfalls of love—Mariya had reported her dislike of Tanya, evaluating her as a strange girl and flirt—Shostakovich penned home a thoughtful letter on 3 August 1923 that reveals the young man to have ingested, if not entirely digested, the idealism of the liberated sexual mores of the era:

> ... Of course the best thing imaginable would be the total abolition of the institution of marriage, with all its fetters and constraints on love. But that, of course, would be Utopia. If marriage doesn't exist, then the family won't exist, and then that would be really terrible. But, in any case, love is free, there can be no debate about that. And, mamochka dear, I warn you that it is possible that if someday I fall in love, it may not be with the aim of contracting a marriage. But if I do marry and my wife falls in love with someone else, I will not say a word; if she needs a divorce I will give it to her, taking the blame on myself.... But at the same time, there exists the sacred vocation of motherhood and fatherhood. So that, when you think about it all, your head fairly starts to explode. In any case, love is free! [15]

The attachment between Mitya and Tanya took root deeply; weathering the uncertainties of long separations, other romantic interests, and his mother's meddling, it endured for many years. Although they lived in different cities and saw each other only rarely, they sustained an active correspondence. They spent a month together in the summer of 1926—Mitya rented a room nearby her parents' summer place—at Anapa on the Black Sea. Late in her life, Glivenko reminisced that Mitya found it difficult to commit himself. But he continued to pursue her even after she announced her marriage to another man in 1929, aiming to convince her to leave her husband to come and live with him in Leningrad. He accepted that the relationship was finally over only after the birth of her first child in 1932. [16]

As the summer of 1923 drew to a close and Tanya and other companions departed, Shostakovich grew impatient to get back home to his mother, his teachers, and the rich cultural life of his beloved "Peter." He began to compose a trio for piano, violin, and cello—incorporating in its second subject material from a discarded piano sonata he had composed three years earlier—and asked Tanya's permission to dedicate it to her. He was also eager to start making a contribution to the family finances and promised his mother: "Just wait, mamochka, soon I will return, I'll give concerts and make money and then just see how we'll live. Just let me stay healthy." [17] Many sources, relying on Shostakovich's own 1927 autobiographical sketch,[18] pinpoint the autumn of 1923 as the time when he first took employment as a cinema pianist. Evidence from extant letters and other sources, however, shows his dating to be in error; he began to work in the cinema only in the autumn of 1924.

Shostakovich did play in many recitals and concerts that fall. On 8 November 1923—with a program combining Liszt's transcription of Bach's Organ Prelude in A Minor and Beethoven's *Appassionata* Sonata with his own *Preludes, Fantastic Dances,* and *Theme and Variations*—he presented his first solo recital at the Circle of Friends of Chamber Music. Critic V. Valter was impressed: "I shall be so bold as to greet this youth with the same words I greeted the young Heifetz. In Shostakovich's playing one is struck by that same joyously serene confidence of genius. My words relate not only to the exceptional playing of Shostakovich, but to his works as well. What wealth of fantasy and astonishing conviction, confidence in one's own work (especially in the *Variations*)—at just seventeen years old!" [19] Among other engagements that December, Shostakovich substituted for Nikolayev on piano in Bach's Brandenburg Concerto no. 5 in a concert at the Conservatory conducted by Glazunov.[20] Also at the Conservatory, he and two colleagues successfully presented his recently completed Trio (provisionally renamed Poem) for Violin, Cello, and Piano, in a concert of music by student composers.

When not performing himself, Shostakovich attended and raved about performances by Vladimir Horowitz, Nathan Milstein, and Egon Petri. He was a habitué of the State Academic Theater of Opera and Ballet (as the Mariyinsky Theater was now officially named) and an especially avid fan and discerning critic of classical ballet. As Bogdanov-Berezovsky recalled, this was the period of Mitya's serious infatuation with the scores of Chaikovsky.[21] Unfortunately, no trace has been found of a ballet on Hans Andersen's "Little Mermaid," which Shostakovich reported working on during the summer of 1923. He was less attracted to the artistry of modern dance, although in the winter of 1923–1924 he collaborated with and accompanied Mariya Ponna on her choreography of his *Three Fantastic Dances.* (Ponna, a swimming champion turned acrobatic dancer styled after Isadora Duncan, would become extremely popular soon afterward in a duet team with Alexander Kaverzin.) On 1 December 1923, Shostakovich accompanied Ponna's rendering of works by Schubert, Mozart, and Rachmaninoff and his own *Fantastic Dances* at the Circle of Friends of

Chamber Music. Presumably, this was the same scantily clad, "expression-istic" choreography of the *Fantastic Dances* that mortified the composer's unsuspecting mother when it was performed before her late husband's distinguished colleagues and their families at the Bureau of Weights and Measures.[22]

Shostakovich's studies at the Conservatory continued. He made progress in the "form" class and even started violin lessons. In late December 1923 and the first two weeks of January 1924, he composed, in white heat, *Three Pieces* for Cello and Piano; he actually wrote four but destroyed the fourth immediately. As an assignment for Steinberg's class, he began to compose a symphony. He reported what happened when he brought the beginnings of a third movement, a scherzo, to his teacher:

> ... He tore it to shreds. He said, "I cannot say anything about such music. What is this enthusiasm for the Grotesque? There were already Grotesque bits in the Trio. All the cello pieces are Grotesque and finally this Scherzo is also Grotesque! What is this!" ... I have a great deal of respect and love for him, as he's a very good person and musician. For this reason I am rather upset about his attitude to the cello pieces and to the symphony scherzo. But he gets on with me superbly well. Admittedly, he's in a bit of a huff with me because I haven't done anything for more than six months. Besides he is too conservative: "the inviolable foundations of the *kuchka*," the "sacred traditions of Nikolai Andreyevich [Rimsky-Korsakov]" and other such pompous phrases. Unfortunately, I can no longer indulge him with my music.[23]

Despite his criticisms of the scherzo, Steinberg nevertheless instructed Shostakovich to proceed with the composition.

In what remains an enigmatic episode in Shostakovich's biography, his career at the Leningrad Conservatory very nearly came to an abrupt end shortly thereafter. In a letter to Nikolayev dated 12 March 1924, Sofya bemoaned Mitya's exclusion, ostensibly on grounds of youth and immaturity, from the Academic course (as the graduate program was then named). She confessed bewilderment that the Conservatory could turn away such a talented youngster.[24] Although the rebuff—believed to have been motivated by internal political intrigues—presumably related chiefly to the continuation of Dmitriy's studies in piano, it impelled mother and son to pursue plans for him to transfer to the Moscow Conservatory. On 3 April 1924, Shostakovich filed his application for transfer, citing Leningrad's harmful climate as the grounds. While in Moscow, he attended to practical and financial arrangements. He was accepted by pianist Konstantin Igumnov for study without ceremony. On 8 April, he auditioned for Nikolai Myaskovsky and other members of the composition faculty, who accepted him straightaway into the "free composition" class.[25] Shostakovich eagerly anticipated studying with Myaskovsky, whom he rated "100,000 times better than Oats

['Ovyosïch'—a pun on Steinberg's patronymic 'Oseyevich']," but he was loath to part from Nikolayev.[26]

Moscow was attractive for many reasons. Tanya Glivenko lived there. As importantly, Shostakovich was already thick with a spirited group of Myaskovsky's students at the Moscow Conservatory—Lev Oborin, Mikhaíl Kvadri, Vissarion Shebalin, Mikhaíl Starokadomsky, Yuriy Nikolsky, and Mikhaíl Cheremukhin—who proudly branded themselves the Moscow "Six." Kvadri, a brash and enterprising youth, drew Shostakovich into their orbit and, on the latter's trips to Moscow, included him in their activities. Back home, Shostakovich corresponded actively with members of the group with lively exchanges of opinions on music, each other's compositions, and the performances and performers they heard. Kvadri and his friends were eager to facilitate Shostakovich's transfer to Moscow. Shostakovich was also impressed with what he perceived as the more flexible and liberal academic environment at the Moscow Conservatory in contrast to the "stupid formalists" in Leningrad.[27] In the end, however, it seems that Sofya's reluctance to let her seventeen-year-old son out of the nest, coupled with a successful campaign to reinstate him as a piano student in the Academic course at the Leningrad Conservatory, prevented Shostakovich from concluding the transfer.

He set his sights instead on completing the composition course. After recuperating in the Crimea again in the summer of 1924, Shostakovich returned to Leningrad and, in October 1924, began to compose a symphony: "Now I'm writing a symphony (Conservatory task for this year), which is quite bad, but I have to write it so that I can have done with the Conservatory this year." [28] In the meantime, the family's material situation showed no improvement. When an official lending program was discontinued, his piano was removed, leaving Dmitriy to compete with Mariya and her students for the use of an old one that sounded like a "saucepan." Dmitriy was constantly broke. He suffered regularly from colds and bronchitis. In the hope of alleviating the poverty and buying peace of mind for his composing, he sat the qualifying exam for the job of cinema pianist; here he recalled that his lessons in improvisation of the summer of 1919 stood him in good stead.[29] In November 1924 he took a job at the Bright Reel cinema for 100 rubles a month, against the protests of his mother and sisters. He was optimistic initially about being able to keep the drudgery from affecting his creative exertions or his health. By early December he had completed the first two movements of his symphony, the second identified as a "scherzo," in piano score. Exactly how much he was able to salvage from his earlier exercises, from the movement criticized by Steinberg back in February, for instance, is unknown. He had been working simultaneously on another scherzo, orchestrating a work originally dating from 1923 referred to in some correspondence as his "Officer's scherzo," the Scherzo in E-flat Major, op. 7. The autograph score of this work is dated 15 October 1924. Shostakovich, however, underscored the grotesque in the two movements he had already completed of his symphony: "In general I am satisfied with the symphony. Not bad. A symphony like any other, although it really ought to be called a symphony-grotesque." [30] Shostakovich's designation on an autograph score dates the beginning of work on the composition as 1923;[31] another manuscript, however, dates the beginning of work as 1924, as does the composer in a 1926 letter.[32]

Shostakovich eagerly anticipated the visit of Kvadri, Oborin, Shebalin, and other of his Moscow chums to Leningrad at the end of December, even though he knew that his nightly job would prevent him from accompanying them to concerts and the theater. He had them over to share their music late one afternoon, after which he invited them to join him and attend the film; to their utter amazement, during his stint that evening Shostakovich reproduced precisely a complex piano sonata one of them had introduced an hour earlier.[33] Shostakovich also arranged for Lev Oborin to present a piano recital, his first public appearance in Leningrad, at the Circle of Friends of Chamber Music on 31 December 1924. Plans were launched to present a concert of Shostakovich's music in Moscow.

Shostakovich completed the slow, third movement of his symphony by mid-January 1925. Pleased with the result, he nonetheless succumbed to bouts of despair, worrying that his symphony would never get a performance, that it "will go into my bag and no further." [34] Overwork was taking its toll. The fourth movement did not come easily. On 15 February he confessed to Bogdanov-Berezovsky that he had made no progress with the finale, that he was "written out" after three movements.[35] Instead, he began to orchestrate the first movement and copy parts for the scherzo, hoping for a reading by the student orchestra. His mood was not improved by the unexpected unpleasantness of having to take his former boss at the Bright Reel cinema to court for nonpayment of salary: "I never thought I would have to sue someone, all the more so Volïnsky, whom I used to respect and whom I now see is just an exploiter and a cheat." [36]

In early March Shostakovich departed for three weeks to Moscow, where a joint concert of his chamber works with those of Shebalin was scheduled. His spirits were buoyed by the acceptance of several of his works for publication and the anticipated honorarium, as well as by the arrangement of other paying concerts. He reported home that Kvadri was "fattening him up" and that other friends were supplying him with good seats to the opera, Meyerhold's Theater, and the Moscow Art Theater. When there was time, he went to the circus.[37] In what was the first public performance of his music in Moscow, the concert he shared with Vissarion Shebalin on 20 March

1925 in the Small Hall of the Moscow Conservatory proved less than a resounding triumph for Shostakovich. Featured on his half of the program were performances of the Piano Trio, op. 8, *Three Fantastic Dances*, op. 5 (performed by the composer), *Three Pieces* for Cello and Piano, op. 9, and the Suite for Two Pianos, op. 6 (played by Oborin and the composer). Shebalin's music on the first half of the program, including a string quartet performed by the Moscow Conservatory Quartet (renamed in 1931 the Beethoven Quartet, this ensemble would later forge a close bond with Shostakovich in the creation of his own string quartets), was received more enthusiastically than that of the visiting composer from Leningrad, which upset Shostakovich. Preparing his mother to expect negative reviews, he adopted a defiant tone: "Let them write that Shostakovich doesn't have talent, that his works—excuse the expression—are dogs—. Just let them. We'll show them." [38]

Overriding the disappointment of the public reception of his music in Moscow, Shostakovich made the acquaintance and won the respect of valuable new friends, most significantly Boleslav Yavorsky. Yavorsky, a music theorist, pianist and teacher distinguished by his reputation for encyclopedic brilliance, artistic insight, and disdain for academic routine, was, at the time, a teacher at Moscow's First Musical Technical School and the chairman of the Music Section of the State Scientific Council. Taking the young composer under his wing, he played a formative role in Shostakovich's development over the next several years, serving as mentor, confidant, and friend. At critical junctures he exerted his influence unstintingly to further his protégé's career.

It was also at this time that Shostakovich was introduced by Kvadri to Mikhaíl Tukhachevsky, the Civil War hero who happened to be a passionate music-lover, amateur violinist, and violin-maker. After hearing some of Shostakovich's music, he offered to facilitate his relocation to Moscow. Invigorated by his acquaintance with Yavorsky, and freshly resolved to dedicate his life to music ("For me there is no joy in life other than music. All life for me is music" [39]), in April 1925 Shostakovich took Tukhachevsky up on his offer and renewed his efforts to transfer to Moscow, this time with the goal of studying with Yavorsky. His mother indicated her readiness to permit the move by autumn, if she could be assured that Mitya's welfare and health would be adequately safeguarded. Whether or not it was her reluctance that proved decisive the second time around, once again the plan to move to Moscow ultimately came to nothing.

In the meantime, contact with Yavorsky had given Shostakovich the encouragement he needed to complete his symphony. He took up the finale on his return to Leningrad and, juggling the heady intoxication of composition with his grief over the terminal illness of a friend, the young poet

Vladimir Kurchavov—which he blamed for the gloomy cast of the finale—
he completed the piano score of the symphony by the end of April. (He told
Yavorsky that he composed the finale "in a single breath" in less than a
week.[40]) Shostakovich dedicated his Symphony no. 1 to Mikhaíl Vladimirovich Kvadri.[41] On 6 May 1925, assisted by his friend Pavel Feldt, he performed his two-piano arrangement of the symphony for Glazunov,
Steinberg, and the rest of the Conservatory's composition faculty and students in the final exam for the composition course. Reactions varied.
Shostakovich reported, for instance, that Glazunov did not like the third
and fourth movements, but that overall his symphony was well received.
He expressed his own satisfaction with the entire work; he was especially
pleased with the finale.

On a trip to Moscow shortly after the exam, Shostakovich showed the
symphony to his friends. He was taken to meet Myaskovsky and reported
that the latter admired everything but the first movement of the symphony.
In June, he toiled at finishing the orchestration and making a fair copy of
the score. He affixed the official date of completion as 1 July 1925.[42]

A number of creative projects were put on hold by the tedious task of or-
chestrating and copying the symphony. In mid-June he had confided to
Yavorsky he was eager to begin a large piano sonata patterned after the Liszt
Sonata and that there were already ideas for a Second Symphony floating
around in his head. Later in the summer, as he vacationed in Oranienbaum,
on the outskirts of Leningrad, and then for two months in Slavyansk in the
Donbass region, Shostakovich picked up one of his interrupted projects, a
Suite for String Octet. In December 1924, parallel with the composition of
the First Symphony, he had completed a prelude and part of a fugue for four
violins, two violas, and two cellos. Abandoning the fugue, in the spring of
1925 he reformulated the concept into a Suite for Octet and began composing a scherzo, relishing the increasing modernism and astringent harmonies of his style. Work on the scherzo, which he touted as the "very best
thing I have ever written," was completed in Slavyansk. Although he started
a third movement and projected a suite consisting of a total of five movements, in the end only the prelude and scherzo were completed and paired
as *Two Pieces* for string octet, op. 11. They were dedicated to the memory of
his friend, Volodiya Kurchavov, who had died in the Crimea in June. Reluctant at first to show the newly written scherzo for string octet to Steinberg,
when he finally did, Shostakovich reported that the latter "made a sour face
and expressed the hope that, when I turn thirty, I will no longer write such
wild music." [43]

In mid-September, Shostakovich returned to the Leningrad Conservatory, where he was officially registered as a student of the "free composition" class on the Academic course. He may have been reluctant to share his

more radical compositional efforts with Steinberg, but he was still eager to benefit from the latter's expertise and practical advice on the orchestration and sound of his symphony. His skepticism of the reactionary musical tastes of Steinberg and Glazunov had not diminished his respect for their musicianship and orchestral authority. Shostakovich reported that Steinberg was satisfied with the first two movements, but they bickered over the third, and the teacher tried to persuade his pupil that the finale would be unperformable in tempo. Shostakovich, to the contrary, became increasingly convinced that only a live performance of his symphony would resolve others' misgivings and vindicate his own choices. To secure such a performance became his obsession during the winter of 1925–1926; his mood during this period seesawed frequently between self-confidence and insecurity, between optimism and despair.

His finances, meanwhile, showed no improvement. To pay off creditors, he was obliged in October to take a replacement position at the Splendid Palace cinema. He was pleased that at least this job did not require him to improvise as much as the one he had held the previous year and at 134 rubles a month, that the pay was also significantly improved, but he complained that playing the same music over and over again drove him crazy, preventing him from composing and practicing the piano. And he still managed to rub patrons the wrong way. One evening, while illustrating the evocatively titled film *Swamp and Water Birds of Sweden*, he was carried away in transports of evocative bird imagery when he heard a noisy eruption of clapping and sporadic catcalls from the audience. Puzzled, Shostakovich assumed that the film must be terrible. Afterward he was told that the audience had not been impressed by his flights of creative fancy and had thought he must be drunk. Far from being stung by the criticism, Shostakovich expressed his pride in having distracted their attention from the film.[44]

The urgent petition of Glazunov and the Conservatory directorate to contrive a trip abroad for the young composer on medical grounds ("in view of student Shestakovich's [sic] absolutely exceptional gifts") came to nothing.[45] Shostakovich may not even have known about the effort. By mid-December, he had liberated himself from the Splendid Palace and was optimistic that he might be able to start composing again. By the end of the month he reported having started work on a Second Symphony. Still in debt, however, he allowed himself to be flattered into accepting another film job, at the Picadilly cinema, where he drudged on reluctantly until March 1926. By then his prospects had improved and he was able to leave the cinema pit for good.

At the Conservatory, Shostakovich took up conducting classes with Nikolai Malko, the eminent conductor recently returned to Leningrad after

a seven-year absence to take up the duties of chief conductor of the Philharmonic. Although Shostakovich made fun of his prattling and name-
dropping in class, he gave him credit for knowing his craft. What would ultimately prove more important for their relationship, though, was the fact
that Malko was one of the most sympathetic and energetic propagandists of
new music in Russia. Thinking initially that the best he could hope for his
symphony was a student reading, Shostakovich considered conducting the
scherzo himself at one of the regular sessions on Fridays. Instead, he tremu-
lously screwed up his courage to ask for Steinberg's support and to show
the First Symphony to Malko. Yavorsky's enthusiastic recommendation
helped smooth the way for Malko's acceptance, in November 1925, of the
symphony for performance. And to Shostakovich's pleasant surprise,
Steinberg arranged to have the Conservatory cover the copying costs.

Additional backing came eventually from Boris Asafyev, a prominent figure in Leningrad new music circles, an influential arbiter of taste, and an associate and champion of the most progressive Western composers. Asafyev
had expressed interest in hearing Shostakovich's symphony as early as the
previous summer. He repeatedly put off the eager youngster, however,
which led Shostakovich to gripe about his conceited behavior. Nonetheless,
Shostakovich was greatly relieved and gratified by the praise Asafyev lav-
ished on his First Symphony when he finally heard it in December and by
his endorsement of the need both for performance and publication.

Asafyev subsequently forfeited Shostakovich's trust by staying away from
the premiere of the First Symphony. The putative excuse—Asafyev's petty
quarrel with the leadership of the sponsoring organization—offended the
young composer.[46] Very quickly, Shostakovich realized that Asafyev did not
measure up to his deep-seated conviction that "a truly great person is always simple, always modest, and always has his feet planted firmly on the
ground."[47] In 1927, he quipped that Asafyev was the most vulgar person
(*samïy bol'shoy poshlyak*) he knew.[48] In light of this information and
Asafyev's craven reaction to the savage attacks on Shostakovich in 1936 and
1948, as well as in the context of Asafyev's career as revered elder statesman
of Soviet musicology, Shostakovich's subsequent assertions—about the
formative role played by Asafyev on his artistic worldview, for instance, and
his influence on the composition of both *The Nose* and the piano suite *Aphorisms*[49] (works later appraised among the most flagrant of his "formalist"
aberrations)—were most likely indictments concocted ex post facto.[50]

The year 1926 began auspiciously. On New Year's Eve, Shostakovich
dreamed that he was walking in a desert when suddenly an old man appeared before him and predicted that he would have a lucky year.
Shostakovich resolved to finish his Second Symphony quickly; he claimed
he could already hear the whole work in his head. He also kept himself busy

correcting the parts for his First Symphony and gratifying a passion for chess. He was delighted when Yavorsky helped expedite a professional trip to Moscow in early February, all expenses paid, to promote his music and that of other Leningrad student composers at the Moscow Conservatory, and he was pleased with his reception there. He reported that Myaskovsky and other luminaries of the Association of Contemporary Music (ASM) had promised to include his symphony in their programs, that Yavorsky and Myaskovsky were determined to put pressure on Leningrad musicians to find him more suitable employment than film accompaniment, and that Tukhachevsky had found him a room and a job in Moscow, if he wanted it.[51] When he showed the symphony, the *Two Pieces* for octet, and the *Three Fantastic Dances* to the music panel of the State Music Publisher on 9 February 1926, he was thrilled that everything was accepted for publication.[52] He was finally beginning to make his mark in the world.

Shostakovich could no longer stomach the grind at the Picadilly, and on his return to Leningrad he submitted his resignation. Relishing his freedom, he resumed attendance at concerts and other entertainments. He was impressed by Fritz Stiedry's performance of Chaikovsky's Serenade for Strings and Stravinsky's *Rite of Spring*. He judged Prokofiev's *Love for Three Oranges*, which received its Russian premiere in Leningrad in February 1926, exceptionally good. The jazz band of Sam Wooding and the Chocolate Kiddies—who performed what was billed as a "negro operetta" at the Leningrad Music Hall during a three-month Russian tour—was, to Shostakovich, a musical revelation of America. The vitality and enthusiasm of the performers also made an indelible impression. And he was awestruck by the twelve ferocious Bengal tigers that formed a pyramid, rolled balls, and leaped through flaming hoops at the circus.

Early in March, Shostakovich collared the necessary players to give his octet a live reading and was so ecstatic with the result that he went around in a delirium for days. In April, he was unanimously selected for the newly reorganized graduate program in composition at the Leningrad Conservatory. In his testimonial, Steinberg indicated that Shostakovich had shown himself to be an unusually conscientious and diligent student, and that "Shostakovich is unquestionably the most talented representative of Leningrad's young composers."[53] But the major event of the spring was the long-awaited premiere of his First Symphony. In what was the first orchestral concert to be sponsored by the Leningrad Association for Contemporary Music (LASM), and the closing concert of the Philharmonic season, the program scheduled for early May also featured works by two other young composers: Joseph Schillinger's *March of the Orient* for large orchestra, and Yuliya Veysberg's cantata for chorus and orchestra, *The Twelve*. Shostakovich the perfectionist fretted for months in advance over every particular.

To his dismay, after the posters had already gone up the performance date was shifted from 8 May to 12 May, because on the earlier date a number of the brass players were required for a performance of *Salome* at the State Academic Theater of Opera and Ballet. Immediately after the first rehearsal, the composer phoned home in relief to report that everything was all right. Steinberg, who also attended the rehearsal, recorded that Mitya "is in indescribable raptures from his own music and the sound; I found it hard to restrain him from an unbridled display of his feelings." [54]

The success of Shostakovich's First Symphony, the first of his orchestral works to be performed, exceeded the composer's wildest expectations. Having stubbornly resisted the changes advised by older and more experienced composers, Shostakovich felt that his creative instincts and convictions had been vindicated conclusively. He was immensely satisfied with the way the work sounded, with all of its instrumental detail, and with the superb quality of the performance under Malko's direction. The enthusiastic reception accorded both the work—by popular demand the scherzo had to be repeated—and its nineteen-year-old composer was also cause for rejoicing. After the concert, a proud Mitya celebrated his success until the wee hours of the morning with family and guests, including Malko, Nikolayev, and Steinberg. The date of his triumphal debut as a symphonic composer, 12 May 1926, was an anniversary that Shostakovich commemorated for the rest of his life.

Contemporary critics of the First Symphony were somewhat more sober in their evaluation of the work than the first-night audience. Identifying the symphony's traditional style and accessible musical language, N. N. Strelnikov pointed to the fresh ideas, their versatile development, and the genuine talent permeating every measure as the unquestionable strengths of the work. But he was disappointed by the composer's inclination to substitute technique and external effect for any probing of emotional depth or psychological insight.[55] In singling out, in particular, the failure of the slow movement to fulfill its expressive mission, Strelnikov was not alone. Malko, too, found the third movement weak, and the critic M. M. Sokolsky thought it sounded a bit artificial. He concluded that "lyricism is not yet Shostakovich's domain." [56] But even the harshest criticisms of the symphony were framed relative to the composer's youth and exceptionally bright potential. Many recognized the parallel with the legendary debut of the sixteen-year-old Alexander Glazunov with his own First Symphony in 1882. Few left the concert without a keen awareness of having participated in a very special event, the debut of a major new symphonic composer.

1926–1928

3

Spreading Wings

I can't remember why now, but for a certain brief period after completion of the Conservatory I was suddenly terror-struck with misgivings about my call-ing as a composer. I couldn't compose a thing and in a fit of "disillusionment," I destroyed almost all my manuscripts. I regret that now, because among the burned manuscripts was, among other things, the opera The Gypsies *on the poem of Pushkin.*

Shostakovich was both exhilarated and exhausted after all the anticipation and anxiety of the months preceding the premiere of his First Symphony.[1] In the weeks following the debut, he was at loose ends; he longed to go south to Anapa for the summer to rest but griped that the Conservatory was only giving him eighty rubles for the trip, scarcely enough to cover the cost of "papirosï"[2] (the distinctive Russian cardboard-tipped cigarettes he smoked), and counted instead on the advance promised for the publication of his symphony. He started to write a piano concerto but abandoned it in disgust: "I am waiting for inspiration from above."[3] The fickleness of his muse was a source of ongoing concern to him.

In early July, Shostakovich departed for Kharkov, where Malko had pro-grammed a performance of his First Symphony for a summer park concert with the resident orchestra and had also prevailed, against local resistance, in having the unknown young composer-pianist invited as soloist in a per-formance of Chaikovsky's First Piano Concerto. In what was his first major concert tour, Shostakovich was depressed by the conditions he discovered; at the first rehearsal of his symphony, he found that the orchestra did not have the proper complement of performers, that there was a bad violin soloist, and that, instead of a grand piano, there was a "vile, tinkling upright." The performance, on 5 July, was humiliating for the inexperienced composer. As if the wretchedness of the provincial orchestra and the awful outdoor acoustics were not enough, as soon as Malko mounted the podium, a nearby pack of dogs began to bark loudly and long, to the great amusement of the audience. Shostakovich was mortified; he confessed that he felt as if he had watched ten hooligans rape his girlfriend without being able to do anything about it.[4] Nevertheless, there was a silver lining: money. Anticipating his impending performance with the orchestra under the same atrocious conditions, Shostakovich contemplated the harsh reality of engaging in musical "prostitution," something he believed he had forsaken forever when he gave up playing in movie houses. But although the dogs were again in attendance for his performance of the Chaikovsky concerto on 12 July, Shostakovich was pleased with the way he played. The success of this performance also led to an additional invitation (and an additional honorarium) for a recital on 15 July, at which, in addition to works by Liszt, a number of his own compositions (the *Eight Preludes, Fantastic Dances,* Piano Trio, and *Two Pieces* for string octet) were performed.

From Kharkov, Shostakovich traveled to Anapa on the Black Sea coast, where he and Tatyana Glivenko were reunited for a month of rest and recreation. He stopped in Moscow to visit Yavorsky on the return trip, and, home by the end of August, he reported that he had completed a big chunk of a piano sonata. Shostakovich made relatively rapid progress on the new work, even though he sometimes found it difficult to block out the sound of Czerny etudes played by Mariya's students in the next room. Completing his First Piano Sonata on 20 October 1926, Shostakovich played it to some of his Conservatory friends the same day; they found blood on the piano keys after he was done. When Shostakovich showed the sonata to Steinberg, the latter's disapproval of the modernist idiom was predictable; he was astounded to discover that Shostakovich could actually hear what he had written. Shostakovich gave the premiere of his Piano Sonata, op. 12, on 2 December 1926 at a concert in the Small Hall of the Philharmonic sponsored by the Leningrad Association of Contemporary Music. He rated the sonata's reception as more successful when he performed it again a week later before a smaller and more discriminating audience at the Circle of Friends of Chamber Music. Before giving the Moscow premiere in January 1927, he arranged to perform the brief work twice in the same concert.

Stylistic affinities between the sonata and *To October, a Symphonic Dedication,* op. 14, did not pass unnoticed when the latter work was first performed in 1927, which perhaps accounts for the attribution of a subtitle, "October" or "October Symphony," to the Piano Sonata by some of Shostakovich's contemporaries.[5] However no such subtitle is mentioned in Shostakovich's correspondence, nor did it appear in the program of the first performance, on the first publication of the work by Muzgiz in 1927, or in period worklists. Late in life, Shostakovich firmly denied ever having attributed a subtitle to this work.[6]

As a graduate student registered at the Leningrad Conservatory, Shostakovich was awarded a modest stipend. (Although his enrollment appears to have involved little more than an annual progress report, Shostakovich managed to extend his graduate status, and his stipend, until January 1930.) In the autumn of 1926 the composer also took up teaching. A reluctant instructor of score reading at the Central Music Technical School two days a week, Shostakovich groused that one group of his students was less advanced, the other even *less* advanced, and that many could not even play the piano.[7] He continued to perform in public, both as soloist and accompanist; one of his more extended partnerships was with the chamber singer Lidiya Vïrlan. And Shostakovich was especially thrilled to perform, on 12 December 1926, as one of the pianists in the Russian premiere of Stravinsky's *Wedding*.

The most significant development of the end of the year was the selection, engineered by Yavorsky, of Shostakovich to be one of five pianists representing the Soviet Union in the Chopin Competition set to take place in Warsaw in January 1927. The honor and responsibility of competing for the Soviet Union in its first appearance at an international piano competition were enormous. Shostakovich was not one of the most obvious candidates. He expressed ambivalence about competitions as such; what excited him about this particular one was the opportunity it afforded him to go abroad. Traveling, exploring new places, was something that stimulated the composer throughout his life. With less than a month to prepare his program, Shostakovich went into virtual seclusion.

There was one additional hurdle for Shostakovich to clear before going to Warsaw. As part of the newly reorganized curriculum at the Conservatory, graduate students were required to pass an exam in Marxist methodology. When notified of the date of the exam in late December, Shostakovich despaired in a letter to Yavorsky; he felt certain he would fail, resulting in 1) shame, 2) the loss of his stipend, and 3) being labeled a political unreliable. But that he did not take the matter very seriously is evidenced by the fact that in this same letter he lined out—thereby drawing attention to it—his initial designation of "Scriptures" as the discipline in question, substituting instead "Marxist methodology," and he joked about his pianistic versus political reliability.[8]

Most available information points to the conclusion that, as a youth, Shostakovich was not especially active politically, although he followed current events and was innately patriotic and civic-spirited. In letters to Tanya Glivenko, he revealed a supportive stance toward communism, as well as a disdain not uncommon among the intelligentsia for the fruits of the New Economic Policy (NEP). He greeted the news of Lenin's death in January 1924 with grief—according to his sister Mariya, their father used to tell them that they were distantly related to Lenin[9]—but he was indignant about the plan to rename the city on the Neva in his honor, reasoning that Lenin, a man opposed to ceremony, would have opposed it.[10] (He mailed more than one letter in 1924 from "St. Leninburg.") To his musical correspondents, however, he rarely mentioned politics at all; the possibility cannot be ruled out that his comments to Tanya were responsive to her own interests and convictions. There is little credible evidence, for instance, to suggest that the figure of Lenin was a meaningful influence behind the creation of the First Symphony, as has been claimed.[11]

Viewed in retrospect, the story of Shostakovich's exam in Marxist methodology in the last week of December 1926 seems an ominous prescription for early martyrdom, although the still politically naive Shostakovich recounted it to Yavorsky simply as an amusing anecdote. The exam was conducted orally for a group of five students by a commission. When one of the students was asked to explain the difference, from the sociological and economic standpoints, between the work of Chopin and Liszt, his answer induced prolonged fits of hysterical laughter from Shostakovich and another classmate. Offended by the outburst, an "elegant" Marxist quizzed Shostakovich about his reading preparation, concluding that the student could in no way be prepared to answer questions about the sociological principle of Bach's system of temperament and Scriabin's timbral aggregates. Shostakovich was summarily dismissed from the exam. When he realized that, in fact, he had been dismissed without even being given the opportunity to answer a single question, Shostakovich successfully appealed to the secretary of the commission for re-examination, demanding also the re-examination of the student whose exam his behavior had disrupted. Both were tested again the next day. Both passed without further consequence.[12]

Shostakovich was in Moscow to attend the premiere, on 9 January 1927, of his *Two Pieces* for octet and to give the local debut of his Piano Sonata. Five days later, together with the other designated competitors—Muscovites Yuriy Bryushkov, Grigoriy Ginzburg, and Lev Oborin and Leningrader Iosif Shvarts—Shostakovich presented his Chopin competition program (Polonaise in F-sharp Minor, Nocturnes in F-sharp Major and C-sharp Minor, Mazurkas in B Minor and C-sharp Minor, Etudes in C-sharp

Minor and A-flat Major,[13] and Ballade in A-flat Major) to a discriminating audience in the Large Hall of the Moscow Conservatory. At first, Shostakovich was nervous. He could not anticipate the level of competition, and he did not want to embarrass himself or his supporters. But in his letter home he reported his triumph, the enthusiastic response of the audience, and the protective pride of Yavorsky.[14] The critics were more guarded in their evaluations of Shostakovich's performance, some finding his playing still technically unpolished.

Shostakovich's train trip to Warsaw was trouble-free. Of the thirty-one competitors (seventeen Polish and fourteen foreigners), he was fortunate to draw the penultimate lot because, after attending the opening of the competition on 23 January, he was forced to return to his hotel because of a stomach ache. His ailment was diagnosed as appendicitis, a fact he wanted kept secret from his overanxious mother. With medication and rest, he recovered from the attack in time to make his first appearance in the competition on 27 January. Even in the short period since his Moscow concert, he had refined his technique and polished his program discernibly. He performed well enough to make the final round of eight competitors, playing Chopin's First Concerto with orchestra.

Despite what he felt was the overwhelming success of his appearances, the enthusiastic public ovations, and his self-confident assessment that the choice for top honors was between himself and Oborin, Shostakovich was left out of the prizes, receiving only an honorable mention. His friend Oborin was awarded first prize and another of the Russians, Ginzburg, finished in fourth place, but in an outcome as controversial as it was unexpected, the all-Polish jury awarded the second and third prizes to Polish pianists. Shostakovich subsequently consoled his mother with the news that a sympathetic jury member had slipped him their tally, according to which he should have received third prize behind Oborin and Ginzburg. However, when the jury members contemplated the national disgrace should all the prizes be awarded to the Russians, they apparently juggled the results.[15] Shostakovich did his best to master his disappointment. In an autobiographical essay written later in the year, he blamed his lack of success on the pain from appendicitis.[16] Following another serious attack, Shostakovich's appendix was removed in Leningrad on 24 April 1927.

Shostakovich's success with the public and press at the Chopin competition did not go unrewarded. An extra concert appearance was arranged for Oborin and Shostakovich in Warsaw on 5 February 1927, at which, in addition to works by Chopin and Beethoven's *Appassionata*, Shostakovich played his own sonata, reporting that the audience applauded it warmly and that the concert was a colossal success.[17] His pride was intact. And the honorarium from this concert provided Shostakovich the means to realize one of his secret ambitions for the trip: to travel to Berlin ("a magical city ... I could not have imagined anything like it" [18]), where he and Oborin spent a week. Unfortunately, neither time nor finances proved sufficient for the hoped-for visit to Vienna as well.

Back home, Sergey Prokofiev was in the midst of a triumphant homecoming tour, appearing in Moscow, Leningrad, and Ukrainian cities for the first time since his departure from Russia in 1918 after the Revolution. Shostakovich was a devoted admirer of the thirty-five-year-old musician. On Shostakovich's twentieth birthday in 1926, Nikolai Malko presented Shostakovich with the score of Prokofiev's First Piano Concerto, which became a staple of his concert repertory. And when Shostakovich learned that Prokofiev was expected to visit Leningrad in January 1927, he was very excited: "I would love to hear how he plays, and I have an immodest desire to meet him. For all that, this is one of my favorite composers and not only of contemporaries, but overall. I don't know whether I will succeed in making his acquaintance." [19] The young composer did not leave a meeting to chance; on 30 October 1926, Prokofiev acknowledged and returned the greetings Shostakovich had enclosed with one of Yavorsky's letters.[20]

Shostakovich arrived back in Leningrad in time to hear Prokofiev's performance of his Second Piano Concerto with Malko on 19 February 1927, as well as his solo recital on 22 February. Shostakovich thought Prokofiev performed brilliantly, but he did not care for the Overture for Seventeen Instruments (op. 42), and when Malko introduced the two at intermission at the first of the concerts, he did not warm to Prokofiev as much as he had expected to. The next evening, Vladimir Shcherbachov hosted a gathering of young composers in Prokofiev's honor, providing them the opportunity to introduce their music to the distinguished guest. Shostakovich, the second person to perform—after Joseph Schillinger—played his recently composed sonata. Prokofiev recorded in his diary:

> The second person to play is Shostakovich, a very young man who is not only a composer but also a pianist. He gives me the score and plays boldly, by heart. His sonata starts with lively two-part counterpoint in Bach-like style. In the second movement, which follows without a break, the harmonic style is quite mellow and there is a melody in the middle—nice enough, but diffuse and a bit too long. This Andante changes into a fast Finale which, compared to the rest, is disproportionately short. And yet, after Schillinger, it is so much more lively and interesting that I am happy to start praising Shostakovich. Asafyev laughs at me, saying I like Shostakovich so much because the first movement is so clearly influenced by me. [21]

Shostakovich recorded that Prokofiev had asked him to play the beginning slower, finding it hard to understand. And Nikolayev told him that Prokofiev had liked the sonata, especially the first movement.[22]

(The young Shostakovich had the opportunity to meet other musical luminaries visiting Leningrad in the 1920s. He played his trio for Franz Schreker in October 1925, his First Symphony for Darius Milhaud in the spring of 1926 and for Bruno Walter in early January 1927; the latter undertook to conduct its first foreign performance in Berlin the following year.[23] Shostakovich was introduced to Alban Berg at the premiere of *Wozzeck* in June 1927; after hearing a performance of the First Symphony in Vienna a year later, Berg sent him a congratulatory letter. In 1928, Shostakovich encountered Artur Honegger during his Russian visit. Although Shostakovich attended Bela Bartók's concerts in January 1929, he did not have the opportunity to meet him.)

It is not surprising, perhaps, after his intensive immersion in the music of Chopin for the Warsaw competition, and still elated from his exposure to Prokofiev, that when Shostakovich resumed composing, his initial efforts took the form of a suite of piano miniatures. In quick succession, between 25 February and 7 April 1927, Shostakovich produced a series of ten laconic genre studies. Stylistic expectations evoked by the commonplace designations (Recitative, Serenade, Nocturne, Elegy, Funeral March, Etude, Dance of Death, Canon, Legend, and Lullaby) were belied by the composer's unconventional approach. The pieces were all extremely short; the Elegy had only eight measures and the Nocturne used no bar lines at all. With brittle linearity and dissonance the composer continued to shake off academic shackles. Initially intending to produce a suite of twelve pieces, Shostakovich discarded two of them, and on Yavorsky's advice he titled the completed collection *Aphorisms*.

While producing the *Aphorisms*, Shostakovich received his first commission. In late March he accepted the invitation of the Agitotdel (Propaganda Division) of the State Publishers' Music Section to compose a symphonic work in honor of the tenth anniversary of the Revolution. He wrote Tanya Glivenko of a preliminary whim that had found encouragement from the Propaganda Division: "at the very end I have decided to introduce factory hooters tuned to a certain key." [24] In early June, when he had written about twelve minutes of music and reached the appropriate spot in his score, he went to a factory to test hooters and determine the precise specifications.[25]

In the periodic progress reports he made to friends, Shostakovich betrayed a notable lack of enthusiasm for work on his "patriotic" score (other nicknames he employed were "revolutionary" music, "October" and "Oktyabrina"). Although he found enjoyment in tackling the purely musical challenges, he had to keep prodding himself in order to meet the 1 August deadline. Whether the decision to append a choral section was stipulated in the original commission is unclear, as is how the selection of the poet was made, but from the moment he saw them, the composer was

mortified by the poor quality of Alexander Bezïmensky's verses,[26] which
trace over four stanzas the progression from the suffering and oppression
of prerevolutionary workers ("We came, we begged for work and bread.
Our hearts were gripped in the clutches of despair") to their unity in
the struggle led by Lenin ("We understood, Lenin, that our fate bears the
name: struggle!") to the ultimate triumph of the October Revolution
("October! It is the herald of the awaited sun. October! It is the will of
rebellious ages"). Shostakovich found the verses "repulsive" and was not
optimistic about his ability to redeem them musically. In May, fresh from
reading Maupassant, he devised an effective motivational strategy to keep
himself toiling: he vowed he would take the 500 rubles he was to receive for
the commission and invest them in a trip to Paris. Unfortunately, by early
July, Shostakovich's application for travel authorization had been rejected.
But by then he was over the hump and the composition was nearly
complete.

   This was a hybrid work, consisting of a single, episodic movement with
concluding chorus executed as a graphic musical "placard," an aural counterpart to the revolutionary mass spectacles and allegorical dramatizations
popular during the early Soviet period. The title was fixed belatedly. Early
sources referred to the composition formally as "Symphonic Poem" or
"Symphonic Dedication to October"; it was published in 1927 under the title *To October, a Symphonic Dedication*, op. 14. It was only christened a
"symphony"—Symphony no. 2, *Dedication to October*, op. 14—considerably later. In a promotional flyer issued by the State Music Publishers in
mid-1929,[27] the work is still identified simply as "Dedication 'to October'
for Orchestra and Chorus, op. 14."[28] The legend that Shostakovich transformed his own memory of witnessing the killing of a boy during a worker's
uprising on Nevsky Prospect in July 1917 into the episode in the Second
Symphony that precedes the entry of the chorus[29] is complicated by information in one of his letters to Yavorsky. There Shostakovich tags the just-
written passage, which he judges successful, with the unofficial title "Death
of a Child."[30] Offering no explanation, he plunges directly into a lengthy
encomium for Pyotr Voykov—the Soviet ambassador to Poland, assassinated there on 7 July 1927—expressing his deep distress and personal grief
at the loss of someone who had gone above and beyond the call of duty
looking after him during his stay in Warsaw.[31] There appears, incidentally,
to be no connection at all between this work and the "Second Symphony"
Shostakovich had reported embarking on in January 1926, a work evidently
abandoned soon thereafter.

   The family's financial situation was still far from comfortable. It was just
as well that his Parisian fantasy unraveled; after his sister lost her job in the
summer of 1927, the entire family was dependent on his income and his

honorarium was needed to pay debts. Still, Shostakovich's wanderlust did not disappear. Tantalized, no doubt, by the travel stories of Yavorsky and others, Shostakovich applied and was rejected again the following summer for a foreign travel grant. His mother's repeated scheming, however, to establish her talented but still sickly son in America—in 1923, her sister, Nadezhda, had emigrated with her husband to the United States, where a brother-in-law had also settled after fleeing the Revolution—appears to have received no encouragement from her son.

Another distraction Shostakovich devised for himself while laboring on *To October* was the inception of a new and more stimulating project, his first opera. On 12 June 1927—coincidentally, the day before the Leningrad premiere, in the presence of the composer, of Alban Berg's *Wozzeck*—Shostakovich alerted Yavorsky that as soon as he finished his symphonic poem he intended to get to work on an operatic setting of "The Nose," Nikolai Gogol's tale of the preposterous misadventure of a tsarist civil servant, to a libretto he would write himself.[32] Reacting to Yavorsky's understandable incredulity about the subject matter, on 2 July Shostakovich reiterated his intention to compose an opera on "The Nose" and, while acknowledging that he could not yet devote himself to it full time because *October* was not done, he admitted he had already composed the overture and several bits of the opera itself.[33] Ultimately, he sought some assistance for the libretto; while he took responsibility for the bulk of Acts I and II himself, he shared responsibility for Act III with Georgiy Ionin and Alexander Preys. Although Yevgeniy Zamyatin received billing as one of the librettists, the extent of his contribution is unclear; in print, Shostakovich credited him with the authorship of a single scene in Act I, but shortly before the premiere of the opera the composer declared that he had deemed Zamyatin's contributions unsuccessful and discarded them.[34]

The genesis of Shostakovich's opera coincided with the beginning of the closest friendship of his life. The composer later reminisced that he remembered having being introduced to Ivan Ivanovich Sollertinsky first in 1921, but their second meeting in 1926 was unforgettable. It obviously took place just before that same exam in Marxist methodology in December 1926 that nearly proved the composer's undoing:

> A large number of Leningrad students were taking an exam in Marxism-Leninism in order to qualify for graduate study. Among those waiting to be called before the examination commission was Sollertinsky.
>
> Before the exam I was extremely nervous. We were examined in alphabetical order. Presently, Sollertinsky was called in by the commission. He came out again very quickly. I plucked up courage and asked him: "Please would you tell me, was the exam very difficult?" "No, not at all," he answered. "What did they ask you?" "The simplest of questions: the origins of materialism in Ancient Greece; the po-

etry of Sophocles as an expression of materialist tendencies; English seventeenth-century philosophers and something else as well."

Need I add that Ivan Ivanovich's account of the exam instilled me with terror?[35]

Sollertinsky's extraordinary intellect, encyclopedic erudition, and passion for music were already well known in Leningrad. His mischievous sense of humor was but another trait Shostakovich would soon come to appreciate.

Born in 1902 in Vitebsk, Sollertinsky's interests, expertise, and phenomenal memory encompassed disciplines ranging from philosophy, linguistics, and languages, ancient and modern, to the history of the literature and drama of numerous cultures and periods. He lectured on these topics and others at many academic institutions in Leningrad. Although largely self-trained, Sollertinsky developed an intense commitment to music and was an inveterate concertgoer. From the mid-1920s, he began to assert himself as one of Leningrad's most learned and perceptive critics, initially with a concentration on theater and ballet and subsequently, especially after his acquaintance with Shostakovich, with a focus more on the symphonic literature and music theater. From 1929 he served as the extremely popular concert lecturer at the Leningrad Philharmonic, functioning increasingly as an influential artistic adviser there as well as in Leningrad's music theater circles.

The fast friendship between Shostakovich and Sollertinsky dates from the spring of 1927. Nikolai Malko claimed to have introduced them;[36] undoubtedly this took place at his birthday celebration on 4 May 1927. As Shostakovich recalled:

> There were few guests, maybe four including Sollertinsky and myself. The time passed quickly, without our noticing. I was utterly amazed when Sollertinsky turned out to be an unusually merry, simple, brilliantly witty, and entirely "down-to-earth" person.... Our excellent host kept us until late, and Sollertinsky and I walked home.... During the conversation it emerged that I didn't know a single foreign language, while he couldn't play the piano. So the very next day Sollertinsky gave me my first lesson in German and I gave him a lesson on the piano.[37]

The exchange of lessons did not last long; Shostakovich never mastered German, nor did Sollertinsky learn to play the piano, but the two men became absolutely inseparable: "They had an insane friendship. Sollertinsky came to see us every day in the morning and stayed until the evening. They spent the whole day together, laughing and chuckling.... On the days they didn't meet, Mitya and Ivan Ivanovich wrote to each other." [38]

Shostakovich and Sollertinsky were kindred spirits uniquely able to challenge and divert each other. Sollertinsky's effortless command of languages, literature, and cultural history unlocked new doors for a composer-pianist whose academic education had been cut short on his entry into the Conservatory. Even in the sphere of music, Shostakovich credited his friend with "always trying to expand my world-view.... Sollertinsky cultivated my interest in music, as they say, 'from Bach to Offenbach.'" [39] Shostakovich's exploration of the music of Mahler was but one of the more fruitful pursuits nourished by his contact with Sollertinsky. For his own part, Sollertinsky recognized and treasured the creative genius of his friend, to whom he offered an invaluable source of stimulus and support. Insecure with words, as early as mid-1928 Shostakovich turned to his articulate associate for help in framing his ideas for publication. It seems likely that Sollertinsky continued to cast a beneficent editorial eye over his friend's published writings at least until 1936. For that matter, it seems equally likely that the aesthetic positions reflected in Sollertinsky's criticism owed at least something to Shostakovich's impeccable musical ear and professional acumen.

It is noteworthy that shortly after Shostakovich befriended Sollertinsky, the number of letters from the composer to Yavorsky (or at least those preserved) dropped off sharply. It is difficult to avoid the conclusion that Sollertinsky, who was only four years older than the composer and lived in the same city, quickly came to replace Yavorsky as Shostakovich's mentor and confidant. With shared tastes and enthusiasms in intellectual and artistic matters as well as in amusements and social pursuits, with shared indifference to material comforts and a shared sense of humor, Sollertinsky was an almost ideal companion for and alter ego to Shostakovich.

In the fall of 1927, after a six-week vacation in Detskoye Selo, where he met the woman, Nina Varzar, who would eventually become his wife, Shostakovich resumed work on his opera *The Nose* and prepared for the premiere of his *October*. The conductor Malko, who was increasingly disturbed by the young composer's stubbornness and vanity, noted that Shostakovich had almost unreasonable expectations of the performers at rehearsals, demanding very fast tempi. Extremely reluctantly, Shostakovich was persuaded to compromise by substituting *spiccato* for *pizzicato* in one spot. After the first performance—by the Leningrad Philharmonic and Academic Capella under Malko, at 11:45 PM on 5 November, in conclusion to a concert-meeting honoring educational workers (the performance was repeated the following evening at a similar event honoring scientific workers)—Shostakovich sent a lengthy list of expressive nuances and refinements to Konstantin Saradzhev, the conductor scheduled to lead the Moscow premiere.[40]

"In *To October* I tried to convey the pathos of struggle and victory," declared the composer in a contemporary report; he classified the manner in which the predominantly polyphonic composition unfolds as "dialectically linear."[41] Shostakovich was proud of the technical prowess he was able to display, manifest most imposingly at the climax of the instrumental portion of the score with the superimposition of thirteen independent instrumental cadenzas climaxing in overlapping waves of chromatic scales and twenty-two-voice "ultra-polyphony." Already in the summer, he had tested the score on "four workers and one peasant," musically untutored. Understandably, they found the "ultra-polyphony" tough going. But the composer claimed they went into ecstasies over the chorus—diatonic and securely tonal, it contrasts sharply with the instrumental section—and attempted to sing it.[42]

Shostakovich registered his satisfaction with the public reception of *To October*, and the critics reacted positively to its embodiment of the revolutionary theme. At a repeat performance on 26 November, a "storm of enthusiastic applause" propelled the composer out to take ten bows.[43] Steinberg, Shostakovich's erstwhile teacher, was skeptical: "Shostakovich's piece *October* is the absolute emancipation from any kind of 'verticality.' If one eliminates memories of music, then some spots sound relatively imposing. But surely this can't really be the 'new art.' Perhaps it is just a youngster's mischief."[44] Nikolai Myaskovsky, who had approved Shostakovich's prospective transfer to his class at the Moscow Conservatory three-and-a-half years earlier, confided his own view in a letter to Boris Asafyev: "You know I don't like his [Shostakovich's] music. But he touches a raw nerve; you don't admire him and follow his stunts with as much interest as you do Popov's, but his music simply and spontaneously thrills you. I spat at the rehearsals of *To October*—it was just as disgusting as rehearsals of Stravinsky—but in concert the piece simply stunned me; everything was so forceful, everything in the right place, so concise and yet so interestingly and consummately laid out. He's a disagreeable boy, but a really major talent."[45] Despite the generally favorable critical regard for what was one of the first expressions of the revolutionary theme in music, and its receipt of a prize in a contest sponsored by the Leningrad Philharmonic,[46] Shostakovich's *To October* did not establish itself in the repertory.

Early in 1928, Shostakovich embarked on a new adventure. He moved to Moscow—arriving in time to hear the Moscow premiere of his First Symphony on 8 January—to assume a temporary position as pianist at the Meyerhold Theater. Shostakovich had long been fascinated with Vsevolod Meyerhold's uniquely innovative approach to the dramatic stage and with the fundamental role it assigned to musical principles; he saw Meyerhold's productions when the company toured in Leningrad and took advantage of his own trips to Moscow to attend performances there. His conception for an opera on "The Nose" was deeply indebted to the work of Meyerhold, most particularly to his landmark production of Gogol's *Inspector General* in 1926. His predecessor as pianist at the Meyerhold Theater was his friend Leo Arnshtam, who claimed he recommended Shostakovich for the job as his replacement. However, Shostakovich's name was not unknown to Meyerhold. Nikolai Malko, diligent champion of the young composer, had introduced the First Symphony to the director the previous summer.

In Leningrad in the fall of 1927, Meyerhold phoned Shostakovich and invited him out to supper to make his acquaintance. He and his wife, the actress Zinaída Raikh, persuaded the young composer to stay with them on his next trip to Moscow. In a thank you note written after his return from this trip, Shostakovich gushed: "I remember my entire stay with you with delight. I've never had such a wonderful time in Moscow as on my last trip. As for your theater, it is the most remarkable thing I have ever seen in my life." [47] Shostakovich was flattered and excited by Meyerhold's interest in *The Nose*. Nevertheless, when Meyerhold extended an invitation to the composer shortly afterward to come to work in the Meyerhold Theater temporarily, Shostakovich—proud and ever mindful of his own worth— held out for a generous salary: "I will not sell my freedom cheaply." [48]

While he worked at the theater, Shostakovich lodged in the Meyerhold household, where he completed Act I and sketched Act II of *The Nose* under the encouraging eye of his host. One incident made an indelible impression on the composer: "A serious fire once broke out at his [Meyerhold's] flat. I was out at the time, but he gathered up all my manuscripts and returned them to me in perfect condition. I was amazed, after all, there were far more valuable things that could have burned." [49] Despite his enthusiasm for Meyerhold's theater, Shostakovich's duties as head of the music division— chiefly supervisory and performing onstage or in the pit during performances—left no room for creative initiative and were not calculated to sustain his interest for long. Meyerhold's musical instincts were less venturesome than his dramatic ones, and he probably kept the young composer on a tight leash. [50]

For his own part, Shostakovich lampooned the self-absorbed conceits of his hosts when he wrote home to Sollertinsky: "I am living here in an environment of geniuses (a genius director, 'a genius actress,' 'Akh, Zinka! How well you acted yesterday. It was genius'), a 'genius' composer and a 'genius' poetess. The last two are the offspring of the 'genius' poet Yesenin and the 'genius' actress." [51] After two months in Meyerhold's employ, Shostakovich left the theater and returned to Leningrad. The opportunity to collaborate with the director in a more creative capacity would come soon.

In the meantime, the composer's major task was to complete his opera, which he accomplished in the summer of 1928. In May, he auditioned the first two acts of *The Nose* before the Artistic Council of the Leningrad opera houses. The opera was accepted for production at the Malïy Opera Theater and initially scheduled for the 1928–1929 season. Urgently in need of an "experimental" production to rejuvenate its own repertory and finding Shostakovich's opera suitably "leftist" in its musical potential, Moscow's Bolshoy Theater also auditioned and accepted *The Nose* for staging.[52] The Bolshoy hired Meyerhold to mount this production, but it was repeatedly postponed and never got off the ground. Anxious to hear something of his new opus in live performance, Shostakovich quickly fashioned a suite of seven numbers from *The Nose*, which was first performed by Malko in Moscow on 25 November 1928.

Shostakovich subsequently calculated that, although work on *The Nose* had been spread out over a year, it took him a month to compose Act I, two weeks to write Act II, and three to write Act III. Zoya recalled that her brother encountered difficulty when working on the third act: "It simply wouldn't come. But then I remember him coming into our living room one morning and telling us that he had heard the whole of the third act in a dream; he there and then sat down and wrote it all out."[53] His mother later relayed the essence of the dream in more detail. Under deadline pressure and creatively blocked, Shostakovich dreamed that he was late for the dress rehearsal of his opera and managed to arrive at the theater only in time to hear the performance of the third act from the back of the hall. The audience responded enthusiastically. On waking, the excited composer hastened to write down what he had heard in his dream, finishing the opera in a matter of days.[54]

Even if somewhat romanticized, this instance of subconscious musical revelation was not isolated. For Shostakovich composition was not something that typically came as the result of conscious struggle or painstaking application. Most often he was able to conceptualize a work in its entirety and produce his music quickly, as the inspiration struck him, without detailed sketches or corrections. Contemporaries marveled at his total concentration, his ability to block out everything around him, his discipline, his speed. "I always found it amazing that he never needed to try things out on the piano. He just sat down, wrote out whatever he heard in his head, and then played it through complete on the piano.... He never demanded or appeared to need silence in order to compose."[55] As a lodger in the Shostakovich apartment on Marat Street for five years beginning in 1929, film director Sergey Yutkevich recalled that he never observed the composer "working."[56] Later in life Shostakovich described his aversion to revising: "If it turns out badly, let the work remain as is—I will try to avoid my earlier mistakes in the next.... When I find out that a composer has made eleven versions of one symphony, I think involuntarily, how many new works might he have written in that time?" [57]

Shostakovich's facility was also a source of pride. Legend has it that on a dare from Malko he was given an hour to orchestrate from memory the foxtrot "Tea for Two" from Vincent Youmans's musical *No, No, Nanette*, popularized in Russia under the name "Tahiti Trot." He dashed it off in forty-five minutes. This incident must have taken place sometime before October 1927.[58] Malko was so pleased with the result that after giving the premiere at the same Moscow concert in November 1928 with the suite from *The Nose* and another trifle, the transcription for winds of *Two Pieces by Scarlatti*, he included it in numerous concerts. Shostakovich subsequently incorporated the number in his ballet, *The Golden Age*. As we will see, by 1930 Shostakovich would have cause to regret the celebrity of his hasty arrangement.

1929–1932 **4**

Pioneer

Shostakovich's professionalism and facility were to prove indispensable during a period of intensive, pioneering activity as composer for the dramatic theater, ballet, and film that began in late 1928. That summer, the directors of Leningrad's Sovkino had fielded a bold new proposal: to hire a professional composer to furnish music designed expressly to complement and enhance a specific silent film. The benefits of such an enterprise were by no means self-evident; the mediocre conductors who routinely stitched together patchworks of musical clichés for their theater orchestras, together with legions of theater pianists, were almost guaranteed to fight the incursion into their domain. There were myriad practical problems to be dealt with as well. Nevertheless, Sovkino announced that directors Grigoriy Kozintsev and Leonid Trauberg were already scouting for a composer to provide the musical scenario for their upcoming film, *The New Babylon*, a story of the Paris Commune of 1871. By late December they had picked the composer they wanted to launch the experiment. For a fee of 2,000 rubles, Shostakovich contracted to deliver the piano score for *The New Babylon* on 1 February 1929, and full score and parts for a normal fourteen-piece theater orchestra on 1 March 1929. Trauberg recalled that Shostakovich studied the editing sheets carefully, requested the chronometer timings for each scene, watched each part of the film twice and "two weeks later brought us the finished music for the whole film (an hour and a half of music)." [1] On 20

February, the day after the completed film had passed muster, Shostakovich's music was screened and accepted by the artistic panel at Sovkino,
which concluded, "This music is distinguished by its considerable closeness
to the style and rhythm of the film, by great emotional strength and
expressivity. The effect of the picture is greatly heightened. Furthermore,
despite the originality and freshness of the form, the music is sufficiently
simple and can be appreciated by the mass viewer." The panel recommended that the necessary measures be taken to ensure the performance of
Shostakovich's score during screenings of the film.[2]

When the film was released on 18 March, the effort met with humiliating
failure. Liberal errors in the distributed scores and parts, insufficient rehearsals, lack of ensemble coordination, plus a certain amount of hostility
(and perhaps outright sabotage) among conductors led to the ousting of
Shostakovich's music in the majority of Leningrad theaters by the second or
third day. Part of the explanation for the disaster stemmed from the fact
that less than three weeks before the release, the directors had been obliged
by the censors in Moscow to re-edit the film, leaving Shostakovich the task
of substantially rewriting his score and recopying the parts. Working day
and night despite a case of the flu, he was unable to stem the large number
of mistakes in the materials.[3] In an article that argued the merits of music
written specially for film, Shostakovich had hinted at another danger facing
live film scores when he attacked the scandalous practice of projectionists
speeding up films in order to squeeze two showings into a single evening: to
change the speed of a film was a sure way to ruin its music.[4] Trauberg recalled of the premiere of *The New Babylon*: "The orchestra, unused to the
harmonies and rhythms of the young composer, became separated from
the screen. On screen a frenzied dance seethed, while in the orchestra there
was a funeral march."[5] A sympathetic critic complained that the music had
been performed abominably everywhere.[6] Shostakovich came to his own
defense, recruiting Sollertinsky's support as well, but to no avail. The experiment was stillborn.

Far from forswearing work in films after this experience, Shostakovich
soon accepted Kozinstev and Trauberg's invitation to contribute to one of
Russia's first dramatic sound-films, *Alone*, which was completed in mid-
1930 as a silent film, with soundtrack added the next year (it was released in
October 1931). Shostakovich was given considerable creative autonomy in
what was essentially a nonspeaking film, dramatizing through his music the
contemporary story of a young Leningrad schoolmistress sent to work in
the depths of Siberia. Equally adventurous was his score for *Golden Mountains* (released in November 1931), a talking film directed by Yutkevich
about the transformation of a Russian peasant into a revolutionary worker,
which had also been started as a silent film. Unfortunately, the state of the

technology was not yet up to the sophisticated expectations; because of Moscow's overloaded power circuits, at the premiere of *Golden Mountains* the film ran sluggishly and the soundtrack "wheezed and gurgled in an inconceivably low bass register!" [7] This accident, however, did not forestall eventual appreciation of the uncommon expressive role played by the music in assuring the film's success.

At precisely the same time as he was realizing the fleeting potential of live film scores with *The New Babylon*, another opportunity presented itself that Shostakovich could not refuse. After Prokofiev telegrammed Meyerhold from Paris on 3 January 1929 declining the invitation to write the music for his staging of Vladimir Mayakovsky's new play, *The Bedbug*, Meyerhold turned to Shostakovich. The composer later conceded that he had not especially liked the play, but he had been swayed by Meyerhold's conviction and authority. [8] He also recalled that the eccentric poet had quite distinct ideas about the kind of music he wanted for his "magical comedy": "Mayakovsky asked me: 'Do you like firemen's bands?' I said that sometimes I do and sometimes I don't. And Mayakovsky answered that he liked firemen's music best and that firemen's music was the kind I should write for *The Bedbug*." [9] Shostakovich's flair for the grotesque allowed him to hold his own in what must have been intimidating company. He contributed an appropriately impish musical component to the scathing satire of the new bourgeois spirit. Describing the effect of the lengthy instrumental entr'acte that concluded part one of the play, a witness reported: "The cacophony was indescribable! Some people covered their ears from such music, others—they were in the majority—construed the intermezzo as a purely comic effect and laughed wholeheartedly." [10] Meyerhold was heard to comment of the music, "That'll clean out brains!" [11] *The Bedbug* opened successfully in Moscow on 13 February 1929,[12] generating a spirited critical debate that, by revealing an increasingly intolerant critical stance toward satire, foreshadowed the rapidly encroaching dictatorship of proletarian cultural watchdogs.

As if working on *The New Babylon* in Leningrad and commuting to Moscow to deliver numbers for *The Bedbug* were not enough, among other activities during the first two months of 1929 Shostakovich also began teaching at Leningrad's Choreographic Tekhnikum (where Galina Ulanova remembered him as an instructor of music theory), played Prokofiev's Piano Concerto no. 1 in a Philharmonic concert (3 February), and—performing a favor for the team who were continuing to prepare the production of his own opera—contributed two numbers, an interlude and finale, for the Malïy Opera Theater's production of Erwin Dressel's opera *Der arme Columbus* (staged as *Columbus*), a comically revisionist interpretation of Columbus's discovery of America, that premiered on 14 March.

Shostakovich's contribution stood out by its superior quality. The interlude, which incorporated music jettisoned from *The Bedbug* and was performed before the sixth scene, was encored. The finale, or epilogue, to the
opera was designed to accompany an animated film depicting contemporary America of the day.

In the summer of 1929, Shostakovich took a leisurely cruise along the
Black Sea coast and vacationed in Gudauta, where he worked on a new symphony. On the way home he traveled inland along the Georgian Military
Highway. He forewarned Sollertinsky of his plan to go by airplane from
Pyatigorsk to Moscow, cautioning him not to breathe a word of this to his
mother: "If this reaches mama, she'll go crazy with fright." [13] As it turned
out, in a comedy of errors, he managed to fly only to Tikhorets, where he
became stuck for days trying to secure a train ticket out. [14]

By the end of the summer Shostakovich reported that he was exhausted
and had not stopped working during his six-week trip; he had written his
"May First" Symphony and was working on a ballet, *Dinamiada*. The former he rated good, the latter worse. [15] Previewing the coming season, a
Leningrad newspaper announced the premieres of three major works by
Shostakovich: the opera *The Nose*, the ballet *Dinamiada* (subsequently
renamed *The Golden Age*), and the *First of May* Symphony. It indicated that
the completion of the symphony was being held up by the absence of the
text—to be supplied by the poet Demyan Bedny—for the concluding
chorus. [16]

Little has been uncovered about the background to the composition of
Shostakovich's Third Symphony, which mirrored the Second (*Dedication
To October*) in its episodic, single-movement framework with concluding
chorus and in its broadly programmatic approach. That it was not conceived of a piece, however, can be deduced from the fact that not only was
the instrumental portion composed before the concluding text had been
written, but also because, in the end, that text was supplied not by Bedny
but by Semyon Kirsanov. Shostakovich indicated that it was intended to
form the second part, or movement—after the symphonic *Dedication To
October*—of a projected cycle of symphonic compositions dedicated to the
revolutionary calendar. [17] He submitted the *First of May* Symphony as part
of his graduate student requirement: "Whereas in the 'Dedication' [*To October*] the main content is struggle, the 'May First Symphony' expresses the
festive spirit of peaceful construction, if I may put it that way." [18] The con-
trapuntal pyrotechnics of the former gave way to a simpler, more
homophonic style in the latter. The composer emphasized the optimistic
spirit of the work, acknowledging the influence of Beethoven's Ninth Symphony on his choral finale, a paean to the annual observance of workers'
solidarity. At the time he was composing his Third Symphony,

Shostakovich confided in Shebalin that he was intrigued by the notion of a symphony in which not a single theme is repeated.[19] It was a revealing confession. For all the surfeit of melodic material in this symphony, there is virtually no repetition of themes.

Even without an explicit program, Soviet listeners found the idiom of the *First of May* Symphony immediately accessible, its topical allusions less abstract than those of *To October*. The music relies heavily on familiar inflections from the contemporary urban musical soundscape and public ritual, from mass and workers' songs and pioneer marches to the uplifting strains of brass instruments, oratorical flourishes, and massed choral perorations. Also readily apparent are the bonds with Shostakovich's music of the period for film, theater, and music hall. With only minor changes, he would soon appropriate the seven-measure coda of the *First of May* Symphony to serve double-duty as the coda to the finale of the music to the film *Golden Mountains* (as in the Suite, op. 30a).

A contemporary recalled that Shostakovich initially included in this symphony a part for "machine gun"—a specially constructed wooden ratchet—but when the score was published that part was omitted.[20] The premiere of the *First of May* Symphony—on 21 January 1930, by the orchestra of the Leningrad Philharmonic and the chorus of the Academic Capella conducted by Alexander Gauk—was timed to coincide with the anniversary of Lenin's death. The symphony received a repeat performance the next day in a concert presented to Komsomol youth. Its success was markedly greater than that of the other two choral-symphonic works that shared the bill: *Dark City* and *Komsomoliya*, both by Moscow composer Nikolai Roslavets.[21]

The premiere of the *First of May* Symphony was overshadowed by an event of greater significance to Shostakovich. After over a year of preparation, publicity, and mounting expectations, the Malïy Opera Theater finally unveiled its production of *The Nose* on 18 January 1930. Contributing to the mood of anticipation was the widespread recognition that, despite much discussion and isolated experiments, the venerable tradition of Russian opera had thus far failed to find any promising direction in the Soviet period. While bold, fresh, and distinctively "Soviet" strides had been made in the dramatic theater, film, and other creative arenas, and the productions of a number of modern Western operas in Leningrad—Schreker's *Der ferne Klang*, 1925; Prokofiev's *Love for Three Oranges*, 1926; Berg's *Wozzeck*, 1927; and Krenek's *Der Sprung über den Schatten*, 1927, and *Jonny spielt auf*, 1928—had sharpened the debate, the crisis in contemporary Soviet opera was perceived as acute.

Written before Shostakovich had any practical experience in the theater, the great originality and talent of *The Nose* nevertheless became evident im-

mediately. The creative team at the Malïy Opera Theater, especially director Nikolai Smolich and conductor Samuíl Samosud, envisioned the future
of Soviet opera as the consequence of bold innovation and experimentation. They threw their energy and the resources of the Malïy Opera Theater
solidly behind the realization of Shostakovich's vision:

> With the staging of Shostakovich's opera *The Nose*, the Malïy Opera Theater and
> its Artistic-Political Council are embarking on the path of the decisive Sovietiz-
> ation of the operatic repertory.... Soviet opera should not arise by means of the
> lowering of artistic quality in comparison with operatic works of the past. The
> form of Soviet opera should be different from the forms incorporating bourgeois
> ideology. Our goal, therefore, is to lend every possible assistance to the task of
> raising the cultural level of the proletarian masses. [22]

Sollertinsky, too, became an enthusiastic and energetic proponent of the
opera.

That the creators realized that *The Nose* might prove controversial can be
deduced from the care taken in preparing the public. Shostakovich felt
obliged to justify his choice of a libretto that was neither Soviet nor revolutionary. He complained that his overtures to Soviet authors had been re-
buffed for one reason or another, that he had found nothing suitable for an
opera in the contemporary literature, and that, therefore, he had been
compelled to turn to the classics. His attraction to this particular story by
Gogol he explained by its powerful satire on the period of Tsar Nicholas I,
its clear and expressive language, and its interesting potential for theatrical
spectacle.[23]

As early as the summer of 1928, articles assessing the innovative significance of the opera had begun to appear. The performance of the suite from
The Nose by Malko in Moscow in November 1928 helped to generate interest, as did lecture-demonstrations for composers' groups. On 16 June 1929,
a concert performance of the opera was held during the All-Russian Musical Conference in Leningrad. Shostakovich had protested this performance
vehemently beforehand. Without the scenic component, he felt his conception of the work would lose all meaning and substance:

> Rimsky-Korsakov in the introduction to his operas wrote that "opera is, first of
> all, a musical work." If one takes that position, then all opera theaters should be
> closed and operas should be performed in tuxedos in the Philharmonics. When I
> wrote *The Nose*, it seems to me that I was coming from quite a different position
> than Rimsky-Korsakov. That's why *The Nose* loses all sense to me if it is viewed
> only from the musical standpoint. For its musical component is derived exclu-
> sively from the action.... I repeat once more: the presentation of *The Nose* in con-
> cert performance will be its death.[24]

The equal balance between the elements of music and theatrical action in
the opera, the attempt to "musicalize" the pronunciation of Gogol's words,

and his unusual concept of the work as a "theater symphony" were aspects that Shostakovich repeatedly stressed in interviews and articles.

Shostakovich's principled protest notwithstanding, the June 1929 presentation went ahead as scheduled. It provoked heated debate. The opera was harshly criticized by the proletarian wing for its avoidance of a Soviet theme, its musical complexity, and its inaccessibility to the masses. One composer pointed out its lack of social and ideological relevance to students and workers and warned ominously that "with his opera Shostakovich, without a doubt, has strayed from the main road of Soviet art. If he does not accept the falsity of his path, then his work will inevitably arrive at a dead end." [25] For all the criticism, Shostakovich's prediction of the "death" of his opera was premature. *The Nose* still had enough committed advocates to keep the production on track.

On 14 January 1930, four days before the staged premiere of the opera in Leningrad, three scenes were performed with piano accompaniment to an audience of Leningrad workers. Shostakovich (who apparently did not object this time to the absence of orchestra, scenery, and costumes), Sollertinsky, and other speakers provided introductions and explications. The questions and comments from the audience afterward revealed a range of opinions, some perplexed, some critical, although the drift of the debate was constructive. Asked what spectator he had written this for, Shostakovich commented, "I live in the USSR, work actively and count naturally on the worker and peasant spectator. If I am not comprehensible to them I should be deported." Sollertinsky concluded optimistically: "It is evident that the majority are for the opera. I am satisfied that it will not be difficult for the working class viewer. It will be difficult for the opera buff accustomed to Italian opera, but understandable to the worker." [26]

Unfortunately, on its public premiere, the opera was immediately subjected to ruthless criticism that focused not so much on the quality of performance or production as on the opera's serious ideological flaws, esoteric style, and rejection of classical operatic values. Sollertinsky's attempt to defend the experiment, its originality, and its implicit promise for the future development of Soviet opera was rejected militantly. *The Nose* was branded "the infantile sickness of leftism." [27] Notwithstanding the tabulated results of questionnaires distributed to working-class spectators at two performances that registered a 100 percent approval rating,[28] the pretensions of *The Nose* as an opera accessible to, suitable for, and worthy of the masses were repudiated unequivocally by the proletarian critics.

Shostakovich was upset by the published criticism: "The articles are doing their work and those who read them won't go to see *The Nose*. I will suffer over this for a week, for two months I will tolerate the schadenfreude of 'friends and acquaintances' that *The Nose* failed, and then I will calm down and begin to work again, only on what, I don't know." [29] His worry that the production might not even survive to its third performance proved unfounded. But when *Tosca* was substituted unexpectedly for the fourth scheduled performance of his opera on 4 February, Shostakovich complained to the director of State Theaters in Leningrad, Zakhar Lyubinsky, because the reason for the substitution—the illness of a lead actor—had not been announced and the rumor circulating in Moscow was that no one was buying tickets to *The Nose*.[30] On 16 April, having concluded that his opera was a failure, Shostakovich secretly petitioned Lyubinsky to effect the immediate withdrawal of *The Nose*: "I am convinced that *The Nose* is one of my most successful works.... The path taken by *The Nose* is the correct path. But if *The Nose* is not perceived the way I would like, then it is necessary to withdraw it."[31] Shostakovich was inordinately fond of his first opera; he judged people by whether they were "for" or "against" it.[32]

Lyubinsky did not accede to the composer's request. *The Nose* received a respectable fourteen performances between January and June 1930 and played two more times in the next season before disappearing from the repertory.[33] The Maliy Opera Theater did not lose confidence in its young protégé, nor did Shostakovich think of abandoning the field of opera. In the summer of 1929, before *The Nose* had even reached the stage, the Maliy Opera Theater announced it had commissioned Shostakovich to write a new, Soviet opera, *The Carp*, to a libretto written by Nikolai Oleynikov (the "Zoshchenko of poetry"), the author of a satirical poem of the same name. It was scheduled to be mounted the following season as the Maliy's second (after *The Nose*) "experimental" operatic venture. By late in the year, Moscow's Bolshoy Theater had followed suit and also reached agreement with Shostakovich to produce *The Carp*.[34] In late January 1930, while *The Nose* was embroiled in controversy, Shostakovich expressed his eagerness to be working on the new opera. Oleynikov's failure to deliver the libretto explains Shostakovich's lack of progress, as well as the eventual collapse of the project.

What galled Shostakovich the most in the dispute surrounding *The Nose* was the hypocrisy of the critics. In April 1929, in the context of a debate on the state of musical criticism, Shostakovich had lamented the incredible polarity of opinions to be found in the contemporary press. He argued for objective, musically competent evaluations capable of explaining—both to the reader and to the composer being reviewed—why something is good or bad and how shortcomings could be avoided.[35] In the wake of the operatic debacle, he was justifiably bitter about the volte-face of critics who had repressed their enthusiastic support of only a year or two earlier for his opera. He felt they should be obliged to disclose and explain their conversion publicly. What these defections and the tone of the critical rhetoric reflected, as the composer well knew, was the increasingly militant hegemony of a narrowly defined "proletarian" cultural agenda.

From the time of its founding, early in 1926, Shostakovich had been a member of the Leningrad Association of Contemporary Music (LASM), an organization modeled on but independent of its Moscow counterpart, the Association of Contemporary Music (ASM), founded in 1924, and it was under LASM auspices that his First Symphony and his Piano Sonata received their premieres. But Shostakovich remained aloof from the intrigues and the cliques that plagued Leningrad's musical life, from the competition that sprang up between the self-appointed leadership of LASM and the less formal Circle for New Music. Shostakovich supported wholeheartedly the merger of LASM and the Circle proposed in autumn 1926, but when it appeared that this union might be scuttled, he staged a walk-out from LASM, along with a number of other young members, and switched his support to the Circle for New Music because that was where he felt the high-quality musicians had congregated. These defections undoubtedly hastened the unification, in February 1927, of the two groups under new leadership at LASM. After a short period of renewed activity, however, the organization quietly disintegrated in 1928.[36]

Despite his past allegiance with Leningrad's defunct new music groups, the radical modernism of some of his works (the Piano Sonata, for instance, and *Aphorisms*), his association with the "leftist" director Meyerhold, and the failure of his operatic experiment, Shostakovich proved somewhat less vulnerable than many of his colleagues to the virulent attacks and harassment by the extremists of the Russian Association of Proletarian Musicians (RAPM) during the cultural revolution of the late 1920s and early 1930s. He was not dependent for his livelihood on a single institution; he had negotiated contracts to provide music to order with a broad range of theaters (both musical and dramatic), film projects, and other organizations. His concert appearances also brought in income. His adaptability and the wide assortment of his enterprises probably helped insulate him from the loss of work and of publication and performance opportunities that ruined many careers. Even while dismissing *The Nose*, proletarian critics were able to praise Shostakovich's contribution in other areas, most particularly his work with the Theater of Working-Class Youth (TRAM).

TRAM was a Leningrad theater that had been organized in 1925 by Mikhaíl Sokolovsky on the basis of the amateur dramatic groups of young workers who presented topical skits, songs, and dances in their factory clubs. TRAM was conceived as a collective; the agitprop plays were written and performed by amateurs, young workers who drew directly from their everyday life for the theatrical action. The immediacy of the themes and the freshness and spontaneity of the productions (their independence from

the professional theater and professional actors was a founding tenet of
TRAM) made them extremely popular with young viewers as well as with
the press. Similar theaters sprang up in other cities, and by the late 1920s
the "TRAM movement" had become an influential force in the Soviet
theater.

By 1929, Sokolovsky himself had branched away from the original concept. The Leningrad TRAM had become a professional theater; its actors
and actresses left their factory jobs for full-time work on the stage. In 1929,
for the first time, Sokolovsky produced a play by a professional dramatist,
The Shot by Alexander Bezïmensky (the very author of those unfortunate
verses for "To October"). A versified satirical comedy exposing bureaucracy in socialist construction and championing the young shock-workers
of the First Five-Year Plan, *The Shot* was staged simultaneously by
Meyerhold at his theater in Moscow. Shostakovich was recruited to supply
the music for the TRAM production. Judging by contemporary accounts,
Shostakovich's music added much to the impact of Bezïmensky's comedy,
which premiered in Leningrad on 14 December 1929. Shostakovich went
on to write music for two more TRAM productions over the next year and a
half: *Virgin Soil*, op. 25, on a theme of collectivization (premiered 9 May
1930), and *Rule, Britannia!*, op. 28, on the class war abroad (premiered 9
May 1931).[37]

For Shostakovich, collaboration with TRAM undoubtedly represented
something more positive than simply a defense against the onslaught of
proletarian values, although to at least one other composer trying to camouflage his own allegiances, Andrey Balanchivadze, Shostakovich's example
offered a model.[38] Shostakovich was the same age as the young actor-
workers and undoubtedly sympathized with their energy and commitment; while vacationing in Slavyansk in the summer of 1925 he had kept
company with factory youth and participated in their amateur theatricals.[39]
In his graduate student report for the fall of 1929, he expressed the desire to
write a Soviet opera on a Soviet subject and explained the attraction of
TRAM, in part, as the only place where real workers' art was being forged.[40]
He took active part in TRAM's debates, outspokenly defending the crite-
rion of quality for the future development of proletarian musical culture.
On the question of ideology in music, he defined it not as the subject matter
of a work but the expression of the composer's attitude toward the subject.[41] In *The Shot*, a number of the memorable musical moments involved
actors in dual roles as musicians. The creators underlined the significance
of music: "The 'external technique' of the TRAM actor is not limited to
movement and words. His future development will lead to the mastery of
musical instruments.... The conversion of a musician into an actor and an
actor into a musician marks the increasing musical richness of the specta-

cle." [42] Significantly, in *The Nose*, Shostakovich had been approaching the same ideal from another direction, stimulating conventionally trained operatic singers to enhance their dramatic skills.

Not all of Shostakovich's public reactions to the cultural revolution were so constructive. In response to a March 1930 survey by the RAPM journal *Proletarskiy muzïkant* (Proletarian Musician) in the campaign to stifle the publication and performance of "light music" as well as to purge the ranks of professional organizations of those musicians guilty of disseminating it, the reply published over Shostakovich's signature classified him among the enthusiastic supporters of the battle against the "light genre" in music, especially gypsy music (exemplifying the degenerate legacy from the bourgeois past) and the foxtrot (subsuming jazz and decadent influences from the West). Echoing orthodox RAPM prescriptions to deal with the problem, he advocated censorship, expulsion of offenders from composers' societies, and active propaganda through the Party and other social organizations: "Only together with all of Soviet society, leading widespread educational work on the class essence of the light genre, will we succeed in liquidating it." [43] Knowing he had been guilty of the very outrages he was decrying, Shostakovich added a postscript in which he acknowledged his own political mistake in having granted permission to Malko to make use of his instrumentation of "Tahiti Trot," claiming that it was intended as a number from his ballet *The Golden Age* and that, played out of context, it might create the erroneous impression that Shostakovich was a proponent of the "light genre." [44] Although the fact that Malko was out of the country might have made him seem a convenient scapegoat, Shostakovich's shifting of the blame for his popular arrangement was neither honest nor fair, as the conductor protested in a subsequent letter to the editor. At the very least, Shostakovich's orchestration of Youmans's foxtrot had been composed years before the ballet *The Golden Age* had even been conceived, and it had been extensively performed with Shostakovich's permission. The editors of the journal persisted in holding both men accountable for the dissemination of this "pearl" of the light-music genre. [45]

When this exchange of recriminations took place, *The Golden Age* had not yet reached the stage. Alexander Gauk, who conducted the premiere of the ballet in October 1930, later claimed that it was at his request that Shostakovich included the popular transcription of "Tahiti Trot" in the ballet, as the entr'acte to Act III. [46] Above and beyond the issue of the role of "Tahiti Trot" in the *The Golden Age*, the ballet itself represented one of the most frustrating theatrical ventures of Shostakovich's career.

By the end of the 1920s, Soviet ballet was no better off than Soviet opera. The need to invigorate new forms and fresh choreographic impulses to impart revolutionary realities and to replace the stodgy, classical repertoire was pressing. In an attempt to remedy the situation, early in 1929 the Directorate of the State Academic Theater of Opera and Ballet (GATOB) in Leningrad sponsored a competition for a ballet libretto on a contemporary theme to be based ideally on mass scenes; the possible inclusion of assemblies, demonstrations, fights, station throngs, and street crowds was suggested.[47] First prize was awarded, reluctantly, to the film director Alexander Ivanovsky for his *Dinamiada*, a libretto on the confrontation between a squad of upstanding Soviet sportsmen and their fascist opponents during an industrial exhibition in a bourgeois country. By May 1929, despite his ambivalence about the libretto, Shostakovich had been recruited as composer for the ballet.[48]

The gestation of the production was long and painful. Conceived as a collective, experimental effort—a "choreographic spectacle" to showcase the fresh idioms and insights of young choreographers—the makeup of the production team went through many changes. So, too, did the libretto. On 17 September 1929, at a meeting of the Artistic Council for Ballet of the State Theaters, a reworked libretto was presented along with Shostakovich's music to Act I. The contrived plot still gave cause for concern (one participant called it "insipid"), and it was accepted with provisos.[49] Among other changes, the ballet was subsequently renamed *The Golden Age* and the action was shifted from "Faschlandia" to an unnamed Western capitalist city. Shostakovich based his score on the juxtaposition of two types of music to represent the opposing dramatic poles: music of "unhealthy eroticism" derived from Western bourgeois culture (foxtrot, tango, cancan, and popular Western salon dances); and music of the Soviet proletariat (marches, pioneer songs, etc.), to emphasize robust physical health and athleticism. The composer adopted a polemical stance toward music in the theater; he aimed not simply to write music that was an illustrative backdrop for the dance, "but to dramatize the very musical essence, to give the music real symphonic tension and dramatic development."[50] Sollertinsky, who served on the Artistic Council, reported that the members had reacted enthusiastically to Shostakovich's music: "a brilliant example of the combination of the greatest technical expertise of musical artistry with complete accessibility." He raved that it marked a new step, after Chaikovsky and Stravinsky, in the history of Russian ballet music.[51]

Tentatively scheduled for premiere in late January 1930, the production was delayed. In early February 1930, Shostakovich vigorously protested the outline for the ballet proposed by the newly appointed director, Emmanuíl Kaplan, at a meeting of the Artistic Council, and he grouched about his bad luck with the way the ballet was being produced all spring. Not surprisingly, Shostakovich's music encountered resistance. The choreographers[52] conceded that the sounds and rhythms were difficult for the ballet troupe of the former Mariyinsky Theater, a sentiment echoed by Galina Ulanova, whose performance of the Komsomol girl was among the first roles of her professional career. Confused about the many discrepancies she perceived between staging and music, Valentina Khodasevich, who designed the production and costumes, remembered her awkward and ultimately futile discussion with the composer. Balletomanes certified that the music "did not repose on the ears." [53]

The symphonic depth and unusual orchestration of the ballet posed technical problems for the orchestra as well. In his reminiscences, conductor Gauk noted the composer's intransigent stance against his suggested changes in the difficult scoring.[54] But when, in June 1930, the announcement was made that the production of *The Golden Age* was being postponed until the next season chiefly due to the difficulty of Shostakovich's music for the musicians, nineteen members of the orchestra issued a swift rebuttal, supported by Shostakovich and Gauk, insisting that blame for the postponement ought to be assigned elsewhere.[55]

After all the frictions and frustrations, the day after the public premiere of *The Golden Age* (a paid matinée preview took place on 25 October 1930 as a benefit, followed by a closed performance on 26 October and the public premiere on the 27th), Shostakovich reported to Lyubinsky that, judging by audience response, the ballet had enjoyed great success and that, as a result, scenes from it were to be included in the holiday gala of the Leningrad Soviet on 6 November.[56] In a letter to Smolich, however, Shostakovich downgraded the success to "lukewarm" and confessed that in his own eyes it was a humiliating failure: "In any musical spectacle, music plays the primary and not a servile role, and if this is not taken into account in the production of the spectacle, then the spectacle will not succeed." [57] Shostakovich was satisfied with his own music, but he could not defend his participation in what he deemed an anti-artistic enterprise. He vowed henceforth to work only on subjects that really excited him. Almost as an afterthought, he mentioned that he had begun work on a new opera (although he did not name it, he was referring to *Lady Macbeth of the Mtsensk District*). Shostakovich's negative appraisal of *The Golden Age* was seconded by the savage reviews of proletarian critics, who judged it much more harshly than did its audiences. The ballet ran for ten performances in 1930 and eight in 1931. Productions prepared with the composer's supervision were also mounted in Kiev (1930) and Odessa (1931).

Shostakovich's principled resolution to work only on projects that genuinely excited him was premature. He was overloaded with commissions—his old friend Oborin had been concerned about this when he saw him in Moscow in early September 1930, describing him as thin, worn out, looking bad[58]—including a deadline of 1 January 1931 for delivery of another ballet score, *The Bolt*, for the same theater (GATOB). That he had accepted this project without any great "excitement" can be deduced from the way he summarized for Sollertinsky the preliminary scenario, by Viktor Smirnov, right after receiving the commission in February 1930: "The content is very topical. There's a machine. Then it breaks down (problem of wear and tear on equipment). Then they fix it (problem of amortization), and at the same time they buy a new one. Then everyone dances around the new machine. Apotheosis. All this takes three acts." [59] After the humiliation of his first ballet, Shostakovich seems to have become less involved with the production of the second, which was choreographed by Fyodor Lopukhov. Despite substantial revision, which focused the theme of *The Bolt* as a tract against hooliganism and industrial sabotage, the libretto was not significantly improved: "*Raymonda* and *Coppelia* seem like works of Shakespeare compared to the dramaturgy of *The Bolt*." [60] Like its predecessor, *The Bolt* was peopled with caricatured social types; the action was archetypal agitprop. Even though Shostakovich's music elicited some admiration, the complete failure of the ballet after its premiere on 8 April 1931 came as no surprise. It was withdrawn within two weeks—standard references indicate it was performed only once, though Gauk's recollection was that it was performed twice—ostensibly to undergo necessary revision. By 21 June, no work at all had been begun on revising the production, and *The Bolt* was removed from the repertory entirely.

Shostakovich's music outlived the ballets. Even before *The Golden Age* was staged, a suite of seven numbers from the ballet was performed on 19 March 1930 by the Leningrad Philharmonic Orchestra conducted by Gauk. (For its publication, as op. 22a, the composer subsequently condensed the suite to four numbers.) This suite gained a place in the international symphonic repertory. The witty Polka (a satirical vignette of Western bourgeois prattle about disarmament and world peace entitled "Once upon a Time in Geneva ... (Angel of the World)," from Act III of the ballet) became one of the composer's most recognized gems in his own transcription for piano and innumerable other arrangements. The suite of eight numbers compiled from *The Bolt* in 1931 (op. 27a; for publication in 1934, the composer condensed it to six numbers) went on to supersede its predecessor in popularity after its premiere on 17 January 1933. Shostakovich salvaged other music from his failed ballets for future projects, including his third ballet.

Perhaps Shostakovich's most unusual theatrical experiment was his contribution to the repertory of the music hall. The music hall—dazzling vaudeville revues blending popular song, dance, comedy, and circus acts—was a relatively recent phenomenon in the Soviet Union (Leningrad's Music Hall was opened in 1928). Proletarian critics made the music hall a conspicuous target of their attacks, among other reasons because of its lack of political or socially redeeming virtues. In 1931, Shostakovich was persuaded to join in and add class to the initial attempt by the Leningrad Music Hall to consolidate the normally unrelated acts of a program into a dramaturgically unified show, *Declared Dead*—with a "composed" score and a pragmatic underlying instructional purpose. The show, which featured popular singer-actor and jazz band leader Leonid Utyosov, was dedicated to civil defense preparedness. Standard English renditions of the title of the revue (including *Conditionally Killed, Conditional Death, Allegedly Murdered,* and *Hypothetically Murdered*) are all misleading in light of the actual premise of the plot, which revolved around the character played by Utyosov being inadvertently "declared dead" during an air raid drill. The ambiguous status of the "dead" protagonist set the stage for spectacular diversions. Among the advertised attractions of the show were flying trapeze and equestrian acts, a trained German shepherd, acrobats, clowns, film, and a dream sequence in Paradise with "rejoicing seraphims" (the Music Hall ballet ensemble), God, the Devil, and the Twelve Apostles (Utyosov's hallmark "theatrical jazz" band).

Shostakovich was a great fan of pageantry and the circus.[61] He had a high opinion of Utyosov, with whom he had spent time in Odessa in the summer of 1930 while working on the film *Alone.* He was also well qualified to compose the score. Indeed, one of the critical flaws detected in *The Golden Age* had been its implicit glorification of the bourgeois music hall and its decadent dances (part of the first and the entire third act had actually been set in a music hall). And the musical style of the ballet—with the accent on fashionable dance idioms, musical satire, and the grotesque in sharply differentiated, theater-style orchestrations—carried over from his work in the dramatic theater and film, as well as from *The Nose.* Still, it is difficult to imagine how the edifying lessons of *Declared Dead* could conceivably have meshed with the more established demand for eye-catching spectacle, variety, and light entertainment. Despite an impressive cast, the critics were not persuaded.

Shostakovich was not in Leningrad for the premiere of *Declared Dead* on 2 October 1931 (not 20 October, as in some sources). He had taken a two-month sabbatical, traveling along the Black Sea coast, and then inland to Tiflis (renamed Tbilisi in 1936). He swam, played volleyball, and, most importantly, worked on his new opera, *Lady Macbeth of the Mtsensk District.* But he kept up with the steady campaign in the press against cultural "fellow travelers" (*poputchiki*),[62] commenting sardonically in his letters home to Sollertinsky. On his return home he issued an extraordinary manifesto, "Declaration of a Composer's Duties," a scathing attack on the state of music in the theater world. Cataloguing all the scores he had composed over the past three years—eleven works in all, of which ten had been written for stage and film—he denounced all his theatrical and film music, grading only the *First of May* Symphony a worthy contribution to the development of Soviet music culture: "It is no secret to anyone that, at the fourteenth anniversary of the October Revolution, *the situation on the musical front is catastrophic.* We composers answer for the situation on the musical front. And I am deeply convinced that it is precisely the universal flight of composers into the theater that has created such a situation." [63] Among other things, he lamented the low status accorded music in the theater as contributing to the low quality of performance, the pathetic state of recording technology in the cinema, and the dependence on stock "illustrative" musical clichés. Citing *Declared Dead* as an example, he deplored the role of music diminished to "naked accommodation" with the appalling tastes of some theaters, and he censured the utterly outrageous methods used in staging music theater works (*The Golden Age, The Bolt*). The one exception he made to his litany of disgrace and failure was *The Nose*, precisely because it had been composed independent of any collaboration with a theater. With impassioned rallying cries, he summoned composers to accept responsibility for their art form and turn away from subordination to theatrical institutions in the creation of works for the stage. And although he promised to fulfill his contract, reluctantly, to provide incidental music to a production of *Hamlet* at the Vakhtangov Theater in Moscow, he vowed to return the advances and cancel his contracts for a film, *The Cement Sets*, and an operetta, *The Negro.* To set an example, he swore to reject all future theatrical commissions for a period of five years.[64]

Shostakovich knew that his bold stand and deliberately defiant tone would unleash controversy. After publication, he sent a copy of his "Declaration" to Shebalin—undoubtedly he distributed it to other potential sympathizers as well—asking him to respond in print: "The discussion in connection with the aforementioned article promises to be lively." [65] The response of proletarian critics was swift and harsh. Shostakovich was upbraided for shifting the blame for his own failures and for confusing what was in fact his personal creative crisis (evidenced by his impassioned defense of the failed "formalist" experiment, *The Nose*) with a crisis in musical theater and film. Shostakovich's call for composers to disengage themselves from the theater was perceived as a renunciation of the collective principle of socialist construction: "Thus … you drape yourself in a toga of proud solitude declaring that only in isolation from the spheres of artistic construction is it possible to create the magnificent edifices of the musical future." [66] The critics averred that his appeal would find no support among Soviet composers, that he had branded himself an ideological outcast. As it happens, dissatisfaction among musicians with the repressive state of affairs in Soviet musical life had already begun to intensify. Whether or not

Shostakovich had any intimation when he issued his "Declaration," the stifling domination of the field of music by the dogmatists of RAPM was about to come to an end. In the meantime, Shostakovich covered himself by announcing that he was at work on—and had already completed the introductory movement of—a five-movement, full-evening symphonic poem with soloists and chorus devoted to the life of Karl Marx.[67]

On 23 April 1932, Shostakovich was one of six representatives from Leningrad in attendance with other composers in Moscow at a two-day (April 23 and 25) conference held by Anatoliy Lunacharsky's successor as cultural commissar, Andrey Bubnov. Along with other speakers, Shostakovich analyzed the unhealthy situation in Soviet musical life, cataloguing the abuses of RAPM's despotic stranglehold on Soviet music and its vindictive persecution of ideological opponents and fellow travelers. That same day, in what was clearly a carefully conceived step, a resolution of the Communist Party, "On the Reconstruction of Literary-Artistic Organizations," was issued. Recognizing that the proletarian arts organizations had outlived their usefulness, the resolution called for the liquidation of the Russian Association of Proletarian Writers and its sister organizations in the other arts (including RAPM) and mandated the consolidation of all Soviet writers, composers, and so forth—supporters of Soviet power and socialist construction—into unified creative organizations.

Like many of his professional colleagues, Shostakovich hailed the resolution with relief and enthusiasm, seeing in it a vindication of composers who had not knuckled under to RAPM's demagoguery. He appealed for the immediate formation of a Union of Soviet Composers, and when the Leningrad branch was organized in August 1932 he was elected to its governing board, taking an active role in its future development. That the Party and Soviet society seemed to be demanding of its composers a wider and more sophisticated spectrum of musical attainments—from symphonies and operas to chamber and variety music—than the marches and mass songs that had been condoned almost exclusively by RAPM, came as heartening news to Soviet musicians. The creative atmosphere improved perceptibly.

1932–1936 5

Tragedy-
Satire

When Shostakovich took on the status quo in the Soviet musical theater in late 1931 with his "Declaration of a Composer's Duties" and swore off theatrical commissions for five years, what he had not yet acknowledged publicly was that he was already hard at work on a new opera, *Lady Macbeth of the Mtsensk District*, a project undertaken independent of any commission or planned production. With what was by now wide-ranging experience as a composer of music for film and theater, and with convictions honed by an arduous apprenticeship, Shostakovich was ready to reassert control over his creative destiny and try his hand at another opera.

Shostakovich began work on the new opera in autumn 1930. In choosing his subject, he turned once again not to a contemporary author or topic but to nineteenth-century Russian literature:

All the librettos offered to me were extremely schematic. The heroes inspired in me neither love nor hate, they were all stereotyped. I appealed repeatedly to highly qualified writers but, for a number of reasons, they rejected "petty" work of the kind of an opera libretto....

Taking into consideration the specifics of the operatic theater, the character of the heroes should be outlined in exceptionally bold relief and forcefully. One shouldn't write an opera "in general" about the Five-Year Plan, "in general" about socialist construction, one should write about living people, about the builders of the Five-Year Plan. Our librettists have not yet come to grips with this circumstance. Their heroes are anemic, impotent. They (the heroes) inspire neither sympathy nor hate; they are mechanical. That is why I turned to the classics (Gogol, Leskov). Their heroes make it possible to laugh uproariously and to cry bitter tears.[1]

Nikolai Leskov's 1864 story, *Lady Macbeth of the Mtsensk District*, is a lurid tale about Katerina Izmailova, a merchant's young wife. Bored, sexually unfulfilled, and frustrated by her provincial life, Katerina is overwhelmed by passion conceived for a brash, handsome employee of her husband. To sustain her liaison, she is impelled to commit a series of murders with her lover, which lead eventually to their exposure, capture, and exile to Siberia. Spurned there by her lover, the still-obsessed Katerina hurls herself into the deadly waters of the Volga River, dragging a rival with her.

In a 1940 interview, the composer claimed that Asafyev had advised him to read Leskov's story, providing the stimulus for the composition of the opera.[2] It seems unlikely that it would have required such an express recommendation to introduce Shostakovich—who was in any event an indefatigable reader—to Leskov's well-known story. He had been acquainted with it at least since the early 1920s, when, at the home of family friend Boris Kustodiyev, he could have seen the latter engaged in creating the illustrations for an edition of Leskov's tale eventually published in 1930 in Leningrad, after Kustodiyev's death.[3] Shostakovich enlisted Alexander Preys, one of the collaborators on his previous opera, to work with him in fashioning the libretto.

The chronology of composition spanned more than two years. Act I of the opera was begun in Leningrad on 14 October 1930. Shostakovich made more sustained progress in the autumn of 1931, during the two-month sabbatical mentioned earlier. On 7 October 1931 he wrote to Sollertinsky from Gudauta that he had completed the second scene of his opera, announcing from Batumi on 30 October that he had finished the first act in piano score.[4] While engaged in the orchestration, overnight on October 31 he tossed off arrangements for string quartet of Katerina's aria from Act I scene 3—one of the lyrical centerpieces of the opera—and the "Polka" from *The Golden Age*, which he presented the next morning to delighted fellow hotel guests, the Vuillaume Quartet. The orchestration of Act I of *Lady Macbeth* was completed in Tiflis on 5 November 1931.

Act II of the opera was begun in Leningrad on 19 November and completed in Moscow on 8 March 1932. Shostakovich was eager to test the still-unfinished opus with discriminating critics, to pave the way for eventual production. In late October 1930, having barely begun the composition but sure of its promise, he had already been anxious to acquaint Smolich with his new opera, deeming him the only director to whom he could entrust the work. He also confided at this very early stage his plan to compose a cycle of three operas, a plan he would subsequently expand and amplify.[5] While in Moscow in March 1932, he demonstrated the completed two acts of *Lady Macbeth* independently to directors Smolich of the Bolshoy Theater and to Boris Mordvinov of the Nemirovich-Danchenko Musical Theater. The latter recalled, "It became apparent to everyone in attendance that we were dealing with a phenomenon of the most interesting and highest creative order. The silence that lasted several minutes after the conclusion was a sign of general agreement about our high assessment…. The opera was accepted without any qualms and, proud and happy to be the first to confer such recognition, we signed a contract with Dmitriy Dmitriyevich almost the very next day."[6] Shostakovich subsequently concluded negotiations for productions at both the Bolshoy Theater in Moscow and the Maliy Opera Theater in Leningrad.

Back in Leningrad, Shostakovich began the third act of his opera on 5 April 1932, completing it in Gaspra, while on his honeymoon, on 15 August. In mid-October, he went public with his work-in-progress, elucidating the differences in his vision from that of Leskov's literary original:

> I have been working on *Lady Macbeth* for about two and a half years. *Lady Macbeth* is the first part of a projected trilogy devoted to the condition of women of various epochs in Russia. The subject of *Lady Macbeth of the Mtsensk District* is drawn from Leskov's essay of the same name … a most truthful and tragic portrait of the fate of a talented, clever, and exceptional woman perishing in the nightmarish conditions of prerevolutionary Russia….
>
> I resolve the opera in a tragic vein. I would say that *Lady Macbeth* could be called a tragi-satirical opera. Despite the fact that Ekaterina Lvovna is the murderer of her husband and father-in-law, I sympathize with her nonetheless. I have tried to impart to her whole way of life and her surroundings a gloomy satiric character….
>
> The musical material of *Lady Macbeth* differs sharply from my previous operatic work, the opera *The Nose*. It is my deep conviction that in opera there should be singing. And all the vocal parts in *Lady Macbeth* are melodious, lyrical.[7]

The composer would subsequently stress this last point: "In the opera I have arias, duets, trios, large choruses. Recitative—in its old, traditional guise—is almost totally absent. I devoted great attention to achieving the singability and melodiousness of each part. My orchestra does not accompany but plays a leading role together with the singers."[8]

Although Shostakovich projected completion of the opera in another three or four months, the fourth and final act, begun in late October, was finished well ahead of schedule, on 17 December 1932. Shostakovich dedicated *Lady Macbeth of the Mtsensk District* to his new bride, Nina Varzar. (To her he had also dedicated his *Six Romances on Texts by Japanese Poets*, op. 21—settings of love lyrics for tenor and orchestra—the first three of which had been composed in 1928, the fourth in 1931, and the last two in April 1932.)

A vivacious brown-eyed blonde, Nina Vasilyevna Varzar—"Nita," as her family nicknamed her—was the youngest of three daughters of a professional couple: Vasiliy Vasilyevich Varzar, a lawyer; and his wife, Sofya Mikhailovna (née Dombrovskaya), an astronomer. Nina caught Shostakovich's eye while on vacation outside Leningrad in the summer of 1927, when she was a gifted eighteen-year-old student in the Physics and Mathematics Department of Leningrad University. (She subsequently specialized in experimental physics and pursued a professional career in research.) With his new friend Sollertinsky, Shostakovich began to frequent the regular Varzar family "Thursdays" that fall. There he rubbed shoulders with the young artists, architects, and scientists of the Varzar sisters' acquaintance, indulged his proclivities for puns, yarns, and mild mischief, and supplied foxtrots and tangos for dancing.[9] The young Nina was stylish and athletic. She loved music and the dance and took extracurricular instruction in singing and ballet.[10]

The courtship was unhurried. There were serious obstacles, in any case, to developing romance. Nina's mother wanted her daughter to finish university. Shostakovich's mother, exceptionally protective of her young prodigy and concerned first and foremost with assuring his professional and financial security, did not warm to the Varzar family or to the prospect of losing her son to another woman. Not surprisingly, relations within the Shostakovich household became strained. The composer canceled wedding plans at least once. On his part, Shostakovich did not abandon hope for a relationship with Tatyana Glivenko, even after her marriage in 1929. In his final preserved letter to her, in 1931, he expressed bitterness toward his family, claiming they had poisoned his life.[11]

On 13 May 1932, assisted by Sollertinsky but without informing his mother, sisters, or the bride's family, Shostakovich and Nina registered their marriage in a civil ceremony in Detskoye Selo, outside Leningrad. Shostakovich's sister Mariya wrote to her aunt in America shortly afterward:

> I feel I cannot tell you properly what has happened—but what composed and made up our happiness has ended.... Vsevolod Constantinovich [Frederiks, Mariya's husband.] always said that one should not spoil a boy the way we did Mitya. Perhaps he is right, but after all it was Mother who created and nourished his talent.... Our greatest fault is that we worshipped him, all three of us. But I don't regret it. For, after all, he is a really great man now. Frankly speaking, he has a very difficult character—he is rough with us, hardly speaks to us, and at the same time he is terribly attached to Mother. Toward those close to him his character is just impossible."[12]

The new bride moved into the rooms in the communal apartment on Marat Street with her husband and mother-in-law, successfully adapting herself to their routine; in early 1934 Shostakovich was able to acquire a private cooperative apartment on Dmitrovsky Lane with the honorarium from *Lady Macbeth*. This apartment became a convivial gathering place for the artistic and scientific intelligentsia.

Shostakovich fulfilled his reluctant promise to provide the music for Nikolai Akimov's production of *Hamlet* at the Vakhtangov Theater in Moscow, but Akimov's eccentrically revisionist, almost parodistic treatment of the Shakespearean classic, casting Hamlet as a portly schemer intent only on seizing power, fared badly with the critics at its premiere on 19 May 1932. Shostakovich's music was better received. The high opinion of Jury Jelagin, a member of the theater orchestra, was shared widely: "The music Shostakovich wrote for *Hamlet* was magnificent. Though it was very modern, it came closer to Shakespeare's *Hamlet* than anything else in Akimov's production." [13] From the music provided for the production, Shostakovich salvaged a suite for small orchestra, op. 32a.

While still at work on the music to *Hamlet*, Shostakovich announced that following its completion he would devote himself to a work dedicated to the fifteenth anniversary of the October Revolution, a grand symphonic poem with soloists and chorus on the theme "From Karl Marx to Our Days," using as its leitmotiv Marx's words "Philosophers only explained the world, we must recast it." Shostakovich outlined his plan to the press in detail, identifying Nikolai Aseyev as the librettist of the projected five-movement, evening-long work and claiming that he had already completed the introductory movement and expected to complete the work by September and the premiere to be performed by the Leningrad Philharmonic conducted by Gauk. Yet no trace of this work seems to have survived. [14]

Shostakovich's "five-year plan" proclaimed in late 1931—to reject, for that period, all new commissions for work in the theater and film—proved short-lived. After the Central Committee Decree of 23 April 1932, perhaps Shostakovich felt the conditions he had denounced earlier would no longer conspire to stifle creative initiative. Strict compliance with his resolution, on the other hand, as high-minded as the intent might have been, would certainly have caused considerable hardship for the Shostakovich family by eliminating the composer's primary source of income. Whatever the reason, even before he had completed work on *Lady Macbeth of the Mtsensk District*, Shostakovich undertook to provide the music for a new film, *Counterplan*, directed by Sergey Yutkevich and Fridrikh Ermler.

With a scenario closely modeled on contemporary life in a Leningrad turbine factory, the creators of *Counterplan* aimed to evoke the revolutionary romanticism of the massive industrialization drive and to put a sympa-

thetic human face on the working class. *Counterplan* was targeted for
release on 7 November 1932, the fifteenth anniversary of the Revolution,
thus work on the film had to advance at an unforgiving pace, not unlike the
momentum of its subject matter, the factory workers' strenuous push to
meet the Five-Year Plan. Shostakovich was accustomed to the pressure of
deadlines; some of the music was composed on the set as scenes were being
shot. His most significant contribution to the film, however, was the product of considerably more calculation. The directors asked for a theme song,
a contemporary workers' anthem with broad appeal. As preserved sketches
and variants demonstrate, Shostakovich worked hard to refine just the
right melodic profile and spirit for his mass song, "The Song of the
Counterplan."[15] His labor was well rewarded; the cheery "rise and shine"
song, with a text by Boris Kornilov, scored an instant hit on release of the
film and was soon being sung by millions.[16] The popularity of the tune
endured. In its best-known Western incarnation, Shostakovich's melody
was published in 1942, arranged with a new text by Harold J. Rome, as
an inspirational song, "The United Nations."[17] Shostakovich revived the
tune himself in subsequent works: in *Poem of the Motherland*, op. 74, the
film score to *Michurin*, op. 78, and his operetta *Moscow, Cheryomushki*,
op. 105.

During the next three years, Shostakovich's projects in the dramatic theater and movies hardly diminished at all. He wrote incidental music for a
production of Pavel Sukhotin's play *The Human Comedy* (based on Balzac's
Comédie humaine) at the Vakhtangov Theater that premiered on 1 April
1934. He provided music for the film *Maxim's Youth* (released 27 January
1935)—the first in what would become an extremely popular trilogy
of "Maxim" movies directed by Kozintsev and Trauberg—as well as for
the films *Love and Hate* (released 1935) and *The Girlfriends (released 1936).*

Two weeks after the completion of *Lady Macbeth*, Shostakovich came
back for the first time in five years to his own instrument, the piano. He began composing a set of *Twenty-four Preludes*, op. 34, an omnibus of miniatures ranging from the insouciant to the somber. Although he could not
quite sustain the pace of composing one prelude a day, he managed to complete the set on 2 March 1933. Meanwhile, on 17 January a concert devoted
to his music, including first performances of the suite from *The Bolt* and the
passacaglia (organ version) from *Lady Macbeth*, was presented successfully
at the Large Hall of the Leningrad Philharmonic. The occasion was festive;
afterward, friends were entertained to supper at the Shostakovich home
with the slightly tipsy composer supplying the dance music.

A few days after completing his cycle of preludes, Shostakovich embarked on a concerto for piano not unrelated in style and spirit to the more
playful of the solo preludes. This marked not simply the composer's initial

essay in the concerto genre but also his first venture in the realm of traditional symphonic structures since the completion of his First Symphony eight years earlier. Scoring the four-movement work for the unusual accompaniment of trumpet and string orchestra, the composer completed work on 20 July 1933. The composer subsequently divulged to a student that he had initially conceived the work as a concerto for trumpet; the difficulty of writing for that solo instrument and the addition of the piano had transformed it into a double concerto, and finally the piano had eclipsed the trumpet.[18]

Fusing his identities as composer and performer, the new piano works eased Shostakovich's return to concert performance. Until 1930, he had been relatively active as a concertizing pianist, playing combined solo programs of his own music and that of other composers, as well as appearing with orchestra chiefly with the two Chopin concertos and the First Concertos of Chaikovsky and Prokofiev. For two and a half years, however, his public appearances virtually ceased, until 17 January 1933, when he included eight of the new preludes on his concert. In memoirs—committed to paper more than thirty-five years later—Levon Atovmyan recalled that Shostakovich's mother told him she attributed her son's abandonment of an active performing career to his humiliation at the Chopin competition in 1927. Atovmyan also recalled that shortly before the composition of the op. 34 preludes, Shostakovich had indicated to him his desire to give up composing and return to concert performance.[19]

On 24 May 1933, Shostakovich gave the premiere of the complete cycle of *Twenty-four Preludes* in Moscow. On 15 October, on the opening concert of the Leningrad Philharmonic's season, he performed the premiere of his Piano Concerto in C Minor, op. 35. The orchestra was conducted by Fritz Stiedry. Thereafter he resumed a more frequent schedule of public appearances, although, excepting as accompanist, he appeared henceforth only as an interpreter of his own music. After the Moscow premiere of his concerto on 9 December 1933, Shostakovich's opinion was reported: "What is the basic artistic theme of this concerto? I consider it absolutely superfluous to follow the example of a number of composers, who take the line of least resistance and always try to decode the content of their compositions with extraneous definitions drawn from some related field of art. I cannot describe the content of my concerto with any means other than those with which the concerto is written." [20]

The concerto would become a repertory staple, a guaranteed crowd-pleaser, brimming with youthful ebullience. If the music was nowhere near as modernist or "wild" as that of the immediate post-Conservatory period, Shostakovich's former teacher Steinberg was shocked nonetheless by the brashness, the irreverent hodge-podge of styles, which range from paraphrases of Beethoven and snippets of Haydn and Mahler to a saucy Odessan song and undercurrents from jazz and the music hall.[21] After hearing the Moscow premiere, Myaskovsky tersely noted in his diary: "Piano Concerto—brilliant, with philistinism."[22]

Revived interest in the piano notwithstanding, Shostakovich still devoted much of his energy at this point to the theater. Reviewing his ultimately futile search for contemporary libretti, the composer conceded that Nikolai Aseyev had provided him with a libretto for a comic opera, *The Great Lightning*, but said it had not suited him.[23] Actually, Aseyev and the composer had been paired in one of the Malïy Opera Theater's creative "brigades" mustered to produce operas on contemporary Soviet themes. Their particular assignment was to deliver an opera on "the class struggle in the West."[24] Shostakovich's operetta-like setting, dating from 1932, of fragments of the Aseyev libretto was discovered and performed only after his death. (The complete libretto has not resurfaced but evidently centered, not unlike *The Golden Age*, on the clash of cultures between a delegation of Soviet workers and their hosts in a capitalist country.)

From the advent of sound in film, Shostakovich began to contemplate the creation of a new hybrid medium, the film-opera, a fancy he would return to regularly during his career. Perhaps the closest he actually came to the realization of the new, synergistic medium he envisaged was his collaboration, beginning early in 1933, with film director Mikhaíl Tsekhanovsky[25] on a full-length animated version of *Tale of the Priest and His Worker, Blockhead* after Pushkin, for which the musical setting preceded the animation. The satirical theme and grotesque characterizations greatly appealed to Shostakovich, who worked on the score in spurts but continued even after the film's contract had been canceled. A suite from his music to the unfinished project (most of the completed film footage was destroyed during the Leningrad blockade) was evaluated as "brilliant in its orchestration and clever in its musical language" after its performance in 1935.[26]

For the moment, however, any contemplation of new dramatic projects took a back seat to shepherding *Lady Macbeth of the Mtsensk District* to the stage. In April 1933, Shostakovich traveled to Sverdlovsk to demonstrate *Lady Macbeth* to the management and musicians of the local opera theater (in what he regarded a cultural backwater, he found himself pleasantly surprised by the quality of their production of *Tsar Saltan*), and in August he signed a contract with the Bolshoy Theater. Copyists had trouble keeping up with the demand for scores. One of the most significant events on the Moscow musical scene in May 1933, as Myaskovsky relayed to Prokofiev in Paris, was the preliminary run-through of the opera with orchestra at the Nemirovich-Danchenko Musical Theater. The audition had been organized for the purpose of vetting by Commissar Bubnov; while recommending that the language of the libretto be sanitized, he gave his blessing for work on the production to proceed.

The production of *Lady Macbeth* at the Malïy Opera Theater in Leningrad reunited the same collaborators—Samosud, Smolich, and Dmitriyev—who had created *The Nose* four years earlier. Smolich commenced his staging of the opera on 10 October, completing it on 28 November 1933. Shostakovich, characteristically tense and reserved, together with the more demonstrative Sollertinsky, took part in the selection of singers. Both were attentive observers of the rehearsals. Meanwhile, Shostakovich also commuted to Moscow to be present at rehearsals at the Nemirovich-Danchenko Theater. In mid-November he wrote to Sollertinsky that during his current Moscow stay he had been kept busy from morning to night attending rehearsals and correcting proofs of the opera.

Rivalry between Leningrad's Malïy and Moscow's Nemirovich-Danchenko Theaters was intense. The production in Moscow, where the demands of Shostakovich's score strained the technical and musical resources of the company, was prepared more as a team effort than that in Leningrad. The collaborators there, including conductor Grigoriy Stolyarov, director Mordvinov, and Vladimir Dmitriyev (who designed both the Leningrad and Moscow productions), assembled and refined their dramatic interpretation through a painstaking process of trial and error, with Nemirovich-Danchenko joining the team in the autumn to put the finishing touches on the production. Nemirovich-Danchenko took a different reading of the opera from that of Smolich—polemicizing "with Shostakovich's narrow understanding of Shostakovich himself for the true Shostakovich" [27]—one that emphasized the tragedy and soft-pedaled the satire. The differences in their approaches were underscored by Nemirovich-Danchenko's adoption of *Katerina Izmailova*, the heroine's name, as the title for his production. Scheduled dates for the premiere were repeatedly postponed, conceding to the Malïy Opera Theater the privilege of unveiling its production of *Lady Macbeth of the Mtsensk District* first, on 22 January 1934. Nemirovich-Danchenko's *Katerina Izmailova* opened in Moscow two days later.

Expectations for Shostakovich's new opera ran high. Well before its premiere, extensive coverage in the press promoted the significance of the event for Soviet opera. Even the most skeptical of critics, concerned chiefly with issues clarifying the proper social ramifications of the drama or lamenting its lack of a moral force for good (and not, incidentally, bristling with puritanical indignation at the carnal excesses that later became an issue), were swayed by the undeniable originality and power of Shostakovich's music. Myaskovsky, never one of Shostakovich's most active boosters, pronounced the opera "stunningly wonderful" after his first hearing, despite some objections to the orchestration. [28] Composer Yuriy

Shaporin, in what was perhaps an excess of enthusiasm for the work of a composer who was still, after all, under the age of thirty, appraised *Lady Macbeth* as "the apex of Shostakovich's creative work." Another Leningrad composer and colleague, Gavriil Popov, confided in his diary after attending a rehearsal of the opera at the Malïy Opera Theater with Prokofiev: "*[Lady] Macbeth* is a remarkable, deep, and brilliantly orchestrated composition."[29] Samosud proclaimed Shostakovich's opera a masterpiece, the best in the Russian operatic literature of the past half-century.[30]

The reception of Shostakovich's opera, critical and especially popular, did nothing to confute the anticipation. It left no doubt that *Lady Macbeth of the Mtsensk District* represented a proud milestone in the history of Soviet music. The day after the premiere, the press blazoned its exceptional success; the creators, and most notably the composer, had been summoned on stage not just at the end of acts but in between individual scenes as well. The Malïy Opera Theater's show was instantaneously predicted to become "one of the most beloved of the mass viewer."[31]

This does not mean that more circumspect views were not voiced. At roundtable discussions devoted to the opera in Leningrad from 16 to 20 February, for instance, the rhetoric was heated. Conservative speakers, chiefly political functionaries from the Union of Composers, carped at the lack of restraint and critical balance in the extravagant praise of Shostakovich's composition, as well as at the proper assessment of the composer's development and its relationship to Russian tradition. Sollertinsky, who had provided a comprehensive and controversial article on Shostakovich's creative development for the program booklet of the Malïy production, came in for direct attack. It was in response to these critics that Shostakovich blithely quipped in a letter on 24 February, in what would prove to be prescience as ironic as it was naive: "Basically this is all boring. All the same, I hope that if RAPM didn't grind me into powder, that the SSK [Union of Soviet Composers] will not succeed in doing so either."[32]

Shostakovich's frustration with critics was longstanding and his disdain for the tendencies and quality of critical discourse no secret: "When a critic writes that in such-and-such a symphony Soviet civil servants are represented by the oboe and clarinet and Red Army soldiers by a group of brass instruments, it makes you want to scream, 'It's not so!'"[33] "Journal criticism is of assistance to me personally in those instances when the critical article or review in question is written by a highly qualified critic. Unfortunately, this is rarely the case in the journal *Worker and Theater*."[34] Full of self-confidence from his operatic triumph, Shostakovich even attempted preemptive strikes:

> Maybe, after *Tale of a Priest* is released, I will be rebuked again by some musical critics for superficiality, for mischievousness, for the absence of the real human

emotions that "finally" surfaced in my *Lady Macbeth*. But what can be considered human emotions? Surely not only lyricism, sadness, tragedy? Doesn't laughter also have a claim to that lofty title? I want to fight for the legitimate right of laughter in "serious" music. When a listener laughs loudly during my symphonic concert, it doesn't shock me a bit, on the contrary, it pleases me.[35]

Shostakovich continued to grouse about those who claimed that only in *Lady Macbeth* did he achieve a musical language of depth and humanity.

In the immediate aftermath of the premiere of *Lady Macbeth*, an opera both more realistic in its dramaturgy and more accessible in its musical idiom than *The Nose*, Shostakovich showed more interest in its popular than in its critical reception. It had been targeted, after all, not at the intellectual elite but at the broad masses. On 27 February 1934, after the tenth performance of *Lady Macbeth* in Leningrad, the composer communicated his satisfaction to Smolich: "The show is going fine. The public listens very attentively and begins to run for its galoshes only after the final curtain. There is very little coughing. In general there are quite a number of pleasant things that make my composer's heart rejoice." He was pleased that the performances were selling out and that the audiences were enthusiastic in their demand for curtain calls. "As a whole it must be said that in your production, Lady Macbeth has 'reached' the spectator. There is tension, there is interest, and there is sympathy for Ekaterina Lvovna." [36] In the two-plus years of the opera's run, the Malïy Opera Theater tallied eighty-three performances of *Lady Macbeth*; for the forty-nine performances through the end of 1934 the average attendance was calculated at an impressive 92.8 percent of capacity, and the show reaped an enormous profit.[37] Within five months of its premiere, the opera had already been broadcast on the radio five times from the Nemirovich-Danchenko Theater and once from the Malïy.[38]

Even with its shift of focus, Nemirovich-Danchenko's production proved no less successful with audiences than its Leningrad rival. There are indications that, of the two, Shostakovich personally favored his hometown's production. In places he felt Nemirovich-Danchenko's motivation stemmed more from Leskov's story than from the opera libretto, and he appreciated the high musical quality of Smolich's production and the stronger roster of singers. Nevertheless the composer remained both gracious in his appreciation of the Moscow production and attentive to its continued welfare. This production ran for ninety-four performances through the winter of 1936; in the summer of 1934 it scored a hit on tour in provincial Voronezh. Word about the sensational new Soviet opera quickly spread abroad. Within two years of its unveiling, staged or concert versions of *Lady Macbeth* had been performed in the United States, Argentina, Czechoslovakia, Sweden, Switzerland, and England.

With the success that had eluded him for so long under his belt, Shostakovich grew more ambitious. His plan for a trilogy of operas expanded to a tetralogy:

> I want to write a Soviet *Ring of the Nibelungs*. It will be an operatic tetralogy about women, in which *Lady Macbeth* will take the place of *The Rhinegold*. The driving image of the next opera will be a heroine of the People's Will movement. Next, a woman of our century. And, finally, I will portray our Soviet heroine, embracing collected features of women from the present and the future, from Larisa Reysner to Zhenya Romanko, the best female concrete worker on the Dneprostroy Dam project. This theme is the leitmotiv of my daily reflections and of my life for the next ten years. [39]

At the end of 1934 he announced that Alexander Preys was at work on the libretto for the second opera of the cycle, utilizing works of Saltïkov-Shchedrin and Chekhov as sources. [40]

In mid-July 1934, Shostakovich announced himself ready to write an opera-farce, the chief allure being that "it starts as a farce and ends as a bloody tragedy." [41] A month later the composer had cooled to the idea. Numerous other operatic collaborations were explored. In September 1935 it was announced that Shostakovich had agreed to write an opera on Mikhaíl Sholokhov's *Virgin Soil Upturned* to a libretto to be written by the author. [42] In early 1936, Shostakovich was so impressed with Mikhaíl Bulgakov's reading of his play *Pushkin* that he requested a copy; Bulgakov's wife recorded her opinion that, of the choice between Prokofiev—who had also expressed interest in the subject—and Shostakovich to write the opera, the latter should be chosen. [43]

Shostakovich became highly prized as an expert in opera. In April 1934 he participated at a conference at the Nemirovich-Danchenko Theater exploring future directions in Soviet opera; in December 1935 he was selected to conduct a conference in Leningrad on the Malïy Opera Theater's experiences as a laboratory for Soviet opera. He was called upon to counsel young composers on their theater works. The most successful of his protégés was Ivan Dzerzhinsky. It was through Shostakovich's intervention, considerable technical assistance, and continued support that Dzerzhinsky's first opera, *The Quiet Don* (based on Sholokhov's novel about the suffering and heroism of Don Cossacks during the Civil War), made it to the stage—after its dismal failure in an opera competition—in a production that premiered at the Malïy Opera Theater on 22 October 1935. In gratitude, Dzerzhinsky dedicated the opera to his mentor.

Shostakovich was thrust increasingly into the limelight. His creative plans and progress were routinely tracked in the press, his pronouncements on topics musical and nonmusical were solicited, and he was in demand for committees, competition juries, and organizational posts. In 1934, he was elected a deputy of Leningrad's October District,[44] inaugurating the pattern of public service and official responsibilities that would endure throughout the rest of his life. In 1933 he joined a city commission on jazz.

The Resolution of April 1932 and the consequent disbanding of RAPM had vented an explosive surge in the popularity of and craving for jazz, as Shostakovich observed: "The former holy terror of the word 'jazz' has given way to a veritable 'jazz-bacchanalia.'"[45] Shostakovich's catholic tastes in music "from Bach to Offenbach," in gypsy music, street songs, and the music hall, were well established. Jazz-derived rhythms, textures, and instrumental color had been assimilated into much of his music, from the ballets and theatrical scores to his Piano Concerto. In February 1934, Shostakovich composed a suite of three dances for jazz band, first performed in Leningrad the next month. But Shostakovich, acutely sensitive to good taste and professional quality, irrespective of musical style, perceived danger in the jazz fad: "I am not against jazz as such. But I am against those ugly forms in which the universal, almost mindless enthusiasm for the genre has manifested itself."[46] "The matter is a serious one: here and there vulgarity (*poshlost'*) and philistinism are rearing their heads."[47]

In late May 1934, Leningrad played host to a ten-day international music festival. Shostakovich's music was prominently featured. *Lady Macbeth* was performed, Dmitri Mitropoulos conducted the suite from *The Golden Age*, and the composer played his Piano Concerto under Alexander Gauk, in a concert that also included the suite from *The Bolt*. The occasion proved consequential in ways more than strictly professional; Shostakovich fell in love with one of the interpreters engaged for the festival, Yelena Konstantinovskaya, a twenty-year-old university student.

Shortly after meeting her, in mid-June, Shostakovich was obliged to depart on a concert tour. On the train trip south, he made the acquaintance of composer Aram Khachaturyan. From Baku, Shostakovich traveled to Batumi and by steamer along the Black Sea coast to Yalta, where he met up with Nina. Husband and wife vacationed together at a rest home belonging to the Bolshoy Theater in Polenovo, near Tarusa. Chronicling all the symptoms of his lovesickness, Shostakovich sent almost daily missives to his sweetheart in Leningrad. He was unable to compose. He occupied his time by knocking off "boring" fugues, one a day, and by reading Turgenev. (While in Baku, however, he had reported taking pleasure in two successive late-night sessions of gypsy music.)

In mid-August, on their way home through Moscow, Nina initiated a separation, to which the composer reacted badly. Shostakovich loathed confronting unpleasantness. When he followed her to Leningrad a few days later, he patched things up with his wife. But he continued to see Yelena, escorting her openly to concerts and public events in 1935 and toying for some time with the idea of marriage to her. Approached by an intermediary, Nina agreed to a divorce. Writing to Sollertinsky from Moscow on 10 March 1935, Shostakovich told him it was possible he would never return to Leningrad; the issue of his move to Moscow was being actively mooted about the highest reaches of the government and he had already seen the apartment being prepared for him. That the initiative for this move likely came from him is evident from the complaints about how badly he has been treated in Leningrad, especially with respect to obtaining a separate room for Nina. He reasons, in this letter, that as much as he hates the prospect of leaving Leningrad, if he moves with his mother to Moscow he will be able to relinquish the apartment to Nina.[48] During a trip to Moscow some months later, Shostakovich showed Atovmyan his divorce certificate. After he returned to Leningrad to fetch his belongings, Atovmyan received a telegram: "Remaining in Leningrad. Nina pregnant. Remarried. Mitya."[49]

In the fall of 1935, by which time he knew his wife was pregnant, Shostakovich confessed to Sollertinsky: "There can be no question of a divorce from Nina. I have only now realized and fathomed what a remarkable woman she is, and how precious to me."[50] They moved that fall into a new apartment on Kirovsky Prospect, ceding their old apartment to the composer's mother. Their first child, a daughter, was born in May 1936. Shostakovich's firm conviction of the necessity of preserving the family for the sake of the children cemented the relationship: "Even when he goes out himself, he likes to know that we're all at home, so that he returns to find his wife and children waiting for him."[51] Nina later indicated that it was only after their reconciliation that she adopted her husband's name.[52]

In the wake of the initial estrangement from his wife, in mid-August 1934 in Moscow Shostakovich began the composition of the Sonata for Cello and Piano in D Minor, op. 40, a work of classical dimensions that scarcely hints at the turmoil in his personal life. By 17 August, the first movement of the sonata was almost complete and by 13 September the third movement was done. The final, fourth movement was completed on 19 September in Leningrad. Viktor Kubatsky—forty-three-year-old former principal cellist at the Bolshoy Theater and organizer of the Stradivarius Quartet, friend of the composer and promoter of his career since the 1920s—had persuaded Shostakovich to undertake the sonata while vacationing with him at Polenovo. Kubatsky, to whom the composer dedicated the work, gave the premiere of the new sonata in Leningrad on 25 December 1934 accompanied by the composer. Although it was not an instant success, the cello sonata steadily attracted new adherents.

Shostakovich related the simplification of style in the cello sonata, which he regarded as a step forward, to the influence of Maxim Gorky's articles on the "purity of language."[53] He spoke frequently during the early months of

1935 about his search for a simple, expressive musical language all his own, repudiating the striving for originality at any cost that had marked some of his earlier music.[54] But he drew a sharp distinction between simplicity and oversimplification: "Sometimes the struggle for a simple language is understood somewhat superficially. Often 'simplicity' turns into epigonism. But to speak simply doesn't mean one should speak as they spoke fifty to a hundred years ago. This is a trap many composers fall into, afraid of accusations of formalism. Both formalism and epigonism are the worst enemies of Soviet musical culture."[55]

The other major work of the period was the score for a ballet, Shostakovich's third. After the failure of *The Bolt*, choreographer Fyodor Lopukhov had been obliged to leave his job at the State Academic Theater of Opera and Ballet. He was invited to organize a new company at the Malïy Opera Theater to replace its corps de ballet, with a brief to present alternative fare to that of the State Academic Theater. Still motivated to create a ballet on a theme of contemporary relevance—a comic entertainment with a lyrical rather than the grotesque and satirical emphasis of *The Bolt*—Lopukhov developed with Adrian Piotrovsky a libretto about events on a collective farm in the region of the Kuban River in southern Russia. Lopukhov's invitation to Shostakovich to write the music was, at least in part, an attempt to exculpate the failure of *The Bolt*, to show that they could realize positive heroes and celebrate the joyful, uplifting spirit of labor on a collective farm. It also offered the opportunity to blend choreographic styles from classical ballet and folk genres. Shostakovich summarized the premise of the three-act ballet:

> A group of Soviet artists goes to the Kuban, where they meet with Kuban collective farmers. This meeting marks a first. The collective farmers, initially taking the artists for people from some other, unknown sphere, don't know how to relate to them. And the artists don't immediately find a common language with the collective farmers.
>
> Quickly, however, both sides discover lots of common points of contact. Both sides are constructing socialist life: the one on a collective farm, the other on the artistic front. The romantic peripeteia that transpires in the open air of the Kuban countryside bring the two brigades—collective farmers and artists—even closer together.[56]

That Shostakovich was genuinely inspired by the libretto's potential, despite his admiration for Lopukhov, seems improbable. The nature of the project, its development, and the method of collaboration did not suggest great improvement over his previous ballet experience, offering the composer virtually no scope for independent creative vision. In the winter of 1934 he had already backed out of a contract to create a new ballet from the music of *The Golden Age* and *The Bolt* for the Nemirovich-Danchenko

Theater in Moscow. A certain portion of the music for Lopukhov's new ballet, which was substantially completed by the end of 1934, was drawn, in fact, from *The Bolt*.

Financial exigencies may have motivated Shostakovich to take on the project: in the wake of his separation from Nina, two months after signing the contract for the ballet with the Malïy Theater on 13 June 1934,[57] the composer told Konstantinovskaya that he wanted to buy a dacha outside Leningrad and for that purpose had taken a job for 20,000 rubles.[58]

Nevertheless, Shostakovich bent over backward to meet the choreographer's needs. New musical material was dictated by and sometimes created momentarily in response to Lopukhov's explanations and demonstrations. The composer subsequently described his goal: "The music in this ballet is, in my opinion, happy, light, entertaining and, most important, danceable. I deliberately tried to find a clear, simple language here, equally accessible to the viewer and the performer." [59]

Work on the production of the new ballet dragged on. By early April 1935, having discarded "Two Sylphides" and "Kuban," they still had not settled on a name and Shostakovich was using the working title "Whimsies" (*Prichudï*). In mid-April, the composer left on a five-week tour of Turkey, performing his music and attending meetings and receptions as a member of an official delegation of Soviet performing artists that included, among others, pianist Lev Oborin and violinist David Oistrakh, singers Valeriya Barsova and Mariya Maksakova, and dancers Natalya Dudinskaya and Asaf Messerer. As Shostakovich informed Sollertinsky, his wardrobe was vastly enriched. Before departure he was outfitted with custom-made suits, tails, a dinner jacket, overcoats, boots, and so on.[60] His initial misgivings about making the trip were largely dispelled by the historic sights, scenic beauty, and warm hospitality he experienced. When he returned home in late May, he was just in time to participate in the final rehearsals for his ballet, now definitively titled *The Limpid Stream*, from the name of the collective farm on which the action takes place. The premiere took place on 4 June 1935.[61]

Critical response to *The Limpid Stream* was decidedly mixed. The dramatic superficiality of the libretto and the contrived characters and situations came in for especially harsh attack. But even Shostakovich's music did not escape unscathed. Although some saw the music as interesting, as "saving" the ballet by elevating its tone, no less a critic (and best friend) than Sollertinsky blasted that presumption: "There is no inner unity even in the music of Shostakovich. To a significant degree, it is constructed of bits from the score of the previous ballet *The Bolt*.... *The Limpid Stream* is not musically among the best ballets of Shostakovich; at any rate, it is inferior to the remarkably masterful score of *The Golden Age*." [62]

Nonetheless, *The Limpid Stream* went over considerably more success-fully with its audiences, and Lopukhov was invited to adapt and mount the ballet at the Bolshoy Theater the following autumn. Shostakovich faced the prospect with no little trepidation. On the basis of rehearsals at the Bolshoy in October and November, he was fully expecting the ballet to be pulled be-fore reaching public performance. Shortly before its Moscow premiere on 30 November 1935, he confided with evident anxiety to Sollertinsky, who had protested unavailingly the serious defects in the musical dramaturgy of the ballet from the outset: "I think it is clear to you that *The Limpid Stream* is my shameful failure. And that I have felt that way about it from the very beginning. I only want you to believe my attitude and by believing, to un-derstand, and by understanding, to forgive."[63] Critical reaction to the Bolshoy production was more positive. Ironically, even Sollertinsky revised his opinion after experiencing the improved musical performance of *The Limpid Stream* in Moscow: "For the first time *The Limpid Stream* began to sparkle with the richest of orchestral colors. The patchwork quality disap-peared.... Moreover, conjunctions of symphonic development of the musi-cal action were revealed that, it seems, were previously missing from the score of *The Limpid Stream*."[64] The ballet played eleven times in Moscow during the two months after its premiere.

On 17 November 1935, Shostakovich's attendance at a critical rehearsal of *The Limpid Stream* at the Bolshoy Theater was curtailed, as he described wryly in a letter to Sollertinsky:

> Today I had the enormous good fortune of attending the concluding session of the Congress of Stakhanovites. In the presidium I saw Comrade Stalin, Com-rades Molotov, Kaganovich, Voroshilov, Ordzhonikidze, Kalinin, Kosior, Mikoyan, Postïshev, Chubar, Andreyev, and Zhdanov. I heard the speeches of Comrades Stalin, Voroshilov, and Shvernik. I was captivated by Voroshilov's speech, but after hearing Stalin I completely lost any sense of moderation and shouted "Hurrah!" along with the whole hall and applauded endlessly. You will read his historic speech in the newspapers so I won't reproduce it for you. Cer-tainly, today is the happiest day of my life: I saw and heard Stalin.
>
> The Congress began today at 1 PM. That is why I left the rehearsal.[65]

On 26 December 1935, a new production of *Lady Macbeth of the Mtsensk District* received its premiere on the second stage of Moscow's Bolshoy Theater. Conducted by Alexander Melik-Pashayev, whose artistry Shostakovich greatly admired, the production directed by Smolich was modeled on the latter's successful Leningrad production of the opera. It joined Nemirovich-Danchenko's Theater's *Katerina Izmailova*, which was still playing regularly, in Moscow's theatrical repertory. From 5 to 17 Janu-ary 1936, Leningrad's Malïy Opera Theater brought its own production of Shostakovich's opera on tour to the capital, along with its recent staging of

Dzerzhinsky's *The Quiet Don* and several other works. Thus, during the space of a few weeks in early 1936, a visitor to Moscow could have attended three different productions of Shostakovich's opera.

On 17 January, accompanied by Vyacheslav Molotov, Andrey Bubnov, and other high-ranking government officials, Stalin attended a performance of *The Quiet Don* by the touring Malïy company. Before the final act, Dzerzhinsky, Samosud, and the director were summoned to the leader's box for a conversation, widely reported in the press, during which Stalin and Molotov, in addition to identifying some flaws in the production, gave their blessing to "the work of the theater in the sphere of the creation of Soviet opera, noting the considerable ideological-political value of the production of the opera *The Quiet Don.*" [66]

Nine days later, on 26 January, Stalin and his entourage went to the opera once again, this time to see a performance of the Bolshoy's new production of *Lady Macbeth of the Mtsensk District.* Shostakovich happened to be in Moscow that evening, and obviously anticipating something analogous to what had transpired at the performance of Dzerzhinsky's opera, the director of the Bolshoy summoned him to the theater. According to the composer, the show went well and at the end he was given a good reception by the audience. He regretted, however, not having paid his respects to the dignitaries after the third act; not only was the Dzerzhinsky episode not repeated, but Stalin and his associates departed before the end of the opera. With heavy heart, Shostakovich went to catch his train for Arkhangelsk, where he was scheduled to appear in concert with Kubatsky, himself recently fired from the Bolshoy Theater. Shostakovich was left to ponder the ominous signals for the next twenty-four hours or so.

On 28 January 1936, the Soviet artistic community was stunned by the appearance of an unsigned editorial, "Muddle Instead of Music," in *Pravda* (the official newspaper of the Central Committee of the Communist Party):

> Several theaters have presented to the culturally maturing Soviet public Shostakovich's opera *Lady Macbeth of the Mtsensk District* as a novelty, as an accomplishment. Fawning musical criticism extols the opera to the heavens, trumpeting its fame. Instead of practical and serious criticism that could assist him in his future work, the young composer hears only enthusiastic compliments.
>
> From the very first moment of the opera the listener is flabbergasted by the deliberately dissonant, muddled stream of sounds. Snatches of melody, embryos of a musical phrase drown, struggle free and disappear again in the din, the grinding, the squealing. To follow this "music" is difficult, to remember it is impossible....
>
> At the same time as our critics—including musical critics—swear by the name of Socialist Realism, in Shostakovich's work the stage presents us with the coarsest naturalism. [67]

In the crudest of terms ("The music quacks, hoots, pants, and gasps in order to express the love scenes as naturally as possible"), the editorial censured the opera's deliberate rejection of the principles of classical opera and of a "simple, accessible musical language." Its flaws were equated with the petty bourgeois formalist distortions found in the theater (the specter of "Meyerholdism" was specifically invoked), literature, and other spheres. This was contrasted to the "genuine," simple art demanded by the Soviet masses. Shostakovich was accused of having almost deliberately pandered to the unwholesome tastes of "aesthete-formalists"; the opera's success with bourgeois audiences in the West was adduced as proof. That the views expressed represented something much more crucial, and much more official, than an individual expression of aesthetic values was clear. No attempt was made to disguise the threat: "This is a game ... that may end very badly." [68]

Lest the gravity of the cultural situation be lost on Soviet artists, on 6 February 1936 a second unsigned editorial, "Balletic Falsity," appeared in *Pravda*. Here Shostakovich and his collaborators on *The Limpid Stream* were upbraided for their unrealistic, uninformed portrayal of life on a collective farm. They were criticized for their arrogant avoidance of the folk songs, games, and dances that would have contributed authenticity to the ballet. Although the music of *The Limpid Stream* was conceded to be less dissonant and contrived than that of *Lady Macbeth*, the facts that it had "absolutely nothing in common either with collective farms or with the Kuban" and that the composer had recycled music from his "industrial" ballet *The Bolt*, were perceived as damning: "The authors of the ballet— both producers and composer—evidently reckon that our public is undemanding, that it will swallow everything that nimble and impertinent people cook up for it. In actuality, it is only our musical and artistic criticism that is undemanding. It frequently extols works that do not deserve it." [69]

It would take some time for the full meaning and ramifications of these articles to sink in. Over the succeeding days and months the shock waves rippled steadily outward in Soviet culture. For Shostakovich, who was cast down overnight from the summit as the brightest star among young Soviet composers to the abyss as pernicious purveyor of cultural depravity, things would never again be the same.

1936–1937 6
Crisis

On 28 January 1936, when the pivotal "Muddle Instead of Music" appeared in *Pravda*, Shostakovich was in Arkhangelsk. His schedule there was not unduly disrupted by its appearance; he gave his chamber recital with Kubatsky and performed the Piano Concerto with the resident orchestra. On 3 February, he met with young composers. In a lively exchange, he questioned them about their studies, offered advice on the acquisition of musical technique, and encouraged them to study the classics. He brought the enjoyable evening to a close by playing excerpts from his ballet, *The Limpid Stream*, not yet censured in the second *Pravda* editorial.[1]

But the gravity of his predicament did not escape Shostakovich. From Arkhangelsk he instructed Isaak Glikman—Leningrad dramaturg and theater historian who was a devoted friend and sometime assistant to Shostakovich from the early 1930s until the composer's death—to sign up immediately for a newspaper clipping service. He began to compile scrapbooks of relevant material. One gauge of just how quickly the repercussions of the *Pravda* editorials mushroomed into a sweeping cultural crusade is the fact that by 23 February Shostakovich had run out of room in his first, seventy-eight-page, scrapbook.[2]

The assault on *Lady Macbeth* was by no means the first time the debate over formalism had been engaged. Soviet musicians, like their colleagues in the other arts, had for some time paid lip service to the aesthetic ideal of So-

cialist Realism. The meaning of the concept, however, was poorly understood with respect to music, exemplified by the fact that the vast majority of
musicians and critics had concurred wholeheartedly with the advancement
of *Lady Macbeth* as a shining example of the best of Soviet art. As recently as
April 1935, Shostakovich had declared confidently, "At one time I was subjected to fierce critical attacks, principally for formalism. I did not and do
not recognize such reproaches to the slightest extent. I have never been and
never will be a formalist. To disparage any work whatsoever as formalist on
the grounds that the language of the work is complicated and sometimes
not immediately understandable is unacceptable foolishness."[3] Perhaps
even more revealing were his comments at a conference on Soviet symphonic composition in February 1935, when Shostakovich had remarked
on the thorny issue of "content" in music: "There was a time when this was
all greatly simplified. If you set verses, it would seem, there's your content,
if you don't—there's your formalism."[4] In the same forum he had gone on
to urge more thorough study of Western music: "In order to study such
leading masters as Alban Berg, Weill, and others, the Union of Soviet Composers ought to organize a seminar. We need to become more deeply, seriously acquainted with the musical culture of the West, for there is much of
instructive interest there."[5]

In his high-profile role as model young Soviet composer during the year
leading up to the condemnation of *Lady Macbeth*, Shostakovich had been
candid about the influence the music of such contemporary composers as
Berg, Schoenberg, Krenek, Hindemith, and especially Stravinsky had exerted on his development, especially in the three years after completing
Conservatory.[6] Just a few weeks before "Muddle Instead of Music" appeared, Shostakovich commiserated with Sollertinsky on the recent death
of Alban Berg: "His passing grieved me no less than you. The deceased was a
genius. I am convinced that sooner or later he will be appreciated."[7]
Shostakovich had been equally frank, at the same time, in cataloguing the
limitations of his own Conservatory education, voicing his opinion of the
technical inferiority of the new crop of Soviet composers—including that
of his successful protégé Ivan Dzerzhinsky[8]—and the pressing need to
study the "masters" of contemporary Western music. To Shostakovich, a
lack of professionalism in one's craft was inexcusable; appropriating the
best the West had to offer was not incompatible with the lofty mission of a
Soviet composer.[9]

Once *Lady Macbeth* had been singled out and denounced as "formalist"
by *Pravda* and its modernistic defects and "coarse naturalism" linked indis-
solubly with what were perceived as the decadent tastes of the bourgeois
West, Shostakovich found himself in an untenable position. The idealistic
vision of a Soviet music informed by cosmopolitan sophistication was no

longer viable. Taken together with the endorsement of Dzerzhinsky's *The Quiet Don* and the attack on *The Limpid Stream*, whose chief musical sin consisted not in stylistic "formalism" but rather in its willful disregard for the genuine folk sources proper to its subject matter, an approved recipe for Socialist Realism could be deduced by example. The only musical art deemed worthy of the working classes, and thus the only music demanded by the Soviet state, was to be defined by its accessibility, tunefulness, stylistic traditionalism, and folk-inspired qualities. It was to be optimistic, aspiring to heroic exhilaration.

It was hardly a coincidence that on 17 January 1936, the same day Stalin attended the performance of Dzerzhinsky's opera, the establishment was announced of an All-Union Committee for Artistic Affairs (subsequently transformed into the USSR Ministry of Culture) to oversee all artistic organizations, including theaters and educational institutions. On 10 February, in one of his first speeches at the helm of the new organization, Platon Kerzhentsev made it explicit that the larger reach of the *Pravda* editorials extended well beyond Shostakovich and the field of music to all spheres of the arts. To the beleaguered composer, whose fundamental stature as a composer he did not question, Kerzhentsev, a veteran Bolshevik cultural official, offered the following public advice:

> If up to this point Shostakovich composed in privacy under the influence of such sorry excuses for critics as Sollertinsky, then now his work should proceed first and foremost from our country's abundant repertory of folk song. It would not be a bad idea for Shostakovich to take a page from the book of Rimsky-Korsakov. Contact with the abundance of the folk musical heritage had a beneficial effect on his whole work. Only Shostakovich should not restrict himself to the songs of the Russian people as Rimsky-Korsakov did but should travel around the whole Soviet Union and become acquainted with the rich mine of musical folklore of the peoples of the Soviet Union. [10]

The ramifications of the *Pravda* attacks, however, were not instantly apparent to everyone. After their regular meeting on 5 February, Leningrad music critics were assailed by the press for their insufficiently thoughtful attention to the issues raised by the "Muddle" editorial. In Leningrad especially, some musicians expressed disagreement with the tendentious article, mistakenly assuming that the position advanced by *Pravda* might leave room for debate.[11] Brutal attacks on Ivan Sollertinsky were published.

Ironically, in the scramble for scapegoats to explain the monumental lapse in the field of Soviet musical culture, Shostakovich's own sins paled before those of music critics who had praised and encouraged him to pursue his incorrect path, failed to alert him to his "formalistic" mistakes in time, and stimulated, directly or indirectly, other composers to emulate his example. Even now, the immensity of Shostakovich's talent and creative potential was not cast in doubt, and pleas were issued not to turn him into a "living corpse." Chief among the villains held accountable for the situation was Shostakovich's *eminence grise*, Sollertinsky, branded as apologist for and active propagandist of Western bourgeois tendencies, denigrator of native Russian traditions, abhorrent aesthete, and the primary agent of Shostakovich's perversion from the true course of Socialist Realism. That the precocious, charmed pair, Shostakovich and Sollertinsky, had managed to generate no small degree of alienation and envy among some of their peers—their cocky attitude and irreverent, sometimes insensitive humor could be hard to stomach—inevitably contributed to the pitch of their debunking.

By the time Moscow musicians convened for the first of three days of deliberations on 10 February, the participants had acquired a more compliant appreciation of the *Pravda* editorials. Notwithstanding protests against unkind personal remarks directed at Shostakovich, there was little deviation from the ritual justifications, indignant recriminations, and effusive thanks for the far-sighted wisdom of—and timely intervention by—the Party on behalf of the Soviet mass listener. At a second round of meetings in Leningrad, the participants put up less resistance to the inevitable. Analogous sessions were promoted in Kharkov, Kiev, Tiflis, Yerevan, Tambov, and all around the country; the *Pravda* editorials served as catalyst to expose local formalists and their sympathizers and compel a leveling submissiveness. Ideological vigilantes, assisted by additional *Pravda* editorials, ensured that the lessons of Shostakovich's disgrace were not lost on the other arts and that the struggle for conformity to the precepts of Socialist Realism was elevated to a warlike footing.

Shostakovich himself was spared the humiliation of a public expiation. He declined to attend the discussions and issued no public statement, but he read the press with morbid fascination and received detailed reports about the proceedings from friends. At his request, on his way home from Arkhangelsk he was received by Kerzhentsev in Moscow. Shostakovich indicated to him his acceptance of the Party's guidance, albeit somewhat conditionally, and his desire to prove it in his creative work. He was anxious to know whether he needed to write some sort of letter. The chief of the Committee for Artistic Affairs outlined to him the steps that would be required for his rehabilitation, including rejection of his formalist mistakes and the influence of critics like Sollertinsky, the production of music accessible to the masses, and, in future, the submission of any proposed opera or ballet project to advance screening by the Committee for Artistic Affairs. At the end of the audience, Shostakovich asked Kerzhentsev to convey to Comrades Stalin and Molotov the earnest desire of Soviet composers to be granted a meeting with Stalin.[12]

The end of February found Shostakovich back in the capital, sitting by the phone waiting for it to ring. Judging by his remarks in a letter to "his dear and only friend" Sollertinsky, he had applied and was hoping to be received by Stalin. In the meantime, of his friends, he reported that only Shebalin stopped by from time to time. The only other "incident" he had to report since arriving in Moscow was that he had made an implacable foe of Nikolai Golovanov, influential conductor at the Bolshoy Theater, by criticizing him in the discussion after a routine rehearsal of *The Quiet Don*.[13]

Not all colleagues sought to distance themselves from him. The faintheartedness of Asafyev, formerly eloquent exponent of *Lady Macbeth* who deferred forthwith to the superior wisdom of *Pravda*, cannot have surprised the composer. Other prominent figures demonstrated more backbone. In March, Maxim Gorky—influential cultural and social figure and, significantly, the chief literary conceptualizer of Socialist Realism—used his personal access to Stalin to express his indignation at the destructive campaign:

> Shostakovich is young, twenty-five [sic] years old, an unquestionably talented man, but very self-assured and quite high-strung. The *Pravda* article hit him just like a brick on the head, the chap is utterly crushed.... "Muddle," but why? What does this so-called "muddle" consist of? Critics should give a technical assessment of Shostakovich's music. But what the *Pravda* article did was to authorize hundreds of talentless people, hacks of all kinds, to persecute Shostakovich. And that is what they are doing.... You can't call *Pravda*'s attitude to him "solicitous," and he is deserving precisely of a solicitous attitude as the most talented of all contemporary Soviet musicians.[14]

Stalin did not acknowledge Gorky's appeal. Nor did he summon Shostakovich.

Passed over by this particular cultural purge, Boris Pasternak privately identified with Shostakovich and its other victims. He was not alone in experiencing a tragic epiphany: "Everything has become confused, no one understands anything and everyone fears something.... You know what I regret? The past five years we all affected ridiculous naiveté, we, the Bulgakovs of all stripes, the Fedins, the Shostakoviches. No one will return those years to us. And there is little time. But what is to be done?"[15]

On 14 March, in a lecture to a packed hall in Leningrad, Vsevolod Meyerhold, whose own name had been invoked scathingly in "Muddle Instead of Music," spoke up boldly and unexpectedly in defense of Shostakovich and the rehabilitation of his creative work. A spectator recalled the moment: "The hall freezes. An outburst of applause is addressed to Shostakovich, and all heads, as if by command, turn in his direction. Dmitriy Dmitriyevich fidgets, mops his forehead with a handkerchief. Again stormy applause, this time for Meyerhold."[16] Later in the year,

Meyerhold continued to counsel the young composer to be brave, cheerful, and not give in to his sorrow. He expressed his confidence that once Shostakovich heard his new symphony, he would "throw himself once again into the struggle for new monumental music" that would reduce his "spleen" to ashes.[17]

Shostakovich found support from other friends as well. In Moscow that spring, he visited his patron Tukhachevsky, then deputy to Voroshilov and one of the highest-ranking officers in the Red Army. An observer recalled: "I met him [Shostakovich] in the Tukhachevskys' apartment, dispirited, confused. You had to see with what sympathy Mikhaíl Nikolayevich treated him! The two of them closeted themselves for a long time in the study. I don't know what they talked about, but Shostakovich came out a renewed man. He strode resolutely to the piano and began to improvise."[18] Tukhachevsky, too, tried to intercede on Shostakovich's behalf with Stalin, but with no more success. Glikman recalled that at one point that spring Shostakovich confided, "If they cut off both hands, I will compose music anyway holding the pen in my teeth."[19] In a similar vein, Shostakovich wrote in April to his friend Andrey Balanchivadze, one of the few composers to have defended Shostakovich publicly:

> I have suffered and done a great deal of thinking in the recent past. So far I have come to the following conclusion: *Lady Macbeth*, for all her enormous flaws, is for me the kind of work that I could never stab in the back. I could be wrong and it could be that my courage is insufficient, but it seems to me that one needs courage not only to murder one's own things but also to defend them. Since the latter is currently impossible and useless, I am not undertaking anything in that direction.... If you find out sometime that I have "dissociated myself" from *Lady Macbeth*, then know that I did it 100 percent honestly. But I think that this won't happen very soon. Not at least for five or six years; after all, I am slow-witted and very honest in my work.[20]

By early June, just after the birth of his first child, Shostakovich was able to joke with Sollertinsky and a group of his Leningrad compatriots about whether he should name his daughter "Sumburina" or "Falshetta" (feminine names derived from the key words in the titles of the two *Pravda* editorials).[21]

The most therapeutic means for coping with the crisis for Shostakovich was to immerse himself in composition. Nearly forty years later the composer reflected back on that period: "After 'Muddle Instead of Music' the authorities tried to persuade me to repent and expiate my sin. But I refused to repent. What helped me then was my youth and physical strength. Instead of repenting, I wrote my Fourth Symphony."[22]

As long ago as November 1934, the composer disclosed that he had begun, but set aside temporarily, the first movement of his Fourth Symphony.

Subsequently projecting its completion to be one of his main tasks for 1935, along with the composition of the second opera of his tetralogy, he envisaged the symphony as a "monumental, programmatic piece of great ideas and great passions." He indicated that the work had been gestating for many years, but dissatisfied with the sketches made until then he planned to begin over again from scratch.[23] A surviving autograph manuscript of a fully orchestrated opening for the Fourth Symphony that bears no relation to the finished work probably represents some of this discarded material.[24] In April 1935, Shostakovich announced, with the same self-assurance manifested in his simultaneous repudiation of the "formalist" label, that his Fourth Symphony would embody the "credo" of his creative work.[25]

At this point, however, Shostakovich had no progress to report. In an article published in mid-April, on the eve of his departure for Turkey, he admitted he was still uncertain what shape his future symphony would take; as groundwork, he was planning to write some chamber music and instrumental works.[26] He mentioned a string quartet already in progress and a violin sonata. Neither of these works was executed. What was realized in the way of preparatory work were the *Five Fragments* for orchestra, op. 42, all drafted in one day on June 9. The beginning of work on the definitive Fourth Symphony is usually dated from mid-September 1935. At the end of October, Gavriil Popov heard the first movement up until the recapitulation, describing it as "very astringent, strong, and noble," and by early December word of the "grandiose (thirty-minute!)" first movement, completed and dazzlingly orchestrated, had traveled to Moscow.[27] On 6 January 1936, Shostakovich notified Sollertinsky from Moscow, where he was involved with the Bolshoy Theater's ill-fated production of *Lady Macbeth* as well as with the Malïy Opera Theater's tour, that he had finished the second movement of his symphony a few days previously: "It has the character of an intermezzo in tempo Allegretto. It's ten minutes long. I'm pleased with how it has turned out." [28]

The *Pravda* scandal interrupted his progress, but by mid-February 1936 Shostakovich was impatient to get back to work. In mid-April he wrote to friends that he had almost completed orchestrating the third and final movement; he told Shebalin he was at such loose ends that he was dragging out finishing it. The completion date of the Fourth Symphony is conventionally given as 20 May 1936, although Shostakovich wrote to Kubatsky on 27 April that he had completed it the day before,[29] which accords with the projections the composer had made to other friends.

The Fourth Symphony revealed Shostakovich's active, if maverick, engagement with the post-Beethoven symphonic tradition, especially with the music of Mahler. It is in scope and scale, above all, where the shadow of Mahler looms largest. Though not Shostakovich's longest symphony (the

Seventh would claim that honor), the Fourth was his most ambitious and wayward, most prodigal of material, sandwiching a relatively brief "scherzo" between sprawling outer movements, each lasting nearly half an hour. Shostakovich's expressivity here was couched in monumental terms, in the confrontation of extremes ranging from the banal to the sublime, the trivial to the tragic. With a scoring for twenty woodwinds, seventeen brass, and large complements of percussion and strings, the orchestra of the Fourth was the largest required by any of Shostakovich's symphonies.[30]

On one of his periodic conducting tours to Russia, Otto Klemperer made a date to see Shostakovich and hear his new symphony. The evening before the scheduled appointment on 30 May 1936, Klemperer and Sollertinsky turned up unannounced at the Shostakovich apartment. They socialized until after midnight. Early the next morning, Nina gave birth to the couple's first child, Galina. When Klemperer, along with Sollertinsky, Stiedry, Gauk, and others, arrived for the scheduled appointment at noon, they celebrated the birth with champagne and sent a congratulatory telegram to the hospital. Domestic euphoria, however, did not deter Shostakovich from the business at hand of demonstrating his Fourth Symphony to the assembled musicians. As Glikman recalled, the symphony made an enormous impression; both Stiedry and Klemperer were inspired to pledge performances the coming season, the former in Leningrad and the latter in South America. The composer politely but firmly rejected Klemperer's request to reduce the number of flutes (six) required by the score.[31]

Acceptance of the symphony by distinguished musicians could not extinguish Shostakovich's fears, now compounded by the natural anxieties of a man who took the responsibilities of fatherhood exceptionally seriously. He composed little that summer and spent much of September in Odessa as musical supervisor for the Kozintsev and Trauberg film, *Maxim's Return*. He hustled up contracts for several other film projects as well, but he confided to an old friend that one of the consequences he had anticipated from the "historic" days of January 1936 had indeed come to pass: his income had decreased sharply. The *Pravda* campaign had exacted a predictable toll on the number of performances of his works and his concert appearances. Where he used to make 10,000–12,000 rubles a month, he was now barely able to scrape together 2,000–3,000 and had been obliged to cut back on expenses.[32] At times he was reduced to living in debt, reminiscent of his poverty-stricken student days.

His expenses had increased considerably since then. Besides his mother, wife, and infant daughter, Shostakovich's household had expanded in 1935 to include both a cook-housekeeper, Fedosya Kozhunova ("Fenya") and, after the birth of his daughter, his wife's former nanny, Praskovya Demidova ("Pasha"). He never developed expensive tastes—beyond fastidious cleanliness, he was as indifferent to his clothing and appearance as he was to exotic cuisines and creature comforts—but he was not parsimonious. He could not refuse anyone who came to him for assistance, and there were many.

Among Shostakovich's revenue-producing efforts in the autumn of 1936 was his music for a production of Afinogenov's *Salute, Spain!*, a play about the Spanish Civil War conceived in the heat of the moment and brought to the stage at the Pushkin Theater in Leningrad on 23 November, barely a month after its inception. Three other productions of the play were mounted almost simultaneously. Shostakovich had agreed to collaborate reluctantly; one listener took note of the vast gulf between this music— simple, warm, unpretentious, infused with stylized Spanish folklore—and that of *Lady Macbeth*.[33]

The premiere of the Symphony no. 4 in C Minor, op. 43, with the Leningrad Philharmonic conducted by Stiedry was scheduled for 11 December 1936. In anticipation, Shostakovich admitted that he was "trembling with fright."[34] His apprehension was well founded. The concert did not take place. That morning, a brief announcement appeared in *Sovetskoye iskusstvo*: "Composer Shostakovich appealed to the Leningrad Philharmonic with the request to withdraw his Fourth Symphony from performance on the grounds that it in no way corresponds to his current creative convictions and represents for him a long outdated phase."[35]

Isaak Glikman, who attended rehearsals with the composer, recalled the circumstances of the Fourth Symphony's withdrawal:

I don't know about Dmitriy Dmitriyevich, but I sensed suspicion in the hall's atmosphere. Rumors had been circulating in musical and, more importantly, in fringe circles, that, disregarding the criticism, Shostakovich had written a devilishly difficult symphony, jam-packed with formalism.

And then one fine day the secretary of the Union of Composers V. E. Iokhelson showed up at a rehearsal along with an official type from Smolnïy [headquarters of the city's Party apparatus], after which the director of the Philharmonic, I. M. Renzin, a pianist by profession, invited Dmitriy Dmitriyevich to his office.... Fifteen to twenty minutes later Dmitriy Dmitriyevich returned for me and we departed on foot....

I was confused and disturbed by the prolonged silence of my despondent companion. Finally, in a flat, almost expressionless voice, he said that the symphony would not be performed, that it had been withdrawn at the insistent recommendation of Renzin; not wanting to resort to administrative measures, the latter had prevailed upon the composer to refuse consent for the symphony's performance himself.[36]

After the suppression of the Fourth Symphony, rumors explaining its disappearance began to spread. Alexander Gauk, who came from Moscow to attend a rehearsal, observed that Stiedry clearly did not understand the work and was poorly prepared, the orchestra playing was muddy, and the impression produced was atrocious. Kirill Kondrashin, who conducted the premiere twenty-five years later in 1961, embellished the legend of a cancellation motivated chiefly by Stiedry's incompetence.[37] Shostakovich himself lent credence to this explanation in later years and, in 1956, spoke disparagingly of the unknown symphony—before it had been rehabilitated—as imperfect in form, long-winded, and suffering from "grandiosomania."[38]

Stiedry himself later recalled that, after rehearsing the first and second movements without incident, the orchestra made its resistance felt the day they began rehearsing the third movement; the musicians were deliberately not putting forth their best efforts. Noticing this, Shostakovich took Stiedry aside at the break. He pondered whether pressing ahead with a performance of the symphony under the circumstances might provoke a public scandal. Stiedry's impression was that it was Shostakovich who took the initiative in canceling the rest of the rehearsal and the performance.[39] The story Shostakovich subsequently related to Rodion Shchedrin—of having picked up the score and walked out after a noisy, indignant convocation by the orchestral players—is consistent with Stiedry's version.[40] Others also pointed to the opposition mounted by musicians in the orchestra, as well as that of Philharmonic administrators, as the cause for the withdrawal of the Fourth Symphony.[41] When asked the reason in a 1973 interview, Shostakovich's response was terse: "I didn't like the situation. Fear was all around. So I withdrew it."[42] As a consequence of withdrawing it Shostakovich was obliged to pay back his 300-ruble advance.[43]

Perhaps the fact that Stiedry had left the Soviet Union in 1937 and was safely out of harm's way furnished a handy scapegoat to account later for the embarrassingly glaring and audible rift in the composer's catalogue between the Third and Fifth Symphonies. Given the political and aesthetic climate of the time, there seems very little doubt that even in a flawless performance the massive, "Mahlerian" work would have been construed as the epitome of formalism, an act in arrogant defiance of the Party's benevolent guidance.

Indeed, the more intriguing question is not why it was withdrawn but how it came as close to public performance as it did. The symphony had been conceived on an ambitious scale, as the artistic "credo" of an enlightened modernist; the final movement, written after the launching of the *Pravda* campaign, made no conspicuous acknowledgment of or concession to the critical furor. Those who heard the Fourth Symphony then—it was widely studied in professional circles in piano reduction—were awed by its depth, its measure, its "colossal breath." In the mind of at least one of his colleagues the real reason for Shostakovich's withdrawal was shamefully clear. Myaskovsky recorded in his diary on 11 December 1936: "Shosta-kovich was so persecuted by the discussions that he canceled the perfor-mance of his new (Fourth) Symphony—monumental and dazzling. What a disgrace for us, his contemporaries."[44] In 1945, after hearing Shosta-kovich and Moisey Vainberg give a powerful reading of the Fourth Sym-phony in the composer's arrangement for two pianos, the composer's student Yevgeniy Makarov was left in no doubt why the work had been deemed unsuitable for performance ten years earlier. Samosud, Atovmyan, and others present on this occasion brainstormed, exploring options to procure a performance of the Fourth Symphony. They discarded as im-practical the suggestion to renumber it (by then it would have been his Ninth Symphony) in order to avert awkward explanations for its long dis-appearance because too many people already knew the work. Makarov re-mained skeptical about the wisdom of a performance even then.[45]

Shostakovich kept a low profile. The interviews, statements, and articles that had appeared regularly in the press before the *Pravda* attacks disap-peared. In 1937 some semblance of security, financial and professional, re-turned to his life when he was appointed to the faculty of his alma mater, the Leningrad Conservatory. (Sollertinsky, whose career had also taken a nose dive after January 1936, had been recruited a few months earlier by the far-sighted and courageous director of that institution, Boris Zagursky.) Al-though standard sources indicate that Shostakovich's teaching duties started only in the autumn of 1937, he was already teaching instrumenta-tion there from the beginning of 1937.[46]

Above and beyond his own personal and professional crisis and the broader aesthetic campaign against "formalism" in the arts, Shostakovich, who was interested in and stayed informed about current affairs, was not indifferent to or immune from the horrifying developments that were en-veloping Soviet society as a whole. The rising tide of paranoia and isola-tionism, the intensifying threats of conspiracies, the arrests and trials, and the disappearances were inescapable facts of life. On 18 June 1936, Maxim Gorky died (his death was subsequently pinned to "Trotskyites" and "fas-cists" but is now believed to have been on Stalin's orders). In August, the show trial of Zinovyev and Kamenyev and others took place with macabre fanfare. The duly convicted conspirators were shot. The laxness of the secu-rity service in exposing the Trotskyite-Zinovyevite conspiracy led to the ap-pointment of Yezhov as head of the NKVD[47] in September 1936; his name would become synonymous with the worst excesses of the Great Terror. In January 1937 the second Moscow show trial of the "Trotskyite anti-Soviet Center" yielded fourteen more death sentences. And this was just the tip of the iceberg.

Shostakovich's family was not left untouched by the expanding web of

Stalin's purges. Many friends and colleagues disappeared. By the spring of 1937, the composer's brother-in-law, Vsevolod Frederiks, had been arrested, his sister Mariya exiled to Central Asia, and his mother-in-law, Sofya Varzar, sent to labor camp. When he did not receive a letter from Sollertinsky for almost a month while in Gaspra in May 1937, the composer panicked, obviously fearing his best friend might have been arrested, too.[48] Shostakovich may have believed that his friendship with a high-ranking officer in Leningrad's NKVD, Vyacheslav Dombrovsky—a violinist and music-lover—would insulate him from harm, but by the summer of 1937 Dombrovsky had himself fallen victim to the purges, and his wife, Genrietta, was sent to a labor camp.[49] Such were the circumstances under which Shostakovich was expected to produce a work to serve as a public yardstick of the success of his ideological rehabilitation.

With the exception of film and incidental music, in the months that followed the completion of his Fourth Symphony the composer produced only the *Four Romances on Texts of Pushkin* in late 1936—for the hundredth anniversary of the poet's death—completing them on 2 January 1937. (A setting of another Pushkin poem, "The Demons," sketched earlier on 1 August, was left incomplete.) However, he did not submit the songs for performance at that time, insisting that they formed only the initial installment of a planned cycle of twelve Pushkin settings. The premiere of the *Four Romances*, performed by Alexander Baturin accompanied by the composer, took place in Moscow on 8 December 1940.

Reporting on a six-day gathering of members of the Union of Soviet Composers in April 1937, the press duly noted that although in the wake of the *Pravda* editorials Shostakovich was clearly in need of serious criticism and comradely assistance, the leadership of the Union and music critics were colluding in avoiding any mention of Shostakovich's recent work.[50] In fact, nothing new by Shostakovich had been presented to the concert-going public for the past two years.

A week after this report, Shostakovich began the composition of his Fifth Symphony. By early May, when he traveled south with Nina to Gaspra, he had at least the first movement in a form finished enough to play for composer Tikhon Khrennikov and separately, to Khachaturyan and Shebalin. He reported that his new symphony had been very well received by all three.[51] On the way home, in early June, Shostakovich visited in Moscow with respected musician, editor, and long-time mutual associate of Mikhail Tukhachevsky, the theorist Nikolai Zhilyayev.[52] He played for him and for the young composer Grigoriy Frid, who was also in attendance, the *Four Romances* and the two completed movements of his Fifth Symphony. On his departure for the train station at the end of the evening, Shostakovich left behind the first movement and had to return to retrieve it. Frid recalled that, although he understood the romances poorly at the time, the symphony made an enormous impression on him. Zhilyayev's assessment was that the romances still retained traces of "hooliganism" but that the symphony was marvelous, its composer a genius.[53]

In late May 1937, Marshal Tukhachevsky was arrested in Kuybïshev. On 11 June, *Pravda* announced that he and other high-ranking Red Army commanders had been charged with treason. After a summary trial, they were shot the next day. A few days later, when Frid visited Zhilyayev again, he noticed that he had taken down his portrait of the military hero. A few months later, Zhilyayev disappeared.[54] The arrest and execution of Tukhachevsky struck dangerously close to Shostakovich as well. He later confided to a younger colleague that he had been summoned for interrogation at the NKVD headquarters in Leningrad to probe his connections with Tukhachevsky and the ostensible plot to assassinate Stalin; according to this account, he was miraculously spared from the dire consequences of further inquisition by the fortuitous arrest of his own interrogator.[55] Whether or not this particular incident actually took place as described, there is no question that many of Shostakovich's contemporaries perished for crimes much less grave than their close contacts with one of the country's leading military figures convicted and executed for treason. Shostakovich knew well that his life was in peril.

Shostakovich's completion of the Fifth Symphony is routinely dated as 20 July 1937, just three months after it had been begun, although more than five weeks later, on 29 August, the news that he was currently in the process of finishing the fourth movement was circulated.[56] (The composer claimed to have written the third movement, Largo, in three days.[57]) On 8 October, with the work already slated for performance in November by the Leningrad Philharmonic, the composer finally played his new work for his colleagues at the Composers' Union. Shcherbachov, who had also come under fire the previous year for his "formalistic" leanings, found the music on this hearing "remarkable, but sickeningly depressing." He took note of its very strict, ascetic tone as well as of the unusual concentration and emotional integrity of the whole, features he and other contemporaries perceived as unquestionably new in the music of Shostakovich.[58]

In an atmosphere taut with anticipation, Shostakovich's Symphony no. 5 in D Minor, op. 47, received its public premiere on 21 November 1937, performed by the Leningrad Philharmonic Orchestra conducted by a relative unknown, Yevgeniy Mravinsky. The significance of the occasion was apparent to everyone. Shostakovich's fate was at stake. The Fifth Symphony, a nonprogrammatic four-movement work in a traditional, accessible symphonic style, its essence extrapolated in the brief program note as "a lengthy spiritual battle, crowned by victory," scored an absolute, unforgettable triumph with the listeners. One witness recalled that men and women cried openly during the Largo,[59] another that as the finale progressed, the listeners began to rise to their feet, one by one, giving release at the end to a deafening ovation as Mravinsky waved the score over his head.[60] Another listener recorded in her diary: "The whole audience leapt to their feet and erupted into wild applause—a demonstration of their outrage at all the hounding poor Mitya has been through. Everyone kept saying the same thing: 'That was his answer, and it was a good one.' D. D. [Shostakovich] came out white as a sheet, biting his lips. I think he was close to tears."[61] Veniamin Fleyshman, one of the new students in Shostakovich's class, wrote home to the provinces in excitement: "The greatest event of these days was the performance in the Philharmonic of the Fifth Symphony of our teacher, D. D. Shostakovich, which immediately won over all musicians and nonmusicians by the depth of the music, the sincerity and singular talent of its orchestral writing."[62]

The effusive show of support for Shostakovich and his new work was not cause for unqualified jubilation. Among a number of colleagues who traveled from Moscow to attend the premiere, Vissarion Shebalin recalled that the enthusiasm was so great and Shostakovich was called to the stage so many times that the ovation threatened to turn into a demonstration, obviously an ominous development in light of *Pravda's* criticisms of the composer. Sollertinsky and Shebalin's wife did their utmost to remove the composer from the provocative scene as quickly as possible.[63] Mikhaíl Chulaki, then the director of the Leningrad Philharmonic, confirmed that bureaucratic functionaries did, in fact, interpret the unrestrained uproar at the premiere as a challenge to the Party's aesthetic leadership.[64] Two officials from the Committee for Artistic Affairs were dispatched to Leningrad to attend a subsequent performance of the work and investigate how the concert organizers had arranged such a commanding triumph. They concluded, against all the manifest evidence of the symphony's tremendous success with the public, that the audience did not consist of ordinary concertgoers but of plants, hand-picked to assure the success of the work.[65] Alexander Gauk, who also attended the Leningrad premiere of the Fifth Symphony, helped quash the spread of similar disinformation on his return to Moscow the next day when he happened to overhear—and stepped in to overrule—one official attempting to downplay the success of the work to Kerzhentsev, the head of the Committee for Artistic Affairs, as having been fomented by a claque of Shostakovich's friends imported for the purpose from Moscow.[66]

When he conducted the premiere of Shostakovich's Fifth, the thirty-four-year-old Mravinsky was an unsung staff conductor on the roster of the Kirov Theater of Opera and Ballet.[67] He would later allow that he had not fully grasped the nature of the responsibility he had shouldered: "To this day I can't understand how I dared to take on such a proposition without much dithering or hesitation." [68] It was his success introducing this work, nevertheless, that paved the way for his taking top prize in the First All-Union Conducting Competition in October 1938 and landing the post as chief conductor of the Leningrad Philharmonic Orchestra the same year. It also earned him the respect and loyalty of Shostakovich and the privilege of conducting the premieres of many of his subsequent symphonic works.

Mravinsky prepared the Fifth Symphony with a fastidiousness that alarmed even the composer, who was not one to meddle or intrude in the rehearsal process. What the composer remembered as a veritable inquisition, Mravinsky recalled as his own frustrating attempt to enlist the author's help in order to interpret his intentions correctly: "As much as I pestered the composer, I succeeded in 'extracting' virtually nothing from him." [69] Shostakovich's tight-lipped reluctance to talk about his Fifth Symphony went deeper than a simple conflict of rehearsal techniques. For nearly twenty months after the appearance of the *Pravda* editorials in January 1936, Shostakovich's name had virtually disappeared from the press; before then his opinions and information about works-in-progress had been featured regularly and prominently. He had demonstrated no reticence in speaking about his music. Before the first performance of the Fifth Symphony, by contrast, his only published statement about it acknowledged only the simple fact of its completion. Even after its apparently successful unveiling, Shostakovich's unwillingness to speak about the work continued.

On 29 December 1937, more than a month after the premiere, Mravinsky presented a detailed musical analysis of Shostakovich's Fifth Symphony to a gathering at the Composers' Union in Leningrad as part of a continuing peer review process. At their previous session, the members had implored the composer to explain to them what he had meant to say in his new symphony; the latter, pointing to the score, indicated he had "explained" it three or four times already, through its performances. Mravinsky described to them the cunning and chiefly nonverbal means he had used to compel Shostakovich to show him what he intended and averred that his own interpretation bore the exclusive stamp of authorial approval. He offered his own analysis as a surrogate for Shostakovich's; the composer provided musical illustrations from the piano.[70]

After a cautious start, critics embraced the new symphony enthusiastically. The review of Alexey Tolstoy—prominent writer, long-time fan of Shostakovich's music, and, coincidentally, sometime social companion—set a standard in its passionate tone and rhetoric that many subsequent critics would emulate. Advancing an interpretation of Shostakovich's Fifth

Symphony as an exemplar of the loftiest ideals of Socialist Realism, Tolstoy popularized the catch phrase "formation of a personality" (*stanovleniye lichnosti*) as a metaphor to explain the work's dramatic essence and social significance.[71] Evaluation of the new symphony took place in the broad public forum and was not limited to music professionals. Many critics were not entirely convinced by the authenticity of the joy and "optimism" evinced in the finale, particularly after the emotionally charged, funereal Largo, the unquestionable center of gravity of the work. Despite some misgivings, however, almost everyone conceded publicly that Shostakovich, if not yet there, was at least firmly back on the track toward Socialist Realism.

Only after his Fifth Symphony had been successfully vetted through repeat performances to Party officials, the professional music community, and the general public and the readings on the barometer of critical opinion indicated a consensus of support, did Shostakovich finally break his silence. Then, in mid-January 1938, he hazarded the observation that his Fifth Symphony was, to a certain extent, autobiographical, its subject the "suffering of man, and all-conquering optimism. I wanted to convey in the symphony how, through a series of tragic conflicts of great inner spiritual turmoil, optimism asserts itself as a world-view."[72] His desire to be accepted back into the Soviet cultural fold was signaled in yet another statement released the same day: "There is nothing more honorable for a composer than to create works for and with the people. The composer who forgets about this high obligation loses the right to this high calling.... The attention to music on the part of our government and all the Soviet people instills in me the confidence that I will be able to give everything that is in my power."[73]

A few days before the Moscow premiere of his symphony played by the USSR State Symphony under Alexander Gauk, a more expansive, if still cautiously formulated, gloss on the Fifth Symphony, "My Creative Answer," was issued over Shostakovich's signature. In it he underscored the classical antecedents of his symphony, declared special pride with his attainment in the third movement, and rejected the notion that the last movement differed stylistically from the first three. He embraced Tolstoy's metaphor of the "formation of a personality" and his rationalization for the tragic impulse behind the symphony: "It was man, with all his sufferings, that I saw at the center of this work, lyrical from start to finish. The finale of the symphony resolves the tragically tense moments of the opening movements in a life-affirming, optimistic plan."[74] It was here, too, that the composer mentioned that among the many critical interpretations of his symphony, "one gave me special pleasure, where it was said that the Fifth Symphony is the practical creative answer of a Soviet artist to just criticism."[75] This passive appreciation of an unidentified critic's remark is the source of one of the most enduring myths about Shostakovich, that the composer used the phrase as a subtitle for his Fifth Symphony. Shostakovich never accepted the criticism leveled at him and his opera in 1936. The symphony showed no signs that he had taken Kerzhentsev's paternal advice to study Russian folklore or followed any of the other most obvious recipes for rehabilitation. He neither affixed nor endorsed any subtitle to his Fifth Symphony, nor does any appear on the published score. While many of his peers did feel an urgent, perhaps even guilty, need to reclaim Shostakovich into the community of Soviet composers, the conceit of a "subtitle" was seized upon and propagated not so much in the Soviet Union as in the West.[76]

Although broad public reaction to the Fifth Symphony was generally positive—its terms of expressivity, sincerity of feeling, "human" vulnerability, and tragic pathos were perceived as new for a composer best known to date for trenchant satire and acerbic wit—some colleagues who had already heard and admired the Fourth Symphony were somewhat less taken with its successor. In his Fifth Symphony, Shostakovich consciously scaled back his ambition to more manageable, more traditional dimensions, to a clarity of design and execution instantly grasped by the listener because it plays off against familiar paradigms of the symphonic tradition from Beethoven to Chaikovsky and Mahler. Attending the rehearsals for the Moscow premiere, Myaskovsky noted in his diary: "Best of all are the first and third movements, the second is Mahlerian (in the character of minuets and *Ländlers*), the fourth is pungent, the middle is good, but the end is bad. D-major formal reply. The instrumentation is devilish." [77] While finding points in it to admire, after five hearings Myaskovsky had to admit that the Fifth Symphony was not growing on him.[78] Not every listener, at any rate, was immediately won over by Shostakovich's Fifth Symphony. Sollertinsky, Shostakovich's best friend and chief booster, is said to have maintained that the Fifth Symphony was created from the "waste matter" of the Fourth.[79] Yet another who experienced a palpably negative reaction was the poet Osip Mandelstam. On 10 March 1938, less than two months before his fateful arrest, he commented on the Fifth in a letter: "Tedious intimidation.... I cannot approve." [80]

Conductor Boris Khaikin recalled that, after one of the early performances of the Fifth Symphony, Shostakovich remarked to him, "I finished the symphony *fortissimo* and in the major. Everyone is saying that it's an optimistic and life-affirming symphony. I wonder, what would they be saying if I had finished it *pianissimo* and in the minor?" [81] Only years later, after hearing the Fourth Symphony (which ends *pianissimo* and in the minor), did Khaikin fully comprehend the implications of the question.

Whether the finale of the Fifth Symphony succeeds ultimately in balancing the gravity of the preceding movement and the symphony as a whole and whether the *Bildungsroman* scenario (in which "the tragically tense

moments of the opening movements" are resolved in a "life-affirming, optimistic plan") is here convincingly executed are questions that have not
abated since the Fifth Symphony's premiere. The "finale problem" in
Shostakovich's symphonic works was an issue that would crop up again,
notably in connection with his Tenth Symphony. In the light of comments
attributed to the aging, embittered composer in *Testimony*,[82] the suggestion has gained wide currency that Shostakovich may have deliberately set
himself up to fail in crowning the Fifth Symphony with a genuinely jubilant
finale, intending instead to convey the sense of rejoicing under duress.[83]

Shostakovich's reluctance to describe and discuss his music publicly in
any terms but the most sweeping platitudes, a trait that would endure for
the rest of his life, was born of common sense and a survival instinct. It also
proceeded from a natural disinclination to circumscribe the multiplicity of
meanings music harbors. Shostakovich preferred to let his music "speak"
for itself and inevitably directed the curious to his scores. (In a fit of annoyance late in life, Shostakovich equated talking about one's music with blab-
bing about a lover.[84]) No one was in a position to predict where the whims
of Stalin might lead. As the *Lady Macbeth* affair had demonstrated, enormous popularity and critical approbation were no protection, rather the
opposite. That the immediate acclaim and widespread acceptance of the
Fifth Symphony suggested ominous analogies with the history of the reception of *Lady Macbeth* did not go unnoticed. In Leningrad, on 29 January
1938, the same day that Shostakovich was attending the triumphant Moscow premiere of his Fifth Symphony, the pragmatic chairman of that city's
branch of the Composers' Union, composer Isaak Dunayevsky, issued a
statement in which he used Shostakovich's Fifth Symphony as the chief example of the risks posed by the organization's lack of leadership and control
over the promotion of musical works: "Unhealthy instances of agitation—
even of psychosis to a certain extent—are taking place around this work. In
our circumstances this might do both the work and its composer a bad
turn.... Because of the chatter and the sensation we may let the most important thing slip through our fingers: a healthy influence on the composer
and his education in the spirit of the tasks confronting Soviet music.... One
does not need to be a great prophet to foresee what this might lead to." [85]

Fortunately, Shostakovich's Fifth Symphony did not become, at this
juncture, the victim of an unexpected political backlash or critical inversion. Composed under such coercive circumstances, it was a remarkable accomplishment, a work of indisputably outstanding creative originality and
quality. At a defining moment in the history of Soviet music, Shostakovich's
Fifth Symphony set the bar for musical Socialist Realism very high. Within
a few months it was being actively promoted worldwide as a proud Soviet
contribution to the international symphonic literature. Western listeners

did not find Socialist Realism an impediment to their appreciation of the Fifth Symphony's very considerable musical merits; its composer was acknowledged as one of the most significant symphonists of the century. Late in 1938, when the Fifth Symphony was performed at Moscow's Bolshoy Theater in the final concert of a *dekada*, a showcase of Soviet music, Shostakovich was forewarned that Stalin might attend. He did not. In any case, as the composer noted years later, by that point his fortunes had already righted themselves.[86]

Unfortunately, in 1948, Dunayevsky's unheeded warning would echo again all too prophetically.

1938–1941 **7**

Reprieve

"For a whole year after submitting my Fifth Symphony I did almost nothing." [1] The success of his Fifth Symphony earned Shostakovich a creative reprieve, a respite from enormous pressure and stress. It restored his name to favor and removed him, for the time being, from the roster of ideologically suspect artists. The 1936 *Pravda* editorials, however, and the campaign they inflamed, left indelible scars on the composer. Although it is impossible to guess what creative directions he might have pursued and how his music might have developed without external interference, some of the unfortunate consequences are indisputable. A plan in the works for Shostakovich to collaborate with Sollertinsky on a ballet treatment of *Don Quixote* was scuttled. [2] Shostakovich never again undertook an original score for the ballet. Even more unfortunately, at the age of twenty-nine, Shostakovich's career as an operatic composer came to an abrupt and untimely halt. He abandoned his ambition to create a Soviet "Ring" cycle. Though there was rarely a time during the rest of his life when there was not at least one operatic project simmering on a back burner, in what was an incalculable loss for the musical stage, he never completed another opera. [3]

His two-year ordeal had left Shostakovich restless and disoriented. After visiting with Yavorsky in Moscow in May 1938, he resolved to accomplish what he had been unable to do back in his Conservatory days; he wrote to his former mentor requesting to be accepted as his student. Underscoring the utter seriousness of his intent, Shostakovich scheduled an appointment to meet with Yavorsky in late June, promising to give him a full picture of his output and to acquaint him with his unperformed, unpublished works including the Fourth Symphony and the *Four Romances*.[4] Late that year, an understandably distressed Sollertinsky lamented that Shostakovich was planning to pack up his family and move to Moscow for good.[5] Whether or not these two aims were related, neither was carried out at this time.

Insecurity in his own new job as teacher may have had a little to do with Shostakovich's desire to revert to the role of student. As a teacher, Shostakovich did not feel the same innate self-assurance he did as composer or pianist; he was uncomfortably aware that he was not a natural. But Shostakovich was conscientious in everything he set his mind to, and he took his teaching duties extremely seriously, devoting a great deal of time and attention to his students. Although he did not attempt to develop a distinctive methodology or system, he worked hard to impart what he felt they ought to know. He put no restrictions on the type or style of music students might write, demanding from them only integrity and the highest possible quality, an approach that was commended in one of his teaching evaluations. He was tactful and circumspect in framing his comments about new compositions, but students quickly learned to "read" from his behavior whether he really liked something or not. Teaching through professional example with generously shared expertise and sensitivity earned him the devotion of his students. In 1939, they helped Shostakovich celebrate his promotion to the rank of professor at the Leningrad Conservatory.

Orest Yevlakhov and Georgiy Sviridov became Shostakovich's first composition students, joined later in the class by Veniamin Fleyshman, Yuriy Levitin, Galina Ustvolskaya, and others. They were all awed by their teacher's phenomenal musical memory, laserlike insight into compositional flaws, outstanding sight-reading ability, and encyclopedic command of the literature. Shostakovich was exacting in his expectation that his students observe the discipline of regular composing; laziness, alien to his own nature, was not a quality he tolerated in others either. When he assigned in-class exercises to develop compositional skills, he would invariably take part himself. On one occasion when, to drill in speed writing, the students were given a text by Heine to set for voice and piano, Fleyshman observed that "Shostakovich wrote his in five minutes and it was the best of all."[6] Such hands-on demonstrations of Shostakovich's effortless mastery were by no means uncommon.

A central element in Shostakovich's pedagogical approach—as it was a cherished memory of his own professional upbringing—was the exploration of music literature through arrangements for piano four-hands. Shostakovich expected young composers to command keyboard skills and sight-reading facility competent for this purpose, although he tried to wean them from dependence on the piano for composing. In addition to the classics of Western and Russian literature—Mozart, Beethoven, Schumann, Chaikovsky, and so on—Shostakovich shared many of his personal favorites with his students: the Mahler symphonies and *Das Lied von der Erde,* Verdi's *Otello,* and, in his own four-hand arrangement, Stravinsky's *Symphony of Psalms.* Shostakovich also routinely brought his own new compositions to his class, as well as his older works, like *The Nose.*

Shostakovich took a supportive, long-term view of his best students' welfare. On occasion, he discreetly supplied material assistance, as when the ailing Yevlakhov, for instance, was in desperate need of treatment in the Crimea in 1940. He became extremely concerned in the late 1940s when rumors reached him that his former student Sviridov was addicted to the bottle. On learning that Fleyshman had been killed defending Leningrad during the early days of World War II, Shostakovich arranged to have Fleyshman's unfinished one-act opera, *Rothschild's Violin* (based on a short story by Chekhov), sent to him in evacuation. He took it upon himself to complete Fleyshman's promising opus in 1944, and pushed for its publication and performance in the 1960s. Students of subsequent generations would benefit similarly from his personal and professional solicitude.

On 10 May 1938, Shostakovich's second child, a son, Maxim, was born. In the fall, the family moved to a more spacious apartment on Bolshaya Pushkarskaya Street, their last permanent home in Leningrad. The composer was up at six; the morning was generally reserved for composing, with dinner served promptly at two. Always punctual himself, Shostakovich did not countenance tardiness in others any more than he did laziness. He was a considerate friend and a meticulous correspondent, answering his mail promptly and remembering to send birthday and new year's greetings to his friends and acquaintances. Shostakovich's appetite for music was voracious; many of those close to him observed that his need for the sustenance of composing, playing, and listening to music was on a par with his need for food. When unable to attend live performances he followed musical broadcasts on the radio, and he was quick to acquire a record player. He socialized willingly. He liked to drink with friends, but his capacity for both was limited. On occasion, he would appear to withdraw into an inaccessible inner world.

Shostakovich was not a man who suffered idleness or boredom well; he appeared a bundle of nervous energy, given to restless fidgeting and squirming. From his mother he inherited the penchant to wile away idle moments laying out games of solitaire. He was not driven solely by artistic pursuits. From childhood, he was an indefatigable reader of fiction, classic and contemporary. Chess was chiefly a youthful infatuation; although he followed match play, he was never as serious a competitor as Prokofiev or David Oistrakh. In old age one of the favorite yarns he liked to retell was how, as a callow teenager, he had challenged and lost to Alexander Alekhine,[7] something which could have taken place only before the future world champion left Russia for good in the spring of 1921. Shostakovich enjoyed billiards and cards, and during the 1930s he played poker regularly.

One of Shostakovich's poker group was author Mikhaíl Zoshchenko,[8] whose trenchant sense of humor he greatly admired, perhaps because it so uncannily mirrored his own. Zoshchenko characterized the composer's cardplay as "venturesome, severe, and enthusiastic."[9] Shostakovich was obviously a risk-taker. While in Odessa in September 1936, in straitened circumstances and surviving on credit, he sat down twice to play and dropped 1,000 rubles, prompting a sleepless night spent musing on the theme, "unlucky in cards, unlucky in love, unlucky in profession."[10] In December that same year, Gavriil Popov logged an all-night poker game in which Shostakovich played "brilliantly" but nonetheless managed to wind up losing more than anyone else.[11] Zoshchenko, by contrast, was evidently not much of a bluffer. Shostakovich's memory of him at the card table was not charitable, as he reminisced after Zoshchenko's death with writer Anatoliy Mariengof, who with his wife, the actress Anna Nikritina, also figured in the composer's social set: "He played poker abominably! I couldn't stand playing with him. He played like a fool. Always lost."[12] Despite deep mutual admiration for each other's art—and at least cursory exploration of a possible collaboration on a comic opera—Shostakovich and Zoshchenko never really found common ground for a close friendship.[13]

Although he liked to bicycle and enjoyed playing volleyball in the summer, Shostakovich was not particularly dexterous as a sportsman, but he was a passionate fan of soccer: "Shostakovich was a rabid fan. He comported himself like a little boy; leapt up, screamed, gesticulated."[14] With his soccer buddies—a circle of professional players and sports writers largely distinct from his musical friends—Shostakovich closely followed the fortunes of his favorite teams, attended matches as often as possible, and traded detailed descriptions and analyses. His interest in the sport was not casual; he planned ahead when he traveled to take advantage of playing schedules and, on at least one occasion, interrupted a vacation in a remote, idyllic spot in order to return to Leningrad to attend a match.[15] He even enrolled in a school for referees, but could not find enough time to devote to the profession.[16] What fired Shostakovich's passion, judging from his soccer correspondence, was not so much the competitive urge as his love for the beauty of the game, its artistry. He took strong exception to sloppy play and poor sportsmanship. What he may also have admired were the agility and sheer physical grace of players in peak form, qualities he himself always lacked. Reflecting an actuarial streak in his nature, Shostakovich maintained a neat log of soccer scores inscribed in a notebook—championship play arranged in pyramids—for many years both before the war and after. (He used the same notebook to log the results of chess tournaments, to inscribe his worklist by opus number, and, at least initially, to catalogue the scores in his library.[17]) Soccer offered Shostakovich an escape, both from music and from the cares of daily life.

Shostakovich's interests also included public service. Although in later years, as his official obligations mounted, it would become virtually impossible to distinguish between those activities he engaged in willingly and those he simply found himself incapable of declining, as early as the fall of 1925, when he was elected to the academic council at the Leningrad Conservatory for the third year, he maintained that he was attracted to, and interested in, public service.[18] He routinely served on artistic advisory panels and competition juries as well as on various boards of the Union of Composers from its inception. Having become a district deputy in 1934, in 1939 he was elected a representative to the Leningrad City Council. Little research has been conducted on this aspect of his public service, but it does not appear to have involved him actively in decision-making or governance. As in all his endeavors, Shostakovich was scrupulous in executing his responsibilities faithfully.

The year after completion of the Fifth Symphony was not totally barren in the creative sphere. Shortly after the birth of his son, Shostakovich began work on a string quartet. Although he had frequently stressed the necessity for composers to work in a wide range of genres, including chamber music, and had even lamented the shortage of new Soviet works enriching the instrumental repertory, beyond a handful of student compositions the only chamber work Shostakovich had in his portfolio, by age thirty-one, was the Cello Sonata. The medium of the string quartet, however, was not entirely virgin territory for the composer. In 1932, we recall, he had arranged two of his popular tunes for the Vuillaume Quartet and he had also included twelve preludes scored for quartet in his music for the film *Girlfriends* (1934–1935). But no trace has been found of the string quartet he had announced "in progress" in 1935 as preparation for his Fourth Symphony.

Despite all his good intentions—and the persistent needling of members of the Glazunov Quartet, Shostakovich's eager colleagues on the faculty of the Conservatory—the inception of his String Quartet no. 1 in C Major, op. 49, on 30 May 1938 was tentative and its completion, in mid-July, fortuitous:

> I began to write it without special ideas and feelings, I thought that nothing would come of it. After all, the quartet is one of the most difficult musical genres.
> I wrote the first page as a sort of original exercise in the quartet form, not think-

ing about subsequently completing and releasing it. As a rule, I fairly often write things I don't publish. They are my type of composer's studies. But then work on the quartet captivated me and I finished it rather quickly.[19]

Soon after, the composer confided to Sollertinsky, "I have also completed my quartet, the beginning of which I played you. In the process of composition I regrouped in mid-stream. The first movement became the last, the last first. Four movements in all. It didn't turn out particularly well. But, you know, it's hard to compose well. One has to know how." [20]

In anticipation of its first performance, Shostakovich felt obliged to forestall comparison between his First Quartet and his previous work, the Fifth Symphony: "Don't expect to find special depth in this, my first quartet opus. In mood it is joyful, merry, lyrical. I would call it 'spring-like.'" [21] (Years later Shostakovich would expand on the conceptual "program" of his First Quartet: "I tried to convey in it images of childhood, somewhat naive, bright, springlike moods." [22]) He need not have worried. Audiences and critics required no excuse for the composer's "lyrical intermezzo." They were uniformly charmed by the unexpectedly fresh, childlike simplicity of the unpretentious work on its premiere in Leningrad on 10 October 1938 by the Glazunov Quartet.

On 16 November, Shostakovich attended the Moscow premiere[23] of his First Quartet played by the Beethoven Quartet, a group with whom Shostakovich had first come in contact in 1925. They too had been waiting impatiently for a work from the composer. Their performance of Shostakovich's new opus on this occasion was so successful with the public that they were obliged to repeat it in its entirety as an encore. The creative collaboration inaugurated with these performers in 1938 would prove uncommonly productive: the Beethoven Quartet were afforded the privilege of unveiling all but the first and the last of Shostakovich's fifteen quartets. Together with the composer, they also gave the first performance of his Piano Quintet.

Shostakovich did not tally film work in his creative furlough. On completion of the Fifth Symphony, in late 1937 Shostakovich worked on music to the film *Volochayev Days* (directed by the Vasilyev "brothers," Georgiy and Sergey, and released in early 1938), discarding ten drafts, or so he claimed, before being satisfied with the heroic "Partisan Song," which formed the musical backbone.[24] Even before beginning work on the film, Shostakovich had contracted with the Kirov Theater for an opera on the same subject—the defense by partisans against Japanese interventionists in the Far East during the Civil War—and had made sketches toward this end. The operatic project eventually collapsed, early in 1940, ostensibly for lack of a suitable libretto. Also completed by the end of 1937 was Shostakovich's music for part one of *The Great Citizen* (released in February 1938), the first of Fridrikh Ermler's propagandistic two-part series inspired by the career and murder of Sergey Kirov. Shostakovich also provided the music for the second part of the series (released in November 1939). Apparently Shostakovich also briefly contemplated an opera on this subject. Other film music completed during this period included the score for *Friends*, directed by Arnshtam (released in October 1938), Yutkevich's *The Man with a Gun* (released in November 1938), and *The Viborg Side* (released in 1939), the final installment of Kozintsev and Trauberg's popular "Maxim" trilogy.

Father now of two youngsters, Shostakovich contributed music in 1939 to his only children's film, the animation of Samuíl Marshak's *Tale of the Silly Little Mouse* (released in 1940), directed by Tsekhanovsky. The central musical component of the film—animated only after Shostakovich's score had been recorded—was a lullaby designed by the composer to vary according to the personality of each different animal singing it. While working on the score, in April 1939, Shostakovich again communicated his interest in writing a film-opera and sent out feelers to potential librettists and directors.[25]

In autumn 1938, Shostakovich was approached with a paying proposition to compose something for the USSR State Jazz Band, then in the process of formation as an official instrument to regulate the public's taste in popular culture. After hearing a rehearsal of the new ensemble, Shostakovich pledged to create for it a small thematic suite, "à la Musorgsky's *Pictures at an Exhibition*." He claimed, quite disingenuously, that he had never composed anything specifically for jazz ensemble but saw in it a bright future; he promised that his second [sic] jazz work would be a concerto for piano and jazz band.[26] Matvey Blanter recalled that when Shostakovich played his suite for him and the conductor Viktor Knushevitsky they agreed that its instrumentation sounded fine, but the music was not jazzy. After sitting in on a rehearsal, Shostakovich reworked the instrumentation and everyone was satisfied.[27] Shostakovich's three-movement suite—Scherzo, Lullaby, and Serenade—was performed at the ensemble's inaugural public concert on 28 November 1938, on a program that included a transcription of Rachmaninoff's C-sharp Minor Prelude, a rendition of the Georgian folk song "Suliko" (widely rumored to be Stalin's favorite), and the premiere of what would shortly become Blanter's hit song, "Katyusha."[28] Contrary to the information in many sources,[29] Shostakovich's "Suite no. 2 for Jazz Orchestra" is still lost; the eight-movement work frequently misidentified as his "Second Jazz Suite" is actually a compilation of arrangements, chiefly from film music, for variety orchestra.

At a time when Shostakovich was able to appreciate a recess from the glare of the public eye and a modicum of professional stability, many of his colleagues in the arts were not as fortunate. After prolonged attacks in the press, on 8 January 1938 Meyerhold's theater in Moscow was finally shut down by order of Kerzhentsev. Just three months earlier, Shostakovich, claiming overwork, had backed out of his agreement to provide music for a play based on Nikolai Ostrovsky's novel *How the Steel Was Tempered* that Meyerhold was preparing to stage.[30] In the days preceding the closing, while Shostakovich was in Moscow preparing for the local premiere of his Fifth Symphony, he took part in the Meyerhold family council desperately seeking a way to salvage the situation. If the composer had sometimes made catty remarks in letters to Sollertinsky about the director, and his outsized ego, that had changed after Meyerhold's principled public stand in Shostakovich's defense against the persecution fomented by *Pravda* in 1936.

On 25 May 1938, accompanied by Meyerhold, Shostakovich was the honored guest of Konstantin Stanislavsky at his Musical Studio for a demonstration (*The Merry Wives of Windsor*) and consultations aimed at convincing the composer to produce a new opera. A few weeks later, Meyerhold revealed that he was planning to write an opera libretto for Shostakovich based on Mikhaíl Lermontov's *A Hero of Our Times*.[31] (At the same time as Meyerhold hatched this plan, it was publicized that the composer was planning to write a ballet, *Lermontov*, for the Kirov Theater.[32] Five months later, in November 1938, Shostakovich noted that he was thinking of writing an opera on Lermontov's *Masquerade*.[33] None of these designs came to fruition.) In an address on repertory to Stanislavsky's troupe on 4 April 1939, Meyerhold stressed the importance of encouraging the nation's best composers, Shostakovich and Prokofiev among them, to bring their operatic works to the company.[34]

Meanwhile, the purges continued. In early March 1938, the highly publicized "wrecking" trial of Nikolai Bukharin and a score of other prominent figures began. Later that month a counterrevolutionary writers' organization was exposed in Leningrad, implicating a number of prominent writers. In May 1938, Osip Mandelstam was arrested (he was sentenced to five years at hard labor and perished in a transit camp in late December). In May 1939, they came for Isaac Babel (he was shot in January 1940). On an evening in mid-June 1939, Shostakovich and Glikman were on their way home from a soccer match when they bumped into Meyerhold by chance on the staircase of the composer's apartment house. They invited the director in for a cup of tea.[35] The next morning Meyerhold was arrested in his Leningrad apartment. Before her own brutal murder, Zinaída Raikh began collecting signatures on a letter in Meyerhold's defense; Shostakovich was said to have been one of those who signed.[36] To no avail. Meyerhold was summarily tried on 1 February 1940 and shot a day later. Shostakovich only learned the full truth about Meyerhold's fate in 1955, when he took a strong stand supporting the director's rehabilitation at a time when his own situation was none too secure.[37]

Signaling the end of his creative hiatus, Shostakovich announced in late September 1938 that he was anxious to get down to work on his Sixth Symphony, a monumental composition for soloists, chorus, and orchestra employing the poem "Vladimir Ilyich Lenin" by Mayakovsky. Admitting that the declamatory nature of Mayakovsky's verses made them difficult to set, he indicated that over the summer he had made many sketches, largely unsatisfactory, and that hard labor still lay ahead.[38] He returned to the theme of his "Lenin" symphony in published interviews several more times before the end of the year, expanding the conception to incorporate other literary sources, including folktales and songs about Lenin.[39] But by late January 1939, in a radio address, Shostakovich spoke about the Sixth Symphony he was "getting ready to write" with no mention of Lenin or any extramusical associations whatsoever.[40] There was no more talk of text, soloists, or chorus. The relationship between the Sixth Symphony and the "Lenin" symphony had been severed.

On 27 August 1939, Shostakovich played excerpts from the two recently completed movements of what was now his purely instrumental Sixth Symphony to colleagues in Leningrad, creating an "enormous impression" on the listeners. The composer projected completion of the third and final movement of the symphony within a month.[41] A day later his comments were quoted in the press: "The musical character of the Sixth Symphony will differ from the mood and emotional tone of the Fifth Symphony, in which moments of tragedy and tension were characteristic. In my latest symphony, music of a contemplative and lyrical order predominates. I wanted to convey in it the moods of spring, joy, youth."[42] As he was putting the finishing touches on the symphony in October 1939, Shostakovich reiterated its intended moods of "spring, joy, youth, lyricism."[43] He was particularly pleased with the finale when he played the new work for Sollertinsky and Glikman: "This is the first time I have written such a successful finale. It seems to me not even the sternest of critics will be able to find fault with it."[44]

On 21 November 1939, under much less fraught circumstances than had accompanied the unveiling of Shostakovich's Fifth Symphony exactly two years to the day earlier, Mravinsky conducted the premiere of the Symphony no. 6 in B Minor, op. 54, in Leningrad.[45] Glikman recalled that the performance was enormously successful and that the finale was encored.[46] A local critic quickly hailed the new work, confirming that since his previous symphony Shostakovich had made further progress in freeing himself from formalistic influences, and pronounced it to have been written in a clear language accessible to every listener of symphony concerts. He predicted a bright future for the work.[47]

Nonetheless, critical reception of the Sixth Symphony on the whole was decidedly less enthusiastic. The symphony was unveiled during a ten-day festival of Soviet music that also showcased patriotic cantatas by Prokofiev (*Alexander Nevsky*) and Shaporin (*On the Field of Kulikovo*). The deliberately lopsided, unusually ordered three movements of the nonprogrammatic symphony did not square with most critics' expectations of the genre; they could not fathom the underlying conception. Shostakovich's "youthful, joyful" score displayed none of the childlike innocence and charm of the First Quartet; some critics heard in the solemn first movement only shallow pretentiousness and, in the subsequent movements, a reversion to the cold and superficial technical "coquetry" of his formalist days. In the inevitable comparisons with the Fifth Symphony (also performed during the festival), the Sixth emerged the sure loser. The Fifth Symphony, admittedly, was a tough act to follow, and Shostakovich was never a composer to replicate formulas, no matter how successful. He needed to set himself new compositional challenges.

Shostakovich was unable to attend the Moscow premiere of his symphony on 3 December 1939, conducted by Mravinsky—he heard the radio broadcast—but the malicious gossip of Moscow musicians got back to him; "Atovmyan wrote me that all (sic!) the composers are indignant with my symphony. What can be done: I didn't oblige, evidently. As much as I try not to be distressed by this circumstance, all the same my heart is heavy. Age, nerves, all this tells." [48]

If the Sixth Symphony left many critics perplexed and disillusioned, Shostakovich's next major work, the Piano Quintet in G Minor, op. 57, elicited uniformly enthusiastic responses from listeners and critics alike.[49] They immediately recognized it to be a splendid continuation of classical tradition (with polyphonic mastery worthy of Bach in the fugue), a work of beguiling clarity, melodic charm, and vitality, indelibly suffused with the imprint of Shostakovich's individuality. Begun during the summer of 1940 while Shostakovich was vacationing in Luga and completed on 14 September that year, the Piano Quintet received its premiere in Moscow on 23 November in a performance by the Beethoven Quartet with the composer at the piano, during another showcase festival of Soviet music.

After the success of Shostakovich's First Quartet, the Beethoven and Glazunov Quartets kept the pressure on him to provide additional works. Dmitriy Tsïganov, first violinist of the Beethoven Quartet, remembers that Shostakovich, flush with the success of his First Quartet in late 1938, promised to write a piano quintet to play with them, joking that he would write harder parts for the quartet than for himself.[50] The composer confided to

Glikman that he wrote himself into the work as performer on purpose, so that when the Beethoven or Glazunov Quartets wanted to take it on tour they would be obliged to take him along, giving him an excuse to travel.[51] The stratagem paid off handsomely. He rehearsed extensively. The Piano Quintet was nominated for a Stalin Prize by Leningrad's Union of Composers and performed for the prize committee even before its premiere. In the wake of its public triumph, the demand for repeat performances was heavy. The work quickly established itself among Shostakovich's most popular works, and the composer was presented frequent opportunities to perform it at home and on tour.

Such acceptance was by no means routine or inevitable. How precarious the position of the creative artist was in Stalinist Russia is emphasized by a recently published denunciation sent to Stalin on 7 January 1941 by cultural functionary and Communist Party stalwart Moisey Grinberg, in which he condemned consideration of the Piano Quintet for such a prestigious honor as a Stalin Prize:

> An atmosphere of unhealthy sensation has been created around the Piano Quintet by D. Shostakovich. Yet in its essence this is a composition of profoundly Western orientation (I mean the work of contemporary Western composers). The editors of *Pravda* made a mistake by publishing an article ... in which the quintet is touted as "unquestionably the best composition of 1940," and Shostakovich as a neoclassic who has contributed "practical clarity to our debates about the mastery of classical experience." The first movement of the quintet, it is true, is constructed in a classical, Bachian scheme. But how much there is in this quintet of stilted, singular new sounds resulting from abstract formal quests. And how little there is of genuine beauty and strength, emanating from an awareness of genuine life, from the realization in music of great human feelings.... This is music that does not connect with the life of the people.[52]

Grinberg likened the "atmosphere of unhealthy sensation" surrounding Shostakovich's new quintet to the veneration of *Lady Macbeth* in the days preceding the appearance of *Pravda*'s "Muddle Instead of Music." [53] But these grievances went unheeded. In March 1941, when the first recipients of Stalin Prizes were announced, Shostakovich received a "category one" award for his Piano Quintet.

The list of abortive projects—those contracted or announced but not produced, for whatever reason—is particularly long at this point in Shostakovich's career. In addition to those projects already mentioned, Shostakovich considered a number of other operatic ventures, including one in 1939 to a libretto by V. G. Bragin set during the Civil War, and an opera-ballet the same year on Yevgeniy Shvarts's *The Snow Princess*.[54] At least one of his projects was doomed by the censors. In late 1940 the Kirov Theater contracted with Anatoliy Mariengof (librettist) and Shostakovich for an opera based on Lev Tolstoy's *Resurrection*, titled *Katyusha Maslova*, after Tolstoy's heroine. Mariengof got down to work quickly but in early 1941 requested and was granted a deadline extension because Shostakovich had not been available for consultations. *Katyusha Maslova* was included in the list of state commissions for 1941. By 8 March, Mariengof's libretto was complete and Shostakovich notified the Kirov that it was well written and formed a good foundation to begin composition of the music. Later that month, the composer participated in the review of the libretto at the Kirov, pronouncing his approval with only minor reservations. The review panel accepted the libretto and forwarded it for official acceptance to Glavrepertkom, the government agency in Moscow in charge of theater censorship. On 10 May, Glavrepertkom telegraphed its response: "The libretto for the opera *Katyusha Maslova* has been banned." [55]

Shostakovich also flirted with operetta. In July 1939, he announced that he had recently begun work on an operetta, *The Twelve Chairs*, after the popular tale by Ilya Ilf and Yevgeniy Petrov, for inclusion in the repertory of the Leningrad Theater of Musical Comedy. In October 1939 he targeted its completion by the end of the year, but the work never materialized. In the summer of 1940, Shostakovich contemplated orchestrating Offenbach's *La belle Hélène*, confessing he "loves it madly," but he quickly abandoned the idea. [56] When Boris Khaikin—from 1936, artistic director and principal conductor of Leningrad's Malïy Opera Theater—was in the process of mounting a production of Johann Strauss's *The Gypsy Baron* (premiered on 22 February 1941), it was decided to interpolate an extra dance number, a polka, in the final act. Only after the polka had been selected and choreographed did it transpire that there were no orchestra materials available. In desperation, Khaikin called Shostakovich, who orchestrated "The Excursion Train Polka" overnight and with such flair that, as Khaikin recalled, it was invariably encored at every performance. At a certain point they tried to substitute for the encore another choreographed polka, this one in Strauss's own orchestration. The audience's disappointment was discernible, and Shostakovich's singular gem was quickly reinstated as the encore. [57] In May 1941, Khaikin proposed to Shostakovich the more ambitious project of overhauling Strauss's *Wiener Blut*. The composer responded that he liked the operetta and would be pleased to participate, in fact, he wanted expressly to take part in the editing and to orchestrate selected material, [58] but he was unable to start work on it right away. The Nazi invasion of Russia a month later rendered this project another of the casualties of war. Shostakovich's plan to orchestrate Offenbach's *Barbe-bleue* for Khaikin in the summer of 1943 similarly came to nothing. [59]

Unquestionably, the most mysterious and intriguing of Shostakovich's inventions of the period is his work commemorating Lenin, explicated elaborately in more than a dozen interviews spanning two and a half years. Even after his Sixth Symphony took a different direction, he did not abandon the "Lenin" symphony. In August 1939, he outlined the content of his next symphony: "First movement—Lenin's youthful years, second—Lenin at the head of the October storm, third—the death of Vladimir Ilyich and, fourth—without Lenin on the Leninist path. A series of musical fragments are already ready, which will subsequently be incorporated in this, my most significant work of late, the Seventh Symphony in memory of the genius leader of humanity." [60] In a number of interviews released in January 1940, Shostakovich claimed that much material for the first and second movements was already done and that he was expecting to finish that year.[61] In December 1940, he admitted that he had overreached himself and failed in his attempt to write a Lenin cantata on Mayakovsky's text,[62] but reports of his work on his "Lenin" symphony continued well into 1941,[63] and in late May Shostakovich's Seventh Symphony—presumably as yet incomplete— was included in the repertory plan for the Leningrad Philharmonic's 1941–1942 season. Once Germany invaded Russia, Shostakovich's pledges to deliver a "Lenin" symphony vanished abruptly. The Seventh Symphony that materialized consummated a very different agenda. Tangible evidence of his labor on this "Lenin" symphony has not been found; it is hard not to conclude that the enterprise afforded a convenient public relations smokescreen.

The date 21 March 1939 marked the centenary of Musorgsky's birth. Shostakovich chaired the committee charged with organizing activities to commemorate the occasion in Leningrad and delivered the opening remarks at the gala concert honoring the great Russian composer. For three days in mid-April he sat on the jury of a vocal competition for best performance of a work by Musorgsky. Shostakovich's active involvement with the legacy of his predecessor bore fruit. In late 1939, at the instigation of Samuíl Samosud, since 1936 artistic director and principal conductor of the Bolshoy Theater, Shostakovich embarked on the reorchestration of Musorgsky's operatic masterpiece, *Boris Godunov*.

Of all his musical forebears, Musorsgky was the Russian composer to whom Shostakovich felt spiritually closest by this time; in a December 1940 interview he listed him as his favorite composer.[64] The influence of the nineteenth-century composer on his Soviet descendant had not thus far been terribly conspicuous in Shostakovich's music—excepting perhaps in the final act of *Lady Macbeth of the Mtsensk District*—but it would henceforth assume steadily increasing importance. Reorchestrating *Boris* was a potentially foolhardy venture, as Shostakovich well knew. Rimsky-Korsakov's was the standard performing version of the opera. In 1928, accompanied by much fanfare, Musorgsky's original version had been revived

in Leningrad, but it had left doubts about its viability for the modern operatic theater. As work on his own reorchestration was nearing completion in
the spring of 1940, after six months of intensive labor, Shostakovich confessed to Sollertinsky, "The more I work on this, the more I doubt the practical expedience of this work. Everyone will curse me for it. Both the
devotees of Musorgsky and the devotees of Rimsky-Korsakov. The former
for 'infringing,' the latter for my impertinence in 'counterposing.' Both the
former and the latter will find a whole slew of defects.... All the same I am
doing it." [65]

Shostakovich's approach to the reorchestration was dictated on the one
hand by his innate respect for Musorgsky's unique compositional abilities
and, on the other, by the recognition that Musorgsky had been technically
ill equipped to realize the full orchestral potential of his own music.
Shostakovich took exception to Rimsky-Korsakov's extensive "improve-
ments" to Musorgsky's score; in his own version he tried, as far as possible,
to change not a single note of the composer's original. (In the summer of
1940, Shostakovich approached his orchestration of Musorgsky's "Song of
the Flea"—made for but not finally included in the comic film *The Adventures of Korzinkina*— with the same reverence, refusing to "trick it up." [66])
He was called upon to defend his policy of noninterference in the reorchestration of *Boris*, as his comments in a letter to director Nikolai Smolich attest: "I am only instrumenting it. As you can see, the work is of a purely
technological order. I did not set myself other goals. Nor did my client
Samosud.... If I were to follow your directions, then I would be obliged to
recompose a great deal. And that I absolutely don't want to do, even though,
for a composer, it is a task interesting to the highest degree." [67] Many years
later, in 1953, Shostakovich summarized his dissatisfactions with the competition more bluntly: "Rimsky-Korsakov groomed, waved, and sluiced
Musorgsky with eau de cologne. My orchestration is crude, in keeping with
Musorgsky." [68]

Ironically, Shostakovich's orchestration of *Boris* proved as ill-fated as his
own operas. Originally announced for production in 1940, Shostakovich
delivered his reorchestration of Musorgsky's opera to Samosud in late May
that year. Meanwhile the Kirov Theater also entered negotiations with a
view toward producing the new version. That fall, Shostakovich's repeated
attempts to retrieve his score—or even a copy—from the Bolshoy, in order
to fulfill his contractual obligation to the Kirov, produced only the response
that the Bolshoy was intending to stage it in December 1941. When finally
the composer was obliged to travel to Moscow himself he found that
Samosud's commitment to the new version was wavering. Shostakovich's
manuscript had been altered with cuts, massive changes, and rearrange-
ment; he estimated it would take two or three months to restore it to its

original state.[69] The composer took a stern view of Samosud's inclination to compromise (especially marked with respect to the "Polish" scenes): "As far as the opera as a whole is concerned, I remain convinced that Musorgsky did it better than Rimsky-Korsakov did. Obviously, in the given instance, our tastes differ.... Habit is a powerful force. I think that, having conducted Rimsky-Korsakov's version in its day you have become accustomed to his fountain [scene], and a certain asceticism in [the original] Musorgsky and in my orchestration of it shocks you."[70]

How composer and conductor resolved their differences is unclear. Soon afterward, in April 1941, Shostakovich heard Samosud conduct an orchestral rehearsal of his orchestration. He announced that he was looking forward to the premiere with great anticipation. An official from the Committee for Artistic Affairs who vetted the new orchestration was left with no qualms about the propriety of staging the centerpiece of the Russian operatic canon in Shostakovich's version. Unfortunately, the war intervened. When the Bolshoy Theater returned to Moscow from evacuation in 1943, Shostakovich fully expected the production of Musorgsky's opera in his orchestration to be resumed. However, Samosud was soon replaced at the helm of the company by Ariy Pazovsky, who, as former chief at the Kirov had been preparing to mount Shostakovich's version of the opera there before the war but who now elected, or was compelled, to revert to the Rimsky-Korsakov edition. As it transpired, Shostakovich had to wait sixteen more years for the premiere of his orchestration of *Boris Godunov*, on 4 November 1959, at the Kirov Theater in Leningrad.

In response to a plea in early 1941 from his colleague and friend, the writer Marietta Shaginyan, who was newly infatuated with the Piano Quintet and its creator, Mikhaíl Zoshchenko drafted for her a thoughtful portrait of the Shostakovich he knew, a deeply complex individual:

> It seemed to you that he is "frail, fragile, withdrawn, an infinitely direct, pure child." That is so. But if it were only so, then great art (as with him) would never be obtained. He is exactly what you say he is, plus something else—he is hard, acid, extremely intelligent, strong perhaps, despotic and not altogether good-natured (although cerebrally good-natured).
>
> That is the combination in which he must be seen. And then it may be possible to understand his art to some degree.
>
> In him, there are great contradictions. In him, one quality obliterates the other. It is conflict in the highest degree. It is almost a catastrophe.[71]

For Shostakovich, 1941 got off to a good start. As chronicled in the press, he spent the first working day teaching at the Conservatory and performing his quintet that evening with the Glazunov Quartet at the Philharmonic in a concert capped by Mravinsky conducting the Fifth Symphony.[72] On 16 March, the announcement of his Stalin Prize for the Piano Quintet was published. At the time, Shostakovich was busy preparing for the premiere of Kozintsev's production of *King Lear* at the Bolshoy Dramatic Theater in Leningrad on 24 March, for which he provided music. Shakespeare's tragedies were of more than passing interest to Shostakovich: "From the poetry and dynamics of these tragedies music is born.... It is difficult to write music to Shakespeare's plays. The author of *Hamlet* and *King Lear* absolutely does not tolerate banality. It seems to me that when one speaks of the magnitude of Shakespeare then one needs to keep in mind the inner magnitude and the breadth of spirit, not the external pomp and circumstance." [73] In tackling *King Lear* at this point in his career, what interested the composer most was the character of the fool: "With amazing mastery the fool illuminates the gigantic figure of Lear; the difficulty of realizing him in music is enormous. The fool's wit is prickly and sarcastic, his humor magnificently clever and black. The fool is very complicated, paradoxical, and contradictory. Everything he does is unexpected, original, and always wise." [74] Shostakovich may have identified with the fool; as Zoshchenko appreciated, he certainly shared many of the characteristics he describes. His setting of the "Ten Songs of the Fool" formed the centerpiece of his incidental music for Kozintsev's production. In 1942, the composer set Shakespeare's Sonnet 66, including it in his *Six Romances on Texts of W. Raleigh, R. Burns, and W. Shakespeare*, op. 62. Later in life he returned to both *Hamlet* and *King Lear* again, to collaborate with Kozintsev on his celebrated films of the plays.

In early April 1941, Shostakovich went on tour to Rostov-on-Don. Later that month, together with Nina, he departed for a month-long vacation in Gaspra. On the way home, a shocking incident took place. Traveling on the same train to Moscow from Simferopol, Shostakovich encountered violinist Miron Polyakin in the next-door compartment. The two stayed up late playing cards. When the train pulled into the station the next morning, it was discovered that Polyakin had died in his compartment. Shostakovich had been the last person to see him alive; in what can only have been traumatic circumstances, he was interrogated by the militia before being released. [75]

The month of June was occupied with state exams—this year Shostakovich was chairman of the piano commission, as well as a member of the composition jury—and the end-of-year rituals at the Conservatory. The composer eked out a few hours to attend soccer matches. On Sunday, 22 June 1941, at the peak of Leningrad's legendary "white nights," Shostakovich planned to attend a double-header with Glikman and go out to dinner afterward. On their way to the stadium they heard Molotov's radio broadcast proclaiming Germany's invasion of the Soviet Union.

1941–1944 **8**

The War Years

In the week that followed the declaration of war, activities at the Conservatory proceeded almost as if nothing had happened. Exams were completed, students were graduated, and stipend recipients for the next year were selected. Shostakovich had immediately volunteered for the army but was told, "We'll call you when we need you."[1] Another application to join, dated 2 July 1941, also met with rejection. The impatient composer signed up with the Home Guard, then in the process of formation: "I am going to defend my country and am prepared, sparing neither life nor strength, to carry out any mission I am assigned."[2] Shostakovich spent the next few weeks— with a brigade of volunteers from the Conservatory—digging ditches and throwing up weapon emplacements and antitank barriers around Leningrad. Later in the month he was assigned to the firefighting brigade at the Conservatory to protect the roof against incendiary attacks. He never actually had occasion to extinguish an incendiary; Conservatory official Aron Ostrovsky confessed to him toward the end of the war that they had deliberately devised excuses to get him off the roof, especially when danger was imminent, exploiting the pressing need for musical arrangements for frontline performance.[3] But posed photographs of the helmeted composer steadfastly standing guard on the roof of the Conservatory, shot on 29 July and disseminated around the globe, served as potent symbols of Leningraders' heroic resistance.

When not on guard duty, Shostakovich made arrangements of twenty-seven popular songs and operatic arias—predominantly for solo voice accompanied by violin and cello—by composers ranging from his contemporaries Dunayevsky and Blanter to Glinka, Dargomïzhsky, Musorgsky, Beethoven, Rossini, and Bizet. He was named music director of the Home Guard's summarily organized theater and worked on satirical skits for its shows. He set a poem by an acquaintance in the Guard, "The Fearless Regiments Are on the Move" (later popularized at the front as "The Fearless Guard's Regiments Are on the Move" and also known under the title "Song of a Guard's Division") to give the Home Guard its own marching anthem.

Among the patriotic songs most Soviet composers were dashing off on the irresistible impulse of the moment, Shostakovich too penned rousing exhortations to the defense of his homeland. One of these, the "Oath to the People's Commissar," on a text by Vissarion Sayanov, was singled out as one of the best songs of the first months of the war. Initially, it did not meet with unmixed approval. When the composer submitted his simply harmonized tune to the Leningrad branch of Muzgiz, members of the submissions committee charged Shostakovich with having swung from one extreme to the other, from formalism to primitivism. Their harsh evaluation was overruled by the director, an old school friend of the composer, who ordered publication and payment of ten times the normal honorarium. Shostakovich explained his motivation for writing such an uncharacteristically straightforward song with the words: "I want everyone to sing it." [4] In the late 1950s—after Khrushchev's denunciation of Stalin—Sayanov revised the text and the song acquired a new title, "A Great Day Has Come." References to the "people's commissar" were amended, as was the final line of the original song: "The great hour has come, Stalin leads us to battle, his order is law! Go boldly into dread battle!" [5]

Shostakovich began a big work for soloist, chorus, and orchestra on the Psalms of David. [6] He abandoned it after a few days. Then he tried writing his own text but, again, was dissatisfied. On 19 July 1941, he began the composition of a work that would soon occupy a unique place in the history of music, the Seventh Symphony. [7] He composed with feverish intensity; it was so hard to tear himself away that he even took the score with him to the roof of the Conservatory. [8] He later recalled: "I wrote my Seventh Symphony, the *Leningrad*, quickly. I couldn't not write it. War was all around. I had to be together with the people, I wanted to create the image of our embattled country, to engrave it in music." [9]

In early August, noticeably leaner, Shostakovich played the exposition of the first movement and the theme for the central variation episode depicting the Nazi invasion to his friend Glikman. As yet unsure of the eventual outcome of his work and anticipating inevitable accusations of his having imitated Ravel's *Boléro*, he remarked: "Let them accuse me, but that's how I hear war." [10]

Shostakovich completed the draft sketch of the first movement of his Seventh Symphony on 29 August (the fair copy of the score was completed on 3 September 1941) as the Nazi blockade of Leningrad was being consolidated. By then, the personnel of Leningrad's main artistic and intellectual institutions had already been evacuated out of the path of the advancing German army. Shostakovich saw the Sollertinskys off at the train station on 22 August, when they departed with the Philharmonic for the eventual destination of Novosibirsk. Glikman departed with the Conservatory to Tashkent. To the consternation of his friends, Shostakovich himself resisted evacuation. On 29 August he wrote to Sollertinsky that he was planning to evacuate with his family along with Lenfilm to Alma-Ata in two days. Shostakovich did not leave. On 4 September, the Nazis began shelling Leningrad.

On 14 September, together with many of the performing artists who remained in the city, Shostakovich participated in a benefit concert for the defense fund. Three days later, on 17 September, his voice was broadcast over Leningrad Radio: "An hour ago I finished the score of two movements of a large symphonic composition. If I succeed in carrying it off, if I manage to complete the third and fourth movements, then perhaps I'll be able to call it my Seventh Symphony. Why am I telling you this? So that the radio listeners who are listening to me now will know that life in our city is proceeding normally." [11] That evening, some colleagues gathered at the Shostakoviches' apartment to hear the completed movements. One of those present recorded the incredible emotional intensity and immediacy of the impact the performance produced on its audience. At one point, when the airraid sirens sounded, Shostakovich proposed that they continue the music-making after a short break so that he could escort his wife and children to the shelter. [12] A week later Shostakovich celebrated his thirty-fifth birthday modestly, with just a few guests, in a city over which the specter of starvation already hovered.

On 29 September, Shostakovich completed the score of the third movement of his symphony. The next evening the call came from local Party headquarters ordering Shostakovich to evacuate. To the enormous relief of his many friends, on 1 October 1941 he was flown with his wife and two children to Moscow. They were obliged to travel light: the only scores Shostakovich took with him were those of *Lady Macbeth*, his Seventh Symphony, and Stravinsky's *Symphony of Psalms* (the score and his own piano arrangement). [13] When he was finally able to return to Leningrad in the fall of 1944, he was touched to discover that his other manuscripts had been carefully preserved at the Leningrad Philharmonic. Of more immediate concern was the fact that he was forced to leave behind the other members of his family, his mother, sister, and nephew and his wife's relatives.[14] He left with the understanding that they would be evacuated directly.

In the capital, Shostakovich and his family put up at the Hotel Moscow. Boris Khaikin ran into the composer in the hotel shortly after their arrival. At a time when air raid alerts were a frequent occurrence, he recalled observing the composer anxiously pacing in the basement muttering to himself, "Wright brothers, Wright brothers, what have you wrought, what have you wrought?" [15] Shostakovich's stay in Moscow was crowded with interviews and appearances. His made a compelling story, that of a courageous young composer resisting evacuation to defend his native city not only by physical deeds but also through one of the most venerated of human endeavors—one inherently antithetical to the destructive impulse of war—the creation of art. It was a heady propaganda weapon, evoking both inspiration and defiance, and its publicity was exploited skillfully almost from the moment of the work's conception.

On the morning of 15 October, Shostakovich was told to report with his family to the Kazan railway station for evacuation eastward. They were assigned places in a carriage reserved for the Bolshoy Theater. The scene at the station was chaotic; Shostakovich looked so forlorn that others felt compelled to assist the composer—never an aggressive individual—in helping his wife and two small children board and find spots on the seriously overcrowded train, which finally departed at 10 PM, in the darkness of blacked-out Moscow. Traveling on the same train were friends and acquaintances—composers including Vissarion Shebalin, Reinhold Glière, Dmitriy Kabalevsky, and Aram Khachaturyan, as well as Lev Oborin, Boris Khaikin, numerous Bolshoy artists, and luminaries from other cultural spheres. In the turmoil of departure two suitcases of the Shostakoviches' clothing and personal effects were left behind. During the journey, Shostakovich was the shy but grateful recipient of donated pieces of spare clothing. For a time, it was feared that the carefully bundled quilt containing the score of the Seventh Symphony had been lost as well, but during one of the interminable station stops it was found.[16] Among the chief topics of conversation during the journey was the debate over where it would be best to get off: Sverdlovsk, Kuybïshev, Tashkent, or other destinations. Everyone had advice for Shostakovich.[17] When, after an arduous seven-day trip they arrived in Kuybïshev on 22 October, Shostakovich detrained with his tired and hungry family. His intention was to move on to Tashkent eventually (where the Leningrad Conservatory had been sent), but he was held up in Kuybïshev—the seat of the evacuated government, the diplomatic corps, and the central press—and settled down there.

Initially, the Shostakoviches were housed in a school assigned to the

Bolshoy Theater, sleeping on the floor of a cramped classroom. At the beginning of November, the chairman of the Committee for Artistic Affairs arranged for the Shostakoviches to receive a room of their own and for the composer to get a piano. The composer mused about his situation to a colleague:

> When we boarded that dark train compartment with the children in Moscow, I felt like I was in paradise! ... But after seven days of travel I felt like I was in hell. When they billeted me in the school classroom—on a rug no less, and surrounded by suitcases—I once again felt myself in paradise. But three days later the situation already grated; it was impossible to dress, surrounded by masses of strangers.... Once again I perceived it as hell. And then they moved us to this separate room, gave us reasonable conditions.... And what do you think? Soon I felt that I needed a piano. I was given a piano. Everything seemed to be going well and once again I thought, "This is paradise!" But I began to notice that a single room is terribly inconvenient for working; the children are noisy and intrude. They need to make noise, they're children after all, but unfortunately, it makes it impossible for me to work.[18]

What lies behind the manifest frustration is the fact that, in all the disruption of the double evacuation, Shostakovich had lost his composing momentum, something that invariably upset him even in the best of times. Although he had announced in Moscow that the conception, if not the actual composition, of the fourth movement of his Seventh Symphony was well in hand ("Currently I am completing the last, fourth, movement. I have never worked so quickly as now"; [19] "In the finale I want to describe a beautiful future time when the enemy will have been defeated" [20]), on 29 November 1941, exactly two months after the completion of the third movement, he complained in a letter to Sollertinsky that the fourth movement was not going well. A day later, in a letter to Glikman, he admitted that he had not even begun it yet.[21] On 9 December, the Shostakovich family was moved into a separate two-room apartment in Kuybïshev, providing the composer with that "paradise" of creative space he needed. The very next day he reported that he had begun composition of the finale of his symphony.[22] News of the first significant Soviet military successes, the liberation of the cities of Elets and Kalinin,[23] had undoubtedly bolstered his spirits as well.

By this point, Shostakovich had decided to remain in Kuybïshev, partly because he was still working to secure the evacuation from Leningrad of his mother and sister and thought he could best accomplish the task in place. To his great relief, he had tracked down his closest friends scattered in far-flung exiles and also found ways to compensate for the boredom and lack of musical stimulation by playing four-hand piano arrangements with Oborin and listening to a neighbor's limited record collection. Early in

December he was instrumental in organizing a branch of the Union of Composers in Kuybïshev, of which he was elected chairman. On Wednesdays, the members gathered to listen and discuss each others' music; at the first creative gathering, on 10 December, Shostakovich demonstrated the three completed movements of his Seventh Symphony.[24]

On 27 December 1941, the Shostakoviches threw a party. For Flora Litvinova (Yasinovskaya-Litvinova), an impressionable young neighbor whom Nina had recently taken under her wing, it was an unforgettable evening of food, vodka, noisy chatter, and music. When she arrived Shostakovich and Oborin were regaling the guests, drinking, and singing along with a tune from an operetta. Shostakovich was in good spirits, funny and charming at the keyboard, and there was dancing in the corridor. Amid all the merriment, the composer quietly announced that earlier that day he had completed his Seventh Symphony.[25]

Soon afterward, Shostakovich played the completed symphony to musicians and friends, among them Lev Oborin and Samuíl Samosud, the artist Pytor Vilyams and his wife Anna, and the harpist Vera Dulova. Litvinova recalled the occasion:

> When Dmitriy Dmitriyevich finished playing, everyone rushed up to him. He was tired, agitated. Everyone spoke at the same time. About this theme [the "invasion" episode of the first movement], about fascism. Someone immediately dubbed the theme "ratlike." They spoke about the war, struggle, and Victory.... Samosud predicted enormous success for the symphony: it will be played everywhere.
>
> Later that evening ... I looked in again on the Shostakoviches to drink tea. Naturally, they were talking about the symphony again. And then Dmitriy Dmitriyevich said reflectively: "Fascism, of course. But music, real music, is never attached literally to a theme. Fascism isn't simply National Socialism. This music is about terror, slavery, the bondage of the spirit." Later, when Dmitriy Dmitriyevich became used to me and began to trust me, he told me directly that the Seventh (and the Fifth as well) are not only about fascism but about our system, in general about any totalitarianism.[26]

As much as it reveals the possibility of a much broader, and less particular, agenda behind the composition of his Seventh Symphony (and, perhaps even more significantly, his conviction about the impossibility of a literal attachment between music and any narrow theme), this incident also helps to illustrate how completely and unconditionally his contemporaries— close friends and strangers alike—embraced Shostakovich's Seventh as a direct consequence of, and response to, the war. Shostakovich did nothing to disabuse them. His detailed explications of the programmatic basis for the first three movements of his symphony were being widely circulated long before the work was even finished:

The exposition of the first movement tells of the happy, peaceful life of people sure of themselves and their future. This is the simple, peaceful life lived before the war by thousands of Leningrad militiamen, by the whole city, by our country.

In the development, war bursts into the peaceful life of these people. I am not aiming for the naturalistic depiction of war, the depiction of the clatter of arms, the explosion of shells, and so on. I am trying to convey the image of war emotionally.... The reprise is a funeral march or, rather, a requiem for the victims of the war. Simple people honor the memory of their heroes. How much I needed words for this episode! But I couldn't find them anywhere. There was even a moment when I set out to write them myself. But now I am even glad that there aren't any words, because it would complicate the score too much. After the requiem there is an even more tragic episode. I don't know how to characterize this music. Maybe what is here are a mother's tears or even that feeling when grief is so great that there are no tears left. These two lyrical fragments lead to the conclusion of the first movement, to the apotheosis of life, of the sun. At the very end distant thunder appears again reminding us that the war continues....

The second and third movements are not associated with a specific program. They are intended to serve as a lyrical respite.... The second movement of the symphony is a very lyrical scherzo. There is a little humor in it, but for me it is somehow connected with the scherzo of the quintet. The third movement is a passionate adagio, the dramatic center of the work.[27]

In his notes for the premiere of the work, the composer expanded his description of the second and third movements: "The second movement is a scherzo, a fairly well-developed lyrical episode, recalling pleasant events and past joys. The atmosphere is of gentle sadness and reverie. Joy of life and the worship of Nature are the dominant moods of the third movement."[28] Later, the composer admitted that he had considered attaching descriptive titles to each movement—"War," "Memories," "The Country's Wide Expanses," and "Victory"—but found them too restrictive and dropped them.[29]

On completion of the symphony, Shostakovich reported to Sollertinsky: "Three movements turned out successfully. The fourth movement is still much too fresh and thus I can't treat it sufficiently critically, but it seems that everything is also fine. The first three movements (especially the first and third) have stood the test of time and still continue to please me."[30] Some critics found fault with the finale, with its brevity and "insufficient" optimism. Samosud, drafted by the Committee for Artistic Affairs to conduct the premiere of the Seventh Symphony (within days of its completion already being promoted for a Stalin Prize), tried to persuade the composer that to make the finale really effective what he needed was to include soloists and chorus to sing the praises of Stalin. As Shostakovich told Glikman, "There are a whole host of other valuable remarks occasioned by the fourth movement; I take them under consideration, but not into practice, because as far as I am concerned there is no need for a choir and soloists in this movement and the optimism is entirely sufficient." [31]

Beyond the issue of a choral apotheosis, Shostakovich was troubled at first by the prospect of the premiere conducted by Samosud. He knew and respected him highly as an operatic conductor but had misgivings about his competence in the symphonic sphere. What Shostakovich really wanted was to hear Mravinsky conduct the work, but wartime conditions and the enormous propaganda value of the symphony outweighed personal and aesthetic concerns. By late January, the Seventh Symphony was already in rehearsal in Kuybïshev, with Samosud conducting the Bolshoy Theater Orchestra. After hearing the first full run-through of the first two movements on 5 February, Shostakovich was pleased with his own handiwork, with the sound of the orchestra, and with Samosud's masterly execution; he predicted that the symphony would fare well. [32]

The satisfaction Shostakovich might have derived from the preparation of a major new work was undermined by his consuming anxiety over the fate of his loved ones in Leningrad. From the occasional letter, he knew about the desperate hardships his family was enduring in blockaded Leningrad, where the food situation was critical. He was told that his dog had been eaten and that there were no more cats and dogs in the city. Several of his relatives there were suffering from malnutrition. Shostakovich was greatly frustrated that his time-consuming efforts and all the promises of assistance he had received had as yet failed to produce any results, especially since he had been promised when he left Leningrad that his mother, sister, and nephew would follow in a day or so. His agitation was compounded by his less than ideal situation in Kuybïshev. The apartment was freezing. Shostakovich was desperately lonely for his friends and missed the stimulation of an active cultural life. He could not get hold of enough paper, writing or manuscript. By February 1942, he noted that many people were beginning to return to Moscow and himself toyed with the idea of going on to Tashkent, but he decided it was best to stay put until he could ensure the safety of his relatives. At a rehearsal on 14 February, he was given the news that his family would be evacuated from Leningrad without waiting in line, which cheered him up for "two or three hours." [33]

On the evening of 5 March 1942, Shostakovich's Seventh Symphony received its premiere in Kuybïshev in a performance broadcast nationwide and transmitted abroad. It was a musical event of unprecedented significance, offered in an atmosphere charged by months of anticipation. Before the concert, as was his tendency before the premieres of his music, Shostakovich was a nervous wreck: "Dmitriy Dmitriyevich was in a state of acute agitation and tension. He ran from one room to another, mumbling a greeting in passing. He looked pale, and he was clenching his fists." [34]

Shostakovich addressed the audience, live and radio, before the performance, explaining how he came to write the piece, describing its character and content. In an inspirational article published in *Pravda* three weeks later, he reinforced the deeply patriotic impulse behind his Seventh Symphony:

> The war we are fighting against Hitler is an eminently just war. We are defending the freedom, honor, and independence of our Motherland. We are struggling for the highest human ideals in history. We are battling for our culture, for science, for art, for everything we have created and built. And the Soviet artist will never stand aside from that historical confrontation now taking place between reason and obscurantism, between culture and barbarity, between light and darkness....
> I dedicate my Seventh Symphony to our struggle with fascism, to our coming victory over the enemy, and to my native city, Leningrad.[35]

The emotional response to, and inspirational impact of, Shostakovich's Seventh Symphony surpassed all expectations. Even in its dimensions it was unwieldy, a work of defiant determination. It made no compromises or concessions either in length, lasting approximately eighty minutes (and performed at its premiere with an intermission after the first movement), or in scale, with scoring for unusually large orchestra, including eight horns, six trumpets, and six trombones. The resonance of its reception and the immediacy and universality of its morale-boosting effect turned it almost overnight into a potent national—and even international—symbol of just cause and steely resolve in the war against fascism. It anchored itself in the popular consciousness as an instantaneous cultural icon, something totally unprecedented for a serious symphonic work.

On 20 March, Shostakovich flew to Moscow with the principals of the Bolshoy Theater Orchestra to prepare for performances of the Seventh Symphony in the capital. A day before his departure, he was finally reunited with his mother, sister, and nephew in Kuybïshev. Although he reported that his mother was all skin and bones, he was relieved to see that Mariya and her son had survived their ordeal tolerably well. In Moscow, Shostakovich found his in-laws—also recently evacuated from Leningrad—and sent them on to Kuybïshev. Although a few weeks earlier Shostakovich had moved with his family to a more spacious four-room apartment in Kuybïshev, the composer was acutely aware of the burden of his responsibility to feed and restore to health his newly arrived relatives.

The Moscow premiere of Shostakovich's Seventh Symphony, an event no less eagerly anticipated than the performance in Kuybïshev, took place on 29 March 1942 in the Columned Hall of the House of Unions. Samosud was once again the conductor, leading the combined forces of the Bolshoy Orchestra and the All-Union Radio Orchestra. Ilya Erenburg, one of many listeners in whose memory the experience became indelibly inscribed,

recalled that the audience listened in rapt attention to the music of the finale, unconscious of the drone of air-raid sirens on the street outside: "The
public was told of the alert when the concert was over, but people didn't
rush to the shelter. They stood, hailing Shostakovich, they were still in the
grip of the sounds." [36] On 11 April 1942, the announcement was published
that Shostakovich had been awarded a Stalin Prize (category one) for his
Seventh Symphony.

The clamor for performances of the *Leningrad* Symphony was enormous, both at home and abroad. In April, the microfilmed score was flown
to Teheran on the first leg of its circuitous journey to the West. On 22 June
1942, Henry Wood conducted the London Symphony in the Western
broadcast premiere and, on 29 June, in the concert premiere at a Proms
concert at the Royal Albert Hall. Leopold Stokowski, Serge Koussevitzky,
and Artur Rodzinski all vied for the privilege of presenting the American
premiere. Koussevitzky secured the rights for the American concert premiere (which he conducted in Lenox, Massachusetts, on 14 August 1942).
However, the National Broadcasting Company, which had initiated negotiations as early as January, before the symphony had even begun rehearsals
in Kuybïshev, and locked up the first performance rights for the Western
Hemisphere by April, offered the premiere to Arturo Toscanini, who conducted the NBC Orchestra in a studio concert broadcast nationwide on 19
July 1942. The 20 July issue of *Time* magazine, which reached the stands the
week before the broadcast, featured a cover portrait of Shostakovich, bespectacled in his fireman's helmet and in heroic profile. Hundreds of performances followed in the West. In January 1943, it was announced that
Shostakovich (together with Prokofiev) had been elected an honorary
member of the American Academy of Arts and Letters.

During the course of the war, virtually every Soviet city that could mobi-
lize sufficient instrumental forces to tackle the work gave it at least one performance. Of special significance for Shostakovich personally were the
performances by Mravinsky and the Leningrad Philharmonic, still in evacuation. The composer spent most of the month of July 1942 in Novosibirsk,
where in addition to attending Mravinsky's rehearsals and performances of
the Seventh Symphony he was joyfully reunited with Sollertinsky and other
friends displaced from Leningrad. He also performed his Piano Quintet
and the *Four Romances on Texts of Pushkin* at a concert of his music.

Without question, the most remarkable wartime performance of the
Seventh Symphony was the one on 9 August 1942 in blockaded Leningrad,
an event of legendary import all by itself. At the end of the first winter under
siege, city authorities went to extraordinary lengths to revive the city's cultural life. The surviving members of the Radio Orchestra (the only symphony orchestra remaining in Leningrad) who were still capable of

performing were joined by players from other institutions; some were even called back from the trenches. Special rations were granted so that they might regain sufficient strength to perform. Even before the ragtag group of forty or fifty players had made its first concert appearance on 5 April 1942, conducted by the Radio Orchestra's Karl Eliasberg (who had played chamber music with Mitya twenty years earlier when they both studied at the Petrograd Conservatory), the determination to perform Shostakovich's *Leningrad* Symphony was already firm.

The obstacles to performance in the devastated city were enormous. Overcoming them became a matter of civic, even military, pride. In early July, the score of Shostakovich's symphony was flown by night to the blockaded city. A team of copyists worked day and night—despite shortages of paper, pencils, and pens—to prepare the parts. More serious was the insufficiency of brass players to tackle Shostakovich's score; most had to be tracked down at the front. By the end of July the orchestra was rehearsing full time. The concert hall on 9 August 1942 was packed, and the audience applauded with all the strength they could muster. The concert was also broadcast on loudspeakers throughout the city and, in psychological warfare, to the German troops stalled outside the city. They had been targets of an intensive artillery bombardment in advance ordered by the commander of the Leningrad front to ensure their silence during the performance of Shostakovich's Seventh.[37]

Immediately after the completion of the Seventh Symphony, Shostakovich embarked on a composition of a totally different stripe, an operatic setting of Gogol's comic play, *The Gamblers*. (Extreme emotional and stylistic dislocations between successive works were not uncommon in Shostakovich's creative output.) The seeds may have been planted already in late 1938, when Shostakovich read about the Munich pact and apparently noted the similarities between the participating world leaders and Gogol's wily cardsharpers.[38] For his second Gogol opera, the composer set himself the task of setting Gogol's play word for word, without cuts or alterations, as he told Shebalin on 10 June 1942, requesting that he keep it a secret.[39] Although very much in the public eye at this time, Shostakovich informed only his closest friends about his latest work-in-progress, perhaps because, as he remarked in a letter to Sollertinsky, it was "devoid of any point."[40] By 11 November 1942, despite the pleasure he professed to be experiencing writing the opera, the composer had realized the task he had set himself was unrealistic; he had already written thirty minutes' worth of music accounting only for about one-seventh of the opera. On 27 December, he announced that he had dropped work on *The Gamblers* because of the utter senselessness of the enterprise.[41] But in March 1943 Shostakovich told Sollertinsky he was making a piano score and—although he doubted the feasibility of finishing the opera—he was continuing to work on it.[42] A year later, he played and sang the completed portion to three of his students at the Moscow Conservatory, producing a strong impression on them. In outlining its weaknesses and the reasons he did not expect to complete the setting, he cited the problem of length as well as the lack of female roles and a chorus.[43] More than thirty years later, Shostakovich based the second movement of his last composition, the Sonata for Viola and Piano, op. 147, on themes from his abandoned opera.

On 7 May 1942, just in time for Maxim's fourth birthday, his father started a setting for bass and piano of Walter Raleigh's poignant text, "To My Son," in Boris Pasternak's translation, and set it aside. Shostakovich confessed he was busy attending meetings, writing articles, making radio addresses, writing film music—the struggle to find the means to support the extended family under his protection was an ongoing concern—and obviously did not have time to compose.[44] He managed to eke out time to attend the Sunday soccer matches between local squads, but the quality of play was not really up to his standards. In September, Shostakovich left on a three-week trip to Moscow. Fulfilling a commission for the NKVD Song and Dance Ensemble[45] to write a suite of music, *Native Leningrad,* for a patriotic show entitled *Native Country* that premiered in Moscow on 7 November, detained him there for two months.

While in Moscow, Shostakovich met with writer Samuíl Marshak, who provided him with translations of three poems by Robert Burns ("In the Fields," "MacPherson before His Execution," and "Jenny"), which the composer set for bass and piano. On his return to Kuybïshev, Shostakovich performed the three new songs with Alexander Baturin on 4 November. Ten days later he informed Shebalin he had composed three more songs, making a total of six. One of these was actually his Raleigh setting, begun early the previous summer. On 18 November he sent the additional songs, including settings of Shakespeare's Sonnet 66 and "The Royal Campaign," an English children's folk song, to Levon Atovmyan in Moscow with instructions on how they should be correlated with the three Burns songs. He wanted to dedicate these settings to his friends—Atovmyan, Shebalin, Sviridov, Glikman, and Sollertinsky—but had not yet decided which one to whom.[46] By the time Muzfond published Shostakovich's *Six Romances on Texts of W. Raleigh, R. Burns, and W. Shakespeare* for bass and piano, op. 62, in February 1943, Shostakovich had made his selections, adding another friend, his wife, as the sixth dedicatee.[47] He quickly set about orchestrating his "British" songs, completing work on 18 March. Although this very personal work did not establish itself in the repertory, some of its chilling poetic themes would resonate in Shostakovich's late vocal music; a literal reminiscence of "MacPherson before His Execution" appeared in the second movement of his Symphony no. 13, *Babiy Yar*, op. 113 (1962). In 1971, Shostakovich made a new version of the cycle for bass and chamber orchestra, op. 62/140.

As difficult as the war years were for the losses and material hardship, what bothered Shostakovich as much was the dislocation; he missed the contact with his friends, who were scattered all around the country. In the fall of 1942, Shostakovich traced his respected former mentor, Boleslav Yavorsky, to his exile in Saratov. Hearing that Yavorsky's circumstances were appalling, Shostakovich interceded with local authorities and with the Composers' Union in Moscow to improve his situation and support his research. He was deeply distressed by the news of Yavorsky's death in Saratov on 26 November. He had been equally saddened to hear of the death of his former teacher, Leonid Nikolayev, on 11 October in Tashkent, from typhoid fever.

In early February 1943, as Shostakovich was himself beginning to recover from a bout of typhoid, he began to think about a new piano sonata. When he finished the first movement on 18 February, he was contemplating the sonata as a four-movement work, but a month later, on 17 March, he put the finishing touches on the final, third movement. Soon after, he played the new work for the Committee for Artistic Affairs and the Composers' Union. A critic found it an affecting work, a work profoundly influenced by the classical canon in the composer's search for positive themes and profoundly optimistic ideological content (like the quartet and quintet), unquestionably the composer's most significant piano work.[48] Shostakovich dedicated his new piano sonata to the memory of Nikolayev—he later reminisced about him to his own students as a wonderful composition teacher—and gave its public premiere in Moscow on 6 June 1943. At the same concert he accompanied Efrem Flaks in the first complete performance of his *Six Romances on Texts of W. Raleigh, R. Burns, and W. Shakespeare*.

Begun in Kuybïshev, the Piano Sonata no. 2 in B Minor, op. 61, had been completed at a sanatorium near Moscow during a three-week stay at the beginning of March. For almost a year Shostakovich had deliberated moving to Moscow, where he felt it would be easier to live and work, but application to various authorities had failed to yield suitable housing. On this trip, Shostakovich was determined to resolve the issue. Even before he and Nina were able to find an apartment, Shostakovich accepted a professorship at the Moscow Conservatory, where his old friend Shebalin had been named director in November 1942. He started teaching in April—initially he had only one student—and he and Nina moved into their new apartment, on Kirov Street, at the end of the month. The rest of the family joined them in June. They had to make do without furnishings for some time, but even without furniture, Shostakovich found life more interesting in Moscow than in Kuybïshev: "In addition to questions of sustenance, here musical questions crop up." [49] He prepared for the anticipated production of *Boris Godunov* at the Bolshoy and announced plans to orchestrate Offenbach's *Barbe-bleue* for Leningrad's Malïy Theater, to contribute incidental music to a Kozintsev production of Shakespeare's *Otello*, and to compose a children's ballet on Alexey Tolstoy's tale, "The Golden Key." [50]

To Marietta Shaginyan, who visited on 27 May 1943, Shostakovich admitted that, as busy as he was, he had not been able to compose for some time; he complained of a headache he routinely suffered when he was not composing. Dismissing his recent piano sonata as a trifle, he said that he was feeling revulsion toward his own music. What was gnawing at him was the desire to write his Eighth Symphony, [51] an ambition he was soon to realize.

Shostakovich began work on the Eighth Symphony in early July, completing the first movement in Moscow on 3 August 1943. The second and third movements were completed in Ivanovo, on 18 and 25 August, respectively. In the summers of 1943 and 1944, many of the composers recently returned from evacuation made use of a composers' retreat outside Ivanovo, situated on the grounds of a former poultry farm. Working in a converted henhouse, Shostakovich found the surroundings conducive to the submersion in composition that had so recently eluded him. On 9 September, he wrote to Sollertinsky, "Nothing special to write about myself. I have just (literally) finished my Eighth Symphony. There's a certain vacuum in my soul, the kind that's always there when a big work has been completed." [52]

Written quickly, in a little over two months, the Eighth Symphony was not attended by the same fanfare and publicity that accompanied the genesis of the Seventh. Shostakovich showed the work-in-progress to colleagues, but its existence was revealed to the public only after its completion, in an interview published on 18 September 1943:

> I completed work on my new, Eighth Symphony, a few days ago. I wrote it very quickly, in a little over two months. I didn't have any preconceived plan for this symphony. When I completed my Seventh Symphony, I intended to write an opera, and a ballet, and I began to work on a heroic oratorio about the defenders of Moscow. But I set aside the oratorio and started work on my Eighth Symphony. There aren't any concrete events described in it. It expresses my thoughts and experiences, my elevated creative state, which could not help but be influenced by the joyful news connected with the victories of the Red Army. My new composition is an attempt to look into the future, into the postwar era.
>
> The Eighth Symphony contains many inner conflicts, both tragic and dramatic. But, on the whole, it is an optimistic, life-affirming work. The first movement is a long adagio which generates significant dramatic tension at its climax. The second movement is a march with scherzo elements, the third a very forceful,

dynamic march. And, despite its marchlike form, the fourth movement has a sorrowful character. The final fifth movement is bright, joyful music of a pastoral quality with various dance elements and folk tunes....

To compare this symphony with my previous works, in mood it is closest to my Fifth Symphony and the quintet.... I can sum up the philosophical conception of my new work in three words: life is beautiful. Everything that is dark and gloomy will rot away, vanish, and the beautiful will triumph.[53]

Mravinsky undertook to conduct the premiere of the Eighth Symphony, which went into rehearsal in Moscow on 20 October. A student who sneaked into the hall during the initial run-through recorded that Shostakovich was very nervous, sometimes getting up and approaching Mravinsky's back before sitting down again without having spoken. When subsequently asked how the rehearsal went, the composer's answer was "Terribly! ... A wasted day." Five days later, when rehearsals were in full swing, Shostakovich pronounced himself satisfied; he was especially pleased that certain risky spots sounded well, justifying his hopes.[54] During the course of rehearsals, Shostakovich decided to dedicate the symphony to Mravinsky. The premiere of the Eighth Symphony took place in the Large Hall of the Moscow Conservatory on 4 November 1943.

The unprecedented success of the Seventh had created impossible expectations for Shostakovich's next symphony. Critical opinion did not fall in line unanimously behind it. On the one hand, after hearing it for the first time in September, Sollertinsky immediately pronounced the Eighth significantly better than the Seventh. On his own first hearing, Myaskovsky found the symphony tragic despite its pellucid ending.[55] Similarly, Asafyev was overwhelmed by the "incarnation of the tragic greatness of suffering and the inexorability of the human will" in the work and compared its initial impact on him to that of Chaikovsky's Sixth Symphony.[56] Even its most fervent admirers admitted that the Eighth was a challenging work, lacking the instantaneous popular appeal of the Seventh. Poet and dramatist V. M. Gusev, who attended the dress rehearsal on 3 November, noted in his diary that he did not understand everything on first hearing and wanted to hear it again, but he also registered his relief that he had not found the symphony as boring as Khrennikov had forecast.[57] The reviews that appeared—and they were few in number—were generally positive, but their enthusiasm was qualified by caveats about the length of the work and the difficulty of the language. Sollertinsky alerted his wife that one of his upcoming lectures (on the topic of Shostakovich's "creative path") scheduled in Moscow three weeks after the premiere was taking on added consequence because of the controversy surrounding the Eighth.[58] He also attributed the success of the premiere more to Shostakovich's name and stature than to the symphony itself: "It makes an enormous impression, but the music is significantly tougher and more astringent than the Fifth or the Seventh and for that reason it is unlikely to become popular.... And it has some fierce enemies, headed by Yu. A. Shaporin." [59]

Shostakovich was obviously disappointed by the reception of his new symphony. On 8 December 1943 he wrote to his friend Glikman:

> I am sorry you didn't hear my Eighth Symphony. I am very happy with how it went. Mravinsky has played it here four times; on 10 December he will play it for the fifth. The discussion that was to have taken place in the Union of Composers was put off on account of my illness. It will now take place and I have no doubt that valuable critical observations will be articulated in the discussion that will inspire me in my future work, in which I will reexamine my previous work and, instead of one step backward, I will take one step forward.[60]

The Eighth Symphony did, in fact, generate much comment at the Plenum of the Organizing Committee of the Union of Composers (28 March to 7 April 1944) devoted to a survey of the work of Soviet composers during the war years, at which Shostakovich presented the keynote address. Prokofiev, for instance, voiced his own disappointment with the work, criticizing it above all for its excessive length and the weakness of the melodic material. But a central problem in the contemporary reception of Shostakovich's Eighth Symphony was pinpointed by N. A. Timofeyev: "What is the reason for the somewhat chilly reception of the Eighth Symphony? I think it is because these tremendous experiences, these sufferings brought about by evil are not overcome, are not vanquished, instead they are, as it were, replaced by a passacaglia and a pastorale. Evidently, listeners sensed that the weakness of this work is in the transition to its last movements." [61] At a time when the presentiment of impending victory over the Nazis was becoming palpable in the Soviet Union, Shostakovich's failure to limn the psychological climate—to provide an optimistic, even triumphant finale—was a letdown to those inclined to read the symphony, like its predecessor, as an authentic wartime documentary. In a speech to the Stalin Prize Committee on 16 March 1944, actor-director Solomon Mikhoels defended Shostakovich: "I am deeply convinced that the music of Shostakovich belongs to the future near at hand.... Many don't understand Beethoven and Chaikovsky; all that signifies is that the listeners are not sufficiently cultured. In the musical sense they are illiterate.... Their contemporaries didn't understand Beethoven, Stendahl, Mayakovsky.... We, the builders of the future, should be especially attentive to those artists who are able to sense the future, who outstrip their time. Shostakovich is just such an artist." [62] Despite the support of Myaskovsky and others on the prize committee, the opinion expressed by the chairman of the Committee for Artistic Affairs, Mikhaíl Khrapchenko, prevailed: Shostakovich's Eighth

Symphony was recidivous and too individualistic, its language intentionally complicated and inaccessible, its mood exceptionally pessimistic.[63]
Shostakovich did not receive a Stalin Prize for his Eighth Symphony.

Mravinsky continued to promote the Eighth Symphony, performing it
with the Leningrad Philharmonic in Novosibirsk and later at home in
Leningrad, soon after the return from evacuation. The American premiere
was presented by Artur Rodzinski and the New York Philharmonic on 2
April 1944, and the British premiere, in a studio broadcast, by Henry Wood
and the BBC Orchestra on 13 July 1944. But unlike its predecessor, the
Eighth Symphony was not immediately taken up and championed by many
conductors.

While writing his Eighth Symphony, Shostakovich took time out to participate in the competition for a new national anthem to replace the
"Internationale," which had been in use since 1917. Like many of the nearly
200 competitors, Shostakovich penned multiple anthems; one was on a text
by Yevgeniy Dolmatovsky, another used a variant of the winning text by
Sergey Mikhalkov and El-Registan. At some point during the competition,
Marshal Voroshilov suggested that Shostakovich and Aram Khachaturyan
collaborate to submit a joint entry. Their joint anthem, in addition to their
individual entries, made it to the third and final round, which was adjudi-
cated in the Bolshoy Theater. The Red Army Chorus and the Bolshoy Theater Orchestra presented each anthem separately, and then with combined
forces, for consideration by members of the Party and government. During
one of these screenings, in late autumn 1943, Shostakovich and
Khachaturyan were summoned to Stalin's box.[64] The story has undoubtedly been embellished in the retelling,[65] but its main issue is clear. In the
course of the conversation, Stalin expounded his ideas about the ideal national anthem. He praised the entry by A. V. Alexandrov, which adapted the
Mikhalkov-El-Registan text to a well-known song, "Hymn of the Bolshevik
Party," composed in 1939. When Stalin criticized the orchestration of this
anthem and Alexandrov tried to shift the blame for his orchestration to
Viktor Knushevitsky, who had in fact orchestrated many of the entries,
Shostakovich challenged Alexandrov and accused him of lying. Afterward
he explained the reason for his incautious outburst: "But why did he try to
ruin Knushevitsky? After all, Knushevitsky is in the military. They could
dispatch him the devil knows where." [66] This incident notwithstanding,
when the announcement was made in late December, it was Alexandrov's
music that had been chosen for the new national anthem.[67]

On request, Shostakovich willingly played his anthem to his students in
the fall of 1943, showed them the text and encouraged them to compose
music to it. With a text substitution, the Shostakovich-Khachaturyan anthem became the "Song of the Red Army." Shostakovich recycled the song

he had originally written on the Mikhalkov-El-Registan text into the score of another review for the NKVD Song and Dance Ensemble, *Russian River*, op. 66, that premiered in Moscow on 17 April 1944. (Its opening melodic phrases later served as the basis for *Novorossiisk Chimes*, composed in 1960.) This was not the end of Shostakovich's career as a composer of patriotic anthems; his archive includes an anthem for the Russian Federation composed in 1945, and in 1948 he was an unsuccessful contestant in the competition for a hymn to Moscow.

Shortly before his death in 1942, Yavorsky wrote Shostakovich optimistically: "I hope we will soon hear the Fourth [Symphony]. The Rapmovtsï will be no more, the Patriotic War should sweep them away.... Now they won't be able to shut us up, their despotic time has passed when they prescribed for composers the etiquette of permissible respectably joyful 'emotions.'" [68] We do not know whether Shostakovich ever shared in this optimism. By late 1943, however, with the prospect of victory considerably closer, Shostakovich contemplated the future with a characteristic touch of irony:

> It is now the last day of 1943, 4 PM. A blizzard is raging outside my window. 1944 approaches. A year of happiness, a year of joy, a year of victory. This year will bring us much joy. Freedom-loving peoples will finally cast off the yoke of Hitlerism and peace will reign all over the world. We will once again begin to live a peaceful life under the sun of the Stalinist constitution. I am convinced of this and therefore experience extreme joy. You and I are separated temporarily; I wish you were here so that together we could celebrate the glorious victory of the Red Army led by the great commander Comrade Stalin.[69]

The next day, when some students came for their lesson, Shostakovich told them his new year had gotten off to a bad start because he had become stuck in the elevator between the third and fourth floors for ten minutes. He reiterated this often enough to provoke the suspicion that he might be superstitious.[70]

Any disposition Shostakovich might have had toward superstition was soon validated. On 11 February 1944, his closest friend and companion, the person he respected most, Ivan Sollertinsky, died suddenly in Novosibirsk at the age of forty-one—in preceding days he had been complaining of heart pains. The separation from Sollertinsky had been hard on Shostakovich during the war years. No sooner had he secured his own niche in Moscow in the spring of 1943 than he started plotting unremittingly for his friend to join him in the capital. Shostakovich eagerly awaited Sollertinsky's visits to Moscow in September, when he played him his just-completed Eighth Symphony, and again in November, when, among his other activities, Sollertinsky gave a nationally broadcast address commemorating the fiftieth anniversary of Chaikovsky's death. When he returned to

Novosibirsk in mid-December, plans for his permanent move to Moscow had been finalized. Only a few days before his death, on the nights of 5 and 6 February 1944, Sollertinsky introduced the premiere performances of Shostakovich's Eighth Symphony in Novosibirsk.

Shostakovich's loss was incalculable. He offered his condolences to Sollertinsky's widow: "It is impossible to express in words all the grief that engulfed me on hearing the news about Ivan Ivanovich's death. Ivan Ivanovich was my very closest and dearest friend. I am indebted to him for all my growth. To live without him will be unbearably difficult." [71] His published eulogy was no less personal and poignant, as were subsequent reminiscences. More than twenty years later, Shostakovich confessed in a television interview, "When I work on new compositions, I always think, And what would Ivan Ivanovich have said about this?" [72]

If Shostakovich felt unequal to the task of adequately paying tribute to his friend in words, he proved more than eloquent in music. He dedicated the first major work completed after Sollertinsky's death, the Piano Trio no. 2 in E Minor, op. 67, for piano, violin, and cello, to the memory of his friend. Actually, he had started composing the trio late in 1943 and worked on it concurrently with his completion of the orchestration of Fleyshman's opera, *Rothschild's Violin*.[73] In one of his routine briefings on forthcoming works that October, he mentioned he had started writing a piano trio "on Russian folk themes," [74] and in a letter dated 8 December Shostakovich alerted Glikman that he was working on a trio, so it seems more than likely he had also briefed Sollertinsky before he left Moscow two days earlier. In early January, he responded to a questionnaire elucidating his views on chamber music: "Chamber music demands of a composer the most impeccable technique and depth of thought. I don't think I will be wrong if I say that composers sometimes hide their poverty-stricken ideas behind the brilliance of orchestral sound. The timbral riches which are at the disposal of the contemporary symphony orchestra are inaccessible to the small chamber ensemble. Thus, to write a chamber work is much harder than to write an orchestral one." [75] As a demonstration of his commitment to chamber music, Shostakovich noted that he was currently writing a trio. Its first movement was completed in Moscow on 15 February, four days after Sollertinsky's death.[76]

Progress on the trio then ground to a halt. During the spring, Shostakovich experienced bouts of depression and illness. In April he wrote to Glikman: "I can't work. I'm not composing anything. Because of that I am suffering, since it seems to me that I will never be able to compose another note again." [77] His teaching responsibilities continued; in July, when he was finishing up music to the film *Zoya*—about a young wartime heroine—he presided over the final examinations in piano at the Moscow Conservatory. When they were over, he left to join his family at the Ivanovo artists' retreat.

At Ivanovo, Shostakovich finished his trio quickly, dating completion of the second movement on 4 August 1944 and the final (fourth) movement on 13 August. Soon after, he began the composition of his Second String Quartet, completing the score on 20 September. On 6 September, Shostakovich greeted Vissarion Shebalin on the occasion of the twentieth anniversary of their acquaintance: "Yesterday I finished the second movement of the quartet that I began composing while here. I started the third movement (penultimate) without a pause. To commemorate the aforementioned anniversary, I would like to dedicate the quartet to you." [78] In sharp contrast to his recent complaint about artistic impotence, now Shostakovich fretted about his creative profligacy: "The process of music composition gives me no little concern and unrest. What bothers me is the lightning speed with which I compose. Without a doubt, it isn't good. One shouldn't compose as quickly as I do.... It is exhausting, not particularly pleasant and, on conclusion, one has no confidence whatsoever that the time hasn't been wasted. But the bad habit reasserts itself and, as before, I compose too quickly." [79] His companions, in the meantime, were hard pressed to figure out when he found the *time* to compose so much; at Ivanovo, Shostakovich was a regular at soccer matches and other social activities. [80] Late in life, in response to a questionnaire, Shostakovich indicated that for him the compositional process always began with an instantaneous grasp of the future work, a vision of the whole. [81] He estimated that when engrossed in work—and with only lunch to distract him—he averaged twenty to thirty pages of score a day. [82]

Shostakovich had told Dmitriy Tsïganov about the trio in the spring, when only the first movement was done. He had the parts sent to Tsïganov and to Sergey Shirinsky (respectively, the first violinist and cellist of the Beethoven Quartet) as soon as the work was finished. From late September, Shostakovich rehearsed the trio with them assiduously and supervised the full Beethoven Quartet in rehearsals of his Second Quartet, painstakingly working out interpretive details. The rehearsals were sometimes attended by friends (Oborin, Shebalin) and sometimes by the composer's children, Maxim and Galya. After listening to the first movement of the trio, six-year-old Maxim went to the keyboard and accurately picked out the theme with one finger: "Maxim announces that he likes the quartet less well because it doesn't have such 'jolly tunes' as this one and, singing this theme, he moves off, smiling happily." [83]

The public premieres of the Second Piano Trio (performed by the composer with Tsïganov and Shirinsky) and the Second Quartet (performed by the Beethoven Quartet) took place in Leningrad on 14 November 1944. The

trio was received especially warmly and was quickly taken up by other performers. That it furnished a worthy addition to the distinctively Russian
tradition of musical memorials composed for piano trio—capped by the
trios of Chaikovsky and Rachmaninoff—did not escape remark by his contemporaries. Sollertinsky's sister recognized in the second movement "an
amazingly exact portrait of Ivan Ivanovich, whom Shostakovich understood like no one else. That is his temper, his polemics, his manner of
speech, his habit of returning to one and the same thought, developing
it." [84] In 1946, the trio was awarded a Stalin Prize (category two).

1945–1948
"Victory" 9

Glory to the helmsman of our country, to the genius leader and commander,
to the great Stalin!

As the tide of World War II gradually turned and the military successes of the Allied forces on the Western front and the Soviets on the Eastern made the defeat of Hitler's army ever more certain, the pressure increased proportionately on Soviet artists to blazon triumphantly the approaching victory, the national salvation, and, above all, to exalt the genius and brilliant leadership of the conquering hero, Stalin.[1] In October 1943, on the eve of the premiere of his Eighth Symphony, Shostakovich was already publicizing his intent to write his Ninth Symphony—"about the greatness of the Russian people, about our Red Army liberating our native land from the enemy"—a symphony dedicated to the Victory.[2] A year later, in a ritual deposition on the occasion of the twenty-seventh anniversary of the Revolution, Shostakovich affirmed:

> Now that the Great Patriotic War is coming to an end, its historical significance is ever more clearly apparent. It is a war of culture and light against darkness and obscurantism, a war of truth and humanism against the savage morality of murderers.... What are my dreams today, reflecting on the future of our creative art? Undoubtedly like every Soviet artist, I harbor the tremulous dream of a large-scale work in which the overpowering feelings ruling us today would find expres-

sion. I think that the epigraph to all our work in the coming years will be the single word "Victory." [3]

David Rabinovich recalled a conversation he had with Shostakovich in 1944 when the latter indicated he was already thinking about his next, ninth, symphony: "I would like to write it for a chorus and solo singers as well as an orchestra if I could find suitable material for the book and if I were not afraid that I might be suspected of wanting to draw immodest analogies." [4] Meeting with his students at his apartment on 16 January 1945, Shostakovich informed them that the day before he had begun work on a new symphony and that he had completed the exposition. When asked about his progress a week later, he had reached the middle of the development section but complained that the going was slow because he was writing straight into full score and the work opened with a big *tutti*.[5] In February, the composer was quoted in the press: "On the threshold of approaching victory, we must honor with reverence the memory of the brave soldiers who have died, and glorify the heroes of our army for eternity." [6] During the winter of 1945, it was well known to Soviet musicians that Shostakovich was at work on his Ninth Symphony. Rabinovich reported: "Some musicians even had an opportunity to listen to the beginning, powerful, victorious major music in a vigorous tempo. Shostakovich told friends he was working with enthusiasm." [7] Glikman was one of those who heard ten minutes or so of the music Shostakovich had written for the first movement ("majestic in scale, in pathos, in its breathtaking motion") when he visited the composer in Moscow in late April. Shostakovich allowed then that he was troubled by much in the symphony, not least of all by its ordinal, which was inducing in many the temptation to compare it with Beethoven's Ninth.[8]

Whether intimidated by the possibility of "immodest analogies" with Beethoven's Ninth, oppressed by the widespread anticipation of a "Victory" symphony to cap his wartime trilogy, or simply dissatisfied with what he had written, Shostakovich dropped work on this symphony. When Shostakovich resumed composing his Ninth Symphony in late July 1945—after the victory over the Nazis was firmly in hand, hailed with festive rejoicing on Red Square on 9 May 1945—it was an entirely new work. Completed on 30 August, the five-movement symphony lasting barely twenty-five minutes bore no resemblance whatsoever to the monumental symphonic apotheosis everyone had been expecting. Lacking a chorus, lacking a program, lacking all pretensions to gravity and majesty (also lacking a big *tutti* opening), it was almost the antithesis of expectations. Shostakovich forewarned listeners: "In character, the Ninth Symphony differs sharply from my preceding symphonies, the Seventh and the Eighth. If the Seventh and the Eighth symphonies bore a tragic-heroic character, then in the

Ninth a transparent, pellucid, and bright mood predominates." [9] After Shostakovich and Svyatoslav Richter played the Ninth Symphony in a four-hand arrangement to musicians and cultural officials in early September, one critic observed: "It seems that in his Ninth Symphony Shostakovich is taking a breather, a creative diversion from those great philosophical-ethical problems that formed the content of his Seventh and Eighth Symphonies.... The Ninth Symphony is like a symphony-scherzo, separating Shostakovich's two preceding orchestral tragedies from the concluding Victory symphony the composer conceived long ago and which, undoubtedly, he will eventually write." [10]

Though many were caught off guard, the initial reaction of his peers to Shostakovich's Ninth Symphony was generally favorable. Myaskovsky took a dislike to it, describing it as "shrill," [11] but Gavriil Popov was charmed: "Transparent. Much light and air. Marvelous *tutti*, fine themes (the main theme of the first movement— Mozart!). Almost literally Mozart. But, of course, everything very individual, Shostakovichian.... A marvelous symphony. The finale is splendid in its joie de vivre, gaiety, brilliance, and pungency!!" [12] Semyon Shlifshteyn rated it one of the most harmonious creations in Shostakovich's music. [13] Khachaturyan predicted a great future for the symphony.

The premiere of the Ninth Symphony, conducted by Mravinsky, took place on 3 November 1945, sharing the program with Chaikovsky's Fifth Symphony, on the opening concert of the twenty-fifth season of the Leningrad Philharmonic, carried around the country in a live radio broadcast. Shostakovich's new symphony was well received; by popular demand, the last three movements were repeated. The Moscow premiere took place two weeks later, on 20 November, with Mravinsky conducting the USSR State Symphony. It was no less successful. Reviewing the new symphony, critics assessed its achievement as more directly comparable to the composer's chamber scores and to the humor and spirit of his early works than to the philosophical weightiness of his more recent symphonies. Daniil Zhitomirsky emphasized: "For all the surface simplicity and accessibility of its content, the Ninth Symphony possesses that degree of artistic beauty and spirituality that permits contact with the precious vital sources of art. This is the significance of Shostakovich's new symphony." [14] That critical opinion did not coalesce unanimously in support of the Ninth Symphony, however, was evidenced by revived accusations of the "grotesque" in Shostakovich's music, of the paradoxical contrasts of the "serious" with the "trifling," afflictions associated with his youthful, now discredited, style.

When members gathered at the Union of Composers in Moscow to discuss Shostakovich's new symphony in early December, Zhitomirsky found himself obliged to defend it from the deep disappointment of those who found it an inappropriate reflection of the self-congratulatory national mood, as well as from literal, oversimplified interpretations of the content of the symphony. He urged his colleagues not to insist on reducing this music to a formula.[15] When the next issue of the union's journal, *Sovetskaya muzïka*, reported on the discussion, however, it published not the critiques but the views of one of the Ninth Symphony's professed admirers. Nikolai Timofeyev, a composer who had known Shostakovich since 1925, concluded his article with a conciliatory comment: "I think that after a few years have passed, we will hear this music very differently.... And then we will come especially to love this work notwithstanding its few flaws, perhaps even for the presence of those very qualities that now occasionally seem to us paradoxical."[16] Unfortunately, his hopeful prediction did not come true. Two years later, it would be alleged that the negative reviews of the Ninth Symphony originally submitted to *Sovetskaya muzïka* had been suppressed on the personal directive of the chairman of the Committee for Artistic Affairs, Mikhaíl Khrapchenko.[17] Nominated for the Stalin Prize in 1946, Shostakovich's Ninth Symphony failed to win it.

Having been a reluctant evacuee from his native Leningrad in 1941, Shostakovich frequently evinced his longing to return home during the war years. He was intensely proud of his native city, its people, and its cultural institutions. When he was visited in Moscow in the summer of 1943 by Ostrovsky, emissary from the Leningrad Conservatory, still domiciled at that time in Tashkent, Shostakovich pointed to a copy of Riemann's *Musik-Lexikon* and pronounced: "If I am ever judged worthy of inclusion in this book, I want it to read that I was born and died in Leningrad."[18] He wrote to his former colleagues then that he expected they would all soon be back in their classrooms. The blockade of Leningrad was lifted on 27 January 1944. In late August of that year, Shostakovich attended the final soccer match in Moscow and proudly rooted for his home team, Leningrad's Zenith, in their triumphant quest for the national championship.[19] The next month, the Leningrad Conservatory returned home and, in early October, Shostakovich and his wife visited Leningrad for the first time since their evacuation three years earlier.

Shostakovich made regular visits to Leningrad, where his mother had already resettled, but he did not hasten to resume his teaching or residence there. In February 1946 he wrote a letter in English to Fritz Stiedry, advising him of the circumstances of Sollertinsky's death and informing him: "My family lives in Moscow now, but we miss Leningrad and intend to return there."[20] To Stiedry, and others, Shostakovich touted the pre-eminence of the Leningrad Philharmonic among Soviet orchestras. Shostakovich continued to accept major new responsibilities in Leningrad. He continued to consign his major new works to premieres there. But for all that, he did not move back. In January 1947, the family moved into a new apartment—actually into two adjoining apartments with separate entrances—on Mozhaiskoye Shosse (renamed Kutuzovsky Prospect in 1957), where Shostakovich would remain until 1962. Arnshtam contended that the Shostakoviches were provided this apartment, as well as a dacha, at the personal direction of Stalin, an arrangement that was communicated to Shostakovich by Lavrentiy Beria.[21] If so, then the choice of where Shostakovich would reside was taken out of his hands. By November 1947, Shostakovich's mother had finally given up hope for her son's permanent return: "I still can't get accustomed to the idea that Mitya has abandoned his city. But in all probability it was necessary."[22]

In December 1944, eight-year-old Galina Shostakovich, her feet dangling above the piano pedals, performed a newly composed march at a public concert of music for children organized by the Union of Composers. She was followed at the keyboard by the composer, her father, who demonstrated another new children's piece, a waltz.[23] Years later, Galina recalled that her father wrote pieces for her one by one, as she progressed on the piano, and she would labor over each one for a couple of months.[24] Six of them were published as his *Children's Notebook*, op. 69. A seventh piece, "Birthday," written for his daughter's ninth birthday in 1945, was later appended to the collection. When a new weekly children's radio show about music was inaugurated in June 1945, Shostakovich was recruited as editor-in-chief, actively throwing his weight behind the task of propagandizing good music and cultivating the tastes of the nation's youth. On the first broadcasts, Shostakovich spoke about the importance of music and played his cycle of children's piano pieces.[25]

Beginning in 1946, Shostakovich spent summers with his family in Kellomäki (renamed Komarovo in 1948), a resort in the Karelian Isthmus fifty kilometers northwest of Leningrad. Until 1950, when the privilege was rescinded, they lived in a dacha supplied by the state and thereafter on the second floor of a dacha built by his father-in-law. Shostakovich was generally most productive during these idyllic summer stints, but his work never stopped him from attending as many soccer games as possible, or from socializing with family and friends.

During a winter break beginning in late February 1946, Shostakovich and his family vacationed at Ivanovo, along with Prokofiev, Khachaturyan, and other musicians. This was not a working vacation for Shostakovich. Clumsy on skis, he nevertheless went out every day with his children. After supper in the communal dining room, the guests engaged in music-making or charades. Shostakovich threw himself into these leisure activities with no less intensity than he would invest in more serious pursuits.

Relaxing with the Shostakovich family on this occasion was Mstislav

Rostropovich. In December 1945, the eighteen-year-old cellist had captured first prize at the All-Union Competition for Performers. Rostropovich has credited Shostakovich, who chaired the jury for the instrumentalists, with principled intervention in the political crosscurrents of the competition to assure that the prize was awarded on merit.[26] In Ivanovo, Shostakovich subsidized the purchase of the young performer's first concert outfit. They celebrated the acquisition with some local, nearly lethal, moonshine.[27]

During the war years, strict regimentation of Soviet artists and intellectuals had inevitably slipped from the list of top priorities. In the euphoria immediately following victory, faith that the loosening of constraints and repressive control over the arts would translate in peacetime into a more relaxed and enlightened cultural atmosphere was shared widely by Soviet intellectuals. Their hopes were quickly deflated. Perceiving threats to his power both from within the country and—as a consequence of the contacts between Soviet and Allied forces—from the capitalist West, a paranoid Stalin moved with a sense of fresh urgency to reassert his domination over the intelligentsia as a whole.

Early in 1946, Stalin picked Andrey Zhdanov as his ideological watchdog. On 14 August 1946, the Central Committee of the Communist Party issued a resolution, "On the Journals *Zvezda* and *Leningrad*," publicly triggering a wave of cultural purges that would eventually become known as the "Zhdanovshchina." The resolution censured the two Leningrad-based journals (and shut down *Leningrad* entirely) for their publication of works by Mikhaíl Zoshchenko and Anna Akhmatova, branding the former writer as exemplifying vulgarity, lack of moral principle, and an apolitical attitude and the latter as the exponent of bourgeois-aristocratic aestheticism and decadence ("art for art's sake"). The importance of Soviet literature for the political education and training of new generations, its obligation to deal with issues of relevance to contemporary life, and its total subservience to the interests of the people and the state were underscored.[28] Zhdanov's subsequent speech to Leningrad writers and Party activists, in which the implications of the resolution were interpreted and amplified, became a no less influential document. Both resolution and the text of the speech were widely distributed. Additional resolutions soon followed: "On the Repertory of Dramatic Theaters and Measures to Improve It" on 26 August; and "On the Film *A Great Life*" on 4 September. The same day, Akhmatova and Zoshchenko were expelled from the USSR Writers' Union.

Just as in 1936, the creative intelligentsia from all spheres was expected to respond energetically to the resolutions, applying the admonitions and prescriptions directly to their own disciplines. On 24 September, the day before his fortieth birthday, Shostakovich wrote to Glikman that he was awaiting, "with interest," the beginning of the expanded Plenum of the Composers' Union Orgkomitet (Organizational Committee), scheduled to start at the end of the month. With unmatched personal experience in these matters, Shostakovich could have harbored no illusions and surely felt some trepidation about what might transpire. He was deeply distressed by Zoshchenko's plight after the initial resolution had appeared and, according to a number of reports, discreetly provided the proud writer with material assistance.

Since the appearance of his Ninth Symphony, Shostakovich had written only one work of substance, his Third String Quartet. After finishing its second movement in late January 1946, progress on the work slowed during the winter months. Shostakovich completed the remaining four movements between 9 May (first movement) in Moscow, and 2 August in Kellomäki, a few days before the appearance of the first of the Central Committee resolutions on cultural affairs. Experiencing the rush of creative consummation, the composer wrote to Vasiliy Shirinsky: "It seems to me that I have never been so pleased with one of my works as with this quartet. Probably I am mistaken, but for the time being this is exactly how I feel." [29]

Shostakovich dedicated his new quartet to the Beethoven Quartet— Dmitriy Tsïganov, Vasiliy Shirinsky, Vadim Borisovsky, and Sergey Shirinsky—an ensemble of musicians whose friendship and collaboration with the composer stretched back more than twenty years and to whom he was deeply grateful. (Just a few days before the premiere of his new quartet Shostakovich helped the ensemble celebrate the milestone of its five thousandth rehearsal![30]) Zhitomirsky rated the work highly: "In the wealth and versatility of its ideas, the Third Quartet surpasses everything the composer has composed in the sphere of chamber music." [31] For all the considerable strengths of the quartet, however, the cultural crisis that erupted between the time of its completion and its first performance, on 16 December 1946 in Moscow, effectively eclipsed its reception. Even after its unofficial censure in 1948 as "formalist," Shostakovich continued to regard the Third Quartet as one of his most successful compositions, singling it out as such to the young Edison Denisov in 1950.[32]

On 30 September 1946, a highly critical article by musicologist Izraíl Nestyev, "Remarks on the Work of D. Shostakovich: Some Thoughts Occasioned by His Ninth Symphony," was published. The timing of its appearance, on the eve of the Composers' Plenum, and its context, alongside the transcript of Zhdanov's speech in *Kul'tura i zhizn'*, the recently founded organ of the Central Committee's Directorate for Propaganda and Agitation, spoke volumes. Acknowledging Shostakovich's best scores as the pride of Soviet music, a puzzled Nestyev nevertheless sought satisfactory explanations for the appearance of the Ninth Symphony with its playful and grotesque humor: "What remains to be proposed is that the Ninth Symphony is a kind of respite, a light and amusing interlude between Shostakovich's significant creations, a temporary rejection of great, serious problems for the sake of playful, filigree-trimmed trifles. But is it the right time for a great artist to go on vacation, to take a break from contemporary problems?" Not for the first time in Shostakovich's career, his music was separated into two sharply contrasting tendencies. The first, and admittedly most prominent over the past ten years, was characterized by Nestyev as the striving for high principles and the humanism of art. The second was characterized by its "cynical, pernicious grotesquerie, the tone of relentless mockery and ridicule, emphasis on the ugliness and cruelty of life, the cold irony of stylization." Stravinsky ("an artist without a country, without belief in progressive, elevated ideals and deep ethical principles") was invoked as the unrivaled master of this latter tendency, one stemming from the decline of bourgeois art. The article concluded with a clear charge to Shostakovich: "For a whole generation of Soviet people who have grown up over the past twenty years, Shostakovich is their favorite composer, their pride and hope. This generation believes in Shostakovich, seeing in him the expression of the noblest ideals and strivings, a singer of life's truths. It expects this truth from the composer in his future work." [33]

It fell to Khachaturyan, as keynote speaker at the Plenum, which took place from 2 to 8 October 1946 and gathered together representatives from all across the country, to frame the issues for discussion, to outline the implications of the Central Committee resolutions for the world of Soviet music and musical life. The appearance of Nestyev's article obliged him to tackle the problem of Shostakovich's Ninth Symphony. Khachaturyan deftly postponed judgment by acknowledging that after the heroic Seventh and the tragic Eighth Symphony, "We were entitled to expect a different Ninth Symphony, more monumental, more associated with great contemporary images. For now the symphonic trilogy promised by Shostakovich remains unfinished, and the present Ninth Symphony evades the task of completing that trilogy." [34] He was firm in his defense of Shostakovich from accusations of insidious influence from the West, describing him as a Soviet patriot bred from Russian national traditions and as the pride of Soviet music. Several subsequent speakers attempted to tarnish this image, to tear down the composer from his lofty pedestal, but they were counterbalanced by equally ardent defenders. More threatening were attacks on Shostakovich's "imitators," young composers including Moisey Vainberg and Yuriy Levitin, whose music was thought to manifest the strong influence of Shostakovich's music with insufficient discrimination. It did not escape notice that when Shostakovich finally spoke to the assembly, he did not bother to address the criticisms leveled at his own music. He made no concessions, no apologies. Beyond his comments on the broad significance of the Central Committee resolutions, he rose only to the defense of the younger composers.

In the circumstances, the composers and musicologists at the Plenum took the high road, generally interpreting their task as constructive and forward-looking rather than as a destructive, recriminating enterprise. Most of the perceived failings were traced not to individuals but to dissatisfactions with the Composers' Union and other musical institutions, to the indifference or administrative incompetence of the Orgkomitet—of which, incidentally, Shostakovich was a member—and to the inadequacy of musical criticism. The Orgkomitet was charged with a radical restructuring of its activities. Composers and musicologists bought themselves a reprieve with their declaration of allegiance to the principles of the Central Committee resolutions and with the promise they could and would live up to the pressing demands of the Soviet people.

On 12 October 1946, laid up with a serious case of the flu, Shostakovich wrote to Glikman that he had been forced to miss the last two sessions of the Plenum because of his illness. He summed up the earlier sessions in one word: "interesting." He betrayed a sense of world weariness belied by his still youthful years when he remarked, "All the same, I notice that illnesses and all manner of ordeals now come harder: the years are passing." [35]

Shostakovich's prestige remained substantially unaffected by these events. Earlier in the year he had been awarded his third Stalin Prize (for the Second Piano Trio).[36] In December 1946, as part of the largesse distributed during the celebration of the eightieth anniversary of the Moscow Conservatory, Shostakovich was awarded the Order of Lenin as one of its most distinguished professors. Meanwhile, after the death in Leningrad of his teacher, Maximilian Steinberg, in December 1946, Shostakovich was invited to take over his composition class, and on 1 February 1947, he was reregistered as professor at the Leningrad Conservatory. That same month, still residing in Moscow, Shostakovich was unanimously selected chairman of the Leningrad branch of the Composers' Union and was also elected to the RSFSR Supreme Soviet as representative from Leningrad's Dzerzhinsky District. On the eve of the thirtieth anniversary of the October Revolution, he—together with Khachaturyan, Prokofiev, Shebalin, and Shaporin—was named a People's Artist of the RSFSR.[37] Shostakovich's standing and visibility as a leading Soviet composer and dedicated public servant had never been greater.

In light of the recent Central Committee resolutions and the discussions concerning the proper civic role of the arts, commemorating the thirtieth anniversary of the Revolution conspicuously with newly composed, appropriately ceremonial musical works became a matter of no small importance in the Soviet music world. No composer could afford to ignore the obligation. Shostakovich, however, got off to a rather late start. At the end of August 1947, the composer disclosed that he had written a *Festive Overture* for the upcoming celebrations, but even though it was slated for performance by Mravinsky in Leningrad, as well as in Moscow and other cities around the country, the work failed to materialize.[38] On 14 October, it was announced that a few days earlier he had finished a new work written for the thirtieth anniversary, *Poem of the Motherland*. The "solemn, heroic poem-cantata"—scored for mezzo-soprano, tenor, two baritones, and bass, with chorus and full orchestra—was a relatively straightforward medley of six well-known songs spanning the history of the Revolution: "Boldly, Comrades, Keep Step," "O'er Hills and Dales," Alexandrov's "Sacred War," Shostakovich's own "Song of the Counterplan," Dunayevsky's "Song of the Motherland," and Vano Muradeli's prize-winning 1945 paean to victory, "The Will of Stalin Led Us." Shostakovich explained: "These songs give rise in the listener's soul to feelings and images dear and unmistakable to every Soviet person. The main thing all these images give rise to is the passionate and selfless love of Soviet people for their country, the firm determination to sacrifice oneself for the Motherland."[39]

On 15 October 1947, Shostakovich informed Atovmyan that Muzfond would be assuming responsibility for copying the parts.[40] Just how high a priority, and what human and material resources were invested, in bringing *Poem of the Motherland* to the public is attested to by the fact that two weeks later the parts were not only ready but the work had already been rehearsed and recorded for imminent release (on 78 rpm) by soloists, chorus, and orchestra of the Bolshoy Theater conducted by Konstantin Ivanov.[41] Although it was certainly broadcast on the radio at the time, whether the *Poem of the Motherland* also received live performances during the thirtieth anniversary festivities has not been established. In subsequent months it would be pronounced a dismal failure with the public, the feeble effort of a composer who had not been able to come up with anything more significant for the celebration.[42]

On 5 January 1948, Stalin and members of the Politburo attended a "dress rehearsal" at the Bolshoy Theater of Vano Muradeli's opera *The Great Friendship*, the most heralded of the musical offerings rendered for the thirtieth anniversary of the Revolution. The opera dealt with a historical subject that should have been dear to Stalin's heart, the consolidation of Communist power in the northern Caucasus during the Civil War period. The dignitaries, however, were not pleased by what they saw. The matter might have ended there, with the quiet suppression of the production, had it not already been publicly unveiled, amid great fanfare, at the Bolshoy, the premiere stage of the country, in performances on 7 and 9 November 1947.

Productions had also been mounted in more than a dozen regional theaters.

We now know that indications of an impending offensive on the musical front had surfaced earlier. In mid-December 1947, functionaries of the Agitprop Department had submitted to Zhdanov and other Central Committee secretaries a brief surveying the "shortcomings" in the development of Soviet music.[43] The purpose of this document was to frame the major ideological issues and goals for the forthcoming First All-Union Congress of Soviet Composers, scheduled for February 1948. In the context of the perceived grave dearth of Soviet operas, Muradeli's The Great Friendship was characterized there as flawed by serious political errors. That despite these errors the opera had managed to reach the stage revealed an embarrassing lack of vigilance on the part of the Committee for Artistic Affairs and responsible organs of the Party bureaucracy.[44] The failure of Muradeli's opera notwithstanding, the chief thrust of the Agitprop brief lay elsewhere:

> The First Congress of Soviet Composers must evaluate the situation in Soviet music—its successes and serious defects—correctly. It must subject formalistic, individualistic tendencies to decisive criticism and serve as the basis for the decisive turning point of Soviet music toward democratic, genuinely realistic forms in all genres. The Congress of Composers must decisively reject the pernicious "theory" according to which complex, untexted instrumental-symphonic music ought to occupy the leading and defining position in Soviet music.[45]

At a conference convened by the Central Committee of the Communist Party at the Bolshoy Theater on 6 January 1948, the librettist and participants in the production of The Great Friendship mounted a spirited defense of their efforts. Muradeli, however, truckled, casting the net of blame for his personal transgressions over the Soviet music establishment as a whole and supplying Zhdanov with the ammunition needed to escalate the inquiry into a wholesale purge of the country's leading musicians. Summoned to a second conference at the Kremlin beginning on 10 January 1948, more than seventy Soviet composers, conductors, musicologists, and others were confronted by Andrey Zhdanov with the Central Committee's condemnation of Muradeli's opera. Zhdanov compared its flaws directly to those exposed twelve years earlier in Shostakovich's Lady Macbeth of the Mtsensk District, deploring the lack of advancement in Soviet opera during the intervening period. Zhdanov encouraged the musicians to unmask the unhealthy elements in their ranks. After eliciting three days of complaints, recriminations, and justifications from the musicians, Zhdanov required no more evidence to conclude that the flaws in Muradeli's opera represented only the tip of the iceberg. Soviet music was in a deep state of crisis:

Indeed, even though it is outwardly concealed, a fierce struggle is taking place be-tween two directions in Soviet music. One represents the healthy, progressive as-pects in Soviet music, based on the recognition of the immense role of the classical heritage and, in particular, on the traditions of the Russian musical school, on the combination of high idealism and substance in music, its truthful-ness and realism, and on the deep, organic connection with the people and their legacy of music and folk song, combined with high professional mastery. The other direction produces formalism alien to Soviet art. Under the banner of illu-sory innovation, it conveys a rejection of the classical heritage, of national char-acter in music, and of service to the people in order to cater to the purely individualistic experiences of a small clique of aesthetes.[46]

Recent research indicates that the transcript of this conference, published in March 1948 in an edition of 50,000 copies, presents a "revised" account of what actually took place there. For instance, when Zhdanov summed up the names of the group of "leading" composers (Shostakovich, Prokofiev, Myaskovsky, Khachaturyan, Kabalevsky, and Shebalin), he actually identi-fied them only as the "leading group, which presently holds the reins and keys to the 'executive committee on artistic matters.'" In the published tran-script, a sentence was appended to Zhdanov's statement, ominously refo-cusing its purpose from one of administrative description to a political indictment: "We will consider that it is these comrades namely who are the principal and leading figures of the formalist direction in music. And that direction is fundamentally incorrect." [47]

As Shostakovich greeted the new year of 1948 with his family and friends, a feeling of foreboding was in the air.[48] News of the debacle at the Bolshoy Theater spread quickly through the artistic community, so when Shosta-kovich was among those summoned to the convocation with Zhdanov, he could have had no illusions about the gravity of the situation. As a one-time convicted formalist who had been nurtured back into the fold and elevated to the pinnacle of prestige in the world of Soviet music—one, furthermore, whose successes since the Seventh Symphony had all been equivocal—Shostakovich was a prime target for accusations of recidivism. Speaker after speaker raised questions about the complex language of the Eighth Sym-phony and the widespread disillusionment with the Ninth. That Shostakovich—along with his most eminent peers—was perceived to be above criticism, that as composer and teacher he exerted enormous influ-ence on rising generations of Soviet composers, that as a leader in the Com-posers' Union he wielded inordinate control over the welfare of Soviet music and musicians, made him all the more vulnerable.

Shostakovich was the only participant, besides Zhdanov, to address the assembly twice, briefly at the end of the first day of deliberations and once again after Zhdanov's speech on the final afternoon. Shostakovich's comments were general, for the most part, his manner reflective and a trifle awkward. After reproaching Muradeli for not accepting responsibility for his failures, he addressed the issue of his own during his final statement:

> In my work there have been many failures and serious setbacks, although throughout the entire course of my compositional career I have thought about the people, those who listen to my music, about the people who raised me, educated and reared me. I always strive to make my music accessible to the people. I have always listened to criticism addressed to me and have tried my best to work harder and better. I am listening now, too, and will listen in the future. I will accept critical instruction. And I call upon our musical organizations to engage in the widest possible development of criticism and self-criticism." [49]

Years later, in 1965, Shostakovich objected to the way Ilya Erenburg had described the proceedings in his memoirs: "At the beginning of 1948, S. S. Prokofiev and D. D. Shostakovich related that Zhdanov had invited the composers and—in an attempt to demonstrate what 'melodic' music was, in contrast to the flawed works—had played something on the piano." [50] After reading this, Shostakovich immediately mailed a letter of protest to Erenburg, saying that no such thing had ever taken place, but that he, Shostakovich, had witnessed the creation of the legend of Zhdanov as performer-pedagogue: "In actual fact this never happened. Zhdanov did not sit down at the piano, he instructed the composers using the methods of his oratory." In response to Shostakovich's request that, in future editions of his memoirs, he correct this mistake, Erenburg agreed to substitute Shostakovich's description of Zhdanov's methodology.[51]

In a tragic coincidence, on the final day of the conference, 13 January 1948, the same day Shostakovich was obliged to humble himself before Zhdanov and his peers, the body of the distinguished Jewish actor Solomon Mikhoels was discovered in Minsk. Suspicions that he had been murdered were later confirmed. Shostakovich, who was a family friend, visited the grieving relatives after the Central Committee meeting had ended. As he conveyed his condolences over the loss of her father, Mikhoels's daughter recalled that Shostakovich remarked, "I envy him." [52] When he subsequently described the conference proceedings to Glikman, he observed, "Twelve years ago I was younger and better able to cope with all sorts of rebukes. I'm getting old. I'm giving out." [53]

On 10 February 1948, the Central Committee issued its resolution, "On V. Muradeli's opera *The Great Friendship.*" The cause of the failure of Muradeli's opera was traced to the "formalistic" path he had pursued, a tendency that was observed to have thoroughly contaminated contemporary Soviet music. In one of the preliminary drafts of the resolution, specific works—including Shostakovich's Eighth and Ninth Symphonies, Prokofiev's Sixth Symphony and piano sonatas, Khachaturyan's Symphony-Poem,

Popov's Third Symphony, the piano sonatas of Myaskovsky, and the quartet of Shebalin—were singled out as exemplars of the formalistic trend, but in the final version the wording was more sweeping: "The situation in the realm of the symphony and opera is especially bad. The problem is one of composers who are adherents of a formalistic, anti-people direction. This direction has found its fullest expression in the works of such composers as comrades D. Shostakovich, S. Prokofiev, A. Khachaturyan, V. Shebalin, G. Popov, N. Myaskovsky, and others, whose works show particularly clear manifestations of formalistic distortions and antidemocratic tendencies in music that are alien to the Soviet people and its artistic tastes." [54] (For reasons as yet undetermined, the name of Dmitriy Kabalevsky, originally indicted in Zhdanov's list of "leading" Soviet composers, was removed from the list published in the resolution, while that of Popov was added.) In its conclusions, the Central Committee's resolution condemned the formalist direction in music, commanding the appropriate Party and government organs take all necessary measures to liquidate the defects and promote the development of a realistic direction in Soviet music.

Shostakovich did have something to distract him as this terrible ordeal unfolded. He continued with the composition of his First Violin Concerto. He told Glikman that he worked on its third movement when he returned home each evening after the vile sessions with Zhdanov. [55]

Shostakovich had begun work on the concerto in the summer of 1947. That May, while participating in the Prague Spring Festival (among other highlights, Mravinsky conducted the Czech Philharmonic Orchestra in memorable performances of the Eighth Symphony), Shostakovich had teamed up with David Oistrakh and Czech cellist Miloš Sádlo to perform his Second Piano Trio, which they also recorded. Shostakovich had first heard Oistrakh play in 1935, when the latter captured top prize in the Second All-Union Competition. They had the opportunity to become better acquainted a few months later when they were colleagues in the delegation of Soviet performing artists that toured Turkey. More recently, Shostakovich had heard Oistrakh's Moscow concert cycle, "The Development of the Violin Concerto," during the 1946–1947 season.

Shostakovich did not release bulletins about this particular work-in-progress. Having sketched the first movement ("Nocturne") in late July in Kellomäki, he completed it in Moscow on 12 November 1947. The second movement ("Scherzo") was completed in the first week of December. The "Passacaglia," the movement he was working on during the Central Committee conference, was completed on 19 January 1948. On 5 February, five days before the Central Committee issued its resolution, Shostakovich played the first three movements plus the cadenza of the concerto for Gavriil Popov, who found it "very fine, a little reminiscent of the Sixth Symphony (in its spirit and its orchestral texture)."[56] What still remained to be composed was a quick finale ("Burlesque"). A month later, in mid-March 1948, the composer played the concerto to his students in Leningrad.[57] They were enormously impressed. Shostakovich dated the completion of the composition as 24 March 1948. One composer recalls that Shostakovich was able to identify precisely where he had been in the score (in the middle of a passage of sixteenth notes for the violin) when the resolution of 10 February was published. No change in style is discernible.[58]

The violin lessons of his student days notwithstanding, Shostakovich was not a violinist. After introducing the concerto in Leningrad, he asked one of those present, Veniamin Basner, an accomplished violinist, to assist him by trying out the work on his violin. Shostakovich was unsure whether certain passages were feasible. Basner declared that everything was playable as written.[59] David Oistrakh concurred when Shostakovich acquainted him with the concerto later in 1948. Igor Oistrakh recalled that his father was extremely excited in anticipation of a violin concerto by Shostakovich and that the composer's performance on this occasion made a strong impression: "How he managed to play the whole texture of the scherzo on the piano without missing a single note remains a mystery to me to this day."[60] The composer later recalled, "When I showed the First Concerto to Oistrakh, to my great surprise he said: 'There is nothing to correct here, everything is playable.'"[61] Shostakovich credited his lessons in instrumentation from Steinberg for his proficiency. Oistrakh did not postpone learning the concerto; he repeatedly invited Oborin over to accompany him. In hindsight, he reflected sadly that it is possible he could have persuaded Shostakovich to sanction the work's premiere then. As it turned out, they would have to wait seven years.[62]

In the spring of 1948, Shostakovich's position in Soviet society was unenviable. Even had he been able to find the performers imprudent enough to take the risk, there could be no question of a hospitable reception for a concerto that would certainly have been deemed "formalist" according to the criteria so recently articulated by Zhdanov. Despite the fact that Shostakovich publicized the recent completion of his Violin Concerto to colleagues assembled for the First All-Union Congress of Soviet Composers in April 1948, indicating then that he would soon submit it to audition,[63] he wisely shelved his new work. As soon as he acquired his first tape recorder in the summer of 1952, he dusted off the score and made a meticulous arrangement of the orchestral accompaniment for two pianos, eight-hands, not skipping a single note. He persuaded Oistrakh to make him a tape of this version. Finally, in 1955, more than two years after Stalin's death, Shostakovich's Violin Concerto received its first performance.

In the twelve years that had elapsed since the condemnation of *Lady*

Macbeth, the mechanisms of Stalinist cultural repression had been finely honed. In 1948, there could be no question that Shostakovich—a principal target of the Central Committee's censure and, furthermore, a repeat offender—might be permitted to evade with impunity the civic obligation to recant his sins publicly. In the wake of the Central Committee resolution, Glière, Khachaturyan, Shostakovich, and the other "formalist" composers were stripped of their positions of authority in the Composers' Union. Although Boris Asafyev was made titular chair of the organization, the real power devolved to the newly appointed general secretary, thirty-four-year-old composer Tikhon Khrennikov, whose first assignment was to organize the First All-Union Congress of Soviet Composers, postponed two months by the recent discussions and the appearance of the Central Committee resolution.

At a conference of composers and musicologists convened in Moscow between 17 and 26 February, Khrennikov set the tone for the proper appreciation of the Central Committee's intervention in a keynote address. As subsequently reported in *Sovetskaya muzïka*, most of the participants manifested complete solidarity with the insights recently imparted by Zhdanov during the January conference and with the Central Committee resolution. The few who refused to capitulate—Shebalin, for instance—were reprimanded severely. In what by this time had become a ritual practice, the gathered musicians sent an open letter to Stalin, the Great Leader and Teacher, replete with effusive expressions of gratitude for his solicitude and wisdom.[64]

At the February meeting, Shostakovich struggled to put a brave face on his own capitulation to the inevitable. In his remarks he conceded that whenever the Party had interceded in artistic matters, it had always brought benefit to Soviet art. Having taken the criticisms of *Lady Macbeth* in 1936 seriously to heart, he reflected that in recent years he had thought his work had begun to evolve in a different direction, only to realize now that his music had once again lapsed into a formalist language incomprehensible to the masses: "When, today, through the pronouncements of the Central Committee resolution, the Party and all of our country condemn this direction in my creative work, I know that the Party is right. I know that the Party is showing concern for Soviet art and for me, a Soviet composer."[65] He promised: "I will try again and again to create symphonic works that are comprehensible and accessible to the people, from the standpoint of their ideological content, musical language and form. I will work ever more diligently on the musical embodiment of images of the heroic Russian people." He vowed also to write more mass songs and concluded his remarks with a rallying call to all composers to the task of realizing this "marvelous" resolution.[66]

The campaign against the formalist composers was fanned by the press. Citizens and patriotic music-lovers vented their indignation, publicly and privately, at the state of affairs in Soviet music that had been checked, thanks to the timely intervention of Comrade Zhdanov and the Central Committee. (Its lessons were subsequently simplified and reinforced by the publication and production at the Moscow Art Theater in 1949 of a contemporary play about the downfall and eventual redemption of a "formalist" composer; the protagonist was widely perceived to represent Shostakovich.[67]) In 1953, shortly after Stalin's death, Shostakovich reflected back on this period of his life: "When they criticized me for formalism, you won't believe how many poison-pen letters I received from absolute strangers, scarcely literate in music. These were the kind of expressions to be found in them: 'You ought to be executed, killed, exterminated, you scoundrel,' and so on." [68]

The exhibition of slavish homage to the tenets articulated by Zhdanov and the Central Committee was capped by the First All-Union Congress of Soviet Composers, attended by delegates from all across the country and held in Moscow from 19 to 25 April 1948. The "honor" of delivering the opening two-part address to the Congress, "Thirty Years of Soviet Music and the Tasks of Soviet Composers," was split between Asafyev and Khrennikov, although, due to illness, Asafyev's speech was read for him in his absence. The proceedings were monitored by Party observers. Shostakovich was reported to be teaching in Leningrad and thus missed the opening session, but thereafter he was seen to be a regular and attentive participant at the Congress, in sharp contrast to other discredited composers who either did not attend or were perceived to be spending most of their time socializing or smoking in the hallways. Events did not unfold quite as smoothly and predictably as the organizers would have wished. A report to Zhdanov and the Central Committee indicated that, as of the end of the day on 23 April, not one of the "composer-formalists"—with the conspicuous exception of Muradeli—had deigned yet to address the assembly. Urgent measures needed to be taken to improve this situation and raise the critical level of the discourse. A letter directed to the presidium of the Congress from the Leningrad delegation condemning the "conspiracy of silence" by the formalists was received sympathetically by the hall.[69]

The next day Shostakovich rose to address the Congress. He reiterated his belief in the correctness, and his acceptance, of the Party's guidance. Elucidating his future plans, he pledged that melody would become the driving impulse behind his new compositions, melody infused by the national ethos. He professed increased understanding of the need for programmatic music and music connected with literary images for the Soviet audience, with an emphasis on contemporary themes. He embraced the injunction for continuous peer evaluation at all stages of the compositional process. Among projects already in progress, he mentioned music for the film *The Young Guard* and an opera on the same subject. He expressed the desire to write songs and short symphonic pieces and to try his hand at an operetta.[70]

One of those present recalled that after Shostakovich descended from the tribunal, everyone avoided him in the hallways, and he looked dispirited and dismayed.[71] His contrite example was widely publicized and vaunted to those "formalists" (including Myaskovsky, Prokofiev, Shebalin, and Popov) who were seen as scorning the imperative to make obeisance publicly.[72] That not everyone found it entirely convincing, however, is evidenced by the quite sensible observation made by artist Nadezhda Udaltsova in her diary on 28 April: "Well then, Shostakovich has repented and his repentance has been accepted, it has proved satisfactory. Oh, stupid people, they should understand that the whole matter is not in the words, but in the work. They should *all* understand that!"[73]

Shostakovich's tribulations did not end with public purgation. By order of Glavrertkom, the central censorship board, on 14 February a long list of works by the "formalist" composers was officially proscribed for performance and removed from the repertory. The roster of Shostakovich's banned works included Symphonies nos. 6, 8, and 9, the Piano Concerto, *Two Pieces* for String Octet, the Second Piano Sonata, *Six Romances on Texts by W. Raleigh, R. Burns, and W. Shakespeare*, and *Aphorisms*. Only a few works of unquestioned stature—the First, Fifth, and Seventh Symphonies, for instance, and the Piano Quintet—were conspicuously omitted from the list.[74] It made little difference. With notable exceptions,[75] cautious performers and concert managers found it more prudent to strike from their programs all works by the condemned composers.

As of 1 September 1948, Shostakovich was dismissed from his professorships at the Moscow and Leningrad Conservatories. In a cartoon published in *Sovetskaya muzïka*, a line of identical little bespectacled Shostakoviches in short pants was shown emerging from the inset portals of the two educational institutions.[76] Within their walls, the battle was engaged to eradicate the disease of formalism, and with it Shostakovich's pernicious influence on young Soviet musicians. His ten-year-old son was made to vilify his father during a music school exam.[77] The extraordinary pressure exerted on students to denounce him encountered, however, at least small pockets of resistance.[78] One of the few humiliations Shostakovich and the other disgraced composers were spared was expulsion from the Composers' Union.

That Shostakovich and his formalist colleagues had been able to wreak so much havoc in Soviet music, and to go undeterred for so long, was as much an indictment of the state of Soviet music criticism as it was of the composers themselves. To place a pseudoscholarly veneer on the inversion of values

Который год из этих славных стен
Идет чреда бесславных смен.
Идут, идут —
Хоть караул кричи!
Всё маленькие шостаковичи!

"Pedagogical humor" by A. Kostomolotsky from Sovetskaya muzïka 4 (1948). [The line of figures is shown emerging from the portals of the Leningrad and Moscow Conservatories.] Rough translation:

Year after year these glorious portals
Disgorge a stream of inglorious mortals.
They keep on coming—
in vain one bemoans
All the Shostakovich clones!

that had officially taken place in the assessment of Shostakovich's career and compositions, the new editor of *Sovetskaya muzïka*, Marian Koval (one of those mediocrities elevated abruptly by the Zhdanovshchina into a position of influence) provided a three-part survey of Shostakovich's career that was published during the summer.[79] It was a highly tendentious tract exposing the clear trail of backsliding in the composer's creative evolution. Shostakovich's flirtation with the "decadent" modernistic devices characteristic of the bourgeois West, his attraction to disharmony, ugliness, and the grotesque, his propensity for empty abstractionism and extreme individualism, and his studied avoidance of the folk roots and healthy virtues of the Russian classical tradition were analyzed in work after work. Even a composition as sacrosanct as the Seventh Symphony was found to have deluded its original audience: "The listener of that time heard in the Seventh Symphony more than was actually there; the listener of the present day hears in it only what it contains." [80] The "lies" of complicit critics who had been apologists for Shostakovich were scathingly debunked. (Soviet musicologists would be subjected to a more sweeping purging of ranks in 1949.)

The full measure of the anguish and misery Shostakovich experienced during this period can only be guessed. There are indications that he contemplated suicide. Indeed, it would be surprising if he had not. There is also testimony, as yet unconfirmed, that he and his family were under NKVD surveillance. As in 1936, Shostakovich sought what solace he could within a small circle of family and loyal friends. There was no money. Fenya, the family's housekeeper, and her niece spent their own savings to feed them.[81]

In a dedication inscribed in a volume of his verse on 22 April, Boris Pasternak, who, although not close to the composer was able to appreciate his situation better than most, counseled him to bear up stoically: "Take courage, Dmitriy Dmitriyevich, preserve, through all of this, your clarity of spirit and health. Remember that even if it were the case that there was just a shadow of truth behind all of this, it is not our business to be clever and show off, and break and spoil the best in ourselves that man is given by nature at birth—his wholeness. Calmly and joyfully accept everything that greets you on your path, may you be helped in these days from a distance, by your great future." [82]

In a letter to Smolich on 3 April, Shostakovich hinted at a more ambiguous vision of his future—resigned to a survival with ambition only for the eventual promise of a heavenly paradise—with his quotation of a phrase ("We shall see the whole sky shining like diamonds") from Sonya's poignant closing monologue in Chekhov's *Uncle Vanya*. He signed off this letter to the man who had mounted the original productions of both of his operas: "The to-this-day grateful author of the justifiably censured operas (*The Nose* and *Lady Macbeth of the Mtsensk District*) D. Shostakovich." [83] In mid-August, the composer's anxious mother reported that her son was "holding up like a trouper. He is working, although his nerves are making themselves felt."[84]

If music was Shostakovich's best refuge in times of crisis, ultimately it too would prove his best revenge. His commentary on the events of 1948 would be preserved as a trenchant satire, the *Antiformalist Rayok*[85]—a caricature in music of an official convocation on "the struggle of the realistic and formalistic directions in music"—the antecedents of which come directly out of Musorgsky. Its existence long rumored, the score of *Rayok* finally surfaced in 1989 and has been the object of continued controversy ever since, chiefly over the dates of composition and the authorship of the sung libretto. The dating debate concerns whether Shostakovich actually wrote a sizable portion of his lampoon in the summer of 1948, while the events were still fresh but the peril from discovery all too real. Isaak Glikman is the lone witness who claims that Shostakovich played it to him, in secret, that summer.[86] Other witnesses maintain that Shostakovich actually undertook the composition only in 1957, in conjunction with the Second All-Union Congress of Soviet Composers—the proceedings of which furnished additional grist for the satirical mill—when he enlisted the help of Lev Lebedinsky as librettist.[87] The concluding portion of the work is believed to have been added in the mid-1960s.

Contemplating *Rayok* primarily as a "composed" work, with fixed dates of composition, may not be the most helpful approach. The spoof bears all the hallmarks of the Russian genre of *kapustnik*, a party skit, a diversion that might have been improvised, expanded, and embellished through many private "performances" over a long period of time. Shostakovich was an entertainer. Satire was his natural expressive outlet. Whether he started *Rayok* in 1948 or later, the impulse to place his own wicked spin on those long hours of pompous pontificating he had been forced to stomach in 1948—and to share the travesty with his closest friends—would sooner or later have proved irresistible.

1948–1953

Public and Private

10

On 24 April 1948, facing his colleagues at the Composers' Congress, Shostakovich had pledged to place melody at the heart of his future works, melody infused with the essence of folklore. He had promised to produce romances and songs. In May, the composer began querying a Jewish friend about the pronunciation of certain Yiddish words and the rhythmic flow of folk texts that he knew only in Russian translation.[1] What he was studying was a collection of translated texts, *Jewish Folk Songs*, that had been published in Moscow in 1947.[2]

By August 1948, which Shostakovich spent in Kellomäki, he had selected texts from this volume and, between 1 and 29 August, he completed settings of eight of the poems for soprano, contralto, tenor, and piano. On his return to Moscow, Shostakovich played the score to soprano Nina Dorliak and her husband, Svyatoslav Richter. Both were moved. At Shostakovich's suggestion, Dorliak recruited other singers to perform the composition.[3] They unveiled the eight songs for a private gathering of musicians and friends at Shostakovich's birthday party on 25 September 1948. Dorliak recalled: "The new work was striking and profound, and everybody was moved by its intense and simple sincerity."[4] Among those present was Nataliya Mikhoels: "On this occasion Shostakovich, rubbing his hands together nervously, introduced the recently written songs with the words: 'I have here, you might say, some new songs.'"[5]

In October, Shostakovich added three more settings to *From Jewish Folk Poetry*, completing the work on 24 October. Even before doing this, he orchestrated the first eight songs. On 30 November, Shostakovich visited Myaskovsky, to whom he played "marvelous songs and ensembles on Jewish texts and a very interesting violin concerto."[6] Shostakovich and his vocalists had regular rehearsals during the fall. As musicologist Daniil Zhitomirsky recorded in his diary, the "dress rehearsal" of *From Jewish Folk Poetry*—performed by Richter, Dorliak, Tamara Yanko, and the tenor Nikolai Belugin—was held at Shostakovich's apartment on 18 December 1948 in the presence of his wife and two children, Yuriy Levitin, Kara Karayev, Levon Atovmyan, Zhitomirsky himself, and "some unknown young chap in a military uniform. Before beginning, D. D. asks us to take note of all shortcomings in the performance. They discuss in detail where and how all the performers should stand. Atovmyan is quick on the uptake and removes the chairs. The complete cycle is performed twice. The singers are fired up, as—for all his reserve—is the author.... After the performance there is general, animated conversation and collective devising of new names for the songs."[7]

Shostakovich showed his guests the published collection from which he had taken the texts, praised it, and recommended that all composers exploit the resource. The occasion wrapped up with a modest celebration. As Zhitomirsky also noted in his diary, the performance they were all so eagerly anticipating—slated for 20 December at the Union of Composers—was canceled, with the result that the song cycle could not be auditioned before the Second Plenum of the leadership of the Composers' Union, which opened 21 December 1948.[8]

On 22 January 1949, Shostakovich wrote to his former student Karayev, one of those in attendance at the dress rehearsal a month earlier: "I haven't yet demonstrated my Jewish songs. I expect to do so in about ten days. Since you are interested in their fate, I'll write you in detail about that presentation."[9] The only thing Shostakovich could have meant by this was that he had not yet submitted the cycle to the peer review process at the Union of Composers. This explains, in part, why it was not unveiled at the Plenum a month earlier, at which keynote speaker Khrennikov had reprimanded Prokofiev harshly for defiantly withholding his latest opera from the collective evaluation process.[10] Whether Shostakovich did submit his cycle to such scrutiny has not come to light. *From Jewish Folk Poetry* would have to wait six more years for its first public performance, when it was premiered by the composer, Nina Dorliak, Zara Dolukhanova, and Alexey Maslennikov on 15 January 1955 in Leningrad. In the meantime, Shostakovich could not and did not conceal its existence. Students at the Moscow Conservatory knew it,[11] as did professional musicians within and without the composer's inner circle. The guests attending the composer's birthday party in 1950 were treated to a performance of the cycle.[12]

Shostakovich's interest in Jewish music was of long standing, revealing itself through his painstaking completion in 1944 of the opera *Rothschild's Violin* by his student Fleyshman and developed further in the composition of his own Piano Trio no. 2, op. 67, which incorporated a Jewish tune in its concluding movement, and in the Violin Concerto, with the conspicuously "Jewish" inflections of its scherzo. The appearance of these works at a time when appalling revelations about the Holocaust were filtering out and when homegrown anti-Semitism was assuming more menacing dimensions is hardly coincidental; Shostakovich's aversion to anti-Semitism in any form was deeply rooted. Nevertheless, the deeply aesthetic nature of his engagement with Jewish folklore and music should not be underestimated. The inflected modes of Jewish music went hand in hand with his own natural gravitation toward modes with flattened scale degrees. Shostakovich was attracted by the ambiguities in Jewish music, its ability to project radically different emotions simultaneously. As he later observed to the poet Aron Vergelis: "It seems I comprehend what distinguishes the Jewish melos. A cheerful melody is built here on sad intonations.... The 'people' are like a single person.... Why does he sing a cheerful song? Because he is sad at heart." [13]

In most studies of Shostakovich, the composition of *From Jewish Folk Poetry* is treated as the composer's deliberate, principled protest against the anti-Semitic crusade that erupted during Stalin's final years, a protest that Shostakovich's innate survival instinct dictated remain private. This is a view reinforced by comments attributed to the aging composer in *Testimony*.[14] In reality, when Shostakovich turned to Jewish folk texts for his first major work in the aftermath of the resolution of 10 February 1948 and set them even as the final installment of Koval's diatribe on his music was rolling off the press,[15] he was in all likelihood approaching the project in a constructive attempt to satisfy the "public" promises he had just made. None of them had precluded the composition of music of quality or of exploiting folk material that genuinely ignited his creative imagination. Shostakovich was not a composer who willingly composed "for the drawer." [16] He had a strong need to connect, to communicate with listeners, to hear his music performed. And in the summer of 1948 he was under intense pressure to redeem himself publicly.

As a musicologist specializing in the Jewish facet of Shostakovich's creativity perceptively observed, *From Jewish Folk Poetry* is an example of stylized urban folk art; its texts are genuine folk texts, its melodic writing is simple and highly accessible: "This was the sort of music required by the

resolution of February 1948—'democratic,' 'melodious,' and 'understandable for the people.'" [17]

Despite increasingly menacing incidents of anti-Semitism that had occurred in the country since the end of the war, by the summer of 1948
Shostakovich, like the majority of his countrymen, could not yet have
known about Stalin's monstrous plan for the eventual containment or
eradication of Soviet Jewry. On the other hand, before he investigated Yiddish texts and their pronunciation, Shostakovich would have already become acquainted with the new Sinfonietta based on Jewish themes by his
protégé, Moisey Vainberg, a work that Myaskovsky characterized at the
time as "striking and pointed" [18] and that had been positively vetted by the
Union of Composers. Recruiting performers and unveiling his new song
cycle to friends and colleagues in late September, Shostakovich had no
compelling reason to believe there might be any undue risk involved, that it
might actually be perilous to publicize this composition. Even by late December 1948, when Stalin's campaign against Jewish institutions and intellectuals was already gaining momentum, the particular ethnic focus of
Shostakovich's song cycle cannot have been what prevented its public performance; Vainberg's Sinfonietta, performed at the opening concert of the
Plenum and dedicated to "the friendship of the peoples of the USSR," was
vaunted by Khrennikov as shining proof of the benefit to be reaped by
shunning the ruinous influence of modernism, turning to folk sources, and
following the path of realism: "Turning to the sources of Jewish folk music,
Vainberg created a striking, cheerful work dedicated to the theme of the
bright, free working life of the Jewish people in the Land of Socialism." [19]

By late January 1949, however, shortly after Shostakovich sent his letter
to Karayev, Stalin's campaign against "rootless cosmopolitans" escalated
rapidly into a virulent campaign against Jewish culture and Zionism in the
press.[20] Shostakovich's near-disastrous timing, the tragic irony of his attempt to redeem his recent promises by favoring the folklore of the "wrong"
ethnic group, must have become appallingly clear to him. To contemplate
public performance of *From Jewish Folk Poetry* then became absurd.
Shostakovich prudently shelved the work.

The ill-fated opus would continue to divulge its eerie ironies. After January 1953, for instance, with the exposure of the so-called Doctors' Plot—the
trumped-up conspiracy to murder Stalin by a group of predominantly
Jewish doctors—and the deliberate instigation of anti-Semitic terror on a
massive scale, the translators' decision years earlier to substitute "doctors"
for "engineers" in the final poem of the cycle, "Happiness," in which the
blessings of an old Jewish shoemaker's wife are exalted ("The star shines
over our heads ... our sons have become doctors"),[21] took on chilling new
significance.

With his two most important works of the recent past now consigned to the drawer unperformed, and with so many professional avenues closed to him, Shostakovich had to rely on film music to support his family during this difficult period. He confided to colleagues: "It's unpleasant that I have to do this. I advise you to do it only in the event of extreme poverty, extreme poverty." [22] His daughter, Galina, recalled that he referred to this labor at this period as his "bride price" but executed it honestly, quickly, and with his accustomed efficiency.[23] It was in connection with his work on film scores, specifically on *Encounter at the Elbe*, that Shostakovich complained to his friend Glikman on 12 December 1948, the end of one of the most difficult years of his life, that he was feeling poorly, suffering from frequent headaches, and observing himself in the shaving mirror aging rapidly: "The physical aging, unfortunately, is also bringing about a loss of spiritual youth. But perhaps this is all this a result of overwork. After all, in the past year I have written a lot of film music. It supports me but is extraordinarily exhausting." [24]

Between 1947 and 1952 Shostakovich produced symphonic scores to seven films. Their subject matter fell into three categories: film biographies of prominent individuals (*Pirogov*, op. 76, 1947; *Michurin*, op. 78, 1948, released 1949; *Belinsky*, op. 85, 1950, released 1953); World War II films (*The Young Guard*, op. 75, in two parts, 1947–1948; *Encounter at the Elbe*, op. 80, 1948, released 1949; *The Fall of Berlin*, op. 82, in two parts, 1949, released 1950); and a film about the Civil War (*The Unforgettable Year 1919*, op. 89, 1951, released 1952). It is a measure of their political orthodoxy that five of these films (excepting only *Belinsky* and *The Unforgettable Year 1919*) were awarded Stalin Prizes. As Shostakovich observed in connection with his work on *Encounter at the Elbe*: "Here a circumstance that I have previously observed made itself strongly felt—that for a composer the cinema is not only schooling for mastery but often a political seminar as well." [25]

The promised opera on *The Young Guard* never materialized. Shostakovich indicated that the music intended for the opera had been diverted into the film instead. For public consumption at least, he revived the notion of composing a film-opera, an operatic work designed specifically for the screen.[26] For all the effort expended on the music to *Encounter at the Elbe*, two of the songs Shostakovich wrote for the film, "Homesickness" and "Song of Peace"—both to texts by Yevgeniy Dolmatovsky—became very popular. They bolstered the composer's credibility as a producer of mass songs.

A year after his well-publicized disgrace, Shostakovich's fortunes took an unexpected turn. In 1949, he was prevailed upon to represent the Soviet Union as a member of its official delegation to the Cultural and Scientific Congress for World Peace in New York. The story of his acceptance of this mission is another of those that has become legendary. It was apparently after Shostakovich had turned down Foreign Minister Molotov's request that he join the delegation, probably in mid- to late February 1949,[27] that Shostakovich was alerted to expect an important phone call:

> At the appointed time, Nina Vasilyevna and Anusya Vilyams took up their posts at extensions, just in case. When I was told that Comrade Stalin would speak with me, I took fright. I don't remember the conversation exactly, but Stalin proposed that I travel to the United States with a delegation. I imagined with horror how I would be pestered there with questions about the recent resolution and blurted out that I was sick, that I couldn't go, and that the music of Prokofiev, Myaskovsky, Khachaturyan, and myself was not being performed.
>
> The next day a brigade of doctors arrived, examined me, and really did pronounce me sick, but Poskrebïshev said he would not relay that to Comrade Stalin.[28]

On 16 March 1949, by Stalin's personal instruction, Glavrepertkom order no. 17, dated 16 February 1948, which had banned from performance and removed from the repertory the works of formalist Soviet composers, was rescinded.[29] Four days later, on 20 March, Shostakovich departed for New York as a member of the delegation: "So I went to the United States, whence we were swiftly evicted as undesirable elements." [30]

Shostakovich's apprehensions about making the journey, his first to America, were well founded. The Congress unfolded, from 25 to 27 March 1949, in a swirl of cold-war hyperbole and controversy. For the duration of the Congress, its main venues were picketed by protesters. A rival meeting was mounted concurrently. As the most famous member of the seven-man Soviet delegation—among the others were Alexander Fadeyev, head of the Writers' Union, and film directors Sergey Gerasimov and Mikhaíl Chiaureli—Shostakovich was in the glare of the media spotlight. His words and actions made headlines both in Russia and in America. He was presented with a scroll signed by forty-two representatives of the music world and everywhere was greeted with enthusiastic ovations.[31] ("A shy, stiff-shouldered man with a pale, wide forehead, Shostakovich was painfully ill at ease. To the repeated ovations he received he ducked his head abruptly again and again, like a small boy after a commencement speech. He cringed visibly from the photographers' flashbulbs, mopped his brow, twiddled his spectacles. During speeches, his long fingers seemed to be tapping out some nameless composition on his forearm." [32]) Doing nothing to aggravate his still precarious situation at home, he comported himself as a model representative of his country.

The composer's prepared speech, which was read by an interpreter to a session attended by 800 people on 26 March 1949 at the Waldorf-Astoria Hotel as the composer looked on, "appearing nervous and uneasy," confounded some by the stridency of its tone and its scarcely veiled accusations of American imperialism and warmongering. To the consternation of others, Shostakovich reaffirmed unequivocally his acceptance of the criticisms and constructive guidance he had recently received from the Soviet government: "The criticism brings me much good. It helps me bring my music forward." [33] Among composers, Stravinsky was singled out for denunciation: "[He] betrayed his native land and severed himself from his people by joining the camp of reactionary modern musicians.... Stravinsky's moral barrenness reveals itself in his openly nihilistic writings, proclaiming the meaninglessness and absence of content in his creations." [34] Shostakovich's performance on piano of the Scherzo from his Fifth Symphony before an audience of 18,000 people in Madison Square Garden at the conclusion of the Congress's final session produced a tremendous ovation.

Back home, Shostakovich, who as a callow youth in the late 1920s had made light of mandatory political training, was assigned a private instructor in Marxism-Leninism to remedy the manifest deficiencies in his education. To help the composer familiarize himself with the "classics of Marxism-Leninism," he studied conspectuses prepared for him by his friend Glikman.[35]

Though he was handpicked by Stalin as an official Soviet spokesman for the Cultural and Scientific Congress for World Peace in New York in 1949, we can be sure that the politically deficient Shostakovich was not entrusted with writing the speech delivered in his name there. That the speeches and published writings—not of Shostakovich alone but of prominent figures from all walks of life—that touched even remotely on matters of state policy or image were closely monitored and regulated by appropriate levels of the Party apparatus was accepted procedure. In an accommodation initially dictated by a keen instinct for survival, Shostakovich inured himself to the dutiful reading of the speeches and the signing of articles placed in front of him. His distasteful predicament was by no means exceptional. He expected others to pay as little heed to the numbing clichés of Soviet public discourse as he did himself.

While it would be foolish to accept at face value all the statements and writings ascribed to Shostakovich, it does not follow that he shared none of the sentiments or opinions expressed in this way. Similarly, if much of what was published over his signature was ghosted by others—and there is ample evidence to confirm that sometimes Shostakovich did not even bother to read what was thrust under his nose—it still does not follow that he abdicated responsibility for everything attributed to his pen.[36] The matter is not so simple. As handwritten documents in his archives and recorded responses in interviews and press conferences attest, Shostakovich became fluent in the language of officialese. He was so fluent that he could spin off exquisite parodies in his letters. The archives contain drafts of talking points for official speeches in his own hand.[37] Shostakovich willingly accepted some commissions to provide articles and reviews on topics—usually musical—of special interest to him. He routinely commissioned experienced and trusted colleagues to ghostwrite for him, outlining for them his guidelines, carefully screening the finished product, and duly passing along the fees thus earned.[38] He was even capable of manipulating the media for his own shrewd purposes.[39]

Although his writing, particularly that in a satirical vein, emphatically belies his modesty, Shostakovich was habitually dismissive of his literary skills. He recruited Sollertinsky to assist him in framing and polishing his earliest public statements, and he always felt more comfortable communicating through his music than with words. After the death of Stalin, Shostakovich's affected ambivalence toward the "public" word, his refusal to clarify his genuine views and repudiate statements in conflict with them, would eventually drive a wedge between him and the post-Stalin generation of Soviet intellectuals.[40]

His success with film music notwithstanding, Shostakovich could not postpone indefinitely his reckoning with the clear mandates of the 1948 resolution. Everyone anxiously awaited his creative response. While praising Shostakovich's music for the film, *The Young Guard*, screened during the Second Plenum of the Composers' Union in December 1948, Khrennikov had also been unambiguous in his warning that Soviet society was still expecting from him works in other genres, "imbued with the spirit of realism, embodying the vital images of our reality." [41] It was imperative for Shostakovich to demonstrate both the sincerity of his commitment to the principles of Socialist Realism and the sureness of his footing on the road to rehabilitation. In the spring of 1949, a chance meeting with the poet Yevgeniy Dolmatovsky on the Red Arrow train from Moscow to Leningrad offered him a solution to his predicament.

Dolmatovsky had already distinguished himself as a dependable lyricist of mass and patriotic songs. Indeed, Shostakovich had employed his lyrics for one of his entries for the national anthem contest in 1943, and his recent settings of two Dolmatovsky poems in *Encounter at the Elbe*, as well as that of "A Beautiful Day" in *The Fall of Berlin*, had gained wide currency independent of the films. During their train trip, the poet later recalled, he regaled his new acquaintance with his observations about the preliminary efforts then taking place in the implementation of Stalin's "Great Plan," unveiled in October 1948, for the afforestation and drought protection of the nation's countryside so ravaged by the recent war. Shostakovich listened attentively and asked for more details, remarking that the names of the various trees sounded musical. At a second meeting, Shostakovich asked

Dolmatovsky if he would write verses for an oratorio about the future forests. Shostakovich planned the oratorio together with Dolmatovsky; it was apparently at the composer's suggestion that the subject for the fourth movement, "Pioneers Plant the Forests," was included. He began writing the music only after the verses were ready.[42]

Shostakovich composed the seven-movement oratorio, *Song of the Forests*, op. 81, for tenor and bass soloists, boys' chorus, mixed chorus, and orchestra, at Komarovo during the summer of 1949, completing it on 15 August. From a postcard to Atovmyan dated 9 August, it is evident that some mix-up had occurred with the authorization of a contract for the oratorio proffered by the Committee for Artistic Affairs and that the composer had initially undertaken the composition without even soliciting a contract.[43] Although it may not accurately convey his feelings while composing the oratorio, sometime later Shostakovich confessed to a former student: "I sat down at night and, within a few hours dashed off something 'haphazardly.' When I submitted what I had written, to my amazement and horror, they shook my hands and paid me." [44] Yevgeniy Mravinsky presented the premiere of the new oratorio in Leningrad on 15 November 1949.[45] According to Galina Ustvolskaya, who accompanied him, after the performance Shostakovich returned to his room at the Hotel Europe and began to sob, burying his head in a pillow. He sought consolation in vodka.[46]

Song of the Forests was among 200 new works by Soviet composers performed in Moscow during a Plenum of the Union of Composers from 26 November to 10 December 1949, an event summed up in Myaskovsky's diary as "a very sorry picture. One would think that the composers have forgotten how to write. Heaps of cantatas, one worse than the next." [47] For Myaskovsky, nevertheless, Shostakovich's *Song of the Forests* stood out as one of the few redeeming highlights in this dismal panorama: "Heard Shostakovich's new cantata [sic] 'Of the Forests.' It is very simple, but fresh and vivid; it sounds delightful for the voices and, needless to say, in the orchestra." [48]

Fortunately, those chiefly concerned with policing observance of the aesthetic guidelines outlined in the 1948 resolution were also favorably impressed by Shostakovich's oratorio. Speaker after speaker at the Plenum rejoiced in the composer's tuneful, folk-inspired, uplifting treatment of the timely theme—"infused with the genuine zeal of Soviet construction, the zeal of Soviet patriotism" [49]—finding it profound and convincing. The press followed suit. Self-congratulation on the successful rehabilitation of the wayward composer was even deemed to be in order: "I want to congratulate everyone assembled in that now we no longer, and I hope we will never again, call Shostakovich a representative of the formalistic direction." [50] In 1950, *Song of the Forests* was awarded a Stalin Prize (category one). After Stalin's death and discrediting, Dolmatovsky revised portions of the texts of the first, fifth, and seventh movements to eliminate all references to the leadership and genius of Stalin, including the triumphal concluding paean: "Glory to the Party of Lenin! Glory to the People forever! Glory to the wise Stalin, Glory." [51] As Shostakovich commented sarcastically in 1957: "The poet, a slave of honor, has corrected the text in the spirit of the times. Unlike his colleague Pushkin—also a slave of honor—he has not perished and has no intention of perishing." [52]

While in New York in March 1949, Shostakovich had attended a concert by the Juilliard Quartet at which the First, Fourth, and Sixth Quartets by Bartók were performed. In his published travelogue, Shostakovich reported disliking the Fourth but being very taken with the Sixth. [53] Shortly after returning home, he embarked on a new quartet of his own, his Fourth in D Major, op. 83. Between the composition of the second and third movements, Shostakovich interrupted work to write *Song of the Forests*. He dated the completion of the final, fourth movement on 27 December 1949 and dedicated the score to the memory of a close friend, the artist and scenic designer Pyotr Vilyams, who had died two years earlier at the age of forty-five. [54]

As Dmitriy Tsïganov recalled thirty years later, when he had completed his Fourth Quartet, the composer invited the violinist over, alone. Shostakovich said his friends had been advising him that it would be a mistake to perform this work immediately, that it might receive an unfriendly reception. He wanted Tsïganov's opinion. After listening to Shostakovich play the Fourth Quartet on the piano, Tsïganov recommended they put it into rehearsal before taking any decision. [55]

The Beethoven Quartet began rehearsing Shostakovich's Fourth Quartet on 10 February 1950. On 15 May—in the presence of Alexander Kholodilin, the head of the music division of the Committee for Artistic Affairs, the composer, his wife, and a handful of composers—they played it twice. [56] This, evidently, was when the decision to withhold the quartet was reached. Shostakovich's friends had been right. Even without considering the "Jewish" intonations in the last movement, the current climate was distinctly inhospitable to nonprogrammatic chamber compositions. Shostakovich made an arrangement of the work for two pianos. Along with *From Jewish Folk Poetry*, the Fourth Quartet was performed at Shostakovich's birthday soirees. And Valentin Berlinsky, cellist of the Borodin Quartet, recalls that their ensemble also performed Shostakovich's Fourth Quartet—presumably at some later date—for the Ministry of Culture in order to secure an official commission, with the money it entailed, for the composer. Their effort was successful. [57] (Throughout these difficult years, Shostakovich continued to perform his Piano Quintet publicly with the Beethoven Quartet, as well as with the Borodin and Komitas Quartets.) The Fourth Quartet would finally receive its public premiere, in a performance by the Beethoven Quartet, on 3 December 1953.

In July 1950, Shostakovich found himself in Leipzig imbibing musical impressions from the celebrations of the two-hundredth anniversary of the death of Johann Sebastian Bach and serving on the jury for the First International Bach Competition. Among the contestants was a twenty-six-year-old pianist from Moscow, Tatyana Nikolayeva. Though not required by competition regulations, she had come prepared to play any of the forty-eight preludes and fugues of the *Well-Tempered Clavier* on request and was encouraged by a very impressed Shostakovich to exercise her advantage. She took first prize. At a subsequent festival concert in Berlin, Shostakovich filled in for the indisposed Mariya Yudina in a performance of Bach's D Minor Concerto for three pianos, together with Nikolayeva and Pavel Serebryakov.

The savor of Bach's music lingered. In mid-October 1950, Shostakovich invited Nikolayeva to his home and played for her preludes and fugues he had just composed in the keys of C major and A minor. Over the next few months he continued composing preludes and fugues, sharing them with Nikolayeva, among other colleagues, as each was completed.[58] Initially it was not his intention to create a cycle. He told his former student Yuriy Levitin that he had decided to begin working again by writing a prelude and fugue a day, "so as not to lose my qualifications."[59] After completion of the cycle he told another colleague that he had decided to compose them on behalf of all of them: "No one here knows how to write fugues."[60]

Shostakovich had not always found the fugue appealing. As a tyro composition student in 1925, he had rejected writing a fugue to pair with the prelude in his octet (op. 11): "It's not my business to engage in stunts."[61] While traveling in the summer of 1934, lovesick for Yelena Konstantinovskaya, he had complained to her that since he was unable to compose he had taken to writing a fugue a day.[62] Now, in addition to the invigorating example of Bach, Shostakovich attributed his renewed attention to the fugue in 1950 as a "technical exercise with the aim of perfecting mastery in the polyphonic genre (along the lines of the polyphonic studies undertaken by Rimsky-Korsakov or Chaikovsky in their time)."[63]

The focus on technique soon shifted to a focus on the artistic, however, when Shostakovich determined to write a complete cycle, *Twenty-four Preludes and Fugues*, op. 87, proceeding around the circle of fifths alternating major and minor keys. Between 10 October 1950, when the Prelude in C Major was dated, and 25 February 1951, when the Fugue in D Minor, and the cycle, was completed, Shostakovich's progress was fairly steady, averaging either a prelude or a fugue every three days or so. Nikolayeva reported that Shostakovich wrote out the pieces without corrections and that only once, in the B-flat Minor prelude, he was dissatisfied with what he had begun and replaced it.[64]

Concurrent with his work on preludes and fugues, Shostakovich composed his *Ten Poems on Texts by Revolutionary Poets of the Late Nineteenth and Early Twentieth Centuries*, op. 88, for mixed chorus. This was his first concert work for unaccompanied chorus. He later credited its genesis to the intensive study of revolutionary songs he had made while writing music for historical revolutionary films. While he described the underlying theme of the choruses as the 1905 Revolution—and he would make conspicuous use of some of the music six years later in his Eleventh Symphony, *The Year 1905*, op. 103—some contemporaries, at least, had no trouble divining current relevance in the texts.[65] Early in 1951, Shostakovich submitted his new choruses to obligatory peer evaluation by the choral section at the Union of Composers: "Everyone was a bit nonplussed by Dmitriy Dmitriyevich's announcement that he was still inexperienced in *a cappella* choral writing and wanted as much critical feedback as possible. Although we all decided that this was some kind of coyness on the part of the universally recognized composer, there were actually a fair number of comments. Imagine the amazement of the participants of the choral section when, before long, Shostakovich brought back the score of this vocal cycle, significantly reworked." [66] The composer reported to Glikman that the "musical community" had received the choruses warmly.[67] The *Ten Poems on Texts by Revolutionary Poets*—Shostakovich's choice of "Poems" instead of "Choruses" was deliberate—were given their premiere in Moscow by the State Choir of Russian Song and the Boys' Choir of the Moscow Choral School conducted by Alexander Sveshnikov on 10 October 1951. They were widely perceived to mark a step forward, even from the success of *Song of the Forests*, in Shostakovich's ascent toward the heights of great realistic art. For them, the composer was awarded a Stalin Prize (category two) in 1952.

Shostakovich was not so fortunate with the reception of his *Twenty-four Preludes and Fugues*. On 31 March 1951, he played the first half of the cycle to a large gathering at the Union of Composers. He was scheduled to present the second half on 5 April, but discussion of the composition was evidently postponed until 16 May. By all accounts, the composer played very badly and did not show off his new opus to its best advantage. But the poor performance alone did not merit the fierce critical onslaught that greeted the work.[68] That the *Twenty-four Preludes and Fugues* represented a fundamentally different direction in the composer's output from the approved "realistic" line of *Song of the Forests*, his recent film scores, and even the new choral work, *Ten Poems on Texts by Revolutionary Poets*, was immediately apparent. Party-line activists determined that in his cycle of preludes and fugues, Shostakovich had failed to revive the Russian polyphonic tradition by infusing it with contemporary vitality. Instead, the composer had succumbed to constructivist complexity, gloomy moods, and individualistic aloofness. In short, the appearance of this polyphonic cycle fueled lingering suspicions "that Shostakovich has not wholly overcome all his previous errors and that some serious contradictions are still impeding his creative rehabilitation." [69]

Some voices were raised in defense of Shostakovich's new opus, most passionately that of Mariya Yudina, whose advocacy of artistic ideals in evaluating the significance of Shostakovich's accomplishment—as opposed to ideological yardsticks—was noteworthy in the context both for its sincerity and for its utter incongruity. These rare voices of reason were overpowered by the self-important enforcers of the 1948 cultural credo, those eager to demonstrate their unrelenting vigilance and to "instruct" the recalcitrant composer in the error of his ways. Neither public performance nor publication of the cycle was endorsed. Still, the music circulated widely in manuscript. In December 1951, Emil Gilels included three of the *Twenty-four Preludes and Fugues* (nos. 1 in C Major, 5 in D Major, and 24 in D Minor) in his recital programs in Helsinki, Oulu, and Lahti, Finland, as well as in Minsk. On 5 January 1952, Gilels performed them in Moscow in a concert evidently missed by the composer, who wrote him a few days later: "I've been hearing from all quarters about your brilliant performances of my preludes and fugues. I thank you warmly." [70] (Gilels repeated his performances of the three numbers in Stockholm and Göteborg in February 1952.) In February 1952, Shostakovich himself played a selection of the *Preludes and Fugues* at concerts in Baku; the first concert on 28 February—to an undersold hall papered with unappreciative soldiers from the local garrison—proved a great trial for the composer. [71]

In May 1952, the eminent pianist Heinrich Neuhaus wrote a colleague that he only had six of Shostakovich's *Preludes and Fugues* and that he had not yet found time to arrange to copy the rest: "Marvelous music, and those of us who love not just 'feeling' but 'intellect' in music are simply in clover! ... What they call the 'broad' (evidently, in distinction to the 'elite') public doesn't grasp it for the moment, and there is nothing exceptional in that, of course. It will always remain great nourishment for the professionals, like Bach, at any rate." [72]

Later that summer, Nikolayeva took it upon herself to perform the cycle again at the Committee for Artistic Affairs, making sure first that Shostakovich was out of town. The result this time was positive and publication was authorized. On 13 August, Shostakovich wrote to Atovmyan that Nikolayeva was in ecstasy about performing twelve of the preludes and fugues but expressed his deep skepticism about her intention to perform all twenty-four.[73] Despite these reservations, she gave the public premiere of the complete cycle on 23 and 28 December 1952 in Leningrad. Later in her life, Nikolayeva—who established a special niche for herself as authorized interpreter of the complete cycle—insisted that Shostakovich had always intended this work to be played in its entirety,[74] but her assertion is not supported by his own (or her earlier) statements, or by performance practice during the composer's lifetime. On the publication of *Twenty-four Preludes and Fugues* in late 1952, Neuhaus pronounced it an event of rare magnitude in the musical world and phoned the composer to tell him that pianists were counting on him to compose a second set. He reported Shostakovich's laughing reply: "Never."[75]

Money continued to be a pressing problem for Shostakovich. He had a large household to maintain; in addition to the children's nurse and domestic help, he employed a driver. He sent money regularly to his mother and sister in Leningrad. He fantasized about procuring a patroness along the lines of Chaikovksy's Madame von Meck. His choral arrangements of *Ten Russian Folksongs* in the summer of 1951 were for quick sale to the Committee for Artistic Affairs. As soon as he read that the recording of *Song of the Forests* had been released that same summer, he alerted Atovmyan—to whom he confessed he was on the verge of financial catastrophe—to find out about the honorarium.[76] The symphonic "pops" arrangements prepared by Atovmyan of three suites from Shostakovich's ballet music probably fall into the gainful category as well.[77] Practical considerations may also have motivated Shostakovich's decision to set *Four Songs on Texts of Dolmatovsky* in 1950–1951. Dolmatovsky recalled that, in 1950, when he was working on a play in verse, he sent Shostakovich texts for a number of songs he needed, including one that was an "aeronautical beacon," a song designed to help a pilot navigate across the Alps during a storm.[78] Though the play was never staged, Shostakovich's popular setting of "The Motherland Hears" acquired legendary status on the report that Yuriy Gagarin, the first man in space, had sung it as he returned to earth on 12 April 1961.

Throughout this period, Shostakovich retained a prominent civic profile.[79] As his appearance at the Cultural and Scientific Congress in New York had underscored, he stood out among Soviet cultural figures for the recognition he enjoyed at home as well as for the enormous respect which he and his creative work enjoyed in the West. This dual acknowledgment—and his apparently unresisting acquiescence to manipulation by the Party and state—made Shostakovich a useful symbol and spokesman for Soviet propaganda. In October 1950, Shostakovich was one of three musicians (along with Composers' Union chief Khrennikov and Dmitriy Kabalevsky) elected to the Soviet Committee for the Defense of Peace. He participated in the National Congresses and in November 1950 and December 1952 he was a

member of the Soviet delegation to International Peace Congresses in Warsaw and Vienna respectively. His speeches at these events—standard
boilerplate all—were widely distributed.

That his attendance at such congresses and conferences proved a burdensome distraction is confirmed by Ilya Erenburg's reminiscences, expunged
from the original publication of his published memoirs, of one such
occasion:

> I remember that on one dreary day I spotted Shostakovich with earphones on;
> his face was very gloomy. I went up to him. He whispered that they had torn him
> away from work and now he was forced to listen.... I told him, "Don't listen, take
> off the earphones." Dmitriy Dmitriyevich refused: "Everyone knows I don't
> know foreign languages, they'll say it was disrespect to the assembly." ... The next
> day I saw him again with earphones on, this time happy. He explained: "I figured
> it out—I unplugged them. Now I can't hear anything. It's absolutely
> marvelous! [80]

Years later, Shostakovich would impart another useful tip for dealing with
such circumstances to the young poet Yevgeniy Yevtushenko: "I have my
method, Yevgeniy Alexandrovich, to avoid applauding. I pretend that I am
writing down these great thoughts. Thank heavens, everyone sees that my
hands are occupied." [81]

In February 1951, Shostakovich was re-elected as deputy to the RSFSR
Supreme Soviet from Leningrad's Dzerzhinsky District. Although this facet
of his public life remains to be studied, judging from a sampling of his official correspondence, his most important function was probably as interme-
diary and advocate for needy constituents. In a city devastated by blockade
and war, not to mention the repressive policies of its own government, the
petitions Shostakovich fielded—pleas for improved living space, residence
permits, apartment repairs, access to special medical services, invalids'
pensions—were often heartrending in the tragedy of the stories they told.
With his customary conscientiousness, Shostakovich steered these requests
through the labyrinths of bureaucracy, tracking their progress and
disposition.

It was in this sphere, in extending a helping hand to others in need, that
the lofty status—the public positions, the plethora of awards, titles, and
honors—of an otherwise unpretentious man justified its utility. Shostakovich routinely traded on his prestige and connections to come to the aid
of friends, colleagues, and even strangers, often with selfless disregard for
the possible consequences to himself and his family. He did not turn his
back on the families of the victims of Stalin's purges. In a number of cases,
he agitated to restore urban residence permits to survivors released from
the Gulag after the war. When Lina Prokofiev (the composer's first wife)
was arrested in 1948, her sons turned to Shostakovich, then under a cloud

himself. Although he wanted to help them, there was nothing he could do.[82] Such appeals were by no means unusual. Shostakovich could no more spurn the entreaties of the persecuted and the powerless than he could resist the blandishments of political functionaries.

His intercessions were deeply appreciated. Following the revelation of the Doctors' Plot in January 1953, Moisey Vainberg, Shostakovich's friend and, coincidentally, the son-in-law of Solomon Mikhoels, was arrested in the early morning hours of 7 February on the charge of "Jewish bourgeois nationalism." Shostakovich quickly fired off a testimonial on his behalf to Lavrentiy Beria.[83] Anticipating the imminent arrest of Vainberg's wife as well, Nina Shostakovich had her sign a power-of-attorney so that their daughter would be cared for. Two months later, after the death of Stalin, Vainberg was released and rehabilitated. The two families joined in celebrating the event and consigned the unused power-of-attorney to the flames.[84]

Although Shostakovich had been stripped of his teaching positions, he remained accessible to those who genuinely valued his professional opinion. In June 1948, after withstanding months of vile public abuse, he diligently responded to a letter from a nineteen-year-old mathematics student at Tomsk University who aspired to become a composer: "I am very glad that you love music and are excited by all kinds of questions about this art form which is so dear to me, and without which, more than likely, I couldn't live a day." [85] He became a responsive correspondent of the young Siberian, Edison Denisov, extending a sympathetic ear and ample encouragement, critiquing his early compositional efforts, and giving him practical counsel about his career options. As mentor, Shostakovich tried to impart the benefit of his hard-earned wisdom: "A few words about your grievances. I advise you to envy Mozart, Beethoven, Chaikovsky. To envy Koval, Muravlyov, and so on, really and truly isn't worth it, no matter how successful these failures sometimes may be.... P.S. I repeat: envy of Mozart will lead you forward. Envy of talentless losers will take you backward." [86]

Shostakovich's major public submission for 1952 was a cantata for boys' choir, mixed chorus, and orchestra on a text by Dolmatovsky, *The Sun Shines Over Our Motherland*, op. 90. The work was initially titled "Cantata about the Party," in anticipation of the Nineteenth Communist Party Congress in the fall of 1952, and it went through several textual revisions. Shostakovich composed this apparently earnest hosanna to the radiant Communist future in the summer of 1952 at Komarovo, completing it on 29 September 1952. The cantata was unveiled in Moscow on 6 November 1952 during the celebrations for the thirty-fifth anniversary of the Revolution. It was also featured on the opening concert of the Sixth Plenum of the Composers' Union on 31 January 1953. Mixed opinions about Shostakovich's new cantata were revealed during the deliberations at the Plenum. Some found it merely mediocre, stilted. Ivan Dzerzhinsky, the harshest—and most perceptive—critic of the work, lambasted it as "primitive, cold, ritually festive, devoid of sincere feeling and inspiration." [87] Its most passionate defender, Aram Khachaturyan—in what only in hindsight sounds like withering sarcasm—extolled *The Sun Shines Over Our Motherland* as "the apotheosis of a major triad." [88]

For public consumption, Shostakovich hailed the advent of the Nineteenth Communist Party Congress.[89] In private, he spent the first four days of the Congress, 5 to 8 October 1952, setting a Pushkin poem each day, as if continuing the cycle he had begun back in 1936–1937. Like so much of his vocal music, the *Four Monologues on Texts of Pushkin* for bass and piano, op. 91, are illumined by intimate purpose distant from the composer's public mask. Also on the "private" side of the ledger was the composition of a new quartet, his Fifth, completed on 1 November 1952. In it he paid homage to a former student, Galina Ustvolskaya, for whom he sheltered profound professional respect and tender personal feelings, by conspicuously incorporating a melody from one of her compositions, the Trio for Clarinet, Violin and Piano of 1949. Though rehearsals began in early 1953, it would not be until the following autumn before the Fifth Quartet in B-flat Major, op. 92, would receive its first public performance, on 13 November 1953 in Moscow. Shostakovich dedicated it to the artists of the Beethoven Quartet in honor of their thirtieth anniversary. Not long afterward, Denisov visited Shostakovich and recorded that the composer was deeply attached to this quartet (dismissing the Fourth, by comparison, as merely "entertaining"). He also told Denisov that it was unlikely the Fifth Quartet would be published because "musical circles react to it negatively." [90]

On 5 March 1953, both Joseph Stalin and Sergey Prokofiev died. Years earlier, Shostakovich's youthful infatuation with Prokofiev's music had dissipated not long after he first met his idol, and the relationship between the two men never went beyond polite, though not uncritical, exchanges of opinion about each other's music. Through the tribulations of 1948, however, Shostakovich certainly came to appreciate that they had much more in common with each other than with their philistine persecutors. On 12 October 1952, the day after the premiere of Prokofiev's Seventh Symphony, Shostakovich sent the ailing composer his enthusiastic congratulations, concluding his letter: "I wish you at least another hundred years to live and create. Listening to such works as your Seventh Symphony makes it much easier and more joyful to live." [91] In recognition of the musical watershed created by the deaths of Prokofiev and Myaskovsky (in 1950), conductor Nikolai Golovanov was probably voicing the hopes of many—as well as extending an olive branch to a one-time adversary—when he addressed

Shostakovich: "I believe that you remain a serious, unbending, always strictly principled musician. All the genuine workers on the front of our musical art understand and value this well.... Please accept my wishes for your happiness, health, and, naturally, your creativity; may your artistic path be strewn with roses (and fewer thorns, which are unavoidable in the life of every great artist)." [92]

Shostakovich's "official" sentiments on the death of Stalin—deep grief, appreciation for all that the leader had done to prevent a new war and foster friendship among the workers of the world, and an enduring faith that nothing could prevent the triumph of communism—were promptly publicized.[93] With respect to the political watershed intimated by Stalin's death, Shostakovich in private remained sober about prospects for the future. Flora Litvinova recalls that while he exhibited a sense of relief, he felt no euphoria.[94] And when the young Denisov asked him if whether he thought there would now be changes for the better, Shostakovich replied: "Edik, the times are new, but the informers are old." [95]

1953–1958

The Thaw

In April 1953, Shostakovich traveled to a sanatorium in Kislovodsk in the foothills of the Caucasus for a month of rest and recuperation. His health had never been robust since childhood, and his letters chronicle a steady stream of afflictions and hospitalizations. On one occasion, after the whole family had been stricken with various illnesses, Shostakovich quipped that God must have allocated the good health and beauty to his in-laws.[1]

In early June 1953, Shostakovich was a member of a cultural delegation sent to Vienna and Graz. He attended a concert of music by Berg, Honegger, and Stravinsky and confided in a colleague that the Austrian composer who had exerted the most influence on him from his earliest years was Gustav Mahler. He surprised his travel companions with his impulsive insistence on riding a daredevil roller-coaster at the Prater. He returned exhilarated: "I love the madcap, it gave me great pleasure. You've undoubtedly forgotten that I am the author of the opera *The Nose!*"[2] The composer rated the "hell-train," on which he also took a spin, "cheap and primitive."

Back home in the summer of 1953, Shostakovich set his sights on composing a new symphony. For all his evident success in recasting himself in the image of a dutiful "Socialist Realist" composer during Stalin's final years, Shostakovich's conspicuous avoidance of the symphony, the genre that had brought him such wide fame and had also defined the terms of his disgrace in 1948, had not gone unnoticed. He was not alone in avoiding nonprogrammatic symphonic scores in the period after 1948. The threat to the proud Russian symphonic tradition of continued abstinence by Soviet composers was perceived as real: "Several prominent masters—for instance, Shostakovich, Khachaturyan, Shaporin, Khrennikov, Kabalevsky, Muradeli—have, in the recent past, demonstrated no creative activity in the symphonic genre even though they know that Soviet listeners expect from them monumental, heroic symphonies on stirring contemporary themes. Is it not time for them to overcome this timid lethargy in the resolution of great creative tasks?" [3]

There is evidence that Shostakovich actually *had* made a timely start, years earlier, on a Tenth Symphony as the climax of the wartime trilogy begun with the Seventh and Eighth Symphonies, but at least by early summer 1947—shortly before he began working on his Violin Concerto—he had become dissatisfied with what he had done and indicated he would start over.[4] In a number of interviews conducted late in her life, pianist Tatyana Nikolayeva remained firm in her conviction that the composer actually completed his Tenth Symphony in 1951, interrupting his work on the *Twenty-four Preludes and Fugues* to play her the exposition of the first movement then in progress.[5] It is conceivable that Shostakovich may have continued thinking about a new symphony and even done some sketching in 1951. Nevertheless, the preponderance of both external and internal evidence illuminating the process of the Tenth Symphony's composition suggests that, Nikolayeva's claim notwithstanding, the symphony was substantially composed—as the composer indicated on his manuscript score, in letters, and in interviews—in the summer and fall of 1953.

On 27 June 1953, Shostakovich alerted Kara Karayev from Komarovo: "I am trying to write a symphony. Although nothing is holding me back, work proceeds so-so. When 'creative potential' is at its peak, then nothing disturbs composition. But when it is middling or low, then neither creative retreats nor similar conveniences can help.... For the moment I am dragging out the first movement with difficulty, and how it will fare beyond that, I don't know." [6] Composition of the first movement was still dragging along three weeks later.[7] Shostakovich dated its completion on 5 August 1953.

Shostakovich worked on the symphony on the veranda of his dacha at Komarovo. He related an amusing incident to friends: One day a sparrow had flown in through the window and, during the commotion as they tried to shoo it out, the frightened bird had relieved itself on the score of Shostakovich's symphony. Glikman's family saw it as a lucky omen for the symphony's future success.[8] The composer commented to another correspondent: "Well, if a sparrow dirties your creative work with his ... it's not that bad. Much worse when it is done by more significant personalities than a sparrow." [9]

Having completed the second movement on 27 August, Shostakovich indicated to Glikman that he was dissatisfied with it.[10] Two days later, he wrote Elmira Nazirova, a twenty-four-year-old pianist living in Baku, that he had finished the second movement and was writing the third but was not satisfied with the results. More strikingly, he revealed a source of private inspiration: he had transcribed her name, Elmira, into musical pitches, E-A-E-D-A. He provided her with a detailed explanation of just how he had derived the transcription of this arresting motto played by the French horn twelve times during the third movement, where it is interleaved with appearances of Shostakovich's own personal cipher.[11]

This was not Shostakovich's first letter to Elmira. As a student at the Moscow Conservatory in the late 1940s, she had taken a few composition lessons from him in 1947. She saw him infrequently thereafter. Between 12 April 1953 and 13 September 1956, Shostakovich sent her at least thirty-four letters. The vast majority of these date from the summer and fall of 1953, when he was hard at work on the Tenth Symphony. In reminiscing about their relationship later in life, Nazirova described Shostakovich's as an opportunistic infatuation. She had the distinct sensation that Shostakovich had needed her most as a muse and that, after the premiere of the Tenth Symphony, her "mission" had been accomplished.[12] After that, Shostakovich's dispatches to her dropped off abruptly.

Curiously, on 10 August 1953, when he was still engrossed in work on the second movement of his symphony, Shostakovich wrote to Elmira that he had heard the third movement in a dream, had remembered a bit, and was intending to use it in his future work.[13] Nearly six weeks later, on 17 September, Shostakovich told her he had replayed one of his favorite works, Mahler's *Das Lied von der Erde*, the day before and had recognized the ominous cry of the monkey (which he described to her as a Chinese symbol of death, cruel fate, and unhappiness) in "Das Trinklied vom Jammer der Erde" as identical to the horn theme—that is, to the transcription of her name—of his Tenth Symphony. He thought it might constitute an interesting topic for musicological research.[14]

Shostakovich's own musical monogram made its conspicuous debut in the third movement of the Tenth Symphony.[15] The German transcription of the initials of his first and last names, D. Sch., have been converted into the German pitch names D Es C H, which correspond to the pitches D E♭ C B♮.

Shostakovich was musically fortunate in his name, as he obviously appreciated. The intervallic relationship of the four pitches is at once semantically distinctive and teeming with harmonic and melodic ambiguity. The composer would explore the rich potential of his motto most extensively in 1960 in his "autobiographical" quartet, the Eighth. In the latter part of his life he often "signed" his compositions—sometimes conspicuously, sometimes discreetly—with his musical monogram.

Before Shostakovich had even finished the Tenth Symphony, Mravinsky came from Leningrad to discuss the work-in-progress. On the completion of the fourth movement on 25 October 1953, Shostakovich and Moisey Vainberg went to Leningrad to demonstrate the symphonic opus in the composer's four-hand arrangement; Mravinsky undertook to prepare for the prompt premiere of the new symphony. When they played the four-hand version of the Tenth Symphony at the Moscow Conservatory, Shostakovich commented to Vainberg, "It would be great if they [i.e., the Leningrad orchestra] could play it as well as we do." [16]

The last weeks of 1953 were hectic. In a sign of the easing of intellectual and cultural constraints that had begun to make itself felt after the death of Stalin, Shostakovich was now confident enough to risk the public premieres of two works, the Fourth and Fifth String Quartets, heretofore deferred. The premiere that attracted the most attention, however, was the unveiling of Shostakovich's Tenth Symphony in Leningrad on 17 December 1953 by the Leningrad Philharmonic Orchestra under Mravinsky. Gavriil Popov recorded in his diary that after the third movement some timid applause broke out but that at the conclusion the author was summoned to the stage for many bows.[17] Edison Denisov, who came from Moscow for the event, attended the festive post-concert supper that the composer held in his hotel suite for family and friends, including Khachaturyan, Glikman, Levitin, Nikolayeva, and Atovmyan. The toasts flowed liberally.[18] The success was repeated when Mravinsky conducted the Moscow premiere of the Tenth Symphony with the USSR State Symphony on 29 December.

Not for the first time in Shostakovich's career one of his works now became embroiled in controversy, at the center of the renewed struggle to define Soviet aesthetic policy. In fact, Mravinsky claimed that the whiff of intrigue reached him even before the Moscow premiere. He took the initiative to invite the Minister of Culture, Panteleymon Ponomarenko, to the concert and made an end run around Composers' Union officials attempting to swamp the hall with Shostakovich's opponents. Ponamarenko's expressed appreciation of the work after hearing it neutralized this "administrative" line of attack.[19]

Rumblings of discontent with the state of affairs in the arts—with the stifling rigidity of ideologically-driven aesthetic criteria and the banal creative stereotypes they fostered—had begun to surface in artistic circles already in 1953. A *Pravda* review (signed by an anonymous "Viewer") of a new theatrical production published on 27 November 1953,[20] gave an encouraging boost to the proponents of cultural liberalization by underscoring the artist's fundamental right to creative freedom and bold experimentation. By drawing from this review in his own new year's message for 1954, Shostakovich thus armed himself for the impending debate of his Tenth Symphony:

> One of the worst misfortunes for art is its homogenization, its accommodation to a single model, no matter how good. That kind of approach to work on a composition wipes out individuality and breeds stereotypes and blind imitation. It arrests the development of the creative idea and deprives art of the joy of discovery.
>
> Socialist Realism opens up extraordinary scope for the artist's ideas. It grants the greatest liberty for the emergence of creative personality, for the development of the most varied genres, directions, and styles. That is why it is so important to support the artist's daring, to examine his creative signature and—understanding the merits and shortcomings of one or another artistic choice—to allow for the artist's right to independence, to audacity, to quests for the new.[21]

Even before the advent of increased official tolerance for artistic diversity had been signaled by *Pravda*, Aram Khachaturyan—condemned of formalism alongside Shostakovich in 1948—had lamented the sorry state of recent Soviet music, with its surfeit of mediocre scores camouflaged by pompous patriotic programs and with the persistent meddling of incompetent bureaucrats in the creative process.[22] When, in the spirit of encouraging constructive debate and greater diversity of opinion, *Sovetskaya muzïka* opened its pages to unprecedented coverage, beginning with its March 1954 issue, of the discussion of Shostakovich's new symphony, Khachaturyan led off with his ringing endorsement. Shostakovich's Tenth Symphony, he asserted, was a fresh and original work, dramatic and multifaceted, a "new step toward the affirmation of the high principles of realism in Soviet symphonic work,"[23] a symphony relevant to and worthy of the contemporary listener, a memorable milestone in the Soviet symphonic legacy. Acknowledging its sharp conflicts, its stormy passions, and—in tacit recognition of the most controversial aspect of the symphony—its tragic cast, Khachaturyan dubbed Shostakovich's Tenth Symphony "an optimistic tragedy, infused with a firm belief in the victory of bright, life-affirming forces."[24]

Others were more circumspect in their evaluations. The lack of a concrete program enabling them to "read" the symphony, for instance, left some critics skeptical. At least one doubted the success of Shostakovich's emancipation from dense psychologism and the obscure musings of modernism.[25] The bluntest criticism was couched as the view of an ordinary, untutored listener. Expecting the fourth movement to resolve, somehow, the gloomy hopelessness of the first, the frightening, "fateful" force of the second, and the spiritual despondency of the third, this disappointed listener instead found the finale too lightweight: "The tragic questions and doubts troubling the author of the symphony were left unanswered. I left the concert in a depressed state.... Negative, gloomy, at times depressing images dominate in the symphony. The composer did not create the image of a positive hero capable of battling and overcoming the dark, gloomy forces."[26]

For three days, 29–30 March and 5 April 1954, a vigorous debate on the Tenth Symphony was held at the Union of Composers.[27] In what was his first public statement about his new symphony, Shostakovich opened the proceedings with an informal introduction to the work. His remarks were excessively self-deprecating; he allowed to having written the work too quickly, to having failed in his goal of creating a genuine symphonic allegro in the first movement. He fretted that perhaps the second movement might be too short and the proportions of the third unbalanced. He vouchsafed no program, adding only; "In this work I wanted to convey human feelings and passions."[28]

The most vocal opponents of the Tenth Symphony evaluated it from the narrow perspective of the "realistic method" propagated since the time of Zhdanov. They necessarily found it wanting; it was insufficiently optimistic and uplifting, insufficiently melodic, too complex for immediate appreciation by the masses, an inaccurate reflection of contemporary Soviet reality. By contrast to comparable convocations of the recent past, however, the number of speakers impatient with the dogmatic intransigence and parochial aesthetic formulas of the guardians of ideological orthodoxy was sizable. The work's proponents openly extolled its virtues, its stunning mastery and invigorating originality, rallying support for a more accommodating view of the diverse needs and tastes of the Soviet listener. Shostakovich was apparently satisfied. At any rate, he reported to Glikman on 7 April that the outcome of the debate had been in his favor.[29]

Matters stood differently at the session of the selection committee for the Stalin Prize that took place on 1 April, while the Composers' Union debate was still ongoing. Chaired by Khrennikov, the music panel considered three nominated works of Shostakovich: the Tenth Symphony, the *Twenty-four Preludes and Fugues*, and the patriotic cantata, *The Sun Shines Over Our Motherland*. Khrennikov spearheaded the rejection of the Tenth Symphony from consideration, contending that it was far from—even antipathetic to—the ideals of Soviet music. He did advocate rewarding Shostakovich, as one of the hardest working and most talented of Soviet composers, and to this end he advanced the candidacy of the cantata, even though most in attendance recognized it was considerably inferior musically. There were panelists who voiced strong support for the selection of the Tenth Symphony. In a rueful admission, the admiring Alexander Goldenveyzer allowed that even though he did not know whether the future would afford it wide acclaim, he would be ashamed to feel that he had been one of those who had spoken out against the symphony. Vladimir Zakharov—songwriter, music director of the Pyatnitsky Folk Chorus, and one of Zhdanov's faithful lieutenants in the 1948 campaign against formalism—zeroed in on the crux of the problem: "All the same, what the Stalin Committee represents is politics in the sphere of music. What the award of a Stalin Prize indicates is that this is the correct path, this is the path along which, in this instance, symphonic composition should develop."[30] The hardliners were unwilling to cede this imprimatur to Shostakovich's Tenth Symphony. In a compromise, consideration of the symphony for a Stalin Prize was postponed for a year, and Shostakovich never received any award at all for his Tenth Symphony.

A year later, when Soviet symphonic composition was the featured topic of the Eighth Plenum of the Composers' Union, Shostakovich's Tenth Symphony once again loomed large in the discussion, rated by many as the best work performed at the Plenum. In his closing comments, Khrennikov reiterated his conviction that the Tenth Symphony was an unconvincing musical reflection of the truth of their life—significantly less satisfying than *Song of the Forests*—and expressed his hope that in a subsequent work Shostakovich would find the means of expression and corresponding forms to embody successfully the "great truth" of Soviet life.[31] Continuing controversy did not hinder the dissemination of the Tenth Symphony. By mid-1955, in addition to the continued advocacy and a first recording by Mravinsky, the symphony had been published, taken up by several other Russian conductors, and given successful foreign premieres in New York and London. That the implications of the popular reception of this work continued to rankle in some circles is evidenced by the fact that in April 1957, three years after the debate had flourished, one of the sternest of its original critics deemed it expedient to revisit the Tenth Symphony and recapitulate its dangerous flaws. In so doing, musicologist Yuliy Kremlyov inadvertently offered a plausible explanation for its tremendous resonance and impact:

> We know all the difficulties that workers have endured in capitalist countries. We survived the most brutal world war with its incalculable human toll. At home in the USSR, we were witnesses to the enormous harm caused by the cult of personality.
> For the past ten years, world history has developed in a way that has led for

some people to the repression of simple, natural, joyful, and bright feelings, mental acuity, and harmony.

This repression and distraction of feelings, which fragments and splinters them, is temporary, of course, yet it is serious and deep. It is precisely this kind of repression that is conveyed in a number of Shostakovich's works (the Tenth Symphony, in particular), and it is precisely in this that the music of the Tenth Symphony, with its psychological depression and imbalance, is a true document of the era.[32]

Denied the Stalin Prize for his Tenth Symphony, Shostakovich was nevertheless rewarded for his hard work and contributions to Soviet music. In August 1954, together with Shaporin and Khachaturyan, he was awarded the title "People's Artist of the USSR." Earlier in the summer, it had been announced that Shostakovich was to receive the International Peace Prize, an honor that was formally bestowed at a ceremony in Moscow on 4 September with lavish tributes, a thundering ovation, and a concert of the composer's music. Late in the year, it was announced that Shostakovich had been elected an honorary member of the Swedish Royal Academy of Music.

The summer of 1954 was the last Nina Shostakovich would spend together with her husband and children at Komarovo. Later, friends and relatives would recall noticing Nina's off-color complexion, but no one seems to have suspected anything seriously amiss with her health. During the summer, Shostakovich composed *Five Romances on Texts of Dolmatovsky* ("Songs of Our Days"), op. 98, and fretted whether his eighteen-year-old daughter would be successful in negotiating university entrance exams. To his great relief, she was accepted. In the fall, he sent his newly composed romances to bass Boris Gmïrya in Kiev.

Nina had returned to her profession after the war, joining the laboratory of the eminent physicist and former Leningrad University classmate Artyom Alikhanyan, pursuing research in cosmic radiation. Alikhanyan became a family intimate. That his relationship with Nina went beyond the professional was an open secret, but, like the composer's periodic amours, it did not upset the domestic tranquility of the Shostakovich household. (Beyond a close personal relationship fireproofed by the tribulations they had braved together over the years, the birth of Nina and Dmitriy's two children had sealed a family bond uncannily presaged in the letter from the sixteen-year-old Shostakovich to his mother.[33]) Nina's work required her to spend several months each autumn at the cosmic research station on Mount Alagez in Armenia. She spent the fall of 1954 there as usual.

In early November, Shostakovich responded to a last-minute request from the Bolshoy Theater, where he had signed on as musical consultant,[34] for a curtain raiser to ornament its concert celebrating the thirty-seventh anniversary of the Revolution. He dashed off his *Festive Overture*, op. 96, in a matter of days. Couriers sent from the theater fetched the pages of manuscript with ink still wet on the page. After its first performance on 6 November 1954, by the Bolshoy Theater Orchestra conducted by Melik-Pashayev, Shostakovich's *Festive Overture* quickly established itself as his most durable piece of occasional music.

Two days later, on 8 November 1954, in an event that must have reminded him of his Moscow debut nearly thirty years earlier, Shostakovich shared a chamber concert with his old friend Vissarion Shebalin at the Small Hall of the Moscow Conservatory. Among the works featured on Shostakovich's half of the program was the premiere of his Concertino for Two Pianos, op. 94, performed by his sixteen-year-old son, Maxim, with one of his classmates from the Central Music School, Alla Maloletkova.[35]

This was not the first time Shostakovich had turned his attention to pedagogical literature for his children. When his daughter had been a fledgling pianist in the mid-1940s, he had penned a number of children's pieces for her, published as his *Children's Notebook*, op. 69. Although Galina's interests soon led her away from music, Maxim showed an inclination to pursue it seriously as a career, initially concentrating on piano performance. As contemporary critics noted, although the ebullient one-movement Concertino had been written with young performers in mind, allowances for age were not conspicuous. It was a work that might well appeal to adult pianists. A proud father marveled at the wonders of training after Maxim and his partner repeated their success with another performance of the Concertino at a concert of Shostakovich's music in January 1955. Sadly, Maxim's mother did not survive to hear it.

On the evening of 3 December 1954, Shostakovich was called out of a concert in Moscow with the news that Nina had been hospitalized in Yerevan. He rushed to join her, but by the time he arrived the next day, she was in a coma following an emergency operation on a cancerous tumor in the colon. She died shortly afterward. In his characteristically purposeful fashion, the distraught Shostakovich checked his grief as best he could, busying himself with the details of making the funeral arrangements and transporting his wife's body back to Moscow. On 10 December, Nina was buried in Novodevichy Cemetery in Moscow.

It did not take Shostakovich long to fathom the extent of his loss. Nina had braved his most humiliating defeats and terrors together with him. A woman of spirit, strong-willed, intelligent, and pragmatic, Nina had shielded him from many of the nuisances of day-to-day affairs and from the importunate supplicants and sycophants who clustered around him, creating for him a comfortable home and working environment. As Shostakovich confessed to Denisov shortly after her death, among other things he had depended on her as a secretary. She would answer the phone and tell people he was away for two months. Without her, he was reduced to talking to everyone himself.[36] He felt alone and unprotected, apprehensive about the blows that might now strike him. Even his young son realized immediately how defenseless his father had been left. When Shostakovich broke the news of his mother's death to him on the phone from Armenia, Maxim is reported to have remarked, "Now they'll devour him," and burst into tears.[37]

Shostakovich felt inadequate to the task of raising two teenagers alone. He was a loving and indulgent father but not a caregiver. He obsessed about their welfare and felt ill equipped to supervise their upbringing properly. Not a few observers at the time regarded Galina, and particularly Maxim—growing up in what was by Soviet standards an environment of rare privilege—as spoiled and undisciplined. Their father was no more skilled at refusing them than he was at refusing others. Galina recalled that one of the rare occasions on which their normally reserved father opened up to them occurred shortly after the death of their mother, when Shostakovich sounded them out about his idea of marrying Galina Ustvolskaya, someone already well-known to them.[38] He besieged her with letters and attention, but Ustvolskaya refused his marriage proposal.[39] Shostakovich acquired the services of a secretary, but for the time being he coped with the domestic situation by himself.

To assuage his grief in the days after Nina's death, Shostakovich dusted off the score he had dedicated to her, the opera *Lady Macbeth of the Mtsensk District*, and made some revisions. It was a work fraught with associations and memories, one that had always remained close to his heart. As he informed Glikman at the time, he was little concerned with whether the opera would be staged again or not.[40] In March 1955, however, he was energized by a successful audition of the new version of his opera and the prospect of an imminent production at Leningrad's Malïy Theater to initiate a comprehensive revision of the libretto. His chief objective was to clean up what he now regarded (from the perspective of an older, more discreet man than the youth who had penned the opera more than twenty years earlier) as the vulgarity of its language and its naturalistic excesses.[41] Revisions or no, restoring to the stage the work that for nearly two decades had epitomized the most pernicious heresy in the history of Soviet music promised to be no simple matter. It would not be accomplished quickly.

After the completion of the Tenth Symphony, Shostakovich was frustrated by the inability to compose. Among the distractions he complained about was a heavy concert schedule; in April 1955, for example, on a tour of the Baltics with Rostropovich and vocalists, he played seven concerts in eight days in five cities. That fall, he confided to Karayev: "To this day I have not become accustomed to the stage. It causes me much anxiety and nervousness. As soon as I reach the age of fifty I will cease concert activity."[42] In March 1956, he fretted, "I will soon start to feel like a Rossini. As everybody knows, that composer wrote his last composition at the age of forty, after which he lived until the age of seventy without composing another note. That's small comfort for me."[43] The death, in November 1955, of Shostakovich's doting mother, who had put the nurturing of her son's great gift above all else, made it all the harder to put grief behind him.

That Shostakovich experienced a lengthy creative drought was not literally true, of course, even if he chose to discount the functional and "populist" works composed during this period: the Concertino, the *Festive Overture*, the Dolmatovsky romances, his arrangements of *Six Spanish Songs*, op. 100[44] (1956) and scores to the propaganda documentary *Song of the Great Rivers (Unity)* (1954), and the films *The Gadfly* (1955) and *The First Echelon* (1955–1956). No creative hiatus or decline was apparent to the outside world, in any event, which was generously served by the public unveiling in 1955 of two major works that had been cached for many years.

On 15 January 1955, Nina Dorliak, Zara Dolukhanova, Alexey Maslennikov, and the composer gave the first public performance of *From Jewish Folk Poetry* in Leningrad. In the seven years since it had been written, during which official anti-Semitism had escalated to the brink of a new holocaust barely averted by virtue of Stalin's death, the cycle had acquired tragic resonances and a poignancy the composer could never have imagined when he wrote the cycle. Glikman recorded that its success was stunning, exceeded only, in Shostakovich's own humble estimation, by its success at the Moscow premiere five days later.[45] Listeners could not miss the contemporary relevance of the texts; the insistence of the announcer in explaining that the Siberian exile alluded to in the "Lullaby" took place in tsarist times evoked titters from the audience.[46] The immediacy and dramatic intensity of the scenes led critics to fantasize about what might rightfully be expected from another opera by Shostakovich. Initial reactions to this opus, however, were not uniformly constructive. Shostakovich was very upset, in early February, by two anonymous letters he received and what he perceived as an anti-Semitic campaign targeted against the cycle.[47] Happily, a month later he was able to report that the unpleasantness had passed.[48] The cycle was included in the programs of Shostakovich's Baltic tour and published a few months later.

David Oistrakh gave the first performance of Shostakovich's Violin Concerto in A Minor, op. 77,[49] in Leningrad on 29 October 1955 with the Leningrad Philharmonic under the baton of Mravinsky. There are hints that the delay in bringing this work to the concert hall may have been due, at least in part, to the soloist. Shostakovich had earlier announced the premiere for the 1954–1955 concert season. Oistrakh, who did not master contemporary scores without effort, wrote to a friend while on vacation in August 1955: "I have learned some things for the new season, polished some, applied finishing touches, not least of which I have mastered Shostakovich's concerto, which I now play quite effortlessly. ... Thanks to a free head and time I have plumbed it thoroughly. I have come to understand only now that it is a marvelous work; I have fallen in love with it with all my soul."[50]

After the first rehearsal with orchestra on 25 October, Shostakovich leafed through the score of the work that he had completed under such monstrous conditions in 1948 and reflected thoughtfully that he really was deserving of respect after all.[51] The premiere proved a jubilant triumph, tidings of which were carried on the front page of *Sovetskaya kultura*.[52] Oistrakh and the composer were greeted with wild applause and ovations. While noting correspondences between the Tenth Symphony and the concerto in preliminary assessments, critics heard only positive things to recommend the concerto, nothing to produce reservations. Oistrakh made up for his initial foot-dragging by becoming an ardent champion of the concerto. Only two months after the first performance—even before introducing it to Moscow audiences—the violinist included it in his repertory for his first concert tour of the United States. He gave the Moscow premiere on 4 February 1956. In July 1956, impatient with the absence of serious critical writing about the concerto—and admonishing the leadership of the Union of Composers for its willful negligence—Oistrakh published his own appreciation of the piece.[53]

In the early morning hours of 25 February 1956, Nikita Khrushchev delivered his "secret" speech to a closed session of the Twentieth Congress of the Communist Party, with its unexpected denunciation of Stalin and revelations about the ghastly consequences of the "cult of personality." While this event marks a turning point in political history, the slow process of releasing prisoners from labor camps and rehabilitating victims of the Stalinist terror had actually been under way for some time. Shostakovich participated actively in this endeavor, agitating persistently on behalf of the most varied victims, including old family friends from Leningrad, Genrietta Dombrovskaya and her sons.

Vsevolod Meyerhold was also among those for whose rehabilitation Shostakovich campaigned. The prosecutor in charge of reviewing his case immediately regretted having summoned Shostakovich in the summer of 1955; when he told Shostakovich the truth about Meyerhold's death, the composer took quite ill and was scarcely able to make it out of the office.[54] On 13 September 1955, employing his loftiest official titles—Deputy of the RSFSR and People's Artist of the USSR—Dmitriy Shostakovich wrote in defense of Meyerhold a lengthy letter to the prosecutor, testifying forcefully to the director's artistic genius, his patriotism, and his incomparable creative contribution to the nation.[55] Meyerhold was rehabilitated on 26 November 1955, and Shostakovich soon joined the commission established to preserve his artistic legacy. When, in December 1955,[56] Shostakovich saw cause to invoke a phrase from one of Anton Chekhov's letters—"It is the duty of writers not to accuse, not to prosecute, but to champion even the guilty once they have been condemned and are enduring punishment.... Great writers and artists ought to take part in politics only so far as they have to protect themselves from politics. There are plenty of accusers, prosecutors and gendarmes without them." [57] —he was almost certainly articulating it as a position of principle.

The path to rehabilitation was neither straightforward nor assured. On the afternoon of 12 March 1956, by instruction of Vyacheslav Molotov, First Deputy Chairman of the USSR Council of Ministers, an "expert" commission representing the Ministry of Culture gathered at Shostakovich's Moscow apartment to evaluate the revised version of his opera, *Lady Macbeth of the Mtsensk District*, to determine whether the opera could be permitted to be staged again. Shostakovich was not particularly sanguine about the prospect; he was obliging colleagues from Leningrad's Malïy Theater who were insistent about producing the opera. After listening to Shostakovich perform the opera at the piano, members of the commission—chaired by Dmitriy Kabalevsky and including Georgiy Khubov and Mikhaíl Chulaki—proceeded to subject it to harsh criticism matching in spirit and substance the attacks of twenty years earlier. The vote to recommend against production of *Lady Macbeth*, in view of its serious ideological-artistic defects, was unanimous.[58] Two weeks after the delivery of Khrushchev's "secret" speech, it was still too early to contemplate rehabilitation and revival of *Lady Macbeth of the Mtsensk District*, the most notorious cultural casualty of the Stalinist period.

In what is surely one of the most curious episodes in his life, in the summer of 1956 Shostakovich remarried suddenly. During June, evidently, Shostakovich served on the jury judging mass songs for a Komsomol contest.[59] Involved in the proceedings was a Komsomol activist and instructor, Margarita Kainova, a young woman thirty-two or thirty-three-years old, who caught the composer's eye. Evidently too shy to forge her acquaintance on his own, Shostakovich asked for help in effecting an introduction. Khentova says that Shostakovich asked Dolmatovsky—a plausible candidate—to introduce them; the very next day the composer phoned her up and proposed.[60] Lebedinsky's version of the incident differs. He claims that the composer asked him to deliver one of a pair of opera tickets to her. Shostakovich's plan was to use the other himself and thereby make her acquaintance. The stratagem failed when he found her "seat" at the opera occupied by a strange man. Soon afterward, nonetheless, Shostakovich invited Lebedinsky over to meet Margarita and allowed that he had pro-posed impulsively at their first meeting.[61] The two tales may not be irrecon-cilable. What is clear is that their marriage in late July—disclosed only after the fact to most of his friends and relatives as well as to his children—came as a huge surprise to everyone.

Shostakovich's choice of bride was as puzzling as the precipitancy of their nuptials. Little is known about Kainova. Although Shostakovich tried to in-troduce her into his circle of friends and family, no one seems to have un-derstood or approved of the match. Fond memories of Nina probably did not make it any easier for Margarita to find her own niche in the tightly knit family. Shostakovich described his intended in a letter to Flora Litvinova: "She is a kind woman, and I hope she will be a good wife to me and a good mother to my children."[62] He told Atovmyan that the children had taken the news well.[63] It does appear that even though she demonstrated little ap-preciation for her husband's music or special genius, she tried to restore some semblance of domesticity and order to his household, a front on which Shostakovich had been fighting a losing battle since the death of his first wife. But Margarita was never able to win the support of the children or the domestic staff. After three years of marriage, in the summer of 1959, Shostakovich terminated the relationship—designating his son as interme-diary to effect the break—and divorced her, settling her in an apartment with a monthly stipend.

But that was later. In Komarovo in August 1956, Shostakovich was a man on his honeymoon. He was also composing again. Having made sketches as early as June, he wrote his Sixth String Quartet, op. 101, during August, completing it on the thirty-first. For the first time since the composition of the Tenth Symphony, he was able to report he was satisfied with something he had composed.[64] The premiere of his new opus was presented by the Beethoven Quartet in Leningrad on 7 October 1956.

Before that premiere took place, however, Shostakovich had passed his fiftieth birthday, an event observed with more pomp and circumstance than he would have liked. On the eve of the anniversary, 24 September 1956, at the conclusion of a concert featuring performances of *The Sun Shines Over Our Motherland*, the Violin Concerto, and the Fifth Symphony, Shostakovich was obliged to sit on stage amid buckets of flowers (he loathed cut flowers) and endure the public torture of speeches, testimoni-als, and an ensemble of young Pioneers singing their rendition of "Song of the Counterplan" in his honor. The announcement that Shostakovich had been awarded the Order of Lenin was greeted with a thunderous ovation. For a composer still officially branded with the stigma of the 1948 decree—and to whom such ritual displays were distasteful anyway—listening to ful-some praises must have been trying indeed. On 26 September,

Shostakovich threw a banquet at the Prague Restaurant for 140 guests. According to Glikman, officialdom was not invited and the atmosphere was relaxed.[65]

In conjunction with Shostakovich's fiftieth birthday, an autobiographical sketch, the first retrospective by the composer to appear in twenty years, was published in *Sovetskaya muzïka*.[66] Wrapping up a survey of his career retrofitted to conform to current values, Shostakovich announced: "I am presently working on my Eleventh Symphony, which, undoubtedly, will be ready by the winter. The theme of this symphony is the Revolution of 1905. I love this period in the history of our Motherland, which found clear expression in workers' revolutionary songs. I don't know whether I will quote these songs extensively in my symphony, but its musical language, undoubtedly, will be close in character to the Russian revolutionary song." [67] Shostakovich had been making periodic disclosures about his forthcoming Eleventh Symphony, and its intended relationship to the First Russian Revolution, since at least April 1955. In an article timed to coincide with the opening of the Twentieth Communist Party Congress in February 1956, Shostakovich had stated, "I am now writing my Eleventh Symphony, dedicated to the First Russian Revolution, to its unforgettable heroes. And I would like in this work to reflect the soul of the people who first paved the way to socialism." [68]

These bulletins were premature. From the Eleventh Symphony eventually completed, we know that Shostakovich did in fact lean heavily on the legacy of the Russian revolutionary song. In early January 1957, the composer told Glikman he was beginning work on it, and in an outline of his creative plans for 1957 he indicated that he expected to finish the symphony that year: "I announced my intention to write the Eleventh Symphony, dedicated to 1905, quite a while ago. However, I have put aside this work thus far because I wasn't yet satisfied with how work on this symphony was progressing." [69]

One of the obstacles that impeded the symphony's headway was the composition of the Second Piano Concerto, op. 102. A week after its completion on 5 February 1957, Shostakovich pooh-poohed it in a letter to Denisov as a work with no redeeming artistic merits.[70] What he did not say was that the concerto—a pedagogical sequel to the Concertino for Two Pianos—had been written as a vehicle for his son Maxim, then in his final year of study at the Central Music School. In his first appearance with orchestra, Maxim Shostakovich performed the premiere on 10 May 1957, his nineteenth birthday, with the USSR Symphony Orchestra conducted by Nikolai Anosov in Moscow. Critics were greatly taken with the concerto's charming simplicity, carefree spirit, and lyrical warmth. Notwithstanding any reservations the senior Shostakovich may have retained about its artistic significance, performances of the Second Piano Concerto quickly became a staple of his own concert schedule.

On 24 February 1957, Shostakovich informed Glikman that he had completed the first movement of his Eleventh Symphony; he thought it would be more accurately characterized as the "introduction." On 31 March, he reported that life was very busy; he was wasting a lot of time and was unable to devote himself properly to work on the symphony.[71] He was distracted now by daily attendance at sessions of the Second All-Union Congress of Soviet Composers held in Moscow from 28 March through 4 April 1957.[72]

The Second Congress had been two years in the making. Originally scheduled to convene in March 1956, it was postponed a year, undoubtedly to allow ample time to digest all the implications of the Twentieth Communist Party Congress. The groundwork was painstakingly prepared with convocations and position papers. Unlike its predecessor of 1948, this Congress did not unfold under crisis conditions. It did not function as a forum to root out "formalism" or any other latent threat to the welfare of Soviet music. The consensus was that, on the whole, Soviet composers had risen admirably to the challenges the Party and the people had set before them, that the substantial accomplishments of Soviet music were the envy of the entire progressive world. There were certainly problems and issues of contention, but they chiefly concerned organizational and bureaucratic matters, not the appraisal of ideological or stylistic purity. This was a time for stocktaking, for realignment with shifting political realities, and, most importantly, for a collective reaffirmation of allegiance to the creative method of Socialist Realism and the sound leadership of the Communist Party.

It became evident quickly that the Central Committee of the Communist Party, which was represented at the Congress by Dmitriy Shepilov, broadly supported the moves toward greater tolerance and flexibility that had been gaining influence within the composers' organization over the past several years. The militancy of Yuliy Kremlyov, for instance, who pressed his demand to wage unremitting war against formalism and decried the level of musical complexity to be found in Shostakovich's Violin Concerto, sounded distinctly out of tune with prevailing sentiment. Even Khrennikov was scolded for his disparaging reference to Shostakovich's Tenth Symphony in his keynote address, a subjective judgment patently invalidated by the successful history of the work. By no coincidence, three of Shostakovich's works were among the select group featured on the concerts of the Congress: the Fifth and Tenth Symphonies and the Violin Concerto.

Shostakovich's stature at the Second Congress was very different from the position of unmitigated disgrace he had occupied nine years earlier. The significance of his contribution to Soviet music was unassailable. His comments to the Congress delivered on 1 April (for which Daniil Zhitomirsky later claimed authorship[73]) were plainspoken and self-assured. His call to eliminate a surviving remnant of the "cult of personality," the practice of stifling constructive creative discussion by means of ideological discreditation, was greeted with applause.[74] Judging from his letters to absent colleagues, Shostakovich was alert to lingering vestiges of Zhdanov-era rhetoric, but he was generally satisfied with the course of the Congress and the newly elected composition of the leadership of the Composers' Union. Shostakovich himself was one of thirteen secretaries elected to the union's highest governing body, the Secretariat. Khrennikov won re-election as first secretary.

Shostakovich's attention to the language of the Congress paid off in an unexpected fashion. He was evidently hugely tickled by Shepilov's flagrant mispronunciation of "Rimsky-Korsakov"; the secretary of the Central Committee exhorted Soviet musicians "to preserve and actively develop the traditions of Glinka and Chaikovsky, Musorgsky and Rimsky-KorSAkov, Mozart and Beethoven, Chopin and Smetana."[75] According to Lebedinsky, it was right after the conclusion of this session of the Congress on 3 April that Shostakovich whisked him away to his dacha at Bolshevo and constrained him to compose the libretto for the satire, *Antiformalist Rayok*,[76] in which the character "Troikin" was modeled directly on Shepilov. Although there is considerable contention about whether the satire was composed in its entirety at this time, as well as about the extent of Lebedinsky's contribution, there is no question that the Second Composers' Congress spurred Shostakovich to activity on his satire in the spring of 1957. He amused close friends by playing it for them.

In the summer of 1957 Shostakovich was able to return to and finish his Eleventh Symphony, *The Year 1905*, op. 103, which he had undertaken to deliver in time for the fortieth anniversary of the October Revolution. He wrote to Denisov from Komarovo on 22 July that he had been sitting for days on end in his "creative laboratory" writing the symphony and would soon finish.[77] Its completion was dated 4 August 1957. Performing piano four-hands with Mikhaíl Meyerovich, Shostakovich played his new symphony in Leningrad and Moscow in September. Mravinsky, Shostakovich's collaborator of choice, expected to unveil the symphony as he had all the composer's symphonic works over the past twenty years, but in view of the significance of the anniversary, a decision was made to present the premiere in the capital. Shostakovich's Eleventh Symphony was first performed there on 30 October 1957 by the USSR State Symphony Orchestra conducted by Natan Rakhlin. Mravinsky conducted the Leningrad Philharmonic in the local premiere four days later, on 3 November.

Ten years earlier, Shostakovich's failure to pay appropriate musical homage to the thirtieth anniversary of the October Revolution had added impetus to his disgrace in 1948. The four-movement Eleventh Symphony, with its manifest program about the abortive Russian Revolution of 1905 graphically realized through a breathtaking symphonic canvas, scored, by contrast, a brilliant triumph for the composer. A more monumental, accessible, or effective tribute in commemoration of the fortieth anniversary could scarcely have been imagined. Such kudos as the Eleventh Symphony produced had not been heard for one of Shostakovich's works since his Seventh Symphony. At the discussion of the symphony at the Union of Composers in Moscow on 28 November, speakers were unanimous in awarding it highest marks as "a work of enormous realistic power." [78] One critic illuminated its appeal: "Thanks to its extensive use of the revolutionary song heritage, the language of this symphony proved to be simpler and more accessible than in previous major works of the composer while remaining, at the same time, deeply individual." [79] Shostakovich's Eleventh Symphony was awarded a Lenin Prize in 1958.

Whether it was Shostakovich's true purpose to project a concealed, "Aesopian" subtext through his Eleventh Symphony is a debate that was engaged posthumously. [80] The explicit program of the symphony depicts the legendary events of "Bloody Sunday," 9 January 1905, when police fired on a group of workers bearing petitions to Tsar Nicholas II in the Winter Palace in St. Petersburg (the composer's own father was said to have walked among them that day [81]), killing and wounding several hundred people. Analogies with the crushing in the autumn of 1956 of the Hungarian "counterrevolution" by Soviet troops are not difficult to draw. Glikman has recorded that on 10 January 1957, when Shostakovich told him he was beginning work on the Eleventh Symphony, he indicated that "it wouldn't be anything like *Song of the Forests*." [82] Put simply, Shostakovich did not approach his Eleventh Symphony as a propagandistic potboiler. The evils of tyranny and oppression with which the symphony deals are a pervasive theme in his music, one he well knew is timeless and universal. The fresh proof of their universality in 1956 would not have escaped the composer. This does not mean, however, that delivering a personal commentary on the events in Hungary was the motivating impulse behind the composition of the Eleventh Symphony. Available evidence does not corroborate this conclusion. [83]

As appalled as the Soviet intelligentsia may have been by its government's bloody suppression of the Hungarian uprising, Shostakovich actually provided listeners in 1957 little incentive to explore this connection or to delve any deeper than the manifest content of his score. By the late 1950s, the larger-than-life public image of the most distinguished of Soviet composers—conveyed through the inescapable profusion of speeches, articles, testimonials, photo opportunities, and so forth—was as a sincerely reclaimed

loyalist, a cultural pitchman for the causes of the Communist Party and Soviet state. Most of Shostakovich's contemporaries accepted, or rejected, the
Eleventh Symphony at face value. Aleksandr Solzhenitsyn, for example,
failed to discern any redeeming contemporary message behind the Eleventh Symphony. Reflecting on the moving experience of hearing an in-
ternee in a concentration camp sing the revolutionary song, "Listen" (a
song employed by Shostakovich in the first movement of his symphony
Palace Square), Solzhenitsyn observed in part 5 of *The Gulag Archipelago*:
"It is a great shame that, before his Eleventh Symphony, Shostakovich did-
n't hear that song here! Either he wouldn't have touched it at all or he
would have expressed its modern instead of its extinct significance." [84]
Anna Akhmatova, on the other hand, defended the work against its detrac-
tors, precisely because she found the rendering of its manifest substance so
moving: "His revolutionary songs sometimes spring up close by, sometimes float by far away in the sky... they flare up like lightning.... That's the
way it was in 1905. I remember." [85]

On 8 February 1958, just two days shy of the tenth anniversary of the
1948 Central Committee resolution condemning Shostakovich and his colleagues as formalists, Nikita Khrushchev and the members of the Central
Committee of the Communist Party hosted a reception for prominent
members of the Soviet intelligentsia, the scientific and cultural elite, in the
Kremlin Palace. In what amounted to a well-publicized pep rally for the ongoing task of building communism, Khrushchev and his comrades toasted
the splendid accomplishments of Soviet research and medical scientists,
writers, filmmakers, musicians, visual artists, and theater workers. The
privilege of the answering toast on behalf of Soviet musicians was bestowed
on Shostakovich. Stressing the marvelous creative conditions enjoyed by
Soviet musicians and the paternal, sensitive, and considerate guidance
given them by Party and government, Shostakovich raised his glass "to the
Communist Party of the Soviet Union and its Leninist Central Committee,
to our own Soviet government, to the great Soviet people." [86]

As chairman of the organizing committee that had been planning the
event since August 1956, Shostakovich was on hand to welcome the competitors and guests to the First International Chaikovsky Competition for
violinists and pianists in Moscow in March 1958. At the conclusion of competition in April, he presented the prizes to the winners, Russian violinist
Valeriy Klimov and American pianist Van Cliburn.

Shostakovich's own honors and awards kept pouring in. Accompanied
by Margarita, in mid-May Shostakovich traveled first to Rome to be inducted as honorary member of the Accademia di S Cecilia and then to Paris
for concert appearances and recordings of the two piano concertos with
André Cluytens. In Paris he was inducted as Commandeur de l'Ordre des

Arts et des Lettres. At the end of June he traveled to England, where he was awarded an honorary doctorate by Oxford University; he was also made an honorary member of the Royal Academy of Music. In October, he accepted the Sibelius Prize in Helsinki and caused a stir by donating the prize money of 7 million Finnmarks to the Finnish Russian Society. (A few months earlier, in June, he had been made chairman of the recently founded Soviet-Austrian Society.)

While Shostakovich was being honored abroad, on 28 May 1958 the Central Committee of the Communist Party adopted an extraordinary resolution (not published until nearly two weeks later), "On the Correction of Errors in the Evaluation of the Operas *The Great Friendship, Bogdan Khmelnitsky,* and *From All My Heart.*"[87] Contained in this document was the official admission that the resolution of 10 February 1948 had contained incorrect and unfair evaluations of leading Soviet composers' contributions: "Gifted composers, Comrades Prokofiev, Shostakovich, Khachaturyan, Shebalin, Popov, Myaskovsky, and others, who demonstrated faulty tendencies at times in some of their works, were indiscriminately denounced as representatives of the formalist, anti-people trend."[88] As far as the admission of mistakes went toward rehabilitating the good name and reputation of the country's leading composers—two of whom in the interim, Prokofiev and Myaskovsky, had died still officially in disgrace—it is significant that the new document did not actually rescind the 1948 resolution. It affirmed that the earlier resolution had been correct and timely in denouncing formalist tendencies in music and had, on the whole, played a positive role in the further development of Soviet musical art. It reconfirmed the prerogative of Socialist Realism.

Although Marina Sabinina recounts that as early as February or March 1956 Shostakovich told her that he had been approached by a high official exploring the possibility of "correcting" the 1948 resolution (she vividly describes the composer's incensed response to the very notion[89]), progress toward this moment had been slow and cautious. In December 1956, Party officials had reaffirmed the fundamental validity of the Zhdanov resolutions on the arts.[90] Nor, despite an auspicious remark in the speech of Dmitriy Shepilov, had its essential validity been challenged during the Second All-Union Congress of Soviet Composers in 1957. Khrushchev's policy was to keep a tight rein on the creative intelligentsia.

On 11 June 1958, Moscow's composers and musicologists gathered to discuss the "historic" development. Shostakovich's public response was stiff and strangely impersonal: "Removing the unfair, peremptory evaluations from a number of Soviet composers, [the resolution] reveals an excellent perspective for the future advancement of Soviet music along the realistic path."[91] Shostakovich's personal reaction was reserved for intimates like

Rostropovich and his wife, soprano Galina Vishnevskaya, whom he summoned imperiously to come drink with him while he crooned his favorite Zhdanov admonition to write music that is "beautiful and refined" to the tune of a lezginka and marveled: "A historical, don't you know, decree on abrogating the historical decree…. It's really so simple, so very *simple*." [92]

For all practical purposes, nevertheless, the 1958 resolution was a mere formality for Shostakovich's career, an official imprimatur on accomplished fact. The prestige and stature he had lost in 1948 had already been more than recouped. Just two days before it was published he pocketed his latest prize, the Lenin. Shostakovich's stature in the global arena, which in the xenophobic isolationism of the late Stalin years had constituted a dangerous liability, had become a matter of profound national pride in the race to catch and overtake capitalism with the attendant cultural one-upsmanship of the Khrushchev era. The works that had been at the center of the maelstrom in 1948 had already eased their way back into the concert hall. By the summer of 1955, the Ninth Symphony was being performed and broadcast. In his 1956 autobiographical sketch, the composer said how much he regretted that the Eighth Symphony had not been performed in so many years. [93] It was, by his own admission, a work invested with deep feeling and significance. After ten years without a performance, Shostakovich's Eighth Symphony was rehabilitated in October 1956, in a performance by the Moscow Philharmonic Orchestra conducted by Samosud. [94] And Shostakovich was in the audience in Leningrad, on 2 December 1956, when Mravinsky once again conducted the symphony the composer had dedicated to him thirteen years earlier.

1958–1961

Consolidation 12

In March 1957, the news that Shostakovich was at work on his first operetta, *Moscow, Cheryomushki*, dealing "with the life of young builders in Moscow" spread around the globe.[1] From the composer's standpoint, the announcement was probably premature. He had not yet completed his Eleventh Symphony. But the keen anticipation at the prospect of Russia's preeminent composer of "serious" music crossing over into the popular theater could not be denied. It was a source of special pride for the Moscow Theater of Operetta, which recruited the composer with the help of chief conductor Grigoriy Stolyarov, whose association with Shostakovich stretched back a quarter century to the Moscow premiere of *Katerina Izmailova*. Another veteran of that Nemirovich-Danchenko Theater production, Vladimir Kandelaki (he created the role of Boris Timofeyevich), was also now associated with the Moscow Theater of Operetta. He undertook the direction of Shostakovich's operetta.

The libretto of *Moscow, Cheryomushki* (*cheryomushki* are bird cherry trees), written in three acts by the experienced team of Vladimir Mass and Mikhaíl Chervinsky, dealt with a topical theme geared to one of most pressing concerns of urban Russians, the chronic housing shortage and the difficulties of securing livable conditions. The model apartment complexes then going up in the "New [Noviye] Cheryomushki" district of southwest Moscow, especially the widely publicized construction of an experimental housing project in the years 1956–1957, gave the work its topical slant as a tangible manifestation of the universal dream for modern, attainable, noncommunal housing.

Shostakovich sent preliminary numbers for the operetta to Stolyarov for his consideration in October 1957, but most of its composition dates from 1958. On 7 August 1958, Kandelaki indicated that the Moscow Operetta Theater had already started work on the production, intended to be its first of the coming season. He classified *Moscow, Cheryomushki* as an "operetta-revue" and described its music as "singable and melodic."[2] Shostakovich's work, however, was far from complete. From late September until the end of October—handicapped by a weakened right hand, which had him hospitalized for the entire month of September—Shostakovich was still hastily orchestrating the score, cutting and recomposing as he went along. He fired off the finished numbers to Stolyarov every few days, along with detailed instructions on how to incorporate them.

On 19 December, Shostakovich reported to Glikman that he was diligently attending rehearsals of his operetta: "I am mortified with shame. If you are thinking about coming to the premiere, I advise you to reconsider. It makes no sense wasting time just to gape at my disgrace. It's boring, insignificant, silly."[3] For the press he put on a braver face:

> The composition of an operetta is something new for me. *Moscow, Cheryomushki* is my first and, I hope, not my last experience in this appealing genre. I worked on it with great enthusiasm and lively interest. I think that what should result from our collaborative efforts ... should be a cheery, upbeat show.... There is lyricism in it, and "gags," assorted interludes, dances, and even an entire ballet scene. Parodistic elements are suggested at times in the musical design, the quotation of popular motives from the not-too-distant past and even from several songs by Soviet authors.[4]

The affection Shostakovich professed for the genre and his admiration of the mastery of Offenbach, Johann Strauss, and Lehár were sincere sentiments of long standing.

Interest in Shostakovich's new operetta was widespread. Even before it was unveiled, theaters from the Malïy in Leningrad to the Volksoper in Vienna and the Komische Oper in Berlin were exploring the possibility of mounting their own productions. The open dress rehearsal of *Moscow, Cheryomushki* on 20 January 1959 at the Moscow Theater of Operetta was packed with journalists, critics, and musicologists, both Soviet and foreign. According to a veteran of the operettic stage who attended, there were lively arguments during the intermissions; some viewers were nonplussed by the sheer amount of musical quotation in the score, in particular by the conversion of a popular urban ditty of highly questionable pedigree, "There Used to Be Merry Days," into the winsome theme waltz, "Song of

Cheryomushki." Nevertheless, he observed that professionals and ordinary spectators alike reacted with smiles and evident enjoyment to most of the numbers.[5] The public premiere of *Moscow, Cheryomushki,* op. 105, took place on 24 January. After the performance the following evening, Shostakovich feted his collaborators and friends at a late-night party.

Critics, on the whole, were enthusiastic about the show, finding it clever, lighthearted, visually engaging. They agreed that Shostakovich's music was the chief source of its appeal. Those who had worried that the famed composer of complex symphonic masterpieces might have trouble adapting to the comparatively guileless requirements of the operettic medium were relieved and delighted by his natural flair. Those who remembered Shostakovich's youthful ballets and theater music were not surprised. Indeed, dance numbers had actually been appropriated from *The Bolt* and *The Limpid Stream,* and the tune of "Song of the Counterplan" also found its way into the score. The wit, the finely honed satirical edge—rendered in deft parodies of music from Chaikovsky and Borodin to traditional and urban folklore to "pop" songs—and the superb orchestration were widely admired. *Moscow, Cheryomushki* was judged to mark an auspicious debut for the composer, one that significantly elevated the quality of the contemporary musical theater. There was some debate about whether it was most accurately classified as an operetta. Some were more comfortable with the designation "revue" or "vaudeville." When the piano-vocal score of *Moscow, Cheryomushki,* op. 105, was published in 1959, Shostakovich designated it a "musical comedy."

Complaints about the show chiefly focused on the book by Mass and Chervinsky. Despite some clever comic strokes, the quality of the libretto was embarrassingly inferior to that of the music. That both music and drama fizzled in the last act and that, in order to unravel the plot intrigues and resolve the romantic dilemmas, the authors stooped to the ploy of a "magic garden," also disappointed many. According to Glikman, Shostakovich was nauseated by the vulgarity and primitive jargon of the dialogues.[6] Any misgivings of critics or composer were not serious enough to deter a spate of productions both regional (from Odessa to Magadan) and foreign (from Bratislava and Prague to Rostock and Zagreb). In 1961, when Lenfilm undertook to make a film version directed by Gerbert Rappaport, Shostakovich was reluctantly persuaded to provide additional music. The film, *Cheryomushki,* was released in late 1962. Despite its initial success, *Moscow, Cheryomushki* did not establish itself in the repertory. Shostakovich continued to regard it as one of his lesser accomplishments, chalking it up in the Socialist Realism column.[7] He never returned to the genre.

Shostakovich's progress in the late summer and early fall of 1958 had been hampered by the debility of his right, writing, hand. The loss of strength and mobility was severe. His hand tired easily when he wrote. He recalled now that even in Paris in May he had been barely able to play the piano but had not paid attention. Now he could manage to play only slowly and *pianissimo*. After examination, three specialists confirmed that the ailment was serious, but they were unable to put a name to it. Treatment consisted of hand massages and injections three times a day that left him barely able to sit.[8] By the end of his month in the hospital, he was reporting some improvement in his ability to write, but he doubted he would soon be ready to resume concertizing.[9] What this exposed was the onset of a chronic condition, a source of persistent annoyance and frustration that would be diagnosed definitively only eleven years later.

As Shostakovich was steeling himself to make his much heralded debut as a composer of operetta, he was also making quiet progress on another theatrical front. In his public accounting at the outset of 1959, he reported that the previous year he had been busy not only with the composition of *Moscow, Cheryomushki*, but also with the orchestration of Musorgsky's opera, *Khovanshchina*.[10] This was a project long in gestation. In the 1951–1952 season, Boris Khaikin, then chief conductor of Leningrad's Kirov Theater, had determined to undertake a new production of Musorgsky's "national music drama" in Rimsky-Korsakov's edition, supplemented with additional material from Lamm's restoration of the composer's piano-vocal score. Shostakovich's orchestration of *Boris Godunov* had remained unperformed.[11] Whether Khaikin knew it is unclear. Still, he turned to the composer who had come to his rescue years earlier with a show-stopping orchestration of a Strauss polka. Shostakovich accepted the job with alacrity. His devotion to the music of Musorgsky notwithstanding, this was a period of acute financial hardship, and Khaikin secured him the maximum allowable fee (6,000 rubles) for the job.[12] When the composer examined the work to be undertaken, nevertheless, he made it clear to Khaikin that he had no intention of compromising or prettifying Musorgsky's original. He delivered his orchestration of the required extracts within a couple of days.[13] The revival of *Khovanshchina*, with Shostakovich's contributions, was premiered at the Kirov on 13 July 1952.

This was probably what whetted Shostakovich's appetite to tackle a reorchestration of the complete opera along the same lines as his earlier work on *Boris Godunov*. Unlike *Boris*, however, Musorgsky had left *Khovanshchina* incomplete at his death. The only viable performing edition remained Rimsky-Korsakov's. Shostakovich undertook his edition of *Khovanshchina* initially for a film version of the opera. In mid-1955, he wrote to a colleague: "With *Khovanshchina* matters are still unsettled. It hasn't been included in the schedule yet. I have my doubts about the scenario.... Regardless how the issue is resolved in the Ministry of Culture, I will work on the score of *Khovanshchina* in any event. Rather, I am already working on it." [14] He did not give his full attention to the project until 1958, when the practical arrangements for the film, directed by a well-respected specialist in filmed operas, Vera Stroyeva, were more or less firmly in hand. The composer collaborated on the scenario.

Shostakovich finished his orchestration of the first act of *Khovanshchina* in March 1958. In mid-July, evidently in response to a request from abroad for his orchestration of *Boris*, the justifiably cynical Shostakovich advised them to study the Lamm piano-vocal score first:

> No one has made use of my work here. Singers have been especially aggressive in their opposition. They swear that Musorgsky is "impossible to sing" and that in this respect Rimsky-Korsakov's edition is just fine.... The "opinion" about Musorgsky's unsingability should be put down to habit and familiarity.... Essentially the same thing is happening now with *Khovanshchina*, on which I am currently working. I am already receiving signals from Moscow that it is inconceivable to perform *Khovanshchina* in such a form. Singers, apparently, are the same the world over. [15]

Objections were vehement enough that the Bolshoy Theater management even considered the possibility of forbidding the participation of its singers in the film version. [16] But by the new year, Shostakovich was able to report that although the singers had not originally found his version of *Khovanshchina* to their liking, having relearned their parts they were now participating enthusiastically in the making of the film. He hoped it would put an end to the absurd talk about an "incompetent" Musorgsky. [17] The film of *Khovanshchina*, starring Mark Reyzen as Dosifey and conducted by Yevgeniy Svetlanov, was released in May 1959.

The hex on Shostakovich's Musorgsky orchestrations was finally lifted. The Kirov Theater, which had been actively wooing Shostakovich to collaborate on new projects and had already announced its imminent production of *Lady Macbeth of the Mtsensk District* for the 1959–1960 season, undertook the premiere production of Shostakovich's orchestration of *Boris Godunov* on 4 November 1959, with Boris Shtokolov in the title role, conducted by Sergey Yeltsïn. A year later, on 25 November 1960, the staged premiere of Shostakovich's orchestration of *Khovanshchina* was given there under the same conductor.

On 6 June 1959, Shostakovich made the unexpected announcement that his next major work would be a cello concerto. He indicated that the first movement, an allegretto in the character of a humorous march, was already done and that he expected the work would be in three movements. [18] When he finished the full score, in Komarovo on 20 July, [19] the work had taken its final shape in four movements (the final three performed without pause).

After completing the piano reduction, he alerted Mstislav Rostropovich in Moscow.

Years earlier, dreaming of just such an outcome, Rostropovich had been counseled by the composer's first wife that if he really wanted Shostakovich to write a work for him, he should *never* mention it, an injunction he had observed with the greatest difficulty.[20] When he heard the welcome news, Rostropovich marshaled his accompanist, Alexander Dedyukhin, and hastened to Leningrad. He received the score on the evening of 2 August 1959. Four days later, on 6 August, Rostropovich and Dedyukhin went out to Shostakovich's dacha for a first run-through. To Shostakovich's astonishment, Rostropovich already had the concerto memorized. As Yevgeniy Chukovsky (Shostakovich's prospective son-in-law) recalled, this first performance was celebrated with a festive repast on the downstairs veranda. Afterward, he drove the composer back to Leningrad and, after stopping to pick up vodka and snacks, they congregated at the apartment of the composer's sister, where Shostakovich, Rostropovich, and Dedyukhin discussed details of the new concerto and the composer penned in its dedication to Rostropovich.[21]

The concerto was unveiled at the Composers' Union on 21 September. Five days later, Shostakovich celebrated the marriage of his daughter to Chukovsky. On 4 October 1959, Rostropovich gave the premiere of Shostakovich's First Cello Concerto in E-flat Major, op. 107, with the Leningrad Philharmonic Orchestra conducted by Mravinsky. The huge success was repeated five days later in Moscow, when Rostropovich performed the concerto with the Moscow Philharmonic Orchestra under the baton of Gauk. Just a month after these premieres, Rostropovich gave the first foreign performance of Shostakovich's latest opus, on 6 November, with the Philadelphia Orchestra under Eugene Ormandy. Vaunted as an "historic occasion," the Philadelphia concert was attended by a long list of notable American composers, critics, and performers. Most importantly, it was attended by Shostakovich himself, who was also on hand to supervise the first recording of the concerto by the same forces.

Some months before commencing work on the Cello Concerto, Shostakovich had waxed enthusiastic about Prokofiev's Symphony-Concerto to Denisov, and it was this work that he credited with inspiring the creation of his own concerto.[22] He told Rostropovich—who had been an active collaborator with Prokofiev in reworking his First Cello Concerto into the Symphony-Concerto at the end of the composer's life—that he had played his record of the work so many times he had worn it out. The connections with Prokofiev's work were evident to Rostropovich. Less evident was the grotesque distortion, which Shostakovich took perverse pleasure in drawing to his attention, of the opening phrase of the Georgian folk melody

"Suliko," in the last movement.[23] Proverbial as Stalin's favorite folk tune, not surprisingly "Suliko" figured prominently in the satirical *Rayok*. What few noticed, however, is the fact that Shostakovich had adapted the distinctive four-note motif that opens the first movement of the concerto and forms the basis for its "humorous" march, from a procession of a very different cast, the "Procession to Execution" from his film music to *The Young Guard* (1948).[24]

The unveiling of the Cello Concerto was sandwiched between two significant foreign excursions. In September, Shostakovich was a guest at the Third Warsaw Autumn Festival. In a radio interview given there, he said he was not entirely happy that his First Piano Concerto had been featured on the opening concert; he wished they had selected a different, "more representative" work.[25] On a subsequent program, his Fifth and Sixth Quartets were performed by the Beethoven Quartet, but the trip served more to give him an intensive dose of contemporary European musical trends, including performances of works by composers ranging from Bacewicz, Berio, Boulez, Britten, and Gorecki, to Nono, Pousseur, Pierre Schaeffer, Xenakis, and Varèse. Sidestepping any prompting to assess the latest trends in his radio interview, Shostakovich expressed himself pleased to have had the opportunity to hear works by the older generation of twentieth-century composers, Bartók, Stravinsky, Hindemith, and Szymanowski.[26] As we will see, he was more forthcoming with his opinion on the state of contemporary music later.

From 22 October to 21 November 1959, Shostakovich was a member of the Soviet delegation that toured seven American cities (Washington, D. C., San Francisco, Los Angeles, Louisville, Philadelphia, New York, and Boston) as part of a high-profile cultural exchange program of the U.S. State Department. Traveling with composers Khrennikov, Kabalevsky, Konstantin Dankevich, and Fikret Amirov and musicologist Boris Yarustovsky, Shostakovich was propelled through a nonstop whirl of receptions, banquets, entertainments, institutional inspections, and press conferences. In addition to the premiere of his Cello Concerto in Philadelphia, Shostakovich presided at performances of his Tenth Symphony in Washington and his First Piano Concerto in Louisville. (On their departure from the United States, Shostakovich and Kabalevsky flew on to Mexico City, where, on 27 November, Alexander Gauk conducted the Orquestra Sinfónica Nacional in a performance of Shostakovich's Fifth Symphony.) The glitter and warmth of the reception everywhere was in stark contrast to that of his first trip to the United States ten years earlier, when, though invited to participate in additional cultural activities at the conclusion of the Peace Congress, he had been peremptorily ordered to leave the country together with the rest of the Soviet delegation by the U.S. State Department.

What had not changed was the drift of the questions. Shostakovich was repeatedly queried about his attitude to the criticisms that had been leveled at him by the Communist Party. Not surprisingly, he regurgitated what by now were polished phrases about his embrace of that criticism. Especially by contrast to the joviality and ebullience exhibited by some of his colleagues, what struck observers about the most famous member of the delegation was his dourness, his reticence, his nervous fidgeting, his chain-smoking. Attempts to draw him out were unsuccessful. The scheduled appearance of Shostakovich and Kabalevsky on the nationwide television broadcast *Face the Nation* was canceled by the network as unworkable when the leader of the group, Khrennikov, demanded that the entire delegation be allowed to appear on the allotted half-hour segment.

Another theme raised repeatedly during their American visit, according to an account attributed jointly to Shostakovich and Khrennikov, was the Soviet attitude toward dodecaphony, with the (preposterous, so they claimed) allegations that not only was it not performed in the Soviet Union but Soviet composers were officially forbidden to compose dodecaphonic music and, therefore, were denied artistic freedom.[27] The opening of channels for cultural exchange had ushered in a new era of cultural competition. On his return from Italy and France the previous year, Shostakovich had reported that "the leading French masters are deeply troubled about the future of music in the West. They are troubled by the dissemination of false 'avant-garde' trends—like the notorious dodecaphony or 'concrete music'—among their youth. This still-born art gains no recognition from the broad public, it attests to the ideological impasse, the crisis of bourgeois culture."[28] Such phrases, coupled with tributes to the adherents of genuinely "progressive" music responsive to the needs of the broad listening public, figured increasingly in Shostakovich's lexicon, as mouthpiece of official Soviet aesthetic policy.

In an interview given to a Polish journalist during the Warsaw Autumn Festival but published subsequently in *Sovetskaya muzïka*, Shostakovich preached at length of the perils of dodecaphony, which he felt had unreasonably monopolized the programs of the festival:

> I am firmly convinced that in music, as in every other human endeavor, it is always necessary to seek new paths. But it seems to me that those who see these new paths in dodecaphony are seriously deluding themselves. The narrow dogmatism of this artificially invented system rigidly fetters the creative imagination of composers and deprives them of individuality. It is no accident that in the entire legacy of Schoenberg's dodecaphonic system there is not a single work that has gained wide acceptance.... Dodecaphony not only has no future, it doesn't even have a present. It is just a "fad" that is already passing.[29]

Soviet music, he asserted by contrast, was evaluated not by its degree of experimentation or by its deviation from tonality but by whether it was good, that is, whether it was rich in substance and artistically consummate.

This is not the place to debate the Soviet failure to acknowledge the aesthetic "inevitability" of the so-called Second Viennese School and Serialism. In hindsight, the stance, though dogmatic, seems considerably less wrong-headed and regressive than it was then thought to be in the West. At least in Shostakovich's case, it should not be assumed that he was ignorant of the musical styles he was condemning. Nor can it be taken for granted that the official line he was obliged to toe was completely alien to his real preferences and convictions. Shostakovich was an exceptionally sensitive and literate musician. In Warsaw, in America, and on his frequent foreign jaunts, he was provided with ample opportunity to meet composers, listen to their music, and assess the international picture. He stocked up on recordings whenever he traveled.

His son Maxim has recalled that scores sent by composers or musical organizations could always be found in their home and that Boulez's *Le marteau sans maître*, the late works of Stravinsky, and a couple of pieces by Xenakis were among those works he admired.[30] In March 1959, as it happens, Shostakovich presented his old friend Shebalin with a score of *Le marteau* for his birthday. Denisov recorded in a diary entry for 1957 Shostakovich's private comments about his dislike of the music of Schoenberg and his feeling that Messiaen's *Trois petites liturgies* were rather saccharine.[31] After having been singled out in one of Shostakovich's speeches as the "arch-representative of 'decadent capitalist culture,'" Karlheinz Stockhausen subsequently received a private letter from the composer professing admiration for his music and encouraging him to visit.[32] Still, if his tastes in music were more catholic than his sometimes strident rhetoric might suggest, Shostakovich nonetheless favored more conservative contemporary idioms, the music of Benjamin Britten, for instance. His distaste for dry, inexpressive music and his opposition to composition by rational system or mathematical formula were genuine. Direct engagement with his listener, the need to connect through his music with ordinary people, remained a central concern for Shostakovich.

In February 1960, Shostakovich found himself, bored and lonely, back in the hospital for further treatment of his right hand. He entertained himself by rereading a period novel of the 1920s and penning long missives of sardonic political commentary to friends. He may also have used this period of enforced isolation to resume work on a string quartet, his Seventh, which was completed in March 1960. The previous summer, at the same time he announced the forthcoming Cello Concerto, he had divulged that he had also completed one and a half movements of a new quartet. Perhaps waxing a trifle sentimental at a time when he had just extricated himself from his unsuccessful second marriage, Shostakovich dedicated his Seventh Quartet in F-sharp Minor, op. 108, to the memory of his first wife, Nina. (Had she lived, she would have turned fifty in May 1959). By late April 1960, he was able to report that he was deriving great pleasure from rehearsals of the new quartet. The brief "life-affirming" work was unveiled to a receptive audience by the Beethoven Quartet in Leningrad on 15 May. It was, incidentally, during the rehearsals of the Seventh Quartet that Shostakovich disclosed to Dmitriy Tsïganov his firm intention to compose twenty-four string quartets, one in every major and minor key.[33]

Shostakovich's creative accomplishment was overshadowed by new advancement as a public servant. In the first week of April 1960, the First Constituent Congress of Composers of the Russian Federation (RSFSR) took place in Moscow. Although this marked the formal establishment of a Composers' Union on the republic level, its organizing committee had been functioning since early 1958 and had sponsored a number of official plenums. Meanwhile, a composers' organization for the city of Moscow had been created in June 1959. Highlights of the First Constituent Congress included a reception at the Kremlin hosted by the USSR Council of Ministers and a grand concert in the Kremlin theater attended by the Soviet leadership and the diplomatic corps that began with a performance of *The Sun Shines Over Our Motherland*. On 9 April 1960, Shostakovich was elected first secretary, the highest leadership position, of the newly founded Union at the initial convocation of its directorate.[34] On 30 April, his was one of the May Day salutations to the nation published in *Pravda*: "We are reaching communism. To hymn the fairest human society in history is a worthy and absorbing mission for composers.... On May Day 1960 I already hear the music of communism. And, looking ahead, I want to summon all Soviet composers, my dear friends, to even more intense labor and new creative successes. Onwards friends, to communism!"[35]

In private, Shostakovich was frequently much more cynical about the aspirations and promise of communism. In conversation in 1956, he flatly contradicted Flora Litvinova's presumption (a presumption revealing in itself, given her own family history and long association with the composer) that, in general, he shared her belief in the idea of communism: "No, communism is impossible."[36] His unanticipated application for membership in the Communist Party in 1960, a move he discussed with neither friends nor family, remains one of the most puzzling episodes of his biography.

In late June 1960, Shostakovich found himself in Leningrad, where he suffered an emotional breakdown. What brought it on was the prospect of an imminent convocation in Moscow to set in motion his initiation as a Party member. The tales he told Glikman and Lebedinsky—both of whom bore witness to his collapse—are contradictory. According to the version related to Glikman, Khrushchev's decision to make Shostakovich head of the newly founded Union of Composers of the Russian Federation had been coupled with the requirement that he become a Party member. The composer maintained he had resisted the blandishments of a persistent Central Committee member delegated to ensure his recruitment but had been outmaneuvered and obliged eventually to capitulate.[37] Lebedinsky, himself a Party member since 1919, claims that there was no grand plan to recruit Shostakovich, that the pressure to join actually came from low-level functionaries looking to feather their own caps with such a trophy. He noted that Shostakovich did not actually name those who had forced him to sign the application but gave him to understand, shamefacedly, that he had succumbed while under the influence of alcohol.[38]

Shostakovich was guarded, secretive even with his most trusted friends. Although Glikman and Lebedinsky were not confident they had gotten to the bottom of their friend's distress, they were able to ward off the immediate crisis by detaining Shostakovich in Leningrad so that he missed the scheduled Party convocation. A few days later Shostakovich traveled to Dresden, ostensibly to collaborate with his old friend Leo Arnshtam on a film commemorating the World War II devastation of the city, *Five Days—Five Nights*. He viewed the graphic film footage, toured the ruins of the devastated city, and then repaired to the tranquility of Gohrisch, in "Saxon Switzerland."[39] Instead of scoring the film, however, in a white heat he wrote a new string quartet, his Eighth, completing it on 14 July 1960. On his return to Moscow, he was among the guests invited to another of the highly publicized "get-togethers" between Khrushchev and the Central Committee and representatives of the intelligentsia on 17 July, this one a Sunday picnic set in idyllic natural surroundings outside Moscow. The guests indulged in swimming, fishing, boating, tennis, and other recreational activities in addition to the requisite speech-making. Once again the honor of presenting the return toast to the Central Committee on behalf of the Soviet musical world fell to Shostakovich's lot. His toast, and his reflections on the significance of the meeting, were circulated widely.

Two days later, on 19 July, Shostakovich wrote to Glikman about his recent trip to Dresden: "However much I tried to draft my obligations for the film, I just couldn't do it. Instead I wrote an ideologically deficient quartet nobody needs. I reflected that if I die some day then it's hardly likely anyone will write a work dedicated to my memory. So I decided to write one myself. You could even write on the cover: 'Dedicated to the memory of the composer of this quartet.'"[40] Shostakovich outlined for Glikman the numerous themes—taken from his own works and those of others—he had employed in the quartet. Describing the "pseudo-tragicality" of the quartet, he measured the tears its composition had cost him as the volume of urine after a half-dozen beers. By the time of writing the letter, he was already beginning to get beyond its pseudo-tragicality to admire the perfection of its form and to look forward to rehearsing it with the Beethoven Quartet.[41] Galina Shostakovich, too, remembers her father announcing when he returned from Dresden that he had written a quartet dedicated to himself, an auto-biographical quartet.[42] Although his claim has not been substantiated, Lebedinsky contends that Shostakovich meant the Eighth Quartet to be his final work; he planned to commit suicide after his return from Dresden, a plan foiled when his stash of sleeping pills was removed surreptitiously.[43]

The composer did not mention it, but both Glikman and Lebedinsky naturally ascribe Shostakovich's alarm about his impending admission into the Communist Party as the motivating force and key to the composition of the Eighth Quartet. Glikman had already realized that, despite his initial show of determination in Leningrad, Shostakovich did not possess the courage of his convictions. He would not be able to muster sufficient will-power to resist his fate.[44] (His infernal cowardice was a character trait Shostakovich bewailed in recurrent bouts of self-loathing.) Without further ado, on 14 September 1960, Shostakovich attended his formal induction as a candidate member of the Communist Party, by unanimous vote, at a meeting of the Moscow composers' Party organization. One year later, his provisional status was officially upgraded to full membership.

This was a development that left many of Shostakovich's friends and colleagues mystified. It left many other intellectuals disappointed, even disillusioned. Few seriously entertained the possibility that, by this date, a Damoclean sword still dangled over Shostakovich or his family, as had certainly been the case during the Stalin era. It is true that, in a move to improve and liberalize the image of the Communist Party under Khrushchev, there was a campaign to recruit into its ranks fresh blood from the intelligentsia. Nevertheless, the chronology of events, among other factors, renders the excuse of "quid pro quo" for his appointment as first secretary of the RSFSR Union of Composers implausible; by the time he joined the Party, he had already occupied the post for five months.[45] That some degree of coercion was brought to bear is evident. Notwithstanding the assertions of Khentova—based on her archival research and the testimony of Aram Khachaturyan[46]—and others, Shostakovich did not submit his application for membership in the Communist Party voluntarily. It remained a sore spot. He confided little to Irina Supinskaya, whom he encountered initially at about this time and whom he married in 1962, except that it was black-mail and that if she loved him she would not pry.[47] Different explanations were offered for his behavior. Lebedinsky, who occasionally demonstrated impatience with his friend's needless compromises and his socializing with stooges and other unsavory types, chalked it up to the paradoxical, even neurotic, impulses in his nature. More commonly, Shostakovich's capitulation has been rationalized as the product of chronic fear, the terror that had warped his life.

When Shostakovich informed Galina Serebryakova (a friend of his youth recently returned from the camps) that he had joined the Party, she was astounded; she had assumed he was a Communist as far back as the 1920s.[48] Khachaturyan, Oistrakh, Karayev, Kondrashin, and many other friends and artists he respected had long belonged to the Party. Indeed, it should be remembered that to all appearances Shostakovich was already a "loyal son" of the Communist Party when he joined. He had ceded unconditionally his signature, his voice, his time, and his physical presence to all manner of propaganda legitimizing the Party. Especially since the Tenth Symphony, he had even devoted a disproportionately large portion of his music to the greater glory of Socialist Realism. He was a role model for the status quo, a malleable symbol of the fusion of civic responsibility with artistic genius, of popularity with professional respect. As an actual member of the Party he could give nothing more. But this episode—with his distraught reaction, escape, and creative catharsis—strongly suggests that the demons Shostakovich wrestled with were his own, that he had crossed his own line in the sand. He was neither the first nor the last to realize, too late, that the path of accommodation with the Soviet system was one of no return.

In late September 1960, Shostakovich traveled to London and Paris for performances by the touring Leningrad Philharmonic Orchestra. When Rostropovich played his Cello Concerto in London on 21 September, Shostakovich made the acquaintance of Benjamin Britten. An hour before his departure for London, Shostakovich had given an interview about his summer's work, including his stay in Dresden: "The terrors of the bombardment that the inhabitants of Dresden lived through, which we heard about in the words of the victims, suggested the theme for the composition of my Eighth Quartet. I found myself under the influence of the scenes being filmed, reproducing the way it used to be. I wrote the score of my new quartet in the space of a few days. I am dedicating it to the victims of war and fascism." [49] With the dedication slightly reformulated—"To the memory of the victims of fascism and war"—this became established as the "official" legend of the Eighth Quartet.

The Eighth Quartet in C Minor, op. 110, was unveiled by the Beethoven Quartet at the opening chamber music concert of the new season in Leningrad on 2 October 1960. The performance was repeated in Moscow the next day for the musical community at the Composers' Union, and the first public performance in Moscow took place on 9 October. Under the extraordinary impact of the new work, Heinrich Neuhaus wrote to a colleague, "It's music of absolute genius! I was shaken and cried." [50] The critics were no less affected. Even though they were misdirected in their understanding of the sum and substance of the quartet, they were stunned by its tragic depth and raw passion even as a broader expression of protest and resistance, a true humanistic document of its era. That the Eighth Quartet was destined to become a classic of both Soviet and Western music was confidently predicted.[51] That it was "autobiographical" in its essence did not escape attention either, even if the pervasive use of Shostakovich's personal motto and the numerous quotations from his earlier scores were believed to underscore his lifelong "struggle against the dark forces of reaction." [52]

The Eighth Quartet was not the only composition completed by Shostakovich during the summer of 1960. On 15 September he sent off tape and score of a brief musical tribute commemorating the victims who died in the World War II battle to liberate Novorossiisk (for which he recycled material from one of his abandoned wartime attempts at a national anthem). City authorities, who had originally turned to him hoping he would supervise the selection of suitable excerpts from the classics, were overwhelmed by the gift of a specially written homage. *Novorossiisk Chimes* established itself as a model for memorial installations. As of 27 September 1960, the tape plays hourly at the eternal flame in Novorossiisk's Heroes Square. The first two phrases were also adapted as the musical cue for the late evening news on Moscow Radio.

Even before his flight to Leningrad and his unexpectedly productive sojourn in Dresden, on 19 June Shostakovich had quietly completed a song cycle for soprano and piano—*Satires*, op. 109—settings of five poems by turn-of-the-century social satirist Sasha Chyorny.[53] Well aware what an odd contrast this opus would present to the quartets whose composition framed it, Shostakovich reasserted his right to creative diversity and his mischievous streak, explaining the attraction of the verses: "Caustically, with great sarcasm [Chyorny] makes fun of the philistines from the period of reaction that set in after the 1905 Revolution. He writes witheringly about people who have fallen into the embrace of mysticism, who have tried to escape into a parochial, personal orbit." [54] Most likely it was the 1960 publication of a collection of Chyorny's poetry that provided the spark for Shostakovich's composition, although Flora Litvinova remembered hearing Shostakovich recite Chyorny's *Satires* in Kuybïshev during the war.[55]

Among the first to hear the new vocal cycle were Vishnevskaya and Rostropovich. After playing it for them, Shostakovich admitted to the thrilled soprano that he had written it for her in the hope she would agree to sing it, and he inscribed its dedication to her. According to Vishnevskaya, it was at her suggestion that—in anticipation of the likely threat of censorship—the composer added the subtitle "Pictures of the Past" to mask the contemporary relevance of the texts. (The third of the five poems, "Our Posterity," was particularly transparent. As if in direct challenge to the omnipresent slogans exalting the bright Communist future, the poet took aim at the ageless injunction to sacrifice personal fulfillment so as to assure paradise for one's descendants; sentencing any descendants to fend for themselves, the poet peevishly demands a little reward from his own life on earth.) Vishnevskaya, joined by her husband in his first appearance as piano accompanist, gave the premiere of *Satires* as the finale of her Moscow recital, on 22 February 1961, a concert that also included performances of works by Dargomïzhsky and Prokofiev and Musorgsky's *Songs and Dances of Death*. The concert was one of the high points of the concert season. Still, the reviewer for *Sovetskaya muzïka* found Shostakovich's new cycle the least of its appeals, a frivolous diversion, its music slight but of considerably more interest than its texts.[56] The audience was more appreciative and demanded an encore of the complete cycle.[57] Vishnevskaya continued to perform the cycle, but it was not taken up by other singers. With incisive wit so redolent of his youthful spunk, the *Satires* remained dear to Shostakovich. As he confessed to Glikman, he sensed that his difficult life was making him lose his natural sense of humor.[58]

By the summer of 1959, at the same time as he publicized his forthcoming Cello Concerto, Shostakovich had revived expectations that he would write a major work devoted to Vladimir Ilyich Lenin: "What form my idea will take, whether it will be an oratorio, a cantata, a symphony, or a symphonic poem, I don't want to predict. One thing is clear: the effort to embody the mighty image of the greatest man of our most complex epoch will demand the exertion of all creative resources. I would really like to complete it in time for the ninetieth anniversary of Vladimir Ilyich's birthday."[59] With this announcement, Shostakovich picked up a thread he had abandoned eighteen years earlier at the outbreak of the war. That the form his musical "Lenin" tribute would now take would be a symphony became evident quickly, but by the time the ninetieth anniversary of Lenin's birth arrived in April 1960, Shostakovich's Twelfth Symphony was still no more than a promise. That summer, he announced that the forthcoming plenum of the Russian Composers' Union would be dedicated to the theme "Lenin—the Party—the People." Under the circumstances, he could no longer postpone redeeming his pledge.

In a radio broadcast on 29 October 1960, Shostakovich discussed his progress on the Twelfth Symphony with uncharacteristic volubility. He had conceived the idea for the composition while completing his Eleventh Symphony, as a programmatic continuation dedicated to the events of the October Revolution, as well as to the memory of the great leader of the laboring masses, Lenin. Reporting that two of its four movements were almost ready, he offered a synopsis of the individual movements: "I have conceived the first movement as a musical account of the arrival of V. I. Lenin in Petrograd in April 1917 and of his meeting with the toiling masses, the working class of Petrograd. The second movement reflects the historical events of 7 November. The third movement tells about the Civil War, and the fourth about the victory of the Great October Socialist Revolution." [60] Shostakovich also "disclosed" here for the first time that his memories as an eyewitness to events in Petrograd in 1917—he cited Lenin's memorable speech on his arrival at Finland Station—were serving as a source of profound inspiration. [61]

A few days before this information was broadcast, in what was another manifestation of his still undiagnosed condition, Shostakovich had stumbled and unexpectedly broken his left leg at his son Maxim's wedding. He spent the rest of 1960 in hospital, which may help explain why progress on the Twelfth Symphony temporarily came to a standstill. He later specified that intensive work on the score took place only in the spring and summer of 1961, when he targeted its delivery for the Twenty-second Congress of the Communist Party in October. On 15 August 1961 he wrote Glikman from Zhukovka (where in 1960 he had purchased a dacha to replace the one in Bolshevo, which he returned to the state) that he was expecting to complete the Twelfth Symphony in a week or two: "For the most part, the first movement has succeeded, the second and third almost completely. The fourth, undoubtedly, won't come off. I am writing it with difficulty." [62] He put the finishing touches on the symphony a week later, on 22 August. On 25 August he had the reduction for piano four-hands ready to give to Vainberg and Boris Chaikovsky, who had agreed to be ready to perform it in three or four days. Shostakovich's Twelfth Symphony in D Minor, *The Year 1917*, op. 112, dedicated to the memory of Vladimir Ilyich Lenin, went into rehearsals in Leningrad on 25 September; in a performance that was broadcast on Leningrad radio and television, what has been billed as its official premiere, attended by the composer, was given there on 1 October 1961 by the Leningrad Philharmonic Orchestra conducted by Mravinsky. In actual fact, two hours earlier the first performance had already been presented by the local orchestra in Kuybïshev, conducted by Abram Stasevich. [63] The Moscow premiere took place two weeks later.

On 26 August, Shostakovich had informed Lebedinsky that the symphony was done: "The symphony is programmatic, but I don't know what to call the movements (there are four of them). When I see you, I'll show it to you and we'll confer, if you find it possible. I'll then tell you the program of the symphony, too. I'm not going to write any more symphonies. I've grown old. I'll write easy little pieces for wind instruments." [64] Lebedinsky later claimed, incredible as it sounds, that Shostakovich originally intended his Twelfth Symphony to be a satire of Lenin and could not be persuaded of the foolhardiness of the venture. On the eve of the first rehearsal he phoned Lebedinsky in a panic and summoned him to Leningrad. He told him then that he had finally realized how badly he had miscalculated; he had rewritten the symphony in the space of three or four days, but was convinced the result was terrible. He swore Lebedinsky to secrecy.[65] In another account Lebedinsky specified that Shostakovich did this hasty rewriting in Leningrad two weeks before the premiere.[66] Even if one accepts the notion that—with his phenomenal facility, and notwithstanding a debilitated writing hand—Shostakovich could rewrite a forty-minute symphony in three or four days, what this tale does not account for is the fact that Vainberg and Chaikovsky had played the new symphony at the Union of Composers on 8 September. A detailed appreciation—based on a study of both piano reduction and full score—of what was recognizably the symphony as we know it had already been published on 16 September.[67] As it was, the one-month interval between the symphony's completion and its first rehearsal was exceptionally brief, especially for the copying of performance materials for large symphony orchestra. Substantial changes between the symphony's completion and its simultaneous premieres in two far-flung cities could not have failed to attract considerable attention and comment.

Although only a detailed study of the manuscript sources can confirm it, what seems more likely is that if Shostakovich radically reconsidered his conception of his symphony, this took place between the summer of 1960 and the following summer, when he completed it. The family archive is said to contain sketches for the Twelfth Symphony that apparently date from early summer 1960; interpolated on page 26 is a large chunk from the *Satires*.[68] And although the focus on events of 1917 remained constant, the underlying programmatic basis of the four movements Shostakovich had described on the radio in October 1960 is significantly different from that of the finished symphony, to whose movements Shostakovich attached the descriptive titles "Revolutionary Petrograd," "Razliv," "Aurora," and "The Dawn of Humanity."

The much-anticipated work commemorating Lenin and the Bolshevik Revolution by the most eminent living Soviet composer—newly clasped to the bosom of the Communist Party—was unfurled with great fanfare on the eve of the twenty-second Party Congress, which took place during the last two weeks of October 1961. Shostakovich was invited to attend the Congress as a guest. That the Twelfth Symphony might turn out to be anything less than a brilliant masterpiece was unthinkable. So it is hardly surprising that critics rallied zealously behind the new symphony, hailing the Twelfth a worthy successor to the Eleventh, a balancing pendant to a diptych of "revolutionary" symphonies. That there were significant differences between the two works was acknowledged. The programmatic impulse behind the Twelfth Symphony, for instance, was perceived to be more generalized and suggestive, less concrete and dynamic than the Eleventh, leading one critic to counterpose the two symphonies as a "folk music drama" (the Eleventh) and a "folk-heroic epic" (the Twelfth).[69] Everyone noted the profoundly Russian qualities of the symphony, especially in its thematic writing; Borodin and Musorgsky were invoked as its spiritual forebears.

As befitting a work of such lofty purpose, the Twelfth Symphony was rapidly disseminated throughout the country in performances for workers, miners, students, and collective farmers, who were reported to respond enthusiastically. Conductor Stasevich said that after one regional performance, a miner had confessed to him that many of his ilk had considered Shostakovich to be an "incomprehensible" composer but thanks to the vivid revolutionary imagery of the Twelfth Symphony they now appreciated him in a different light.[70] That seasoned critics—musical and political—were less convinced of its genuine excellence can be gauged from the fact that, unlike the Eleventh, the Twelfth Symphony was not graced with the Lenin Prize or any other.

1961–1966

Renewal

Three months after the premiere of the Twelfth Symphony, the long post-poned premiere of Shostakovich's Fourth Symphony finally took place in Moscow on 30 December 1961. Kirill Kondrashin had been appointed chief conductor of the Moscow Philharmonic Orchestra the previous year. The idea of resurrecting Shostakovich's mysterious "missing" symphony origi-nated with the Philharmonic's artistic administrator;[1] after Kondrashin studied the reduction for piano four-hands and agreed to conduct it, they broached the idea to Shostakovich and solicited his permission.

As late as 1956, Shostakovich had felt compelled to maintain the fiction of a Fourth Symphony "discarded" by a dissatisfied composer. In the hospi-tal in Moscow in September 1958, he wrote to Glikman that he was spend-ing his ample spare time thinking about his opera, *Lady Macbeth*, and his Fourth Symphony, about how much he would like to hear them, in the meantime playing them through in his inner ear. While skeptical about how much pleasure a performance of the former might now afford him, he felt confident that the symphony could be successfully played.[2] When the pros-pect of a live performance finally surfaced in 1961, Shostakovich admitted that much in this score remained dear to him even after all these years.[3] And, after hearing a piano run-through, an effusive Shostakovich told Lebedinsky that it was the very best thing he had ever written, even better than his Eighth Symphony: "Here I wasn't thinking about anything—not about the form, not about anything." [4] Offered the chance to revise the score before its premiere, he refused to change a single note. [5]

Any lingering doubts about the viability of Shostakovich's Fourth Symphony were dispelled by its triumphant premiere, performed by the Moscow Philharmonic Orchestra under Kondrashin. Shostakovich observed to Glikman that in many respects his Fourth Symphony was better than his most recent symphonies. It was a sentiment widely shared. Flora Litvinova addressed her diary after hearing the premiere: "Why do Dmitri Dmitrievich's later works lack those qualities of impetuosity, dynamic drive, contrasts of rhythm and colour, tenderness and spikiness?" [6]

Soviet critics, while excited by the find of a major, missing "link" in Shostakovich's creative biography, refrained from value-laden contemporary comparisons. They located the Fourth Symphony firmly in its chronological context and explored its significance as a stepping stone to the more polished Fifth and subsequent symphonies. Western critics were considerably more blunt. The back-to-back British premieres of the Fourth and Twelfth Symphonies at the 1962 Edinburgh Festival, where the critical success of the former was inverse in proportion to the dismal failure of the latter, led inevitably to speculation that Shostakovich's genius might be on the wane. [7]

The year 1962 was an eventful year for Shostakovich. The early months were dominated by official activities. In mid-January he presided over the Third Plenum of the governing board of the RSFSR Composers' Union in Moscow, delivering a keynote speech that, among its other points, once again denounced the gloomy, self-absorbed artistic tendencies of the West, the antihumanistic "avant-garde" techniques totally divorced from the pulse of life. [8] In March, Shostakovich, who had served as a deputy to the RSFSR Supreme Soviet since 1947, was elected a deputy to the Council of Nationalities of the USSR Supreme Soviet representing Leningrad. At the end of March, he was a delegate to the Third All-Union Congress of Composers. As soon as the Congress ended, Shostakovich presided, in his capacity as president of the Organizing Committee, at the opening ceremony of the Second International Chaikovsky Competition on 1 April.

In 1961, at the request of his former student Orest Yevlakhov, now chair of the Leningrad Conservatory Composition Department, Shostakovich had resumed teaching at his alma mater, so he was now also faced with a monthly commute to Leningrad to supervise his class of graduate students. He began spending time at the Composers' Union artists' retreat at Repino, outside Leningrad, where many of his late works would be written. Boris Tishchenko, Gennadiy Belov, Alexander Mnatsakanyan, Vyacheslav Nagovitsïn, German Okunev, and Vladislav Uspensky were among those who reaped the benefits of his guidance after his reinstatement as educator.

(After his dismissal from both the Moscow and Leningrad Conservatories in 1948, he never resumed teaching at the Moscow Conservatory.)

This was a busy time in Shostakovich's personal life, too. Even before the birth of his third grandson in January 1962 (Galina's two boys, Andrey and Nikolai, were born in 1960 and 1962, and Maxim's son Dmitriy was born in 1961), living space in the apartment on Kutuzovsky Prospect where the extended family had resided since 1947 had become impossibly cramped. Having been allocated an apartment in a Composers' Union building on Nezhdanova Street in the center of Moscow, Shostakovich moved there in the winter of 1962, turning over the Kutuzovsky apartment to his daughter. At the same time, new romance blossomed in his life. In the summer of 1962, Shostakovich began living with Irina Antonovna Supinskaya. Their marriage was officially registered in November, after Supinskaya's divorce had been finalized.

Lebedinsky, once again, claims to have facilitated Shostakovich's introduction to the young woman, who worked under him as a literary editor at Sovetskiy Kompozitor publishers.[9] Although it is often assumed that they met early in 1962, when Shostakovich broke the news of his marriage to Glikman in June, he indicated he had known Irina more than two years. Supinskaya had been one of the literary editors of the vocal score of *Moscow, Cheryomushki*, published in 1959, and the two also came into contact at concerts.[10] The actual decision to remarry, however, was no less impulsive than his immediately previous venture into matrimony; Glikman says Shostakovich had sworn to him just a month before he announced it that he would never marry again.[11]

Shostakovich introduced his new bride to his friends cautiously; he seemed concerned that at the age of twenty-seven, only slightly older than his daughter, she might be considered too young for him. But he was clearly happy with his young bride, whose intelligence, humility, and background made her a more obviously compatible match for the composer than his second wife. As he succinctly summarized in a letter to Glikman: "She is nearsighted. She can't pronounce r's and l's. Her father was a Pole, her mother Jewish. They are both dead. Her father suffered from the personality cult and the infraction of revolutionary legality. Her mother died. She was raised by her aunt on her mother's side.... She also spent time in a *det. dom* and in a *spets. det. dom* [orphanages for the children of 'enemies of the people']. In short, a girl with a past."[12]

With the conspicuous exception of Lebedinsky, who soon grew away from the composer, most of Shostakovich's friends were delighted that Shostakovich had decided to remarry and readily approved his choice of Irina. Industrious, efficient, and devoted, Irina finally brought stability and tranquility back into his life, relieving him of the domestic cares that he found so burdensome. And as his physical condition and health steadily deteriorated during the remaining years of his life, Irina was his indispensable companion and helpmate. The view that Irina's care and ministrations might have been responsible for prolonging the composer's life for several years was widely shared.

Shostakovich's interest in composition was also reinvigorated.

On 19 September 1961, the poem "Babiy Yar," a forthright condemnation of anti-Semitism by the young Russian poet Yevgeniy Yevtushenko, had been published in *Literaturnaya gazeta*, igniting intense public debate and a campaign of vilification against him. He was accused of trying to drive a wedge between nationalities, of inciting ethnic hatred by elevating the wartime suffering of Jews above that of Russians. Shostakovich responded deeply to the verses, which mirrored his own aversion to anti-Semitism so closely. In 1962, the embattled poet was stunned to receive a phone call from the famous composer. With his peculiar deference and humility, Shostakovich begged his permission to set the poem to music, which Yevtushenko granted with alacrity. It was only at this point in the conversation that Shostakovich confessed, with relief, that the setting was already done. He invited Yevtushenko to come over and hear it.[13] According to Glikman, who claims to have given the composer the poem a day or so after its publication, Shostakovich's decision to set the text had been taken immediately.[14]

Much about the composition was unusual for Shostakovich. He departed from his custom of composing straight into full score,[15] completing the piano score of *Babiy Yar* on 27 March 1962 and the full score on 21 April. He was also uncharacteristically forthcoming in his correspondence with information about his further progress. Initially, he intended the setting for bass, bass chorus, and orchestra to stand alone as a symphonic poem. But in a newly published volume of Yevtushenko's verse, *Vzmakh ruki* (A Wave of the Hand), presented to him by the poet, the composer found three additional poems he wanted to set and began to contemplate the idea of a "symphony" of Yevtushenko settings. Lively exchanges between poet and composer led Shostakovich to request the writing of a new poem, "Fears," which was revised with the composer's involvement. As different in substance and style as the five poems were, what linked them was their bold engagement with social and political ills in contemporary Soviet life. Shostakovich subsequently pinpointed the underlying theme of his symphony: "In the Thirteenth Symphony I dealt with the problem of civic, precisely 'civic,' morality."[16]

In late June 1962, Shostakovich entered the hospital for more treatment on his right hand. He spent his spare time there working on his Yevtushenko settings, announcing to Shebalin on 1 July:

Since landing in the hospital, I have begun composing a Thirteenth Symphony. More likely, it will be a vocal-symphonic suite of five movements.... For this composition I have used the words of the poet Yevgeniy Yevtushenko. On closer acquaintance with this poet, it has become clear to me that he is a great and, most importantly, a thinking talent. I have met him. I liked him a lot. He is twenty-nine years old (sic!). It is very nice that such young people are appearing among us.

The Symphony consists of five movements. I. Babiy Yar, II. Humor, III. In the Shop, IV. Fears, V. A Career. The first three movements are all done. The fourth and fifth movements are coming along, the fourth less well. Yevtushenko hasn't finished "Fears" yet.[17]

In his score, Shostakovich dated the completion of the movements as follows: "Humor," 5 July; "In the Shop," 9 July; "Fears," 16 July. The final movement of the symphony, "A Career," was dated 20 July 1962, a date that— together with the anniversary of the premiere of his First Symphony— Shostakovich would commemorate for the rest of his life.

Shostakovich found himself obliged to defend his choice of poet to many of his friends. Even without the flap over "Babiy Yar," Yevtushenko was a controversial figure. The composer explained to Glikman, "What I like in his work is the presence of ideas and its indisputable humaneness. The talk about him as a *stilyaga*, a 'boudoir poet,' is provoked, to no small degree, by envy. He is considerably more talented than many of his colleagues who occupy correct positions."[18] In 1965, defending Yevtushenko from the criticisms of his student, Boris Tishchenko, Shostakovich revealed a great deal about himself and the impulse behind the Thirteenth Symphony:

I am offended for my favorite poet, or for one of my favorite poets—for Yevtushenko. Let's leave aside such things as stylistic beauty, rhythmic elegance, et al., in which I am poorly versed.

You don't like it that he collared you and preaches what you know: "Don't steal honey," "Don't lie," etc. I also know that one shouldn't behave that way. And I try not to. However, it doesn't bore me to hear it over and over again. Perhaps Christ said it better, probably even best of all. But that doesn't deprive Pushkin, Lev Tolstoy, Dostoyevsky, Chekhov, J. S. Bach, Mahler, Musorgsky, and many others of the right to speak about it. Moreover, I believe they have an obligation to speak about it, as does Yevtushenko.

To remind us of it over and over again is the sacred obligation of man....

As for what "moralizing" poetry is, I didn't understand. Why, as you maintain, it isn't "among the best." Morality is the natural sister of conscience. And because Yevtushenko writes about conscience, God grant him all the very best.

Every morning, instead of morning prayers, I reread—well, recite from memory—two poems by Yevtushenko, "Boots"[19] and "A Career." "Boots" is conscience. "A Career" is morality. One should not be deprived of conscience. To lose conscience is to lose everything.

And conscience needs to be instilled from earliest childhood.[20]

Shostakovich was anxious to secure his new symphony the best possible performance. He was particularly concerned with securing an "intelligent" singer as soloist. On 19 June, when only the setting of "Babiy Yar" was as yet in existence, he wrote to the bass Boris Gmïrya in Kiev (a singer to whom he had also entrusted his Pushkin settings, opuses 46 and 91) asking if he would take a look at his new symphonic poem. Shostakovich volunteered to come to Kiev to play it for him: "It seems to me that I have been singularly successful with this work. True, there are people who consider 'Babiy Yar' Yevtushenko's failure. I cannot agree with them. Not in the slightest. His lofty patriotism, his passionate love for the Russian people, his genuine internationalism captivated me completely and I 'embodied' or, as they say nowadays, 'attempted to embody' all these feelings in a musical composition." [21]

As soon as he got out of the hospital, in late July, Shostakovich traveled with Irina to Gmïrya's dacha outside of Kiev to acquaint the singer with the finished symphony. He then sought out Yevgeniy Mravinsky at his summer retreat outside Leningrad to enlist his services. Shortly afterward, under the impression that Mravinsky was already committed to the performance of his new symphony, Shostakovich attempted to assuage Gmïrya's evident misgivings: "Regarding your concern about possible 'repercussions' from the performance of the Thirteenth Symphony, as my very rich experience demonstrates, all the lumps will fall on the composer. It seems to me that these circumstances need not trouble you." [22] However, after consulting with the Ukrainian Communist Party leadership, who informed him that performances of Yevtushenko's poem "Babiy Yar" were categorically forbidden in Ukraine, on 16 August, Gmïrya sent Shostakovich his refusal.[23] Mravinsky would also turn down the composer, a rebuff that was an especially bitter pill for Shostakovich to swallow. But it would be some time before Shostakovich would find out about either of these rejections.

From late July to mid-August, Shostakovich traveled with Irina to Solotcha, near Ryazan, to meet the maternal aunt who had raised her. While there, he made an arrangement of his Thirteenth Symphony for piano four-hands and made tempo corrections to the score. He proofread the score of *Khovanshchina* and also orchestrated Musorgsky's *Songs and Dances of Death*. On completion of the orchestration on 31 July 1962, he mailed the unexpected gift to Galina Vishnevskaya, to whom he inscribed the dedication. On 16 August, Shostakovich flew with Maxim to England for a month. The chief purpose of this trip was to attend the Edinburgh Festival, where Shostakovich's music was to be featured. This was not the first festival Shostakovich had attended that year; in mid-June, he had traveled to Gorky to participate in the highly successful First Festival of Contemporary Music, whose guiding spirit had been Rostropovich. Together with performances there of the Cello Concerto, the Eighth Quartet, the *Satires*, and arias and entr'actes from *Lady Macbeth*, the local premiere of Shostakovich's Fourth Symphony (by Kondrashin and the Moscow Philharmonic Orchestra) had been rated a triumph, the central event of the festival.[24]

However, if not necessarily in quality then certainly in quantity, the presentation of Shostakovich's music in Edinburgh was on an entirely different scale; it amounted to the first comprehensive retrospective of his creative career. Among the works performed during the three-week festival by a wide assortment of performers were all eight of the string quartets; the Fourth, Sixth, Eighth, Ninth, Tenth, and Twelfth Symphonies; the violin and cello concerti; arias and entr'actes from *Lady Macbeth*; the *Satires*; and other works from all periods. The Belgrade Opera brought its production of *Khovanshchina* in Shostakovich's orchestration. Shostakovich later conceded that the whole experience was stressful. His energy was drained by the punishing concentration of rehearsals and concerts, and not all the performances met his exacting standards for quality. On the other hand, he admitted that hearing so many of his works in such a short span gave him the opportunity to reevaluate some of them critically.[25] Some of them—the very early *Two Pieces* for string octet, op. 11, for instance—he had not heard, most probably, in more than thirty years. Though he did not discuss it in numerous interviews, Shostakovich cannot have failed to notice the frigid reception given his Twelfth Symphony.

What spare time remained to Shostakovich in Edinburgh seems to have been consumed by thoughts of his Thirteenth. As he wrote to Lebedinsky on 26 August: "Everything is fine here. Many concerts, rehearsals, receptions, etc. I'm terribly homesick for you, for Irina, and for the whole family. The Thirteenth Symphony possesses me the whole time. I consider everything else trivial. I await impatiently the moment I will hold the score in my hands again, play it, re-experience it. I want to see you. I want to learn your opinion of the symphony. It is constantly on my mind. I think about it all the time." [26] With prying journalists, Shostakovich was not especially forthcoming about his latest symphony, hinting only that it would be somewhat unorthodox in form. After the conclusion of the Edinburgh Festival, Shostakovich's reunion with the score was delayed another week while he attended two concerts in London.

Shostakovich returned home just before Igor Stravinsky arrived for his landmark visit, the first to his homeland since before the revolutions of 1917. For the duration of his three-week trip, Stravinsky, who had been reviled for much of the Soviet period as a renegade and a leading apostle of bourgeois aesthetics, was dogged by an entourage of well-wishers and fawning officials. Not the kind of person to force himself on others, Shostakovich had little contact with the man whose music he had admired for so many years.[27] It is not even clear which of Stravinsky's concerts Shostakovich attended. They met at two formal events, the first a reception on 1 October, when they were seated flanking the hostess, Minister of Culture Ekaterina Furtseva. Shostakovich was observed to behave with his habitual nervous discomfort. He also attended the farewell banquet on 10 October and engaged in somewhat desultory conversation with Stravinsky, bashfully admitting that he had been so overwhelmed when he first heard the *Symphony of Psalms* that he had made an arrangement of it.[28]

That Shostakovich attended at least one of Stravinsky's concerts is clear because the experience gave him the courage to try something he had long wanted to do, to conduct his own music. He confessed to Stravinsky that he would like to follow his example, "except that I don't know how not to be afraid." [29] Shostakovich was soon offered the opportunity to test himself in this role, one he had not seriously attempted since his student days.[30] On 12 November, he conducted the Gorky Philharmonic Orchestra in performances of the *Festive Overture* and the Cello Concerto in the first part of a concert devoted to his music. Rostropovich, in addition to appearing as cello soloist, conducted the second part of the program in what was one of his own early appearances on the podium, which included the premiere of the orchestration of Musorgsky's *Songs and Dances of Death* sung by Vishnevskaya and four entr'actes from *Lady Macbeth*. The orchestra had been meticulously prepared in advance. Still, Shostakovich was very nervous. He persuaded Rostropovich to split a half-liter of vodka with him before attending his first rehearsal.[31] For a concert that was justifiably regarded as a musical "event," critical assessment of Shostakovich's debut was generous, notwithstanding the unevenness of his technique. The participants celebrated the success of their outing with a festive supper. But for Shostakovich this remained a one-time venture; he later said it was the weakness of his hand that kept him from conducting his own music.

It was none of these things, not his conducting debut, not the visit of Stravinsky, not even the Fourth Plenum of the Russian Composers' Union (devoted to the problem of jazz and popular music), which he was responsible for organizing and over which he presided in mid-November, that was at the forefront of Shostakovich's attention in the autumn of 1962. What occupied him most were preparations for the impending premieres of his Thirteenth Symphony and his revised version of *Lady Macbeth of the Mtsensk District.*

Shostakovich received the letter from Gmïrya turning down his request to perform the solo part in the Thirteenth Symphony on his return from Edinburgh and quickly set about finding a suitable replacement, canvassing Vishnevskaya and others for their recommendations. As late as 7 October, however, after more than two months with no word on the matter from Mravinsky, Shostakovich asked Glikman to ascertain whether the conductor was prepared to accept the score.[32] Mravinsky was evasive, non-committal, a shocking development no one expected. After all, this was Shostakovich's preferred interpreter. Since braving the risky premiere of his Fifth Symphony in 1937, he had enjoyed the privilege of "creating" five more of his symphonies, not to mention other scores. His unwillingness to conduct the Thirteenth, a work whose importance to the composer he cannot have failed to note, was all the more difficult to understand since he was neither anti-Semitic nor a Party stalwart.

Mravinsky's rejection of the Thirteenth Symphony is most often attributed to the deleterious influence of his young, second wife, Inna, who had worked as a Communist Party activist and who has been credited with devising the lame (and patently untruthful) excuse that Mravinsky did not conduct choral music, only "pure" music. Mravinsky's third wife and surviving widow, Alexandra Vavilina, has branded this story a malicious lie. She claims that the diagnosis of Inna's terminal illness had already been made and that Mravinsky simply did not have the strength to undertake the enormous responsibility of preparing Shostakovich's Thirteenth Symphony while he was caring for his beloved, dying wife.[33] Mravinsky's motivations remain unclear. Vavilina's assertion that Shostakovich understood the situation and did not take offense, however, is strongly contradicted by his letters. As a youth, Shostakovich had confided in his mentor, Yavorsky, that he was terribly afraid of rejection.[34] He lost none of this sensitivity as an adult. Blessed with and grateful for the enduring loyalty of exceptional performers, ranging from Rostropovich, Vishnevskaya, and Oistrakh to the Beethoven and Borodin Quartets, Shostakovich felt deeply hurt and betrayed by the unanticipated defection of Mravinsky. Eventually, the two would be able to reestablish professional contact, but the loss of trust was never repaired.

After its rejection by Mravinsky, Shostakovich offered the first performance of his Thirteenth Symphony to Kondrashin, who accepted without reservations. A bass from the Bolshoy Theater, Viktor Nechipailo, was engaged to sing the solo part. Kondrashin simultaneously coached a singer affiliated with the Moscow Philharmonic, Vitaliy Gromadsky, as his alternate. The premiere was set for 18 December.

The atmosphere seemed auspicious. There were the autumn visits of Stravinsky and later Balanchine with the New York City Ballet. Yevtushenko's cautionary poem, "Stalin's Heirs," was published in *Pravda* on 21 October 1962. On the same day, "Fears," the only previously unpublished poem used in Shostakovich's symphony—the one written specifically for it—was published.[35] And, with the personal authorization of

Khrushchev, the November 1962 issue of *Novïy mir* contained Solzhenitsyn's extraordinary memoir of the Stalinist camps, *One Day in the Life of
Ivan Denisovich.*

Then, on 1 December 1962, Khrushchev's intemperate outburst at the
sight of abstract modernist works displayed at the Manezh exhibition,
"Thirty Years of Moscow Art," lit the fuse of a new campaign for "ideological purity" in the arts. Shostakovich was one of the seventeen prominent
artists and scientists who signed an appeal to Khrushchev to "stop the
swing in the figurative arts to previous methods, which are alien to the
whole spirit of our times." [36] On 17 December, just one day before the advertised premiere of Shostakovich's Thirteenth Symphony, a meeting of
Party leaders with members of the artistic intelligentsia took place in Moscow. The "untimely" allegation of Russian anti-Semitism contained in
"Babiy Yar," its publicity accentuated by having been set to music, sparked
an ominous exchange between Yevtushenko and Khrushchev.[37]

Even without the added political tension and rumors surrounding the
event, anticipation was running high for the premiere of Shostakovich's
new symphony. Its nature, and the Yevtushenko texts, were already well
known, and the musical community had become acquainted with
Shostakovich's score. After hearing it, Aram Khachaturyan had been moved
to proclaim, early in November, "There is not a shadow of exaggeration
here, this is indeed a great composition by a great artist," asserting that the
Thirteenth Symphony was a work dedicated to the moral code of Soviet
people and affirming their high ethical standards.[38] The upcoming
premiere was touted as an event eagerly anticipated by the entire musical
world.[39]

Accounts of the premiere of the Thirteenth Symphony differ. What is
clear is that—either because of illness or because he had been summoned
peremptorily to the Bolshoy Theater—the scheduled bass soloist,
Nechipailo, failed to appear for the dress rehearsal on the morning of 18
December. The hall was full; in addition to Conservatory students and
teachers, Party and government officials were conspicuously in attendance.
Whether his alternate, Gromadsky, would turn up or be prepared to perform was uncertain.[40] When, after Gromadsky's arrival, the rehearsal finally
got under way and it became clear that performance glitches would not suf-
fice to scuttle the premiere, Shostakovich was called on the carpet from on
high.[41] The principals withstood all the pressures put to bear on them to
cancel the performance voluntarily. Tactics of repression had changed significantly since the death of Stalin; cultural bureaucrats shrewdly calculated
that the consequences of banning the performance would be more damag-
ing than of letting it proceed. In a city rife with rumors of a possible last-
minute cancellation, the premiere went ahead on schedule, minus, how-

Portrait of thirteen-year-old Mitya Shostakovich by Boris Kustodiyev (1919)

DS, Nina Varzar, and Ivan Sollertinsky (1932)

Dmitriy Shostakovich (1935)

DS with his son Maxim at Ivanovo (summer 1943)

DS with his daughter Galina at Ivanovo (summer 1943)

DS attending a soccer match

Shostakovich at work (1940s)

DS presiding over the drawing of lots for violinists at the first Chaikovsky competition in Moscow (1958). Seated from left to right: jury members Galina Barinova, Dmitriy Tsiganov, David Oistrakh

DS consulting with Tikhon Khrennikov

Shostakovich in rehearsal

DS with Mstislav Rostropovich and Yevgeniy Mravinsky after a performance of the First Cello Concerto in Leningrad (1959)

DS with his second wife Margarita in Paris (1958)

DS with the Beethoven Quartet. From left to right: Dmitriy Tsiganov, DS, Sergey Shirinsky, Vasiliy Shirinsky, Vadim Borisovsky

DS with his son Maxim on arrival at London airport en route to the 1962 Edinburgh Festival

DS with his third wife Irina

ever, the planned television transmission. A repeat performance, on 20 December, also went ahead as scheduled.[42]

By all accounts, the audience response to the symphony's first performance was extraordinary; extroverted poet and introverted composer were enveloped in a tumultuous ovation with the unmistakable overtones of a political demonstration. Yevtushenko recalled:

> At the symphony's premiere, the audience experienced something rare: for fifty minutes they wept and laughed and smiled and grew pensive.... What astonished me first of all in the Thirteenth Symphony was that if I (a total musical ignoramus) had suddenly developed an ear, that would be the music I would have written. Moreover, Shostakovich's reading of my poetry was so exact in intonation and sense that it felt as if he had been inside me when I was writing the poem and he had composed the music as the lines were born. [43]

It is commonly accepted that the premiere of the Thirteenth Symphony was ignored by the Moscow press. This is not literally true. A brief, preliminary assessment appeared the morning after,[44] as did Kondrashin's enthusiastic endorsement of the work.[45] Still, the official tactic was to disregard the Thirteenth Symphony. The only critical response of any significance came in the form of an unsigned editorial that, while naming no names, censured such talented, authoritative, and genuinely popular masters for devoting a major multi-movement musical work to rummaging in the dustbins at the fringes of Soviet life, under the banner of the struggle against the cult of personality: "If, let's say, a composer writes a symphony about our reality, basing it chiefly on gloomy, evil, sarcastic-parodistic or tearful, pessimistic images, then, whether the author desires it or not, what results is the denigration of our life, its mistaken, distorted portrayal." [46]

After the premiere performances, the collaborators were issued an ultimatum: either changes must be made to the text of the first movement to reflect the fact that Russians and Ukrainians died alongside Jews at Babiy Yar, or further dissemination of the symphony would be prohibited. To save the symphony, Yevtushenko provided eight substitute lines for the text before departing on a trip to Germany and France in early January.[47] Kondrashin helped persuade Shostakovich to swallow the compromise, which required no substantive changes in his music. It was the words—and not just those of the first movement—that were deemed unsatisfactory. Indeed, amid all the brouhaha that enveloped the Thirteenth Symphony, Shostakovich's music was rarely even mentioned. (On its own, Shostakovich's music defied no stylistic taboos and was hardly controversial.) The widespread allegation that, without consulting with Shostakovich, Yevtushenko *published* a new, politically correct, variant of "Babiy Yar" is untrue. Though Yevtushenko may have offered Shostakovich other draft corrections, no version of the poem twice as long as the original,[48] or containing forty new lines,[49] has come to light. Judging by his comments in a letter dated 15 February 1963, Shostakovich obviously felt he had been placed in an awkward position: "I don't like Yevtushenko's new verses. However, the matter stood as follows: either the new verses, or without any. I evidently lost heart. But Yevtushenko dispatched these verses to me and went abroad for two months." [50]

Yevtushenko's original and replacement verses for "Babiy Yar," a total of four lines near the beginning of the poem and another four lines near the end, translate as follows:

Original:

I imagine now that I am a Jew.
Here I wander through ancient Egypt.
And here, I am crucified on the cross and die,
And still bear the marks of the nails.
***
And I become like a long, soundless scream
Above the thousand thousands here interred.
I am each old man shot dead here,
I am each child shot dead here.

Replacement:

I stand there as if at a wellspring,
That gives me faith in our brotherhood.
Here lie Russians and Ukrainians
With Jews they lie in the same earth.
***
I think about Russia's heroic feats,
In blocking fascism's path.
To the very tiniest dewdrop,
Her whole essence and fate is dear to me.

Shostakovich did not inscribe the new text in his manuscript score.

The Thirteenth Symphony, with the eight substitute lines interpolated in the first movement, was performed again in Moscow by Kondrashin on 10 and 11 February 1963. In mid-March, after attending a two-day meeting at the Kremlin between Party leaders and members of the cultural intelligentsia, which cast an ominous pall over the process of artistic de-Stalinization, Shostakovich traveled to Minsk for the first of two performances of the Thirteenth Symphony—using the original text—presented there by conductor Vitaliy Katayev.[51] A local critic offered the only extended critical appraisal of the work, determining that notwithstanding Shostakovich's good intentions and the undeniable power of his music, the ideological sense of his symphony was flawed and he did not understand the Party's requirements for art.[52] While further performances of the symphony were not expressly prohibited, it was clearly understood that they were not encouraged.[53]

If the whole experience of launching his Thirteenth Symphony was fraught with disillusionment, after patiently waiting more than twenty-five years, Shostakovich finally enjoyed the satisfaction of seeing his second opera recapture its legitimate place in the repertory. Even after the official rejection of the revised *Lady Macbeth* in March 1956, efforts to rehabilitate Shostakovich's opera had not stopped. The Kirov Theater expressed interest in the work, and after screening it in March 1957, they included it in their repertory plan for 1958, then kept pushing it back from season to season. There was a revival of interest in the West as well. Determined to produce the opera, La Scala scheduled it for its 1958–1959 season even though Shostakovich indicated to them his revisions were still incomplete. (He was hedging; he had already told people at home that he had completed the revisions.) The Deutsche Oper am Rhein in Düsseldorf went ahead and presented the German staged premiere of the original *Lady Macbeth* in November 1959, billing it as the last time the work would be shown in its original version.[54]

After the publication of the 1958 "corrective" resolution, the rehabilitation of *Lady Macbeth* became just a matter of time. By 1959, Shostakovich was assured that his opera would be mounted by the Kirov Theater in the spring of 1960; while in the United States in the fall, he invited critics to come to Leningrad to attend the premiere. He wrote to Glikman from a Moscow hospital at the end of February 1960 that he expected to come to Leningrad after his release in about two weeks to participate in rehearsals and preparations for the production.[55] It did not materialize. By the end of the season, Shostakovich's opera had reverted to being "held in reserve" at the Kirov.[56] According to Glikman, it was canceled by order from local Party bureaucrats as unsuitable for the preeminent operatic stage of the city.[57]

In June 1961, after Khrennikov had made a case to the Central Committee that continued prohibition of the opera would be extremely awkward, Shostakovich's revised *Lady Macbeth* received another official screening at the Union of Composers in Moscow.[58] On this occasion, no longer able to cope with the pianistic demands, the composer asked his friend Vainberg to perform the opera, who then left before the discussion. Two hours later, Vainberg was flabbergasted and touched when Shostakovich arrived on his doorstep to inform him that the opera had passed muster and would be staged.[59] Shortly afterward, they played the opera for the opera troupe of the Stanislavsky-Nemirovich-Danchenko Theater. Despite the enthusiasm of the theater management and the director, Lev Mikhailov, it took some effort to overcome the inherent resistance to Shostakovich's opera of many members of the company. They had been brought up, after all, with the absolute certainty that this opera was the epitome of pernicious musical "formalism." [60]

Shostakovich supervised the preparations for the revival carefully. He had a great deal at stake. At least in the early stages, he did not entirely trust the grasp and vision of the director, who, in an excess of enthusiasm early on suggested that in order to warm the image of the heroine, Katerina, Shostakovich should compose another two or three arias about her dream of becoming pregnant by her seducer, Sergey.[61] Shostakovich did no such thing.

From the spring of 1962, as we have seen, arias and entr'actes from the opera were already being performed regularly in concert, as if to test the waters. By September 1962, progress on the production was being chronicled in the press. In an interview, Shostakovich initially pinpointed the unveiling of the new production for 20 December, two days after the premiere of his Thirteenth Symphony.[62] In the end, it was postponed because of the conflict. The closed rehearsal of the opera on 21 December was followed by an evaluation session, duly reported to the ideological commission of the Central Committee, which gave its go-ahead for a preview performance to proceed.[63] On 26 December, the "unofficial" premiere, a probationary public preview of Shostakovich's revised opera—definitively renamed *Katerina Izmailova* and given a new opus number, op. 114—took place as a substitution for an advertised performance of *The Barber of Seville*. The substitution, however, was not last-minute; Shostakovich had time to send out printed invitations.[64]

Yevtushenko was among those who attended. He was inspired to write a poem about the experience, "Second Birth,"[65] which he dedicated to the composer and delivered before his departure for Europe. Shostakovich was deeply touched by the gesture and by Yevtushenko's verses, but he took exception to the title: "My music never died, and therefore it didn't need to be born a second time." [66]

The "official" premiere of *Katerina Izmailova* went ahead on 8 January 1963. In commemorating its passage, *Pravda* conceded that the opera had been unfairly discredited during the years of the personality cult and forgotten.[67] Monitored closely after the recent controversy surrounding the Thirteenth Symphony, the successful rehabilitation of Shostakovich's martyred masterpiece—and with it the confirmation of Shostakovich's continued good standing—was reported worldwide. It inaugurated a spate of new productions of Shostakovich's opera. Shostakovich invested a significant amount of his time over the next several seasons supervising many of them, including those in Riga and London in late 1963, Zagreb in 1964, Vienna,

Kazan, Kiev, Ruse (Bulgaria), Leningrad, and Budapest in 1965. He was anxious to forestall any unauthorized musical and directorial liberties with his creation (he was especially sensitive to excessive erotic displays). When he heard, in 1964, that La Scala intended to mount his opera using the old version, he was very upset, insisting that they use the revised version or not stage it at all. In the score of *Katerina Izmailova*, published in 1965, Shostakovich included an unequivocal proscription against rearrangements or cuts. Although most Western commentators routinely dismiss Shostakovich's endorsement of the revised version of his opera as the result of political coercion, there is significant evidence to suggest that his preference for the revised *Katerina* was in fact genuine.[68]

Of all the productions, Shostakovich found the one at the Shevchenko Theater of Opera and Ballet in Kiev the most satisfying musically, and thus it was the forces from this theater, under the baton of Konstantin Simeonov, who were recruited to record the soundtrack for the film version of *Katerina Izmailova* (directed by Mikhaíl Shapiro for Lenfilm) in 1965. Galina Vishnevskaya readily accepted Shostakovich's invitation to play the lead. Shostakovich himself prepared the scenario and supervised the taping and editing of the film, which was released in 1967.

Despite the controversy surrounding his Thirteenth Symphony, neither Shostakovich nor Soviet music as a whole became the conspicuous targets of the reactionary cultural backlash against artistic anti-Stalinism in the early months of 1963. Even so, Khrushchev's comments on music in his lengthy speech during the March meeting with the artistic intelligentsia encapsulated the essence of his provincial tastes: "To put it briefly, we stand for melodious music with content, music that stirs people and gives rise to strong feelings, and we are against cacophony." [69] Khrushchev's only reference to Shostakovich was to chide him—not for the first time—for having invited him, during the Composers' Union plenum devoted to jazz and popular music the previous fall, to attend a concert of jazz music at the Kremlin. The invitation had obviously backfired. To Khrushchev, most of this jazz represented the "kind of music that gives you a feeling of nausea and a pain in the stomach." [70] Shostakovich responded publicly to the meeting with well-honed phrases of gratitude for the benevolent and fatherly guidance of the Party. But, in what may have been a sign of solidarity with Yevtushenko—who was under renewed persecution after the publication of his *Precocious Autobiography* in France—in mid-May Shostakovich informed Glikman of his intent to write a new work on Yevtushenko's verse. He did not yet know what form this work might take, but he was already certain that its content would be "dedicated to conscience, to human conscience." [71] Yevtushenko confirms that Shostakovich did indeed propose a symphony on such a subject to him, but all that eventually came of it was his poem, "The Torments of Conscience," which he dedicated to the composer.[72]

In early April 1963, Shostakovich participated in a showcase of Russian music in Moldova. At the beginning of June, he attended a comparable festival in Kyrgyzstan. At both—as, indeed, during similar festivities in Tashkent and in the Don region the following year—he was swept up in a nonstop whirl of concerts, speaking engagements, banquets, and visits to factories, schools, and collective farms. Concerts aside, he estimated that during his ten days in Kyrgyzstan he traveled 3,000 kilometers and had approximately thirty meetings with students, farm workers, and ordinary citizens. In between these trips, Shostakovich spent another month in the hospital in Moscow, for more treatment of his hand. He waxed sentimental about his hospital stay of the previous year, when he was totally engrossed in the composition of his Thirteenth Symphony. Now, by contrast, he said his head was empty; he had no creative energy, no inspiration.[73]

At the artists' retreat in Dilizhan, in the mountains of Armenia, Shostakovich enjoyed conditions during the month of July he hoped would allow him to recoup his creative strength. He could not pass up a trip to Yerevan to attend (twice) the first Soviet production of Stravinsky's *Oedipus Rex*.[74] And on 20 July he toasted the first anniversary of the completion of his "deficient" Thirteenth Symphony. To maintain the skills of his craft, he orchestrated the Schumann Cello Concerto at Rostropovich's request. (The latter performed the premiere of Shostakovich's orchestration of the concerto in Moscow on 5 October.) Shostakovich's orchestration of two choruses by Alexander Davidenko ("At the Tenth Verst" and "The Street Is Aroused"), pieces that he said had revived a sense of nostalgia for the revolutionary romanticism of his youth when he had heard them performed in 1959, were finished in August 1963.[75]

But 1963 was not a productive year for composition. The only original work Shostakovich produced was the *Overture on Russian and Kyrgyz Themes*, op. 115, fulfilling a promise he had made on his recent visit to Kyrgyzstan and commemorating the centenary of Kyrgyzstan's "voluntary incorporation into Russia." Shostakovich had been exposed at first hand to the artistry of at least one of Kyrgyzstan's distinguished folk musicians; he remembered the republic as a place "where everyone sings."[76] For his overture, he used two melodies from a published collection of Kyrgyz folk music. His main Russian theme had been recently collected in the Omsk region of Siberia. Completed early in October, the *Overture on Russian and Kyrgyz Themes* received its premiere in Frunze in November and was first performed in Moscow on 10 November.

Shostakovich spent the last two months of 1963 shuttling between Riga and London in connection with productions of *Katerina*. The early days of

1964 found him in Zagreb for the same purpose. For nine days in February, he was honored as the featured composer at the Second Festival of Contemporary Music in Gorky. More than forty concerts offered a comprehensive showcase of his achievements to date, performed by a superb roster of the finest Soviet artists and ensembles, many of them the dedicatees. Unlike the Edinburgh Festival of 1962, the more compact festival in Gorky was devoted almost exclusively to Shostakovich's music (the exception being a concert of music by Shostakovich's students, planned with his assistance). Maxim Shostakovich, recently graduated from the piano faculty of the Moscow Conservatory and in the process of launching a conducting career, was one of the guest conductors. And the composer himself made what by now—because of his physical disabilities—was a rare concert appearance, performing the Intermezzo from his Piano Quintet with the members of the Borodin Quartet.

Among the musical highlights of the Gorky Festival, Shostakovich listed the premiere, on 19 February, of the orchestral version of the cycle *From Jewish Folk Poetry*, op. 79a. In recapping the events, Shostakovich described this orchestration as his "most recent" work.[77] Actually, he had already orchestrated the first eight songs of the cycle back in 1948; what was "recent" was likely just the orchestration of the final three songs. Another novelty was the performance of excerpts from the composer's music to Kozintsev's film *Hamlet*; in his press conference Shostakovich indicated that work on *Hamlet* was nearing completion and that, while in Gorky, he was busy finishing his contribution to the film so as not to let down the creative team.[78]

Shostakovich had accepted Kozintsev's invitation to write the music for the film early in 1962. His interest in Shakespeare's play was of long standing, as was his artistic relationship with Kozintsev, a director who put great store in the aural aspect of his films. In scoring Kozintsev's film of *Hamlet*, Shostakovich started from scratch; he recycled none of the music he had composed for Akimov's eccentric 1932 interpretation or Kozintsev's own 1954 staging of the play (most of the music for which had in turn been adapted from that for the same director's 1941 production of *King Lear*). The filmed *Hamlet* enjoyed tremendous success on its release in April 1964, a success attributed in no small measure to the psychological shading and symphonic depth of Shostakovich's score. A suite of selections from the film, op. 116a, was quickly assembled by Atovmyan. In December 1965, after viewing the film again, Shostakovich wrote to Kozintsev to congratulate him on his remarkable achievement; he subsequently told him he had seen *Hamlet* eight or nine times.[79]

In the end, the composer was rather less satisfied with his involvement in another film project initiated at around the same time. In numerous interviews, beginning in autumn 1962 and spanning more than two years, prominently listed among Shostakovich's upcoming projects was his music for a biographical film about Karl Marx, based on a novel by Galina Serebryakova, who recruited him for the purpose. When in 1965 he finally set about scoring the film, *A Year Is Like a Lifetime*, work did not go well. As the taping sessions were drawing to an end, Shostakovich accurately foresaw that he would not earn many laurels with this work.[80]

But of all the nascent projects dangled before Shostakovich's ever expectant public, none quickened pulses more than the promise of a new opera. In the summer of 1963, six months after the successful rehabilitation of *Katerina Izmailova*, Shostakovich started dropping increasingly tantalizing hints that he was ready to embark on a new opera; by December, although he was not ready to talk about its subject, he said his dream was to create an opera for the fiftieth anniversary of the Revolution and that he was already doing preliminary work with a librettist.[81] At his press conference in Gorky in February 1964, Shostakovich confirmed rumors that the opera he was planning was based on Mikhaíl Sholokhov's *Quiet Don*.[82] Here, and elsewhere, he emphasized that he would be using different portions of the famous novel from those treated by Ivan Dzerzhinsky in his opera (the very one that had profited from the banishment of *Lady Macbeth of the Mtsensk District* from the stage in 1936). Shostakovich signed off on a libretto and the Bolshoy Theater looked forward to unveiling its production of the new opera during the anniversary season.[83] *The Quiet Don* was also included in the Kirov Theater's long-range plans for the anniversary.

The news of Shostakovich's meeting with Sholokhov in the summer of 1964 received wide exposure, as did periodic status reports. For all the importance he publicly attached to this opera, in January 1966 Shostakovich was still speaking of its composition in the future tense, as his most important project for the coming year.[84]

By the spring, Shostakovich's enthusiasm for *The Quiet Don* had dissipated completely. It disappeared abruptly from his official agenda. Claims by contemporaries that he had completed a substantial portion of the opera are apparently without foundation.[85] In a remarkable memoir, Dmitriy Shepilov—the former high-ranking Central Committee member disgraced as a member of the "anti-Party" group by Khrushchev shortly after his participation in the Second All-Union Congress of Soviet Composers in 1957 and memorably satirized by Shostakovich in his *Antiformalist Rayok*—describes an incident that may shed light on Shostakovich's situation. Shostakovich phoned Shepilov and asked him to visit. He told him that he had been given an assignment to write the opera *The Quiet Don* for the upcoming anniversary and that he had begun work but had run into a dead end and wanted Shepilov's advice. His dilemma was that he was supposed to be writing an opera to celebrate the anniversary of Soviet power about a hero who did not embrace Soviet power! He was concerned that what could be adequately treated in a novel could not be disguised in an opera. Shepilov gave the agitated Shostakovich the reassurance that he was surely hoping to hear: if he found it impossible to write an opera on the subject, he should not feel obliged to do it.[86] A different excuse was advanced to explain Shostakovich's disinclination, two years later, to discuss the project: his disagreement with Sholokhov's interpretation of the character of Grigoriy Melekhov and his unwillingness to exculpate the murders committed by the hero.[87]

During the summer of 1964, Shostakovich more than compensated for the compositional dry spell of the previous year; by mid-September he was referring to his exceptionally prolific streak as "creative diarrhea." [88] The first fruit of this streak was the Ninth String Quartet, op. 117, completed on 28 May in Moscow. Although available evidence suggests that the work was composed quickly, within the space of a month, the quartet was several years in the making. Outlining the upcoming fortieth anniversary season of the Beethoven Quartet, in the summer of 1962 first violinist Dmitriy Tsïganov had noted that they were anxiously anticipating the delivery of Shostakovich's new Ninth Quartet, which they planned to unveil during their Leningrad cycle of performances.[89] In interviews after his return from Edinburgh, Shostakovich stated that he was working on a new quartet; he characterized it on 21 October 1962 as a "children's work (about toys and excursions)," at that point estimating its completion in two weeks.[90] As Tsïganov recalled, in response to his impatient inquiries, the composer promised that he would call the minute the quartet was done. A year later, Shostakovich's position was that completion of his Ninth Quartet might well take another year or even a year and a half.[91] And the call to Tsïganov did not come until the summer of 1964, at which point Shostakovich acknowledged that the Ninth he had just completed was an entirely new quartet; he had discarded the one he had been writing two years earlier.[92] He dedicated the Ninth Quartet to his wife, Irina.

As they had the previous summer, Shostakovich and Irina spent most of the month of July 1964 in Dilizhan. The weather was fine, the surroundings magnificent, and the composer in good spirits. In Dilizhan, Shostakovich composed yet another quartet, his Tenth, op. 118, completing it on 20 July. This one he dedicated to his friend and colleague, Moisey Vainberg, with whom he was engaged in a playful competition; he admitted he had set his sights on overtaking Vainberg's record of nine quartets.[93] The Shostakoviches celebrated completion of the new quartet on the second anniversary of the composition of the Thirteenth Symphony.

In early August, the composer and his wife vacationed on Lake Balaton in Hungary. Shostakovich gave out that he would be spending his time there working on *The Quiet Don*. A month after his return, however, on 14 September 1964, he put the finishing touches on a symphonic poem for bass, mixed chorus, and orchestra, *The Execution of Stepan Razin*, op. 119, based on an as yet unpublished poem by Yevgeniy Yevtushenko.[94] As he wrote Glikman the next day, originally he had thought he might make it into something like the Thirteenth Symphony but had decided against extending it.[95] He also underscored that his approach to Yevtushenko's poetry was different from what it had been in the Thirteenth Symphony; here Shostakovich had found himself taking a polemical stance toward some of the verses, as well as simply discarding those he found weak. He did not expect to be able to convince Yevtushenko to make changes. He did expect that some of the text he had set might cause problems with the censors. And in this symphonic poem ("in the Russian style"), he predicted that critics both well disposed and stern would find plenty to latch on to—the lapses into "coarse naturalism," for instance, not to mention the "depraved conception."[96] Yevtushenko recalls that, while composing *Stepan Razin*, Shostakovich called him several times to probe: "What do you think, Yevgeniy Alexandrovich, was Razin a good man? After all, he killed people, let a lot of innocent blood."[97]

The harvest from Shostakovich's productive summer was quickly reaped. Shostakovich's two new quartets were warmly received at their premieres by the Beethoven Quartet in Moscow on 20 November 1964. On 28 December, also in Moscow, *The Execution of Stepan Razin* was first performed by the Moscow Philharmonic Orchestra and the Choral Capella of the Russian Republic conducted by Kirill Kondrashin. Ivan Petrov, a star of the Bolshoy Theater, had been billed as the bass soloist. But according to Kondrashin, Petrov was unprofessional and unreliable; he attended only two of five orchestral rehearsals and even then did not give his best effort. When he was too indisposed to appear at the dress rehearsal on the morning of the concert, Kondrashin persuaded Shostakovich to let the alternate, Vitaliy Gromadsky, perform the premiere.[98] A repeat performance, with the same forces, was given on 5 January 1965. Performances in Minsk, Gomel, and Gorky soon followed.

Shostakovich's apprehension about censorship problems with *Stepan Razin* proved unfounded. Nevertheless, in the atmosphere of uncertainty following Khrushchev's ouster from power in mid-October 1964 (Shostakovich's reported reaction to this news was the rhetorical question: "Now we will most certainly enjoy an even better life?"[99]), critics did not rush to register their opinion of Shostakovich's disturbingly graphic, allegorical reflection on the fate of Russia's notorious seventeenth-century peasant rebel. Some initial reviewers took objection to his deprecating treatment of the Russian people, but more subtle appreciations soon appeared,[100] placing the work firmly in the continuum of the distinctive tradition of Russian folk drama—with conspicuous homage to Musorgsky—as well as in clear relation to the composer's recent historical and vocal-symphonic interests. In November 1968, nearly four years after its premiere, *The Execution of Stepan Razin* was awarded a State Prize. Shostakovich had anticipated misunderstanding of this opus. That some ambiguity of perception persisted, however, even among those closest to the composer, is evidenced by Shostakovich's disappointment on realizing, in 1966, that he had failed to communicate to Glikman the mood he had intended in a particular passage.[101]

Much of 1965 was occupied with supervising new productions of *Katerina Izmailova* and with work on the film version of the opera. An unexpected source of satisfaction for the composer was the revival of his Thirteenth Symphony—by the original performers—in Moscow in September, followed by performances in December in Gorky and in January 1966 in Novosibirsk. He attended all of these concerts. But beyond finally dispatching the scoring of *A Year Is Like a Lifetime*, Shostakovich completed only one other composition during the year, a contemporary counterpart to the *Satires* of 1960, his *Five Romances* for bass and piano, op. 121, on deliciously mundane personal communications from the 30 August 1965 issue of the popular humor magazine, *Krokodil* (Crocodile). It was dashed off quickly, on the spur of the moment. On 4 September, when Shostakovich informed Glikman that he had completed the cycle and sent him copies of the text, he confessed that it had landed him in something of a domestic jam: his wife was begging him to change the name of the heroine of the fourth number, "Irinka and the Cowherd," lest people think he had written the song about her.[102] In the end Shostakovich did not budge, reasoning that no matter what name he chose he risked offending someone, though when the *Krokodil* romances were published in *Sovetskaya muzïka* in January 1966, he did move the locale of another of the songs, "A Difficult Request," from Petrozavodsk to Moscow. He instructed Yevgeniy Nesterenko, whom he accompanied in a performance in Leningrad on 28 May 1966, to substitute the name of the city where the performance took place.[103]

1966–1969

Jubilees

The new year 1966 got off to a productive start. While reports of his ostensible progress on the opera *The Quiet Don* continued to appear in the press, Shostakovich quietly finished a new quartet—his Eleventh—in F Minor, op. 122, on 30 January. It was dedicated to the memory of Vasiliy Shirinsky, founding second violinist of the Beethoven Quartet, who had died the previous summer.

On 16 February, Shostakovich wrote Glikman that he had begun work on his Fourteenth Symphony; it gave him an excuse to skip the upcoming Composers' Union Plenum in Moscow to go to the retreat at Repino to work on it.[1] A month later, on 20 March, he told Glikman that he was currently writing his Second Cello Concerto and was in the process of finishing up its first movement.[2] That this was one and the same work was clarified in a letter the composer wrote shortly before the concerto's premiere: "It seems to me that the Second Concerto could have been called the Fourteenth Symphony with a solo cello part."[3] By 9 April, Shostakovich had written three movements but claimed that the third was "very bad" and he had decided therefore to rewrite it from scratch.[4] Ten days later, he went to the Crimea for treatment at a sanatorium near Yalta, and it was there that he completed his new cello concerto on 27 April. What he singled out as the most curious feature in the lengthy three-movement work was the appearance (in the second movement and at the climax of the third) of a theme remarkably similar to the lowly Odessan ditty, "Pretzels, Buy My Pretzels!" but he could not explain what had brought it on.[5] Actually, during New Year's Eve festivities celebrated at Zhukovka with Rostropovich and other neighbors four months earlier, the guests had engaged in a game of "My Favorite Melody," and while others had chosen melodies by Beethoven, Mozart, and Chaikovsky, Shostakovich had unexpectedly offered this tune, as if in the grip of youthful nostalgia.[6]

It was Rostropovich's artistry that was in his mind's ear as Shostakovich composed the Second Cello Concerto, just as it had been with his First. And, although the appearance of the concerto came as a surprise, this was the one time in Rostropovich's experience that Shostakovich showed him a work before it was done, perhaps at the moment when he had resolved to rewrite the third movement. Rostropovich was able to offer him a suggestion that subsequently he was delighted to discover the composer had incorporated in the cadenza.[7] On its completion, Shostakovich sent the cellist the piano score from the Crimea. Rostropovich learned the concerto straightaway, traveling to Yalta to play it for Shostakovich before his departure in mid-May.

While the composer immersed himself in composition, plans for the widespread commemoration of his sixtieth birthday were unfolding. By this juncture in his career, Shostakovich had achieved the indisputable status of composer laureate. A projected film biography of the composer fell through, but another film, mixing historical footage with contemporary shots of Shostakovich as he traveled, rehearsed, and performed, was undertaken, as was a volume of testimonials to and essays about him.[8] The prospect of the immoderate celebration of this anniversary—the effusive accolades, the attention, all guaranteed to exceed the hoopla of his fiftieth birthday observance—is surely what prompted Shostakovich to pen the self-deprecating little squib for voice and piano, *Preface to the Complete Edition of My Works and a Brief Reflection apropos of This Preface*, op. 123. Paraphrasing a Pushkin epigram on the impermanence of human creativity, Shostakovich "signed" it with a deadpan recitation of a small portion of his many honorific titles and imposing offices set, naturally, to his musical monogram. Completed on 2 March 1966, Shostakovich included the *Preface* as the opening number in the program for a concert of his works in Leningrad on 28 May 1966.

This chamber concert loomed especially large for the composer. Not only did the program include the premieres of this *Preface*, the *Five Romances on Texts from Krokodil Magazine* (both sung by bass Yevgeniy Nesterenko), and the Eleventh Quartet (played by the Beethoven Quartet), in addition to performances of Shakespeare's Sonnet 66 and "Jenny" from op. 62 and the *Satires* cycle (sung by Galina Vishnevskaya), but Shostakovich, who had not performed in public in more than two years, set his sights on accompanying the two singers himself. As he told Glikman, the thought of performing made him extremely nervous, but he was determined to try, even though he realized he could not command complete control of his right hand.[9] His trepidation communicated itself to the singers. During a rehearsal with Vishnevskaya the day before the concert, he was so nervous he kept repeating the same mistake without realizing it.[10] More than one member of the audience perceived the composer's heightened anxiety when Nesterenko flubbed his part in performance.[11] To compound the stress still further, Leningrad's weather was unseasonably hot and sticky; it was stifling in the packed concert hall.

By most accounts, the concert came off brilliantly and was well received. The Eleventh Quartet was encored. This would turn out to be the composer's final public appearance as a performer. Afterward, Shostakovich was escorted back to his hotel by a throng of well-wishers. At around midnight, an ambulance was summoned because he was feeling unwell, but the diagnosis proved inconclusive. Late the next morning, a heart attack was confirmed and Shostakovich was taken to the Sverdlov Hospital, a facility for privileged patients.

This was not Shostakovich's first brush with heart trouble. He had spent three weeks in a cardiological clinic in January 1965. He was now obliged to spend two months in the hospital followed by another month of recuperation at a sanatorium outside Leningrad. As a result, he was unable to attend the concerts, theatrical events, and exhibitions—including the local premiere of the Thirteenth Symphony—of Leningrad's White Nights Festival at the end of June, fittingly devoted this year to his music. By August, he was reporting to correspondents that he was feeling much better although his legs were wobbly. When Shaginyan visited him in Repino in early September, she recorded in her diary that he was "very pale; flabby, his eyes are restless and don't look straight at one, he has lost most of his hair; his forehead was damp with perspiration, several wisps sticking out in different directions. He walks with difficulty. We embraced. His hands are still shaky and his fingers have become quite weak." [12]

The premiere of Shostakovich's Cello Concerto no. 2 in G Major, op. 126, was scheduled for the jubilee concert celebrating Shostakovich's sixtieth birthday on 25 September 1966 with the USSR State Symphony Orchestra in the Large Hall of the Moscow Conservatory. The morning of the anniversary it was announced that, for his outstanding services in the development of Soviet musical culture, the Central Committee had awarded the composer the title "Hero of Socialist Labor," together with the Order of Lenin and the gold medal "Hammer and Sickle." [13] Shostakovich had not been seen in public since his heart attack, and until the last minute no one could be certain whether he would be well enough to attend the concert. So his appearance in the hall to hear his son, Maxim, conduct the First Symphony and Yevgeniy Svetlanov conduct Rostropovich's performance of the new Second Cello Concerto—and to share with them the acknowledgments onstage—gave genuine impetus to the galvanic ovations.

It had originally been agreed that Rostropovich and Mravinsky would open the season at the Leningrad Philharmonic with the premiere of the new Shostakovich concerto. Somehow, however, what may have been a simple misunderstanding brought about unfortunate consequences. Rostropovich has maintained that Mravinsky announced to him just two weeks before the performance that he refused to conduct the concert because he had not had time to learn the concerto.[14] Elsewhere, he offered a different version of the story. When he arrived in Leningrad during the summer and went to the Philharmonic, expecting to find this concert in its subscription roster, he found nothing listed there. Raising the alarm, he was informed by the Philharmonic's management that Mravinsky had not had time to learn the new score.[15] Rostropovich's disgust over this last-minute cancellation, in addition to his continuing indignation over the affair of the Thirteenth Symphony, led to his break with both the conductor and the Leningrad Philharmonic Orchestra.

To be fair, the phenomenal appetite with which Rostropovich "consumed" and mastered new repertory could not have been more different from the painstaking inquiry and lengthy digestion process with which Mravinsky typically approached new scores. A more benign explanation of the unfortunate incident has been provided by Leningrad conductor Eduard Serov; having been unable to learn the new work in time, Mravinsky decided to move the premiere back until October and instructed the Philharmonic's artistic administrator to advise Rostropovich, which he failed to do. Thus, when the unsuspecting Rostropovich arrived for rehearsals, he was not met at the station and he found no posters or other publicity for the impending concert. He was hurt and offended.[16] To ensure the timely premiere of Shostakovich's new work in his native city, Glikman and Rostropovich arranged for the latter to perform it, in late November, at the Leningrad Conservatory with the student orchestra conducted by Nikolai Rabinovich.[17] Mravinsky's "boorish" behavior over the Second Cello Concerto created another sore spot for the composer.

At the request of the doctor who had been treating his right hand since 1958, Shostakovich returned to hospital in October to attempt to regain the strength in his limbs. The stay brought no relief. The composer summed up his examination by a surgeon and a neuropathologist: "Both of them were extremely satisfied with my arms and legs. In the long run, the facts that I am unable to play the piano and can climb stairs only with colossal difficulty are insignificant. One is not obliged to play the piano and there is no need to climb stairs. One should sit at home, no need to gad about staircases, let alone slippery sidewalks. How true: just yesterday I went for a walk, fell down and banged up my knee. If I had been sitting at home, nothing of the sort would have occurred." [18] After eight years of consultations and treatments that had failed to produce a definitive diagnosis, let alone a cure, his cynicism was understandable. What was more remarkable, for all his afflictions and the steady physical deterioration, was the tenacity with which Shostakovich held on to the hope for improvement. Regularly he submitted to the tedium of lengthy hospital stays, medical consultations, myriad treatments and therapies. He consulted with specialists on his foreign trips. He tried exotic herbal preparations and alternative remedies; he thanked Shaginyan in January 1967, for instance, for her gift of a Japanese magnetic bracelet, saying he would wear it and try to believe in its miracle-working properties.[19]

Shostakovich was well enough to attend the Moscow recital of Peter Pears and Benjamin Britten on 25 December 1966 and to greet the new year 1967 with family and friends at Zhukovka, together with Britten and Pears. Britten was a musician Shostakovich respected deeply. Having made each other's acquaintance in 1960 at the London premiere[20] of Shostakovich's First Cello Concerto, the two maintained contact, in part through their mutual friend Rostropovich, paid each other reciprocal visits, and exchanged letters and music. When he received the score and recording in the summer of 1963, Shostakovich was profoundly affected by Britten's *War Requiem*, recognizing in it a profound work of conscience. Elevating it to rank alongside his beloved *Das Lied von der Erde*, he proselytized the work to students, to colleagues, to all he could persuade to listen. Shostakovich also valued Britten's opinion of his own music more than most. He was touched by the latter's high evaluation of his Second Cello Concerto because "[Britten] is a very fine composer and a good judge of music." [21] As Pears later observed in one of his travel diaries: "I think he [Shostakovich] has not so many listeners whom he can so wholeheartedly respect as Ben." [22] In a 1968 interview on young composers and trends in music, Shostakovich expressed his desire to see "more Brittens. Russian ones, and English ones, and German ones. Various. And of different generations. What attracts me to Britten? The strength and sincerity of his talent, its surface simplicity and the intensity of its emotional effect." [23] The capacity to create music that transforms the listener, having heard it, into a different person—a rare gift he recognized that Britten possessed—was, in Shostakovich's view, the loftiest aspiration any composer could harbor.

Shostakovich's health and handicaps demanded more and more of his attention and energy. He was obliged to give up smoking and drinking after his heart attack, deprivations he suffered out of fear. Unable to compose, he read extensively, but, as ever, the lengthy composer's block made him depressed and anxious. Eight months after his heart attack, in January 1967, he reported that he was trying to compose a little every day, without success.[24] On 3 February, he wrote about his recent reflections on life, death, and his career, fretting that he might be burned out:

> I have become disillusioned with myself. Rather, [I have become convinced] that I am a very dull and mediocre composer. Looking back on "the path traversed" from the vantage of my sixty years, I can say that twice in my life great ballyhoo was made over me (*Lady Macbeth of the Mtsensk District* and the Thirteenth Symphony). Ballyhoo with a very strong effect. However, after everything calms down and returns to normal, it turns out that both *Lady Macbeth* and the Thirteenth Symphony are "fuk," as they say in *The Nose*.... However, the composition of music—an affliction in the nature of a disease—haunts me. Today I completed seven romances on texts by A. Blok. [25]

The completion of the new work went a long way toward reviving Shostakovich's spirits.

Rostropovich had asked Shostakovich for some vocalises that he might perform together with his wife, Vishnevskaya. When the cycle was complete, the composer admitted that after having written the first piece, "Ophelia's Song," for soprano and cello as requested, he realized he did not have sufficient instrumental resources to continue and so added the violin and piano,[26] producing a cycle of seven songs, each with a different combination of accompanying instruments. The verses he set were all from Alexander Blok's early poetry; he explained his choices as the poems that had made the greatest impression on him by their musicality and lyrical feel. His widow later noted that in preparation for his settings Shostakovich had asked her to mark in the collection of Blok's poetry the poems she treasured most; she was initially disappointed to find out that the poems she had selected, ones from Blok's maturity, were not among the ones he had chosen.[27] Shostakovich contributed the title of the final song, "Music"—Blok had left this particular poem untitled—and said he wanted to use that as the title of the cycle as a whole.[28] Ultimately, he gave his vocal-instrumental suite the definitive title, *Seven Verses of A. Blok*, op. 127.[29] He wrote the piano part for himself, taking into account his own physical limitations; he envisioned Vishnevskaya, Oistrakh, and Rostropovich as his ideal collaborators.

A few days after the completion of his song cycle, an ebullient Shostakovich was visited by Veniamin Basner. Shostakovich told him he had conceived the idea for the composition in the hospital but had been unable to realize it. He had begun to doubt himself. The turnabout in his creative fortunes he attributed to a shot of brandy from a bottle he happened to chance upon while his wife was out of the house. The song cycle had then been completed in three days.[30] Shostakovich demonstrated his new cycle to friends and colleagues, but it was not until mid-June, when the schedules of all the designated collaborators coincided, that they rehearsed the work for the first time. The experience afforded the composer a great deal of joy.[31]

In the meantime, Shostakovich continued composing, not without effort. On 13 March he wrote Glikman that he had managed to set another Pushkin romance, *Spring, Spring* (op. 128), but that his umpteenth stab at setting the same poet's famous verse, "Monument," was not working out.[32] In early April, he announced that he was writing a violin concerto very slowly, wringing it out of himself note by note.[33] Cataloguing his recent works for Shaginyan in June 1967, he acknowledged: "I have many and various plans for the future, but little strength or energy. I have begun writing more slowly and with greater difficulty." [34]

Contrary to Shostakovich's usual custom of letting an intended dedicatee in on the secret only after the fait accompli, Igor Oistrakh has indicated that his father was aware of the Second Violin Concerto while it was still in progress.[35] But in a letter from the composer to David Oistrakh written on 20 May, two days after he had completed his new violin concerto in Repino, the announcement sounds very much like a bolt from the blue. Eager to share his new work with Oistrakh, hopeful that the latter would do him the honor of performing it, Shostakovich begged his permission to dedicate the concerto to him.[36] Oistrakh, who accepted the dedication with alacrity, came to believe somehow that Shostakovich had intended the Second Concerto as a present for his sixtieth birthday but had mistakenly bestowed the gift a year early.[37] Perhaps there was some misunderstanding. This was not the kind of error the punctilious Shostakovich was prone to; in his communications with the violinist concerning the Second Concerto the anniversary is not mentioned.

If his recent Second Cello Concerto had been conceived along the lines of a symphony with cello obbligato, by contrast Shostakovich characterized his Second Concerto for Violin, op. 129, as less symphonic than his first one: "In the new concerto virtually everything is set out by the solo violin, everything is concentrated in its part and the orchestra accompanies, as it were." [38] As Oistrakh pointed out, the key Shostakovich selected, C-sharp minor, was an unusual and potentially awkward key for a violinist, but on acquaintance with the concerto he appreciated it as the ingenious stroke of a composer who genuinely understood the expressive capabilities of the instrument.[39]

Shostakovich gave Oistrakh the music in June and rehearsed with him a few days later, at which point he was already amazed by the violinist's inspired performance. They corresponded about interpretive details over the summer. Shostakovich also divulged to Oistrakh that his son, Maxim, was eager to conduct the premiere.[40] Maxim had completed the course in symphonic conducting at the Moscow Conservatory in Gennadiy Rozhdestvensky's class the previous year. In December 1966, at the Second All-Union Conductors' Competition, he had garnered fifth prize. If we are to believe Kondrashin, who chaired the jury, Maxim was not among the strongest competitors and made it to the medal round of six chiefly by virtue of the respect in which the jurors held his father.[41] (Maxim saw events differently; he claimed that his score had been lowered intentionally by "a famous conductor, a great friend of my father" as a "prophylactic" measure, lest Maxim Shostakovich become conceited.[42]) That Shostakovich senior might have had a father's blind spot for his son is understandable, but when it came to a premiere as important as that of the Second Violin Concerto, his judgment was unclouded. He fully appreciated the importance to the future success of new works of recruiting first performers of the highest possible caliber. Clearly, he did not feel his son was up to the challenge yet. Initially he left the decision up to Oistrakh, begging that, in any event, the violinist should have a serious talk with Maxim and impress upon him the enormous responsibility involved in a premiere.[43] He voiced his personal preference for Kondrashin over his still-inexperienced son in a subsequent letter; to avoid offending Maxim, however, he shifted responsibility for the decision to Oistrakh.[44]

As if by way of compensation, Shostakovich entrusted to Maxim the premiere of another new composition, the symphonic poem *October*, op. 131. Completed on 10 August in the Belovezhskaya Forest Preserve in western Belarus, where the Shostakoviches were vacationing, the thirteen-minute *October* was the obligatory tribute to the fiftieth anniversary of the Revolution by a composer whose grander plan of delivering a new opera for the occasion had been quietly scuttled. Shostakovich experienced trouble composing a work to commemorate the jubilee; the stimulus for the symphonic poem *October* had come a few months earlier when he had viewed the film *Volochayev Days*—in preparation by Mosfilm for re-release—to which he had written the music thirty years earlier. He found himself admiring anew the "Partisan Song," over which he had expended so much effort back then, and appropriated it for the second theme of his new symphonic poem.[45] Maxim conducted the USSR State Symphony Orchestra in the premiere of *October* in Moscow on 16 September 1967. Its impact did not outstrip its occasional function.

This was not the only patriotic offering unveiled as the Soviet anniversary approached. During the summer of 1967, Eisenstein's legendary 1928 silent film *October* was prepared for re-release with a soundtrack montage of Shostakovich's music. Although the soundtrack arranged by a trusted colleague met with his basic approval, Shostakovich confessed to Glikman that he did not like the film itself and could not understand why Eisenstein and, for that matter, Dovzhenko, were considered such geniuses.[46] In a situation analogous to that surrounding the genesis of *Novorossiisk Chimes*, Shostakovich fulfilled a request from the city of Volgograd (formerly Stalingrad) for music to be played at their war memorial installation. The brief *Funeral-Triumphal Prelude*, in memory of the heroes of the battle of Stalingrad, op. 130, was recorded, under the baton of Gennadiy Rozhdestvensky, in Moscow in early September; it played in Volgograd in October.

Shostakovich was unable to attend this recording session, or indeed the other premieres of his music that fall, as planned. In the first week of September he broke his right leg and spent the better part of the next several months in hospital. A few weeks after this latest mishap he reported sardonically from the hospital: "I am at 75 percent (Right leg broken, left leg broken, right hand defective. Now I need to damage my left hand and then all 100 percent of my extremities will be out of order)."[47] Under normal circumstances, Shostakovich took an active role in the preparation of his premieres, attending all rehearsals, working with soloists, fine-tuning details of dynamics and tempo. His incapacities now necessitated a different manner of preparation. On 13 September, Oistrakh, accompanied by Kondrashin and the Moscow Philharmonic Orchestra, performed a dry run of the Second Violin Concerto (at the same concert Oistrakh also conducted a performance of the composer's Tenth Symphony) in the Moscow suburb of Bolshevo. A tape was sent to Shostakovich. With score in hand, violinist and composer worked through the interpretive refinements in a series of telephone conversations recorded by Oistrakh. Shostakovich evidently prepared with Kondrashin in the same fashion.

The premiere of Shostakovich's Second Violin Concerto was given by the same forces in Moscow on 26 September 1967.[48] It was received warmly, if not with unrestrained enthusiasm. Oistrakh continued to refine his interpretation and performed the concerto on tour in England in November and in America in January 1968. Shostakovich heard the broadcast of the British premiere on 19 November and, deeply grateful for the marvelous performance, sent a telegram to the violinist the next day. On 6 December, still in the hospital, Shostakovich wrote to Oistrakh again of his gratitude, looking forward to the day he would finally be able to hear the concerto live instead of on radio or tape.[49]

The premiere that attracted the greatest attention that fall was that of the Blok suite on 23 October at the Large Hall of the Moscow Conservatory.[50] Shostakovich was unable to realize his dream of performing the piano part; Vainberg deputized for him in the ensemble with Vishnevskaya, Oistrakh, and Rostropovich. In what was labeled the cultural "event" of the season— the slate of performers alone made it a irresistible ticket—Shostakovich's

vocal-instrumental suite scored a commanding triumph. By popular demand, it had to be repeated in its entirety. Issuing from a composer whose
recent vocal writing had been noteworthy for its satirical detachment, the
confessional intimacy and lyrical, even romantic, warmth of Shostakovich's Blok settings, not to mention the organic integrity of the cycle as a
whole, came as a revelation to critics.

For Oistrakh, the concert was memorable for another reason. The violin
does not play until the third song ("We Were Together"), until which the violinist must sit patiently on stage. Oistrakh felt acutely nervous. As he
waited for his entry, he began experiencing increasingly severe chest pains.
Knowing that Shostakovich was listening to the concert on the radio and
what anxiety it would cause him, he could not bring himself to leave the
stage. He played his part in excruciating pain. Fortunately, when the time
came to perform the encore, his nerves had calmed and his chest pains had
subsided.[51] After the concert, friends gathered at Shostakovich's Zhukovka
dacha for a candlelight supper; the elated composer was assisted downstairs
so he could join in the celebration. Toasting his latest success, he reflected
that he had not composed the romances in vain.[52]

Whiling away his time in the hospital as his bones slowly healed,
Shostakovich read, watched television, and listened to a great deal of music.
He found himself reminiscing about times past, about friends and acquaintances gone forever: "But it's better to have little free time, then memories
don't intrude. Still, my god, what an amazing phenomenon these memories
are."[53] Out of sympathy for his friend Leo Arnshtam, whose wife had just
died, while still in the hospital Shostakovich composed the musical score
for Arnshtam's film, *Sofya Perovskaya*, without having viewed a single
frame of the picture, on the basis of the scenario and the precise
chronometric calculations provided.[54] He was released from the hospital on
the eve of the new year.

Even after his release, Shostakovich's mobility remained significantly im-
paired. He found himself unable to resume his previous gamut of civic and
cultural activities. Cooped up at his Zhukovka dacha in late January 1968,
he complained of boredom and one of his intermittent precipitous drops in
income.[55] Later that spring, in anticipation of the Second Congress of the
Union of Composers of the Russian Federation in mid-May, at which he
delivered opening remarks, Shostakovich asked to be relieved, for health
reasons, of his post as first secretary. In addition to organizational and
administrative responsibilities, during the eight years of his tenure he had
shouldered a grueling schedule of travel around Russia. Although Shostakovich remained on the roster of "secretaries," his former student Georgiy
Sviridov was elected to succeed him at the helm of the organization.

Shostakovich was in Leningrad for the local premieres of his Blok suite, on 20 February, and the Second Violin Concerto, on 3 March 1968. He spent the first three weeks of March living at the Composers' Union retreat at Repino. On 9 March, he told Glikman that he was always anxious that he would not succeed in completing whatever work was then in progress, that he would die and leave it incomplete.[56] Two days later, on 11 March, he completed his String Quartet no. 12 in D-flat Major, op. 133.

On completion of the new quartet, Shostakovich immediately wrote to inform Dmitriy Tsïganov—whose sixty-fifth birthday was on 12 March—to ask him to accept the dedication. When he spoke with Tsïganov ten days later he sounded well satisfied with his new work. In response to the violinist's query about whether the new quartet was "chamber" in its proportions, he retorted: "No, no, it's a symphony, a symphony."[57] On 14 June, the Beethoven Quartet performed the Twelfth Quartet during the first creative convocation of the new secretariat of the Russian Composers' Union, an event deemed significant enough to be reported in the press, along with the commendations of musicians in attendance.[58] The composer himself reported that the performance had been magnificent; he thought it had made an impression.[59] Even more unusual was the appearance of a description and generous appreciation of the Twelfth Quartet, in *Sovetskaya muzïka*,[60] before its public premiere on 14 September in Moscow.

Critics remarked on the novelty in form, language, and technical means of the new quartet, on the composer's unique ability to remain himself while exploring new horizons. There was, indeed, a great deal here that was new and unexpected for Shostakovich's music, not least of which was the considerable dependence on twelve-tone rows for its thematic material, within a broadly tonal context. This was not the cutting edge in Soviet music. Though revered as its elder statesman, a living legend, by now Shostakovich was no longer seen as a pioneer. From the late 1950s through the years of official bluster by the leadership of the Union of Composers—including Shostakovich himself—proclaiming the dangers of dodecaphony and alien avant-garde styles, genuine interest among Soviet musicians in the contemporary trends filtering in from the West had increased steadily, especially among young composers and performers. So had the volume of homegrown "experimental" scores. Shostakovich was not oblivious to these developments. Composer Nikolai Karetnikov even credited him with lending his support and authority to overcome the resistance of the orchestra of the Bolshoy Theater, one of the most conservative bastions of musical tradition, to the staging of Karetnikov's twelve-tone ballet score, *Vanina, Vanini* in 1962.[61]

Shostakovich's adoption of aspects of twelve-tone writing was not an aesthetic volte-face. Isolated examples of twelve-tone rows had already appeared in *Seven Verses of A. Blok* and in the Second Violin Concerto. His propensity for chromatic melodic writing was longstanding. Queried by Tsïganov about the serial elements in his Twelfth Quartet, the composer is said to have commented: "They can also be found in Mozart." [62] In an interview concerning young composers that appeared just before the Twelfth Quartet received its initial screening, Shostakovich's comments highlighted the consistency of his present practice with his lifelong principles:

> As far as the use of strictly technical devices from such musical "systems" as dodecaphony or aleatory is concerned ... everything in good measure. If, let's say, a composer sets himself the obligatory task of writing dodecaphonic music, then he artificially limits his possibilities, his ideas. The use of elements from these complex systems is fully justified if it is dictated by the concept of the composition.... You know, to a certain extent I think the formula "the end justifies the means" is valid in music. All means? All of them, if they contribute to the end objective. [63]

Pressured to name the composers he considered twentieth-century classics, Shostakovich cited Mahler, Prokofiev, Myaskovsky, Stravinsky, Bartók, Berg, and Britten.[64] Nevertheless, he continued to lecture elsewhere on the dangers of "avant-gardism," identified as an antihumanistic, antirealistic direction promoted by a narrow clique of Western musicians.[65]

A few days after the premiere of the Twelfth Quartet, Shostakovich was able to report that it was still producing a strong impression on him. That he had not exhausted the appeal and potential of his new twelve-tone thematicism would become evident when he completed his current work-in-progress, the Sonata for Violin and Piano, op. 134, and subsequent works such as the Fourteenth Symphony and the Thirteenth Quartet. His use of twelve-tone material was one of the symptoms of the increased concentration and austerity, even asceticism, of his late style.

Shostakovich had started composing the Violin Sonata in August at Repino.[66] He hoped to finish it in time to present, tied up with ribbon, to David Oistrakh on his sixtieth birthday, but was late.[67] Not surprisingly, Oistrakh had been fantasizing about a sonata by Shostakovich for some time, but he was not expecting the gift. He figured that after the sixtieth birthday miscue of the previous year, the composer had wanted to make good on his mistake.[68] The Violin Sonata was completed on 23 October 1968.

A month later, Shostakovich sent the touring Oistrakh the violin part and a demonstration tape, anticipating with impatience the moment when he would hear his sonata played with the violinist's unparalleled tone.[69] Oistrakh returned to Moscow in mid-December and the question of a suitable accompanist was broached. Svyatoslav Richter received the nod. Due to scheduling conflicts, however, the public premiere had to be postponed until 3 May 1969 in Moscow. In the meantime, on 8 January, accompanied by Vainberg, Oistrakh unveiled the new sonata to a capacity crowd at a session of the Russian Union of Composers. The response was electric, as it was when Oistrakh and Richter subsequently performed the premieres in Moscow and, on 23 September 1969, in Leningrad.

The previous year, on 24 September 1968, Shostakovich mused in a letter to Glikman: "Tomorrow I will be 62. People at that age love to act coquettish in response to the question: 'If you had it to do all over again would you live your 62 years as you have?' 'Yes, certainly there were failures, there were hardships but, on the whole, I would live these 62 years just the same.' But if that question were to be put to me, I would respond: 'No! A thousand times no!'" [70] Unfortunately, Shostakovich did not expand on what he would have done differently. Surely, though, he would have devoted less of his precious time to the ceremonial functions of public life, like the delivery of opening remarks to the Fourth Congress of the USSR Union of Composers in mid-December 1968. As the Congress wore on, he reported that he was spending days on end attending its sessions, his evenings occupied by the "festive premieres of brilliant new musical compositions." He was not invariably finding the festivities festive. [71]

After the unveiling of his Violin Sonata in January 1969, Shostakovich submitted to another stint in the hospital, a stay made more solitary than usual due to a quarantine for a flu epidemic that kept visitors away. As he informed Glikman on 1 February, he was successfully diverting himself while there by composing an "oratorio" on texts by Federico Garcia Lorca, Guillaume Apollinaire, Rainer Maria Rilke, and Wilhelm Küchelbecker for soprano, bass, and chamber orchestra. [72] From the outset, Shostakovich seems to have envisaged Rudolf Barshai and his Moscow Chamber Orchestra as the medium of choice; without letting on what he was writing, he quizzed Barshai about the possible variables in instrumentation for his ensemble, whether two double basses were manageable, for instance, and how many percussionists. [73] On 16 February, still in the hospital, Shostakovich completed the piano score of his new piece. Reflecting now that "oratorio" was not a suitable designation for a work with no chorus, but that it could not really be called a "symphony" either, Shostakovich admitted that, for the first time in his life, he was in a quandary about what to call a composition. [74] By the time he completed the orchestration of the work's eleven movements, on 2 March 1969, he seems to have resolved the dilemma by designating the work as his Fourteenth Symphony, op. 135.

"It occurred to me that there exist eternal themes, eternal problems. Among them are love and death.... I have never dealt with questions of death. Just before entering the hospital I heard Musorgsky's *Songs and Dances of Death*, and my idea of treating death finally crystallized." Thus Shostakovich described to Glikman, on 19 March, the immediate impulse behind the composition of his Fourteenth Symphony. He reflected additionally that the choice of texts might have been accidental, although he felt they were nonetheless unified by the music.[75] When the composer subsequently made the completion of his new work public, he traced the initial inspiration for his Fourteenth Symphony back even further, to the summer of 1962, when he orchestrated Musorgsky's song cycle. For all the greatness he perceived in Musorgsky's cycle, he said he had been influenced by what he perceived as shortcomings, in particular its brevity.[76] He summarized his underlying motivation, invoking the words of the hero of Nikolai Ostrovsky's hugely successful Soviet novel, *How the Steel Was Tempered*: "Man's dearest possession is life. It is given to him but once, and he must live it so as to feel no torturing regrets for wasted years, never know the burning shame of a mean and petty past; so live that, dying, he might say: all my life, all my strength were given to the finest cause in all the world—the fight for the liberation of mankind."[77] Shostakovich dedicated his new symphony to Benjamin Britten.[78]

As soon as he completed the symphony, Shostakovich summoned Barshai and they began discussing scoring details and vocal casting. Shostakovich suggested Vishnevskaya as soprano, but it took more time to arrive at a decision about the bass soloist. Kondrashin also heard him play the new work. The composer confessed that he had lost several nights' sleep after surrendering it to the copyist, fretting whether he would be able to reconstruct it if it were lost.[79] Shostakovich told Glikman he had written the Fourteenth Symphony very quickly; he had worried that something might happen while he was writing it, that his right hand would finally stop working altogether or he would be struck blind. He felt this work to be one of his landmark compositions, as if everything he had written for the past few years had been leading up to it.[80] Having successfully completed the Fourteenth Symphony, the composer then became fearful he might die before hearing it.

It was Barshai's recollection that the spring and summer were spent in fruitless negotiations with the Moscow and Leningrad Philharmonics, both of which refused categorically to commit their halls for the performance of the Fourteenth Symphony.[81] He offers no explanation for what might have prompted them to take such a stand. Shostakovich's correspondence of the period betrays no undue anxiety about bureaucratic obstacles to the performance. What did occupy the composer during the spring—besides his habitual, if totally unwarranted, apprehension before the successful premiere of the Violin Sonata on 3 May 1969—was supervising the preparation of the performers for his new symphony. As an interim solution, Yevgeniy Vladimirov was chosen as the bass soloist. When, due to her busy touring schedule, Vishnevskaya was unable to learn her part promptly enough for the composer, Shostakovich proposed the substitution of Margarita Miroshnikova. On 10 June, he informed Glikman that rehearsals had begun and the orchestra was sounding marvelous but that the singers were not yet ready and summer vacation was to begin on the 22 June. The musicians would resume work only on 1 September, and they were targeting the premiere date for the end of September.[82] Shostakovich could not wait that long.

At noon on 21 June 1969, a run-through of Shostakovich's Fourteenth Symphony was performed before an overflowing, invited audience in the Small Hall of the Moscow Conservatory. Shostakovich introduced the work, naming and summarizing the import of each of the poems. He also felt the need to explain why he had decided to devote so much attention to such a morbid subject:

> It is not because I am rather old and not because—as an artilleryman would put it—shells are bursting all around me and I am losing my friends and relatives. I should like to recall the words of that remarkable Soviet writer Ostrovsky, who said that life is given to us only once, so we should live it honestly and handsomely in all respects and never commit base acts. In part, I am trying to polemicize with the great classics who touched upon the theme of death in their work. Remember the death of Boris Godunov. When Boris Godunov has died, a kind of brightening sets in. Remember Verdi's *Otello*. When the whole tragedy ends and Desdemona and Otello die, we also experience a beauteous serenity. Remember *Aida*. When the tragic demise of the hero and heroine occurs, it is assuaged by radiant music. I think that even among our contemporaries ... take for instance the outstanding English composer, Benjamin Britten. I would also fault him in his *War Requiem*....
>
> It seems to me that all this stems from various kinds of religious teachings that have suggested that as bad as life might be, when you die everything will be fine; what awaits you there is absolute peace. So it seems to me that perhaps, in part, I am following in the footsteps of the great Russian composer Musorgsky. His cycle *Songs and Dances of Death*—maybe not all of it, but at least "The Field Marshal"—is a great protest against death and a reminder to live one's life honestly, nobly, decently, never committing base acts.... [Death] awaits all of us. I don't see anything good about such an end to our lives and this is what I am trying to convey in this work.[83]

The performance, sung by Miroshnikova and Vladimirov, was superb. Shostakovich reported that it made a strong impression on the audience as well as on himself. The event became indelibly etched in the memories of those who attended, however, not so much because of its musical quality, or because of the impact of Shostakovich's original and profoundly disturbing musical treatment of the theme of death, but because of an incident that took place during the performance. As the fifth movement, "On Watch," was being played, a man sitting near the front of the auditorium rose and noisily made his exit.[84] The composer had requested the audience to be as quiet as possible because the performance was being taped, so the highly disruptive behavior of Pavel Apostolov—specialist in military music and longtime Communist Party functionary—was interpreted by many as a deliberate act of protest. It was only after the performance, when the departing listeners saw the prostrate Apostolov being tended to by a doctor in the foyer, that they realized he must have suffered a heart attack or a stroke. It was generally presumed that he had expired on the spot, or on the way to the hospital, but his actual date of death is recorded as 19 July 1969, almost a month after the symphony's run-through.[85] All the same, in light of the theme of the symphony and the tenor of Shostakovich's introductory remarks, everyone was gripped by the mystical sense that some sort of divine retribution had been visited on one of the "villains" of the Soviet music community.

Shostakovich vacationed with Irina in Dilizhan during July and, in early August, they traveled by train to Irkutsk with Alexander Kholodilin—friend of the composer and his longtime administrative assistant—where they took up residence at a local sanatorium and relished the indescribable beauty of Lake Baikal. At the end of the trip, Shostakovich flew to Ulan-Ude, where he was feted by local musicians and made a People's Artist of the Buryat ASSR. On his return to Moscow, Shostakovich found himself confronted with the disagreeable business of mediating between feuding divas; Vishnevskaya and Miroshnikova were both demanding to sing the official premiere of the Fourteenth Symphony. With Barshai's assistance, they arrived at the amicable compromise of having two pairs of soloists for the two consecutive performances scheduled each in Moscow and Leningrad.[86]

Shostakovich was on hand for the Leningrad premiere of his Violin Sonata on 23 September 1969. Two days later, the composer hosted a supper in Repino—on the occasion of his sixty-third birthday—for a small circle of intimates. Finally, on 29 September, after dozens of rehearsals, the much-anticipated public premiere of the Fourteenth Symphony took place at the Leningrad Capella performed by Galina Vishnevskaya, Yevgeniy Vladimirov, and the Moscow Chamber Orchestra under Barshai's direction. News about the extraordinary work (and perhaps about its "mystical" properties) had spread rapidly. Glikman recalls that the event was surrounded by quite a hubbub and scrambling for scarce tickets. The hall was packed not only with the cream of musical Leningrad but with prominent cultural figures rarely seen at concerts. Performed superbly, the symphony produced an overwhelming impression. The final piercing crescendo slowly evaporated into an intense silence, after which a clamorous ovation erupted.[87] Although the Moscow premiere of the Fourteenth Symphony, which took place on 6 October 1969 in the Large Hall of the Moscow Conservatory, was greeted with equally demonstrative ovations and attracted even greater attention from the national press, Shostakovich was personally disappointed by the lower quality of the performance, sung by Vishnevskaya and Mark Reshetin. He complained that Vishnevskaya had flubbed up badly twice and at one point Barshai had let the orchestra fall apart.[88] For all his devotion to Vishnevskaya, after subsequent performances Shostakovich concluded that he thought Miroshnikova and Vladimirov performed the work better than their doubles, Vishnevskaya and Reshetin,[89] although it was the latter pair who traveled to the Aldeburgh Festival to perform the Western premiere of the Fourteenth Symphony on 14 June 1970 with the English Chamber Orchestra under the baton of the dedicatee, Benjamin Britten.

Shostakovich's dedication of the Fourteenth Symphony was not simply a token of professional respect. In a real sense, it was his creative response to the *War Requiem*, a work he considered "nearly" great. For the nonbeliever Shostakovich, where the genius of Britten's requiem flagged was in its offer of consolation in the hereafter, eternal rest, the promise of "In paradisum deducant te Angeli" (May the angels lead thee into Paradise) contained in the final measures of Britten's score. Once, after listening intently to the recording of the *War Requiem*, Shostakovich had been heard to remark: "You can't achieve anything without God." When asked if he believed in God, his reply was swift and firm: "No, and I am very sorry about it." [90] As unprecedented and unexpected as was this unvarnished musical treatment of death, it is not surprising that some people found (and continue to find) the stark realism of Shostakovich's Fourteenth Symphony and its denial of spiritual redemption profoundly disturbing. Polish composer Krzysztof Meyer, who attended the Moscow premiere of the Fourteenth Symphony, observed that, for all the ovations, the audience seemed a bit dismayed by the work.[91] As improbable as it may sound, it was ostensibly the bleak message of the finale of Shostakovich's Fourteenth Symphony that prompted Lev Lebedinsky to break off his friendship with the composer once and for all.[92] Aleksandr Solzhenitsyn took umbrage not so much at the atheistic position as at the inclusion of the setting of Apollinaire's "In the Santé Jail," because he felt the suffering the French poet endured during his own brief incarceration could not begin to compare with the sufferings of the millions of victims of the Soviet Gulag.[93]

Preoccupation with failing health and intimations of mortality are often adduced as the underlying motives behind the composition of Shostakovich's Fourteenth Symphony. Actually, although he was hospitalized when he set out to compose the symphony, after so many years of steady physical deterioration he had recently found new cause for optimism. The miraculous cure of Olympic and world record high jumper Valeriy

Brumel—sidelined three years earlier with serious compound fractures of his right leg (sustained originally in a motorcycle accident and reinjured forthwith) that the finest surgeons had been unable to heal—gave the composer hope that the little-known Siberian orthopedic surgeon, Gavriil Ilizarov, who had effected this miracle with a pioneering procedure, might be able to help him as well, perhaps restoring the use of his right hand: "I don't want to jump. But I want to board buses, trolleybuses, trams. I want not to die from fright when I step on the escalator in the metro. I want to take staircases with ease. My desires are modest." [94] Shostakovich's wish to consult with the doctor without delay did not work out; while he waited, he brooded over whether his case really fell within Ilizarov's competency.

In the autumn of 1969, when he spent another long stretch in a Moscow hospital, the mysterious ailment that had plagued Shostakovich since 1958—robbing him of the control and mobility of his limbs—was finally diagnosed as a rare form of poliomyelitis. As grateful as he was for the clarity that was finally shed on the situation, it decreased the probable efficacy of Ilizarov's therapy and depressed the composer: "This children's disease sometimes affects even people of advanced age. Now I need to get used to the notion that to cure poliomyelitis is extremely difficult. I must alter my psyche to the psyche of a sick man." [95] Released from the hospital in time to celebrate the new year feeling slightly better, but concerned about how quickly he would weaken and impressed not at all by the wisdom displayed by the "Moscow luminaries" treating him, Shostakovich resolved nonetheless to go to Kurgan in Siberia and consult with Dr. Ilizarov.

Immortality

15

Full of anticipation, Shostakovich flew with Irina to Kurgan at the end of February 1970 and began treatment with Dr. Ilizarov in March, expecting his stay to last about six weeks. He was soon reporting progress to correspondents. By the end of the month he wrote to Shaginyan that he was feeling better, his legs and arms were somewhat stronger, and he was playing the piano, even playing it fast and loud, something he had not been able to manage for three or four years.[1] After having undergone a simple operation, his treatment consisted of a combination of strenuous physical exercise and medication. He provided Glikman with a detailed breakdown of his daily schedule: 7 AM, wake-up; 7–8 AM, washing, shaving, exercises, listening to the news; 8:30, breakfast; 9:15, one-hour walk in the woods; 11–12:30, vigorous gymnastics and massage; 1:30 PM, lunch; 3:30, another walk in the woods; 5 PM, return to hospital. He also was receiving an injection every three days.[2] He raved about the "miracle-working" Dr. Ilizarov to everyone.

By May, Shostakovich's condition was continuing to improve and he had regained enough strength to be given the hope that he could return to Moscow, completely healthy, in June. Among the achievements he now boasted of were climbing staircases, boarding buses (albeit with difficulty), shaving with his right hand, buttoning buttons, and not losing the spoon on the way to his mouth.[3] Being able to play the piano again was an accomplishment with special significance. Although he realized it would take time to recapture his technique, Shostakovich fantasized about the possibility of performing in public again in the upcoming season.

Shostakovich was not released from the hospital in time to exercise his customary ceremonial function, as chairman of the organizing committee, of opening the Fourth International Chaikovsky Competition in Moscow on 2 June 1970. A formal greeting to the participants was published in his name, and since he had not been seen in public in more than three months, a reporter was dispatched to track him down in Kurgan. Ilizarov confirmed that the composer's health was markedly improved and the astonished reporter described a Shostakovich who looked twenty years younger, hale and energetic, with a firm handshake. The first words out of the composer's mouth were, "I can play the piano again!" At this stage he was able to compose in the mornings and was practicing the piano two or three hours a day, expecting to return home in a couple of weeks.[4]

Another milestone that passed while Shostakovich was being treated in Kurgan was the celebration of the one hundredth anniversary of Lenin's birth on 21 April 1970. It was not, however, a milestone overlooked by the composer. As early as December 1968, he had appealed to his colleagues to compose stirring musical tributes for the occasion; he was already thinking about his own contribution for the upcoming jubilee.[5] In April 1969, he declared he was beginning work on an oratorio to commemorate the event.[6] The work he eventually produced was *Loyalty*, eight ballads for male chorus, op. 136, on texts by Dolmatovsky. Exactly when he began composing it is unknown. Dolmatovsky recalled that, having been asked by the composer to reflect on what Lenin meant to them, they met several times in the quiet of Shostakovich's Moscow apartment, after which the poet distilled the essence of their conversations into verse. He remembered that Shostakovich worked on his cycle in Moscow, Leningrad, and Kurgan. (In January 1970, Shostakovich credited Dolmatovsky with having pulled the strings that got him accepted as a patient at Ilizarov's clinic.[7]) Exactly when Shostakovich completed *Loyalty* is also unclear; he informed Dolmatovsky of its completion by letter from Kurgan in April 1970.[8]

Shostakovich dedicated his choral ballads, which elevate Lenin above God, Confucius, Buddha, and Allah as an object of devotion, to Gustav Ernesaks, founding director of the State Academic Male Chorus of Estonia. He had learned that Shostakovich was writing a major work for men's chorus from the newspaper and was flattered by the composer's unexpected attention. Although there was some presumption that the new work should be unveiled at the Lenin jubilee concert, Shostakovich was unwilling to rush the preparation. Ernesaks set the premiere for the end of the year; the composer traveled to Tallinn to assist in the rehearsals and attend the first performance on 5 December 1970. In conjunction with the Moscow premiere of *Loyalty*, on 25 February 1971, Shostakovich was interviewed for television: "It seems to me that Dolmatovsky's words, on which my ballads are based, contain serious, very heartfelt lyrical reflections about Lenin, about the Motherland, about the Party. This is not the first time I have treated this theme.... And I think it will not be my last work about Vladimir Ilyich. In the future I will most certainly strive to embody the image of this great man."[9] In 1974, Shostakovich was awarded a Glinka Prize (the State Prize of the Russian Federation) for *Loyalty* and for his Fourteenth String Quartet, op. 142.

If Shostakovich was comparatively tightlipped during the composition of *Loyalty*, he was more forthcoming about his progress on another concurrent project, the music for Kozintsev's film version of *King Lear*. After the success of their most recent collaboration on *Hamlet*, Kozintsev had invited the composer to work on *King Lear* in 1968, promising the reluctant, ailing composer that less music would be required of him. Shostakovich later admitted that he had wanted to turn down the invitation, but his love of Shakespeare, the cinema, and his friend Kozintsev had swayed his decision.[10] Shostakovich's initial involvement with *Lear* dated from Kozintsev's 1941 stage production; his re-engagement with the subject now may have been spurred by a grander design. In a letter to Shaginyan written in December 1968, just as Kozintsev was gearing up to shoot the film, Shostakovich spoke about his forthcoming collaboration as "the first sketch for my composition about Lear."[11] The ambition of an independent musical work on the Lear theme was never realized.

Shostakovich consulted with Kozintsev in Leningrad in January 1970, before his departure for Kurgan, and once his regimen at Ilizarov's clinic and his energy permitted it, he sent for the *King Lear* materials. When he was interviewed at the beginning of June, he indicated that he had been working all this time on the music for the film and was almost done. Kozintsev kept him supplied with necessary material by post, but the difficult long-distance collaboration was only accomplished at the expense of protracted intercity phone calls between composer and director.[12] In late June, after his release from the clinic, Shostakovich returned to Leningrad to complete his work for the film and supervise the taping of the music.

In a statement issued in mid-June to constituents in the city of Gorky (who had just re-elected him as their deputy to the USSR Supreme Soviet) Shostakovich professed to be in good spirits, with a great desire to work.[13] During July, Kozintsev took note of the difficulty with which Shostakovich made his way from his cottage in Repino to his car, and the stark contrast it made to the energetic and apparently effortless manner with which he threw himself into a grueling nine-hour day once he arrived at the recording studio. The next morning the composer greeted Kozintsev with the comment: "You know, music is my soul, as Glinka said. Yesterday I managed to forget about everything and, you know, I felt really fine. One needs to devote oneself to business."[14]

Even before the successful public release of *King Lear* in February 1971, Shostakovich was able to report to Kozintsev the enthusiastic praise the film generated among viewers at private screenings. Kozintsev and Shostakovich would plan one more collaboration, a film based on Gogol's *Petersburg Tales*, in preparation for which Shostakovich sent the director tape and score of *The Nose* in the spring of 1973. The news of Kozintsev's death that May came as a devastating blow to the composer.

At the end of August 1970, Shostakovich returned to Kurgan for a second round of treatment. Beforehand, on 10 August, he put the finishing touches on another new work, his Thirteenth Quartet, op. 138. Continuing the pattern of dedicating his recent string quartets to the founding members of the Beethoven Quartet, Shostakovich wrote to Vadim Borisovsky, the former violist of the ensemble, asking him to accept the quartet as a belated gift for his seventieth birthday.[15] The composer returned from Kurgan at the beginning of November, in plenty of time to rehearse the new quartet with the Beethoven Quartet as customary and to attend the Leningrad premiere on 13 December, repeated in Moscow a week later. Glikman recalled that the audience in Leningrad remained standing after the initial performance of the Thirteenth Quartet until the musicians repeated the quartet, a stark one-movement work whose prominent role for solo viola and close relationship to the Fourteenth Symphony did not go unremarked. Four months later, when Benjamin Britten and Peter Pears made what would be their last visit to Moscow, they were deeply moved by the private performance in the composer's apartment (repeated on request) of Shostakovich's latest quartet opus.[16]

Shostakovich clung to the promise of a cure. In late September 1970, he wrote Shaginyan from Kurgan that he expected his strength and capacity for work would soon be completely restored. He still had many plans, as he made clear in his last conversation with Flora Litvinova, which took place later that fall in Ruza: "But I myself am not ready to die. I still have a lot of music to write." It was on this occasion, too, in a rare moment of retrospective candor, that Shostakovich speculated how, had circumstances been otherwise, his career might have evolved differently: "You ask if I would have been different without 'Party guidance'? Yes, almost certainly. No doubt the line I was pursuing when I wrote the Fourth Symphony would have been stronger and sharper in my work. I would have displayed more brilliance, used more sarcasm, I could have revealed my ideas openly instead of having to resort to camouflage; I would have written more pure music."[17] That he was still physically weak, tiring easily when he tried to play the piano, was noted by Litvinova. When he saw Shostakovich in Leningrad in December 1970, Glikman observed that he walked with difficulty and his right hand was as weak as ever.[18]

In October 1970, it was announced that Aleksandr Solzhenitsyn had been awarded the Nobel Prize for Literature. Predictably, this was followed by an intensification of the campaign in the Soviet press against the embattled author, who had been expelled from the Union of Writers the previous year. Rostropovich, who with his wife Vishnevskaya had offered refuge to Solzhenitsyn in the guest house at their Zhukovka dacha, felt compelled to send an open letter of protest to four Soviet newspapers. Although his letter was not published in any of them, it leaked out to the West where it made headline news.[19] Interpreted as an anti-Soviet act, it brought its author into direct confrontation with the State. Steps were taken to control the damage. In a letter reporting the reaction of prominent musicians to Rostropovich's deed, an official of the Ministry of Culture advised the Central Committee that, in conversation, Shostakovich had denounced Rostropovich's act in no uncertain terms, taking particular exception to the latter's invocation of his own name and the criticism his music had been subjected to in years past. His words were quoted: "We must do everything possible to save Slava, he is our pride, our country made his name and his world fame." Shostakovich even volunteered to go to West Germany, where Rostropovich was then on tour, to talk to him, but quickly retracted the offer on account of his ill health. His views were deemed to be in complete accord with the "correct, Party position" on the matter.[20]

That Shostakovich's persistent stance of nonresistance to authority—assumed during the Stalinist period—placed him at odds with his natural allies among the increasingly outspoken creative intelligentsia of Brezhnev's Russia was a painful fact that could not escape him. In her memoirs, Vishnevskaya recalls that he often advised them: "Don't waste your efforts. Work, play. You're living here, in this country, and you must see everything as it really is. Don't create illusions. There's no other life. There can't be any. Just be thankful that you're still allowed to breathe!"[21] Although he is reported to have professed deep admiration for Solzhenitsyn's literary art (and after its publication in *Noviy mir* he considered writing an opera on "Matryona's House"), Shostakovich did not establish a friendship with Solzhenitsyn even after the latter became his neighbor at Zhukovka. In 1965, Shostakovich was signatory to a petition requesting an apartment in Moscow for Solzhenitsyn,[22] but he could not support his defiant public exhibition of political dissidence. Conversely, although friends like Rostropovich and Vishnevskaya were able to make allowances for Shostakovich's behavior, Solzhenitsyn manifested scant tolerance for the composer's moral impotence and servile complicity.[23] After the Soviet invasion of Czechoslovakia in the summer of 1968, Solzhenitsyn toyed with the idea of soliciting signatures of prominent Soviet cultural figures on a letter of protest, but he dropped it on realizing how hopeless a task it would be to persuade them to sign: "The shackled genius Shostakovich would thrash about like a wounded thing, clasp himself with tightly folded arms so that his fingers could not hold a pen." [24]

Shostakovich, too, won a prize in autumn 1970. On 10 November, at a festive evening honoring the Soviet militia, his prize-winning opus in a contest cosponsored by the Ministry of Internal Affairs and the Union of Soviet Writers, *March of the Soviet Militia*, op. 139, received its first performance.[25] Another brief ceremonial work, *Intervision*, for orchestra, was broadcast on television in March 1971, on the eve of the Twenty-fourth Congress of the Communist Party of the Soviet Union, to which Shostakovich was a delegate.

When, after a five-month gap, Glikman saw Shostakovich in Moscow in May 1971, he detected neither significant deterioration in his friend's condition nor conspicuous traces of benefit from his Siberian treatments. Together with his wife, Shostakovich returned to Kurgan for the better part of the month of June; he reported to Shaginyan after two weeks there that Ilizarov was helping a great deal, although his right arm still was not working well.[26] After the stifling heat of the capital, Shostakovich found the temperate climate invigorating; in addition to pursuing his therapy, he composed the first movement of a new symphony, his Fifteenth. Although the composer dated its composition to the summer months, Khentova contends its framework had already been sketched on 2 April 1971.[27] The sketches she describes also evidently include the incomplete setting, for bass and piano, of Yevtushenko's then unpublished poem, "Yelabuga Nail," about the suicide of Marina Tsvetayeva. When they got together in May, Shostakovich told Glikman that he had set the poem, but his setting has yet to be published.[28]

Shostakovich pressed forward with the composition of his symphony in Repino, where he spent the month of July. When Glikman visited him there on 13 July, the composer was in elevated spirits, having completed the second and most of the third movement.[29] He felt it necessary to forewarn Glikman that the Fifteenth, his first "pure" symphony—one with neither program nor text—since the Tenth some eighteen years earlier, "is turning out lacking in ideological content, something along the lines of my Ninth." A few days later they discussed the propriety of employing musical quotations, on which the composer was relying extensively in this work. Shostakovich could not explain why, but he found himself wholly unable to resist them.[30] On the eve of his return to Moscow, on 29 July 1971, Shostakovich completed the score of the fourth and final movement of his

Symphony no. 15 in A Major, op. 141. He described to Shaginyan the eyestrain that his intense absorption with its composition had caused and the feeling of creative emptiness left in the wake of its completion.[31] In an interview two years later, Shostakovich identified the Fifteenth Symphony as one of those works that was completely clear to him from the very start, from which he could not tear himself away until it had been written down.[32]

In mid-September—as his sixty-fifth birthday approached, a milestone commemorated by the award of the Order of the October Revolution— Shostakovich suffered a second heart attack and found himself back in the hospital. The concert season at Moscow Conservatory's Large Hall opened without him on 25 September with a concert of his music— Symphony no. 7 and the Second Violin Concerto—conducted by his son, Maxim. The premiere by Maxim of his new, Fifteenth Symphony was advertised as two weeks hence.[33] The composer's medical condition provided reason enough for a postponement.

Shostakovich spent two months in the hospital, missing the Seventh International Music Congress in Moscow in early October, attended by distinguished musicians from forty-three countries. Shostakovich's official contribution to the Congress, "National Traditions and the Precepts of Their Development," was distributed in his absence. On his release from the hospital in mid-November, he transferred to the Barvikha sanatorium for a month, which seemed like heaven by comparison. He reported to Glikman that his heart was doing well, but his legs and arms had weakened noticeably. The benefits of his Kurgan treatments had been lost, and he feared he would have to start all over again from scratch. The good news was that the premiere of his Fifteenth Symphony was now set for early in the new year.[34]

Commuting to the city from the dacha at Zhukovka in late December and early January 1972, Shostakovich attended every rehearsal of his new symphony. This was the first major premiere he had entrusted to Maxim, whose substantial strides as a conductor he had been following closely and with paternal pride. He was pleased with how Maxim was handling the preparation of the symphony with the Large Symphony Orchestra of All-Union Radio and TV and hopeful that the premiere would come off well.[35] After an unforeseen hitch—the late arrival of a replacement musician— that forced a delay in the dress rehearsal in the morning, on the evening of 8 January 1972, the Large Hall of the Moscow Conservatory was packed with "all Moscow" for the unveiling of Shostakovich's latest symphony. Glikman, who sat next to Shostakovich, noted that the composer appeared calm on the surface. During pauses, he whispered that Maxim was doing fine. At the end, the audience gave father and son a prolonged standing ovation.[36]

Even before its premiere, the Fifteenth Symphony had been given an official seal of approval. Union of Composers Chairman Tikhon Khrennikov evaluated it as "one of the most profound of Shostakovich's works. It is full of optimism, the affirmation of life, belief in man's inexhaustible strength." [37] Critics rallied to produce more commentary on the Fifteenth Symphony than had been written about either of Shostakovich's two previous symphonies. Beyond explicating its evident musical merits, its conjunctions with earlier symphonies, as well as the startling contrasts, there was an undeniable fascination with attempts to decode the hidden meaning behind the composer's organic incorporation of musical quotations as disparate as the galop from Rossini's *William Tell Overture* (in the first movement) and the "fate" motive from Wagner's "Ring" cycle (in the last). While Shostakovich vouchsafed no program for the symphony, after the Fifteenth Symphony was screened at the Composers' Union in the fall of 1971, he inflamed speculation by describing the first movement by means of metaphors of childhood, likening it to "a toy store." At least one critic found the implication of carefree innocence here deceptive, concluding that if this was a toy store, at the very least it was one that had been locked up for the night and whose toys were clearly inclined to mutiny against the tyranny of the evil store owner.[38]

The Fifteenth Symphony was soon performed in other Russian cities and around the globe. The Leningrad premiere was of particular concern to Shostakovich. In early April 1972, he asked Glikman to scout out surreptitiously whether Mravinsky was intending to perform the symphony and, if so, when, so that he could plan to attend the final rehearsals. His own relations with the conductor were still strained. He was troubled by the possibility that Mravinsky might not be in complete creative sympathy and might behave as churlishly as he had over the Thirteenth Symphony and the Second Cello Concerto.[39] His misgivings proved unwarranted. Shostakovich went to Leningrad in late April to attend the rehearsals for the local premiere of the Fifteenth Symphony, which took place on 5 May; he marveled at Mravinsky's mastery as a conductor. The latter's performances of the Fifteenth Symphony in Leningrad produced a response no less electric than in Moscow.

Over the past several years, ill health had significantly curbed Shostakovich's ability and desire to travel. In what was his first trip abroad in over six years, in May 1972 the frail composer traveled with Irina to Berlin for the performance of his Fifteenth Symphony by the USSR State Symphony conducted by Yevgeniy Svetlanov, taking in while there a performance of Gershwin's *Porgy and Bess* at the Komische Oper. Then he was welcomed for two weeks of therapy and relaxation in Gohrisch, where twelve years earlier he had composed his Eighth Quartet. Before returning home, Shostakovich attended a performance of Stockhausen's *Hymnen* in

Berlin, reporting later to Glikman that he found it strange and perplexing but with some curious sounds that might be effectively exploited to mysterious effect.[40]

At home, Shostakovich barely had time to unpack before he and Irina were off to Leningrad to board the *Baltika*, sailing on 31 June on a round-trip voyage to England. The composer was an honored, if undemanding, guest on board ship. One of the crew recalled that his only special request was for the repair of his old transistor radio; he wanted to follow the progress of the Spassky-Fischer chess championship set to get under way in Reykjavik.[41] On arrival in London, Shostakovich flew directly to Dublin, Ireland, where he was awarded an honorary doctorate in music by Trinity College. Among other activities scheduled in honor of his visit, Shostakovich was received for an audience by aging Irish President Eamon de Valera. On his return to London, he was received there by British Prime Minister Edward Heath. The real highlight for the composer was his visit with Britten in Aldeburgh—his only visit there—where the Shostakoviches spent two nights. Britten shared with him his work on his as yet incomplete opera, *Death in Venice*.

Loss of health notwithstanding, Shostakovich retained a high public profile. He continued in his longtime ceremonial role as chairman of the Soviet-Austrian Society, extolling the fruits of the nations' cultural cooperation and exchange. He was appointed chairman of the commissions to celebrate the jubilees of Beethoven (1970), Scriabin (1972), and Rachmaninoff (1973), although he can hardly have been motivated by his sense of close aesthetic rapport when he accepted the assignments for the latter two composers. In early October 1972, Shostakovich went to Baku for a celebration of Russian literature and art; his Fifteenth Symphony was performed and he was awarded the title People's Artist of Azerbaijan. A month later he departed once again for London, where on 20 November 1972, as part of an extensive festival of Russian and Soviet music, Maxim conducted the British premiere of the Fifteenth Symphony and Oistrakh performed the First Violin Concerto. In a side trip, Shostakovich traveled up to York to help the young members of the Fitzwilliam Quartet refine their interpretation of his Thirteenth Quartet.

All this traveling came with a price tag. Shostakovich spent the month between his trips to Baku and London in the sanatorium, recouping his strength. He confided to Glikman that the awful heat in Baku had made this stay necessary, that he had little energy and really did not want to go to England. His own desires, however, were not being taken into consideration and he was being forced to go.[42] Shortly after his return, early in December 1972 he found himself back in the hospital, this time complaining of kidney stones. But a routine exam on the eve of his discharge disclosed a cyst in his

left lung, and his doctor confirmed a diagnosis of lung cancer. Shostakovich remained in the hospital until the beginning of February 1973 un-
dergoing radiation treatment.

As depressing as was the experience of his own gradual physical debilita-
tion, Shostakovich clung to life. He suffered the deaths of the valued friends
and colleagues of a lifetime with an undiminished sense of loss: his long-
time secretary, Zinaída Gayamova, and helper Alexander Kholodilin
(1971); composer Gavriil Popov, conductor Nikolai Rabinovich, and violist
Vadim Borisovsky (1972); composer Levon Atovmyan, film director
Grigoriy Kozintsev, and his elder sister Mariya (1973); pianist Lev Oborin,
cellist Sergey Shirinsky, and violinist David Oistrakh (1974). He was increasingly called upon to contribute reminiscences to memorial volumes.
But what upset him more than anything else, nevertheless, was the inability
to compose. "I am almost totally helpless in everyday matters,"
Shostakovich wrote Glikman from hospital on 16 January 1973. "I can't
dress or wash by myself, and so on. Some kind of spring has sprung in my
brain. Since the Fifteenth Symphony, I haven't composed a single note. That
is a dreadful circumstance for me." [43]

Even while unable to compose, he continued thinking about it.
Shostakovich had recently conceived the notion of writing an opera on
Chekhov's story, "The Black Monk." Shostakovich's fondness for Chekhov,
and his partiality for this particular story, had endured since his boyhood. It
was not uncommon for him to spontaneously declaim long passages from
Chekhov's works, or to fashion conversational analogies with reference to
Chekhovian characters and predicaments. In 1943, he pronounced "The
Black Monk" "one of the most musical works of Russian literature, written
almost as a sonata," [44] and at around the same time he suggested it as an operatic subject to his student, Revol Bunin. In 1960, he amplified his remark
about "The Black Monk," saying that he perceived it as a piece written in sonata form. [45] Late in 1971, a literary scholar had jogged Shostakovich's
memory about these observations, [46] and this is possibly what reawakened
his interest in an operatic setting of the story.

At any rate, in September 1972, Shostakovich finally became acquainted
with the *Leggenda Valacca* (Angel's Serenade) by Gaetano Braga, a salon
piece enormously popular around the turn of the century, the performance
of which is specifically mentioned by Chekhov in "The Black Monk." [47]
Visiting with Glikman in Repino on 11 April 1973, Shostakovich told him
that having undertaken to write an opera on Chekhov's story, he had had
someone scout out the music for Braga's piece. He thought that it provided
him with the kernel for his future opera. But he added that *The Black Monk*
would be a hard opera to write because it would have little action. [48]
Whether he made any significant inroads on its composition before his

death is unknown. What he did complete was the arrangement of Braga's "Serenade" for soprano, mezzo-soprano, violin (as specified in Chekhov's story), and piano.

Shostakovich had this discussion with Glikman on the eve of his departure from Repino after a two-and-a-half-week stay. Earlier, on completion of his radiation treatment in February, he and Irina had been whisked to Berlin for the premiere of *Katerina Izmailova* at the Deutsche Staatsoper and to attend other performances, including one of *The Nose*, also at the Staatsoper, during the Fourth Berlin Biennial. Returning home, he had checked into hospital again to monitor the efficacy of the radiation treatments. Once he reached Repino, however, his long creative dry spell finally came to an end and his spirits soared as a consequence. Mravinsky recorded in his diary visiting with the composer the morning of the latter's arrival on 23 March 1973. The anxious composer complained then, as he had frequently in the period since the completion of his Fifteenth Symphony: "For two years I haven't written a single note.... Well, I'm not drinking, lying the whole time in hospitals. I want to start drinking." He proposed they share a drink then and there.[49] Two days later, an ebullient Shostakovich was already toasting the return of his muse.[50] When he returned home to Moscow on 12 April, he had a movement and a half of a new quartet in hand. Completion of the final, third, movement was dated 23 April 1973. Shostakovich dedicated his String Quartet no. 14 in F-sharp Major, op. 142, to Sergey Shirinsky, cellist of the Beethoven Quartet, thus rounding out the series of quartets (nos. 11–14) dedicated to the founding members of the ensemble. Shostakovich personalized this dedication by spelling out the musical equivalent of the dedicatee's name in the opening theme of the third movement, as well as imbedding in it a quote from Act IV of *Katerina Izmailova* ("Seryozha, my fine one").

On completion of his new quartet, Shostakovich was obliged to set it aside to embark on another lengthy foreign odyssey. The month of May was spent in Denmark, where Shostakovich was feted as the winner of the annual Sonning Prize. The composer announced that he was donating the prize money, 60,000 kroner, to the Soviet Peace Fund; in a show of gratitude for this, he was awarded a certificate and medal by the chairman of the Soviet Peace Fund in September. On the musical agenda, Shostakovich attended rehearsals and the premiere performances of the production of *Katerina Izmailova* by Copenhagen's Royal Opera, as well as a performance of his Fifteenth Symphony, conducted by Maxim, in a concert of his music at the Conservatory. He met with Danish composers and listened to their works. He also had time for a little sightseeing; of special interest was the tour of the sites associated with Shakespeare's *Hamlet*.

From Copenhagen, Shostakovich and his wife traveled to Le Havre, where they boarded the liner *Mikhaíl Lermontov* for its maiden trans-Atlantic passage to New York (the first Soviet ship to enter New York harbor in twenty-five years), docking on 11 June 1973. The ostensible purpose of Shostakovich's third, and last, visit to the United States was to accept an honorary doctorate to be awarded by Northwestern University in Evanston, Illinois. While in New York, Shostakovich attended a performance of *Aida* at the Metropolitan Opera as well as the inaugural evening of Pierre Boulez's "rug concerts" with the New York Philharmonic. (He appreciated the quality of the music-making, but thought the spectacle of an audience lounging around on cushions manifested a disrespectful attitude toward the music.) The Shostakoviches traveled by train to Chicago, and on 16 June, in sweltering heat Shostakovich could barely tolerate, he was invested with Northwestern's honorary degree with all due pomp.

All along the way, Shostakovich's hosts and escorts kept a close eye on the precarious state of his health. Medical contingencies were readied. Irina Shostakovich has indicated that there was a hidden agenda behind this trip to America, so visibly stressful for the composer. She had wanted her husband to be examined by American doctors, but Minister of Culture Ekaterina Furtseva and the Russian doctors had screamed that the trip would kill him. When the invitation from Northwestern arrived, Furtseva proceeded to authorize it, forgetting about her earlier tirade. So, when asked by the State Department on arrival if they had any special requests, the Shostakoviches asked to visit the National Institute of Health in Bethesda, Maryland. They were taken there for two days of tests and consultations en route from Chicago back to New York.[51] Publicity surrounding the arrival of Leonid Brezhnev for a state visit on 16 June 1973 helped screen this unscheduled deviation in the itinerary from media scrutiny. Just a few days earlier, Shostakovich had boasted aboard the *Mikhaíl Lermontov* that he was planning to live another 100 years.[52] The American doctors the composer had hoped might offer him a fresh lease on life delivered, instead, the verdict, "incurable": progressive neurological disorder, combined with heart trouble. Shostakovich took the news stoically.[53]

After the long and difficult journey, Shostakovich was eager to get home to rehearse and perform his Fourteenth Quartet. However, due to a serious leg injury sustained by Nikolai Zabavnikov, the second violinist of the Beethoven Quartet, its performance was postponed indefinitely. When the remaining members of the group came over to Shostakovich's place one day to acquaint themselves with the new opus, Shostakovich played the second violin part himself on the piano. As Fyodor Druzhinin recalled, the composer was visibly excited both because of his pleasure at how the work had turned out and because of his unexpected good fortune in playing as part of the Beethoven Quartet, even with one finger.[54] He drew attention to what he called his "Italian" bit in the second movement, a ravishing, if uncharacteristically sentimental duet for cello and violin; its kinship to his arrangement of the Braga "Serenade" is surely not accidental. After introducing the Fourteenth Quartet at the Union of Composers in Moscow on 30 October, the Beethoven Quartet gave the public premiere in Leningrad on 12 November 1973. Two days later they performed it in Moscow during the Third Congress of the Composers' Union of the RSFSR; the Fourteenth Quartet received its "official" Moscow premiere on 18 November 1973.

Shostakovich and his wife had spent the month of August 1973 living peacefully in Pärnu, Estonia. Within his first week there Shostakovich composed a suite of settings for contralto and piano, *Six Verses of Marina Tsvetayeva*, op. 143, completing it on 7 August. His selection of verses was made from the first major Soviet collection of Tsvetayeva's poetry, which had appeared in 1965.[55] In 1970, the composer had become acquainted with Tishchenko's *Three Songs on Verses of Tsvetayeva*, op. 48, and was impressed enough to request a copy, which he played and sang over and over again.[56] Not long after that, it will be recalled, he made a setting of Yevtushenko's reflections on Tsvetayeva's suicide, "Yelabuga Nail." Among the particular poems by Tsvetayeva Shostakovich now chose to set were several that allowed him to intersect with other poets (Shakespeare, Pushkin) and revisit themes (*Hamlet*, the artist versus the tyrant) that had engaged him repeatedly in the past. The words of Tsvetayeva also gave him the opportunity to pay musical homage to a great contemporary poet whose verses he never set: Anna Akhmatova.[57]

Shostakovich began contemplating potential vocalists for his suite, fancying a young Leningrad singer affiliated with the Kirov Theater, Irina Bogachyova, about whom he knew only from a radio broadcast. Early in the fall, he sent her a petition plying the humble suit of his vocal suite, promising that if she would agree to consider singing it, he would come to Leningrad whenever convenient to acquaint her with it.[58] The response was not immediate, but at the end of September, Shostakovich recruited Leningrad pianist Sofya Vakman to accompany Bogachyova, and the two performers came to Moscow to work with the composer toward the end of October. On 30 October 1973, Bogachyova gave the premiere of *Six Verses of Marina Tsvetayeva* in a recital at the Large Hall of the Leningrad Philharmonic. The composer, confined to the hospital, was unable to attend.[59] He was in attendance, however, when Bogachyova and Vakman presented the Moscow premiere on 27 December 1973, in a program that also included performances, by the Beethoven Quartet, of his First and Fourteenth Quartets.

Both new works were well received by the musical community and critics, if without the magnified attention that a symphony might have attracted. But appreciation of Shostakovich's not inconsiderable recent musical accomplishments was undercut by what was widely regarded, among his peers, as an unforgivable act of cowardice and complicity. At the end of August 1973, a massive Soviet press campaign—fomented in what by now was a tried and true, if predictable, manner—was launched against nuclear physicist Andrey Sakharov in the pages of *Pravda* in reaction to his alleged "anti-Soviet" statements to the Western press. Among the many "spontaneous" outbursts of righteous indignation vented at Sakharov in the days that followed was a letter, "He Disgraces the Calling of Citizen," signed by twelve musicians—Shostakovich's name listed among them—condemning the dissident scientist in no uncertain terms.[60] Reaction came swiftly.

On 7 September Lidiya Chukovskaya—Soviet writer, human rights activist, and, coincidentally, related to the composer through his daughter's marriage—issued an "open letter" in defense of Sakharov that was distributed through samizdat and the Western media. In it, she minced no words about her deep disillusionment with the great composer: "Shostakovich's signature on the protest of musicians against Sakharov demonstrates irrefutably that the Pushkinian question has been resolved forever: genius and villainy are compatible."[61] If others were not so outspoken in their criticism, they shared her outrage at the composer's collusion in the slander against Sakharov. At this late date, it was widely believed, there was no conceivable threat or risk to someone of Shostakovich's stature that could have justified his signing such a document. Yuriy Lyubimov admitted snubbing the composer to convey his disapproval.[62] Some sent letters. Some avoided him.

No one believes Shostakovich affixed his signature to this letter by design. Different explanations have been offered for how it was secured. Whether, in fact, he physically signed the letter has even been opened to question.[63] Nevertheless, his conduct suggests that he accepted responsibility and regretted his mistake. The bitter comments about Sakharov ("a potential murderer of millions") in *Testimony*—which, if genuine, must have been dictated very soon after this incident—reverberate with defensiveness.[64] Shostakovich explained to Rostropovich, Sakharov's friend and vocal supporter, the (unsuccessful) excuse he had tried to avoid having to sign: "I'm very weak, ... the only place where I can still take a stroll is around my country house. Unfortunately, that's where Sakharov sometimes walks. How could I look him in the eye if my signature is put at the bottom of this letter?"[65] Shostakovich allegedly told Dr. Lev Kagalovsky, who lived in the same Moscow apartment building and sometimes treated him at home, how he castigated himself for having agreed to place his name on the Sakharov letter: "I won't forgive myself for it until the grave."[66]

A few months after the Sakharov incident, Shostakovich directed

Tishchenko to reread Chekhov's "Ward No. 6" in order to get a clear sense of his self-image: "When I read in that story about Andrey Yefimovich Ragin, it seems to me I am reading memoirs about myself. This especially concerns the description of the receiving of patients, or when he signs 'blatantly falsified accounts,' or when he 'thinks' ... and to a great deal else."[67] Shostakovich's identification with Chekhov's Dr. Ragin, an anti-hero, a nonresister to evil by constitution and conviction, was far from flattering.

Shostakovich and his wife went to Repino right after the turn of the new year in 1974. Though his right hand was in poor condition and he was not succeeding in training himself to write with his left hand, he managed to arrange his Tsvetayeva cycle for contralto and chamber orchestra (op. 143a), completing the orchestration on 9 January. At lunch with Glikman later in the month, they discussed the sad fate of Solzhenitsyn, whose searing indictment of Stalinist repression, *The Gulag Archipelago*, had just been published in Paris. Accused of treason and stripped of his Soviet citizenship, Solzhenitsyn was peremptorily deported to West Germany on 14 February 1974.

In an interview given the previous summer, Shostakovich had disclosed that in conjunction with a planned revival of Strauss's *Die Fledermaus* during the coming season, he would be involved in reorchestrating and re-editing some of the score.[68] What he was undoubtedly referring to was the production by the Moscow Theater of Operetta that his friends Rostropovich and Vishnevskaya had signed on to in desperation after so many professional outlets had been closed to them in the wake of Rostropovich's open letter of 1970 and his manifest support of Solzhenitsyn.[69] It is unclear whether the composer did, in fact, make any contribution to this production, which Rostropovich was still rehearsing when he reluctantly sent his letter to Brezhnev on 29 March 1974, requesting permission to take his family abroad for two years in view of their "artistic quarantine," which effectively throttled their artistic outlets at home. Rostropovich could not bring himself to tell Shostakovich he was leaving; when he and Vishnevskaya came to visit, he handed the composer a copy of his letter to Brezhnev. On reading it, Shostakovich immediately started crying: "In whose hands are you leaving me to die?"[70] Seen off at the airport by Irina Shostakovich, Rostropovich left the country on 26 May 1974, followed two months later by Vishnevskaya and their two daughters, never to see the composer again.

Shostakovich's limbs caused him considerable pain. One consolation his doctors now permitted him was alcohol. Installation of an elevator at the Zhukovka dacha and alterations made for his benefit at the Repino artists' retreat allowed him as much independence of movement as possible. When

Polish composer Krzysztof Meyer visited him for the last time in April 1974, a weak and tired Shostakovich told him: "I know now that I will never be cured. But I have learned not to let it torment me any longer." [71] One can only speculate at what cost, physical and psychological, Shostakovich rose to deliver the opening address—reaffirming the constructive interdependence of Soviet music and Communist ideals—to the Fifth Congress of the USSR Union of Composers at the Kremlin on 2 April 1974.

Shortly before entering the hospital in May, Shostakovich phoned Glikman and told him he was working on a new quartet, his Fifteenth. He completed its composition on 17 May. This was the first quartet since his Sixth, and one of a total of only three, that the composer did not provide with a dedication. The bleak introspection and elegiac cast of its unprecedented succession of six adagio movements left no doubt in his contemporaries' minds that the String Quartet no. 15 in E-flat Minor, op. 144, could be regarded as a personal requiem.

Shostakovich spent the month of June in Repino. In Moscow, the Fifth International Chaikovsky competition, whose organizing committee he had chaired since the competition's inception, got under way without him. The Ministry of Culture sent word that he should return to Moscow to officiate at the awards ceremony. Realizing how ill and weak he was, sympathetic intermediaries in Leningrad tried to persuade him not to cut short his stay at Repino, but Shostakovich returned dutifully to hand out the awards.[72]

The composer was exceptionally productive that summer of 1974. Arnshtam brought a volume of the poetry of Michelangelo Buonarroti to Zhukovka and Shostakovich began composing immediately.[73] His setting of eleven sonnets and poems, the *Suite on Texts of Michelangelo Buonarroti*, for bass and piano, op. 145, was completed on 31 July. In his letter to Glikman dated 23 August 1974, Shostakovich announced not only the recent completion of this suite but that of a subsequent opus as well, *Four Verses of Captain Lebyadkin*, for bass and piano, op. 146, on texts taken from Dostoyevsky's novel *The Devils*. Shostakovich listed the qualities he had found most important in Michelangelo's sonnets: "Wisdom, love, creation, death, immortality." [74] The last four of these were among the titles he assigned to the individual movements. (Arnshtam claims they chose the titles together.) Shostakovich also admitted that he did not think the Russian translations of the poetry by Abram Efros were uniformly successful.[75]

When he returned from his summer vacation at the end of August, Yevgeniy Nesterenko learned that Shostakovich had written the Michelangelo suite with his voice in mind. He received the score, as well as the score of the Captain Lebyadkin songs, soon afterward and began preparing for the premiere. During September, Shostakovich acquainted the members of the Beethoven Quartet with his latest quartet and they began rehearsing it.

Before either of these works were ready for public exposure, a revelation of a different order took place. On 12 September 1974, the Moscow Chamber Music Theater, founded by eminent director Boris Pokrovsky, unveiled its production of Shostakovich's youthful opera, *The Nose*, its first production in Russia in more than forty years. Since the early 1960s, stagings of *The Nose* had been undertaken in Düsseldorf, Florence, Santa Fe, and other cities around the world.[76] Asked what he thought about the prospects for a Russian production, in a 1966 interview, Shostakovich had expressed indifference toward his first opera, claiming neither to remember it well nor to care to return to it.[77] Correcting the vocal score of his opera in 1968 for publication undoubtedly jogged his memory. He enjoyed entertaining friends with the tape he received of the Deutsche Staatsoper production mounted in 1969. And it was evidently with renewed appreciation of his early approach to Gogol that Shostakovich sent Kozintsev score and tape of *The Nose* to launch their prospective collaboration on a film based on Gogolian themes.

Boris Pokrovsky, in the meantime, conceived the determination to revive the opera in Russia. Attempts to interest the Bolshoy Theater in the venture fell on deaf ears. Pokrovsky worked on it with student forces at the State Institute of Theatrical Art (GITIS) in Moscow, who got as far as presenting two-thirds of the opera for their regular exams.[78] Early in 1972, as the Moscow Chamber Music Theater made its debut, the announcement that a production of *The Nose* was in preparation was made public.[79] Once convinced of the continued viability of his first, consciously experimental opera, Shostakovich took lively interest in the preparations for the production, as well as in the fate of the fledgling opera company, notwithstanding the painful effort required of him to descend the steps to the basement auditorium to attend rehearsals. The premiere of *The Nose* was hugely successful. Staged by Pokrovsky and conducted by Rozhdestvensky, it was an event charged with excitement and crowned with interminable ovations for the performers and an exhausted composer. The production effected the enthusiastic, unconditional rehabilitation and long overdue recognition of Shostakovich's early comic masterpiece. It became a signature show of the Chamber Music Theater.

Shostakovich returned to the preparation of his latest compositions. After rehearsing the Fifteenth Quartet with the Beethoven Quartet that morning, Sergey Shirinsky died unexpectedly on 18 October 1974. Mindful of his own mortality, the composer was unwilling to put off the premiere. He invited the young members of the Leningrad-based Taneyev Quartet, whom he had already acquainted with his new work, to become the first performers of his Fifteenth Quartet, an unexpected honor they accepted with alacrity. The composer was in the audience when they gave the first performance in Leningrad on 15 November 1974. With a replacement cellist, the Beethoven Quartet resumed its rehearsals and gave the Moscow premiere of the work on 11 January 1975.

Shostakovich was working concurrently with Nesterenko and pianist Yevgeniy Shenderovich to prepare the premiere of the *Suite on Texts of Michelangelo Buonarroti*, which was received with prolonged ovations in Leningrad on 23 December 1974. The reception was no less memorable when they repeated the performance in Moscow on 31 January 1975. Even before its premiere, Shostakovich had evidently orchestrated the Michelangelo suite as op. 145a,[80] but the premiere of the orchestral version did not take place until after his death.

The composer explicated the attractions of Michelangelo's poetry as its universality, the depth of its philosophical ideas, great humanism, and reflections about creation and love; he saw his particular selection of eight sonnets and three poems as encompassing "lyricism, and tragedy, and drama, and two ecstatic panegyrics in honor of Dante."[81] He also pointed to the five-hundredth anniversary of Michelangelo's birth (in March 1975) as a motivation for having undertaken the settings.[82]

His dissatisfaction with Efros's translations had prompted Shostakovich to enlist the poet Andrey Voznesensky to prepare new ones. But although he advised Nesterenko not to commit it to memory, it was in the Efros version that the work was first performed. On 8 January 1975, Nesterenko and Shenderovich gave a repeat performance at the composer's Moscow apartment for a gathering of colleagues. Later in the evening, Voznesensky arrived with his translations, which he read to the approval of the assembly. Shostakovich found himself confronted with an embarrassing predicament; he had written the music to Efros's translation and, as good as they were, the translations he had commissioned from Voznesensky simply did not fit his music. The composer phoned Dolmatovsky in great agitation, hoping the latter would find a way to salvage the situation.[83] Still perplexed, Voznesensky eventually received a long, "Dostoyevskian" letter of apology from the composer who proposed by way of recompense to set a selection of Voznesensky's own verse.[84] It was a work he would not live to complete.

Even as his friends lamented his visible deterioration, Shostakovich remained active and engaged. In late December 1974, he went to Kiev to oversee the revival of the 1965 staging of *Katerina Izmailova*, conducted by Simeonov and directed by Irina Molostova, a production he continued to regard as exemplary. As one of the team responsible for this production, he was posthumously awarded a Ukrainian State Prize in 1976.

Asked merely to recommend a composer who could orchestrate Beethoven's "Song of the Flea" for a concert of music inspired by Goethe's *Faust* that was being planned by Nesterenko, and finding himself at creative loose ends, Shostakovich volunteered to do it himself in January 1975. Nesterenko performed it at his concert on 1 April. In late March, Shostakovich also supervised the first recording, by Nesterenko and Shenderovich, of the Michelangelo suite.

In mid-February 1975, Shostakovich left for Repino for a month to undertake yet another course of treatment. Evidently, he had not given up hope of a miracle cure. At the beginning of March, he moved into Leningrad proper to receive treatment by the laying on of hands, as Glikman recorded, by some kind of extrasensory healer. Shostakovich nicknamed her "the sorceress."[85] He continued to attend concerts and the theater. He took on a proactive role when the imminent premiere of Vainberg's opera *Madonna and the Soldier* at the Malïy Theater was threatened by a ban imposed by the disgruntled author of the literary original, Vladimir Bogomolov. Shostakovich intervened with the Ministry of Culture, attended the dress rehearsal, and spoke up decisively at the discussion that followed. He wrote for the program booklet and, after the premiere came off as scheduled on 17 March 1975, published a glowing review in *Pravda*.

The premiere of *Four Verses of Captain Lebyadkin*, by Nesterenko and Shenderovich, in the Small Hall of the Moscow Conservatory on 10 May 1975, was the last premiere Shostakovich attended. It was also his last public appearance. When he had informed Glikman about the completion of this work the previous August, the composer had commented that "there is much of the buffoon in Lebyadkin, but much more of the sinister. I have turned out a very sinister composition."[86] Unlike the Michelangelo cycle, which was promptly performed, for months Shostakovich held the Lebyadkin cycle close to the vest, not publicizing its completion and leading many to assume that it had actually been composed in the spring of 1975.

Shenderovich recorded this premiere as another of Shostakovich's triumphant successes, complete with ovations and flowers.[87] Shostakovich reported that songs from the *Krokodil* cycle, also featured on the program, had been encored.[88] At least one member of the audience, however, recalled the occasion in quite a different light. The composer Alfred Schnittke was astonished to find that, notwithstanding a premiere of a new work by Shostakovich, the hall was scarcely more than half full. After Nesterenko performed, Shostakovich stood, made his bows from the audience, and awkwardly exited the hall even though the concert was not over.[89]

For Schnittke this event was symbolic of the decline in interest in Shostakovich's music, at least among musicians of his generation. For the post-Stalin generation of Soviet composers, the music of Shostakovich had marked the approved limit of their academic training. Just as Shostakovich had rejected his academic models in search of his distinctive voice when he graduated from conservatory years earlier, many of them rejected him in turn. He always retained a coterie of devoted former students and legions of admirers, but to many others Shostakovich's significance was as a surviving link to the past and not as a musical bellwether. Esteemed as an elder statesman, his shadow was nonetheless gargantuan and stifling. The ambivalence the younger generation felt toward Shostakovich was only heightened by his all-too-public compromises in the official sphere and his inability to stake out and defend his own moral boundaries, a fearful legacy of the Stalin years that they had been spared. Edison Denisov, whose own first steps as a composer owed much to the support and encouragement of Shostakovich, was one of those who eventually became alienated, even felt personally betrayed, by Shostakovich's pusillanimous behavior.[90]

Immediately following the premiere of the Lebyadkin songs, Shostakovich repaired to Repino for additional sessions with the "sorceress." He left Repino at the end of May, promising to return in August. The ensuing weeks were spent at his dacha in Zhukovka. Late in June, the composer phoned violist Fyodor Druzhinin and told him that he had conceived the idea of writing a viola sonata and wanted to consult with him on technical details.[91] Shostakovich was not allowed visitors, but he consulted with Druzhinin by phone, querying him, for instance, about whether it was possible to negotiate parallel fourths quickly. He was uncommonly informative about his work-in-progress, advising Druzhinin that the first movement was a "novella," the second a scherzo, and the third an adagio in memory of Beethoven. He further characterized the finale as "radiant music."[92] When they spoke on 4 July 1975, Shostakovich had already finished the first two movements and was anticipating admission to the hospital presently, but he buckled down to complete his Sonata for Viola and Piano, op. 147, the very next day.

Before checking into the hospital, Shostakovich sent his new score to the copyist and made arrangements to be in touch with Druzhinin in the coming weeks. He wrote to the violist on 22 July to let him know that the score would not be ready until the beginning of August and that he hoped to check out of the hospital a couple of weeks after that.[93] It appears he actually was released for a day or two at the beginning of the month, but after suffering respiratory seizures that intimated another heart attack, he was readmitted to the hospital on 4 August for tests. By now, the cancer had metastasized to his liver. The condition of his heart and lungs was deteriorating. Druzhinin arranged with Irina to pick up the parts of the Viola Sonata at the composer's Moscow apartment on 6 August. Touched at the discovery that Shostakovich had dedicated the score to him, Druzhinin hurried home to rehearse intensively with his accompanist, Mikhaíl

Muntyan, in anticipation of playing for the composer at the earliest possible opportunity. That opportunity never came.

On the morning of Saturday, 9 August 1975, Shostakovich was feeling better. After breakfast, Irina read him a Chekhov story, "Gusev," and later he chatted with another musician being treated at the hospital, the pianist Yakov Fliyer. Late that afternoon he began to suffocate, and at 6:30 PM he died. The Soviet media, with habitual secretiveness, vouchsafed only that the composer had died after "a protracted, grave illness." The cause of death was reported by foreign journalists as heart failure.[94] His widow confirmed that the proximate cause was lung cancer.[95]

Shostakovich was mourned in a manner befitting his civic stature. His obituary, with eighty-five signatures headed by those of Leonid Brezhnev and the members of the Politburo, emphasized the civic accomplishments of the "great composer of our time" over the musical ones: "A loyal son of the Communist Party, a prominent public figure and statesman, the artist-citizen D. D. Shostakovich devoted his entire life to the development of Soviet music, to the affirmation of the ideals of socialist humanism and internationalism, to the struggle for peace and friendship among nations." [96]

Within the Soviet Union, the announcement of Shostakovich's death was delayed for forty-eight hours without explanation. His funeral was postponed until 14 August, in part to allow time for Maxim, who was on tour in Australia when his father died, to return home. Taking place at the peak of the summer vacation season, when few people and none of the city's orchestras were in Moscow, the funeral was a formal, state ritual accompanied chiefly by taped music. Family members and personal friends gathered for their private farewells at the morgue at 8 AM. The area around the Moscow Conservatory was cordoned off by the police, and the composer's coffin was brought to the Large Hall for members of the public to pay their respects before the memorial service, which commenced at 1:30 PM, with platitudinous speeches by Composers' Union leaders Khrennikov and Shchedrin, Ministry of Culture representative Kukharsky, and others.[97] Many of those present then accompanied the procession to Novodevichy Cemetery, where, to the strains of Chopin's Funeral March and the Soviet National Anthem butchered by a military band, Dmitriy Dmitriyevich Shostakovich was laid to rest, close to the grave of his first wife, Nina, on an unseasonably chilly, drizzly afternoon.

❧ ❧ ❧

The past spring, Shostakovich had requested that his Fourteenth Symphony be performed on his sixty-ninth birthday, a wish that was observed in one of the many memorial concerts on 25 September 1975. After the performance in the Small Hall of the Moscow Conservatory that day, friends gathered at the Shostakovich apartment to hear his last composition, the Viola Sonata, for the first time. Druzhinin and Muntyan gave the public premiere of the sonata in the Small Hall of the Leningrad Philharmonic on 1 October 1975 as the climax of a program that also included, as the composer had stipulated, his cello and violin sonatas. The hall overflowed with rapt listeners. They rose to their feet as one at the conclusion of the performance. Druzhinin solemnly held the score over his head to an intense ovation.

It would be some time before most of them realized that Shostakovich had drawn much of the material in the second movement of the sonata from his unfinished wartime opera, *The Gamblers*.[98] What struck everyone instantly, however, was the suggestion of the theme from the first movement of Beethoven's *Moonlight* Sonata that infused the final adagio. When Shostakovich had told Druzhinin that the last movement would be "in memory" of Beethoven, he had added, "But don't let that inhibit you. The music is bright, bright and clear."[99] It was certainly arresting. As one critic remarked: "It is like the catharsis in tragedy; life, struggle, overcoming, purification by light, exit into immortality."[100] He might have been offering a précis of the composer's life.

Official measures to perpetuate Shostakovich's memory were quickly announced. In the spring of 1975, while he was still alive, a peninsula on Alexander Island in Antarctica had been named after him. A memorial volume of essays appeared and publication of his collected works commenced. Scholarships in his name were instituted at both the Moscow and Leningrad Conservatories. The Leningrad Philharmonic was named in his honor and a commemorative postage stamp was issued for what would have been his seventieth birthday. Composers from all over the globe paid homage to the great composer with musical tributes.

The groundswell of interest in Shostakovich, man and music, was touched off in the West by a political bombshell, the publication of Solomon Volkov's *Testimony*, a provocative book purporting to be the composer's memoirs, in 1979. Appearing shortly before the Soviet invasion of Afghanistan, at the last crest of cold-war tensions, its embittered anti-Soviet message fell on extremely receptive territory. The headline-grabbing defection of the composer's son, Maxim, and his grandson, Dmitriy, in Germany in 1981, kept Shostakovich's name in the limelight. But the fallout from these events was not exclusively political. They occurred at a time when festering dissatisfactions with "serialism" and the academic musical avant-garde had reached a breaking point. Western performers and audiences were ready and eager to explore and embrace more accessible, more obviously "communicative" music, music not ashamed of its audible links to the traditions of the past. Performers and audiences began to "rediscover" the music of Shostakovich—familiar scores and previously unknown works—with new ears. The process of discovery continues. Enjoying ever increasing popularity and critical appreciation, Shostakovich's musical legacy now seems certain to endure well into the future.

Notes

Introduction

1. Among published collections, the following are of exceptional significance: *Pis'ma k drugu: Dmitriy Shostakovich — Isaaku Glikmanu* (Moscow, 1993); *Pis'ma Dmitriya Dmitriyevicha Shostakovicha Borisu Tishchenko: s kommentariyami i vospominaniyami adresata* (St. Petersburg, 1997); M. Kozlova, "'Mne ispolnilos' vosemnadtsat' let ...' (Pis'ma D. D. Shostakovicha k L. N. Oborinu)," *Vstrechi s proshlïm, vïp.* 5 (Moscow, 1984); R. Sadïkhova and D. Frederiks, comp., "Dmitriy Shostakovich: pis'ma k materi," *Niva* 9 (1986); L. Mikheyeva-Sollertinskaya, "D. D. Shostakovich v otrazhenii pisem k I. I. Sollertinskomu. Shtrikhi k portretu," in *D. D. Shostakovich: sbornik statey k 90-letiyu so dnya rozhdeniya,* comp. L. Kovnatskaya (St. Petersburg, 1996); Mikheyeva-Sollertinskaya, "Pis'ma Shostakovicha k Sollertinskomu," *Zhurnal lyubiteley iskusstva* 2, 3, 4 (1996), 1, 4–5, 6–7, 8–9, 10–11 (1997), 1 (1998); "'Khorosho bïlo bï ne dumat' ni o khlebe nasushchom, ni o chyom, a tol'ko zanimat'sya lyubimïm delom ...'; iz pisem D. D. Shostakovicha B. L. Yavorskomu," *Muzïkal'naya akademiya* 4 (1997).

2. The most comprehensive compilations of such materials to have appeared are E. Wilson, *Shostakovich: A Life Remembered* (London, 1994); S. Khentova, *V mire Shostakovicha* (Moscow, 1996).

3. *D. Shostakovich: Sobraniye sochineniy v soroka dvukh tomakh* (Moscow, 1979–87).

4. S. Khentova, *Shostakovich: zhizn' i tvorchestvo,* 2 vols. (Leningrad, 1985–86). This publication actually amounts to a new edition of material originally published in four volumes between 1975 and 1982.

5. A second, "updated" version of Khentova's two-volume biography, published in a run of 100 copies in Moscow in 1996, arrived too late for thorough consideration. Spot-checking, however, reveals that although defectors have made their reappearances, much of the new information published in the ten years since the previous edition has not been consulted, nor have most of its mistakes been corrected. Khentova is the author of numerous other books and scores of articles on the composer, all drawing on the same research base. By far the most useful is *V mire Shostakovicha* (see note 2), which amounts to a source book of interviews she conducted with the composer and more than sixty of his colleagues and family members, plus a selection of the composer's letters to various recipients.

6. S. Volkov, *Testimony: The Memoirs of Dmitri Shostakovich* (New York, 1979).

7. See L. E. Fay, "Shostakovich versus Volkov: Whose Testimony?" *Russian Review* 39, no. 4 (1980): 484–93. In the recently published *Shostakovich Reconsidered* (London, 1998), the attempt by authors Allan Ho and Dmitry Feofanov to "authenticate" *Testimony* by means of third-party endorsements and circumstantial evidence raises as many new questions as it purports to answer. The controversy is far from resolved.

Chapter 1

1. Reminiscence of Mariya Shostakovich in S. Khentova, *V mire Shostakovicha* (Moscow, 1996), 49.

2. V. I. Seroff, in collaboration with Nadejda Galli-Shohat, *Dmitri Shostakovich: The Life and Background of a Soviet Composer* (New York, 1943), 37–39.

3. See the reminiscences of Dmitriy Popov in Khentova, *V mire Shostakovicha*, 59–60; also S. Khentova, *Shostakovich: zhizn' i tvorchestvo*, 1 (Leningrad, 1985), 92, 111.

4. S. Shostakovich, "Moy sïn," *Smena* 18 (1976): 18.

5. V. Smirnov, "O svoyey professii ...; iz besedï s D. D. Shostakovichem," *Teatral'-naya nedelya* 9 (24 February 1941): 11. Shostakovich alludes mockingly here to the famous story of the morbid excitability listening to music aroused in the young Pyotr Chaikovsky. See M. Chaikovsky, *Zhizn' Petra Il'icha Chaikovskogo*, 1 (Moscow, 1997), 42.

6. Khentova, *V mire Shostakovicha*, 17.

7. Shostakovich, "Moy sïn," 18.

8. D. Shostakovich, "Dumï o proydyonnom puti," *Sovetskaya muzïka* 9 (1956): 9. See also, E. Poryadkova, "Violonchelist za stenoy," *Sovetskaya muzïka* 10 (1981): 28.

9. Forty years after the event, Shostakovich would claim that his first opera was *Eugene Onegin*, but this conflicts with his own earlier recollections as well as those of his relatives. See Shostakovich, "Dumï o proydyonnom puti," 10.

10. Autobiographical sketch from 1927, quoted in Khentova, *Shostakovich*, I: 68.

11. Although nine is consistently given as the age at which he commenced his studies, Dmitriy was actually still a few months shy of his ninth birthday.

12. Shostakovich, "Moy sïn," 18.

13. Smirnov, "O svoyey professii," 11.

14. Khentova, *V mire Shostakovicha*, 17.

15. B. Losskiy, "Nasha sem'ya v poru likholetiya 1914–1922 godov," *Minuvsheye: istoricheskiy al'manakh* 11 (1992): 194 .

16. B. Losskiy, "Nasha sem'ya v poru likholetiya 1914–1922 godov," *Minuvsheye: istoricheskiy al'manakh* 12 (1993): 79–80. Shostakovich may have attended another secondary school after leaving this one. In 1966, the composer told Marietta Shaginyan he had been expelled for cutting classes after he enrolled at the Conservatory; see M. Shaginyan, "Fifty Letters from Dmitri Shostakovich," *Soviet Literature* 1 (1984): 77. Conflicting claims notwithstanding, available evidence suggests that Shostakovich did not complete his secondary schooling.

17. L. Mikheyeva, *Zhizn' Dmitriya Shostakovicha* (Moscow, 1997), 20. The actual title of Lermontov's poem is "A Song about Tsar Ivan Vasilyevich, the Young Bodyguard, and the Valorous Merchant Kalashnikov."

18. The composer's contention that he became bored with and left Glyasser's tutelage in February 1917 is contradicted by other evidence and memoirs. See D. Shostakovich, "Avtobiografiya," *Sovetskaya muzïka* 9 (1966): 24.

19. Losskiy, *Minuvsheye* 12:37. Koussevitzky conducted a Beethoven symphony cycle in Petrograd in late September and early October 1918. See O. Dansker, "Muzïkal'naya zhizn' Petrograda-Leningrada: kratkiy khronograf," in *Voprosï teorii i estetiki muzïki, vïp. 6–7* (Leningrad, 1967), 307.

20. E. Wilson, *Shostakovich: A Life Remembered* (London, 1994), 6.

21. Mariya Shostakovich in Khentova, *V mire Shostakovicha*, 51.

22. Seroff, *Shostakovich*, 73.

23. Losskiy, *Minuvsheye* 12:28.

24. Mikheyeva, *Zhizn' Shostakovicha*, 20. It would be easier to dismiss the legend of a revolutionary funeral march composed in 1917 as the product of Soviet hagiography had the story not been reproduced by independent witnesses, including that same Aunt Nadezhda from her eventual emigration in America. As prolific a composer as the youthful Shostakovich was, perhaps he produced more than one funeral march?

25. "Novïy muzïkal'nïy radiozhurnal. D. Shostakovich rasskazïvayet o svoyey rabote nad 12-oy simfoniyey," *Muzïkal'naya zhizn'* 21 (1960): 10.

26. Wilson, *Shostakovich Remembered*, 6. Shostakovich's daughter, however, did not recall ever hearing her father relate this story; ibid. 19.

27. S. Volkov, *Testimony: The Memoirs of Dmitri Shostakovich* (New York, 1979), 7. The adult Shostakovich's assertion to Lev Lebedinsky, that he had gone to Finland Station because he knew "a dictator was arriving," resonates with revisionist hindsight. See Wilson, *Shostakovich Remembered*, 335.

28. B. Losskiy, "Novoye o Shostakoviche," *Russkaya mïsl'* (14 April 1989): 9.

29. M. Grinberg, "Dmitriy Shostakovich," *Muzïka i revolyutsiya* 11 (1927): 17. See also Chapter 3.

30. Losskiy, "Novoye o Shostakoviche," 9.

31. N. Komarovskaya, "Moi vstrechi s B. M. Kustodiyevïm," in *Boris Mikhaylovich Kustodiyev*, ed. V. Kapralov (Leningrad, 1967), 388.

32. The following year, Shostakovich inscribed to the artist a program from his public exam appearance for Leonid Nikolayev's Conservatory class: "For dear Boris Mikhailovich in memory of my first public appearance with my own works. From your loving D. Shostakovich." See *Dmitri Schostakowitsch und seine Zeit: Mensch und Werk*, ed. J. Fromme (Duisberg, 1984), 68.

33. S. Khentova, *Udivitel'nïy Shostakovich* (St. Petersburg, 1993), 100. Kube, whose married name was Shabanova, only found out about this more than a half century later. Shostakovich dedicated the remaining four (nos. 2–5) of the op. 2 preludes to his older sister.

34. A little more than a decade later Bruni's daughter, Tatyana, would design the sets and costumes (with Georgiy Korshikov) for the staging of Shostakovich's second ballet, *The Bolt*.

35. Smirnov, "O svoyey professii," 11. Shostakovich also related the substance of this anecdote to Marietta Shaginyan in a December 1940 interview; see Shaginyan, "Fifty Letters," 71–72.

36. Shostakovich, "Moy sïn," 18.

37. V. Bogdanov-Berezovskiy, *Vstrechi* (Moscow, 1967), 16.

Chapter 2

1. D. Shostakovich, "Dumï o proydyonnom puti," *Sovetskaya muzïka* 9 (1956): 10.

2. V. Bogdanov-Berezovskiy, "Yunost' novoy kul'turï," *Sovetskaya muzïka* 11 (1967): 70–71.

3. I. Shvarts, "Neskol'ko sobïtiy i faktov," in *L. V. Nikolayev: stat'i i vospominaniya sovremennikov, pis'ma* (Leningrad, 1979), 122.

4. V. Val'ter, "Kontsert Dmitriya Shostakovicha," *Zhizn' iskusstva* 29 (15 July 1924): 15. Translation by Richard Sylvester.

5. M. Ozhigova, "Mitya, Dmitriy Dmitriyevich," *Muzïkal'naya pedagogika v ideyakh i litsakh: sbornik statey,* ed. A. Selitskiy (Rostov-on-Don, 1992), 85–86.

6. Most likely, these duplicate preludes are from the now-lost opus 2.

7. Reminiscences of K. Eliasberg, in S. Khentova, *V mire Shostakovicha* (Moscow, 1996), 227.

8. Yu. N. Tyulin, "Yunïye godï D. D. Shostakovicha," in *Dmitriy Shostakovich,* comp. G. Ordzhonikidze (Moscow, 1967), 75.

9. E. Trusova, "Stranitsï vospominaniy," *Sovetskaya muzïka* 9 (1977): 107; translated in D. and L. Sollertinsky, *Pages from the Life of Dmitri Shostakovich* (New York, 1980), 26–27.

10. One of their earliest documented performances of the Suite for Two Pianos took place at a closed concert of the Russian Institute for the History of Art, on 15 January 1923. See A. Kryukov, "K svedeniyu budushchikh letopistsev," *D. D. Shostakovich: sbornik statey k 90-letiyu so dnya rozhdeniya,* comp. L. Kovnatskaya (St. Petersburg, 1996), 161.

11. M. O. Yankovskiy, ed., *Muzïkal'noye naslediye: Glazunov,* 2 (Leningrad, 1960), 462.

12. N. Zelov, "Narkomprosovskiy stipendiat," *Yunost'* 10 (1967): 102.

13. Ibid. While there is no reason to question Glazunov's altruism over the years in aiding the young Shostakovich, his close relationship with the Shostakovich family—which continued even after Dmitriy Boleslavovich's death—was lubricated with illicit alcohol obtained from the Weights and Measures Office. See D. Popov in Khentova, *V mire Shostakovicha,* 61.

14. R. Sadïkhova and D. Frederiks, comp., "Dmitriy Shostakovich: pis'ma k materi," *Niva* 9 (1986): 168.

15. Letter from Shostakovich to his mother dated 3 August 1923, in ibid.

16. Tatyana Glivenko's reminiscences in E. Wilson, *Shostakovich: A Life Remembered* (London, 1994), 85.

17. Letter from Shostakovich to his mother dated 22 September 1923, in Sadïkhova, "Pis'ma k materi," 168.

18. D. Shostakovich, "Avtobiografiya," *Sovetskaya muzïka* 9 (1966): 25.

19. Quoted in L. Kazanskaya, "Kruzhok druzey kamernoy muzïki," *Muzïkal'naya akademiya* 1 (1996): 207.

20. According to a seasoned critic, "The only thing that spoiled the general impression was the wooden sound of the piano playing by D. Shostakovich." See Dmitriy Mazurov (DEM) in *Krasnaya gazeta (vech. vïp.),* 12 December 1923, quoted in Kazanskaya, "Kruzhok druzey," 207–08.

21. V. Bogdanov-Berezovskiy, "Otrochestvo i yunost'," in *D. Shostakovich: stat'i i materialï,* comp. G. Shneerson (Moscow, 1976), 136.

22. D. Popov, in Khentova, *V mire Shostakovicha,* 63.

23. Letter from Shostakovich to Glivenko dated 26 February 1924, in *Fine Printed and Manuscript Music Including the Mannheim Collection,* catalogue for Sotheby's

auction, 6 December 1991 (London, 1991), 148.

24. *L. V. Nikolayev*, 255–56.

25. Sadïkhova, "Pis'ma k materi," 169–70.

26. M. Kozlova, "Mne ispolnilos' vosemnadtsat' let," in *Vstrechi s proshlïm, vip. 5* (Moscow, 1984), 241.

27. Sadïkhova, "Pis'ma k materi," 170.

28. Letter from Shostakovich to Glivenko dated 7 November 1924; Sotheby's catalogue (1991), 148–49.

29. D. Shostakovich, "Avtobiografiya," 25.

30. Kozlova, "Mne ispolnilos'," 244.

31. RGALI f. 2048, op. 1, yed. khr. 1.

32. T. Isakova, "Ozhivshiye notï," *Sovetskaya Rossiya*, 29 July 1984; letter from Shostakovich to Yavorsky dated 8 August 1926, GTsMMK f. 146, yed. khr. 3261.

33. Vl. Vlasov, *Vstrechi* (Moscow, 1979), 165.

34. Letter from Shostakovich to Glivenko dated 13 January 1925, in Sotheby's catalogue (1991), 149.

35. V. Bogdanov-Berezovskiy, *Dorogi iskusstva: kniga pervaya (1903–1945)* (Leningrad, 1971), 62.

36. Letter from Shostakovich to Oborin dated 16 February 1925, in Kozlova, "Mne ispolnilos'," 247.

37. Sadïkhova, "Pis'ma k materi," 170.

38. Letter from Shostakovich to his mother dated 21 March 1925, in ibid., 171.

39. Letter from Shostakovich to Yavorsky dated 16 April 1925, in Kozlova, "Mne ispolnilos'," 233.

40. Shostakovich letter to Yavorsky dated 9 May 1925; "'Khorosho bïlo bï ne dumat' o khlebe nasushchnom, ni o chyom, a tol'ko zanimat'sya lyubimïm delom ...'; iz pisem D. D. Shostakovicha B. L. Yavorskomu," *Muzïkal'naya akademiya* 4 (1997): 30.

41. Although it vanished from subsequent editions (the thirty-two-year-old Kvadri was arrested and allegedly shot in 1929), the dedication appears in the first publication of the full score (Vienna-Leipzig-Moscow, 1927) and in the published two-piano reduction by Yevgeniy Slavinsky (Vienna-Leipzig-Moscow, 1928). Shostakovich amusingly described Kvadri's "proprietorial" behavior at the first Moscow performance of the symphony in a letter to Ivan Sollertinsky dated 10 January 1927; see L. Mikheyeva-Sollertinskaya, "Dmitriy Shostakovich v otrazhenii pisem k Sollertinskomu; shtrikhi k portretu," in *D. D. Shostakovich: sbornik statey k 90-letiyu so dnya rozhdeniya*, comp. L. Kovnatskaya (St. Petersburg, 1996), 89. Shostakovich also dedicated his *Two Fables of Krïlov* to Kvadri.

42. However, in a letter from Shostakovich to Yavorsky dated 2 July 1925, he announced that he had completed work at 2 PM that day; GTsMMK f. 146, yed. khr. 3236.

43. Letter from Shostakovich to Oborin dated 3 October 1925, in Kozlova, "Mne ispolnilos'," 250. When Shostakovich described the same incident to Yavorsky, he quoted Steinberg as having expressed the hope that when he reached the age of thirty, he would cease writing such "terrible" music. Letter from Shostakovich to Yavorsky dated 2 October 1925; GTsMMK f. 146, yed. khr. 3240.

44. Letter from Shostakovich to Oborin dated 28 October 1925, in Kozlova, "Mne ispolnilos'," 252.

45. From protocol dated 23 October 1925; see L. Kovnatskaya, "Shostakovich v protokolakh LASM," in *D. D. Shostakovich: sbornik statey k 90-letiyu*, 55.

46. Letter from Shostakovich to Yavorsky dated 13 May 1926; "'Khorosho bïlo bï ne dumat'," 35.

47. L. Mikheyeva, comp., *Pamyati I. I. Sollertinskogo: vospominaniya, materialï, issledovaniya* (Moscow, 1974), 92.

48. Letter from Shostakovich to Yavorsky dated 6 March 1927; GTsMMK f. 146, yed. khr. 3277.

49. Shostakovich, "Dumï o proydyonnom puti," 11.

50. See L. E. Fay, "Shostakovich, LASM i Asaf'yev," in *D. D. Shostakovich: sbornik statey k 90-letiyu*, 35–47.

51. Letter from Shostakovich to his mother dated 8 February 1926, in Sadïkhova, "Pis'ma k materi," 172.

52. Ibid.

53. "Kharakteristika ot dekana nauchno-kompozitorskogo fakulteta LGK" [20 April 1926]; RGALI f. 2048, op. 1, yed. khr. 66.

54. Steinberg diary, RO RIII, f. 28, yed. khr. 1106.

55. N. Strel'nikov, "Novinki v filarmonii," *Zhizn' iskusstva* 20 (18 May 1926): 12–13.

56. M. Sokol'skiy, "Zakrïtoye sezona v filarmonii," *Rabochiy i teatr* 20 (1926); quoted in Sokol'skiy, *Musorgsky/Shostakovich: stat'i, retsenzii* (Moscow, 1983), 84.

Chapter 3

1. Epigraph taken from D. Shostakovich, "Dumï o proydyonnom puti," *Sovetskaya muzïka* 9 (1956): 11. Fragments from *The Gypsies* actually survived and are preserved in GTsMMK and RGALI.

2. Letter from Shostakovich to S. Protopopov dated 17 June 1926, in S. Khentova, *V mire Shostakovicha* (Moscow, 1996), 292.

3. Letter from Shostakovich to Oborin dated 22 June 1926, in M. Kozlova, "Mne ispolnilos' vosemnadtsat' let," *Vstrechi s proshlim, vip. 5* (Moscow, 1984), 259.

4. Letter from Shostakovich to Yavorsky dated 6 July 1926; "'Khorosho bïlo bï ne dumat' o khlebe nasushchnom, ni o chyom, a tol'ko zanimat'sa lyubimïm delom'; iz pisem D. D. Shostakovicha B. L. Yavorskomu," *Muzïkal'naya akademiya* 4 (1997): 36.

5. See, for instance, GRAVE [pseud. for S. A. Kukurichkin], "Oktyabr'skaya sonata D. Shostakovicha," *Zhizn' iskusstva* 47 (18 November 1928): 18; N. Malkov, "Ob avtore Nosa," in *Nos: polnïy tekst operï* (Leningrad, 1930), 6; also M. Steinberg, *Sovetskaya muzïka* 5 (1936): 38.

6. Interview with Royal S. Brown in New York on 13 June 1973.

7. Letter from Shostakovich to Yavorsky dated 3 November 1926, GTsMMK f. 146, yed. khr. 3269.

8. Letter from Shostakovich to Yavorsky dated 11 December 1926; "'Khorosho bïlo bï ne dumat'," 38.

9. Reminiscences of M. D. Shostakovich in Khentova, *V mire Shostakovicha*, 48.

10. Information summarized in *Fine Printed and Manuscript Music Including the*

Mannheim Collection, catalogue for Sotheby's auction, 6 December 1991 (London, 1991), 151.

11. G. Khubov, "Pervaya geroicheskaya," in *Muzïkal'naya publitsistika raznïkh let* (Moscow, 1976), 8–9; S. Khentova, *Shostakovich: zhizn' i tvorchestvo*, 1 (Leningrad, 1985), 143.

12. Letter from Shostakovich to Yavorsky dated 24 December 1926; "'Khorosho bïlo bï ne dumat'," 38.

13. In a preserved copy of the printed program, the G-flat Major Etude has been scratched out, replaced in pencil by the Etude in A-flat Major; RO RIII f. 94, op. 1, yed. khr. 8. In a letter to Yavorsky from Warsaw, Shostakovich also specifically mentions playing the A-flat Major Etude; "'Khorosho bïlo bï ne dumat'," 39.

14. Letter from Shostakovich to his mother dated 15 January 1927, in R. Sadïkhova and D. Frederiks, comp., "Dmitriy Shostakovich: pis'ma k materi," *Niva* 9 (1986): 174.

15. Letter from Shostakovich to his mother dated 8 February 1927, in ibid., 175.

16. D. Shostakovich, "Avtobiografiya," *Sovetskaya muzïka* 9 (1966): 25.

17. Letter from Shostakovich to his mother dated 8 February 1927, in Sadïkhova, "Pis'ma k materi," 175. While in Warsaw he also played the sonata twice at the home of Polish author Jaroslaw Iwaszkiewicz, breaking the low D-string of his Bechstein. See Krzystof Meyer, *Dmitri Chostakovitch* (Paris, 1994), 96.

18. Letter from Shostakovich to his mother dated 8 February 1927, in Sadïkhova, "Pis'ma k materi," 175.

19. Letter from Shostakovich to Oborin dated 27 September 1927, in Kozlova, "Mne ispolnilos'," 260.

20. Letter from Prokofiev to Yavorsky, in *B. Yavorskiy: stat'i, vospominaniya, perepiska*, 1, ed. by I. Rabinovich, 2nd ed. (Moscow, 1972), 366.

21. *Sergei Prokofiev: Soviet Diary 1927 and Other Writings*, trans. and ed. by Oleg Prokofiev (London, 1991), 106.

22. Letter from Shostakovich to Yavorsky dated 25 February 1927, GTsMMK f. 146, yed. khr. 3276.

23. Most sources incorrectly list 27 May 1927 as the date Walter presented the Western premiere of Shostakovich's First Symphony with the Berlin Philharmonic Orchestra; the actual date of this performance was 6 February 1928. See Peter Muck, *Einhundert Jahre Berliner Philharmonisches Orchester: Darstellung in Dokumenten*, 3 (Tutzing, 1982), 230.

24. Letter from Shostakovich to Glivenko dated 21 March 1927; quoted in Sotheby's catalogue (1991), 149.

25. Letter from Shostakovich to L. Shulgin dated 6 June 1927, in E. Shul'gina, ed., *L. V. Shul'gin: stat'i, vospominaniya* (Moscow, 1977), 58–59.

26. Letter from Shostakovich to Protopopov dated 20 February 1927, GTsMMK f. 329, yed. khr. 592; quoted in Khentova, *Shostakovich*, 1: 186. Judging by internal evidence, this letter is almost certainly misdated; most likely it dates from mid-April.

27. RGALI f. 2048, op. 1, yed. khr. 157.

28. The first unequivocal sign I have been able to find that this had officially become the Second Symphony is the first publication of the score of the Third Symphony, which was submitted to the censor on 6 December 1931 and sent to press on 28 March 1932. In a review of the first performance of the *First of May* Symphony,

however, the critic remarks in passing that Shostakovich is the author of three symphonies. See S. [sic], "Sovetskiye simfonistï: Roslavets, Shostakovich," *Smena* (21 January 1930): 3.

29. M. Grinberg, "Dmitriy Shostakovich," *Muzïka i revolyutsiya* 11 (1927): 17. In *Testimony*, this incident is pinpointed as having taken place in February 1917. See S. Volkov, *Testimony: The Memoirs of Dmitri Shostakovich* (New York, 1979), 7. In the version told by Malko, the incident is located on Letniy Prospect and no mention is made of a workers' uprising; the boy was killed for having stolen an apple. See N. Malko, *A Certain Art* (New York, 1966), 204–05.

30. Here he employs a different word, *mladenets* (infant, baby), which suggests someone of rather younger years than the *mal'chugan* (young boy) of Grinberg's account.

31. Letter from Shostakovich to Yavorsky dated 12 June 1927; "'Khorosho bïlo bï ne dumat'," 40.

32. Ibid.

33. Letter from Shostakovich to Yavorsky dated 2 July 1927, GTsMMK f. 146, yed. khr. 3284.

34. D. Shostakovich, "K prem'ere 'Nosa,'" *Rabochiy i teatr* 24 (16 June 1929): 12; Stenogram of discussion and demonstration of the staging of Shostakovich's opera *The Nose* by the Malïy Opera Theater, Moscow-Narva House of Culture, Leningrad, 14 January 1930, SPgGMTMI kn. 7755/4143, oru. 5365. Shostakovich's comment on this occasion may have been calculated to distance his new opera from a writer recently targeted for public vilification. In a 1942 letter to Ivan Sollertinsky, Shostakovich waxed nostalgic about his librettists for *The Nose*, by then all deceased, listing Zamyatin alongside Ionin and Preys. See L. Mikheyeva, *Zhizn' Dmitriya Shostakovicha* (Moscow, 1997), 240.

35. L. Mikheyeva, comp., *Pamyati I. I. Sollertinskogo: vospominaniya, materialï, issledovaniya* (Moscow, 1974), 91–92. In the Cyrillic alphabet, "Sollertinsky" precedes "Shostakovich."

36. Ibid., 98.

37. Ibid., 92.

38. Zoya Shostakovich, in E. Wilson, *Shostakovich: A Life Remembered* (London, 1994), 64.

39. Shostakovich, "Dumï o proydyonnom puti," 11.

40. G. Geodakyan, "Ideal khudozhnika-grazhdanina," *Sovetskaya muzïka* 9 (1976): 22–23.

41. M. Yakubov, "Ya pïtalsya peredat' pafos bor'bï i pobedï," *Sovetskaya muzïka* 10 (1986): 55, 54.

42. Letter from Shostakovich to Yavorsky dated 2 July 1927, GTsMMK f. 146, yed. khr. 3284.

43. "Na nashem kontserte: vpechatleniya slushatelya," *Smena* (29 November 1927): 4.

44. M. Steinberg diary, 2 November 1927, RO RIII, f. 28, yed. khr. 1106. When Shostakovich had played him the opening of the chorus of his new "revolutionary" piece back in July, however, Steinberg's reaction had been that it was "not bad." See L. Kovnatskaya, "Shostakovich v protokolakh LASM," in *D. D. Shostakovich: sbornik*

statey k 90-letiyu so dnya rozhdeniya, comp. L. Kovnatskaya (St. Petersburg, 1996), 63.

45. Letter from Myaskovsky to Asafyev dated 28 December 1927, in O. Lamm, *Stranitsï tvorcheskiy biografii Myaskovskogo* (Moscow, 1989), 187. Of the current crop of debuting Leningrad composers, a number of critics assessed Gavriil Popov (a student of Vladimir Shcherbachov) as manifesting as much or even greater potential than his coeval Shostakovich.

46. Shostakovich was encouraged to enter his work in the contest by Malko, chairman of the contest committee. He evidently believed that Malko had promised him first prize and took umbrage when he shared second prize (no first was awarded) with another contestant. See Malko, *A Certain Art,* 205, 207–09.

47. Letter from Shostakovich to Meyerhold dated 8 December 1927, in L. Rudneva, "Shostakovich i Meyerkhol'd," *Aprel'* 5 (1992): 221.

48. Shostakovich letter to Meyerhold dated January 1927, in ibid., 222.

49. D. Shostakovich, "Iz vospominaniy," *Sovetskaya muzïka* 3 (1974): 54, quoted in *D. Shostakovich about Himself and His Times* (Moscow, 1981), 321.

50. Meyerhold was obviously concerned that the young composer was on a different musical "wavelength." At a rehearsal for the forthcoming production of Griboyedov's *Woe from Wit* in late November 1927, he deflected his wife's suggestion that they wait for Shostakovich's arrival before settling on the musical selections: "But what if he gives us ultra-contemporary music? Here's what's scary. Shostakovich disapproves of Beethoven. But here's what's strange: I denigrated Rachmaninoff in front of him and Shostakovich stood up for him. He shouldn't have approved of him." See *Meyerkhol'd repetiruyet: spektakli 20-kh godov,* 1, comp. M. Sitkovetskaya (Moscow, 1993), 188–89.

51. Letter from Shostakovich to Sollertinsky dated 10 January 1928, in L. Mikheyeva-Sollertinskaya, "D. D. Shostakovich v otrazhenii pisem k I. I. Sollertinskomu. Shtriki k portretu," in *D. D. Shostakovich: sbornik statey k 90-letiyu,* 89. Before her marriage to Meyerhold, Zinaída Raikh had been married to the poet Sergey Yesenin, by whom she bore a daughter and a son.

52. *Sovetskiy teatr: dokumentï i materialï, Russkiy sovetskiy teatr 1926—1932,* 4, ch. 1, ed. A. Trabskiy (Leningrad, 1982), 134. Shortly after the opera's acceptance, however, officials at Glavrepertkom ruled that the Bolshoy Theater would be permitted to produce it only after fundamental changes to the libretto and music with a view toward "shifting attention from eroticism and mysticism to the socio-political content, that is toward exposing the epoch of Nicholas and of police oppression." See A. Blyum, *Za kulisami "Ministerstva pravdï": taynaya istoriya sovetskoy tsenzurï, 1917–1929* (St. Petersburg, 1994), 169. While there is no indication that Shostakovich ever agreed to countenance any such extensive revisions, this did not prevent the Bolshoy from planning their forthcoming production for more than two years.

53. Zoya Shostakovich, in Wilson, *Shostakovich Remembered,* 73.

54. M. Dolgopolov, *Zvyozdnoye ozherel'ye* (Moscow, 1986), 198.

55. Zoya Shostakovich, in Wilson, *Shostakovich Remembered,* 9.

56. S. Yutkevich, "Vspominaya Shostakovicha," *Muzïkal'naya zhizn'* 2 (1995): 23.

57. D. Shostakovich, "Kak rozhdayetsya muzïka," *Literaturnaya gazeta* (21 December 1965), 3.

58. Although many sources affix a date of 1928 to this orchestration,

Shostakovich's inscription on the score presented to Malko is dated 1 October 1927. See S. Volkov, "Dmitri Shostakovitch and 'Tea for Two,'" *Musical Quarterly* 64, no. 2 (1978): 224; Malko, *A Certain Art*, 213.

Chapter 4

1. L. Trauberg, *Izbrannïye proizvedeniya v 2-kh tomakh,* 1 (Moscow, 1988), 298.

2. "Protokol Muz. Soveshchaniya pri Khud. Byuro k/f," 20 February 1929, RGALI (SPb) f. 257, op. 16, yed. khr. 67.

3. *Iz istorii Lenfil'ma, vïp. 1* (Leningrad, 1968), 256.

4. D. Shostakovich, "O muzïke k 'Novomu Vavilonu,'" *Sovetskiy ekran* 11 (12 March 1929).

5. Trauberg, *Izbrannïye proizvedeniya,* 1: 299.

6. Yu. V., "Muzïka k 'Novomu Vavilonu,'" *Rabochiy i teatr* 14 (1 April 1929): 9.

7. L. Arnshtam, "Zlatïye gorï," in *Muzïka geroicheskogo* (Moscow, 1977), 67.

8. D. Shostakovich, "V 1928 godu ...," *Teatr* 2 (1974): 53. He later claimed his dislike of Mayakovsky's play, *The Bathhouse,* made him decline Meyerhold's subsequent invitation to contribute the music to that production as well. See S. Khentova, *V mire Shostakovicha* (Moscow, 1996), 33.

9. D. Shostakovich, "Novoye o Mayakovskom," *Literaturnaya gazeta* (9 October 1956): 2. Elsewhere, Shostakovich clarified that this was for the first part only; in the second part, set fifty years in the future, Mayakovsky requested emotionless music, "as simple as mooing." See D. Shostakovich, "Iz vospominaniy o Mayakovskom," in *V. Mayakovskiy v vospominaniyakh sovremennikov* (Moscow, 1963), 316.

10. N. Basilov, "Pervaya postanovka," in *Vstrechi s Meyerkhol'dom: sbornik statey* (Moscow, 1967), 378.

11. Kukrïniksï, "V rabote nad 'Klopom,'" in *Vstrechi s Meyerkhol'dom,* 386.

12. In its first three months, it played seventy-nine times and remained a staple in the repertory of the Meyerhold Theater—including its regional tours—for several seasons. See *Sovetskiy teatr: dokumentï i materialï, Russkiy sovetskiy teatr 1926–1932,* 4, ch. 1, ed. A. Trabskiy (Leningrad, 1982), 269–70.

13. L. Mikheyeva, "Istoriya odnoy druzhbï," *Sovetskaya muzïka* 9 (1986): 28.

14. Shostakovich chronicled his misadventures in hilarious detail in a letter he sent to Sollertinsky from Tikhoretsk on 7 August 1929; see Mikheyeva, *Zhizn' Dmitriya Shostakovicha* (Moscow, 1997), 125–27.

15. Letter from Shostakovich to Malko dated 25 August 1929; quoted in S. Volkov, "Dmitri Shostakovitch and 'Tea for Two,'" *Musical Quarterly* 64, no. 2 (1978): 228.

16. N. M. "Nad chem rabotayet D. Shostakovich," *Zhizn' iskusstva* 34 (25 August 1929): 14.

17. "Kompozitor Shostakovich o svoyom proizvedenii: k kul'tpokhodu *Smenï* v filarmoniyu 22 yanvarya," *Smena* (21 January 1930): 3.

18. "Otchyot aspiranta Leningradskoy gosudarstvennoy konservatorii Dmitriya Shostakovicha [31 October 1929]," in M. Yakubov, ed., "... Ya pitalsya peredat' pafos bor'bï i pobedï," *Sovetskaya muzïka* 10 (1986): 56.

19. A. Shebalina, ed., *Vissarion Yakovlevich Shebalin: literaturnoye naslediye* (Moscow, 1975), 41.

20. Viktor Vinogradov, "NB k Tret'yey simfonii Shostakovicha," *Sovetskaya muzïka*

3 (1991): 58. When it was published in 1932, the symphony acquired its definitive designation as Shostakovich's Third Symphony (*The First of May*), op. 20. Curiously, in this edition the author of the choral text was camouflaged as "* * *", an omission all the more conspicuous since the name of the translator into German is supplied. See D. Shostakovich, *Tret'ya simfoniya (pervomayskaya), partitura* (Moscow, 1932).

21. V. Muzalevskiy, "Novïye simfonii (filarmoniya)," *Krasnaya gazeta (vech. vïp.)* 24 January 1930, 4.

22. *Nos. Gosudarstvennïy Malïy Opernïy Teatr* (Leningrad, 1930), 2–3.

23. D. Shostakovich, "Pochemu 'Nos'?," *Rabochiy i teatr* 3 (15 January 1930): 11.

24. Letter from Shostakovich to Smolich dated 7 June 1929, quoted in G. Yudin, "Vasha rabota dlya menya sobïtiye na vsyu zhizn'," *Sovetskaya muzïka* 6 (1983): 90.

25. D. Zhitormirskiy, "'Nos'—opera D. Shostakovicha," *Proletarskiy muzïkant* 7–8 (1929): 39.

26. Transcript of the discussion of the opera *The Nose* at the Moscow-Narva House of Culture on 14 January 1930, SPgGMTMI, kn. 7755/4143 oru. 5365.

27. S. Gres, "Ruchnaya bomba anarkhista," *Rabochiy i teatr* 10 (21 February 1930): 6.

28. "Novosti iskusstva," *Rabochiy i teatr* 8 (10 February 1930): 17.

29. Letter from Shostakovich to Smolich dated 2 January 1930, in Yudin, "Vasha rabota," 91.

30. V. Kiselev, "Iz pisem 1930-kh godov," *Sovetskaya muzïka* 9 (1987): 87.

31. Ibid., 89.

32. A. B. Nikritina, in Khentova, *V mire Shostakovicha*, 145.

33. Mindful of the Malïy Theater's primary mission as an experimental theater, a commission of Narkompros approved a scheduled revival of *The Nose* in March 1933 (after the dissolution of the "proletarian" cultural organizations). This revival did not take place. See "Opera, kotoraya delayet epokhu," *Pro Musica* 7 (September 1996): 4.

34. *Sovetskiy teatr*, 118.

35. D. Shostakovich, "Za muzïkal'nuyu kul'turu," *Rabochiy i teatr* 14 (1 April 1929): 4.

36. L. E. Fay, "Shostakovich, LASM i Asaf'yev," in *D. D. Shostakovich: sbornik statey k 90-letiyu so dnya rozhdeniya*, comp. L. Kovnatskaya (St. Petersburg, 1996), 29–34.

37. Shostakovich retained his sinecure at TRAM until at least the autumn of 1932. He informed Sollertinsky from Gudauta in a letter dated 16 September of that year that, having taken an advance of 400 rubles from TRAM and decamped, he was expecting trouble on his return to Leningrad: "If TRAM kicks me out, I will seek another spot for myself." See L. Mikheyeva-Sollertinskaya, "Pis'ma Shostakovicha k Sollertinskomu," *Zhurnal lyubiteley iskusstva* 1 (1997): 20.

38. A. Balanchivadze in *Dmitriy Shostakovich*, comp. G. Ordzhonikidze (Moscow, 1967), 96–97.

39. E. Sass-Tisovskaya, "Nas utro vstrechayet prokhladoy …," *Muzïkal'naya zhizn'* 10–11 (1995): 18.

40. See M. Yakubov, "Ya pïtalsya peredat' pafos bor'bï i pobedï," *Sovetskaya muzïka* 10 (1986): 56.

41. Balanchivadze in *Dmitriy Shostakovich*, 97.

42. M. Sokolovskiy, D. Shostakovich, R. Suslovich, and I. Vuskovich, "K postanovke 'Vïstrela' v Lngr. Trame," *Zhizn' iskusstva* 50 (1929): 10.

43. D. Shostakovich, "Anketa 'Proletarskogo muzïkanta' o 'lyogkom zhanre,'" *Proletarskiy muzïkant* 3 (1930): 25.

44. Ibid.

45. *Proletarskiy muzïkant* 6 (1930): 39.

46. *Aleksandr Vasil'yevich Gauk: memuarï, izbrannïye stat'i, vospominaniya sovremennikov*, comp. L. P. Gauk, R. V. Glezer, and Ya. I. Mil'shteyn (Moscow, 1975), 125.

47. "Usloviya konkursa na libretto sovetskogo baleta," *Rabochiy i teatr* 2 (1929): 17.

48. The previous year, Shostakovich contracted with the Bolshoy Theater in Moscow to contribute the music for the third act of a four-act collective ballet, *The Four Moscows*, his act to be set at a "communist subbotnik in 1919." Like every other initiative by the Bolshoy to commission Shostakovich throughout his career, *The Four Moscows* was never realized. See I. Barsova, "Mif o Moskve-stolitse (1920–1930)," *Muzïkal'naya akademiya* 2 (1997): 175; *Sovetskiy teatr*, 118.

49. RGALI (SPb) f. 337, op. 1, yed. khr. 65.

50. D. Shostakovich, "Avtor—o muzïke baleta," in *Zolotoy vek* (Leningrad, 1931), 4.

51. I. Sollertinskiy, "Novïy balet 'Dinamiada,'" *Zhizn' iskusstva* 38 (22 September 1929): 14.

52. Kaplan and Vasiliy Vaynonen were ultimately credited as the "authors" of the ballet, while the choreography of individual dances was credited to V. P. Chesnakov and Leonid Yakobson. See *Zolotoy vek*, 1.

53. V. Khodasevich, *Portretï slovami: ocherki* (Moscow, 1987), 244.

54. *Aleksandr Vasil'yevich Gauk*, 124–25.

55. "Pochemu otlozhen 'Zolotoy vek'? (pis'mo v redaktsiyu)," and "Pis'mo v redaktsiyu," *Rabochiy i teatr* 35 (25 June 1930): 7, 16.

56. Kiselev, "Iz pisem 1930-kh godov," 91.

57. Letter from Shostakovich to Smolich dated 30 October 1930, in Yudin, "Vasha rabota," 91–92.

58. Letter from Oborin to Meyerhold dated 4 September 1930, in *Vstrechi s proshlïm, vip. 6* (Moscow, 1988), 246.

59. Letter from Shostakovich to Sollertinsky dated 10 February 1930, in L. Mikheyeva-Sollertinskaya, "D. D. Shostakovich v otrazhenii pisem k I. I. Sollertinskomu," in *D. D. Shostakovich: sbornik statey k 90-letiyu so dnya rozhdeniya*, comp. L. Kovnatskaya (St. Petersburg, 1996), 94.

60. *Rabochiy i teatr* 12 (30 April 1931): 22.

61. Called on to justify his partiality for the circus on more than one occasion, he invariably cited its uncompromising professionalism and artistic mastery. In the 1920s he told Margarita Ozhigova: "If an acrobat performs his stunts the way some of us play the piano he risks breaking his neck." See M. Ozhigova, "Mitya, Dmitriy Dmitriyevich," *Muzïkal'naya pedagogika v ideyakh i litsakh: sbornik statey*, ed. A. Selitskiy (Rostov-on-Don, 1992), 87. To some supercilious students, in the 1940s, Shostakovich offered a different musical analogy: "The circus is the purest of art forms. And note that like any genuine art form it brooks no counterfeit. The director's tone-deaf wife, the committee chairman's aunt or somebody else may sing in op-

era. But only a person expertly trained can perform on the flying trapeze. It is inconceivable to enter the lion's cage simply by 'pulling strings.'" See Ye. Makarov, "Ya bezgranicho uvazhal ego ...," *Muzïkal'naya akademiya* 1 (1993): 151.

62. "Fellow traveler" was an appellation current in the 1920s and early 1930s used to designate creative artists who, without having openly embraced the socialist revolution, were deemed to be in basic sympathy with its ideals.

63. D. Shostakovich, "Deklaratsiya obyazannostey kompozitora," *Rabochiy i teatr* 31 (20 November 1931): 6.

64. Ibid.

65. Letter from Shostakovich to Shebalin dated 29 November 1931, in A. Shebalina, ed., "Eto bïl zamechatel'nïy drug," *Sovetskaya muzïka* 7 (1982): 77. In fact, on more than one occasion that autumn Shostakovich chastised his Muscovite friend for his appeasement of RAPM. See the reminiscences of A. M. Shebalina in Khentova, *V mire Shostakovicha,* 129.

66. M. Yankovskiy, "Kto protiv—edinoglasno," *Rabochiy i teatr* 32–33 (12 December 1931): 10.

67. D. Shostakovich, "Ot Marksa do nashikh dney," *Sovetskoye iskusstvo* (15 February 1932): 1. For more detail, see Chapter 5.

Chapter 5

1. D. Shostakovich, "Plakat' i smeyat'sya," *Sovetskoye iskusstvo* (3 March 1933): 3.

2. M. Shaginyan, "50 pisem D. D. Shostakovicha," *Novïy mir* 12 (1982): 130; English translation in M. Shaginyan, "Fifty Letters from Dmitri Shostakovich," *Soviet Literature* 1 (1984): 72.

3. N. S. Leskov, *Ledi Makbet Mtsenskogo uyezda* (Leningrad, 1930). It is also likely that he had seen the silent film, *Katerina Izmailova,* directed by Cheslav Sabinsky and released by Leningrad Sovkino in 1927.

4. L. Mikheyeva, "Istoriya odnoy druzhbï," *Sovetskaya muzïka* 9 (1986): 31.

5. G. Yudin, "Vasha rabota dlya menya sobïtiye na vsyu zhizn'," *Sovetskaya muzïka* 6 (1983): 92.

6. B. Mordvinov, "Zhivïye lyudi, a ne opernïye maski," *Katerina Izmailova, Opera v 4-kh deystviyakh i 9 kartinakh: libretto* (Moscow, 1934), 15.

7. D. Shostakovich, "Tragediya—satira," *Sovetskoye iskusstvo* (16 October 1932).

8. D. Shostakovich, "Opernïy portfel' kompozitora," *Rabochiy i teatr* 17 (17 June 1933): 22.

9. I. Varzar, "Molodoy Shostakovich—stranitsï iz zhizni," *Niva* 9 (1996): 235.

10. Later, after her marriage to Shostakovich, she confessed she could not summon the courage to sing even her favorite songs in front of her husband; ibid., 238.

11. *Fine Printed and Manuscript Music Including the Mannheim Collection,* catalogue for Sotheby's auction, 6 December 1991 (London, 1991), 151.

12. V. Seroff, in collaboration with Nadejda Galli-Shohat, *Dmitri Shostakovich: The Life and Background of a Soviet Composer* (New York, 1943), 180.

13. J. Jelagin, *The Taming of the Arts,* trans. Nicholas Wreden (New York, 1951), 35.

14. D. Shostakovich, "Ot Marksa do nashikh dney," *Sovetskoye iskusstvo* (15 February 1932): 1. In a 1973 interview, Shostakovich recalled he had selected the verses and had actually begun composing the work some forty years earlier, having in mind to

create something "grandiose." See S. Khentova, *V mire Shostakovicha* (Moscow, 1996), 35.

15. See S. Khentova, *Shostakovich: zhizn' i tvorchestvo*, 1 (Leningrad, 1985), 334–36. The "counterplan" in the film's title alludes to a bold initiative fielded by the factory rank and file.

16. For all the apparent effort invested in the song, however, it triggered more than one accusation of plagiarism. See reminiscences of Abram Ashkenazy and Galina Serebryakova in Khentova, *V mire Shostakovicha*, 125–26, 141; see also V. Zak, *Shostakovich i yevrey?* (New York, 1997), 119.

17. Because of its title, this song has been widely misinterpreted as a hymn for the international organization, which in 1942 was not yet in existence. In fact, it is a World War II song, a rallying anthem for the Allied nations.

18. Ye. Makarov, "Ya bezgranichno uvazhal ego," *Muzïkal'naya akademiya* 1 (1993): 150.

19. L. Atovm'yan, "Iz vospominaniy," *Muzïkal'naya akademiya* 4 (1997): 69–70.

20. D. Shostakovich, "'Ekaterina Izmailova' Avtor ob opere," *Sovetskoye iskusstvo* (14 December 1933).

21. M. Druskin, *Issledovaniya, vospominaniya* (Leningrad, 1977), 225.

22. O. Lamm, *Stranitsï tvorcheskoy biografii Myaskovskogo* (Moscow, 1989), 224.

23. Shostakovich, "Plakat' i smeyat'sya," 3.

24. RGALI (SPb) f. 290, op. 1, yed. khr. 9. Information provided by Lyudmila Kovnatskaya.

25. In a diary entry dating from September 1934, Tsekhanovsky remarked about Shostakovich: "A remarkable kid. Very attentive, very talented.... He is revered as nothing short of a genius. Works with extraordinary speed, but without lessening the quality in the slightest. A real artist. A real master." See S. Khentova, *Shostakovich v Petrograde-Leningrade*, 2nd ed. (Leningrad, 1981), 111.

26. V. Iokhel'son, "Na poroge 4-y godovshchinï L.S.S.K," *Sovetskaya muzïka* 11 (1935): 15.

27. P. A. Markov, *Rezhissura V. I. Nemirovich-Danchenko v muzïkal'nom teatre* (Moscow, 1960), 221.

28. *S. S. Prokof'yev i N. Ya. Myaskovskiy: perepiska* (Moscow, 1977), 403.

29. Z. A. Apetyan, *Gavriil Popov: iz literaturnogo naslediya* (Leningrad, 1986), 252.

30. S. A. Samosud, "Opera, kotoraya delayet epokhu," in *"Ledi Makbet Mtsenskogo uyezda": opera D. D. Shostakovicha* (Leningrad, 1934), 11.

31. *Krasnaya gazeta (vech. vip.)*, 23 January 1934, quoted in "Opera, kotoraya delayet epokhu," *Pro Musica* 7 (1996): 4.

32. Letter from Shostakovich to L. Atovmyan dated 24 February 1934; "Iz pisem," *Muzïkal'naya akademiya* 4 (1997): 71.

33. D. Shostakovich, "Sovetskaya muzïkal'naya kritika otstayot," *Sovetskaya muzïka* 3 (1933): 121.

34. D. Shostakovich in *Rabochiy i teatr* 27 (1934): 7.

35. D. Shostakovich, "Schast'e poznaniya," *Sovetskoye iskusstvo* (5 November 1934): 5.

36. Yudin, "Vasha rabota," 92.

37. RGALI (SPb) f. 290, op. 1, yed. khr. 40. For that period the box office took in

459,087 rubles, against total expenses of 68,035 rubles. Information provided by Lyudmila Kovnatskaya.

38. S. Korev, "Opernïy sezon na radio," *Govorit SSSR* 14 (1934): 19.

39. L. and P. Tur, "Sovremennik budushchego," *Vechernyaya krasnaya gazeta*, 10 February 1934, 3. Many years later, Levon Atovmyan reconstructed from memory the basic scenario of the second opera of the cycle; see Atovm'yan, "Iz vospominaniy," 72–73.

40. D. Shostakovich, "Budem trubachami velikoy epokhi," *Leningradskaya Pravda*, 28 December 1934, 4.

41. S. Khentova, "Zhenshchinï v zhizni Shostakovicha," *Vremya i mï* 112 (1991): 250.

42. "Opera Shostakovicha 'Podnyataya tselina'; libretto pishet Sholokhov," *Smena* (26 September 1935): 4. In the event, it was not Shostakovich but Ivan Dzerzhinsky, following up his success with *The Quiet Don*, who composed a "music drama" on *Virgin Soil Upturned* to a libretto by L. Dzerzhinsky. It was premiered at the Bolshoy Theater in Moscow on 23 October 1937.

43. M. Chudakova, "Zhizneopisaniye Mikhaila Bulgakova," *Moskva* 12 (1988): 59.

44. Though Khentova and other biographers report his election to this post in 1933, period sources point to the following year. See "Znatnïye lyudi teatra," *Rabochiy i teatr* 36 (1934): 2.

45. Shostakovich, "Schast'e poznaniya," 5.

46. Ibid.

47. Shostakovich, "Budem trubachami velikoy epokhi," 4.

48. L. Mikheyeva-Sollertinskaya, "D. D. Shostakovich v otrazhenii pisem k I. I. Sollertinskomu. Shtrikhi k portretu," in *D. D. Shostakovich: sbornik statey k 90-letiyu so dnya rozhdeniya*, comp. L. Kovnatskaya (St. Petersburg, 1996), 92.

49. Atovm'yan, "Iz vospominaniy," 70.

50. Mikheyeva-Sollertinskaya, "D. D. Shostakovich v otrazhenii pisem k I. I. Sollertinskomu," 93.

51. Flora Litvinova in E. Wilson, *Shostakovich: A Life Remembered* (London, 1994), 161.

52. Ibid.

53. D. Shostakovich, "God posle 'Ledi Makbet': beseda s kompozitorom D. Shostakovichem," *Krasnaya gazeta (vech. vïp.)*, 12 January 1935, 2.

54. "D. D. Shostakovich o svoyom tvorchestve," *Sovetskoye iskusstvo* (29 March 1935): 3.

55. D. Shostakovich, "Moy tvorcheskiy put'," *Izvestiya*, 3 April 1935, 4.

56. D. Shostakovich, "Moy tretiy balet," in *Svetlïy ruchey* (Leningrad, 1935), 14.

57. I. Barsova, "*The Limpid Stream* is the third ballet by Dmitri Shostakovich," in D. Shostakovich, *The Limpid Stream, op. 39, piano score* (Moscow, 1997), 219.

58. Khentova, "Zhenshchinï," 252.

59. Shostakovich, "Moy tretiy balet," 15.

60. Letter from Shostakovich to Sollertinsky dated March 1935, in L. Mikheyeva-Sollertinskaya, "Pis'ma Shostakovicha Sollertinskomu," *Zhurnal lyubiteley iskusstva* 6–7 (1997): 47–48.

61. Many sources incorrectly list the date of the premiere as 4 April 1935.

62. I. Sollertinskiy, "*Svetlïy ruchey* v Gos. Malom opernom teatre," *Rabochiy i teatr* 12 (June 1935): 14.

63. Mikheyeva-Sollertinskaya, "D. D. Shostakovich v otrazhenii pisem k I. I. Sollertinskomu," 94.

64. I. Sollertinskiy, "*Svetlïy ruchey*: baletnaya prem'era v Bol'shom teatre," *Sovetskoye iskusstvo* (5 December 1935): 3.

65. Mikheyeva-Sollertinskaya, "D. D. Shostakovich v otrazhenii pisem k I. I. Sollertinskomu," 96–97. This was the concluding session of the All-Union Conference of Stakhanovites, held in the Kremlin from 14 to 17 November, at which Stalin coined the catch phrase "Zhit' stalo luchshe, tovarishchi. Zhit' stalo veseley" [Life has become better, comrades. Life has become more joyful]. See *Sovetskoye iskusstvo* (23 November 1935): 1.

66. "Beseda tovarishchey Stalina i Molotova s avtorami opernogo spektaklya *Tikhiy Don*," *Sovetskaya muzïka* 2 (1936): 3.

67. "Sumbur vmesto muzïki; ob opere 'Ledi Makbet Mtsenskogo uyezda,'" *Pravda*, 28 January 1936, 3. Over the years, while Stalin's role as the compelling force behind this editorial has remained undisputed, there has been much speculation about the actual authorship, with as many as a dozen nominees proposed. Although many questions remain, the recent revelation of his own admission of authorship would seem to tip the scales in favor of one of the principal candidates, David Zaslavsky, a *Pravda* staff journalist. See I. Rïzhkin, "Shest' desyatiletiy Moskovskogo soyuza kompozitorov 1932–1991 gg.," *Moskovskiy kompozitor* (June 1991): 2. Without having considered this confession, but relying on selected archival sources and textual analysis, Leonid Maksimenkov has dismissed Zaslavsky's candidacy in favor of that of Platon Kerzhentsev, head of the newly founded Committee for Artistic Affairs. See L. Maksimenkov, *Sumbur vmesto muzïki: stalinskaya kul'turnaya revolyutsiya, 1936–1938* (Moscow, 1997), 88–112.

68. "Sumbur vmesto muzïki," 3.

69. "Baletnaya fal'sh'," *Pravda*, 6 February 1936, 3.

Chapter 6

1. I. Bragin, "Vstrecha yunïkh kompozitorov s Dm. Shostakovichem," *Severnïy komsomolets* (Arkhangelsk), 6 February 1936. The story that after the appearance of the "Muddle" editorial Shostakovich was run out of town straightaway is untrue. See M. I. Chulaki, "Segodnya rasskazhu o Shostakoviche," *Zvezda* 7 (1987): 189.

2. RGALI f. 2048, op. 1, yed. khr. 159.

3. D. Shostakovich, "Moy tvorcheskiy put'," *Izvestiya*, 3 April 1935, 4.

4. *Sovetskaya muzïka* 5 (1935): 31.

5. Ibid., 33.

6. See, for instance, D. Shostakovich, "Schast'e poznaniya," *Sovetskoye iskusstvo* (5 November 1934): 5; "D. D. Shostakovich o svoyom tvorchestve," *Sovetskoye iskusstvo* (29 March 1935): 3; Shostakovich, "Moy tvorcheskiy put'," 4.

7. L. Mikheyeva, *I. I. Sollertinskiy: zhizn' i naslediye* (Leningrad, 1988), facsimile letter after 160.

8. Shostakovich's public statements about Dzerzhinsky's *The Quiet Don* were not uncritical; he was considerably more derisive in his letters to Sollertinsky. See, for ex-

ample, L. Mikheyeva-Sollertinskaya, "Pis'ma Shostakovicha k Sollertinskomu," *Zhurnal lyubiteley iskusstva* 8–9 (1997), 63–64.

9. Although his reminiscences were recorded more than thirty years after the fact, Atovmyan's recollection—that, in the period in between Shostakovich's return to Moscow from Arkhangelsk and the appearance of the second *Pravda* editorial on 6 February 1936, one of the composer's major concerns was not that his ballet *The Limpid Stream* might fall victim to the same kind of abuse as his opera but rather the *opposite*, that it might be extolled by comparison—sounds plausible. See L. Atovm'yan, "Iz vospominaniy," *Muzïkal'naya akademiya* 4 (1997): 73.

10. "Stroitel'stvo sotsialisticheskogo iskusstva: vïstupleniye P. M. Kerzhentsev na III plenume TsK RABIS," *Sovetskoye iskusstvo* (17 February 1936): 2.

11. After the appearance of the "Muddle" editorial, Shostakovich's opera did not disappear immediately from the boards at any of the theaters where it had been playing. Its last contemporary performance took place at the Nemirovich-Danchenko Musical Theater in Moscow on 7 March 1936.

12. T. Goryayeva, comp., *Istoriya sovetskoy politicheskoy tsenzurï* (Moscow, 1977), 480–81. Kerzhentsev's formula for Shostakovich's rehabilitation also included the advice to travel around the country gathering folk songs; Shostakovich acceded to the concrete recommendation to select and harmonize 100 of the best songs he collected. Neither the collecting trip nor the harmonizations were realized. If Shostakovich did write a "repentant" letter, it has not yet come to light.

13. L. Mikheyeva-Sollertinskaya, "D. D. Shostakovich v otrazhenii pisem k I. I. Sollertinskomu Shtrikhi k portretu," in *D. D. Shostakovich: sbornik statey k 90-letiyu so dnya rozhdeniya*, comp. L. Kovnatskaya (St. Petersburg, 1996), 98. Golovanov's new production of *The Quiet Don* flopped when it was unveiled at the Bolshoy Theater in March 1936. The utter failure of the Bolshoy, the "court" theater, to have made any headway with Soviet repertory, in sharp contrast to the pioneering successes of Leningrad's Malïy Theater, was one of the subtexts of the crisis. In April 1936, Golovanov was fired from the Bolshoy Theater. Named to the newly created post of artistic director was Samosud, who was also rewarded for his achievement at the Malïy Theater with the title "People's Artist of the Russian Federation" and the order "Badge of Honor." See *Sovetskoye iskusstvo* (23 February 1936): 4, (5 March 1936): 1, (11 April 1936): 2.

14. M. Gorkiy, "Dva pis'ma Stalinu," *Literaturnaya gazeta* (10 March 1993): 6.

15. Pasternak letter dated 13 May 1936, in C. Barnes and R. Davis, ed., "'Neotsenimïy podarok': perepiska Pasternakov i Lomonosovïkh (1925–1970)," in *Minuvsheye: istoricheskiy al'manakh* 17 (Moscow, 1994), 394–95.

16. N. Chushkin, "V sporakh o teatre," in *Vstrechi s Meyerhol'dom: sbornik vospominaniy* (Moscow, 1967), 428–29.

17. V. E. Meyerkhol'd: stat'i, pis'ma, rechi, besedï. chast' vtoraya, 1917–1939, comp. V. E. Fevral'skiy (Moscow, 1968), 372.

18. L. V. Guseva, "Ves' dlya lyudey," in *Marshal Tukhachevskiy: vospominaniya druzey i soratnikov* (Moscow, 1965), 156.

19. *Pis'ma k drugu: Dmitriy Shostakovich—Isaaku Glikmanu*, comp. I. Glikman (Moscow, 1993), 9.

20. *Andrey Balanchivadze: sbornik statey i materialov* (Tbilisi, 1979), 16.

21. *V. V. Shcherbachyov: stat'i, materialï, pis'ma*, comp. R. Slonimskaya (Leningrad, 1985), 250. In the event, Shostakovich's daughter was named Galina.

22. *Pis'ma k drugu*, 299.

23. D. Shostakovich, "Budem trubachami velikoy epokhi," *Leningradskaya Pravda*, 28 December 1934, 4.

24. RGALI f. 2048, op. 1, yed. khr. 4.

25. Shostakovich, "Moy tvorcheskiy put'," 4.

26. D. Shostakovich, "Balet i muzïka," *Vechernyaya Moskva*, 11 April 1935, 3.

27. *S. S. Prokof'yev i N. Ya. Myaskovskiy: perepiska* (Moscow, 1977), 444.

28. L. Mikheyeva, "Istoriya odnoy druzhbï; chast' vtoraya," *Sovetskaya muzïka* 9 (1987): 78.

29. S. Khentova, *V mire Shostakovicha* (Moscow, 1996), 296.

30. A page of extracts from Mahler's Third Symphony illustrating "rare cases in orchestration" copied in Shostakovich's hand is presumed to date from this period; RGALI f. 2048, op. 1, yed. khr. 64. Shostakovich's orchestra was also comparable in size and dynamic range, it should be noted, with the First Symphony of Popov—a work harboring Mahleresque aspirations of its own—premiered in Leningrad in 1935 shortly before Shostakovich embarked on the definitive version of his Fourth Symphony.

31. *Pis'ma k drugu*, 11–12.

32. Shostakovich letter to Atovmyan, 23 September 1936 [probably misdated for 23 November]; L. Atovm'yan, "Iz pisem," *Muzïkal'naya akademiya* 4 (1997): 75.

33. A. Glumov, *Nestertïye stroki* (Moscow, 1977), 310.

34. Shostakovich letter to Atovmyan, 23 September 1936 [probably misdated for 23 November]; Atovm'yan, "Iz pisem," 75. Although he committed his memoirs to paper at a distance of more than thirty years, Atovmyan describes visiting Shostakovich in the summer of 1936 and hearing his Fourth Symphony. When he inquired of the composer what he thought *Pravda* would make of it, Shostakovich allegedly bristled: "I don't write for the newspaper *Pravda*, but for myself. I basically don't think about who will say what about my work, but write about what moves me, what has sprouted in my soul and mind. As for how they evaluate the symphony, that is the business of critics, who get paid for it. And money, as everyone knows, doesn't smell." L. Atovm'yan, "Iz vospominaniy," *Muzïkal'naya akademiya* 4 (1997): 74.

35. "Khronika," *Sovetskoye iskusstvo* (11 December 1936): 4.

36. *Pis'ma k drugu*, 12–13. Vladimir Iokhelson, it should be noted, had been instrumental in the suppression of Gavriil Popov's First Symphony—a ban successfully protested by Shostakovich and many other composers—after its only public performance on 22 March 1935. See Z. A. Apetyan, *Gavriil Popov: iz literaturnogo naslediya* (Leningrad, 1986), 362–63.

37. V. Razhnikov, *Kirill Kondrashin rasskazïvayet o muzïke i zhizni* (Moscow, 1989), 182.

38. D. Shostakovich, "Dumï o proydyonnom puti," *Sovetskaya muzïka* 9 (1956): 14. In a 1942 interview, Nina Shostakovich offered an entirely different excuse: "The Fourth Symphony, for example, never saw daylight because the instrumentation of a few bars of the finale failed to satisfy Dmitri and he could not contemplate rewriting

them." See N. Shostakovich, "Mrs. Shostakovitch Writes about Her Husband," *Boston Sunday Globe*, 4 October 1942, sec. 2, 4. Contrary to some reports, Shostakovich made no revisions of any significance at all to the symphony during the years it languished unperformed.

39. R. A. Leonard, "Case of the Missing Bridge," *HiFi & Music Review* 1, no. 7 (October 1958): 25.

40. R. Shchedrin, "Kommentarii k proshlomu," *Muzïkal'naya zhizn'* 10 (1989): 6.

41. See, for instance, the reminiscences of A. Ashkenazy and A. Balanchivadze in Khentova, *V mire Shostakovicha*, 121, 282; also D. Tolstoy, *Dlya chego vsyo eto bïlo* (St. Petersburg, 1995), 107.

42. Khentova, *V mire Shostakovicha*, 35.

43. Ye. Makarov, "Ya bezgranichno uvazhal ego," *Muzïkal'naya akademiya* 1 (1993): 153.

44. O. Lamm, *Stranitsï tvorcheskoy biografii Myaskovskogo* (Moscow, 1989), 255–56.

45. Makarov, "Ya bezgranichno uvazhal ego," 153. Shostakovich's reduction of the Fourth Symphony for two pianos was published in an edition of 300 copies in Moscow in 1946.

46. Shostakovich letter to Atovmyan, 24 March 1937, GTsMMK f. 32, yed. khr. 1760. See also the composer's personnel file at the St. Petersburg Conservatory, LGK arkhiv polka delo no. 254 (84–140).

47. People's Commissariat for Internal Affairs, the state security service.

48. Shostakovich letter to Sollertinsky dated 26 May 1937, in L. Mikheyeva-Sollertinskaya, "Pis'ma Shostakovicha k Sollertinskomu," *Zhurnal lyubiteley iskusstva* 10–11 (1997): 47.

49. See reminiscences of A. Ashkenazy in Khentova, *V mire Shostakovicha*, 122. Shostakovich remained a staunch friend of the Dombrovsky family, looking out for the welfare of their two sons and, in the 1950s, campaigning successfully for the release and rehabilitation of Genrietta and the posthumous rehabilitation of her husband.

50. D. Dubrovskiy, "Strana zhdyot yarkikh proizvedeniy," *Sovetskoye iskusstvo* (11 April 1937): 2.

51. Shostakovich letter to Sollertinsky dated 7 May 1937, in L. Mikheyeva-Sollertinskaya, "Pis'ma Shostakovicha k Sollertinskomu," *Zhurnal lyubiteley iskusstva* 10–11 (1997): 46.

52. G. Frid, "30-ye godï. Konservatoriya. N. S. Zhilyayev," *Sovetskaya muzïka* 3 (1991): 11. Frid's dating of this visit in May is contradicted by other sources.

53. Ibid.

54. Arrested on 3 November 1937, he was executed on 21 January 1938; see I. Vinokurova, "Trizhdï rasstrelyannïy muzïkant," *Muzïkal'naya akademiya* 1 (1996): 82–83.

55. Veniamin Basner in E. Wilson, *Shostakovich: A Life Remembered* (London, 1994), 124–25. The composer evidently also related a version of this story to Krzysztof Meyer. See K. Meyer, *Chostakovitch* (Paris, 1994), 211.

56. *Sovetskoye iskusstvo* (29 August 1937): 4. In a preserved piano sketch, the end of the fourth movement is dated 11 September 1937. See RGALI f. 2048, op. 1, yed. khr. 6.

57. D. Shostakovich, "Moy tvorcheskiy otvet," *Vechernyaya Moskva*, 25 January 1938, 3.

58. *V. V. Shcherbachyov*, 251.

59. *Pis'ma k drugu*, 14.

60. Glumov, *Nestertïye stroki*, 316.

61. Lyubov Vasilievna Shaporina, in *Intimacy and Terror: Soviet Diaries of the 1930s*, ed. V. Garros, N. Korenevskaya, and T. Lahusen (New York, 1995), 356.

62. A. Livshchits, *Zhizn' za rodinu svoyu: ocherki o kompozitorakh i muzïkovedakh, pogibshikh v Velikuyu Otechestvennuyu voynu* (Moscow, 1964), 300.

63. A. Shebalina, *V. Ya. Shebalin: godï zhizni i tvorchestva* (Moscow, 1990), 99.

64. Another Philharmonic administrator later confirmed that the atmosphere surrounding the premiere of the Fifth Symphony had been tense, its success with the authorities by no means assured. See reminiscences of I. G. Admoni in Khentova, *V mire Shostakovicha*, 156.

65. M. Chulaki, "Segodnya rasskazhu o Shostakoviche," 190. Chulaki identifies the two officials as V. N. Surin and the musicologist B. M. Yarustovsky. Both were subsequently lampooned by Shostakovich in his scathing satire, *Rayok*.

66. *Aleksandr Vasil'yevich Gauk: memuariï, izbrannïye stat'i, vospominaniya sovremennikov*, comp. L. P. Gauk, R. V. Glezer, and Ya. I. Mil'shteyn (Moscow, 1975), 129.

67. The prerevolutionary Mariyinsky Theater, which became the State Academic Theater of Opera and Ballet (GATOB) in 1920, was named after Kirov in 1935.

68. Ye. Mravinskiy, "Tridtsat' let s muzïkoy Shostakovicha," in *Dmitriy Shostakovich*, comp. G. Ordzhonikidze (Moscow, 1967), 112.

69. Ibid., 113.

70. Ye. Mravinskiy, "Vïstupleniye v Leningradskom soyuze sovetskikh kompozitorov na diskussii o sovetskoy simfonii s analizom 5-y simfonii D. D. Shostakovicha. Stenogram," 29 December 1937; RGALI f. 2048, op. 3, yed. khr. 404.

71. A. Tolstoy, "Pyataya simfoniya Shostakovicha," *Izvestiya*, 28 December 1937, 3.

72. "Pyataya simfoniya Shostakovicha," *Literaturnaya gazeta* (12 January 1938): 5.

73. D. Shostakovich, "Vmeste s narodom," *Sovetskoye iskusstvo* (12 January 1938): 2.

74. Shostakovich, "Moy tvorcheskiy otvet," 3.

75. Ibid.

76. Russian-language reviews, biographies, and catalogues make no mention of the "subtitle," nor does it feature in concert programs. Exactly how, when, and why it took such firm root in the Western literature remains unclear.

77. Lamm, *Stranitsï biografii Myaskovskogo*, 265.

78. *N. A. Mal'ko: vospominaniya, stat'i, pis'ma*, ed. L. Raaben (Leningrad, 1972), 281.

79. V. Tsukkerman, "Iz kladovoy pamyati," *Sovetskaya muzïka* 10 (1987): 109.

80. See B. Kats, "Shostakovich kak predmet poeticheskogo vnimaniya," in *D. D. Shostakovich: sbornik statey k 90-letiyu so dnya rozhdeniya*, comp. L. Kovnatskaya (St. Petersburg, 1996), 368.

81. B. Khaykin, *Besedï o dirizhyorskom remesle: stat'i* (Moscow, 1984), 89.

82. "I think it is clear to everyone what happens in the Fifth. The rejoicing is

forced, created under threat, as in *Boris Godunov*. It's as if someone were beating you with a stick and saying, 'Your business is rejoicing, your business is rejoicing,' and you rise, shaky, and go marching off, muttering, 'Our business is rejoicing, our business is rejoicing.'" See S. Volkov, *Testimony: The Memoirs of Dmitri Shostakovich* (New York, 1979), 183.

83. Interpreting the intent of this finale has been hampered by widely disparate published tempo markings for the coda (fig. 131)—the final thirty-five-measure flourish of brass fanfares and timpani bringing the symphony to its imposing D-major close. The original edition of the score (Moscow-Leningrad, 1939) gave the brisk marking of quarter note=188, a tempo restored by the editor of volume 3 of Shostakovich's *Collected Works* (Moscow, 1980). This, however, does not account for the fact that in the 1947 Muzgiz reprint of the score, which used the plates from the original 1939 edition with otherwise minor emendations, the tempo at fig. 131 was cut almost in half to eighth note=184, strongly suggesting that the marking in the original engraving was the mistake. The correction to the slower tempo is bolstered by Alexander Gauk and Maxim Shostakovich, among other conductors who worked with the composer. Most Western editions followed the text of the first edition without reference to the 1947 reprint.

That being said, Shostakovich was notoriously cavalier with respect to his published tempo markings; when satisfied with an interpretation he was known to reassure perplexed performers by confessing that his "metronome was broken." Broken metronome or no, Shostakovich persisted in affixing tempo markings to his scores and was not indifferent to unacceptable meddling with them (see, for instance, G. Yudin, "V molodïye godï," *Sovetskaya muzïka* 9 [1986]: 38). Ironically, one instance where he appreciated the radical alteration of a tempo marking was in Leonard Bernstein's performance of the Fifth Symphony with the New York Philharmonic in Moscow in 1959, where the coda was performed at a breathless pace (see Columbia Masterworks MS 6115; re-released on CD in the CBS Great Performances series, MYK 37128). In authorizing Russian conductor Mark Paverman to take comparable license with the score the following year, Shostakovich wrote: "I was very taken with the performance of my Fifth Symphony by the talented Leonard Bernstein. I liked it that he played the end of the finale significantly faster than is customary." From a letter dated 19 July 1960, in Khentova, *V mire Shostakovicha*, 321.

84. T. Grum-Grzhimailo, "Zagadka Shostakovicha," *Smena* 3 (1990): 221.

85. "Deklaratsiya predsedatelya Leningradskogo soyuza kompozitorov I. O. Dunayevskogo prezidiumu soyuza o povïdeniya roli prezidiuma v rukovodstve tvorcheskoy zhizn'yu kompozitorov," 29 January 1938; RGALI f. 2048, op. 1, yed. khr. 160.

86. D. Shostakovich interview, 10 April 1973, in Khentova, *V mire Shostakovicha*, 34.

Chapter 7

1. M. D., "Novïe rabotï kompozitora D. Shostakovicha," *Izvestiya*, 29 September 1938, 4.

2. The inception of this project dated from 1935, not from summer 1936, as claimed in *Pis'ma k drugu: Dmitriy Shostakovich-Isaaku Glikmanu*, comp. I. Glikman (Moscow, 1993), 319.

3. Two months after the appearance of the "Muddle" editorial, the directors of the Malïy Opera Theater announced that, among the nine creative teams it had assembled to produce "Soviet classical opera," it was anticipated that Shostakovich would compose the music for an opera about the revolutionary Baltic fleet in September 1917 to a libretto by O. M. Brik. See B. Rest, "Devyat' sovetskikh oper," *Literaturnaya gazeta* (31 March 1936): 4. Like every other such undertaking initiated in succeeding years, this one was never realized.

4. Shostakovich letter to Yavorsky, 26 June 1938, GTsMMK f. 146, yed. khr. 3290.

5. S. Khentova, *Shostakovich: zhizn' i tvorchestvo,* 1 (Leningrad, 1985), 493.

6. A. Livshchits, *Zhizn' za rodinu svoyu: ocherki o kompozitorakh i muzïkovedakh pogibshikh v Velikuyu Otechestvennuyu voynu* (Moscow, 1964), 299.

7. M. Dolgopolov, "Budem znakomï—Alekhin ...," *Izvestiya,* 17 August 1974, 5. Among others who recall hearing the composer recount versions of this story are Yevgeniy Dolmatovsky and Mstislav Rostropovich.

8. In a 1973 interview, Shostakovich claimed Zamyatin introduced him to Zoshchenko. This must have taken place before Zamyatin's emigration in the fall of 1931. See S. Khentova, *V mire Shostakovicha* (Moscow, 1996), 33.

9. Zoshchenko letter to M. Shaginyan, 4 January 1941, "Mikhail Zoshchenko—Mariette Shaginyan: iz perepiski," *Tallinn* 2 (1989): 99.

10. Shostakovich letter to Sollertinsky, dated 20 September 1936, in L. Mikheyeva-Sollertinskaya, "Pis'ma Shostakovicha k Sollertinskomu," *Zhurnal lyubiteley iskusstva* 10–11 (1997): 45.

11. Z. A. Apetyan, *Gavriil Popov: iz literaturnogo naslediya* (Leningrad, 1986), 104–05

12. A. Mariengof, *Eto Vam, potomki!* (St. Petersburg, 1994), 24.

13. "Mikhail Zoshchenko—Mariette Shaginyan: iz perepiski," 98. The one time Shostakovich visited the author at his Leningrad apartment—he recalled in 1973—Zoshchenko just sat there, as if waiting for him to leave. See Khentova, *V mire Shostakovicha,* 33.

14. L. Chalova, "Takoy on bïl ...," in *Vospominaniya o Mikhaile Zoshchenko,* ed. Yu. Tomashevsky (St. Petersburg, 1995), 339.

15. *Pis'ma k drugu,* 17–18.

16. S. Khentova, *Udivitel'nïy Shostakovich* (St. Petersburg, 1993), 196.

17. This notebook is preserved in the Shostakovich family archive.

18. M. Kozlova, "Mne ispolnilos' vosemnadtsat' let ..." (Pis'ma D. D. Shostakovich k L. N. Oborinu)," *Vstrechi s proshlïm, vip.* 5 (Moscow, 1984)," 250.

19. M. D. "Novïye rabotï," 4.

20. Shostakovich letter to Sollertinsky dated 27 July 1938, in Mikheyeva-Sollertinskaya, "Pis'ma Shostakovicha k Sollertinskomu," 50.

21. M. D., "Novïye rabotï," 4.

22. D. Shostakovich, "O podlinnoy i mnimoy programmnosti," *Sovetskaya muzïka* 5 (1951): 77.

23. Although this performance is consistently credited as the Moscow premiere of the quartet, the Beethoven Quartet had actually performed the work in Moscow for the first time more than three weeks earlier, on 23 October 1938, at a reviewed concert. See N. V. Shirinskaya, "Vospominaniya ob otse," in *V. P. Shirinskiy: stranitsï*

zhizni, tvorchestva i kontsertnoy deyatel'nosti (Moscow, 1996), 63; G. Neygauz, "Strunnïy kvartet Shostakovicha," *Vechernyaya Moskva,* 29 October 1938, 3.

24. D. Shostakovich, "Moi blizhayshiye rabotï," *Rabochiy i teatr* 11 (1939): 24.

25. D. Shostakovich, "Muzïka v kino: zametki kompozitora," *Literaturnaya gazeta* (10 April 1939): 5.

26. M. D., "Novïye rabotï," 4.

27. M. Blanter reminiscences in Khentova, *V mire Shostakovicha,* 158.

28. See S. Skrebkov, "Kontsert Gosudarstvennogo dzhaza Soyuza SSR," *Izvestiya,* 29 November 1938, 4; also A. Kramskoy, "Kontsert Gosudarstvennogo dzhaza SSSR," *Sovetskoye iskusstvo* (16 February 1939): 4.

29. See, for instance, "Editor's Note," *D. Shostakovich: Sobraniye sochineniy v soroka dvukh tomakh,* 10, (Moscow, 1984); D. C. Hulme, *Dmitri Shostakovich: A Catalogue, Bibliography, and Discography,* 2nd ed. (Oxford, 1991), 129–30; E. Meskhishvili, *Dmitriy Shostakovich: notograficheskiy spravochnik* (Moscow, 1995), 111.

30. *V. E. Meyerkhol'd: perepiska 1896–1939* (Moscow, 1976), 348; "Chudesnïy u nas slushatel'; Dmitriy Shostakovich otvechayet na voprosï," *Muzïkal'naya zhizn'* 17 (1966): 7. Despite Meyerhold's evident expectation, in November 1934, that Shostakovich would supply the music for his upcoming production of "Thirty-three Swoons" (based on Chekhov), this did not take place, and late in life Shostakovich denied he had received a commission for this project. See Khentova, *V mire Shostakovicha,* 33. Coincidentally, in the summer of 1938, Shostakovich returned an advance of 1,000 rubles to the Malïy Opera Theater against a contract for an *opera* on *How the Steel Was Tempered.* See Mikheyeva-Sollertinskaya, "Pis'ma Shostakovicha k Sollertinskomu," 50.

31. A. Gladkov, *Meyerkhol'd,* 2 (Moscow, 1990), 163.

32. "Khronika," *Sovetskoye iskusstvo* (2 July 1938): 4.

33. D. Shostakovich, "Zametki kompozitora," *Literaturnaya gazeta* (20 November 1938): 5.

34. *V. E. Meyerkhol'd: stat'i, pis'ma, rechi, besedï. chast' vtoraya 1917–1939,* comp. V. E. Fevral'skiy (Moscow, 1968), 477.

35. I. Glikman, *Meyerkhol'd i muzïkal'nïy teatr* (Leningrad, 1989), 348.

36. K. Yesenin reminiscences in Khentova, *V mire Shostakovicha,* 139.

37. B. Ryazhskiy, "Kak shla reabilitatsiya," *Teatral'naya zhizn'* 5 (1989): 12–13.

38. M. D., "Novïye rabotï," 4.

39. Besides the Mayakovsky text, Shostakovich identified folk poets Suleyman Stalsky and Dzhambul (of Dagestan and Kazakhstan, respectively) as literary sources already selected for the projected four-movement symphony. See "Simfoniya pamyati V. I. Lenina," *Sovetskoye iskusstvo* (20 November 1938): 1.

40. For the text of this radio address, delivered on 26 January 1939, see A. Kryukov, "K svedeniyu budushchikh letopistsev," in *D. D. Shostakovich: sbornik statey k 90-letiyu so dnya rozhdeniya,* comp. L. Kovnatskaya (St. Petersburg, 1996), 164.

41. "6-ya simfoniya D. Shostakovicha," *Vechernyaya Moskva,* 28 August 1939, 3.

42. "Novïye rabotï D. Shostakovicha," *Leningradskaya Pravda,* 28 August 1939, 4.

43. "Operï, simfonii, syuitï, kontsertï. Novïye rabotï leningradskikh kompozitorov," *Kurortnaya gazeta* (Sochi), 20 October 1939.

44. *Pis'ma k drugu,* 19.

45. All secondary sources register the date of the premiere of the Sixth Symphony as 5 November 1939. Reports in the period press, however, as well as a letter from the composer to Atovmyan dated 20 November (GTsMMK f. 32, yed. khr. 1762), make it clear that its premiere performance was anticipated and actually took place on 21 November, the date also recorded in the card file of the St. Petersburg Philharmonic Library and in the concert program. See *Dmitri Schostakowitsch und seine Zeit: Mensch und Werk*, ed. J. Fromme (Duisburg, 1984), 97.

46. *Pis'ma k drugu*, 20.

47. L. Entelis, "Shestaya simfoniya Shostakovicha," *Smena* (23 November 1939): 3.

48. A. Shebalina, "'Eto bïl zamechatel'nïy drug': iz pisem D. D. Shostakovicha k V. Ya. Shebalina," *Sovetskaya muzïka* 7(1982): 78.

49. One notable exception was Prokofiev, whose praise was blunted with quibbles. See "Obsuzhdeniye IV dekadï sovetskoy muzïki," *Sovetskaya muzïka* 2 (1941): 71–72.

50. D. Tsïganov, "Vstrechi s Shostakovichem za dvadtsat' let," *Shostakovichu posvyashchayetsya: sbornik statey k 90-letiyu kompozitora* (1906–1975), ed. E. Dolinskaya (Moscow, 1997), 162. This memoir dates from 1944.

51. *Pis'ma k drugu*, 21.

52. "Proizvedeniye Shostakovich—gluboko zapadnoy orientatsii," *Staraya ploshchad': vestnik* 5 (1995): 156. Grinberg also took exception to the nomination of works by Prokofiev and Khachaturyan. Significantly, by comparison with the Piano Quintet, he found Shostakovich's Fifth Symphony to be "incomparably more serious in scale, more healthy in its tendencies, deeper and more human in its content. The preference of the symphony over the quintet is obvious to every listener."

53. Ibid., 158.

54. "6-ya simfoniya D. Shostakovicha," 3; Khentova, *Shostakovich*, 1: 519.

55. I. Rayskin, "Kak teatr Kirova ne stal teatrom Shostakovicha: dokumental'noye povestvovaniye," *Ars Peterburg: 'Mariinskiy—vchera, segodnya, vsegda'* (St. Petersburg, 1993), 97.

56. Shostakovich letters to Yavorsky, 26 June and 3 July 1940, GTsMMK f. 146, yed. khr. 3292, 3293.

57. B. Khaykin, *Besedï o dirizhyorskom remesle: stat'i* (Moscow, 1984), 90–91.

58. Shostakovich letter to Khaikin, 11 May 1941, RO RIII, f. 94, op. 1, yed. khr. 19.

59. Shostakovich letters to Khaikin, 24 February and 6 May 1943, in Khentova, *V mire Shostakovicha*, 314–15.

60. "Novïye rabotï D. Shostakovicha," 4.

61. See, for instance, D. Shostakovich, "Pamyati vozhdya," *Leningradskaya Pravda*, 22 January 1940, 2.

62. M. Shaginyan, "Fifty Letters from Dmitri Shostakovich," *Soviet Literature* 1 (1984): 72.

63. See, for instance, "Krupneyshiy kompozitor," *Smena* (18 March 1941): 3; "Novïye proizvedeniya sovetskikh kompozitorov," *Leningradskaya Pravda*, 22 April 1941.

64. Shaginyan, "Fifty Letters," 71.

65. L. Mikheyeva-Sollertinskaya, "Pis'ma Shostakovicha k Sollertinskomu," *Zhurnal lyubiteley iskusstva* 1 (1998): 46. In January 1940, Shostakovich's preoccupation with *Boris* came in handy as a polite excuse to deflect a proposal to write a "fes-

tive overture" in honor of Vyacheslav Molotov; he regretted that he did not "feel qualified to recreate the image of Comrade Molotov in music, since that is a very complex task demanding much work, mastery, and, especially, time." Shostakovich letter to Atovmyan, 15 January 1941, GTsMMK, f. 32, yed. khr. 1764.

66. K. Mints reminiscences in Khentova, *V mire Shostakovicha*, 251. *The Adventures of Korzinkina* was released in July 1941.

67. Letter dated 24 February 1940; in G. Yudin, "Vasha rabota dlya menya sobïtiye na vsyu zhizn'," *Sovetskaya muzïka* 6 (1983): 92–93.

68. Yu. Fedosyuk, "Zhivu v serdtsakh vsekh lyubyashchikh ...," *Sovetskaya muzïka* 9 (1991): 34.

69. S. Khentova, "Mnogostradal'naya orkestrovka Shostakovicha," *Muzïkal'naya zhizn'* 19 (1989): 9.

70. Letter from Shostakovich to Samosud dated 13 April 1941, in *S. A. Samosud: stat'i, vospominaniya, pis'ma*, comp. O. L. Dansker (Moscow, 1984), 179–80.

71. M. Zoshchenko letter to Marietta Shaginyan, 4 January 1941, in "Mikhail Zoshchenko—Mariette Shaginyan; iz perepiski," 99–100; trans. in Shaginyan, "Fifty Letters," 73.

72. D. Shostakovich, "V mire zvukov," *Trud*, 3 January 1941, 1.

73. D. Shostakovich, "Korol' Lir," "*Korol' Lir*" v Bol'shom dramaticheskom teatre im. M. Gor'kogo (1941); quoted in *Muzïkal'naya zhizn'* 17 (1976): 10.

74. Ibid.

75. A. Shebalina in Khentova, *V mire Shostakovicha*, 127–28; see also E. Wilson, *Shostakovich: A Life Remembered* (London, 1994), 146.

Chapter 8

1. D. Shostakovich, "V dni oboronï Leningrada," *Sovetskoye iskusstvo* (9 October 1941): 3.

2. D. Shostakovich, "Idu zashchishchat' svoyu Rodinu," *Izvestiya*, 4 July 1941, 2.

3. A. Ostrovskiy, "V godinu ispïtaniy," in *Leningradskaya konservatoriya v vospominaniyakh, 1862–1962* (Leningrad, 1962), 392.

4. M. Ozhigova, "Mitya, Dmitriy Dmitriyevich," *Muzïkal'naya pedagogika v ideyakh i litsakh: sbornik statey*, ed. A. Selitskiy (Rostov-on-Don, 1992), 90–91. Years later, the composer confessed gratefully that the cash influx had rescued him from penury.

5. D. Shostakovich, "*Klyatva Narkomu*" *dlya khora s fortepiano, slova V. Sayanova* (Moscow, 1943).

6. Arnshtam recalled having heard fragments of this setting. See S. Khentova, *V mire Shostakovicha* (Moscow, 1996), 234.

7. Reproducing a mistake in the archival description, some sources incorrectly give the date as 15 July 1941. Allegations that Shostakovich conceived or began the composition of *this* Seventh Symphony before the beginning of the war are not substantiated by the dating on surviving autograph materials. See M. Yakubov, "Preface," in *Dmitri Shostakovich Symphony No. 7, "Leningrad," op. 60: Facsimile Edition of the Manuscript* (Tokyo, 1992), 7.

8. I. Rudenko, "Razgovor s kompozitorom," *Komsomol'skaya Pravda*, 26 June 1973, 4.

9. D. Shostakovich, "Kak rozhdayetsya muzïka," *Literaturnaya gazeta* (21 December 1965): 3.

10. *Pis'ma k drugu: Dmitriy Shostakovich-Isaaku Glikmanu,* comp. I. Glikman (Moscow, 1993), 22.

11. "Iz vïstupleniya po radio. Leningrad. 16 sentyabrya 1941," *Govorit Dmitriy Shostakovich,* Melodiya 33M 40-41705-12. The date given on the record album is incorrect.

12. V. Bogdanov-Berezovskiy, *Dorogi iskusstva* (Leningrad, 1971), 243–46.

13. L. Sollertinskaya, "Shostakovich. Voyennïye godï," *Zvezda* 9 (1986): 173.

14. Shostakovich's sister had been allowed to return from exile to Leningrad before the war.

15. B. Khaykin, *Besedï o dirizhyorskom remesle: stat'i* (Moscow, 1984), 98.

16. As Nina Vasilyevna later told the story, the quilt with the manuscript had been tossed carelessly into the toilet during the struggle of embarkation. When they finally managed to reach it several hours later, it was lying in a puddle. Fortunately, they got to it before the seepage had damaged the manuscript. See D. Zhitomirskiy, "Shostakovich," *Muzïkal'naya akademiya* 3 (1993): 27.

17. N. Sokolov, "O vstrechakh s D. D. Shostakovichem," in *Nabroski po pamyati* (Moscow, 1987), 69.

18. Ibid., 70–71.

19. D. Shostakovich, "Moya Sed'maya simfoniya," *Vechernyaya Moskva,* 8 October 1941; quoted in "Editor's Note," in D. Shostakovich, *Sobraniye sochineniy v soroka dvukh tomakh,* 4 (Moscow, 1981).

20. Shostakovich, "V dni oboronï," 3.

21. *Pis'ma k drugu,* 31.

22. Sollertinskaya, "Shostakovich. Voyennïye godï," 173.

23. Yakubov, "Preface," 8.

24. Sollertinskaya, "Shostakovich. Voyennïye godï," 174.

25. F. Litvinova, "Vspominaya Shostakovicha," *Znamya* 12 (1996): 160; see also E. Wilson, *Shostakovich: A Life Remembered* (London, 1994), 158.

26. Litvinova, "Vspominaya Shostakovicha," 164; see also Wilson, *Shostakovich Remembered,* 158–59.

27. Shostakovich, "V dni oboronï," 3.

28. "Editor's Note," *Shostakovich: Sobraniye sochineniy.*

29. Shostakovich, "O podlinnoy i mnimoy programmnosti," *Sovetskaya muzïka* 5 (1951): 77.

30. Shostakovich letter to Sollertinsky dated 4 January 1942, in L. Mikheyeva, *I. I. Sollertinskiy: zhizn' i nasled.iye* (Leningrad, 1988), 149.

31. *Pis'ma k drugu,* 35.

32. Shostakovich letter to Atovmyan dated 5 February 1942; GTsMMK, f. 32, yed. khr. 1772.

33. *Pis'ma k drugu,* 40.

34. Litvinova, "Vspominaya Shostakovicha," 165; see also Wilson, *Shostakovich Remembered,* 159.

35. D. Shostakovich, "Sed'maya simfoniya," *Pravda,* 29 March 1942, 3; see also Yakubov, "Preface," 9.

36. B. Frezinskiy, "Erenburg i Shostakovich," *Niva* 8 (1989): 205.

37. [K. Eliasberg,] "Artilleristï i muzïkant," *Smena* (25 September 1966): 2.

38. S. Khentova, *Shostakovich: zhizn' i tvorchestvo*, 2 (Leningrad, 1986), 69.

39. A. Shebalina, "Eto bïl zamechatel'nïy drug: iz pisem D. D. Shostakovicha k V. Ya Shebalinu," *Sovetskaya muzïka* 7 (1982): 81.

40. L. Mikheyeva, *Zhizn' Dmitriya Shostakovicha* (Moscow, 1997), 242.

41. Shebalina, "Eto bïl zamechatel'nïy drug," 81.

42. L. Mikheyeva, "Istoriya odnoy druzhbï; chast' vtoraya," *Sovetskaya muzïka* 9 (1987): 82.

43. Ye. Makarov, "Ya bezgranichno uvazhal ego," *Muzïkal'naya akademiya* 1 (1993): 152–53.

44. Shostakovich letter to Atovmyan dated 21 May 1942; GTsMMK f. 32, yed. khr. 1774.

45. The People's Commissariat of Internal Affairs was headed from 1938 to 1946 by Lavrentiy Beria. He established its Song and Dance Ensemble in 1940 to boost the morale of Soviet troops fighting in the war against Finland. During World War II, Yuriy Lyubimov served in it as master of ceremonies. See A. Gershkovich, *The Theater of Yuri Lyubimov: Art and Politics at the Taganka in Moscow* (New York, 1989), 41–42.

46. Shostakovich letter to Atovmyan dated 18 November 1942; GTsMMK f. 32, yed. khr. 1780.

47. The definitive title of the cycle was *Six Romances on Texts of W. Raleigh, R. Burns, and W. Shakespeare*, op. 62. The order of the romances, with their dedicatees, is as follows: 1) "To My Son" (W. Raleigh, trans. Pasternak), dedicated to Levon Atovmyan; 2) "In the Fields" (R. Burns, trans. Marshak), dedicated to Nina Shostakovich; 3) "MacPherson before His Execution" (R. Burns, trans. Marshak), dedicated to Isaak Glikman; 4) "Jenny" (R. Burns, trans. Marshak), dedicated to Yuriy Sviridov; 4) Sonnet 66 (W. Shakespeare, trans. Pasternak), dedicated to Ivan Sollertinsky; 6) "The Royal Campaign" (English folk text, trans. Marshak), dedicated to Vissarion Shebalin.

48. P. Mironov, "Vtoraya sonata Shostakovicha," *Literatura i iskusstvo* (17 April 1943): 4. After studying the Second Sonata closely, pianist Heinrich Neuhaus wrote to Olga Toom on 14 June 1944: "Utmost mastery, novelty, intellect—empty for the soul and severe,—clever and ancient-ancient sorrow consumes and oppresses. But like everything he writes, it is unique of its kind and incomparable." See E. Rikhter, comp., *Genrikh Neygauz: vospominaniya, pis'ma, materialï* (Moscow, 1992), 210.

49. *Pis'ma k drugu*, 58.

50. D. Shostakovich, "Partitura operï Musorgskogo: k postanovke *Borisa Godunova* v Bol'shom teatre," *Vechernyaya Moskva*, 11 May 1943, 3. In the event, none of these projects was realized.

51. Shaginyan, "Fifty Letters from Dmitri Shostakovich," *Soviet Literature* 1 (1984): 75. Unworthy of mention, inter alia, was his recent orchestration of seven British folksongs, performed on a program of English music in Moscow on 25 May 1943 by Mark Reyzen and Larissa Yelchaninova, and, with the addition of an arrangement of "When Johnny Comes Marching Home," published by Muzfond in 1944 as *English and American Folksongs* (see *VOKS Bulletin* 7 [1943]: 44).

52. Mikheyeva, "Istoriya odnoy druzhbï; chast' vtoraya," 83.

53. "Vos'maya simfoniya. Beseda s kompozitorom D. Shostakovichem," *Literatura i iskusstvo* (18 September 1943): 1. While working on the Eighth Symphony, according to Atovmyan, Shostakovich went daily to see a newsreel chronicling the horrors of war and fascist atrocities. L. Atovm'yan, "Iz vospominaniy," *Muzïkal'naya akademiya* 4 (1997): 75.

54. Makarov, "Ya bezgranichno uvazhal ego," 150.

55. O. Lamm, *Stranitsï tvorcheskoy biografii Myaskovskogo* (Moscow, 1989), 302.

56. B. Asaf'yev, "Kompozitor i deystvitel'nost'," *Izbrannïye trudï, vïp. 5* (Moscow, 1957), 50.

57. N. Volkova, "Materialï velikoy otechestvennoy voynï v fondakh TsGALI SSSR," *Vstrechi s proshlïm, vïp. 6* (Moscow, 1988), 448.

58. Mikheyeva, *I. I. Sollertinskiy: zhizn' i naslediye*, 168.

59. Ibid., 166.

60. *Pis'ma k drugu*, 61.

61. *Soyuz sovetskikh kompozitorov SSSR: Informatsionnïy sbornik* 7–8 (1945): 15.

62. K. Rudnitskiy, comp., *S. M. Mikhoels: stat'i, besedï, rechi* (Moscow, 1960), 209.

63. From transcript dated 24 April 1944, "Stenogrammï zasedaniy sektsii muzïki Komiteta po gosudarstvennïm premiyam s obsuzhdeniyami proizvedeniy D. D. Shostakovicha (8-y i 10-y simfonii)," typescript copy, RGALI f. 2048, op. 3, yed. khr. 412.

64. In 1973, Shostakovich told his official biographer simply that the conversation had been businesslike; Stalin had seemed to know something about songs. See Khentova, *V mire Shostakovicha*, 34.

65. Two somewhat different versions of the incident as related by Khachaturyan have been reported. See S. Khentova, "Shostakovich i Khachaturyan: ikh sblizil 48-y god," *Muzïkal'naya zhizn'* 24 (1988): 11; and L. Lebedinskiy, "Iz bessistemnïkh zapisey," *Muzïkal'naya zhizn'* 21–22 (1993): 28. For an English translation of the Khentova interview, see Wilson, *Shostakovich Remembered*, 179–81. The version of the incident attributed to Shostakovich in S. Volkov's *Testimony: The Memoirs of Dmitri Shostakovich* (New York, 1979), is closer to the version related by Lebedinskiy.

66. Lebedinskiy, "Iz bessistemnikh zapisey."

67. Under Stalin's supervision, in 1944 Alexandrov's national anthem was re-orchestrated by Dmitriy Rogal-Levitsky. See D. Rogal-Levitsky, "Gosudarstvennïy gimn; o 281-m avtore gimna," *Nezavisimaya gazeta*, 12 February 1991, 5.

68. I. S. Rabinovich, ed., *B. Yavorskiy: stat'i, vospominaniya, perepiska*, 1 (Moscow, 1972), 607.

69. *Pis'ma k drugu*, 62. It should be noted that this is not simply a generalized parody; Shostakovich was the "author" of many similar hortatory statements published during the war years.

70. Makarov, "Ya bezgranichno uvazhal ego," 152.

71. Mikheyeva, "Istoriya odnoy druzhbï; chast' vtoraya," 78.

72. Mikheyeva, *Pamyati I. I. Sollertinskogo*, 261.

73. Shostakovich dated his completion of the score of *Rothschild's Violin* 5 February 1944 (RGALI f. 2048, op. 1, yed. khr. 57).

74. "Dmitriy Shostakovich rasskazïvayet o svoyey rabote," *Smena* 20 (1943): 15.

75. GTsMMK f. 32, yed. khr. 134.

76. Khentova's claim—subsequently adopted by other authors—that Shostakovich began the trio over again from scratch on 15 February is wrong (Khentova, *Shostakovich*, 1:177). On the autograph score, Shostakovich's dating is found at the *end* of the first movement. Furthermore, changes in ink colors in the manuscript make it possible to surmise that Shostakovich even began notating the second movement at this time, before postponing completion of the work until later that summer. See RGALI f. 2048, op. 1, yed. khr. 28.

77. *Pis'ma k drugu*, 65.

78. Shebalina, "Eto bïl zamechatel'nïy drug," 83.

79. Ibid.

80. M. Meyerovich in Wilson, *Shostakovich Remembered*, 197.

81. M. Aranovskiy, "Zametki o tvorchestve," *Sovetskaya muzïka* 9 (1981): 21.

82. S. Khentova, "Razgovor s Shostakovichem," *Ogonyok* 39 (1966): 6.

83. D. Tsïganov, "Vstrechi s Shostakovichem za dvadtsat' let," in *Shostakovichu posvyashchayetsa: sbornik statey k 90-letiyu kompozitora (1906–1975)*, ed. E. Dolinskaya (Moscow, 1997), 165.

84. Mikheyeva, *I. I. Sollertinskiy: zhizn' i naslediye*, 175.

Chapter 9

1. Epigraph taken from D. Shostakovich, "Istochniki silï," *Sovetskoye iskusstvo* (10 May 1945): 3.

2. "Dmitriy Shostakovich rasskazïvayet o svoyey rabote," *Smena* 20 (1943): 15.

3. D. Shostakovich, "Pod znakom pobedï," *Sovetskoye iskusstvo* (7 November 1944): 3.

4. D. Rabinovich, *Dmitry Shostakovich: Composer* (Moscow, 1959), 96.

5. Ye. Makarov, "Ya bezgranichno uvazhal ego," *Muzïkal'naya akademiya* 1 (1993): 153. Makarov is just a trifle uncertain about the precise date of their meeting at the composer's apartment in mid-January 1945.

6. D. Shostakovich, "V predverii velikoy pobedï," *Komsomol'skaya Pravda*, 13 February 1945, 3.

7. Rabinovich, *Dmitry Shostakovich*, 97.

8. *Pis'ma k drugu: Dmitriy Shostakovich-Isaaku Glikmanu*, comp. I. Glikman (Moscow, 1993), 70.

9. "Devyataya simfoniya D. Shostakovicha," *Sovetskoye iskusstvo* (7 September 1945): 4.

10. R. Davïdov, "O devyatoy simfonii D. Shostakovicha," *Trud*, 16 September 1945, 3.

11. O. Lamm, *Stranitsï tvorcheskoy biografii Myaskovskogo* (Moscow, 1989): 313.

12. Z. A. Apetyan, *Gavriil Popov: iz literaturnogo naslediya* (Leningrad, 1986), 288–89.

13. S. Shlifshteyn, "Devyataya simfoniya Shostakovicha," *Sovetskoye iskusstvo* (26 October 1945): 3.

14. D. Zhitomirskiy, "Pervïye ispolneniya 9-y simfonii D. Shostakovicha," *Sovetskoye iskusstvo* (30 November 1945): 4.

15. D. Zhitomirskiy, "Iz vpechatleniy minuvshikh let," in *D. Shostakovich: stat'i i materialï*, ed. G. Shneerson (Moscow, 1976), 185–87.

16. N. Timofeyev, "Vpechatleniya muzïkanta (o 9-y simfonii Shostakovicha)," *Sovetskaya muzïka* 1 (1946): 69.

17. Speech of Dmitriy Kabalevsky, *Soveshchaniye deyateley sovetskoy muzïki v TsK VKP(b)* (Moscow, 1948), 129–30; T. Khrennikov, "Za tvorchestvo, dostoynoye sovetskogo naroda," *Sovetskaya muzïka* 1 (1948): 61.

18. A. Ostrovskiy, "B godinu ispïtaniy," in *Leningradskaya konservatoriya v vospominaniyakh, 1862–1962* (Leningrad, 1962), 393.

19. They beat the Army team (TsDKA) by a score of 2-1. Zenith was the first non-Muscovite squad to capture the championship and the only one from Leningrad to do so during Shostakovich's lifetime. The composer went to great lengths to secure his ticket to this match, eventually cadging it from the Leningrad team's trainer. See S. Khentova, *Udivitel'nïy Shostakovich* (St. Petersburg, 1993), 256.

20. Shostakovich letter to Stiedry, dated 18 February 1946; GTsMMK f. 32, yed. khr. 152.

21. L. Arnshtam in S. Khentova, *V mire Shostakovicha* (Moscow, 1996), 232–33.

22. Letter from S. V. Shostakovich to Shebalin, dated 14 November 1947, in A. Shebalina, *Pamyati V. Ya. Shebalina: vospominaniya, materialï* (Moscow, 1984), 231.

23. "Muzïka—detyam," *Sovetskoye iskusstvo* (1 January 1945): 4.

24. Reminiscences of Galina Shostakovich, in Khentova, *V mire Shostakovicha*, 83. Despite a dating of 1945 on the autograph, her memory is that the piece "Birthday" dated from 1947.

25. O. Ochakovskaya, "Nado obyazatel'no dat' eto detyam," *Muzïkal'naya zhizn'* 17 (1980): 20–21; O. Chernïy, "Dmitriy Shostakovich," *Novïy mir* 10 (1945): 140.

26. M. Rostropovich in E. Wilson, *Shostakovich: A Life Remembered* (London, 1994), 189.

27. Ibid., 193.

28. "On the Journals *Zvezda* and *Leningrad*," in R. H. McNeal, ed., *Resolutions and Decisions of the Communist Party of the Soviet Union*, 3 (Toronto, 1974), 240–43.

29. Shostakovich letter to V. Shirinsky dated 2 August 1946; "'Goryacho Vas lyubyashchiy ...'; iz pisem D. D. Shostakovicha V. P. Shirinskomu," *Muzïkal'naya akademiya* 4 (1997): 145.

30. V. Shirinskiy, "Iz kvartetnogo zhurnala," *Muzïkal'naya akademiya* 4 (1997): 141.

31. D. Zhitomirskiy, *Dmitriy Shostakovich* (Moscow, 1947); quoted in Koval', "Tvorcheskiy put' D. Shostakovicha," *Sovetskaya muzïka* 4 (1948): 18.

32. Yu. Kholopov and V. Tsenova, *Edison Denisov* (Moscow, 1993), 177. The Third Quartet was not on the list of Shostakovich's works explicitly banned by the Committee for Artistic Affairs on 14 February 1948; see "Proizvedeniye Shostakovicha—gluboko zapadnoy orientatsii," *Staraya ploshchad': vestnik* 5 (1995): 158–59. Nevertheless, it became widely regarded by his contemporaries as one of his "underground" works.

33. I. Nest'yev, "Zametki o tvorchestve D. Shostakovicha: neskol'ko mïsley, vïzvannïkh Devyatoy simfoniey," *Kul'tura i zhizn'* (30 September 1946): 4.

34. "Doklad zamestitelya predsedatelya Orgkomiteta Soyuza sovetskikh kompozitorov SSSR A. I. Khachaturyana," *Sovetskaya muzïka* 10 (1946): 23.

35. *Pis'ma k drugu*, 75.

36. Although the film *Zoya* also garnered a Stalin Prize on this outing, Shostakovich's contribution as composer was not cited. See *Pravda*, 27 January 1946, 4.

37. *Vechernyaya Moskva*, 5 November 1947, 2. Most sources erroneously list the year this honorific was bestowed as 1948.

38. "Prazdnichnaya uvertyura (Beseda s D. Shostakovichem)," *Vecherniy Leningrad*, 29 August 1947, 3. Whether he actually composed something and left it incomplete or destroyed it, or whether he even began composing such a work at that time is unclear. At any rate, there appears to be no connection between this project and the composer's *Festive Overture*, op. 99, composed and first performed in 1954.

39. "'Poema o rodine'; kantata Shostakovicha," *Vechernyaya Moskva*, 14 November 1947, 3. In fact, the score of Shostakovich's *Poem of the Motherland* had been passed by the censors for publication on 11 October.

40. Shostakovich letter to Atovmyan dated 15 October 1947, GTsMMK f. 32, yed. khr. 1792.

41. "Poema o rodine; grammplastinki k 30-letiyu Oktyabrya," *Vechernyaya Moskva*, 31 October 1947, 3.

42. Speech of Tikhon Khrennikov, *Soveshchaniye deyateley sovetskoy muzïki v TsK VKP(b)* (Moscow, 1948), 28.

43. D. Shepilov and P. Lebedev, "O nedostatkakh v razvitii sovetskoy muzïki," in *Tak eto bïlo: Tikhon Khrennikov o vremeni i o sebe*, ed. V. Rubtsova (Moscow, 1994), 185–94.

44. L. Maksimenkov, "Partiya—nash rulevoy," *Muzïkal'naya zhizn'* [pt. 1] 13–14 (1993): 6–8; [pt. 2] 15–16 (1993): 8–10.

45. Shepilov and Lebedev, "O nedostatkakh," 193.

46. Speech of A. Zhdanov, in *Soveshchaniye*, 136.

47. Maksimenkov, "Partiya—nash rulevoy," pt. 2, 8–9. The name of Gavriil Popov was also inserted. For a partial translation of the "revised" transcript of the Central Committee Conference of Musicians, see Alexander Werth, *Musical Uproar in Moscow* (London, 1949), 47–86.

48. F. Litvinova in Wilson, *Shostakovich Remembered*, 202–03. Litvinova may be confusing underlying causes here, and even years; the campaign against "rootless cosmopolitans"—the chief explanation she provides for the sense of foreboding—did not manifest itself until the very end of 1948 and the beginning of 1949. (The *Pravda* editorial she mentions, "About a Certain Anti-patriotic Group of Theater Critics," appeared on 28 January 1949.) Litvinova also describes seeing in the new year 1948 with the Shostakoviches at Ruza, an artists' retreat. Levon Atovmyan describes the same holiday as considerably more jolly and festive, attributing ominous premonitions about the upcoming leap year to Shostakovich alone; L. Atovm'yan, "Iz vospominaniy," *Muzïkal'naya akademiya* 4 (1997): 77. Natalya Popova claims to have celebrated this holiday with the Shostakoviches at their new apartment in Moscow on Mozhaiskoye Shosse; N. Popova, "Novïy god u Shostakovicha," *Nezavisimaya gazeta*, 25 September 1996, 7. Nonetheless, Alexander Werth also registered an unmistakable awareness that "something was up" in the Soviet musical world in the last weeks of 1947: "Inside the Composers' Union, at the Bolshoi Theater and elsewhere, some kind of row was going on. The general public knew little or nothing about it; but musicians, when one talked to them, seemed uneasy"; Werth, *Musical Uproar*, 26.

49. Speech of D. Shostakovich, in *Soveshchaniye*, 163.

50. I. Erenburg, "Lyudi, godï, zhizn'; 6-aya kniga," *Novïy mir* 1 (1965): 123.

51. B. Frezinskiy, "Erenburg i Shostakovich," *Niva* 8 (1989): 207.

52. Nataliya Vovsi-Mikhoels, interviewed in the film *Bol'shoy kontsert narodov*, directed by Semyon Aronovich (1991); see also Wilson, *Shostakovich Remembered*, 228.

53. *Pis'ma k drugu*, 78.

54. Maksimenkov, "Partiya—nash rulevoy," pt. 2, 8.

55. *Pis'ma k drugu*, 78.

56. Apetyan, *Gavriil Popov*, 296.

57. Veniamin Basner dated this occasion as 9 March (Khentova, *V mire Shostakovicha*, 190), and Glikman as 12 March (*Pis'ma k drugu*, 78).

58. M. Meyerovich in Wilson, *Shostakovich Remembered*, 192.

59. V. Basner in Wilson, *Shostakovich Remembered*, 206.

60. V. Yusefovich, *David Oystrakh: besedï s Igorem Oystrakhom* (Moscow, 1978), 220–21.

61. A. Shirinskiy, *Skripichnïye proizvedeniya D. Shostakovicha* (Moscow, 1988), 6. The only alteration of any significance Oistrakh requested—and this was considerably later, during preparations for the premiere—was for the composer to spell the soloist briefly after the cadenza by reassigning the initial statement of the first theme of the finale to the orchestra. Shostakovich, who dedicated the concerto to Oistrakh, was happy to oblige.

62. Reminiscence of D. Oistrakh in Khentova, *V mire Shostakovicha*, 202.

63. *Pervïy vsesoyuznïy s'ezd sovetskikh kompozitorov: stenograficheskiy otchyot* (Moscow, 1948), 346.

64. "Ot kompozitorov i muzïkovedov goroda Moskvï Velikomu vozhdyu sovetskogo naroda tovarishchu Stalinu," *Sovetskaya muzïka* 1 (1948): 27–28. Prokofiev had attended at least a portion of the Zhdanov convocation in January but managed to avoid further public exposure by pleading illness. Instead, he sent an open letter to be read at the Moscow conference, soon published, which on the one hand seemed to welcome the involvement and input of the Central Committee and, on the other, defended his own aesthetic position and legitimate compositional achievements. See *Sovetskaya muzïka* 1 (1948): 66–67.

65. Ibid., 78.

66. Ibid., 79.

67. S. Mikhalkov, "Il'ya Golovin; p'esa v 3-kh deystviyakh, 5-i kartinakh," *Novïy mir* 11 (1949): 112–48.

68. Yu. Fedosyuk, "Zhivu v serdtsakh vsekh lyubyashchikh," *Sovetskaya muzïka* 9 (1991): 36.

69. Rubtsova, *Tak eto bïlo*, 129.

70. *Pervïy vsesoyuznïy s'ezd sovetskikh kompozitorov: stenograficheskiy otchyot*, 343–46. Arnshtam, a lifelong friend of the composer, took responsibility for sketching out Shostakovich's comments for him (Khentova, *V mire Shostakovicha*, 235), although the composer later told Marina Sabinina that a speech prepared for him by a cultural bureaucrat—which he dutifully read like a "puppet"—had been pressed into his hands as he mounted to the podium (Wilson identifies the unnamed bureaucrat as Vasiliy Kukharsky; *Shostakovich Remembered*, 294). Given the tone and specificity

of the text, including, as noted earlier, mention of the recently completed Violin Concerto, Arnshtam's sounds the more plausible claim.

71. Reminiscence of R. Gabichvadze in Khentova, *V mire Shostakovicha*, 283.

72. *Pervïy vsesoyuznïy s'ezd sovetskikh kompozitorov: stenograficheskiy otchyot*, 355. In fact, none of the four—Myaskovsky, Prokofiev, Shebalin, or Popov—actually attended the Congress. In their absence, explained by illness, Shebalin and Popov sent letters that were read to the delegates.

73. N. Udal'tsova, *Zhizn' russkoy kubisti: dnevniki, stat'i, vospominaniya*, comp. E. Drevina and V. Rakitin (Moscow, 1994), 78.

74. "Proizvedeniye Shostakovicha—gluboko zapadnoy orientatsii," 158–59. When this status report was prepared for Stalin a year later, on 15 March 1949, it was noted that two string quartets, Symphonies nos. 2 and 3, and the Piano Trio had not been banned, but that his "best" works—the three symphonies mentioned and the quintet—as well as film music and songs, were being performed in concerts. It did not indicate how often.

75. As Daniil Zhitomirsky recorded in his diary on 27 March 1948, a performance of the Fifth Symphony took place in Moscow not long after the Central Committee resolution appeared. Attended by the composer, it was unadvertised and presented in an out-of-the-way venue, a mediocre performance led by an unknown conductor from Riga; D. Zhitomirskiy, "Shostakovich," *Muzïkal'naya akademiya* 3 (1993): 29. In its German translation, this entry is dated 27 May 1948; D. Shitomirski, *Blindheit als Schutz vor der Wahrheit* (Berlin, 1996), 279–80. More significantly, on 7 December 1948, Mravinsky conducted the Fifth Symphony on a regular subscription concert at the Leningrad Philharmonic. Some "tactless" gesture of defiance by the conductor on stage at the end of the performance (probably elevating the score over his head) came to the attention of Tikhon Khrennikov, who censured the conductor in a major policy address later that month as one of the obstinate, unrepentant champions of "formalist" idols; T. Khrennikov, "Tvorchestvo kompozitorov i muzïkovedov posle Postanovleniya TsK VKP(b) ob opere 'Velikaya druzhba,'" *Sovetskaya muzïka* 1 (1949): 25.

76. A. Kostolomolotskiy, "Pedagogicheskiy yumor," *Sovetskaya muzïka* 4 (1948): 89.

77. A. Abramov, "Maksim Shostakovich o svoyom ottse," *Vremya i mï* 69 (1982): 183.

78. See Wilson, *Shostakovich Remembered*, 215–25.

79. M. Koval', "Tvorcheskiy put' D. Shostakovicha," *Sovetskaya muzïka* 2 (1948): 47–61; 3 (1948): 31–43; 4 (1948): 8–19.

80. M. Koval', "Tvorcheskiy put' D. Shostakovicha," *Sovetskaya muzïka* 4 (1948): 11.

81. Reminiscence of M. Kozhunova in Khentova, *V mire Shostakovicha*, 91.

82. B. Kats, comp., *Muzïka v tvorchestve, sud'be i v dome Borisa Pasternaka* (Leningrad, 1991), 264.

83. G. Yudin, "Vasha rabota dlya menya sobïtiye na vsyu zhizn'," *Sovetskaya muzïka* 6 (1983): 93.

84. Letter to M. Shaginyan dated 22 August 1948; quoted in S. Khentova, *Shostakovich: zhizn' i tvorchestvo*, vol. 2 (Leningrad, 1986), 239.

85. This work has been referred to by many titles and subtitles; the title

Antiformalist Rayok, now commonly adopted, appears on the composer's typed libretto. See M. Yakubov, "'Antiformalisticheskiy rayok' D. D. Shostakovicha: istoriya sozdaniya, istochniki muzïkal'nogo i literaturnogo teksta," in *Antiformalisticheskiy Rayok, score* (Moscow, 1995), 58.

86. Letter from Glikman to Irina Shostakovich dated 27 May 1989, in M. Jakubow, "Dmitri Schostakowitschs 'Antiformalischer Rajok,'" in *Sowjetische Musik im Licht der Perestroika*, ed. by H. Danuser, H. Gerlach, and J. Köchel (Laaber, 1990), 173; see also Yakubov, "'Antiformalisticheskiy rayok' D. D. Shostakovicha," 50.

87. For an overview of the positions in the dating and authorship debate, see Wilson, *Shostakovich Remembered*, 296–99.

Chapter 10

1. J. Braun, *Shostakovich's Jewish Songs: From Jewish Folk Poetry, op. 79* (Tel-Aviv, 1989), 24.

2. I. Dobrushin and A. Yudnitskiy, comp., *Yevreyskiye narodnïye pesni*, ed. Y. Sokolov (Moscow, 1947). This Russian publication was based on a collection of Yiddish texts by the same compilers published in Moscow in 1940.

3. E. Wilson, *Shostakovich: A Life Remembered* (London, 1994), 236.

4. Ibid.

5. Braun, *Shostakovich's Jewish Songs*, 24.

6. O. Lamm, *Stranitsï tvorcheskoy biografii Myaskovskogo* (Moscow, 1989), 328.

7. D. Zhitomirskiy, "Shostakovich," *Muzïkal'naya akademiya* 3 (1993): 29; German translation in D. Shitomirski, *Blindheit als Schutz vor der Wahrheit* (Berlin, 1996), 283–84.

8. Ibid. Elsewhere, Zhitomirsky published a differently worded diary "extract" for 18 December 1948 and situated the context differently; see D. Zhitomirskiy, "Shostakovich ofitsial'nïy i podlinnïy," *Daugava* 3 (1990): 92.

9. L. Karagicheva, ed., *Kara Karayev: stat'i, pis'ma, vïskazïvaniya* (Moscow, 1978), 49.

10. T. Khrennikov, "Tvorchestvo kompozitorov i muzïkovedov posle Postanovleniya TsK VKP(b) ob opere 'Velikaya druzhba,'" *Sovetskaya muzïka* 1 (1949): 25.

11. Wilson, *Shostakovich Remembered*, 225.

12. *Pis'ma k drugu: Dmitriy Shostakovich—Isaaku Glikmanu*, comp. I. Glikman (Moscow, 1993), 90. In 1949, Shostakovich spent his birthday at the "Pravda" sanatorium in Sochi. The claim that *From Jewish Folk Poetry* was performed at his birthday party this year is in error. See Wilson, *Shostakovich Remembered*, 229.

13. A. Vergelis, *Strazh u vorot* (Moscow, 1988), 284.

14. S. Volkov, *Testimony: The Memoirs of Dmitri Shostakovich* (New York, 1979), 157.

15. M. Koval', "Tvorcheskiy put' Shostakovicha," *Sovetskaya muzïka* 4 (1948). This issue was passed by the censor on 3 August 1948.

16. The very conspicuous exception to this generalization is the politically seditious satire, *Antiformalist Rayok*. In stark contrast to the Violin Concerto, *From Jewish Folk Poetry*, and the Fourth Quartet, Shostakovich held this work *very* close to his vest. As mentioned earlier, it surfaced only years after his death, and its dates of composition are still a matter of contention.

17. Braun, *Shostakovich's Jewish Songs*, 27.

18. Lamm, *Stranitsï biografii Myaskovskogo*, 325.

19. Khrennikov, "Tvorchestvo kompozitorov i muzïkovedov," 28.

20. R. Conquest, *Stalin: Breaker of Nations* (New York, 1991), 290–91.

21. Braun, *Shostakovich's Jewish Songs*, 25.

22. V. Razhnikov, *Kirill Kondrashin rasskazïvayet o muzïke i zhizni* (Moscow, 1989), 201.

23. Galina Shostakovich reminiscence in S. Khentova, *V mire Shostakovicha* (Moscow, 1996), 84.

24. *Pis'ma k drugu*, 77.

25. D. Shostakovich, "Kino kak shkola kompozitora," *30 let sovetskoy kinematografii: sbornik statey* (Moscow, 1950), 357.

26. Ibid., 358.

27. Shostakovich's impending participation in the Soviet delegation made front-page news in the United States on 20 February (see the *New York Times*, 20 February 1949, 1). Although they may be in error, most reminiscences place Stalin's phone call to Shostakovich as occurring between late February and mid-March. It is not inconceivable, however, that Shostakovich's participation might have been bruited abroad before his consent had been obtained.

28. D. Shostakovich reminiscences, 10 April 1973, in Khentova, *V mire Shostakovicha*, 34–35. Alexander Poskrebïshev was Stalin's long-time personal assistant.

29. Facsimile reproduced in *Sovetskaya muzïka* 4 (1991): 17. A day earlier, on 15 March 1949, a report on the status of Shostakovich's compositions had been prepared by an official of the Committee for Artistic Affairs. See "Proizvedeniye Shostakovicha—gluboko zapadnoy orientatsii," *Staraya ploshchad', vestnik* 5 (1995): 158–59.

30. D. Shostakovich reminiscences, 10 April 1973, 35.

31. Igor Stravinsky and Arnold Schoenberg, both by now residing in the United States, declined invitations to join in the welcome. Schoenberg responded: "Being scapegoat of Russian restrictions on music I cannot sign. But I am ready to send the following, 'Disregarding problems of styles and politics I gladly greet a real composer. Signed Arnold Schoenberg." P. Lehrman, "A Schoenberg Note about Prokofiev, Shostakovich, Stravinsky and Koussevitzky," *Journal of the Arnold Schoenberg Institute* 11, no. 2 (1988): 177. Stravinsky's snub was well publicized: "Regret not to be able to join welcomers of Soviet artists coming this country. But all my ethic and esthetic convictions oppose such gesture. Igor Stravinsky"; *Stravinsky: Selected Correspondence*, 1, ed. R. Craft (New York, 1982), 358–59.

32. *Time*, 4 April 1949, 22.

33. *New York Times*, 27 March 1949, 44.

34. Ibid., 28 March 1949, 2.

35. *Pis'ma k drugu*, 98.

36. A noteworthy instance occurred in 1964, when, in a lengthy tirade against avant-garde tendencies in modern Western music published over his name, Shostakovich was quoted: "To this day I can't distinguish, say, the music of Boulez from the music of Stockhausen, that of Henze from that of Stuckenschmidt" (D. Shostakovich, "Muzïka i vremya," *Pravda*, 31 May 1964, 6). As it happens, Hans

Stuckenschmidt was an eminent music critic, not a composer. He promptly set the record straight in a letter sent to, but not published in, *Pravda*; see H. Stuckenschmidt, *Zum Hören geboren; ein Leben mit der Musik unserer Zeit* (Munich-Zürich, 1979), 312–13. Judging by a number of reports, Shostakovich was chagrined by the embarrassing gaffe. In an interview published soon after, he went out of his way to redress the error, explaining that a line had been dropped during editing and the passage should have read: "To this day I can't distinguish, say, the music of Boulez from the music of Stockhausen, that of Henze from that music that corresponds to the theoretical conceptions of the music critic Stuckenschmidt" ("Tvorcheskiye planï kompozitora: beseda s D. D. Shostakovichem," *Pravda*, 3 August 1964, 4).

37. See, for instance, RGALI f. 2048, op. 3, yed. khr. 48.

38. See, for instance, *Pis'ma k drugu*, 76, 137, 146–48.

39. For a couple of instances, see L. Fay, "Shostakovich, LASM i Asaf'yev," in *D. D. Shostakovich: sbornik statey k 90-letiyu so dnya rozhdeniya*, comp. L. Kovnatskaya (St. Petersburg, 1996), 29–48.

40. The rift became particularly glaring after his signature appeared on a denunciation of Andrey Sakharov in *Pravda* in 1973. See Chapter 15.

41. Khrennikov, "Tvorchestvo kompozitorov i muzïkovedov," 30.

42. Ye. Dolmatovskiy, "Perepolnennïy muzïkoy," in *D. Shostakovich: stat'i i materialï*, comp. G. Shneerson (Moscow, 1976), 74–75.

43. GTsMMK f. 32, yed. khr. 1794.

44. "Beseda Nelli Kravets s El'miroy Nazirovoy," in *D. D. Shostakovich: sbornik statey k 90-letiyu so dnya rozhdeniya*, comp. L. Kovnatskaya (St. Petersburg, 1996), 242.

45. Some sources incorrectly list the date of first performance as 15 December.

46. S. Khentova, *Udivitel'nïy Shostakovich* (St. Petersburg, 1993), 153.

47. Lamm, *Stranitsï biografii Myaskovskogo*, 331.

48. Ibid., 330.

49. "Tvorcheskaya diskussiya na plenume," *Sovetskaya muzïka* 1 (1950): 43.

50. Ibid., 42.

51. D. Shostakovich, *Pesn' o lesakh*, full score (Moscow, 1950).

52. Letter to E. Denisov, 12 February 1957; original in typescript, German translation in Gojowy, "Dimitri Schostakowitsch: Briefe an Edison Denissow," *Musik des Ostens, Bd. 10*, ed. by H. Unverricht (Kassel, 1986), 198.

53. D. Shostakovich, "Putevïye zametki," *Sovetskaya muzïka* 5 (1949): 21.

54. That the dedication was not included in the published first edition was evidently an oversight; Shostakovich penned it into Tsïganov's copy of the 1954 publication. See Khentova, *V mire Shostakovicha*, 206.

55. Ibid.

56. N. V. Shirinskaya, "Vospominaniya ob otse," in *V. P. Shirinskiy: stranitsï zhizni, tvorchestva i konsertnoy deyatel'nosti* (Moscow, 1996), 85.

57. Wilson, *Shostakovich Remembered*, 245–46. The Ministry of Culture was not established until March 1953; presumably this is a mistaken reference to the Committee for Artistic Affairs.

58. For a not insignificant portion of this time, from approximately mid-December 1950 through at least mid-January 1951, Shostakovich was in residence at

the Composers' Union's artists' retreat in Ruza, outside Moscow, where composer Grigoriy Frid became the sounding board for Shostakovich's daily efforts. See G. Frid, *Dorogoy ranenoy pamyati* (Moscow, 1994), 268–70.

59. Yu. Levitin, "O tom, chto bïlo ...," *Muzïkal'naya akademiya* 3 (1994): 71; see also Wilson, *Shostakovich Remembered*, 211.

60. Matvey Blanter reminiscence in Khentova, *V mire Shostakovicha*, 162.

61. Shostakovich letter to Yavorsky dated 9 May 1925; "'Khorosho bïlo bï ne dumat' ni o khlebe nasushchnom, ni o chyom, a tol'ko zanimat'sya lyubimïm delom ...': iz pisem D. D. Shostakovicha B. L. Yavorskomu," *Muzïkal'naya akademiya* 4 (1997): 30.

62. S. Khentova, "Zhenshchinï v zhizni Shostakovicha," *Vremya i mï* 112 (1991): 250.

63. "K obsuzhdeniyu 24 prelyudiy i fug D. Shostakovicha," *Sovetskaya muzïka* 6 (1951): 55.

64. T. Nikolayeva, "Ispolnyaya Shostakovicha," in *Dmitriy Shostakovich*, comp. G. Ordzhonikidze (Moscow, 1967), 291.

65. *Pis'ma k drugu*, 93.

66. A. Abramskiy, "Na perekryostkakh," in A. Shebalina, *Pamyati V. Ya. Shebalina: vospominaniya, materialï* (Moscow, 1984), 116.

67. *Pis'ma k drugu*, 93.

68. For two accounts of the proceedings, see Wilson, *Shostakovich Remembered*, 248–58. Moisey Vainberg's revelation that Shostakovich made a four-hand arrangement of the complete cycle which the two of them laboriously taped in 1952 on a "Dnepr"—the pioneer of Russian tape recorders—strongly suggests that the composer was dissatisfied with his own proficiency in the performance of his op. 87. Neither the tape nor the score of this arrangement has been found; see L. Nikitina, "Pochti lyuboy mig zhizni—rabota ...," *Muzïkal'naya akademiya* 5 (1994): 19. In a letter to Oistrakh dated 4 July 1952, Shostakovich mentions that he has taped "almost all" of his preludes and fugues (GTsMMK f. 385, yed. khr. 474).

69. "K obsuzhdeniyu 24 prelyudiy i fug D. Shostakovicha," 55.

70. L. Barenboim, *Emil Gilels: tvorcheskiy portret artista* (Moscow, 1990), 171.

71. Shostakovich letter to Atovmyan, dated 29 February 1952; GTsMMK f. 32, yed. khr. 1811.

72. E. R. Rikhter, comp., *Genrikh Neygauz: vospominaniya, pis'ma, materiali* (Moscow, 1992), 246.

73. Shostakovich letter to Atovmyan dated 13 August 1952; GTsMMK, f. 32, yed. khr. 1821.

74. Wilson, *Shostakovich Remembered*, 258.

75. Rikhter, *Genrikh Neygauz*, 126.

76. Shostakovich letters to Atovmyan dated 24 and 28 July 1951; GTsMMK f. 32, yed. khr. 1802 and 1805.

77. A letter from Shostakovich to an official of the Radio Committee dated 18 July 1951 indicates that all three of the ballet suites were complete by this date; GTsMMK f. 32, yed. khr. 1877.

78. *D. Shostakovich: stat'i i materialï*, 75.

79. He gradually reassumed visible roles: he served, for instance, as a member of

the committee preparing to celebrate Stalin's seventieth birthday on 21 December 1949. Having been dropped from the masthead in 1948, Shostakovich was reinstated on the editorial board of the journal *Sovetskaya muzïka* as of March 1950.

80. B. Frezinskiy, "Erenburg i Shostakovich," *Niva* 8 (1989): 206. The passage was restored in the 1990 edition: I. Erenburg, *Lyudi, godï, zhizn'*, 3 (Moscow, 1990), 375–76.

81. Ye. Yevtushenko, "Fekhtovaniye s navoznoy kuchey," *Literaturnaya gazeta* (23 January 1991): 9.

82. Svyatoslav Prokof'yev, "O moikh roditelyakh," in *Sergey Prokof'yev 1891–1991: dnevnik, pis'ma, besedï, vospominaniya* (Moscow, 1991), 237.

83. M. Yakubov, "Mechislav Vaynberg: 'Vsyu zhizn' ya zhadno sochinyal muzïku,'" *Utro Rossii* 7 (16–22 February 1995): 12.

84. Wilson, *Shostakovich Remembered*, 231–32.

85. Kholopova and Tsenova, *Denisov*, 172; Ger. trans. in Gojowy, "Briefe," 181–82.

86. Shostakovich letter to Edison Denisov dated 15 June 1950; Russian in typescript, German translation in Gojowy, "Briefe," 188. Earlier in 1950, Alexey Muravlyov had been awarded a Stalin Prize (category two) for his symphonic poem *Azov-Mountain*.

87. "Tvorcheskaya diskussiya na shestom plenume pravleniya soyuza kompozitorov," *Sovetskaya muzïka* 4 (1953): 46.

88. A. Khachaturyan, "Nad rodinoy nashey solntse siyaet," *Sovetskaya muzïka* 1 (1953): 10.

89. Dm. Shostakovich, "Sozdat' sovetskuyu klassicheskuyu operu," *Sovetskaya muzïka* 10 (1952): 4–5.

90. E. Denisov, "Vstrechi s Shostakovichem," *Muzïkal'naya akademiya* 3 (1994): 91; German translation in Gojowy, "Briefe," 202.

91. "Prokofiev's Correspondence with Stravinsky and Shostakovich," in *Slavonic and Western Music: Essays for Gerald Abraham*, ed. M. Brown and R. Wiley (Ann Arbor, Mich., 1985), 283.

92. Letter dated 22 April 1953, in *N. S. Golovanov: literaturnoye naslediye, perepiska, vospominaniya sovremennikov*, comp. E. Grosheva and V. Rudenko (Moscow, 1982), 130.

93. D. Shostakovich, "Mï sil'nï i yedinï," *Izvestiya*, 9 March 1953, 3.

94. Wilson, *Shostakovich Remembered*, 260.

95. Kholopov and Tsenova, *Denisov*, 11.

Chapter 11

1. *Pis'ma k drugu: Dmitriy Shostakovich—Isaaku Glikmanu*, comp. I. Glikman (Moscow, 1993), 85.

2. Yu. Fedosyuk, "Zhivu v serdtsakh vsekh lyubyashchikh," *Sovetskaya muzïka* 9 (1991): 34. Shostakovich had been a roller-coaster enthusiast since the 1920s.

3. G. Khubov, "Muzïka i sovremennost' (o zadachakh razvitiya sovetskoy muzïki)," *Sovetskaya muzïka* 4 (1953): 20. This essay, published in three parts, was based on Khubov's keynote speech to the Plenum of the Union of Composers leadership delivered on 9 February 1953.

4. Shostakovich letter to Kara Karayev dated 6 June 1947, quoted in L. Karagicheva, "'Pishite kak mozhno bol'she prekrasnoy muzïki'; iz pisem D. D. Shostakovicha K. A. Karayevu," *Muzïkal'naya akademiya* 4 (1997): 207.

5. See, for instance, E. Wilson, *Shostakovich: A Life Remembered*, 257.

6. L. Karagicheva, ed., *Kara Karayev: stat'i, pis'ma, vïskazïvaniya* (Moscow, 1978), 52.

7. Shostakovich letter to Atovmyan dated 18 July 1953; GTsMMK f. 32, yed. khr. 1829.

8. *Pis'ma k drugu*, 102.

9. Shostakovich letter to Elmira Nazirova dated 12 August 1953, quoted in "Beseda Nelli Kravets s El'miroy Nazirovoy," in *D. D. Shostakovich: sbornik statey k 90-letiyu so dnya rozhdeniya*, comp. L. Kovnatskaya (St. Petersburg, 1996), 245.

10. *Pis'ma k drugu*, 104.

11. N. Kravets, "Novïy vzglyad na desyatuyu simfoniyu Shostakovicha," in *D. D. Shostakovich: sbornik statey k 90-letiyu*, 231.

12. "Beseda Nelli Kravets s El'miroy Nazirovoy," 244.

13. Kravets, "Novïy vzglyad," 233.

14. Ibid., 232–33. Considerably more attention has been paid to the sensational revelation attributed to the composer by S. Volkov in *Testimony: The Memoirs of Dmitri Shostakovich* (New York, 1979) of a "hidden" program in the second movement: "The second part, the scherzo, is a musical portrait of Stalin, roughly speaking" (141). I have found no corroboration that such a specific program was either intended or perceived at the time of composition and first performance. Maxim Shostakovich has classified this as one example of the "rumors" reproduced in *Testimony*: "I think some musicologists set this idea forth. Others repeated it.... Father never said it was a portrait of Stalin." See C. Pasles, "Was He or Wasn't He?" *Los Angeles Times/Calendar*, 29 November 1998, 75.

15. Though researchers have detected appearances of the intervallic contours—if not the identical pitches—in earlier works, most notably in the First Violin Concerto (in 1953 still unperformed), this marked the overt confirmation of the personal significance.

16. E. Denisov, "Vstrechi s Shostakovichem," *Muzïkal'naya akademiya* 3 (1994): 91. A performance by Shostakovich and Vainberg of the four-hand arrangement was taped and subsequently issued on recordings.

17. Z. Apetyan, *Gavriil Popov: iz literaturnogo naslediya* (Leningrad, 1986), 320. Popov's appreciation of the new symphony was colored by his perception that Shostakovich had appropriated, perhaps unconsciously, a theme from one of his own works for the main theme of the first movement.

18. Denisov, "Vstrechi s Shostakovichem," 91.

19. Ye. Mravinsky reminiscences in S. Khentova, *V mire Shostakovicha* (Moscow, 1996), 194.

20. Zritel', "Pravo i dolg teatra," *Pravda*, 27 November 1953, 3.

21. D. Shostakovich, "Radost' tvorcheskikh iskaniy," *Sovetskaya muzïka* 1 (1954): 42.

22. A. Khachaturyan, "O tvorcheskoy smelosti i vdokhnovenii," *Sovetskaya muzïka* 11 (1953): 7–13.

23. A. Khachaturyan, "Desyataya simfoniya D. Shostakovicha," *Sovetskaya muzïka* 3 (1954): 25.

24. Ibid., 26. *An Optimistic Tragedy* is the title of a well-known play by Vsevolod Vishnevsky produced in 1933, a heroic saga romanticizing the revolutionary struggle of the Bolsheviks. As an attempt to legitimate the perceived paradoxes in his music, the oxymoron "optimistic tragedy" had earlier been invoked with reference to Shostakovich's Fifth Symphony.

25. P. Apostolov, "K voprosu o voploshchenii otritsatel'nogo obraza v muzïke," *Sovetskaya muzïka* 3 (1954): 38. The author of this article is now best remembered for collapsing during a public run-through of Shostakovich's Fourteenth Symphony in 1969; see Chapter 14.

26. Z. Akimova, "Slovo slushatelya," *Sovetskaya muzïka* 4 (1954): 30.

27. A summary transcript of the proceedings was published in *Sovetskaya muzïka* 6 (1954): 119–34. All references are taken from this source.

28. Ibid., 120.

29. *Pis'ma k drugu*, 107.

30. From transcript dated 1 April 1954, "Stenogrammï zasedaniy Sektsii muzïki Komiteta po gosudarstvennïm premiyam s obsuzhdeniyami proizvedeniy Dmitriya Shostakovicha (8-y i 10-y simfonii …)," typescript copy, RGALI f. 2048, op. 3, yed. khr. 412.

31. "Diskussiya o sovetskom simfonizme," *Sovetskaya muzïka* 5 (1955): 47–48.

32. Yu. Kremlyov, "O desyatoy simfonii D. Shostakovicha," *Sovetskaya muzïka* 4 (1957): 83–84.

33. See Chapter 2.

34. Shostakovich's duties included advising on new repertory and critiquing productions of the classics. He was fired in a staff cutback in the spring of 1959, when the Bolshoy management questioned whether his contributions justified a monthly stipend. See Khentova, *V mire Shostakovicha*, 38, 319.

35. The premiere of this composition is misdated in secondary sources as 20 January 1954. There is no contemporary record of any such concert, although the two did give a performance of the work on 20 January 1955. That 8 November 1954 was the premiere date in fact is indicated in a review of the concert; A. Gotlib, "Kamernïy vecher," *Sovetskaya muzïka* 1 (1955): 105.

36. Denisov, "Vtrechi s Shostakovichem," 91. The diary entry, dated 3 February, has been mistakenly dated 1954 both here and elsewhere. Verifiable internal evidence in the entry makes the 1955 dating incontrovertible.

37. Wilson, *Shostakovich Remembered*, 232.

38. G. D. Shostakovich, "Vspominaya Shostakovicha," *Muzïkal'naya zhizn'* 8 (1994): 35.

39. S. Khentova, *Udivitel'nïy Shostakovich* (St. Petersburg, 1993), 155.

40. *Pis'ma k drugu*, 110.

41. See L. E. Fay, "From *Lady Macbeth* to *Katerina*: Shostakovich's versions and revisions," in *Shostakovich Studies*, ed. D. Fanning (Cambridge, 1995), 178–82.

42. Karagicheva, *Kara Karayev*, 53.

43. Ibid., 54.

44. Mezzo-soprano Zara Dolukhanova turned over to Shostakovich anonymous

songs that a Spanish woman had given her, in the hope that the composer would apply artistic license to transform the thematic material into an original vocal cycle. Expecting greater transformation, she was disappointed with the result and did not sing the premiere or add the set to her repertory. The first performer was evidently Debora Yakovlevna-Nachetskaya; the date has not been established. See S. Yakovenko, *Volshebnaya Zara Dolukhanova* (Moscow, 1996), 114–15. There may have been some misunderstanding. Reminiscing late in life, Shostakovich's recollection was that Dolukhanova had asked him to "harmonize" the tunes. He attributed her disappointment to the realization, once the texts had been translated into Russian, that they should be sung by a man. See Ye. Shenderovich, "V moyey pamyati svetlïy oblik …," *Sovetskaya muzïka* 10 (1981): 33. Notwithstanding this, in his catalogue Shostakovich designated this opus for mezzo-soprano.

45. *Pis'ma k drugu*, 110.

46. Wilson, *Shostakovich Remembered*, 230.

47. Denisov, "Vstrechi s Shostakovichem," 91. See also note 36.

48. Yu. Kholopov and V. Tsenova, *Edison Denisov* (Moscow, 1993), 182.

49. The Violin Concerto was initially assigned opus no. 99, corresponding chronologically to its date of first performance. It was subsequently reassigned opus no. 77, reflecting the actual date of composition. Opus 99 was assigned to the film music for *The First Echelon*.

50. I. Shveytser, "Vspominaya Davida Oystrakha," *Muzïkal'naya akademiya* 4 (1994): 96.

51. *Pis'ma k drugu*, 116.

52. In. Popov, "Skripichnïy kontsert D. Shostakovicha," *Sovetskaya kul'tura* (1 November 1955): 1.

53. D. Oystrakh, "Voploshcheniye bol'shogo zamïsla (O skripichnom kontserte D. Shostakovicha)," *Sovetskaya muzïka* 7 (1957): 3–10.

54. B. Ryazhskiy, "Kak shla reabilitatsiya," *Teatral'naya zhizn'* 5 (1989): 10.

55. Ibid., 12–13.

56. *Pis'ma k drugu*, 117–18.

57. Letter to A. S. Suvorin, 6 February 1898; quoted in Anton Chekhov, *Letters on the Short Story, the Drama, and Other Literary Topics* (New York, 1966), 256.

58. I. Glikman, "Kazn' Ledi Makbet," *Sovetskaya kul'tura* (23 September 1989): 9. Kabalevsky's children have taken issue with Glikman's interpretation of their father's behavior and role in the "second execution" of Shostakovich's opera. See M. Kabalevskaya and Yu. Kabalevskiy, "Kazn' Ledi Makbet: vozvrashayas' k napechatannomu," *Sovetskaya kul'tura* (16 November 1989): 3.

59. Exactly what contest this may have been has not been established. Contrary to some sources, it was not the Sixth World Festival of Youth and Students, which took place in Moscow from 28 July to 11 August 1957. Shostakovich chaired the international jury for its composition competition.

60. Khentova, *Udivitel'nïy Shostakovich*, 157.

61. Wilson, *Shostakovich Remembered*, 273–74.

62. Ibid., 268.

63. Shostakovich letter to Atovmyan dated 25 July 1956; GTsMMK f. 32, yed. khr. 1858.

64. *Pis'ma k drugu*, 124.

65. Ibid.

66. D. Shostakovich, "Dumï o proydyonnom puti," *Sovetskaya muzïka* 9 (1956): 9–15.

67. Ibid., 14.

68. D. Shostakovich, "Nash sovremennik," *Izvestiya*, 14 February 1956, 3.

69. D. Shostakovich, "Planï svoyikh tvorcheskikh rabot v 1957g.," dated 21 January 1957. Autograph ms. RGALI f. 2048, op. 1, yed. khr. 70.

70. Shostakovich letter to Denisov dated 12 February 1957; original in typescript, German translation in D. Gojowy, "Dimitri Schostakowitsch: Briefe an Edison Denissow," in *Musik des Ostens*, 10, ed. H. Unverricht (Kassell, 1986), 197.

71. *Pis'ma k drugu*, 125–26.

72. Widely covered in the daily press, the major speeches, documents, and proceedings of the Second Congress were published in issues of *Sovetskaya muzïka*, May through August 1957.

73. D. Zhitomirskiy, "Shostakovich ofitsial'nïy i podlinnïy: stat'ya vtoraya," *Daugava* 4 (1990): 101.

74. "Vïstupleniye D. D. Shostakovicha," *Sovetskaya kul'tura* (2 April 1957): 4.

75. D. Shepilov, "Tvorit' dlya blaga i schast'ya naroda," *Sovetskaya muzïka* 5 (1957): 8.

76. Wilson, *Shostakovich Remembered*, 298–99.

77. Kholopov and Tsenova, *Denisov*, 183.

78. "Simfoniya '1905 god,'" *Sovetskaya muzïka* 2 (1958): 157.

79. L. Polyakova, "Simfoniya '1905 god,'" *Komsomol'skaya Pravda*, 16 November 1957, 4.

80. See L. Lebedinskiy, "O nekotorïkh muzïkal'nïkh tsitatkh v proizvedeniyakh D. Shostakovicha," *Novïy mir* 3 (1990): 262–63; see also Wilson, *Shostakovich Remembered*, 317–18.

81. Reminiscences of M. D. Shostakovich in Khentova, *V mire Shostakovicha*, 49.

82. *Pis'ma k drugu*, 126.

83. The chronology of composition, specificity of musical materials, and dearth of reliable first-person testimony are among the arguments against it. See also Yu. Levitin, "Fal'shivaya nota, ili grustnïye mïsli o delakh muzïkal'nïkh," *Pravda*, 11 November 1990, 3. For what it is worth, when asked point-blank by his Soviet biographer in 1974 whether it was true that it was the Hungarian uprising that was rendered in the Eleventh Symphony, Shostakovich responded: "No, it is 1905, it is Russian history." See Khentova, *V mire Shostakovicha*, 39.

84. A. Solzhenitsïn, *Arkhipelag Gulag 1918–1956: opït khudozhestvennogo issledovaniya*, 5–7 (Paris, 1975), 54. For unexplained reasons, the published English translation of this passage eliminated the identification of the Shostakovich work in question as the Eleventh Symphony.

85. E. Gershteyn, "V Zamoskvorech'ye," *Literaturnoye obozreniye* 7 (1985): 106. Solomon Volkov, who heard Mravinsky conduct the Eleventh Symphony in Leningrad, has conceded that, though powerfully moved, he suspected no "subtext" when he first heard the work. See M. Pritsker, "Dmitriy Shostakovich: tragediya i zagadka," *Novoye russkoye slovo*, 25 September 1996, 17.

86. "V chest' sovetskoy narodnoy intelligentsii: priyom v Bol'shom Kremlevskom dvortse," *Pravda*, 9 February 1958, 3.

87. "Ob ispravlenii oshibok v otsenke oper 'Velikaya druzhba,' 'Bogdan Khmelnitskiy' i 'Iz vsego serdtsa': Postanovleniye TsK KPSS ot 28 maya 1958 goda," *Pravda*, 8 June 1958, 3.

88. Ibid.

89. Wilson, *Shostakovich Remembered*, 293–94.

90. W. Tompson, *Khrushchev: A Political Life* (New York, 1995), 172.

91. D. Shostakovich, "Mirovoy avtoritet sovetskogo iskusstva," *Pravda*, 13 June 1958, 3.

92. G. Vishnevskaya, *Galina: A Russian Story* (San Diego, 1984), 244.

93. Shostakovich, "Dumï o proydyonnom puti," 14.

94. L. Lebedinskiy, "Proizvedeniya D. Shostakovicha," *Sovetskaya muzïka* 12 (1956): 97–99.

Chapter 12

1. "Shostakovich Doing Operetta," *New York Times*, 20 March 1957, 33.

2. "Pervaya operetta D. Shostakovicha," *Sovetskaya kul'tura* (7 August 1958): 3.

3. *Pis'ma k drugu: Dmitriy Shostakovich—Isaaku Glikmanu*, comp. I. Glikman (Moscow, 1993), 145.

4. D. Shostakovich, "Bït' na vïsote velikikh zadach," *Sovetskaya muzïka* 1 (1959): 10.

5. G. Yaron, *O lyubimom zhanre* (Moscow, 1960), 239–40.

6. *Pis'ma k drugu*, 146.

7. Letter to Karayev dated 6 February 1960; L. Karagicheva, "Pishete ka mozhno bol'she prekrasnoy muziki....'": iz pisem D. D. Shostakovicha K. A. Karayevu," *Muzïkal'naya akademiya* 4 (1997): 206.

8. *Pis'ma k drugu*, 141.

9. Ibid., 143.

10. Shostakovich, "Bït' na vïsote," 9.

11. In the summer of 1951, when a perusal request for *Boris* came from a conductor in Tallinn, Shostakovich was not even sure how to go about tracking down the score. He ended up supplying both his original manuscript and his own annotated copy of the Lamm piano-vocal score. See letters to Atovmyan dated 28 and 31 July 1951; GTsMMK f. 32, yed. khr. 1805, 1806.

12. S. Khentova, *Shostakovich: zhizn' i tvorchestvo*, 2 (Leningrad, 1986), 346.

13. B. Khaykin, *Besedï o dirizhyorskom remesle: stat'i* (Moscow, 1984), 92.

14. Letter to M. Sokolsky dated 17 June 1955, in M. Sokol'skiy, *Musorgskiy/Shostakovich: stat'i, retsenzii* (Moscow, 1983), 131.

15. Letter to G. Shneerson dated 24 July 1958; GTsMMK f. 32, yed. khr. 148.

16. D. Shostakovich, V. Stroyeva, and A. Abramova, "K istorii rabotï nad fil'mom *Khovanshchina*," in *Zhizn' v kino: veteranï o sebe i svoikh tovarishchakh, vïp. 2* (Moscow, 1979), 312.

17. Shostakovich, "Bït' na vïsote," 9.

18. "Tvorcheskiye planï Dmitriya Shostakovicha," *Sovetskaya kul'tura* (6 June 1959): 4.

19. Letter to Atovmyan dated 20 July 1959; GTsMMK f. 32, yed. khr. 1865.

20. E. Wilson, *Shostakovich: A Life Remembered* (London, 1994), 322.

21. Ibid., 325–26.

22. "Tvorcheskiye planï," 4.

23. Wilson, *Shostakovich Remembered*, 323.

24. *Sovetskaya muzïka* 8 (1948): 105.

25. From radio interview with Witold Rodzinski; *Govorit Dmitriy Shostakovich*, Melodiya Mono 33 M 40-41705.

26. Ibid.

27. T. Khrennikov and D. Shostakovich, "Muzïka druzhbï," *Pravda*, 11 December 1959, 6.

28. D. Shostakovich, "Mirovoy avtoritet sovetskogo iskusstva," *Pravda*, 13 June 1958, 3.

29. D. Shostakovich, "Shirokiye massï vernï nastoyashchey muzïke," *Sovetskaya muzïka* 11 (1959): 7.

30. "Prénom Maxime," *Le Monde de la musique* 118 (January 1989): xv.

31. E. Denisov, "Vstrechi s Shostakovichem," *Muzïkal'naya akademiya* 3 (1994): 92.

32. M. Kurtz, *Stockhausen: A Biography* (London, 1992), 94.

33. Tsïganov in S. Khentova, *V mire Shostakovicha* (Moscow, 1996), 207.

34. "Stat' yeshchyo blizhe k zhizni naroda," *Muzïkal'naya zhizn'* 7 (1960): 4.

35. D. Shostakovich, "Vospet' kommunizm," *Pravda*, 30 April 1960, 2.

36. Wilson, *Shostakovich Remembered*, 272.

37. *Pis'ma k drugu*, 160.

38. L. Lebedinskiy, "Iz 'bessistemnïkh zapisey,'" *Muzïkal'naya zhizn'* 21–22 (1993): 27.

39. In transcribing one of Shostakovich's letters, Glikman mistakenly identified the location as "Görlitz" instead of "Gohrisch," although the composer's geographical description clearly pinpoints the latter, as do the memoirs of Leo Arnshtam. See *Pis'ma k drugu*, 159; Khentova, *V mire Shostakovicha*, 236.

40. *Pis'ma k drugu*, 159.

41. Ibid.

42. G. Shostakovich in Khentova, *V mire Shostakovicha*, 85.

43. L. Lebedinskiy, "O nekotorïkh muzïkal'nïkh tsitatakh v proizvedeniyakh D. Shostakovicha," *Noviy mir* 3 (1990): 264.

44. *Pis'ma k drugu*, 161.

45. When asked, in 1974, what had prompted him to take on such an enormous burden as the leadership of the Union of Composers, Shostakovich flared angrily: "What? Everyone should sit at home complaining that their music isn't played, that there are no orchestras.... If you love music, you must serve it." See Khentova, *V mire Shostakovicha*, 38.

46. Khachaturyan in Khentova, *V mire Shostakovicha*, 108.

47. In conversation with the author in Moscow, 22 January 1991.

48. G. Serebryakova, *O drugikh i o sebe* (Moscow, 1968), 307.

49. M. Dolgopolov, "Schast'ye tvorit' dlya naroda," *Izvestiya*, 25 September 1960, 4.

50. E. Rikhter, *Genrikh Neygauz: vospominaniya, pis'ma, materialï* (Moscow, 1992), 275.

51. M. Sokol'skiy, "Surovoye napominaniye," *Izvestiya*, 22 October 1960, 5.

52. Yu. Keldïsh, "Avtobiograficheskiy kvartet," *Sovetskaya muzïka* 12 (1960): 20; Eng. trans. as "An Autobiographical Quartet," *Musical Times* 102, no. 1418 (1961): 226.

53. Sasha Chyorny was the pseudonym of Alexander Mikhailovich Glikberg (1880–1932). *Satires* was the title of a collection of his verse first published in 1910.

54. Dogopolov, "Schast'ye," 4.

55. Wilson, *Shostakovich Remembered*, 341.

56. B. Lyatokhin, "Poyot Galina Vishnevskaya, akkompaniruyet Mstislav Rostropovich," *Sovetskaya muzïka* 4 (1961): 164–65.

57. Vishnevskaya says they were obliged to encore it twice. See G. Vishnevskaya, *Galina: A Russian Story* (San Diego, 1984), 270.

58. *Pis'ma k drugu*, 166.

59. "Tvorcheskiye planï," 4.

60. "Novïy muzïkal'nïy radiozhurnal: D. Shostakovich rasskazïvayet o svoyey rabote nad 12-oy simfoniyey," *Muzïkal'naya zhizn'* 21 (1960): 10.

61. Ibid. That Shostakovich had actually been present to hear Lenin's speech is dubious; see Chapter 1.

62. *Pis'ma k drugu*, 167.

63. "Uspekh dvenadtsatoy," *Sovetskaya muzïka* 4 (1962): 146.

64. M. Konisskaya, "Dusha i maska: pis'ma D. D. Shostakovicha k L. N. Lebedinskomu," *Muzïkal'naya zhizn'* 23–24 (1993): 13.

65. Wilson, *Shostakovich Remembered*, 346.

66. Lebedinskiy, "O nekotorïkh tsitatakh," 267.

67. In. Popov, "Dvenadtsataya," *Sovetskaya kul'tura* (16 September 1961): 1.

68. Khentova, *Shostakovich*, 2: 363.

69. L. Danilevich, "Simfoniya o Lenine, o velikom oktyabre," *Sovetskaya muzïka* 11 (1961): 11.

70. "Uspekh dvenadtsatoy," 146.

Chapter 13

1. V. Razhnikov, *Kirill Kondrashin rasskazïvayet o muzïke i zhizni* (Moscow, 1989), 182. The administrator in question was the same Moisey Grinberg who had condemned the nomination of Shostakovich's Piano Quintet for the Stalin Prize in 1941. See Chapter 7.

2. *Pis'ma k drugu: Dmitriy Shostakovich–Isaaku Glikmanu*, comp. I. Glikman (Moscow, 1993), 143.

3. Razhnikov, *Kondrashin*, 183.

4. Lebedinsky in S. Khentova, *V mire Shostakovicha* (Moscow, 1996), 116.

5. Kondrashin in Khentova, *V mire Shostakovicha*, 196.

6. E. Wilson, *Shostakovich: A Life Remembered* (London, 1994), 348.

7. R. Weitzman, "A Summary of the 1962 Edinburgh International Festival," *Musical Opinion* 1022 (1962): 79.

8. D. Shostakovich, "Nas vdokhnovlyaet partiya," *Muzïkal'naya zhizn'* 2 (1962): 2–3.

9. Wilson, *Shostakovich Remembered*, 352–53.

10. S. Khentova, *Udivitel'nïy Shostakovich* (St. Petersburg, 1993), 163.

11. *Pis'ma k drugu*, 173–74.

12. Ibid., 176.

13. "Rasskazïvayet poet Yevgeniy Yevtushenko," with recording of Shostakovich's Symphony No. 13, Melodiya Stereo A10 00285 000 (1987).

14. *Pis'ma k drugu*, 173.

15. Shostakovich's compositional "method" is a subject requiring additional study, especially in light of the fact that in both the Thirteenth and Fourteenth Symphonies the piano-vocal preceded the full score. It seems not unlikely that it may have changed somewhat over the years; it may also have been different for vocal and instrumental works. The accepted notion that he always composed straight into full score is belied by the sizable number of "sketches" preserved. In a 1996 interview, the composer's widow described Shostakovich's routine—presumably based on her observations over the last fifteen years of his life, when she lived with him—of mentally conceptualizing a future composition, then making a very brief sketch (during which time he could not be disturbed). When he "orchestrated," however, he could carry on a conversation. See M. Vardenga, "Ryadom s geniyem," *Argumentï i faktï* 38 (1996): 3.

16. M. Shaginyan, *O Shostakoviche* (Moscow, 1979), 12.

17. A. Shebalina, *Vissarion Yakovlevich Shebalin: literaturnoye naslediye* (Moscow, 1975), 166.

18. *Pis'ma k drugu*, 175.

19. The poem "Boots" was first published in 1959.

20. *Pis'ma Dmitriya Dmitriyevich Shostakovicha Borisu Tishchenko s kommentariyami i vospominaniyami adresata* (St. Petersburg, 1997), 18. The letter to Tishchenko from which this quotation is taken, dated 26 October 1965, was neither completed nor sent; it was apparently preserved by the composer's wife.

21. S. Khentova, *Shostakovich: zhizn' i tvorchestvo*, 2, (Leningrad, 1986), 426.

22. Khentova, *Udivitel'nïy Shostakovich*, 68.

23. Ibid., 69.

24. Ya. Platek and G. Losev, "Pyat' dney muzïki; zametki o festivale v Gor'kom," *Muzïkal'naya zhizn'* 13 (1962): 4.

25. "Aplodismentï Shostakovichu," *Izvestiya*, 5 September 1962, 1.

26. M. Konisskaya, "Dusha i maska: pis'ma D. D. Shostakovicha k L. N. Lebedinskomu," *Muzïkal'naya zhizn'* 23–24 (1993): 14.

27. His reluctance to engage Stravinsky might have been caused, in part, by embarrassment over his own disparaging "official" statements about the émigré composer over the years and the musical "cold war" fomented around them. In Edinburgh three weeks earlier, he had taken umbrage when his departure from a concert before a performance of the *Rite of Spring* was interpreted by the press as a sign of disrespect. In fact he had left (after Vishnevskaya's performance of two arias from *Lady Macbeth*) merely in order to hear the Borodin Quartet perform his own music at a concurrent concert. See "U telefona—Dmitriy Shostakovich," *Literaturnaya gazeta* (1 September 1962): 1. Then again, the story of their first encounter that spread quickly among Soviet musicians was that it was the nervous but receptive Shostakovich who had been snubbed by a standoffish Stravinsky. See Dmitriy Tolstoy, *Dlya chego vsyo eto bïlo:*

vospominaniya (St. Petersburg, 1995), 440. This might have contributed to Shostakovich's cooling toward the insensitive, egocentric composer. In 1971, he would write, "I worship Stravinsky the composer. I despise Stravinsky the thinker." See *Pis'ma k drugu*, 279.

28. R. Craft, *Stravinsky: Chronicle of a Friendship, 1948–1971* (New York, 1972), 206.

29. Ibid., 207.

30. In 1942, he substituted for an ailing Samosud directing a sectional rehearsal for the woodwinds of his Seventh Symphony but did not report success. See A. Ikonnikov, "Shtrikhi k portretu Shostakovicha," *Nashe naslediye* 4 (1989): 146.

31. Wilson, *Shostakovich Remembered*, 379.

32. *Pis'ma k drugu*, 181.

33. "Smert' ne strashus', no k zhizni privyazan," *Sovetskaya kul'tura* (8 June 1991): 6. Among other performances of "choral" works, Mravinsky conducted the premiere of Shostakovich's *Song of the Forests*.

34. Letter to Yavorsky dated 9 November 1925; "'Khorosho bïlo bï ne dumat' ni o khlebe nasushchnom, ni o chyom, a tol'ko zanimat'sya lyubimïm delom …': iz pisem D. D. Shostakovicha B. L. Yavorskomu," *Muzïkal'naya akademiya* 4 (1997): 33.

35. *Komsomol'skaya pravda*, 21 October 1962, 4.

36. J. Rubenstein, *Tangled Loyalties: The Life and Times of Ilya Ehrenburg* (New York, 1996), 346.

37. B. Zhutovskiy, "Gruppovoy portret v kazyonnom inter'ere," *Literaturnaya gazeta* (5 July 1989): 8. That the authors were explicitly called upon to withdraw the Thirteenth Symphony at this meeting has not been confirmed. See P. Johnson and L. Labedz, eds., *Khrushchev and the Arts: The Politics of Soviet Culture, 1962–1964* (Cambridge, MA, 1965), 12.

38. A. Khachaturyan, "Chuvstvo gordosti za otchiznu," *Sovetskaya kul'tura* (6 November 1962): 4.

39. "Prem'era—vo vtornik: novaya simfoniya Dmitriya Shostakovicha," *Nedelya* 50 (9–15 December 1962): 18.

40. Descriptions of Gromadsky as an "understudy" are inaccurate. The two soloists had been slated to perform in alternate performances and they received equal billing on posters and in the press. According to Vitaliy Katayev, who conducted the two performances of the Thirteenth Symphony in Minsk in March 1963, it was Gromadsky's own understudy for the Moscow premiere, Askold Besedin, who agreed to fill in for the Minsk performances after Gromadsky's late cancellation. See V. Katayev, "Umirayut v Rossii strakhi," *Shostakovichu posvyashchayetsya: sbornik statey k 90-letiyu kompozitora (1906–1975)*, comp. E. Dolinskaya (Moscow, 1997), 173.

41. Kondrashin in Khentova, *V mire Shostakovicha*, 197. This interview dates from the autumn of 1963, less than a year after the events discussed. In an interview recorded more than ten years later, Kondrashin did not mention Shostakovich's summons but recollected instead that he himself had been called backstage for a phone call from the Ministry of Culture. See Razhnikov, *Kondrashin*, 187–88.

42. Gromadsky also sang in this performance, which was recorded and has been released on compact disc: Russian Disc RD CD 11 191.

43. Ye. Yevtushenko, "Genius Is Beyond Genre: Dmitrii Shostakovich (1976–1988)," in *Fatal Half Measures: The Culture of Democracy in the Soviet Union* (Boston, 1991), 294–95.

44. P. Pospelov, "Trinadtsataya simfoniya Shostakovicha," *Moskovskaya Pravda*, 19 December 1962, 3. While providing the titles of the final four movements, Pospelov managed to avoid mentioning the title or the subject matter of the first movement, glossing over it simply as a "mournful requiem."

45. "Dve prem'ery D. Shostakovicha: trinadtsataya simfoniya i opera 'Katerina Izmaylova,'" *Leninskoye znamya* (19 December 1962): 3.

46. "Vïrazhat' pomïslï sovremennikov," *Sovetskaya kul'tura* (25 December 1962): 1.

47. Yevtushenko's claim that he provided only four new lines is inaccurate, as is his description of how they were transmitted to Shostakovich. See Yevtushenko, "Genius Is Beyond Genre," 297.

48. Razhnikov, *Kondrashin*, 189.

49. *Pis'ma k drugu*, 184.

50. M. Shaginyan, "50 pisem D. D. Shostakovicha," *Noviy mir* 12 (1982): 140.

51. In reminiscences of the event, Katayev implicated Kirill Kondrashin as having attempted to scuttle these performances—for reasons unspecified—by recalling the parts five days before the first concert. Overnight, each of the orchestral musicians re-copied his or her own part, thus allowing the performances to proceed as scheduled. See Katayev, "Umirayut v Rossii strakhi," 173–74.

52. A. Ladïgina, "Slushaya trinadtsatuyu simfoniyu," *Sovetskaya Belorussiya*, 2 April 1963, 4; Eng. trans. in Russian Studies Series no. 40 (Chicago, n.d.).

53. Professional deliberation of the Thirteenth Symphony, scheduled for 26 February 1963 in the Moscow Union of Composers, was canceled "for technical reasons." See V. Zak, *Shostakovich i yevrey?* (New York, 1997), 42.

54. *Musik und Szene: Theaterzeitschrift der Deutschen Oper am Rhein*, supplement (Düsseldorf, 1959/60).

55. *Pis'ma k drugu*, 154.

56. I. Rayskin, "Kak teatr Kirova ne stal teatrom Shostakovicha: dokumental'noye povestvovaniye," in *Ars Peterburg: "Mariinskiy-vchera, segodnya, vsegda"* (St. Petersburg, 1993), 100.

57. *Pis'ma k drugu*, 155.

58. A. Bogdanova, *Muzïka i vlast' (poststalinskiy period)* (Moscow, 1995), 366–68.

59. L. Mikhaylov, *Sem' glav o teatre* (Moscow, 1985), 66–67.

60. Mikhaylov, *Sem' glav*, 70.

61. *Pis'ma k drugu*, 170.

62. "Dmitriy Shostakovich o novïkh muzykal'nïkh proizvedeniyakh: kompozitorï—45-y godovshchine Oktyabrya, simfonii, oratorii, pesni molodïkh," *Pravda*, 21 October 1962, 6.

63. Bogdanova, *Muzïka i vlast'*, 370–71.

64. GTsMMK, f. 291, yed. khr. 108.

65. Ye. Yevtushenko, "Vtoroye rozhdeniye," *Kater svyazi* (Moscow, 1966), 196–97.

66. *Pis'ma k drugu*, 184.

67. "*Katerina Izmaylova*: novaya redaktsiya operï D. Shostakovicha," *Pravda*, 9 January 1963, 4.

68. See L. E. Fay, "From *Lady Macbeth* to *Katerina*: Shostakovich's versions and revisions," in *Shostakovich Studies*, ed. D. Fanning (Cambridge, 1995), 178–88.

69. Johnson and Labedz, *Khrushchev and the Arts*, 174.

70. Ibid., 175.

71. *Pis'ma k drugu*, 190.

72. Yevtushenko, "Genius Is Beyond Genre," 297.

73. *Pis'ma k drugu*, 187.

74. Shostakovich had heard *Oedipus Rex* in Leningrad in concert performance in the early 1930s, perhaps even as early as 1928.

75. Most sources misdate the Davidenko orchestrations as 1962. Lebedinsky claimed that the composer undertook them at his request; see Khentova, *V mire Shostakovicha*, 117.

76. D. Shostakovich, "Moyo novoye sochineniye—'Kirgizskaya uvertyura,'" *Literaturnaya gazeta* (12 October 1963): 1.

77. D. Shostakovich, "Bol'shoy prazdnik muzïki," *Pravda*, 25 February 1964, 4.

78. "Shostakovich at Press Conference," *Musical Events* 19, no. 5 (1964), 8.

79. G. Kozintsev, "Spasibo za schast'ye, kotoroye on mne prisnosil," *Sovetskaya muzïka* 9 (1990): 97.

80. *Pis'ma k drugu*, 203.

81. "Novïy zamïsel uvlekayet: rasskazïvayet kompozitor Dmitriy Shostakovich," *Izvestiya*, 14 December 1963, 6.

82. D. Shostakovich, "Svoi novïye proizvedeniya posvyashchayu 50-letiyu velikogo Oktyabrya," *Pravda*, 19 February 1964, 6.

83. M. Chulaki, *Ya bïl direktorom Bol'shogo teatra ... (Moscow, 1994)*, 118.

84. D. Shostakovich, "Rabota dayushchaya vdokhnoveniye," *Izvestiya*, 23 January 1966, 5.

85. S. Khentova, "Razgovor s Shostakovichem," *Ogonyok* 39 (1966): 7.

86. D. Shepilov, "Ya skazal, shto nam nado gotovit' takoy dokument," in V. Rubtsova, *Tak eto bïlo: Tikhon Khrennikov o vremeni i o sebe* (Moscow, 1994), 141–43. It should be noted that Shepilov's sense of chronology is extremely hazy. Whereas all the essentials of his story point clearly to the year 1966, he places the incident in the late Stalin period. That Shepilov and the composer continued to maintain a social relationship by this date is corroborated by the inclusion of two of Shostakovich's letters to him dating from 1966 and 1970.

87. A. Abramov, "Razgovor s Shostakovichem," *Novoye russkoye slovo*, 20 June 1982, 4. The conversation took place in 1967.

88. *Pis'ma k drugu*, 196.

89. A. Kholodkov, "Sorokovoy sezon betkhoventsev," *Sovetskaya muzïka* 8 (1962): 151.

90. "Dmitriy Shostakovich o novïkh muzïkal'nïkh proizvedeniyakh," 6.

91. From a radio interview given on 2 September 1963; *Govorit Dmitriy Shostakovich*, Melodiya Mono 33 M 40-41705.

92. Tsïganov in Khentova, *V mire Shostakovicha*, 209–10. Ironically, in a letter to Glikman dated 18 November 1961, a year before intimations of a new quartet became public, Shostakovich indicated that, having completed a Ninth Quartet with which he was dissatisfied, he had burned it, the first time since 1926 that he had destroyed one

of his manuscripts (*Pis'ma k drugu*, 168). The possibility that this letter has been mis-dated and really dates from 1962, a year later, must be considered seriously. It seems distinctly improbable that Shostakovich could have written, and destroyed, two Ninth Quartets before completing a satisfactory one.

93. *Pis'ma k drugu*, 196.

94. "The Execution of Stepan Razin" is one of the chapters of Yevtushenko's *Bratsk GES*, first published in the April 1965 issue of *Yunost'*.

95. *Pis'ma k drugu*, 196.

96. Ibid., 197.

97. Yevtushenko, "Genius Is Beyond Genre," 295.

98. Razhnikov, *Kondrashin*, 192.

99. S. Slonimsky in Wilson, *Shostakovich Remembered*, 381. The composer's almost identical response to the same question posed by someone else was also recorded. See N. Martïnov, "Pis'ma Shostakovicha. Stranitsï iz zapisnoy knizhki," in *D. D. Shostakovich: sbornik statey k 90-letiyu so dnya rozhdeniya*, comp. L. Kovnatskaya (St. Petersburg, 1996), 287. Shostakovich had delivered his verdict on Khrushchev to Margarita Ozhigova already in February 1964: "For the rehabilitation [of the victims of Stalin's terror], I forgive that dull, marginally intelligent man everything." See M. Ozhigova, "Mitya, Dmitriy Dmitriyevich," in *Muzïkal'naya pedagogika v ideyakh i litsakh*, ed. A. Selitskiy (Rostov-on-Don, 1992), 93.

100. See, for instance, S. Slonimsky, "Pobeda Sten'ki Razina," *Sovetskaya muzïka* 4 (1965): 20–24.

101. *Pis'ma k drugu*, 208.

102. Ibid., 205.

103. Ye. Nesterenko, "Moshch' dukha i moshch' geniya," *Sovetskaya muzïka* 9 (1976): 38.

Chapter 14

1. *Pis'ma k drugu: Dmitriy Shostakovich-Isaaku Glikmanu*, comp. I. Glikman (Moscow, 1993), 209.

2. Ibid., 210.

3. Shostakovich letter to D. Shepilov dated 21 September 1966; in V. Rubtsova, *Tak eto bïlo: Tikhon Khrennikov o vremeni i o sebe* (Moscow, 1994), 142.

4. *Pis'ma k drugu*, 212.

5. Ibid., 213.

6. S. Khentova, *Rostropovich* (St. Petersburg, 1993), 116.

7. C. Samuel, *Entretiens avec Mstislav Rostropovich et Galina Vichnevskaïa sur la Russie, la musique, la liberté* (Paris, 1983), 48; Eng. trans. *Mstislav Rostropovich and Galina Vishnevskaya: Russia, Music, and Liberty/Conversations with Claude Samuel*, trans. E. T. Glasow (Portland, 1995), 58–59.

8. The film, *Dmitriy Shostakovich: Sketches Toward a Portrait*, directed by Albert Gendelshteyn, was released in 1967. The volume, *Dmitriy Shostakovich*, compiled by G. Ordzhonikidze, was published in Moscow in 1967.

9. *Pis'ma k drugu*, 213.

10. G. Vishnevskaya, *Galina: A Russian Story* (San Diego, 1984), 362–63.

11. See, for instance, *Pis'ma k drugu*, 216; N. Martïnov, "Pis'ma Shostakovicha.

Stranitsï iz zapisnoy knizhki," in *D. D. Shostakovich: sbornik statey k 90-letiyu so dnya rozhdeniya*, comp. L. Kovnatskaya (St. Petersburg, 1996), 295; *Pis'ma Dmitriya Shostakovicha Borisu Tishchenko: s kommentariyami i vospominaniyami adresata* (St. Petersburg, 1997), 24.

12. Shaginyan, "Fifty Letters from Dmitri Shostakovich," *Soviet Literature* 1 (1984): 76.

13. *Pravda*, 25 September 1966, 1.

14. E. Wilson, *Shostakovich: A Life Remembered* (London, 1994), 368–69.

15. O. Manulkina, "Mstislav Rostropovich: slishkom mnogo opasnosti dlya moralistov," *Kommersant-DAILY*, 14 September 1996, 12.

16. E. Serov, "Stranitsï pamyati," in *Pamyati N. S. Rabinovich: ocherki, vospominaniya, dokumentï*, comp. D. Bukhin (Washington, D.C., 1996), 147–48.

17. *Pis'ma k drugu*, 222.

18. Ibid., 221.

19. Shaginyan, "Fifty Letters," 87.

20. This performance, by Rostropovich and the Leningrad Philharmonic Orchestra conducted by Gennadiy Rozhdestvensky, took place at the Royal Festival Hall on 21 September 1960. It was not the British premiere, which the same forces presented at the Edinburgh Festival on 9 September.

21. *Pis'ma k drugu*, 220.

22. Entry dated 23 April 1971, in *The Travel Diaries of Peter Pears, 1936–1978*, ed. P. Reed (Aldeburgh, 1995), 165.

23. D. Shostakovich, "Priglasheniye k molodoy muzïke," *Yunost'* 5 (1968): 87.

24. *Pis'ma k drugu*, 224.

25. Ibid., 225–26. As Glikman points out, "fuk"—signifying nonsense, poppycock—is an expression of the character Sobakevich from Gogol's *Dead Souls* that found its way into Shostakovich's opera, *The Nose*.

26. Wilson, *Shostakovich Remembered*, 395–96.

27. E. Petrushanskaya, "Da prebudet s nami!," *Muzïkal'naya zhizn'* 12 (1995): 38.

28. M. Kapustin, "Triumfal'naya prelyudiya: novïye proizvedeniya D. D. Shostakovicha," *Pravda*, 12 September 1967, 6

29. A manuscript edition issued in December 1967 by Muzfond used the designation *Seven Romances*; the first engraved edition, issued by Sovetskiy Kompozitor in 1969, was titled *Seven Verses*.

30. Wilson, *Shostakovich Remembered*, 397–98.

31. *Pis'ma k drugu*, 230.

32. Ibid., 227.

33. Ibid., 229.

34. Shaginyan, "Fifty Letters," 88.

35. V. Yuzefovich, *David Oystrakh: besedï s Igoryem Oystrakhom* (Moscow, 1978), 266.

36. GTsMMK f. 385, yed. khr. 485; partially reproduced in N. Tartakovskaya, "Pisal ego s mïslyami o Vas ...," *Muzïkal'naya akademiya* 4 (1997): 182.

37. D. Oystrakh, "Velikiy khudozhnik nashego vremeni," in *D. Shostakovich: stat'i i materialï*, comp. G. Shneerson (Moscow, 1976), 27. Oistrakh's sixtieth birthday was on 30 September 1968.

38. Kapustin, "Triumfal'naya prelyudiya," 6.

39. Oystrakh, "Velikiy khudozhnik," 28.

40. Shostakovich letter to D. Oistrakh dated 2 July 1967; GTsMMK f. 385, yed. khr. 487.

41. V. Razhnikov, *Kirill Kondrashin rasskazïvayet o muzïke i zhizni* (Moscow, 1987), 195–96. Yuriy Temirkanov eventually took first prize in the competition.

42. M. Shostakovich, "Moy otets," *Smena* 18 (1976): 20.

43. Shostakovich letter to D. Oistrakh dated 2 July 1967; GTsMMK f. 385, yed. khr. 487.

44. Shostakovich letter to D. Oistrakh dated 15 July 1967; GTsMMK f. 385, yed. khr. 488.

45. Kapustin, "Triumfal'naya prelyudiya," 6.

46. *Pis'ma k drugu*, 232.

47. Ibid., 234.

48. A number of sources mistakenly list 26 October as the date of the "official" premiere.

49. Shostakovich letter to D. Oistrakh dated 6 December 1967; GTsMMK f. 385, yed. khr. 490.

50. Some sources erroneously list 28 October as the date of the premiere.

51. Oystrakh, "Velikiy khudozhnik," 30.

52. *Pis'ma k drugu*, 235.

53. Ibid., 237.

54. Arnshtam in S. Khentova, *V mire Shostakovicha* (Moscow, 1996), 236.

55. *Pis'ma k drugu*, 239.

56. Ibid., 240.

57. Tsïganov in Khentova, *V mire Shostakovicha*, 211.

58. "Muzïkantï o novom kvartete Shostakovicha," *Sovetskaya kul'tura* (25 June 1968), 2.

59. *Pis'ma k drugu*, 241.

60. V. Bobrovskiy, "Pobeda chelovecheskogo dukha," *Sovetskaya muzïka* 9 (1968): 31–33. This issue was sent to press on 26 August 1968.

61. N. Karetnikov, "Two Novellas," *Tempo* 173 (1990), 45. Karetnikov mistakenly lists the year of this production as 1961.

62. Tsïganov in Khentova, *V mire Shostakovicha*, 211.

63. Shostakovich, "Priglasheniye k molodoy muzïke," 87.

64. Ibid.

65. D. Shostakovich, "Istochnik tvorchestva—zhizn' naroda," *Pravda*, 14 May 1968, 3.

66. Actually, he had started composing a violin sonata more than twenty years earlier, in June 1945, but abandoned the early effort after the first movement.

67. D. Shostakovich, "Muzïka, rozhdyonnaya segodnya," *Literaturnaya gazeta* (4 December 1968), 8.

68. Oystrakh, "Velikiy khudozhnik," 29.

69. Shostakovich letter to D. Oistrakh dated 22 November 1968; GTsMMK f. 385, yed. khr. 491.

70. *Pis'ma k drugu*, 243.

71. Ibid., 247.

72. Ibid., 249.

73. Wilson, *Shostakovich Remembered*, 413.

74. *Pis'ma k drugu*, 250.

75. Ibid., 252.

76. D. Shostakovich, "Predisloviye k prem'ere: novaya simfoniya D. Shostakovicha," *Pravda*, 25 April 1969, 6.

77. Ibid.; translation from N. Ostrovsky, *How the Steel Was Tempered: A Novel in Two Parts*, trans. R. Prokofieva (Moscow, 1967), pt. 2, 85.

78. The previous year, Britten had dedicated to Shostakovich his church parable, *The Prodigal Son*, op. 81.

79. K. Kondrashin, "Moi vstrechi s D. D. Shostakovichem," in *D. Shostakovich: stat'i i materiali*, 95.

80. *Pis'ma k drugu*, 252.

81. R. Barshay, "Pamyati druga," *Kontinent* 54 (1987): 329.

82. *Pis'ma k drugu*, 257.

83. From tape of Shostakovich's introductory remarks; *Govorit Dmitriy Shostakovich*, Melodiya 33 M 40-41707.

84. Many of the versions disagree about the precise moment when this took place. Shostakovich's letter to Glikman, written just three days after the event, would seem to offer the most reliable account. See *Pis'ma k drugu*, 258.

85. Shostakovich also believed his death had been immediate; see *Pis'ma k drugu*, 258.

86. Wilson, *Shostakovich Remembered*, 417. In fact, however, Yevgeniy Vladimirov performed in both the Leningrad performances. Mark Reshetin sang the bass part for the first time at the Moscow premiere. See "Chetïrnadtsataya simfoniya Shostakovicha," *Leningradskaya Pravda*, 30 September 1969, 4; also *Pis'ma k drugu*, 262.

87. *Pis'ma k drugu*, 262.

88. Ibid., 264.

89. Ibid., 267.

90. L. Lebedinskiy, "Iz bessistemnïkh zapisey," *Muzïkal'naya zhizn'* 21–22 (1993): 27.

91. K. Meyer, *Dimitri Chostakovitch* (Paris: 1994), 507.

92. Wilson, *Shostakovich Remembered*, 352.

93. Ibid., 419.

94. *Pis'ma k drugu*, 249.

95. M. Sokol'skiy, *Musorgskiy/Shostakovich: stat'i retsenzii* (Moscow, 1983), 132. The letter to Sokolsky published here is dated 5 December 1965, the year almost certainly a misprint for 1969.

Chapter 15

1. Shaginyan, "Fifty Letters from Dmitri Shostakovich," *Soviet Literature* 1(1984): 94.

2. *Pis'ma k drugu: Dmitriy Shostakovich–Isaaku Glikmanu*, comp I. Glikman (Moscow, 1993), 270.

3. Ibid., 271.

4. D. Shostakovich, "Ya snova mogu igrat' na royale," *Sovetskaya kul'tura* (2 June 1970), 4.

5. D. Shostakovich, "Muzïka rozhdyonnaya segodnya," *Literaturnaya gazeta* (4 December 1968), 8.

6. D. Shostakovich, "Predisloviye k prem'ere: novaya simfoniya D. Shostakovicha," *Pravda*, 25 April 1969, 6.

7. G. Kozintsev, *Sobraniye sochineniy v pyati tomakh*, 2 (Leningrad, 1983), 438. Rostropovich has also claimed responsibility for organizing the contact with Ilizarov; see E. Wilson, *Shostakovich: A Life Remembered* (London 1994), 423.

8. Ye. Dolmatovskiy, "Perepolnennïy muzïkoy," in *D. Shostakovich: stat'i i materialï*, comp. G Shneerson (Moscow, 1976), 76. The notes in volume 34 of Shostakovich's *Sobraniye sochineniy* list the date and place of completion as 13 February 1970 in Repino, although the composer had actually left Repino and returned to Moscow more than a week earlier.

9. "D. Shostakovich na teleekrane," *Sovetskaya kul'tura* (7 March 1971), 3.

10. M. Dolgopolov, "Budni i prazdniki muzïki," *Izvestiya*, 8 December 1970, 6.

11. Shaginyan, "Fifty Letters," 91.

12. Dolgopolov, "Budni i prazdniki muzïki," 6.

13. *Gor'kovskiy rabochiy*, 18 June 1970; quoted in *D. Shostakovich o vremeni i o sebe: 1926–1975*, comp. M Yakovlev (Moscow, 1980), 319.

14. Kozintsev, *Sobraniye sochineniy*, 2: 438–39.

15. Shostakovich letter to Borisovsky, dated 4 September 1970; in F. Druzhinin, "O Dmitrii Dmitriyeviche Shostakoviche," *Shostakovichu posvyashchayetsya: sbornik statey k 90-letiyu kompozitora (1906–1975)*, comp. E. Dolinskaya (Moscow, 1997), 182. Borisovsky's seventieth birthday was 19 January 1970.

16. *The Travel Diaries of Peter Pears, 1936–1978*, ed. P. Reed (Aldeburgh, 1995), 165.

17. Wilson, *Shostakovich Remembered*, 425–26. In the Russian-language version, Litvinova dates this conversation to 1970 or 1971, though the references to the Fourteenth Symphony, and not to the Fifteenth, would seem to point to the earlier year. See F. Litvinova, "Vspominaya Shostakovicha," *Znamya* 12 (1996): 176.

18. *Pis'ma k drugu*, 275.

19. See, for instance, *Times* (London), 13 November 1970, 1; *New York Times*, 13 November 1970, 1.

20. A. Bogdanova, *Muzïka i vlast' (poststalinskiy period)* (Moscow, 1995), 361–62. To the same official, Shostakovich also implicated Vishnevskaya for having attempted to drag him, at one time, into the scandal over "hitches" with the performance of the *Satires* on texts of Chyorny. Precisely which "hitches" are not identified. In her memoirs, Vishnevskaya accentuates the seditious aspect of the *Satires*, claiming that Shostakovich worried initially that the authorities would not permit the work to be performed and that, following the premiere, a planned television transmission of the cycle did not take place because Vishnevskaya and Rostropovich refused to sanction cuts in the cycle. See G. Vishnevskaya, *Galina: A Russian Story* (San Diego, 1984), 268–70.

21. Vishnevskaya, *Galina*, 399.

22. See *Izvestiya TsK KPSS* 12 (1990): 147.

23. See, for instance, A. Solzhenitsyn, "The Smatterers," in *From under the Rubble* (Boston, 1975), 251.

24. A. Solzhenitsyn, *The Oak and the Calf*, trans. H. Willets (New York, 1980), 221. Ironically, Yevtushenko claims to have been instrumental in convincing the miserable, vacillating composer not to affix his signature to an official letter to the Czech intelligentsia *in support* of the invasion; see Ye. Yevtushenko, "Genius Is Beyond Genre: Dmitriy Shostakovich (1976–1988)," in *Fatal Half Measures: The Culture of Democracy in the Soviet Union* (Boston, 1991), 298.

25. Shostakovich's *March* shared first prize with Vano Muradeli's "Song of a Militiaman's Oath."

26. Shaginyan, "Fifty Letters," 96.

27. S. Khentova, *Shostakovich: zhizn' i tvorchestvo*, vol. 2 (Leningrad, 1986), 540.

28. *Pis'ma k drugu*, 276. Tsvetayeva hanged herself in Yelabuga, a small town in the Tatar Republic, on 31 August 1941.

29. Veniamin Basner's claim that the first three movements were already done by the time Shostakovich arrived in Repino (Wilson, *Shostakovich Remembered*, 436) is contradicted by Glikman, who indicates that only the first movement was in hand (*Pis'ma k drugu*, 277–78).

30. *Pis'ma k drugu*, 278.

31. Shaginyan, "Fifty Letters," 96–97.

32. Interview recorded at WFMT Radio in Chicago, 13 June 1973; *Govorit Dmitriy Shostakovich*, Melodiya 33 M 40-41705-12.

33. *Sovetskaya kul'tura* (25 September 1971): 2.

34. *Pis'ma k drugu*, 280.

35. Ibid., 281–82.

36. Ibid., 282.

37. "Novoye muzïkal'noye proizvedeniye Shostakovicha," *Vechernyaya Moskva*, 8 January 1972, 3.

38. M. Sokol'skiy, "Pyatnadtsataya," *Izvestiya*, 13 January 1972, 5.

39. *Pis'ma k drugu*, 285.

40. Ibid., 288.

41. Ye. Kunitsïn, "Pamyatnïye vstrechi s Dmitriyem Shostakovichem," *Sovetskaya kul'tura* (26 September 1978): 8. As it turned out, the opening game of the chess tournament was postponed from 3 until 11 July 1972, long after Shostakovich had disembarked.

42. *Pis'ma k drugu*, 290.

43. Ibid., 291.

44. D. Shostakovich, "Mïsli o Chaykovskom," *Literatura i iskusstvo* (7 November 1943): 4.

45. D. Shostakovich, "Samïy blizkiy," *Literaturnaya gazeta* (28 January 1960): 3.

46. N. Fortunatov, "Tri neizvestnïkh pis'ma Shostakovicha," *Muzïkal'naya zhizn'*, 14 (1988): 13.

47. Shostakovich letter to Tishchenko, dated 22 September 1972; *Pis'ma D. D. Shostakovicha Borisu Tishchenko: s kommentariyami i vospominaniyami adresata* (St. Petersburg, 1997), 41.

48. *Pis'ma k drugu*, 293.

49. A. Vavilina-Mravinskaya, "Obruchyonnïye muzïkoy," *Muzïkal'naya akademiya* 4 (1997): 100. After his second heart attack, his doctors had forbidden him alcohol and tobacco.

50. *Pis'ma k drugu*, 292.

51. Irina Shostakovich in conversation with the author, 22 January 1991, in Moscow.

52. I. Rudenko, "Razgovor s kompozitorom," *Komsomol'skaya Pravda*, 26 June 1973, 4.

53. D. Baker, "'It *Vas* Premiere': The Night Shostakovich Came to the Met," *Opera News* 59, no. 6 (10 December 1994): 17.

54. Wilson, *Shostakovich Remembered*, 440.

55. *Marina Tsvetayeva: izbrannïye proizvedeniya*, ed. A. Efron and A. Saakiants (Moscow-Leningrad, 1965).

56. Shostakovich letters to Tishchenko, dated 26 January and 6 February 1971; *Pis'ma D. D. Shostakovicha B. Tishchenko*, 39–40.

57. Akhmatova and Shostakovich held each other's work in high mutual regard. Among other attestations to this, in 1958 the poet dedicated her poem "Music" to the composer and inscribed a presentation volume of her verses "To Dmitriy Dmitriyevich Shostakovich, in whose epoch I live on earth." See B. Kats and R. Timenchik, *Akhmatova i muzïka: issledovatel'skiye ocherki* (Leningrad, 1989), 71–72.

58. Khentova, *Shostakovich*, 2: 559.

59. Khentova disqualifies this performance as the premiere because Shostakovich was absent, a condition she does not, however, impose in other instances. See Khentova, *Shostakovich*, 2: 560. Following her lead, a number of sources mistakenly give the date of the first performance in Moscow, 27 December 1973, as the premiere of the suite.

60. "Pozorit zvaniye grazhdanina," *Pravda*, 3 September 1973, 2. The other signatories were D. Kabalevsky, K. Karayev, P. Savintsev, G. Sviridov, S. Tulikov, A. Khachaturyan, A. Kholminov, T. Khrennikov, R. Shchedrin, A. Eshpai, and B. Yarustovsky.

61. L. Chukovskaya, "Gnev naroda," in *Protsess isklyucheniya* (Moscow, 1990), 343. For her defense of Sakharov and other dissidents, Chukovskaya was expelled from the Moscow Writers' Union in 1974. The "Pushkinian question" invoked by Chukovskaya—framed for generations of the Russian intelligentsia in the psychological oppositions of the "little tragedy," *Mozart and Salieri*—was a dilemma that had engaged Shostakovich himself more than once, but he invariably reached the opposite conclusion. In January 1974, he reiterated it to his official biographer: "I have had the fortune to be acquainted with many eminent people. They all distinguished good and evil. Genius and villainy are incompatible, I share that conviction of Pushkin.... Music does not forgive evil." See S. Khentova, *V mire Shostakovicha* (Moscow, 1996), 39.

62. Wilson, *Shostakovich Remembered*, 435. More than twenty years later, Solomon Volkov expressed his continuing puzzlement over the composer's behavior in the affair, as well as the conviction that Shostakovich's refusal to sign would not have brought about untoward repercussions; see M. Pritsker, "Dmitriy Shostakovich: tragediya i zagadka," *Novoye russkoye slovo*, 25 September 1996, 17.

63. I. Shostakovich, "Mnye bïlo strashno vïkhodit' zamuzh za geniya," *Komsomol'-skaya Pravda*, 15 November 1995, 8.

64. S. Volkov, *Testimony: The Memoirs of Dmitri Shostakovich* (New York, 1979), 243.

65. *Mstislav Rostropovich and Galina Vishnevskaya; Russia, Music, and Liberty / Conversations with Claude Samuel*, trans. E. Thomas Glasow (Portland, 1995), 98.

66. A. Gershkovich, "Robert Osborn poyot 'Besov'," *Novoye russkoye slovo*, 23 November 1983, 6.

67. Shostakovich letter to Tishchenko dated 21 February 1974; *Pis'ma D. D. Shostakovicha B. Tishchenko*, 43.

68. D. Mikhaylov, "Dmitriy Shostakovich: muzïka rozhdayetsya v tishine," *Izvestiya*, 7 August 1973, 5.

69. See Vishnevskaya, *Galina*, 447.

70. J. Rockwell, "Rostropovich—I Feel Like a Native," *New York Times*, 18 January 1981, sec. 2, 17.

71. K. Meyer, *Dimitri Chostakovitch* (Paris, 1994), 513.

72. P. Radchik, "K neokonchennomu portretu ...," *Muzïkal'naya zhizn'* 18 (1986): 17.

73. Arnshtam in Khentova, *V mire Shostakovicha*, 237.

74. *Pis'ma k drugu*, 302.

75. Shostakovich's source for his op. 145 settings was *Mikelandzhelo: zhizn', tvorchestvo*, comp. V. N. Grashchenkov (Moscow, 1964).

76. Western productions of *The Nose* required no authorization from, or transactions with, Soviet authorities because, in 1933, Shostakovich conveyed world rights in the work to Universal Edition in Vienna.

77. "Chudesnïy u nas slushatel': Dmitriy Shostakovich otvechayet na voprosï," *Muzïkal'naya zhizn'* 17 (1966): 7.

78. B. Pokrovskiy, "Osvobozhdeniye ot predvzyatosti," *Sovetskaya muzïka* 9 (1976): 37. By 1992, when he turned eighty, Pokrovsky's memory of these distant events had changed; he claimed then to have staged a production with GITIS students and even taken it on tour. See Wilson, *Shostakovich Remembered*, 444.

79. *Sovetskaya muzïka* 4 (1972): 136.

80. The date of completion given in vol. 33 of the Sobraniye sochineniy is 5 November 1974. According to one account, however, Shostakovich told Khachaturyan in response to a query in early January 1975 that he had no current intention to orchestrate the cycle. See Yev. Shenderovich, "V moyey pamyati svetlïy oblik," *Sovetskaya muzïka* 10 (1981): 32.

81. *Leningradskaya Pravda*, 24 December 1974; quoted in *D. Shostakovich o vremeni i sebe*, 347. The citation is misdated here as 1973.

82. Others perceived Solzhenitsyn, not Dante, as the "real" subject of the setting, "To an Exile."

83. Ye. Dolmatovskiy, "Rabota i druzhba," *Sovetskaya muzïka* 10 (1981): 25–26.

84. A. Voznesenskiy, "O," *Novïy mir* 11 (1982): 124.

85. *Pis'ma k drugu*, 306.

86. Ibid., 302.

87. Shenderovich, "V moyey pamyati svetlïy oblik," 33.

88. *Pis'ma k drugu*, 309.

89. A. Ivashkin, *Besedï s Al'fredom Shnitke* (Moscow, 1994), 82–83.

90. Wilson, *Shostakovich Remembered*, 383–84. Another of the disaffected was Nikolai Sidelnikov. See I. Sørbye, "Nikolai Sidelnikov: Vi levde i en fantasi av Kafka ...," *Ballade: Tidsskrift for Ny Musikk* 1 (1993): 12.

91. In contemporaneous interviews the date Druzhinin cited was 25 June 1975; see, for instance, N. Mar, "Shostakovich: posledneye sochineniye," *Literaturnaya gazeta* (27 August 1975), 8. In reminiscences penned considerably later, Druzhinin gave the date as 1 July; see Wilson, *Shostakovich Remembered*, 469; Druzhinin, "O Dmitrii Dmitriyeviche Shostakoviche," *Shostakovichu posvyashchayetsya: sbornik statey*, 188.

92. Mar, "Posledneye sochineniye," 8.

93. Ibid.

94. *New York Times*, 11 August 1975, 1.

95. In conversation with the author, 22 January 1991, in Moscow.

96. *Pravda*, 12 August 1975, 3. The obituary was also published in a number of other newspapers.

97. The texts of these and other eulogies were subsequently published in *D. Shostakovich: stat'i i materiali*, 6–16.

98. The composer had given the manuscript to Galina Ustvolskaya. After the successful revival of *The Nose* in the fall of 1974, he asked for its return. The surviving operatic fragment was first performed, in concert, in 1979.

99. Wilson, *Shostakovich Remembered*, 470.

100. A. Medvedev, "Muzïka bol'shogo serdtsa," *Izvestiya*, 16 October 1975, 5.

List of Works

OPERAS AND BALLETS

op. 15   *The Nose*, opera in three acts (1927–1928)
Libretto by the composer, Yevgeniy Zamyatin, Georgiy Ionin, and
    Alexander Preys, after Nikolai Gogol
First performance: 18 January 1930, Leningrad, Malïy Opera Theater

22   *The Golden Age*, ballet in three acts (1929–1930)
Libretto by Alexander Ivanovsky
First performance: 27 October 1930, Leningrad, Academic Theater of Opera
    and Ballet

27   *The Bolt*, ballet in three acts (1930–1931)
Libretto by Viktor Smirnov
First performance: 8 April 1931, Leningrad, Academic Theater of Opera and
    Ballet

—   *The Great Lightning*, unfinished comic opera (?1931–1932)
Libretto by Nikolai Aseyev
First performance: 11 February 1981, Large Hall of the Leningrad
    Philharmonic

29   *Lady Macbeth of the Mtsensk District*, opera in four acts (1930–1932)
Libretto by the composer and Alexander Preys, after Nikolai Leskov
First performance: 22 January 1934, Leningrad, Malïy Opera Theater
Revised as op. 114

39   *The Limpid Stream*, ballet in three acts (1934–1935)
Libretto by Fyodor Lopukhov and Adrian Piotrovsky
First performance: 4 June 1935, Leningrad, Malïy Opera Theater

—   *The Gamblers*, unfinished opera (1941–1942)
Libretto by the composer, after Nikolai Gogol
First performance: 18 September 1978, Large Hall of the Leningrad
    Philharmonic

105   *Moscow, Cheryomushki*, operetta in three acts (1957–1958)
Libretto by Vladimir Mass and Mikhaíl Chervinsky
First performance: 24 January 1959, Moscow Operetta Theater

114   *Katerina Izmailova* (1954–1963)
First performance: 8 January 1963, Moscow, Stanislavsky and Nemirovich-
    Danchenko Theater
Revision of op. 29

OTHER DRAMATIC WORKS

Incidental Music

19   *The Bedbug*, incidental music to play by Vladimir Mayakovsky (1929)
      First performance: Moscow, Meyerhold Theater, 13 February 1929

24   *The Shot*, incidental music to play by Alexander Bezïmensky (1929)
      First performance: Leningrad, Working Youth Theater, 14 December 1929

25   *Virgin Soil*, incidental music to play by Arkadiy Gorbenko and Nikolai Lvov
      (1930; lost)
      First performance: Leningrad, Working Youth Theater, 9 May 1930

28   *Rule, Britannia!*, incidental music to play by Adrian Piotrovsky (1931)
      First performance: Leningrad, Working Youth Theater, 9 May 1931

31   *Declared Dead*, music for a variety-circus revue by Vsevolod Voyevodin and
      Yevgeniy Rïss (1931)
      First performance: Leningrad Music Hall, 2 October 1931

32   *Hamlet*, incidental music to play by William Shakespeare (1931–1932)
      First performance: Moscow, Vakhtangov Theater, 19 May 1932

37   *The Human Comedy*, incidental music to play by Pavel Sukhotin, after Balzac
      (1933–1934)
      First performance: Moscow, Vakhtangov Theater, 1 April 1934

44   *Salute, Spain!*, incidental music to play by Alexander Afinogenov (1936)
      First performance: Leningrad, Pushkin Theater of Drama, 23 November
      1936

58a   *King Lear*, incidental music to play by William Shakespeare (1941)
      First performance: Leningrad, Gorky Bolshoy Dramatic Theater, 24 March
      1941

63   *Native Leningrad Suite* from *Native Country*; for spectacle of NKVD Song
      and Dance Ensemble (1942)
      First performance: Moscow, Dzerzhinsky Central Club, 7 November 1942

66   *Russian River*, spectacle for NKVD Song and Dance Ensemble (1944)
      First performance: Moscow, Dzerzhinsky Central Club, 17 April 1944

72   *Victorious Spring*, two songs on texts by Mikhaíl Svetlov, for spectacle of
      NKVD Song and Dance Ensemble (1946)
      First performance: Moscow, Dzerzhinsky Central Club, 8 May 1946

—   *Hamlet*, incidental music to play by William Shakespeare (1954)
      First performance: Leningrad, Pushkin Theater of Drama, 31 March 1954,
      Includes music from op. 58a

Film Scores

18   *New Babylon*, for live performance with silent film (1928–1929)
      Sovkino (Leningrad); directed by Grigoriy Kozintsev and Leonid Trauberg

26   *Alone* (1930–1931)
      Soyuzkino (Leningrad); directed by Grigoriy Kozintsev and Leonid
         Trauberg

30   *Golden Mountains* (1931)
      Soyuzkino (Leningrad); directed by Sergey Yutkevich

33   *Counterplan* (1932)
      Soyuzkino (Leningrad); directed by Fridrikh Ermler and Sergey Yutkevich

36   *The Tale of the Priest and His Worker, Blockhead*, unfinished animated film
         (1933–1934)
      Soyuzmultfilm (Moscow); directed by Mikhaíl Tsekhanovsky
      Revised as comic opera by Sofya Khentova (1980)

38   *Love and Hatred* (1934)
      Mezhrabpomfilm (Soyuzdetfilm); directed by Albert Gendelshteyn

41   *Maxim's Youth*, no. 1 in "Maxim trilogy" (1934)
      Lenfilm; directed by Grigoriy Kozintsev and Leonid Trauberg

41a   *Girlfriends* (1934–1935)
      Lenfilm; directed by Leo Arnshtam

45   *Maxim's Return*, no. 2 in "Maxim trilogy" (1936–1937)
      Lenfilm; directed by Grigoriy Kozintsev and Leonid Trauberg

48   *Volochayev Days* (1936–1937)
      Lenfilm; directed by Georgiy and Sergey Vasilyev

50   *The Vyborg District*, no. 3 in "Maxim trilogy" (1938)
      Lenfilm; directed by Grigoriy Kozintsev and Leonid Trauberg

51   *Friends* (1938)
      Lenfilm; directed by Leo Arnshtam

52   *The Great Citizen*, 1st series (1937)
      Lenfilm; directed by Fridrikh Ermler

53   *The Man with a Gun* (1938)
      Lenfilm; directed by Sergey Yutkevich

55   *The Great Citizen*, 2nd series (1938–1939)
      Lenfilm; directed by Fridrikh Ermler

56   *The Silly Little Mouse*, animated film (1939)
      Lenfilm; directed by Mikhaíl Tsekhanovsky

59   *The Adventures of Korzinkina* (1940–1941)
         Lenfilm; directed by Klimentiy Mints

64   *Zoya* (1944)
         Soyuzdetfilm (Moscow); directed by Leo Arnshtam

71   *Simple People* (1945, released 1956)
         Lenfilm; directed by Grigoriy Kozintsev and Leonid Trauberg

75   *The Young Guard* (1947–1948)
         Gorky film studio; directed by Sergey Gerasimov

76   *Pirogov* (1947)
         Lenfilm; directed by Grigoriy Kozintsev

78   *Michurin* (1948)
         Mosfilm; directed by Alexander Dovzhenko

80   *Encounter at the Elbe* (1948)
         Mosfilm; directed by Grigoriy Alexandrov

82   *The Fall of Berlin* (1949)
         Mosfilm; directed by Mikhaíl Chiaureli

85   *Belinsky* (1950, released 1953)
         Lenfilm; directed by Grigoriy Kozintsev

89   *The Unforgettable Year 1919* (1951)
         Mosfilm; directed by Mikhaíl Chiaureli

95   *Song of the Great Rivers (Unity)*, documentary (1954)
         Defa (GDR); directed by Yoris Ivens

97   *The Gadfly* (1955)
         Lenfilm; directed by Alexander Faintsimmer

99   *The First Echelon* (1955–1956)
         Mosfilm; directed by Mikhaíl Kalatozov

106   *Khovanshchina*, reorchestration of Modest Musorgsky's opera (1958–1959)
         Mosfilm; directed by Vera Stroyeva

111   *Five Days—Five Nights* (1960)
         Mosfilm/Defa (GDR); directed by Leo Arnshtam

—   *Cheryomushki* (1962)
         Lenfilm; directed by Gerbert Rappaport
         Arrangement of the operetta, op. 105

116   *Hamlet* (1963–1964)
         Lenfilm; directed by Grigoriy Kozintsev

120   *A Year Is Like a Lifetime* (1965)
         Mosfilm; directed by Grigoriy Roshal

—   *Katerina Izmailova* (1966)
    Lenfilm; directed by Mikhaíl Shapiro
    Film version of opera, op. 114

132   *Sofya Perovskaya* (1967)
    Mosfilm; directed by Leo Arnshtam

137   *King Lear* (1970)
    Lenfilm; directed by Grigoriy Kozintsev

ORCHESTRAL

Symphonies

10   Symphony no. 1 in F Minor (1924–1925)
    First performance: 12 May 1926, Large Hall of the Leningrad Philharmonic
    / Leningrad Philharmonic Orchestra, conducted by Nikolai Malko

14   Symphony no. 2, *Dedication to October*, in B Major (1927)
    Text by Alexander Bezïmensky
    First performance: 5 November 1927, Large Hall of the Leningrad
    Philharmonic / Leningrad Philharmonic Orchestra and Academic Choir,
    conducted by Nikolai Malko

20   Symphony no. 3, *The First of May*, in E-flat Major (1929)
    Text by Semyon Kirsanov
    First performance: 21 January 1930, Leningrad, Moscow-Narva House of
    Culture / Leningrad Philharmonic Orchestra and State Academic Choir,
    conducted by Alexander Gauk

43   Symphony no. 4 in C Minor (1935–1936)
    First performance: 30 December 1961, Large Hall of the Moscow
    Conservatory / Moscow Philharmonic Orchestra, conducted by
    Kirill Kondrashin

47   Symphony no. 5 in D Minor (1937)
    First performance: 21 November 1937, Large Hall of the Leningrad
    Philharmonic / Leningrad Philharmonic Orchestra, conducted by
    Yevgeniy Mravinsky

54   Symphony no. 6 in B Minor (1939)
    First performance: 21 November 1939, Large Hall of the Leningrad
    Philharmonic / Leningrad Philharmonic Orchestra, conducted by
    Yevgeniy Mravinsky

60   Symphony no. 7 ("Dedicated to the city of Leningrad") in C Major (1941)
    First performance: 5 March 1942, Kuybïshev House of Culture / Bolshoy
    Theater Orchestra, conducted by Samuíl Samosud

65   Symphony no. 8 in C Minor (1943)
      First performance: 4 November 1943, Large Hall of the Moscow
          Conservatory / USSR State Symphony Orchestra, conducted by Yevgeniy
          Mravinsky

70   Symphony no. 9 in E-flat Major (1945)
      First performance: 3 November 1945, Large Hall of the Leningrad
          Philharmonic / Leningrad Philharmonic Orchestra, conducted by
          Yevgeniy Mravinsky

93   Symphony no. 10 in E Minor (1953)
      First performance: 17 December 1953, Large Hall of the Leningrad
          Philharmonic / Leningrad Philharmonic Orchestra, conducted by
          Yevgeniy Mravinsky

103   Symphony no. 11, *The Year 1905*, in G Minor (1956–1957)
      First performance: 30 October 1957, Large Hall of the Moscow
          Conservatory / USSR State Symphony Orchestra, conducted by
          Natan Rakhlin

112   Symphony no. 12, *The Year 1917*, in D Minor (1959–1961)
      First performance: 1 October 1961, Large Hall of the Leningrad
          Philharmonic / Leningrad Philharmonic Orchestra, conducted by
          Yevgeniy Mravinsky

113   Symphony no. 13, *Babiy Yar*, in B-flat Minor, for bass soloist, chorus of
          basses, and orchestra (1962)
      Texts by Yevgeniy Yevtushenko
      First performance: 18 December 1962, Large Hall of the Moscow
          Conservatory / Vitaliy Gromadsky, Republican State and Gnesin Institute
          Choirs (basses only), Moscow Philharmonic Orchestra, conducted by
          Kirill Kondrashin

135   Symphony no. 14, for soprano, bass, string orchestra, and percussion (1969)
      Texts by Federico Garcia Lorca, Guillaume Apollinaire, Wilhelm
          Küchelbecker, and Rainer Maria Rilke
      First performance: 29 September 1969, Hall of the Glinka Academy Choir,
          Leningrad / Galina Vishnevskaya, Yevgeniy Vladimirov, Moscow
          Chamber Orchestra, conducted by Rudolf Barshai

141   Symphony no. 15 in A Major (1971)
      First performance: 8 January 1972, Large Hall of the Moscow Conservatory
          / All-Union Radio and Television Symphony Orchestra, conducted by
          Maxim Shostakovich

Concerti, Miscellaneous Symphonic

1   Scherzo in F-sharp Minor (1919)

3   Theme and Variations in B-flat Major (1921–1922)

7   Scherzo in E-flat Major (1923–1924)

23   Two pieces for a staging of the opera, *Der arme Columbus*, by Erwin Dressel
        (1929)

35   Piano Concerto no. 1 in C Minor, for piano, trumpet, and string orchestra
        (1933)
        First performance: 15 October 1933, Large Hall of the Leningrad
            Philharmonic / Dmitriy Shostakovich, Alexander Shmidt (trumpet),
            Leningrad Philharmonic Orchestra, conducted by Fritz Stiedry

42   *Five Fragments*, for orchestra (1935)
        First performance: 26 April 1965, Large Hall of the Leningrad Philharmonic
        / Leningrad Philharmonic Orchestra, conducted by Igor Blazhkov

—   *Solemn March*, in D-flat Major, for military band (1942)

77   Violin Concerto no. 1 in A Minor (1947–1948)
        First performance: 29 October 1955, Large Hall of the Leningrad
            Philharmonic / David Oistrakh, Leningrad Philharmonic Orchestra,
            conducted by Yevgeniy Mravinsky

96   *Festive Overture*, in A Major (1954)
        First performance: 6 November 1954, Bolshoy Theater / Bolshoy Theater
            Orchestra, conducted by Alexander Melik-Pashayev

102   Piano Concerto no. 2 in F Major (1957)
        First performance: 10 May 1957, Large Hall of the Moscow Conservatory /
            Maxim Shostakovich, USSR State Symphony Orchestra, conducted by
            Nikolai Anosov

107   Cello Concerto no. 1 in E-flat Major (1959)
        First performance: 4 October 1959, Large Hall of the Leningrad
            Philharmonic / Mstislav Rostropovich, Leningrad Philharmonic
            Orchestra, conducted by Yevgeniy Mravinsky

—   *Novorossiisk Chimes (The Flame of Eternal Glory)* (1960)

115   *Overture on Russian and Kyrgyz Folk Themes* (1963)
        First performance: 2 November 1963, Frunze Theater of Opera and Ballet

126   Cello Concerto no. 2 in G Major (1966)
        First performance: 25 September 1966, Large Hall of the Moscow
            Conservatory / Mstislav Rostropovich, USSR State Symphony Orchestra,
            conducted by Yevgeniy Svetlanov

129   Violin Concerto no. 2 in C-sharp Minor (1967)
        First performance: 26 September 1967, Large Hall of the Moscow
            Conservatory / David Oistrakh, Moscow Philharmonic Orchestra,
            conducted by Kirill Kondrashin

130   *Funeral-Triumphal Prelude*, in memory of the heroes of the battle of
        Stalingrad (1967)

131   *October*, symphonic poem (1967)
        First performance: 16 September 1967, Large Hall of the Moscow
        Conservatory / USSR State Symphony Orchestra, conducted by Maxim
        Shostakovich

139   *March of the Soviet Militia*, for military band (1970)

Suites

15a   Suite from *The Nose*, for tenor, baritone, and orchestra (1928)
        First performance: 25 November 1928, Large Hall of the Moscow
        Conservatory / Sovfil Orchestra, conducted by Nikolai Malko

22a   Suite from *The Golden Age* (1930)
        First performance: 19 March 1930, Large Hall of the Leningrad
        Philharmonic / Leningrad Philharmonic Orchestra, conducted by
        Alexander Gauk

27a   Suite from *The Bolt* [Ballet Suite no. 5] (1931)
        First performance: 17 January 1933, Large Hall of the Leningrad
        Philharmonic / Leningrad Philharmonic Orchestra, conducted by
        Alexander Gauk

30a   Suite from *Golden Mountains* (1931)

32a   Suite from *Hamlet* (1932)

—   *Suite for Jazz Orchestra*, no. 1 (1934)

—   Suite from *The Tale of the Priest and His Worker, Blockhead* (1935)

—   *Suite for Jazz* Orchestra, no. 2 (1938)

50a   Suite from "*Maxim trilogy*," with chorus, arranged by Levon Atovmyan
        (1961)

64a   Suite from *Zoya*, with chorus, arranged by Levon Atovmyan (?1944)

76a   Suite from *Pirogov*, arranged by Levon Atovmyan (1951)

78a   Suite from *Michurin*, with chorus, arranged by Levon Atovmyan (1964)

80a   Suite from *Encounter at the Elbe*, with voices, arranged by Levon Atovmyan
        (1948)

—   Ballet Suite no. 1, arranged by Levon Atovmyan (1949)

82a   Suite from *The Fall of Berlin*, with chorus, arranged by Levon Atovmyan
        (1950)

75a   Suite from *The Young Guard*, arranged by Levon Atovmyan (1951)

—   Ballet Suite no. 2, arranged by Levon Atovmyan (1951)

— Ballet Suite no. 3, arranged by Levon Atovmyan (1951)

89a Suite from *The Unforgettable Year 1919*, arranged by Levon Atovmyan (1952)

— Ballet Suite no. 4, arranged by Levon Atovmyan (1953)

97a Suite from *The Gadfly*, arranged by Levon Atovmyan (1956)

99a Suite from *The First Echelon*, with chorus, arranged by Levon Atovmyan (1956)

85a Suite from *Belinsky*, with chorus, arranged by Levon Atovmyan (1960)

111a Suite from *Five Days—Five Nights*, arranged by Levon Atovmyan (1961)

114a Suite from *Katerina Izmailova*, for soprano and orchestra (?1962)

116a Suite from *Hamlet*, arranged by Levon Atovmyan (1964)

120a Suite from *A Year Is Like a Lifetime*, arranged by Levon Atovmyan (1969)

CHORAL

— "Oath to the People's Commissar," for bass, chorus, and piano (1941)
Text by Vissarion Sayanov

— "Song of a Guard's Division" ("The Fearless Guard's Regiments Are on the Move"), for bass, mixed chorus, and piano (1941)
Text by Lev Rakhmilevich

— "Glory to Our Soviet Homeland," for mixed chorus and piano (1943)
Text by Yevgeniy Dolmatovsky

— "A Toast to Our Motherland," for tenor, mixed chorus, and piano (1944)
Text by Iosif Utkin

— "The Black Sea," song for bass, men's chorus, and piano (1944)
Text by S. Alïmov and N. Verkhovsky

74 *Poem of the Motherland*, cantata for mezzo-soprano, tenor, two baritones, bass, chorus, and orchestra (1947)

— *Antiformalist Rayok*, for four basses, mixed chorus, piano, and narrator (?1948–?1968)
Text by the composer (with Lev Lebedinsky?)
First performance: 12 January 1989, Kennedy Center, Washington, D.C. / Jonathan Deutsch, Eric Halfvarson, Julian Rodescu, Andrew Wentzel, Members of the Choral Arts Society, Mstislav Rostropovich

— "Our Song," for bass, mixed chorus, and piano (1950)
Text by Konstantin Simonov

—   "March of the Defenders of Peace," for tenor, chorus, and piano (?1950)
Text by Konstantin Simonov

81   *Song of the Forests*, oratorio for tenor, bass, boys' chorus, chorus, and
orchestra (1949)
Text by Yevgeniy Dolmatovsky
First performance: 15 November 1949, Large Hall of the Leningrad
Philharmonic / Vladimir Ivanovsky, Ivan Titov, Leningrad Philharmonic
Orchestra, Leningrad Academic Capella, Boys' Chorus of Choral School,
conducted by Yevgeniy Mravinsky

88   *Ten Poems on Texts by Revolutionary Poets of the Late Nineteenth and Early
Twentieth Centuries*, for unaccompanied chorus (1951)
First performance: 10 October 1951, Large Hall of the Moscow
Conservatory / State Choir of Russian Song and Boys' Chorus of
Moscow Choral School, conducted by Alexander Sveshnikov

—   *Ten Russian Folksongs*, arrangements for soloists, chorus, and piano (1951)

90   *The Sun Shines Over Our Motherland*, cantata for boys' chorus, chorus, and
orchestra (1952)
Text by Yevgeniy Dolmatovsky
First performance: 6 November 1952, Large Hall of the Moscow
Conservatory / USSR State Symphony Orchestra and Chorus, Boys
Chorus of Moscow Choral School, conducted by Konstantin Ivanov

—   "Dawn of October," for chorus and piano (1957)
Text by Vladimir Kharitonov

104   Two Russian folksong arrangements for unaccompanied chorus (1957)

—   "We Cherish October Dawns in Our Heart," for chorus and piano (1957)
Text by Valentin Sidorov

—   "We Sing Glory to Our Motherland," for chorus and piano (1957)
Text by Valentin Sidorov

119   *The Execution of Stepan Razin*, vocal-symphonic poem for bass, chorus, and
orchestra (1964)
Text by Yevgeniy Yevtushenko
First performance: 28 December 1964, Large Hall of the Moscow
Conservatory / Vitaliy Gromadsky, Moscow Philharmonic Orchestra,
RSFSR Academic Choral Capella, conducted by Kirill Kondrashin

136   *Loyalty*, eight ballads for unaccompanied male chorus (1970)
Text by Yevgeniy Dolmatovsky
First performance: 5 December 1970, Estonia Concert Hall, Tallinn /
Estonian State Academic Male Choir, conducted by Gustav Ernesaks

Solo Vocal

4   *Two Fables of Krïlov*, for mezzo-soprano (chorus) and orchestra (1922)

21   *Six Romances on Texts by Japanese Poets*, for tenor and orchestra
      (1928–1932)

—   Impromptu-madrigal, musical joke for soprano and piano (?1930s)

46   *Four Romances on Texts of A. Pushkin*, for bass and piano (1936–1937)
      Nos. 1–3 orchestrated, n.d.

62   *Six Romances on Texts of W. Raleigh, R. Burns, and W. Shakespeare*, for bass
      and piano (1942)
      Texts translated into Russian by Boris Pasternak and Samuíl Marshak
      Orchestrated as op. 62a and op. 140

62a   *Six Romances on Texts of W. Raleigh, R. Burns, and W. Shakespeare*, for bass
      and orchestra (1943)
      Orchestration of op. 62

—   "Patriotic song" (1943)
      Text by Yevgeniy Dolmatovsky

—   "Song about the Red Army" (1942)
      Text by Mikhaíl Golodny
      Composed with Aram Khachaturyan

79   *From Jewish Folk Poetry*, for soprano, contralto, tenor, and piano (1948)
      First performance: 15 January 1955, Leningrad / Nina Dorliak, Zara
         Dolukhanova, Alexey Maslennikov, the composer
      Orchestrated as op. 79a

79a   *From Jewish Folk Poetry*, for soprano, contralto, tenor, and orchestra
      (1948–?1964)
      First performance: 1964
      Orchestration of op. 79

84   *Two Romances on Texts of M. Lermontov*, for voice and piano (1950)

86   *Four Songs on Texts of Ye. Dolmatovsky*, for voice and piano (1950–1951)

91   *Four Monologues on Texts of A. Pushkin*, for bass and piano (1952)

—   *Greek Songs*, for voice and piano (1952–1953)
      Texts translated into Russian by Sergey Bolotin and Tatyana Sikorskaya

98   *Five Romances on Texts of Ye. Dolmatovsky*, for bass and piano (1954)

—   "There Were Kisses," romance on a text by Ye. Dolmatovsky, for voice and
      piano (?1954)

100   *Spanish Songs*, for mezzo-soprano and piano (1956)
      Texts translated into Russian by Sergey Bolotin and Tatyana Sikorskaya

109   *Satires (Pictures of the Past)*, for soprano and piano (1960)
Texts by Sasha Chyorny
First performance: 22 February 1961, Moscow
Galina Vishnevskaya, Mstislav Rostropovich

121   *Five Romances on Texts from Krokodil Magazine*, for bass and piano (1965)
Texts from *Krokodil*, no. 24 (30 August 1965)

123   *Preface to the Complete Edition of My Works and a Brief Reflection apropos of This Preface*, for bass and piano (1966)

127   *Seven Verses of A. Blok*, for soprano, violin, cello, and piano (1967)
First performance: 23 October 1967, Moscow / Galina Vishnevskaya, David Oistrakh, Mstislav Rostropovich, Moisey Vainberg

128   "Spring, Spring," romance for bass and piano (1967)
Text by Alexander Pushkin

140   *Six Romances on Texts of W. Raleigh, R. Burns, and W. Shakespeare*, for bass and chamber orchestra (1971)
Orchestration of op. 62

143   *Six Verses of Marina Tsvetayeva*, suite for contralto and piano (1973)
First performance: 30 October 1973, Leningrad / Irina Bogachyova, Sofya Vakman
Orchestrated as op. 143a

143a   *Six Verses of Marina Tsvetayeva*, for contralto and chamber orchestra (1974)
Orchestration of op. 143

145   *Suite on Texts of Michelangelo Buonarroti*, for bass and piano (1974)
Texts translated into Russian by A. Efros
First performance: 23 December 1974, Leningrad / Yevgeniy Nesterenko, Yevgeniy Shenderovich
Orchestrated as op. 145a

145a   *Suite on Texts of Michelangelo Buonarroti*, for bass and orchestra (1975)
Orchestration of op. 145

146   *Four Verses of Captain Lebyadkin*, for bass and piano (1974)
Texts by Fyodor Dostoyevsky from *The Devils*
First performance: 10 May 1975, Moscow / Yevgeniy Nesterenko, Yevgeniy Shenderovich

Chamber and Instrumental

8   Piano Trio no. 1 in C Minor (1923)

9   *Three Pieces*, for cello and piano (1923–1924, lost)

11   *Two Pieces*, for string octet (1924–1925)

40   Sonata in D Minor for Cello and Piano (1934)
First performance: 25 December 1934, Leningrad / Viktor Kubatsky, the composer

49   String Quartet no. 1 in C Major (1938)
First performance: 10 October 1938, Leningrad / Glazunov Quartet

—   *Three Pieces*, for violin (1940, lost?)

57   Piano Quintet in G Minor (1940)
First performance: 23 November 1940, Moscow / Beethoven Quartet with the composer

67   Piano Trio no. 2 in E Minor (1944)
First performance: 14 November 1944, Leningrad / Dmitriy Tsïganov, Sergey Shirinsky, the composer

68   String Quartet no. 2 in A Major (1944)
First performance: 14 November 1944, Leningrad / Beethoven Quartet

73   String Quartet no. 3 in F Major (1946)
First performance: 16 December 1946, Moscow / Beethoven Quartet

83   String Quartet no. 4 in D Major (1949)
First performance: 3 December 1953, Moscow / Beethoven Quartet

92   String Quartet no. 5 in B-flat Major (1952)
First performance: 13 November 1953, Moscow / Beethoven Quartet

101   String Quartet no. 6 in G Major (1956)
First performance: 7 October 1956, Leningrad / Beethoven Quartet

108   String Quartet no. 7 in F-sharp Minor (1960)
First performance: 15 May 1960, Leningrad / Beethoven Quartet

110   String Quartet no. 8 in C Minor (1960)
First performance: 2 October 1960, Leningrad / Beethoven Quartet

117   String Quartet no. 9 in E-flat Major (1964)
First performance: 20 November 1964, Moscow / Beethoven Quartet

118   String Quartet no. 10 in A-flat Major (1964)
First performance: 20 November 1964, Moscow / Beethoven Quartet

122   String Quartet no. 11 in F Minor (1966)
First performance: 28 May 1966, Leningrad / Beethoven Quartet

133   String Quartet no. 12 in D-flat Major (1968)
First performance: 14 September 1968, Moscow / Beethoven Quartet

134   Sonata for Violin and Piano (1968)
First performance: 3 May 1969, Moscow / David Oistrakh, Svyatoslav Richter

138 String Quartet no. 13 in B-flat Minor (1970)
First performance: 13 December 1970, Leningrad / Beethoven Quartet

142 String Quartet no. 14 in F-sharp Major (1973)
First performance: 12 November 1973, Leningrad / Beethoven Quartet

144 String Quartet no. 15 in E-flat Minor (1974)
First performance: 15 November 1974, Leningrad / Taneyev Quartet

147 Sonata for Viola and Piano (1975)
First performance: 1 October 1975, Leningrad / Fyodor Druzhinin, Mikhaíl
Muntyan

PIANO

— Minuet, Prelude, and Intermezzo, incomplete (?1919–1920)

— Murzilka, n.d.

2 *Eight Preludes* (1918–1920)

— *Five Preludes* (1919–1921)
From a group of twenty-four produced with P. Feldt and G. Klements

5 *Three Fantastic Dances* (1920–1922)

6 Suite in F-sharp Minor for Two Pianos (1922)

12 Piano Sonata no. 1 (1926)
First performance: 12 December 1926, Leningrad / The composer

13 *Aphorisms* (1927)

34 *Twenty-four Preludes* (1932–1933)

61 Piano Sonata no. 2 in B Minor (1943)
First performance: 6 June 1943, Moscow / The composer

69 *Children's Notebook*, seven pieces (1944–1945)

— *Merry March* for two pianos (1949)

87 *Twenty-four Preludes and Fugues* (1950–1951)
First performance (complete): 23 and 28 December 1952, Leningrad /
Tatyana Nikolayeva

— *Seven Dolls' Dances* (arranged from ballet suites) (1952)

94 Concertino for Two Pianos (1954)
First performance: 8 November 1954, Moscow / Maxim Shostakovich, Alla
Maloletkova

— Tarantella for Two Pianos (?1954)

ORCHESTRATIONS

—   "Ya v grote zhdal" [I waited in the grotto], by Nikolai Rimsky-Korsakov (1921)

16   "Tahiti-trot" ("Tea for Two" by Vincent Youmans) (1927)

17   *Two Pieces by Scarlatti* (Domenico), for wind band (1928)

—   "Internationale" by Pierre Degeyter (1937)

58   *Boris Godunov,* opera by Modest Musorgsky (1939–1940)
First performance: 4 November 1959, Leningrad, Kirov Theater

—   "Mephistopheles' Song in Auerbach's Tavern" by Modest Musorgsky (1940)

—   "The Excursion Train Polka" by Johann Strauss (1941)

—   *Twenty-seven Romances and Songs* (transcriptions of classic and popular songs for frontline performance) (1941)

—   *British and American Folksongs,* for bass and chamber orchestra (1943)
Texts translated by Samuíl Marshak, Sergey Bolotin, and Tatyana Sikorskaya

—   *Rothschild's Violin* (completion of Veniamin Fleyshman's one-act opera after Anton Chekhov) (1944)

106   *Khovanshchina,* opera by Modest Musorgsky (originally arranged for film) (1958)
First staged performance: 25 November 1960, Leningrad, Kirov Theater

—   *Songs and Dances of Death* by Modest Musorgsky (1962)

124   *Two Choruses* by Alexander Davidenko (1963)

125   Cello Concerto by Robert Schumann (1963)

—   "Mephistopheles' Song of the Flea" by Ludwig van Beethoven (1975)

Glossary of Names

Afinogenov, Alexander Nikolayevich (1904–1941). Playwright. Author of *Salute, Spain!*, he was a leader of the Russian Association of Proletarian Writers (RAPP) in the early 1930s. In 1937 he was accused of opposing the Party line in literature and expelled from the Party and the Union of Writers, but he was rehabilitated in both a year later. He perished during the bombardment of Moscow.

Akhmatova, Anna Andreyevna [née Gorbenko] (1889–1966). Poet. In *Requiem*, she chronicled clandestinely the sufferings of the Soviet people during Stalin's terror in the 1930s. Together with Zoshchenko, she was officially censured in 1946 and expelled from the Writers' Union.

Akimov, Nikolai Pavlovich (1901–1968). Director, artist. Principal director of the Leningrad Theater of Comedy, 1935–49 and 1955–68. With Vladimir Dmitriyev, he designed the sets for *Declared Dead* at the Leningrad Music Hall. In 1932, Shostakovich supplied the music for his eccentric staging of *Hamlet* at the Vakhtangov Theater in Moscow.

Alekhine, Alexander Alexandrovich (1892–1946). Chess player. He left Russia in 1921 and became a naturalized French citizen. World champion, 1927–35 and from 1937 until his death.

Alexandrov, Alexander Vasilyevich (1883–1946). Composer, conductor. In 1928, he founded the Red Army Ensemble of Song and Dance. Author of patriotic songs, including "Hymn of the Bolshevik Party," in 1943 the winning entry in the contest for the National Anthem of the USSR.

Alexandrov, Georgiy Fyodorovich (1908–1961). USSR Minister of Culture, 1954–55.

Alikhanyan, Artyom Isaakovich (1908–1978). Physicist. A specialist in nuclear physics and cosmic radiation. Member of the Armenian and USSR Academies of Sciences, he was the brother of nuclear physicist Abram Alikhanov (1904–1970).

Amirov, Fikret Meshadi Dzhamil ogli (1922–1984). Composer, music administrator. Director of Azerbaijan Theater of Opera and Ballet, 1956–59. From 1958, secretary of Union of Composers of Azerbaijan; from 1974, of the Union of Soviet Composers.

Anosov, Nikolai Pavlovich (1900–1962). Conductor. Taught conducting at the Moscow Conservatory; conducted the first performance of Shostakovich's Second Piano Concerto.

Apostolov, Pavel Ivanovich (1905–1969). Musicologist, conductor, arts administrator. His speciality was military music. From 1949, he was attached to the Central Committee of the Communist Party. Collapsing during a reading of Shostakovich's Fourteenth Symphony, he died a month later.

Arnshtam, Leo Oskarovich (1905–1979). Film director, scenarist. Shostakovich's fellow student at the Petrograd Conservatory, he subsequently worked at the Meyerhold Theater in Moscow before turning to film. Sound engineer on *Golden*

Mountains, scenarist of *Counterplan,* director of *Girlfriends, Friends, Zoya, Five Days—Five Nights,* and *Sofya Perovskaya,* all with music by Shostakovich.

Asafyev, Boris Vladimirovich [pseud. Igor Glebov] (1884–1949). Musicologist, composer. The most influential musicologist of the Soviet period, in the 1920s he promoted contemporary Western and Soviet music actively. In 1936 and 1948, he deferred to the aesthetic judgment of the Party. Chairman of the Union of Soviet Composers, 1948–49.

Aseyev, Nikolai Nikolayevich (1889–1963). Poet. From early involvement in futurist circles, he gravitated toward agitational poetry. Was paired with Shostakovich in several unrealized projects of the early 1930s. Awarded a Stalin Prize in 1941.

Atovmyan, Levon Tadevosovich (1901–1973). Composer, music administrator. Worked in various managerial jobs, including in the All-Russian Society of Composers and Dramaturgs (Vseroskomdrama), 1929–33, and as director of Muzfond, 1939–48; came under political attack more than once. Trusted by Shostakovich in business and personal matters, as music editor, and as arranger of suites from his ballet and film scores.

Babel, Isaak Emmanuílovich (1894–1940). Writer. A native of Odessa, from 1917 to 1924 he tried his hand at many professions, including in the Red Army Cavalry, about which he published stories. Arrested in 1939, he was tried and shot.

Balanchivadze, Andrey Melitonovich (1906–1992). Georgian composer. Brother of George Balanchine, he became acquainted with Shostakovich while studying at the Leningrad Conservatory in the late 1920s.

Barshai, Rudolf Borisovich (1924–). Violist, conductor. A founding, albeit short-lived, member of the Borodin Quartet, in 1955 he was a founder of the Moscow Chamber Orchestra, which he conducted until his emigration to Israel in 1976.

Basner, Veniamin Yefimovich (1925–1996). Composer. Though not one of Shostakovich's students while at the Leningrad Conservatory in the late 1940s, Basner sight-read scores on violin for his class, and Shostakovich remained a mentor.

Baturin, Alexander Iosifovich (1904–1983). Bass-baritone. Soloist at the Bolshoy Theater in Moscow, 1927–58; professor at the Moscow Conservatory, 1948–83.

Bedny, Demyan [pseud. for Efim Alexandrovich Pridvorov] (1883–1945). Poet. An active Bolshevik from 1912, his work in the postrevolutionary period was markedly agitational and antireligious. In 1938, he was subjected to sharp criticism and expelled from the Party.

Belov, Gennadiy Grigoryevich (1939–). Composer. In 1964, he completed graduate work under Shostakovich at the Leningrad Conservatory.

Belugin, Nikolai Nikolayevich (1903–). Tenor. He sang at the Stanislavsky and Nemirovich-Danchenko Musical Theater in Moscow in the 1940s and 1950s. Took part in domestic performances of *From Jewish Folk Poetry* in 1948.

Beria, Lavrentiy Pavlovich (1899–1953). Party and state figure. Served in the secret police (Cheka) throughout the 1920s. Appointed first secretary of the Georgian Communist Party in 1931. Chief of the NKVD, 1938–46; elevated to full membership in the Politburo in 1946. After Stalin's death, he was tried and executed for crimes against the state.

Berlinsky, Valentin Alexandrovich (1925–). Cellist. A founding member of the Borodin Quartet.

Bezïmensky, Alexander Ilyich (1898–1973). Poet. He joined the Communist Party in 1916, fought in the October Revolution; later became an active member of the Russian Association of Proletarian Writers (RAPP) and a well-published proletarian poet. After it was initially criticized, Stalin came to the defense of his satirical play, *The Shot.*

Blanter, Matvey Isaakovich (1903–1990). Composer. A popular songwriter, he achieved worldwide fame with "Katyusha" (1939). Blanter stood by Shostakovich during his tribulations of 1948.

Blok, Alexander Alexandrovich (1880–1920). Poet. A leading representative of the Russian "Silver Age."

Bogachyova, Irina Petrovna (1939–). Mezzo-soprano. Soloist at the Kirov Theater in Leningrad; in 1973, Shostakovich recruited her as the first performer of his *Six Verses of Marina Tsvetayeva* and dedicated the cycle to her.

Bogdanov-Berezovsky, Valerian Mikhailovich (1903–1971). Musicologist, composer, critic. Shostakovich's closest friend of his Conservatory years, the two later became estranged.

Borisovsky, Vadim Vasilyevich (1900–1972). Violist. Founding violist of the Beethoven Quartet and professor at the Moscow Conservatory; due to ill health, he ceded his position in the quartet to his student Fyodor Druzhinin in 1964.

Brezhnev, Leonid Ilyich (1906–1982). Party and state figure. First secretary of the Central Committee, 1964–66; from 1966 until his death, general secretary.

Bryushkov, Yuriy (Georgiy) Vasilyevich (1903–1971). Pianist. A graduate student of Igumnov at the Moscow Conservatory, he competed in the Chopin Competition in Warsaw in 1927. He enjoyed a concert career and taught at the Leningrad Conservatory, where he was also director from 1951 to 1961.

Bubnov, Andrey Sergeyevich (1883–1938). Bolshevik functionary. In 1929, he succeeded Lunacharsky as Commissar of Enlightenment. Arrested in 1937, he was shot in 1938.

Bukharin, Nikolai Ivanovich (1888–1938). State and Party figure. Editor of *Pravda,* 1918–29; of *Izvestiya,* 1934–37. Member of the Central Committee, 1917–34; candidate member of the Politburo, 1934–37. Arrested on 27 February 1937, he was convicted in the March 1938 show trial of the "Anti-Soviet Bloc of Rightists and Trotskyists" and executed. Rehabilitated in 1988.

Bulgakov, Mikhaíl Afanasyevich (1891–1940). Writer, playwright. The success of his play, *Days of the Turbins,* at the Moscow Art Theater in 1926 was never repeated. In effect, after 1930, he found himself unable to publish or see his plays produced. His masterpiece, the novel *The Master and Margarita,* was published in Russia in 1966–67 in censored form.

Bunin, Revol Samuílovich (1924–1976). Composer. Shostakovich's student at the Moscow Conservatory, 1943–45, and his assistant at the Leningrad Conservatory, 1947.

Chaikovsky, Boris Alexandrovich (1925–1996). Composer. Studied at the Moscow Conservatory with Shebalin, Shostakovich, and Myaskovsky.

Cheremukhin, Mikhaíl Mikhailovich (1900–1984). Composer. Graduated from Myaskovsky's class at the Moscow Conservatory in 1928.

Chervinsky, Mikhaíl Abramovich (1911–1965). Dramatist, poet. Co-librettist of *Moscow, Cheryomushki* (with Vladimir Mass).

Chiaureli, Mikhaíl Edisherovich (1894–1974). Film director, scenarist, actor. A highly decorated Georgian, he directed both *The Fall of Berlin* and *The Unforgettable Year 1919*, with scores by Shostakovich.

Chukovskaya, Lidiya Korneyevna (1907–1996). Writer. A champion of human rights, she protested the trial of Sinyavsky and Daniel, supported Solzhenitsyn, and was expelled from the Moscow Writers' Union in 1974 for her defense of Sakharov. Shostakovich drew her scorn for his signature on an article condemning the latter.

Chukovsky, Yevgeniy Borisovich (1938–). Cinematographer, cameraman. Grandson of author and children's poet Korney Chukovsky and nephew of Lidiya Chukovskaya, he married Shostakovich's daughter, Galina, in 1959.

Chulaki, Mikhaíl Ivanovich (1908–1989). Composer, arts administrator. From 1937 to 1939 he was director of the Leningrad Philharmonic; also served in various capacities in culture ministries. With breaks, he was director of Moscow's Bolshoy Theater from 1955 to 1970.

Chyorny, Sasha [pseud. of Alexander Mikhailovich Glikberg] (1880–1932). Poet. Contributed extensively before 1917 to Russian journals of humor and satire; emigrated in the early 1920s and settled in Paris.

Dankevich, Konstantin Fyodorovich (1905–1984). Ukrainian composer, administrator. Headed Ukrainian Composers' Union, 1956–67; was a member of the delegation of Soviet composers sent to the United States in 1959. Author of the opera *Bogdan Khmelnitsky* condemned in *Pravda* in 1951, subsequently revised and rehabilitated.

Demidova, Praskovya Ivanovna ("Pasha"). Nina Varzar's nanny, she subsequently became nanny to the Shostakovich children.

Denisov, Edison Vasilyevich (1929–1996). Composer, teacher. In 1948, while a student in mathematics at Tomsk University, he initiated a correspondence with Shostakovich, who encouraged his ambition to become a composer and facilitated his move to Moscow and enrollment at the Moscow Conservatory, where he studied under Shebalin; subsequently he became an influential teacher and arbiter of the postwar Soviet avant-garde.

Dmitriyev, Vladimir Vladimirovich (1900–1948). Set designer. Worked in Leningrad and Moscow theaters; in the 1930s, he designed the first production of Shostakovich's *The Nose*, all three Russian productions of *Lady Macbeth of the Mtsensk District* (1934–35), as well as the Bolshoy Theater production of *The Limpid Stream*.

Dolmatovsky, Yevgeniy Aronovich (1915–1994). Poet. Popular chiefly as an author of lyrics for mass songs. From the late 1940s on, he supplied the texts for many of Shostakovich's patriotic vocal works, including *The Song of the Forests*.

Dolukhanova, Zara Alexandrovna (1918–). Mezzo-soprano. A first performer of Shostakovich's *From Jewish Folk Poetry*, she also furnished him the anonymous Spanish songs he harmonized as his op. 100.

Dombrovskaya, Genrietta Davidovna (1903–1961). Literary editor. With her husband, Vyacheslav, a high-ranking officer in the Leningrad Cheka (later NKVD) and amateur violinist, she was friendly with the Shostakovich family from the early 1930s. After her husband was liquidated and she was sent to a labor camp in 1937, Shostakovich remained solicitous about the welfare of her family. In the 1950s, he campaigned successfully for her husband's rehabilitation.

Dorliak, Nina Lvovna (1909–1998). Soprano. Daughter of soprano Xenia Dorliak, wife of Svyatoslav Richter, she was a first performer of Shostakovich's *From Jewish Folk Poetry*.

Dovzhenko, Alexander Petrovich (1894–1956). Film director, writer, scenarist. A pioneer in the Soviet cinema, acclaimed as scenarist and director of *Earth* (1930), he also directed *Michurin* (1949) with music by Shostakovich.

Druzhinin, Fyodor Serafimovich (1932–). Violist. Replaced his teacher, Vadim Borisovsky, in the Beethoven Quartet beginning in 1964; dedicatee and first performer of Shostakovich's Viola Sonata, op. 147.

Dunayevsky, Isaak Osipovich (1900–1955). Composer, administrator. Author of popular songs, operettas, and film scores, he served as music director and conductor of the Leningrad Music Hall, 1929–34; chair of the Leningrad branch of the Composers' Union, 1937–41.

Dzerzhinsky, Ivan Ivanovich (1909–1978). Composer. His first opera, *The Quiet Don*—brought to the stage in 1935 not without significant input from Shostakovich and others—became a role model in 1936 for the Socialist Realist song opera. His many other operas notwithstanding, he was never able to duplicate his original success.

Efros, Abram Markovich (1888–1954). Art and theater historian, literary critic, translator.

Eisenstein, Sergey Mikhailovich (1898–1948). Film director, theoretician. An acclaimed pioneer, in silent films such as *Strike* and *Battleship Potemkin*, he later collaborated with Prokofiev on *Alexander Nevsky* and *Ivan the Terrible*. He and Shostakovich never collaborated, though excerpts culled from the latter's scores were later adapted as soundtracks to *October* (1967) and *Battleship Potemkin* (1976).

Eliasberg, Karl Ilyich (1907–1978). Conductor. From 1937 to 1950, he served as principal conductor of the Leningrad Radio Orchestra; conducted the legendary performance of Shostakovich's Seventh Symphony in blockaded Leningrad on 9 August 1942.

Erenburg, Ilya Grigoryevich (1891–1967). Writer, journalist, memoirist. Spent many years, before and after 1917, living in Europe as a foreign correspondent. During the Spanish Civil War and World War II, he was one of the most popular Soviet war correspondents.

Ermler, Fridrikh Markovich (1898–1967). Film director. He directed *Counterplan* (with Yutkevich) and *The Great Citizen*, series 1 and 2, with scores by Shostakovich.

Ernesaks, Gustav Gustavovich (1908–1993). Choral conductor, composer. Founder, in 1944, and conductor of the Estonian State Academic Male Choir; composer of the National Anthem of the Estonian SSR.

Fadeyev, Alexander Alexandrovich (1901–1956). Writer. One of the leaders of the Russian Association of Proletarian Writers, 1926–32; he later became a leading figure in the Union of Soviet Writers and its general secretary and chairman, 1946–54. He committed suicide after the Twentieth Party Congress.

Fedin, Konstantin Alexandrovich (1892–1977). Writer, cultural official. Member of the literary group "Serapion Brothers" in Petrograd-Leningrad in the 1920s. Though not a Party member, he served as first secretary of the Union of Soviet Writers, 1959–71, and as its chairman, 1971–77.

Feldt, Pavel Emilyevich (1905–1960). Conductor, composer. Studied at the Petrograd-Leningrad Conservatory alongside Shostakovich. He became a ballet conductor at MALEGOT and later at the Kirov Theater in Leningrad; in 1935 he conducted the premiere of *The Limpid Stream*.

Flaks, Efrem Borisovich (1909–). Bass. Soloist at the Leningrad Philharmonic, 1936–42 and 1950–70; at Leningrad Radio, 1943–50.

Fleyshman, Veniamin Iosifovich (1913–1941). Composer. While studying under Shostakovich at the Leningrad Conservatory, he composed *Rothschild's Violin*, a one-act opera. It was substantially complete at the outbreak of World War II, when he volunteered for the front and was killed; Shostakovich completed the opera in 1944.

Fliyer, Yakov Vladimirovich (1912–1977). Pianist. A student of Igumnov at the Moscow Conservatory, he took top honors at the Second All-Union Performers' Competition in 1935; he concertized extensively and taught at the Moscow Conservatory, 1937–75.

Frederiks, Vsevolod Konstantinovich (1885–1944). Physicist, professor. He married Shostakovich's older sister, Mariya, in 1927. In 1937, he was arrested and sent to a labor camp. His wife received a divorce. Released from the Gulag, he died on his way home.

Frid, Grigoriy Samuílovich (1915–). Composer. Studied under Shebalin at the Moscow Conservatory. Beginning in 1965, he created and led the Moscow Youth Music Club, affiliated with the All-Union House of Composers, to facilitate contact between composers, performers, and the educated public.

Furtseva, Ekaterina Alexeyevna (1910–1974). USSR Minister of Culture, 1960–74.

Gauk, Alexander Vasilyevich (1893–1963). Conductor. Conducted at the Leningrad Academic Theater of Opera and Ballet, 1920–31; conducted the Large Orchestra of All-Union Radio, 1933–36 and 1953–61. Founding conductor, 1936–41, of the USSR State Symphony Orchestra. Taught at the Leningrad and Moscow Conservatories; his students included Melik-Pashayev, Mravinsky, Simeonov, N. Rabinovich, and Svetlanov.

Gayamova, Zinaída Alexandrovna (1896–1971). Shostakovich's personal secretary from the 1950s until her death.

Gerasimov, Sergey Apollinariyevich (1906–1985). Film director, scenarist. As an actor, he had roles in the Kozintsev and Trauberg films The *New Babylon, Alone*, and *The Vyborg District*; later directed *The Young Guard*, with music by Shostakovich.

Gilels, Emil Grigoryevich (1916–1985). Pianist. A student of Reyngbald in Odessa and Heinrich Neuhaus in Moscow, he took first prize at the First All-Union

Performers' Competition in 1933 and the Ysaÿe Piano Competition in Brussels in 1938. Taught at the Moscow Conservatory and enjoyed an international concert career.

Ginzburg, Grigoriy Romanovich (1904–1961). Pianist. A student of Goldenveyzer at the Moscow Conservatory, he competed in the Chopin Competition in Warsaw in 1927 where he took fourth prize; concertized and taught at the Moscow Conservatory.

Glazunov, Alexander Konstantinovich (1865–1936). Composer, conductor, administrator. Studied privately with Rimsky-Korsakov and became a member of the Belyayev Circle. A professor at the St. Petersburg Conservatory from 1899, in 1905 he became its director until his departure for Europe in 1928.

Glière, Reinhold Moritsevich (1874/75–1956). Composer. Studied under Ippolitov-Ivanov, Arensky, Konyus, and Taneyev at the Moscow Conservatory; taught there, 1920–41. Chairman of the Organizing Committee of the Union of Soviet Composers, 1939–48.

Glikman, Isaak Davidovich (1911–). Theater historian, dramaturg. Taught at the Leningrad Conservatory. On close terms with Shostakovich from the early 1930s until the composer's death; a volume of more than 300 letters Shostakovich had written to him was published in 1993.

Glivenko, Tatyana Ivanovna (1906–). Daughter of a Moscow academic, in the summer of 1923 she became one of Shostakovich's first sweethearts, with whom he had an on-again, off-again relationship until 1932.

Glyasser, Ignatiy Albertovich (1850–1925). Piano pedagogue. With his wife, Olga, he offered piano courses for children in prerevolutionary St. Petersburg; attended by Shostakovich and his older sister.

Gmïrya, Boris Romanovich (1903–1969). Bass. From 1939, soloist of the Ukrainian Theater of Opera and Ballet in Kiev.

Goldenveyser, Alexander Borisovich (1875–1961). Pianist, composer, educator, administrator. Studied piano and composition at the Moscow Conservatory; enjoyed close contact with Rachmaninoff, Scriabin, and Medtner. One of the most influential pianists and teachers of the Moscow School, he served several stints as vice-rector or director of the Moscow Conservatory, the last in 1939–42.

Golovanov, Nikolai Semyonovich (1891–1953). Conductor, pianist, composer. Fired as conductor of the Bolshoy Theater in 1936 after its unsuccessful production of Dzerzhinsky's *The Quiet Don*, he was rehired as principal conductor there in 1948. Artistic director and principal conductor of the Large All-Union Radio Orchestra, 1937–53.

Gorky, Maxim [pseud. for Alexey Maximovich Peshkov] (1868–1936). Writer, editor, critic, publicist. Conceptualizer of Soviet "Socialist Realism." A founding father of the Union of Soviet Writers, from 1934 he chaired its Presidium.

Grinberg, Moisey Abramovich (1904–1968). Music administrator. Worked in Soviet music publishing, music theater, and radio; he was artistic director of the Moscow Philharmonic, 1958–68.

Gromadsky, Vitaliy Alexandrovich (1928–). Bass. From 1961, soloist of the Moscow Philharmonic. He gave the first performances of Shostakovich's Thirteenth Symphony and *The Execution of Stepan Razin*.

Igumnov, Konstantin Nikolayevich (1873–1948). Pianist. Concertized and, from 1896, became a leading pedagogue at the Moscow Conservatory; in 1924–29, its director.

Ilizarov, Gavriil Abramovich (1921–1992). Orthopedic surgeon. He developed a pioneering procedure to correct deformed bones; in 1970–71, Shostakovich made three trips to his clinic in Kurgan, Siberia, for treatment.

Iokhelson, Vladimir Efimovich (1904–1941). Music journalist, administrator. He was secretary of the Leningrad Association of Proletarian Musicians and later worked in the Union of Soviet Composers and in music publishing there.

Ionin, Georgiy. Writer, dramatist, director. Still in his twenties, he died from scarlet fever not long after collaborating with Shostakovich on the libretto of *The Nose.*

Ivanov, Konstantin Konstantinovich (1907–1984). Conductor. Principal conductor of the USSR State Symphony Orchestra, 1946–65.

Ivanovsky, Alexander Viktorovich (1881–1968). Film director, scenarist. He submitted the winning entry to a competition for a topical ballet libretto in 1929; eventually it was turned into Shostakovich's first ballet, *The Golden Age.*

Kabalevsky, Dmitriy Borisovich (1904–1987). Composer, pianist. Studied with Myaskovsky and Goldenveyzer at the Moscow Conservatory, where he then taught, 1932–80. From 1952, a secretary of the Union of Soviet Composers.

Kainova, Margarita Andreyevna (1924–?). From 1956 to 1959, Shostakovich's second wife. Khentova indicates she died shortly after Shostakovich.

Kamenyev, Lev Borisovich [pseud. for Rosenfeld] (1883–1936). Party and state figure. Allied with Stalin and Zinovyev against Trotsky at the time of Lenin's death, he quickly fell into Stalin's bad graces. Tried and sentenced together with Zinovyev in 1935 for moral complicity in the death of Kirov, they were both retried and executed the following year in the first of the public "show" trials.

Kandelaki, Vladimir Arkadyevich (1908–1994). Bass baritone, stage director. He created the role of Boris Timofeyevich in the Nemirovich-Danchenko Musical Theater production of *Katerina Izmailova* in 1934. While principal director of the Moscow Operetta Theater, 1954–64, he produced Shostakovich's *Moscow, Cheryomushki.*

Kaplan, Emmanuíl Iosifovich (1895–1961). Stage director, singer. He was on staff at the Leningrad Academic Theater of Opera and Ballet, where, in 1930, he directed Shostakovich's first ballet, *The Golden Age.*

Karayev, Kara Abulfaz oglï (1918–1982). Composer. Studied under Shostakovich at the Moscow Conservatory; later became a leading figure in Azerbaijan's music life. From 1962, a secretary of the Union of Soviet Composers.

Karetnikov, Nikolai Nikolayevich (1930–1994). Composer. He studied with Shebalin at the Moscow Conservatory. Influenced by serial techniques, he became one of the leading figures of the post-Stalin avant-garde.

Katayev, Vitaliy Vitalyevich (1925–). Conductor. 1962–71, artistic director and principal conductor of the State Symphony Orchestra of Belarus.

Kerzhentsev, Platon Mikhailovich (1881–1940). Bolshevik cultural official; chairman of the Committee for Artistic Affairs, 1936–38.

Khachaturyan, Aram Ilyich (1903–1978). Composer. Of Armenian extraction, he studied with Myaskovsky at the Moscow Conservatory and became famous for his coloristic ballets and symphonic scores. He met Shostakovich in 1934; the two remained lifelong friends and served together in many official capacities.

Khaikin, Boris Emmanuílovich (1904–1978). Conductor. Artistic director and principal conductor of the Malïy Theater, 1936–43, and the Kirov Theater, 1944–53, in Leningrad; conductor at the Bolshoy Theater in Moscow, 1954–78.

Khodasevich, Valentina Mikhailovna (1894–1970). Artist, costume and set designer. Studied in Moscow, Munich, and Paris. In the postrevolutionary period, designed mass spectacles. Shostakovich's *The Golden Age*, in 1930, was her first experience with ballet.

Kholodilin, Alexander Alexandrovich (1908–1971). Musicologist, cultural official. From 1949, he held positions in the Committee for Artistic Affairs and the USSR and RSFSR Ministries of Culture. In 1964 he was elected a secretary in the RSFSR Union of Composers. He maintained friendly ties with Shostakovich.

Khrapchenko, Mikhaíl Borisovich (1904–1986). Literary historian, government official. From 1939 to 1948, he was chairman of the Committee for Artistic Affairs.

Khrennikov, Tikhon Nikolayevich (1913–). Composer, pianist, administrator. Studied under Shebalin and Heinrich Neuhaus at the Moscow Conservatory, where he then taught from 1961. From 1948 until its demise, general secretary (from 1957, first secretary) of the Union of Soviet Composers, the most influential position in music. From 1976, candidate member of the Central Committee.

Khrushchev, Nikita Sergeyevich (1894–1971). Party and state figure. From 1953 to 1964, first secretary of the Central Committee. Removed from office on 14 October 1964.

Khubov, Georgiy Nikitich (1902–1981). Musicologist, music administrator. Assistant editor, 1932–39, and editor-in-chief, 1952–57, of the journal *Sovetskaya muzïka*. Consultant on music broadcasting to the Central Committee, 1946–52.

Kirov, Sergey Mironovich (1886–1934). Party and state figure. From 1926, first secretary of the Leningrad oblast. Member of the Central Committee from 1923; from 1926, candidate, from 1930, member, of the Politburo. Assassinated in Leningrad on 1 December 1934.

Kirsanov, Semyon Isaakovich (1906–1972). Poet. Also a commentator and war correspondent, he won a Stalin Prize in 1950. In 1954, he joined the directorate of the Union of Soviet Writers.

Klements, Georgiy Lvovich (1906?–1929). Composer, pianist. One of Shostakovich's extremely talented cohorts during their student days at the Petrograd-Leningrad Conservatory, he perished of typhus.

Knushevitsky, Viktor Nikolayevich (1906–1974). Composer, conductor. Artistic director and conductor of the USSR State Jazz Orchestra, 1937–41; of the Variety Orchestra of All-Union Radio, 1945–52.

Kondrashin, Kirill Petrovich (1914–1981). Conductor. Studied with Khaikin. Conducted at the Bolshoy Theater in Moscow, 1943–56. Principal conductor of the Moscow Philharmonic Orchestra, 1960–75, with which he gave the premieres of Shostakovich's Fourth and Thirteenth Symphonies, the Second Violin Concerto, and *The Execution of Stepan Razin*. He defected in 1978.

Konstantinovskaya, Yelena Yevseyevna (1914–1975). Translator, pedagogue. Met

Shostakovich in 1934; they had an affair lasting slightly more than a year. Later she headed the department of foreign languages at the Leningrad Conservatory.

Kornilov, Boris Petrovich (1907–1938). Poet. A former member of the Russian Association of Proletarian Writers (RAPP), in 1935 he came under criticism and was expelled from the Union of Writers. Arrested in 1937 and executed.

Koval (Kovalyov), Marian Viktorovich (1907–1971). Composer. Affiliated with RAPM until its demise, he was one of the organizers of "Prokoll" at the Moscow Conservatory in 1925. In conjunction with the purge of musicians in 1948, he became a secretary of the Union of Composers (1948–57) and editor-in-chief of the journal *Sovetskaya muzïka* (1948–52). Succeeded Zakharov as artistic director of the Pyatnitsky Folk Chorus in 1956.

Kozhunova, Fedosya Fedorovna ("Fenya") (d. 1965). Cook and housekeeper of the Shostakovich family from 1935. After the war her niece, Mariya Dmitriyevna Kozhunova, assumed main responsibility and Fenya supervised the family dacha.

Kozintsev, Grigoriy Mikhailovich (1905–1973). Film director. With Trauberg and Yutkevich was a founder of FEKS in Petrograd; he collaborated with Trauberg on filmmaking through the 1940s. Enjoyed an extended creative relationship with Shostakovich, who provided music to nearly all of his films, from the silent *New Babylon* (1929) to his Shakespearean masterpieces, *Hamlet* (1964) and *King Lear* (1971).

Kremlyov, Yuliy Anatolyevich (1908–1971). Musicologist, composer. Studied with Asafyev and Yudina. Headed the music division of the Leningrad Research Institute of Theater, Music and Cinema, 1957–69.

Kubatsky, Viktor Lvovich (1891–1970). Cellist. Orchestral soloist, 1914–35, and conductor, 1931–35, of the Bolshoy Theater Orchestra and founding member of the Stradivarius Quartet, 1920–30; he was the dedicatee and first performer of Shostakovich's Cello Sonata.

Kukharsky, Vasiliy Feodosyevich (1918–   ). Musicologist, cultural official. Occupied various politically responsible positions; from 1960, he was attached to the Central Committee of the Communist Party. In 1967, he became Assistant Minister of Culture of the USSR.

Kustodiyev, Boris Mikhailovich (1878–1927). Artist, illustrator. Noted for portraits and for his colorful paintings of provincial Russian life.

Kvadri, Mikhaíl Vladimirovich (1897–1929). Composer. As the dominant personality of a group of composition students at the Moscow Conservatory in the mid-1920s, he drew the young Shostakovich into their orbit, presuming the role of his mentor. Shostakovich dedicated *Two Fables of Krïlov* and his First Symphony to him. Kvadri was arrested and allegedly shot in 1929.

Lebedinsky, Lev Nikolayevich (1904–1992). Musicologist. A chief ideologue of the Russian Association of Proletarian Musicians until its demise, he specialized in folk music. Headed the editorial board for folk music at the publisher *Sovetskiy kompozitor,* 1955–65. Though he maintained his distance in the 1930s, Shostakovich became friendly with him in the early 1950s.

Levitin, Yuriy Abramovich (1912–1993). Composer. One of Shostakovich's first students at the Leningrad Conservatory.

Litvinova, Flora Pavlovna (1920–). Biologist. Mother of physicist and human rights activist Pavel Litvinov. Exiled to Kuybïshev during World War II, she became friends with Nina Shostakovich and her husband.

Lopukhov, Fyodor Vasilyevich (1886–1973). Ballet dancer, choreographer. Artistic director of ballet at the Kirov Theater in Leningrad at various periods; organized and directed the ballet company of Leningrad's Malïy Theater, 1931–36. He collaborated with Shostakovich on mounting *The Bolt* and *The Limpid Stream*, of which he was also co-librettist.

Losskiy, Boris Nikolayevich (1905–). Art historian. Son of philosopher Nikolai Losskiy. Shostakovich's schoolmate, 1915–21, at the Shidlovskaya and Stoyunina schools as well as in the piano courses of Glyasser. Expelled from the USSR with his family in 1922.

Lukashevich, Klavdiya Vladimirovna (1859–1937). Children's writer. Popular author and close friend of his parents from their Siberian days, she was Shostakovich's godmother and sometime next-door neighbor. During the Civil War, she petitioned Lunacharsky for improvement in his material conditions.

Lunacharsky, Anatoliy Vasilyevich (1875–1933). Party and state figure, writer, critic. People's Commissar of Enlightenment, 1917–29.

Lyubimov, Yuriy Petrovich (1917–). Director, actor. During World War II, member of the NKVD Song and Dance Ensemble. Artistic director of the Taganka Theater in Moscow, 1964–84.

Lyubinsky, Zakhar Isaakovich (1887–1983). Theatrical administrator. From 1928 to 1930, he was director of Academic theaters in Leningrad.

Makarov, Yevgeniy Petrovich (1912–1985). Composer. Studied with Glière and Shostakovich. Chiefly a composer of band music, he taught at the Institute for Military Conductors, 1947–61, and at the Moscow Conservatory from 1957.

Malko, Nikolai Andreyevich (1883–1961). Conductor. Professor at the Leningrad Conservatory, 1925–28, where Shostakovich took lessons from him. Conducted the premiere of Shostakovich's First Symphony and championed the music of the young composer. From 1929, he lived in the West.

Mandelstam, Osip Emilyevich (1891–1938). Poet. During the Stalin era, most of his works went unpublished. Arrested in 1934 and sent into internal exile, he returned to Moscow only to be arrested again in 1938. He perished in a labor camp.

Mariengof, Anatoliy Borisovich (1897–1962). Poet, playwright. Together with his wife, actress Anna Nikritina, he was a member of Shostakovich's social set in Leningrad before the war. His libretto for an opera to be composed by Shostakovich based on Tolstoy's *Resurrection* was banned by Glavrepertkom in 1941.

Marshak, Samuíl Yakovlevich (1887–1964). Poet, translator. One of the most popular children's writers of the Soviet period.

Maslennikov, Alexey Dmitriyevich (1929–). Tenor. Soloist at the Bolshoy Theater in Moscow, 1956–85. From 1985, an operatic director.

Mass, Vladimir Zakharovich (1896–1979). Dramatist, poet. Co-librettist of *Moscow, Cheryomushki* (with Mikhaíl Chervinsky).

Mayakovsky, Vladimir Vladimirovich (1893–1930). Poet, playwright. The leading spokesman of Russian futurists before World War I, he became a leading champion of the Bolsheviks after 1917. Committed suicide in 1930. Canonized by Stalin in 1935 as "the best and most talented poet of our Soviet epoch."

Melik-Pashayev, Alexander Shamilyevich (1905–1964). Conductor. He studied with Gauk. Conducted at the Bolshoy Theater in Moscow, 1931–64; principal conductor there, 1953–62.

Mendeleyev, Dmitriy Ivanovich (1834–1907). Chemist. Developed the periodic classification of elements. From 1893 until his death, headed the Bureau of Weights and Measures in St. Petersburg.

Meyer, Krzysztof (1943–). Polish composer. He studied with Penderecki and Nadia Boulanger. Made the acquaintance of Shostakovich and published biographies of him in 1973 and 1994; completed Shostakovich's unfinished opera, *The Gamblers* in 1980–81.

Meyerhold, Vsevolod Emilyevich (1874–1940). Actor, theater director. A towering figure in early Soviet culture, from 1920 he headed his own theater in Moscow. Of several proposed collaborations involving Shostakovich, only his production of Mayakovsky's *The Bedbug* was realized. The target of increasingly strident criticism, his theater was closed in 1938; he was arrested in 1939 and executed in 1940.

Meyerovich, Mikhaíl Alexandrovich (1920–). Composer. Studied at the Moscow Conservatory.

Mikhailov, Lev Dmitriyevich (1928–1980). Opera director. From 1960, principal director of the Stanislavsky-Nemirovich-Danchenko Musical Theater in Moscow, where he revived Shostakovich's *Katerina Izmailova* in 1963.

Mikhailov, Nikolai Alexandrovich (1906–1982). USSR Minister of Culture, 1955–60.

Mikhoels (Vovsi), Solomon Mikhailovich (1890–1948). Actor, director. He became artistic director of the State Jewish Theater in Moscow in 1929; in 1941, was named chairman of the Jewish Anti-fascist Committee, which he headed until his murder in January 1948.

Miroshnikova, Margarita Khristoforovna (1932–). Soprano. Soloist of the Moscow Philharmonic, 1966–91.

Mnatsakanyan, Alexander Derenikovich (1936–). Composer. Studied at the Leningrad Conservatory under Yevlakhov; pursued graduate studies there under Shostakovich.

Molostova, Irina Alexandrovna. Stage director. Worked in Kiev, where she directed the highly regarded 1965 production of *Katerina Izmailova* at the Theater of Opera and Ballet. In 1995, she directed the first production of the same opera at the Kirov Theater in St. Petersburg.

Molotov, Vyacheslav Mikhailovich (1890–1986). State and Party figure. Member of the Politburo, 1921–57. Chairman of the Council of People's Commissars, 1930–41; People's Commissar (later Minister) of Foreign Affairs, 1939–49 and 1953–56.

Mordvinov, Boris Arkadyevich (1899–1953). Opera director. From 1930, principal director of the Nemirovich-Danchenko Musical Theater in Moscow; principal director of the Bolshoy Theater, 1936–40.

Mravinsky, Yevgeniy Alexandrovich (1903–1988). Conductor. Studied with Malko and Gauk. Staff conductor on the roster of the Kirov Theater in Leningrad when he was drafted to conduct the premiere of Shostakovich's Fifth Symphony in 1937. In 1938, he took first prize in the All-Union Competition and was appointed principal conductor of the Leningrad Philharmonic Orchestra, a post he retained until his death. Closely involved with the creation of many of Shostakovich's symphonic scores; the Eighth Symphony is dedicated to him.

Muntyan, Mikhail. Pianist, accompanist. Studied with Yakov Fliyer. From 1962, performed with the Large Symphony Orchestra of All-Union Radio; from 1978, soloist with the Moscow Philharmonic Orchestra.

Muradeli, Vano Ilyich (1908–1970). Composer. A Georgian hailing from Stalin's birthplace, he failed to curry favor in 1947 with his opera for the thirtieth anniversary of the October Revolution, *The Great Friendship*, triggering Zhdanov's assault on music in 1948. He quickly rehabilitated himself; chaired the Moscow branch of the Union of Composers, 1959–70.

Myaskovsky, Nikolai Yakovlevich (1881–1950). Composer, pedagogue. Studied alongside Prokofiev at the St. Petersburg Conservatory. From 1918, lived in Moscow and was active in organizing musical life under the Soviets. From 1921, taught at the Moscow Conservatory, where his students included Shebalin, Khachaturyan, and Kabalevsky.

Nagovitsïn, Vyacheslav Lavrentyevich (1939–). Composer. Completed graduate work under Shostakovich at the Leningrad Conservatory in 1966.

Nazirova, Elmira Mirza Riza kïzï (1928–). Composer, pianist. Briefly studied with Shostakovich at the Moscow Conservatory before returning to her native Baku; she corresponded with the enamored composer during the period of composition of his Tenth Symphony.

Nechipailo, Viktor Timofeyevich (1926–). Baritone. Soloist at the Bolshoy Theater in Moscow, 1953–75.

Nemirovich-Danchenko, Vladimir Ivanovich (1858–1943). Theater and opera director. Organized and directed an opera studio attached to the Moscow Art Theater in 1919, named the Nemirovich-Danchenko Musical Theater from 1926 (from 1941, the Stanislavsky-Nemirovich-Danchenko Musical Theater). Directed the Moscow premiere of *Katerina Izmailova* there.

Nesterenko, Yevgeniy Yevgenyevich (1938–). Bass. From 1971, soloist at the Bolshoy Theater in Moscow.

Nestyev, Izrail Vladimirovich (1911–1993). Musicologist. 1945–48, editor-in-chief of music programming for All-Union Radio; 1954–59, assistant editor of *Sovetskaya muzïka*. Taught at the Moscow Conservatory from 1948. In 1960, became a senior fellow of the All-Union Research Institute for Arts History; from 1974, headed section of music of the peoples of the USSR.

Neuhaus, Heinrich Gustavovich (1888–1964). Pianist, pedagogue. A distinguished concert career, 1922–62, was matched by an unparalleled legacy as a teacher at the Moscow Conservatory. Emil Gilels and Svyatoslav Richter numbered among his pupils.

Nikolayev, Leonid Vladimirovich (1878–1942). Pianist, composer. Best known as a leading piano pedagogue at the St. Petersburg-Petrograd-Leningrad Conservatory (1909–42), his graduates included Sofronitsky, Yudina, and Shostakovich, who dedicated his Second Piano Sonata to his teacher's memory.

Nikolayeva, Tatyana Petrovna (1924–1993). Pianist. She studied with Goldenveyser at the Moscow Conservatory. Winning the piano competition at the Leipzig Bach Festival in 1950, her performance helped stimulate Shostakovich to compose his *Twenty-four Preludes and Fugues* (op. 87), a cycle she tirelessly championed.

Nikolsky, Yuriy Sergeyevich (1895–1962). Composer. Studied at the Moscow Conservatory under Myaskovsky; was a member of Kvadri's circle there.

Nikritina, Anna Borisovna (1900–1982). Actress. Together with her husband, Anatoliy Mariengof, she was a member of Shostakovich's social set in Leningrad before the war.

Oborin, Lev Nikolayevich (1907–1974). Pianist. Studied piano with Igumnov and composition with Myaskovsky at the Moscow Conservatory. He was one of Shostakovich's best friends in Moscow even before capturing the first prize at the 1927 Chopin Competition in Warsaw; they remained on close terms.

Oistrakh, David Fyodorovich (1908–1974). Violinist. He studied in Odessa under Stolyarsky and took first prize in the Second All-Union Performers' Competition in 1935, where Shostakovich served on the jury. Shortly after, they toured together in Turkey. His playing supplied fertile inspiration to Shostakovich; the two violin concertos and the violin sonata were written for, and dedicated to, him.

Oistrakh, Igor Davidovich (1931–). Violinist. Son and student of David Oistrakh. Soloist of the Moscow Philharmonic since 1957.

Okunev, German Grigoryevich (1931–1973). Composer. Studied with Yevlakhov and Shostakovich at the Leningrad Conservatory. Wrote extensively for children.

Oleynikov, Nikolai Makarovich (1898–1937). Poet. A member of the Leningrad absurdist group OBERIU ("Union of Real Arts"). In 1930, Shostakovich was eager to turn his satirical poem, *The Carp*, into an opera. However, the poet failed to deliver a libretto and the project went unrealized.

Ostrovsky, Nikolai Alexandrovich (1904–1936). Writer. Seriously wounded during the Civil War, blind and confined to his bed, in 1932–34 he dictated what became a classic socialist realist novel about the Civil War exploits of a young Komsomol activist, *How the Steel Was Tempered.*

Pasternak, Boris Leonidovich (1890–1960). Poet, novelist. Awarded the Nobel Prize for Literature in 1958 for *Doctor Zhivago,* a work that had been published in Italy, he declined the honor. Expelled from the Union of Writers the same year, he was posthumously rehabilitated in 1987.

Pazovsky, Ariy Moiseyevich (1887–1953). Conductor. Artistic director and principal conductor of the Kirov Theater in Leningrad, 1936–43, and of the Bolshoy Theater in Moscow, 1943–48.

Piotrovsky, Adrian Ivanovich (1898–1938). Literary and theatrical critic, dramatist, screenwriter. An influential figure on the Leningrad theater and film scene until he was purged. Author of the play *Rule, Britannia!* and co-librettist of the ballet, *The Limpid Stream.*

Pokrovsky, Boris Alexandrovich (1912–). Opera director. Principal director at the Bolshoy Theater in Moscow, 1952–63 and 1967–82. From 1972, founding artistic director of the Moscow Chamber Music Theater; he directed Shostakovich's *The Nose* there in 1974.

Polyakin, Miron Borisovich (1895–1941). Violinist. Studied under Leopold Auer at the St. Petersburg Conservatory. Toured in the West, 1918–26; thereafter concertized in Russia and taught at the Leningrad and Moscow Conservatories.

Ponna, Mariya Ivanovna. Swimming champion turned modern dancer. In 1923–24, she choreographed Shostakovich's *Three Fantastic Dances* to the composer's accompaniment. Shortly after, she teamed up in duet with Alexander Kaverzin to successfully pioneer the fusion of dance and acrobatics on the variety stage.

Ponomarenko, Panteleymon Kondratiyevich (1902–1984). USSR Minister of Culture, 1953–54.

Popov, Gavriil Nikolayevich (1904–1972). Composer. Shostakovich's contemporary and widely considered his most formidable competitor in Leningrad new music circles in the 1920s. Devoted much of his career to film music.

Poskrebïshev, Alexander Nikolayevich (1891–1965). Stalin's personal secretary and most trusted aide, 1924–52.

Preys, Alexander Germanovich (1906–1942). Dramatist, librettist. He collaborated with Shostakovich on the libretti of *The Nose* and *Lady Macbeth of the Mtsensk District.*

Prokofiev, Sergey Sergeyevich (1891–1953). Composer, pianist. Studied at the St. Petersburg Conservatory. In 1918, he was granted permission by Bolshevik officials to travel in the West, where he concertized extensively and collaborated with Serge Diaghilev. Following brief visits to Russia beginning in 1927, he elected to resettle his family in Moscow in the mid-1930s. After 1938, he was no longer able to travel abroad.

Rabinovich, David Abramovich (1900–1978). Musicologist. Published a biography of Shostakovich in 1959.

Rabinovich, Nikolai Semyonovich (1908–1972). Conductor. Studied conducting with Malko and Gauk. Principal conductor of the Large Symphony Orchestra of Leningrad Radio, 1950–57. He conducted many of the soundtracks for Shostakovich's films.

Raikh, Zinaída Nikolayevna (1894–1939). Actress. The wife of Meyerhold (her previous marriage was to poet Sergey Yesenin) and his leading actress, she was brutally murdered in their Moscow apartment after his arrest.

Rakhlin, Natan Grigoryevich (1906–1979). Conductor. Served as principal conductor of the Ukrainian State Symphony Orchestra and the USSR State Symphony. In 1966, created the Kazan State Symphony, becoming its artistic director and principal conductor.

Rappaport, Gerbert Moritsevich (1908–1983). Film director. He directed the film version of Shostakovich's operetta, *Moscow, Cheryomushki.*

Renzin, Isai Mikhailovich (1903–1969). Pianist, administrator. Director of the Leningrad Philharmonic, 1935–37.

Reshetin, Mark Stepanovich (1931–). Bass. Soloist at the Bolshoy Theater in Moscow, 1956–77.

Reysner, Larisa Mikhailovna (1895–1926). Revolutionary. A famous beauty, she married the revolutionary Fyodor Raskolnikov and became vice-minister of the Bolshevik navy.

Reyzen, Mark Osipovich (1895–1992). Bass. Soloist at the Leningrad Academic Theater of Opera and Ballet, 1925–30; at the Bolshoy Theater in Moscow, 1934–54.

Richter, Svyatoslav Teofilovich (1915–1997). Pianist. Studied with Neuhaus at the Moscow Conservatory; took first prize at the All-Union Performers' Competition in 1945. Noted for his artistic individuality and interpretive insight, he enjoyed a brilliant international career.

Rimsky-Korsakov, Georgiy Mikhailovich (1901–1965). Composer. A grandson of Nikolai Rimsky-Korsakov, he was Shostakovich's fellow student in Steinberg's class at the Leningrad Conservatory. He was a pioneer in acoustical research.

Roslavets, Nikolai Andreyevich (1880/81–1944). Composer. Studied at the Moscow Conservatory. Began to develop an innovative, "posttonal" system of tone organization before 1917. Embracing the Bolshevik Revolution, he became a prominent cultural polemicist in Moscow in the 1920s, furthering the notion of a "revolutionary avant-garde." After 1930, he fell into eclipse.

Rostropovich, Mstislav Leopoldovich (1927–). Cellist, conductor. Studied briefly with Shostakovich at the Moscow Conservatory; subsequently collaborated closely with the composer preparing first performances of his two cello concertos, both of which were dedicated to him. With his wife, Galina Vishnevskaya, he left Russia for political reasons in 1974.

Rozanova, Alexandra Alexandrovna (1876–1942). Pianist, pedagogue. She studied under Balakirev and Malozyomova at the St. Petersburg Conservatory and subsequently taught there; Shostakovich's mother and sister Mariya were among her students as was, from 1918 to 1920, the composer himself.

Rozhdestvensky, Gennadiy Nikolayevich (1931–). Conductor. Conducted at the Bolshoy Theater in Moscow, 1951–60 and 1978–83; principal conductor there, 1965–70. From 1961, artistic director and principal conductor of the Large Orchestra of All-Union Radio and TV; from 1983, of the USSR Ministry of Culture Symphony Orchestra. Principal conductor of the Moscow Chamber Music Theater, 1974–85.

Sabinina, Marina Dmitriyevna (1917–). Musicologist. From 1960, fellow of All-Union Research Institute for Arts History in Moscow. Author of a number of studies of Shostakovich's works.

Sádlo, Miloš (1912–). Cellist. He was a member of the Czech Trio, the Suk Trio, and the Prague Trio, among other ensembles. In 1947, he performed and recorded Shostakovich's Second Piano Trio in Prague with the composer and David Oistrakh.

Sakharov, Andrey Dmitriyevich (1921–1989). Physicist. Worked in the Soviet nuclear weapons program until 1968; in the 1970s, he became an outspoken human rights advocate. Winner of the Nobel Peace Prize in 1975. Exiled to Gorky in 1980, he was allowed to return to Moscow in 1987.

Samosud, Samuíl Abramovich (1884–1964). Conductor. Artistic director of Leningrad's Malïy Opera Theater, 1918–36; he conducted the premieres there of both of Shostakovich's operas. Principal conductor of Moscow's Bolshoy Theater, 1936–43, and of the Stanislavsky-Nemirovich-Danchenko Musical Theater, 1943–50. Also conducted the premiere performances of Shostakovich's Seventh Symphony.

Saradzhev, Konstantin Solomonovich (1877–1954). Conductor, violinist. Studied before 1917 in Moscow, Prague, and Leipzig. Taught at the Moscow Conservatory, 1922–35, and at the Yerevan Conservatory from 1936.

Sayanov, Vissarion Mikhailovich (1903–1959). Writer. An author of civic poems and novels, he won a Stalin Prize in 1949.

Schillinger, Joseph [Moiseyevich] (1895–1943). Composer, theorist. Studied at the St. Petersburg Conservatory, 1914–18, and was active in Leningrad's musical life in the 1920s. In 1928, he emigrated to the United States, where he taught in New York colleges and privately. Noted for his "system" of music theory employed by composers such as George Gershwin.

Schnittke, Alfred Garriyevich (1934–1998). Composer. He studied at the Moscow Conservatory and came to prominence in the 1960s as one of the leading figures of the post-Stalin avant-garde. Though not one of his students, he is widely regarded as the heir to Shostakovich's musical and cultural mantle.

Serebryakov, Pavel Alexeyevich (1909–1977). Pianist and administrator. Studied under Nikolayev at the Leningrad Conservatory; served as director of that institution, 1938–51 and 1961–77.

Serebryakova, Galina Iosifovna (1905–1980). Writer. Published books on Karl Marx and Friedrich Engels. An acquaintance of Shostakovich's youth, they renewed their association after her release from the Gulag in the 1950s.

Serov, Eduard Afanasyevich (1937–). Conductor. From 1975, conductor of Leningrad's Orchestra of Ancient and Contemporary Music; from 1985, conductor of the Orchestra of the Leningrad Philharmonic.

Shaginyan, Marietta Sergeyevna (1888–1982). Poetess, writer. Already a well-established author, in 1940 she conceived an active interest in the music and personality of Shostakovich; corresponded with him and published appreciations of his music.

Shapiro, Mikhaíl Grigoryevich (1908–1971). Film director, scenarist. Worked at Lenfilm from 1928; directed the film version of *Katerina Izmailova* in 1966.

Shaporin, Yuriy Alexandrovich (1887–1966). Composer. In the 1920s, worked extensively as composer for the dramatic theater in Leningrad; was vice-chairman of the Leningrad branch of the Union of Composers, 1932–36. He subsequently moved to Moscow and taught at the Moscow Conservatory, 1939–66. From 1952 until his death, he was a secretary of the Union of Soviet Composers.

Shchedrin, Rodion Konstantinovich (1932–). Composer, pianist, music administrator. A student of Fliyer and Shaporin, he established a close relationship with Moscow's Bolshoy Theater, which produced his operas and ballets.

In 1973, he succeeded Sviridov as chairman of the RSFSR Union of Composers.

Shcherbachov, Vladimir Vladimirovich (1889–1952). Composer. A pupil of Steinberg and Lyadov, he became an influential teacher at the Leningrad Conservatory, where Bogdanov-Berezovsky, Chulaki, Mravinsky, and Popov numbered among his students. Also served in various administrative capacities, including as chairman of the Leningrad branch of the Union of Composers, 1935–37 and 1944–48.

Shebalin, Vissarion Yakovlevich (1902–1963). Composer, pedagogue, administrator. Studied under Myaskovsky at the Moscow Conservatory, where he taught from 1928 (1942–48, its director). His students included Denisov, Gubaidulina, Karetnikov, and Khrennikov. He was a lifelong friend of Shostakovich.

Shenderovich, Yevgeniy Mikhailovich (1918–). Accompanist. Noted for accompanying singers, including Yevgeniy Nesterenko. Formerly a professor at the Leningrad and Moscow Conservatories; in 1991, he emigrated to Israel.

Shepilov, Dmitriy Trofimovich (1905–1995). Party and state official. Served as deputy head, 1947–48, and head, 1948–50, of the Central Committee Propaganda and Agitation Department; 1952–56, editor-in-chief of *Pravda*; 1952–57, member of the Central Committee of the CPSU, from which he was expelled in June 1957 for forming an "anti-Party" group. Although he lampooned him in *Antiformalist Rayok*, Shostakovich sustained cordial relations with him through at least 1970.

Shirinsky, Sergey Petrovich (1903–1974). Cellist. The founding cellist and member of the Beethoven Quartet until his death; Shostakovich dedicated his Fourteenth Quartet to him.

Shirinsky, Vasiliy Petrovich (1901–1965). Violinist, conductor, composer. Brother of Sergey. The founding second violinist and member of the Beethoven Quartet until his death; Shostakovich dedicated his Eleventh Quartet to his memory.

Sholokov, Mikhaíl Alexandrovich (1905–1984). Writer, public figure. His four-part novel about Don Cossacks at the time of the Civil War, *The Quiet Don*, and the two-part *Virgin Soil Upturned* became benchmarks of Socialist Realism. A member of the Organizing Committee of the Union of Soviet Writers from 1933. From 1961, he was a member of the Central Committee. Highly decorated in the USSR, he was awarded the Nobel Prize for Literature in 1965.

Shostakovich, Maxim Dmitriyevich (1938–). Conductor, pianist. Son of the composer. He studied with Fliyer (piano), Gauk and Rozhdestvensky (conducting) at the Moscow Conservatory. Served as assistant conductor of the Moscow Philharmonic Orchestra and the USSR State Symphony Orchestra in the 1960s. Principal conductor of the Orchestra of All-Union Radio and TV, 1971–81. With his son, Dmitriy, he defected while on tour with his orchestra in Germany in 1981.

Shtokolov, Boris Timofeyevich (1930–). Bass. From 1930, soloist at the Kirov Theater in Leningrad.

Shvarts, Iosif Zakharovich (1899–). Pianist. A fellow student of Nikolayev, to whom Shostakovich dedicated his *Three Fantastic Dances*, op. 5. He was also a competitor at the Chopin Competition in Warsaw in 1927.

Siloti, Alexander Ilyich (1863–1945). Pianist, conductor. Studied at the Moscow

Conservatory under Chaikovsky and N. Rubinstein and later with Liszt in Weimar. In 1903 began conducting his own orchestra in St. Petersburg; he emigrated in 1919, eventually settling in New York.

Simeonov, Konstantin Arsenyevich (1910–1987). Conductor. Studied under Ilya Musin and Gauk. Active as a symphonic conductor, 1930–60. Principal conductor of the Ukrainian Theater of Opera and Ballet, 1961–66 and 1975–77; of the Kirov Theater in Leningrad, 1967–75.

Smirnov, Viktor Fyodorovich. Stage director, librettist. At the time of his collaboration as librettist on *The Bolt*, he was director of the second company of the Moscow Art Theater.

Smolich, Nikolai Vasilyevich (1888–1968). Opera director. From 1924, artistic director of the Maliy Opera Theater in Leningrad; directed the first productions of Shostakovich's operas *The Nose* and *Lady Macbeth of the Mtsensk District* there. Later directed at the Ukrainian Theater of Opera and Ballet (1938–47) and the Bolshoy Theater in Moscow (1947–48).

Sofronitsky, Vladimir Vladimirovich (1901–1961). Pianist. Studied under Nikolayev at the Petrograd Conservatory. Enjoyed a distinguished concert career. Professor at the Leningrad Conservatory, from 1936; at the Moscow Conservatory, from 1942.

Sokolov, Nikolai Alexandrovich (1859–1922). Composer, theorist. Studied with Nikolai Rimsky-Korsakov and became a member of the Belyayev Circle. From 1896, he taught at the St. Petersburg Conservatory.

Sokolovsky, Mikhail Vladimirovich (1901–1941). Director. In 1925, he inaugurated in Leningrad the Theater of Working Youth (TRAM), a proletarian theatrical movement "by, of, and for" young workers that swept across the country before fading in influence in the early 1930s. Shostakovich composed incidental music for three TRAM productions.

Sollertinsky, Ivan Ivanovich (1902–1944). Historian and critic of music, theater, dance, literature. An extraordinary polymath and influential arbiter in Leningrad's cultural sphere, from 1927 until his death he was Shostakovich's inseparable friend and closest confidant.

Solzhenitsyn, Aleksandr Isayevich (1918–). Writer. The publication of his memoir of the Stalinist camps, *One Day in the Life of Ivan Denisovich*, in November 1962, was a milestone in the nation's confrontation with the grim reality of Stalin's terror. A camp survivor himself and a principled nonconformist, he came under persistent attack. In 1969, he was expelled from the Union of Soviet Writers; on the announcement in 1970 of his receipt of the Nobel Prize, the criticism redoubled. In 1974, after *The Gulag Archipelago* was published in Paris, he was stripped of his Soviet citizenship and deported.

Stanislavsky, Konstantin Sergeyevich (1863–1938). Actor, director, producer. Founder of the Moscow Art Theater in 1898; he developed a signature acting "method."

Starokadomsky, Mikhail Leonidovich (1901–1954). Composer, organist. As a member of Kvadri's clique at the Moscow Conservatory, where he studied composition with Myaskovsky, he socialized with the young Shostakovich.

Stasevich, Abram Lvovich (1907–1971). Conductor, composer. He conducted, inter alia, the All-Union Radio Orchestra in Moscow, 1944–52, and toured extensively around the Soviet Union. He compiled an oratorio from Prokofiev's music for Eisenstein's film *Ivan the Terrible*.

Steinberg (Shteynberg), Maximilian Oseyevich (1883–1946). Composer, pedagogue. A student, and son-in-law, of Nikolai Rimsky-Korsakov, from 1908 he perpetuated the latter's traditions at the St. Petersburg-Petrograd-Leningrad Conservatory, where Shaporin, Shcherbachov, and Shostakovich numbered among his students.

Stiedry, Fritz (1883–1968). Conductor. He led the Vienna Volksoper, 1923–25, and the Berlin Municipal Opera, 1929–33. From 1933 to 1937, he conducted the Leningrad Philharmonic Orchestra, where he conducted the premiere of Shostakovich's First Piano Concerto. He emigrated to the United States in 1938.

Stolyarov, Grigoriy Arnoldovich (1892–1963). Conductor. Conducted at the Nemirovich-Danchenko Musical Theater, 1930–38, where he presented the Moscow premiere of *Katerina Izmailova*; from 1954, at the Moscow Theater of Operetta, where he conducted *Moscow, Cheryomushki*.

Stravinsky, Igor Fyodorovich (1882–1971). Composer. Although he chose not to repatriate after the revolutions of 1917, his works were disseminated and performed in Soviet Russia through the early 1930s and influenced Shostakovich. Thereafter he became a prime target for vilification by the Soviets, making his well-publicized ceremonial visit to Moscow and Leningrad in 1962 all the more momentous.

Stroyeva, Vera Pavlovna (1903–). Film director. The filming of operas was a notable feature of her career; she directed Musorgsky's *Boris Godunov* (1955) and, having recruited Shostakovich to complete and orchestrate it, *Khovanshchina* (1959).

Supinskaya, Irina Antonovna (1934–). Literary editor. In 1962, she became Shostakovich's third wife.

Sveshnikov, Alexander Vasilyevich (1890–1980). Choral conductor. Founding director of the State Choir of Russian Song, in 1955 renamed the State Academic Russian Choir of the USSR. Also founder of the Moscow Choral School and professor at the Moscow Conservatory.

Svetlanov, Yevgeniy Fyodorovich (1928–). Conductor, composer, pianist. Studied under Gauk and Heinrich Neuhaus. Conducted at the Bolshoy Theater in Moscow 1955–75; he was principal conductor there, 1963–65. In 1965, he became the principal conductor and artistic director of the USSR State Symphony Orchestra. From 1974, he served as secretary of the USSR Union of Composers.

Sviridov, Georgiy (Yuriy) Vasilyevich (1915–1998). Composer, pianist. In 1941, he graduated from Shostakovich's class at the Leningrad Conservatory. A secretary of the USSR Union of Composers, 1962–74 and after 1986; he succeeded his teacher as first secretary of the RSFSR Union of Composers, 1968–73.

Tishchenko, Boris Ivanovich (1939–). Composer, pianist. Studied with Yevlakhov and, as a graduate student, with Shostakovich at the Leningrad Conservatory, where he subsequently taught. Remained personally close to Shostakovich and corresponded with him.

Tolstoy, Alexey Nikolayevich (1882/83–1945). Writer. Lived in emigration,

1918–23; received permission to return to Soviet Russia in 1923. Member of the Organizing Committee of the Union of Soviet Writers from 1933; from 1936, its chairman. Deputy to the USSR Supreme Soviet from 1937.

Trauberg, Leonid Zakharovich (1902–1990). Film director. With Kozintsev and Yutkevich, was a founder of FEKS in Petrograd. With Kozintsev, codirected six films with music by Shostakovich, from *New Babylon* (1929) through *Simple People* (1945).

Tsekhanovsky, Mikhaíl Mikhailovich (1889–1965). Film director, animator. A pioneer of the Soviet animated film, he collaborated with Shostakovich on the unfinished *Tale of the Priest and His Worker, Blockhead,* and *The Silly Little Mouse.*

Tsïganov, Dmitriy Mikhailovich (1903–1992). Violinist. The founding first violinist and member of the Beethoven Quartet until 1977; Shostakovich dedicated his Twelfth Quartet to him.

Tsvetayeva, Marina Ivanovna (1892–1941). Poet. Lacking sympathy for Soviet rule, she left Russia in 1922, eventually settling in Paris. In 1939, she followed her husband and daughter back to the USSR, where she worked on poetic translations. Committed suicide in evacuation during World War II.

Tukhachevsky, Mikhaíl Nikolayevich (1893–1937). Military leader. After distinguished service in the Civil War, became a leader in military reforms and the modernization of the Soviet Army. Made a marshal of the Soviet Union in 1935. Perished in a purge of the Red Army. From 1925, one of Shostakovich's patrons.

Ulanova, Galina Sergeyevna (1910–1998). Ballerina. On completion of her studies at the Leningrad Choreographic Tekhnikum in 1928, she joined the company of the State Academic Theater of Opera and Ballet (in 1935 renamed the Kirov Theater) where she created the role of the Komsomol Girl in Shostakovich's *The Golden Age,* among others. From 1944, she danced at the Bolshoy Theater.

Uspensky, Vladislav Alexandrovich (1937–). Composer. Studied under Boris Arapov and Shostakovich at the Leningrad Conservatory. From 1972, vice-chairman of the Leningrad branch of the Union of Composers.

Ustvolskaya, Galina Ivanovna (1919–). Composer. Shostakovich's student at the Leningrad Conservatory, they sustained an intimate personal relationship although she turned down his marriage proposal after the death of his first wife.

Utyosov, Leonid Osipovich (1895–1982). Singer, band leader, stage and film actor. A native of Odessa and one of the most versatile and popular entertainers and recording artists of the Soviet era, in 1929 he founded one of the first Soviet jazz bands. In later years, he led the RSFSR Variety Orchestra.

Vainberg, Moisey (Mieczyslaw) Samuílovich (1919–1996). Composer, pianist. Studied in his native Poland before escaping to the USSR in 1939, settling in Moscow in 1943. Became one of Shostakovich's most valued musical colleagues. Married to the daughter of Solomon Mikhoels, in February 1953 he was arrested in conjunction with the Doctors' Plot; released in April 1953 after the death of Stalin.

Vakman, Sofya Borisovna (1911–). Accompanist. Concertized widely with instrumentalists and singers; taught at the Leningrad Conservatory from 1946.

Varzar, Nina Vasilyevna (1909–1954). Shostakovich's first wife and the mother of his two children. A student in the sciences at Leningrad University when she met the composer in 1927, they were married in 1932. After World War II, she worked in the laboratory of Alikhanyan, researching cosmic radiation. She died suddenly while on assignment in Armenia.

Vasilyev, Georgiy Nikolayevich (1899–1946) and Sergey Dmitriyevich (1900–1959). Film directors. A duo with the same last name who collaborated under the pseudonym "Vasilyev brothers," they were both students of Eisenstein. Their most famous film was *Chapayev* (1934).

Vavilina, Alexandra Mikhailovna (1928–). Flutist. A member of the Leningrad Philharmonic Orchestra, she became Yevgeniy Mravinsky's third wife.

Vergelis, Aron Alterovich (1918–). Poet, journalist, editor. Founder, in 1961, and editor-in-chief of *Sovetish heymland*, the only Soviet journal in Yiddish.

Veysberg, Yuliya Lazarevna (1879–1942). Composer. Studied under Nikolai Rimsky-Korsakov and Glazunov at the St. Petersburg Conservatory. In 1914, she married Rimsky-Korsakov's eldest son, Andrey, and in the 1920s she was active in the musical organizations of Petrograd-Leningrad.

Vilyams, Pyotr Vladimirovich (1902–1947). Artist, set designer. Principal designer for the Bolshoy Theater, 1941–47. He and his wife, Anna, befriended Shostakovich and his wife in Kuybïshev during the war and the families remained close afterward. Shostakovich dedicated his Fourth Quartet to his memory.

Vïrlan, Lidiya Alexandrovna (1900–1965). Mezzo-soprano. An accomplished recitalist based in Leningrad who concertized from 1925 to 1957 across the Soviet Union; before 1930 Shostakovich frequently performed as her accompanist.

Vishnevskaya, Galina Pavlovna (1926–). Soprano. She sang operetta before joining the Bolshoy Theater in Moscow in 1952. She left Russia with her husband, Mstislav Rostropovich, for political reasons in 1974.

Vladimirov, Yevgeniy Nikolayevich. Bass. The first performer of Shostakovich's Fourteenth Symphony, he sang with the Red Banner Ensemble of the Soviet Army while still a student; from 1966, he was a soloist of Central TV and All-Union Radio.

Volïnsky, Akim Lvovich [pseud. for Khaim Leybovich Flekser] (1861–1926). Art historian, ballet critic. From 1911, Russia's most influential ballet critic; after 1917 he founded and directed a school of Russian ballet in Petrograd.

Voroshilov, Kliment Yefremovich (1881–1969). Military, Party, and state figure. Veteran of the 1905 and 1917 revolutions. People's Commissar of naval and military affairs and of defense, 1925–40. Named marshal of the Soviet Union in 1935. During World War II, member of the State Defense Committee. Member of the Central Committee, 1921–61; of the Politburo, 1926–60.

Vovsi-Mikhoels, Nataliya Solomonovna (1921–). Linguist. A daughter of Solomon Mikhoels, she married composer Moisey Vainberg, through whom she had contact with Shostakovich in the late 1940s and early 1950s.

Voznesensky, Andrey Andreyevich (1933–). Poet. Alongside Yevtushenko, a leading figure of the post-Stalin generation in the late 1950s and early 1960s.

Yarustovsky, Boris Mikhailovich (1911–1978). Musicologist, cultural administrator. Headed the cultural division of the Central Committee, 1946–58. Later served on various boards of UNESCO.

Yavorsky, Boleslav Leopoldovich (1877–1942). Music theorist, administrator, pedagogue. Noted as the architect of the theory of modal rhythm, he was an influential figure in the musical life of Kiev and Moscow and a vigorous patron of the young Shostakovich. Chaired the music section of Narkompros, 1922–30.

Yeltsïn, Sergey Vitalyevich (1897–1970). Conductor. From 1928, conductor of the Leningrad Academic Theater of Opera and Ballet; principal conductor there, 1953–56. He conducted the premieres of Shostakovich's orchestrations of Musorgsky's *Boris Godunov* and *Khovanshchina*.

Yevlakhov, Orest Alexandrovich (1912–1973). Composer. In 1941, graduated from Shostakovich's class at the Leningrad Conservatory, where he subsequently taught.

Yevtushenko, Yevgeniy Alexandrovich (1933–). Poet, writer, playwright. A leading, if highly controversial, figure of the post-Stalin generation who took advantage of the relative liberalization of the late 1950s and early 1960s to push the envelope of the permissible and explore sensitive issues like civic morality. Unlike many of his friends, Shostakovich was genuinely and powerfully moved by Yevtushenko's verses.

Yezhov, Nikolai Ivanovich (1895–1940). Party and state figure. Appointed People's Commissar of Internal Affairs (NKVD) in September 1936, his name became synonymous with the excesses of Stalin's terror. He was replaced by Beria in 1938, arrested in 1939, and shot a year later.

Yudina, Mariya Veniaminovna (1899–1970). Pianist. Studied under Nikolayev at the Petrograd Conservatory; taught there, and later at the Tbilisi and Moscow Conservatories. Enjoyed a successful solo career in Russia, actively propagandizing the cause of new music. Her religiosity, firm principles, and eccentric behavior led to frequent clashes with Soviet officialdom.

Yutkevich, Sergey Iosifovich (1904–1985). Film director. With Kozintsev and Trauberg, he was a founder of FEKS. He roomed with the Shostakovich family in Leningrad, 1929–34, during which period the composer provided music to the films *Golden Mountains* (1931) and *Counterplan* (1932). Their last collaboration was on *The Man with a Gun* (1938).

Zabavnikov, Nikolai Nikolayevich (1937–). Violinist. Studied with Tsïganov at the Moscow Conservatory; after the death of Vasiliy Shirinsky in 1965, he became the second violinist of the Beethoven Quartet.

Zagursky, Boris Ivanovich (1901–1968). Music administrator. Director of the Leningrad Conservatory, 1936–38; during his tenure he appointed Shostakovich and Sollertinsky to the faculty. Subsequently he headed the Leningrad Committee for Artistic Affairs. In 1951, he was named director of the Leningrad's Malïy Theater of Opera and Ballet.

Zakharov, Vladimir Grigoryevich (1901–1956). Composer. From 1932 until his death, he was artistic director of the Pyatnitsky Folk Chorus. A writer of mass songs and a folk song arranger, he was outspoken in his attacks on more "serious" composers, including Shostakovich, in 1948.

Zamyatin, Yevgeniy Ivanovich (1884–1937). Writer. The publication of his anti-utopian novel *We* in the United States in 1924 and his aversion to artistic authority led to his persecution and the banning of his works. In 1931, Stalin granted him permission to leave the Soviet Union.

Zaslavsky, David Iosifovich (1880–1965). Journalist, literary critic. In 1936, he was on the staff of the newspaper *Pravda*; he is widely believed to have been the author of "Muddle Instead of Music," the unsigned editorial attacking Shostakovich's *Lady Macbeth of the Mtsensk District*, published there on 28 January 1936.

Zhdanov, Andrey Andreyevich (1896–1948). Party and state figure. In 1934, he succeeded Kirov as first secretary in Leningrad. He joined the Central Committee the same year; from 1944, he assumed responsibility for ideology. His name became associated with a series of purges in the arts from 1946 to 1948.

Zhilyayev, Nikolai Sergeyevich (1881–1938). Music theorist, composer, editor. Student of Taneyev and Ippolitov-Ivanov and respected pedagogue at the Moscow Conservatory, he was an intimate of Mikhail Tukhachevsky; after the latter's execution, he was himself arrested on charges of monarchism, terrorism, and spying and executed on 20 January 1938.

Zhitomirsky, Daniel Vladimirovich (1906–1992). Musicologist. Initially a RAPM apologist, he outlived this captivation to pursue more conventional avenues of research. He left memoirs of his association with Shostakovich.

Zinovyev, Grigoriy Yevseyevich [pseud. for Radomïlsky] (1883–1936). Party and state figure. United with Kamenyev and Stalin to prevent Trotsky from succeeding Lenin, he soon became one of Stalin's victims. He was tried and sentenced to labor camp in 1935 together with Kamenyev; they were both retried and executed in August 1936 in the first of the public "show" trials.

Zoshchenko, Mikhail Mikhailovich (1894–1958). Writer. After an eclectic early career, he joined the "Serapion Brothers" literary group in 1921; his satirical stories achieved wide exposure during the 1920s. Along with Akhmatova, he was subjected to official criticism in 1946 and expelled from the Writers' Union (readmitted in 1953). During the 1930s, he was a member of Shostakovich's poker circle.

Select Bibliography

Items of chiefly analytical interest have been omitted.

Abraham, Gerald. *Eight Soviet Composers*. London, 1943; reprint ed. 1976.

Abramov, Aleksandr. "Maksim Shostakovich o svoyom ottse" [Maxim Shostakovich on his father]. *Vremya i mï* 69 (1982): 172–84.

———. "Moshch' i infantil'nost' geniya: k vïkhodu v svet memuarov Dmitriya Shostakovicha" [The might and infantility of genius: on the publication of Shostakovich's memoirs]. *Vremya i mï* 58 (1981): 155–71.

———. "Variatsii na temu; k opublikovaniyu vospominaniy Dmitriya Shosta-kovicha 'Svidetel'stvo'" [Variations on a theme: on the publication of Shosta-kovich's reminiscences, *Testimony*]. *Grani* 118 (1980): 158–81

Akopyan [Hakobian], Levon. *Music of the Soviet Age 1917–1987*. Stockholm, 1998.

———. "Zapadnïye avtorï o Shostakoviche: obzor i kommentariy" [Western authors about Shostakovich: survey and commentary]. In *Shostakovichu posvyashcha-yetsya: sbornik statey k 90-letiyu kompozitora (1906–1996)*, comp. E. Dolinskaya, 17–26. Moscow, 1997.

Aleksandr Vasil'yevich Gauk: memuarï, izbrannïye stat'i, vospominaniya sovremennikov [Alexander Gauk: memoirs, selected articles, reminiscences of contemporaries]. Comps. L. P. Gauk, R. V. Glezer, and Ya. I. Mil'shteyn. Moscow, 1975.

Aleksandrov, Andrey. "Yuvenalov bich: o neizvestnom sochinenii D. Shostakovicha" [Juvenalian lash: an unknown work by Shostakovich]. *Sovetskaya kul'tura* (28 January 1989): 4. Eng. trans. in *Music in the USSR* (Jan/Mar 1990): 42–43.

Apetyan, Zarui. *Gavriil Popov: iz literaturnogo naslediya* [Gavriil Popov's literary leg-acy]. Leningrad, 1986.

Aranovskiy, Mark. "Svidetel'stvo" [Testimony]. *Muzïkal'naya akademiya* 4 (1997): 130–32.

———. "Veka svyazuyushchaya nit'" (o syuite dlya basa i fortepiano 'Sonetï Mikelandzhelo Buonarroti' D. Shostakovicha") [The connecting thread of the age (on Shostakovich's Suite for bass and piano "Sonnets of Michelangelo Buonarroti"). In *Novaya zhizn': traditsii v sovetskoy muzïke: stat'i, interv'yu*, 207–72. Moscow, 1989.

Asaf'yev, Boris. "O tvorchestve D. Shostakovicha i ego opere 'Ledi Makbet Mtsenskogo uyezda'" [On Shostakovich's works and his opera *Lady Macbeth*]. In *Ledi Makbet Mtsenskogo uyezda*, 27–31. Leningrad, 1934. Reprinted in *D. Shosta-kovich: stat'i i materialï*, comp. G. Shneerson, 150–59. Moscow, 1976.

———. "Redkiy talant" [A rare talent]. *Sovetskaya muzïka* 1 (1959): 19–23.

———. "Volnuyushchiye voprosï" [Disturbing questions]. *Sovetskaya muzïka* 5 (1936): 24–27. Reprinted in *Izbrannïye trudï*, 5, ed. T. N. Livanova and others, 116–19. Moscow, 1957.

————. "Vos'maya simfoniya Shostakovicha" [Shostakovich's Eighth Symphony]. In *Moskovskaya filarmoniya*. Moscow, 1945. Reprinted in *Izbrannïye trudï*, 5, ed. T. N. Livanova and others, 132–35. Moscow, 1957.

Atovm'yan, Levon. "Iz vospominaniy" [Reminiscences]. *Muzïkal'naya akademiya* 4 (1997): 67–77.

Avrutin, Lilia. "Shostakovich on Screen: Film as Metatext and Myth." *Russian Review* 56, no. 3 (1997): 402–24.

"Baletnaya fal'sh'" [Balletic falsity], *Pravda*, 6 February 1936, 3; and *Sovetskaya muzïka* 2 (1936): 6–8

Barry, Malcolm. "Ideology and Form: Shostakovich East and West." In *Music and the Politics of Culture*, ed. C. Norris, 172–86. New York, 1989.

————. "The Significance of Shostakovich." *Composer* (Winter 1975–76): 11–14; (Spring 1976): 19–22.

Barsova, Inna. "*The Limpid Stream* is the third ballet by Dmitri Shostakovich." *The Limpid Stream*, op. 39 (piano score), 218–22. Moscow, 1997.

————. "Mezhdu 'sotsial'nïm zakazom' i 'muzïkoy bol'shikh strastey'; 1934–1937 godï v zhizni Dmitriya Shostakovicha" [Between "social demands" and "the music of grand passions": the years 1934–37 in the life of Shostakovich]. In *D. D. Shostakovich: sbornik statey k 90-letiyu so dnya rozhdeniya*, comp. L. Kovnatskaya, 121–40. St. Petersburg, 1996.

————. "*Svetlïy ruchey*: k istorii sozdaniya" [*The Limpid Stream*: toward a history of its creation]. *Muzïkal'naya akademiya* 4 (1997): 51–58.

Bartlett, Rosamund. "Shostakovich i Chekhov." In *D. D. Shostakovich: sbornik statey k 90-letiyu so dnya rozhdeniya*, comp. L. Kovnatskaya, 342–58. St. Petersburg, 1996.

Bayeva, Alla. "Shostakovich i sovremennaya otechestvennaya opera" [Shostakovich and contemporary native opera]. In *Shostakovichu posvyashchayetsya: sbornik statey k 90-letiyu kompozitora (1906–1996)*, comp. E. Dolinskaya, 135–42. Moscow, 1997.

Beaujean, Alfred. "'Trauer über eine verlorene Vergangenheit': Zur Romanzen-Suite op. 127 von Dmitri Schostakowitsch." *Bayerische Akademie der Schönen Künste: VI* (1992): 490–96.

Berger, Lyubov', ed. *Chertï stilya D. Shostakovicha* [Stylistic traits of D. Shostakovich]. Moscow, 1962.

————. *Odinnadtsataya simfoniya D. D. Shostakovicha* [D. D. Shostakovich's Eleventh Symphony]. Moscow, 1961.

————. "O vïrazitel'nosti muzïki Shostakovicha" [On the expressiveness of Shostakovich's music]. In *Chertï stilya D. Shostakovicha*, ed. L. G. Berger, 348–73. Moscow, 1962.

"Beseda Nelli Kravets s El'miroy Nazirovoy" [A conversation between Nelli Kravets and Elmira Nazirova]. In *D. D. Shostakovich: sbornik statey k 90-letiyu so dnya rozhdeniya*, comp. L. Kovnatskaya, 236–48. St. Petersburg, 1996.

Biesold, Maria. *Dmitrij Schostakowitsch: Klaviermusik der Neuen Sachlichkeit*. Wittmund, 1988.

Bitov, Andrey. "GULAG i memorial Shostakovicha" [The Gulag and Shostakovich's Memorial]. *Nezavisimaya gazeta*, 29 December 1990, 8. Reprinted in A. Bitov, *Mï prosnulis' v neznakomoy strane: publitsistika*, 78–86. Leningrad, 1991. Eng. trans. in *Shostakovich Reconsidered*, ed. A. B. Ho and D. Feofanov, 521–29. London, 1998.

Blokker, Roy. *The Music of Dmitri Shostakovich: The Symphonies.* London, 1979.

Bobrovskiy, Viktor. "Instrumental'nïye ansambli Shostakovicha" [Shostakovich's instrumental music]. In *D. Shostakovich: stat'i i materialï*, comp. G. Shneerson, 193–205. Moscow, 1976.

————. *Kamernïye instrumental'nïye ansambli Shostakovicha* [Shostakovich's instrumental chamber music]. Moscow, 1961.

————. "O muzïkal'nom mïshlenii Shostakovicha" [About Shostakovich's musical thinking]. In *Shostakovichu posvyashchayetsya: sbornik statey k 90-letiyu kompozitora (1906–1996)*, comp. E. Dolinskaya, 39–61. Moscow, 1997.

————. *Pesni i khorï Shostakovicha* [Shostakovich's songs and choruses]. Moscow, 1962.

————. "Posledneye sochineniye Shostakovicha" [Shostakovich's last composition]. In *Problemï muzïkal'noy nauki, vïp. 6*, 55–71. Moscow, 1985.

————. "Programmnïy simfonizm Shostakovicha" [Shostakovich's programmatic symphonic writing]. In *Muzïka i sovremennost', vïp. 3*, 32–67. Moscow, 1965.

————. "Programmnïy simfonizm Shostakovicha, stat'ya vtoraya (o trinadtsatoy simfonii)" [Shostakovich's programmatic symphonic writing, part 2 (on Symphony no. 13)]. In *Muzïka i sovremennost', vïp. 5*, 38–73. Moscow, 1967.

————. "Shostakovich v moyey zhizni. Lichnïye zametki" [Shostakovich in my life. Personal remarks]. *Sovetskaya muzïka* 9 (1991): 23–30.

Boganova, Tat'yana. *Violonchel'nïy kontsert D. Shostakovicha* [Shostakovich's cello concerto]. Moscow, 1960.

Bogdanov-Berezovskiy, Valerian. *Dorogi iskusstva: kniga pervaya (1903–1945)* [The Journeys of Art, book 1]. Leningrad, 1971.

————. "Operï Shostakovicha" [The operas of Shostakovich]. In *Sovetskaya opera*, 111–43. Leningrad-Moscow, 1940.

————. "Otrochestvo i yunost'" [Adolescence and youth]. *Sovetskaya muzïka* 9 (1966): 26–37. Reprinted in *D. Shostakovich: stat'i i materialï*, comp. G. Shneerson, 132–49. Moscow, 1976.

————. *Vstrechi* [Encounters]. Moscow, 1967.

Bogdanova, Alla. *Muzïka i vlast' (poststalinskiy period)* [Music and power (the post-Stalin period)]. Moscow, 1995.

————. *Operï i baletï Shostakovicha* [Shostakovich's operas and ballets]. Moscow, 1979.

————. "Ranniye proizvedeniya Shostakovicha dlya dramaticheskogo teatra" [Shostakovich's early works for the dramatic theater]. In *Iz proshlogo sovetskoy muzïkal'noy kul'turï*, ed. T. Livanova, 7–34. Moscow, 1975.

————. "Schostakowitschs Musikschaffen für die Bühne." In *Dmitri Schostakowitsch 1984/85: Wissenschaftliche Beiträge. Dokumente. Interpretationen. Programme*, 176–78. Duisburg, 1984.

————. "Shostakovich—znakomïy i neznakomïy" [Shostakovich—familiar and unfamiliar]. *Muzïkal'naya zhizn'* 11 (1979): 8–9.

————. "Sochineniya D. Shostakovicha konservatorskikh let (1919–1925)"

[Shostakovich's compositions during his conservatory years]. In *Iz istorii russkoy i sovetskoy muzïki*, ed. A. Kandinsky, 64–93. Moscow, 1971.

Bolt. *Balet v 3 deystviyakh* [*The Bolt*: A ballet in three acts]. Leningrad, 1931. Article by Sollertinsky and libretto.

Bonfel'd, Moris. "Uroki velikogo mastera" [Lessons of a great master]. *Muzïkal'naya akademiya* 4 (1997): 63–67.

Braun, Joachim. "The Double Meaning of Jewish Elements in Dimitri Shostakovich's Music." *Musical Quarterly* 71 (1985): 68–80. Reprinted in *La musique et le rite sacré et profane*, ed. M. Honegger and P. Prévost, 737–57. Strasbourg, 1986.

———. "Das Jüdische im Werk von Dmitri Schostakowitsch." In *Studien zur Musik des XX. Jahrhunderts in Ost und Ostmitteleuropa*, ed. D. Gojowy, 103–25. Berlin, 1990.

———. *Shostakovich's Jewish Songs: From Jewish Folk Poetry, op. 79*. Tel-Aviv, 1989. Introductory essay with original Yiddish text underlay.

———. "Shostakovich's Song Cycle *From Jewish Folk Poetry*: Aspects of Style and Meaning." In *Russian and Soviet Music: Essays for Boris Schwarz*, ed. M. H. Brown, 259–86. Ann Arbor, Mich., 1984.

Bretanitskaya, Alla. *"Nos" D. D. Shostakovicha* [D. D. Shostakovich's *The Nose*]. Moscow, 1983.

———. "Vtoroye rozhdeniye 'Nosa'" [The second birth of *The Nose*]. In *Muzïka Rossii: muzïkal'noye tvorchestvo i muzïkal'naya zhizn' respublik Rossiyskoy Federatsii, 1973–1974*, 310–23. Moscow, 1976.

Breuer, J., ed. *In Memoriam Dmitrij Sosztakovics*. Budapest, 1976.

Brezhneva, Irina. "Formirovaniye vokal'nogo stilya Shostakovicha na primere rannikh sochineniy ('Basni Krïlova' i shest' romansov yaponskikh poetov)" [The formation of Shostakovich's vocal style on the example of early works ("Two Fables of Krïlov" and Six Romances on Texts of Japanese Poets)]. In *Problemï stilevogo obnovleniya v russkoy klassicheskoy i sovetskoy muzïke*, ed. A. I. Kandinsky, 53–70. Moscow, 1983.

Brockhaus, Heinz Alfred. *Dmitri Schostakowitsch*. Leipzig, 1962; abridged 1963.

Brodjanskaja, Nina. "Schostakowitschs Filmmusiken." In *Dmitri Schostakowitsch 1984/85: Wissenschaftliche Beiträge. Dokumente. Interpretationen. Programme*, 186–88. Duisburg, 1984.

Brown, Malcolm Hamrick. "The Soviet Russian Concepts of 'Intonazia' and 'Musical Imagery.'" *Musical Quarterly* 60 (1974): 557–67.

Brown, Royal S. "An Interview with Shostakovich." *High Fidelity* 23 (October 1973): 86–89.

———. "The Three Faces of Lady Macbeth." In *Russian and Soviet Music: Essays for Boris Schwarz*, ed. M. H. Brown, 245–52. Ann Arbor, Mich., 1984.

Bubennikova, Larisa. "K probleme khudozhestvennogo vzaimodeystviya muzïkal'nogo i dramaticheskogo teatrov" [On the problem of the artistic interaction of musical and dramatic theaters]. In *Problemï muzïkal'noy nauki, vïp. 3*, 38–63. Moscow, 1975.

———. "Meyerkhol'd i Shostakovich: iz istorii sozdaniya operï 'Nos'" [Meyerhold and Shostakovich: from the history of the creation of the opera *The Nose*]. *Sovetskaya muzïka* 3 (1973): 43–48.

Bush, Alan. "Dmitry Dmitrievich Shostakovich." In *Shostakovich: The Man and His Music*, ed. C. Norris, 219–24. London, 1982.

Buske, Peter. *Dmitri Schostakowitsch*. Berlin, 1975.

Chominski, J. M. "24 Preludia i Fugi op. 87 D. Szostakowicza." In *Polsko-rosyjskie miscellanea muzyczne*, ed. Z. Lissa, 287–96. Kraków, 1967.

"Chostakovitch, Lady Macbeth de Mzensk, Le Nez: Livrets, analyses, discographies." *L'Avant-Scène Opéra* 141 (1991).

"Chudesnïy u nas slushatel'; Dmitriy Shostakovich otvechayet na voprosï" [We have a marvelous audience; Shostakovich answers questions]. *Muzïkal'naya zhizn'* 17 (1966): 7

Chulaki, Mikhaíl. "Segodnya rasskazhu o Shostakoviche" [Today I will tell you about Shostakovich]. *Zvezda* 7 (1987): 189–94.

Danilevich, Lev. "Chetïrnadtsataya" [Fourteenth Symphony], *Sovetskaya muzïka* 1 (1970): 14–20

———. *D. Shostakovich*. Moscow, 1958.

———. *Dmitriy Shostakovich: zhizn' i tvorchestvo* [Dmitry Shostakovich: life and works]. Moscow, 1980.

———. *Nash sovremennik: tvorchestvo Shostakovicha* [Our contemporary: the work of Shostakovich]. Moscow, 1965.

Danuser, Hermann. "Dmitri Schostakowitschs musikalisch-politisches Revolutionverständnis (1926–1927); Zur Ersten Klaviersonate und zur Zweiten Sinfonie." *Melos/Neue Zeitschrift* 4, no. 1 (1978): 3–11.

"D. D. Shostakovich o svoyom tvorchestve" [Shostakovich about his creative work]. *Sovetskoye iskusstvo* (29 March 1935): 3.

Dearling, Robert. "The First Twelve Symphonies: Portrait of the Artist as Citizen-Composer." In *Shostakovich: The Man and His Music*, ed. C. Norris, 47–79. London, 1982.

Del'son, Viktor. *Fortepiannoye tvorchestvo Shostakovicha* [Shostakovich's piano works]. Moscow, 1971.

———. "Molodoy Shostakovich (o pianiste 20ïkh i 30ïkh g.)" [The young Shostakovich (about the pianist of the 1920s and 1930s)]. In *Voprosï muzïkal'no-ispolnitel'skogo iskusstva*, vïp. 5, 193–228. Moscow, 1969.

Demosfenowa, G. L. "Der Musiker Schostakowitsch." In *Dmitri Schostakowitsch und seine Zeit: Kunst und Kultur*, ed. K.-E. Vester, 31–38. Duisburg, 1984.

Denisov, Edison. "Vstrechi s Shostakovichem" [Meetings with Shostakovich]. *Muzïkal'naya akademiya* 3 (1994): 90–92.

Devlin, James. *Shostakovich*. Sevenoaks, England, 1983.

Dimitrin, Yuriy. "Muzïkal'naya istoriya" [Musical history]. In *D. D. Shostakovich: sbornik statey k 90-letiyu so dnya rozhdeniya*, comp. L. Kovnatskaya, 269–75. St. Petersburg, 1996.

———. *"Nam ne dano predugadat' ..."*: *razmïshleniya o libretto operï D. Shostakovicha "Ledi Makbet Mtsenskogo uyezda"* [It is not given to us to predict: reflections on the libretto of *Lady Macbeth of the Mtsensk District*]. St. Petersburg, 1997.

Dmitri Schostakowitsch 1984/85: Wissenschaftliche Beiträge. Dokumente. Interpretationen. Programme. Duisburg, 1984.

Dmitriy Shostakovich "Ledi Makbet Mtsenskogo uyezda": vozrozhdeniye shedevra [*Lady Macbeth of the Mtsensk District:* rebirth of a masterpiece], ed. M. Yakubov. Moscow, 1996.

"Dmitriy Shostakovich o novïkh muzykal'nïkh proizvedeniya: kompozitorï—45-y godovshchine Oktyabrya, simfonii, oratorii, pesni molodïkh" [Shostakovich on new musical works: composers for the forty-fifth anniversary of October, symphonies, oratorios, songs of the young]. *Pravda*, 21 October 1962, 6.

Dmitry Shostakovich's Last Compositions. Moscow, ?1976.

"*Dmitriy Shostakovich rasskazïvayet o svoyey rabote*" [*Shostakovich speaks about his work*]. *Smena* 20 (1943): 15.

Dobrïkin, E. "Muzïkal'naya satira v vokal'nom tvorchestve D. Shostakovicha" [Musical satire in D. Shostakovich's vocal works]. In *Problemï muzïkal'noy nauki, vïp.* 3, 17–37. Moscow, 1975.

Dobrïnina, Ekaterina. "'Vernost', tsikl khorovïkh ballad Dmitriya Shostakovicha" ["Loyalty," Shostakovich's cycle of choral ballads]. *Muzïkal'naya zhizn'* 7 (1971): 2–3. Reprinted in *Lyubitelyam muzïki posvyashchayetsya*, 7–13. Moscow, 1980.

Dolgopolov, Mikhaíl. "Kompozitor veka" [Composer of the century]. In *Zvyozdnoye ozherel'ye*, 193–200. Moscow, 1986.

Dolinskaya, Elena. "Moya muzïka nikogda ne umirala" [My music never died]. In *Shostakovichu posvyashchayetsya: sbornik statey k 90-letiyu kompozitora (1906–1996)*, comp. E. Dolinskaya, 157–60. Moscow, 1997.

———. "Pozdniy period tvorchestva Shostakovicha: faktï i nablyudeniya" [Shostakovich's late period: facts and observations]. In *Shostakovichu posvyashchayetsya: sbornik statey k 90-letiyu kompozitora (1906–1996)*, comp. E. Dolinskaya, 27–38. Moscow, 1997.

———. comp. *Shostakovichu posvyashchayetsya: sbornik statey k 90-letiyu kompozitora (1906–1996)* [Dedicated to Shostakovich: collection of articles on the occasion of his ninetieth birthday]. Moscow, 1997.

Dolzhanskiy, Aleksandr. *24 prelyudï i fugi D. Shostakovicha.* Leningrad, 1963; 2nd ed. 1970.

———. "Iz nablyudeniy nad stilem Shostakovicha" [From observations on Shostakovich's style]. *Sovetskaya muzïka* 10 (1959): 95–102. Reprinted in *Chertï stilya D. Shostakovicha*, ed. L. G. Berger, 73–86. Moscow, 1962; and in A. Dolzhanskiy, *Izbrannïye stat'i*, 76–86. Leningrad, 1973.

———. *Kamernïye instrumental'nïye proizvedeniya D. Shostakovicha* [D. Shostakovich's instrumental chamber works]. Moscow, 1965; reprint 1971. Reprinted in A. Dolzhanskiy, *Izbrannïye stat'i*, 120–51. Leningrad, 1973.

Dorfman, Joseph. "Jüdische Elemente im Werk von Dmitri Schostakowitsch." *Neue Berlinische Musikzeitung* 2 (1995): 36–45.

Druskin, Mikhaíl. "O fortepiannom tvorchestve Shostakovicha" [On Shostakovich's piano works]. *Sovetskaya muzïka* 11 (1935): 52–59.

———. *Pervaya simfoniya Dm. Shostakovicha* [D. Shostakovich's First Symphony]. Leningrad, 1938.

———. "Schostakowitsch in den zwanziger Jahren." In *Dmitri Schostakowitsch 1984/85: Wissenschaftliche Beiträge. Dokumente. Interpretationen. Programme,*

50–56. Duisburg, 1984; also in *Dmitri Schostakowitsch und seine Zeit: Mensch und Werk*, ed. J. Fromme, 41–50. Duisburg, 1984. Expanded as "Shostakovich v 20-e godï," in M. Druskin, *Ocherki, stat'i, zametki*, 45–59. Leningrad, 1987.

Druzhinin, Fyodor. "Kvartetï Shostakovicha glazami ispolnitelya. Nekotorïye soobrazheniya i nablyudeniya pri sovmestnoy rabote s avtorom" [Shostako-vich's quartets through the eyes of a performer. Some thoughts and observations occasioned by collaborative work with the author]. In *Shostakovichu posvyashchayetsya: sbornik statey k 90-letiyu kompozitora (1906–1996)*, comp. E. Dolinskaya, 110–15. Moscow, 1997.

———. "O Dmitrii Dmitriyeviche Shostakoviche" [About Dmitriy Dmitriyevich Shostakovich]. In *Shostakovichu posvyashchayetsya: sbornik statey k 90-letiyu kompozitora (1906–1996)*, comp. E. Dolinskaya, 176–205. Moscow, 1997.

DSCH Journal (1994–).

Dubinsky, Rostislav. *Stormy Applause: Making Music in a Worker's State*. New York, 1989.

Durandina, E. "Shostakovich: portret khudozhnika na fone ukhodyashchego veka" [Portrait of an artist against the backdrop of a receding century]. In *Shostakovichu posvyashchayetsya: sbornik statey k 90-letiyu kompozitora (1906–1996)*, comp. E. Dolinskaya, 9–16. Moscow, 1997.

Eberle, Gottfried. "Im Gluckkasten; Dmitri Schostakowitsch und die russische Tradition der musikalischen Satire." *Neue Berlinische Musikzeitung* 3 (1993): 19–26.

———. "Musik und Stalinismus; Dmitri Schostakowitsch und die Entwicklung sowjetische Sinfonik." *Neue Zeitschrift für Musik* 144, no. 4 (1983): 7–10.

Egorova, Tatiana. *Soviet Film Music: An Historical Survey*. Amsterdam, 1997.

"Ein historisches Dokument: Information an das MfS über die sogenannten *Memoiren des Dmitrij Schostakowitsch*." In *Schostakowitsch in Deutschland (Schostakowitsch-Studien, Band 1)*, ed. H. Schmalenberg, 259–62. Berlin, 1998.

Emerson, Caryl. "Back to the Future: Shostakovich's Revision of Leskov's 'Lady Macbeth of Mtsensk District.'" *Cambridge Opera Journal* 1, no. 1 (1989): 59–78.

Eskina, Natal'ya. "Esli eto vsyo zhe neobkhodimo" [If it is absolutely necessary]. *Muzïkal'naya zhizn'* 7 (1997): 38–39.

Fanning, David. *The Breath of the Symphonist: Shostakovich's Tenth*. London, 1988.

———. "Leitmotif in *Lady Macbeth*." In *Shostakovich Studies*, ed. D. Fanning, 137–59. Cambridge, 1995. Russian reprint in *D. D. Shostakovich: sbornik statey k 90-letiyu so dnya rozhdeniya*, comp. L. Kovnatskaya, 103–20. St. Petersburg, 1996.

———, ed. *Shostakovich Studies*. Cambridge, 1995.

Fay, Laurel E. "The Composer Was Courageous, but Not as Much as in Myth." *New York Times*, 14 April 1996, 27, 32.

———. "From *Lady Macbeth* to *Katerina*: Shostakovich's Versions and Revisions." In *Shostakovich Studies*, ed. D. Fanning, 160–88. Cambridge, 1995.

———. "Mitya v myuzik-kholle: yeshcho odin vzglyad na *Uslovno ubitogo*" [Mitya in the music hall: another look at *Declared Dead*]. *Muzïkal'naya akademiya* 4 (1997): 59–62.

———. "Musorgsky and Shostakovich." In *Musorgsky: In Memoriam, 1881–1981*, ed. M. H. Brown, 215–26. Ann Arbor, Mich. 1982.

———. "The Punch in Shostakovich's *Nose*." In *Russian and Soviet Music: Essays for Boris Schwarz*, ed. M. H. Brown, 229–43. Ann Arbor, Mich., 1984.

———. "Shostakovich, LASM i Asaf'yev" [Shostakovich, LASM and Asafyev]. In *D. D. Shostakovich: sbornik statey k 90-letiyu so dnya rozhdeniya*, comp. L. Kovnatskaya, 29–47. St. Petersburg, 1996.

———. "Shostakovich versus Volkov: Whose *Testimony*?" *Russian Review* 39, no. 4 (1980): 484–93.

———. "The Two Katerinas: The Rocky Path of Shostakovich's *Lady Macbeth of the Mtsensk District*." *Opera News* 59, no. 6 (10 December 1994): 12–14, 16.

Fedorov, Gennadiy. "U poroga teatra Shostakovicha" [On the threshold of Shostakovich's theater]. *Teatr* 10 (1976): 26–33.

———. "Vokrug i posle 'Nosa'" [Around and after *The Nose*]. *Sovetskaya muzïka* 9 (1976): 41–50.

Fedosyuk, Yu. "Zhivu v serdtsakh vsekh lyubyashchikh" [I live in the hearts of all lovers]. *Sovetskaya muzïka* 9 (1991): 32–36.

Feuchtner, Bernd. "Erinnerungen von Rudolf Barschai an Dmitri Schostakowitsch." *Neue Berlinische Musikzeitung* 2 (1995): 24–28.

———. *Und Kunst geknebelt von der groben Macht—Dimitri Schostakowitsch.* Frankfurt, 1986.

Finkel'shteyn, Emil. "O Mastere v lichnom tone" [About the master in a personal vein]. *Muzïkal'naya akademiya* 4 (1997): 103–06.

Fitzpatrick, Sheila. "The *Lady Macbeth* Affair: Shostakovich and the Soviet Puritans." In *The Cultural Front: Power and Culture in Revolutionary Russia*, 183–215. Ithaca, 1992.

Frezinskiy, Boris. "Erenburg i Shostakovich" [Ehrenburg and Shostakovich]. *Neva* 8 (1989): 205–08.

Fromme, Jürgen, ed. *Dmitri Schostakowitsch und seine Zeit: Mensch und Werk.* Duisburg, 1984.

Fuchs, Martina. *Ledi Makbet Mcenskogo uezda: vergleichende Analyse der Erzählung N.S. Leskovs und der gleichnamigen Oper D. D. Šostakovič.* Heidelberg, 1992.

Gakkel', Leonid. "Slovo Shostakovicha" [The word of Shostakovich]. *Sovetskaya muzïka* 3 (1980): 14–21.

Genina, Liana. "Razbeg pered propast'yu" [Take-off run before the abyss]. *Muzïkal'naya akademiya* 3 (1992): 13–14.

Gentilucci, Armando. "Šostakovič anno 1925." *Nuova rivista musicale italiana* 3 (1970): 445–62.

Gerasimova-Persidskaya, Nina. "I. S. Bakh i D. Shostakovich" [J. S. Bach and Shostakovich]. In *I. S. Bakh i sovremennost'*, comp. N. Gerasimova-Persidskaya, 33–43. Kiev, 1985.

Gershov, Solomon. "Vstrechi s Shostakovichem" [Encounters with Shostakovich]. *Sovetskaya muzïka* 12 (1988): 79–82.

Gervink, Manuel. "Schostakowitsch aus der Sicht der deutsch-österreichischen Moderne." In *Schostakowitsch in Deutschland (Schostakowitsch-Studien, 1)*, ed. H. Schmalenberg, 1–21. Berlin, 1998.

————. "Überlegungen zur Genese der musikalischen Sprachmittel in Schostakowitschs frühen Streichquartetten." In *Schostakowitsch in Deutschland (Schostakowitsch-Studien, 1)*, ed. H. Schmalenberg, 61–78. Berlin, 1998.

Ginzburg, Lev. "Violonchel'nïye kontsertï Shostakovicha" [Shostakovich's cello concertos]. In *Issledovaniya, stat'i, ocherki*, 158–78. Moscow, 1971.

Glikman, Gavriil. "Shostakovich, kakim ya yego znal" [Shostakovich as I knew him]. *Kontinent* 37 (1983): 361–81; 38 (1983): 319–54. Ger. trans in *Schostakowitsch in Deutschland (Schostakowitsch Studien, 1)*, ed. H. Schmalenberg, 177–207. Berlin, 1998.

Glikman, Isaak. "Kazn' 'Ledi Makbet'" [The Execution of 'Lady Macbeth']. *Sovetskaya kul'tura* (23 September 1989): 9.

————. "'Moya muzïka nikogda ne umirala …': iz pisem D. D. Shostakovicha k I. D. Glikmanu" ["My music never died": from the letters of Shostakovich to I. D. Glikman]. *Znamya* 1 (1993): 134–45.

————. "'Ya vsyo ravno budu pisat' muzïku': introduktsiya k pis'mam Dmitriya Shostakovicha" ["I will write music anyhow": introduction to the letters of Shostakovich]. *Sovetskaya muzïka* 9 (1989): 41–48; 10 (1989): 63–72.

Gojowy, Detlef. "Absurde Szenenfolgen für 2 Violinen, Viola und Violoncello." In *Schostakowitsch in Deutschland (Schostakowitsch-Studien, Band 1)*, ed. H. Schmalenberg, 79–90. Berlin, 1998.

————. "Dimitri Schostakowitsch: Briefe an Edison Denissow." In *Musik des Ostens, 10*, ed. H. Unverricht, 181–206. Kassel, 1986.

————. Dimitri Schostakowitsch mit Selbstzeugnissen und Bilddokumenten. Reinbek bei Hamburg, 1983. Fr. trans., *Chostakovitch* (Arles, 1988).

————. Neue sowjetische Musik der 20er Jahre. Regensburg, 1980.

————. "Das Schostakowitsch-Bild im wissenschaftlichen Schriftum der DDR." In *Schostakowitsch in Deutschland (Schostakowitsch-Studien, 1)*, ed. H. Schmalenberg, 45–60. Berlin, 1998.

————. "Schostakowitsch und die Avantgarde." *Neue Berlinische Musikzeitung* 2 (1995): 3–16.

————. "Schostakowitschs neue Kleider; Beobachtungen an aktuellen Dokumenten zur sowjetischen Musikästhetik und -politik," *Osteuropa* (1987): 505–18.

Goldstein, Michael. "Dmitri Chostakovitch et Evgueni Zamiatine." In *Autour de Zamiatine: Actes du Colloque Université de Lausanne, juin 1987*, ed. L. Heller, 113–23. Lausanne, 1989.

Golianek, R. "Dramaturgia kwartetów smyczkowych Dymitra Szostakowicza." *Muzyka* 39, no. 2 (1994): 94–98.

————. "Dwa spojrenia na twórszość Dymitra Szostakowicza." *Ruch Muzyczny* 34, no. 7 (1990): 1, 5.

"'Goryacho Vas lyubyashchiy …': iz pisem D. D. Shostakovicha V. P. Shirinskomu." ['Yours with warm affection': Shostakovich's letters to V. P. Shirinsky]. *Muzïkal'naya akademiya* 4 (1997): 137–48.

Gres, S. "Ruchnaya bomba anarkhista" [The hand bomb of an anarchist]. *Rabochiy i teatr* 10 (1930): 6–7.

Grigor'yeva, Galina. "Pervaya opera Shostakovicha 'Nos'" [Shostakovich's first opera, *The Nose*]. In *Muzïka i sovremennost'*, vïp. 3, 68–103. Moscow, 1965.

Grinberg, M. "Dmitriy Shostakovich." *Muzïka i revolyutsiya* 11 (1927): 16–20.

Grönke, Kadja. "Komponieren in Geschichte und Gegenwart: Studien zu den ersten acht Streichquartetten von Dmitrij Šostakovič." *Die Musikforschung* 51, no. 2 (1998): 163–90.

———. "Kunst und Künstler in Šostakovičs späten Gedichtvertonungen." *Archiv für Musikwissenschaft* 53, no. 4 (1996): 290–335.

Grum-Grzhimailo, Tamara. "Zagadka Shostakovicha" [The riddle of Shostakovich]. *Smena* 3 (1990): 208–25.

Gubanow, Jakow. "Der Stil Dimitrij Schostakowitschs in den zwanziger Jahren: Harmonik, Polyphonie, Instrumentation." In *Musik der zwanziger Jahre*, ed. W. Keil, 135–65. Hildesheim, 1996.

Gurevich, Vladimir. "Shostakovich—redaktor 'Khovanshchinï'" [Shostakovich, the editor of *Khovanshchina*]. In *Muzïka i sovremennost'*, vïp. 7, 29–68. Moscow, 1971.

———. "Shostakovich v rabote nad 'Khovanshchina'" [Shostakovich at work on *Khovanshchina*]. In *Voprosï teorii i estetiki muzïki*, vïp. 11, 84–108. Leningrad, 1972.

Hellmundt, Christoph, and Krzysztof Meyer, eds. *Dmitri Schostakowitsch Erfahrungen: Aufsätze, Erinnerungen, Reden, Diskussionsbeiträge, Interviews, Briefe*. Leipzig, 1983.

Hitotsuyanagi, Fumiko. "Novïy lik dvenadtsatoy: chto skrïto v nespravedlivo nizko otsenennoy simfonii" [The new face of the Twelfth: what is concealed in the unfairly low-rated symphony]. *Muzïkal'naya akademiya* 4 (1997): 87.

Ho, Allan B., and Dmitry Feofanov, eds. *Shostakovich Reconsidered*. London, 1998.

———. "Shostakovich's *Testimony*: Reply to an Unjust Criticism." In *Shostakovich Reconsidered*, ed. A. B. Ho and D. Feofanov, 33–311. London, 1998.

Hofmann, R-M. *Dmitri Chostakovitch: l'homme et son oeuvre*. Paris, 1963.

Huband, J. Daniel. "Shostakovich's Fifth Symphony: A Soviet Artist's Reply …?" *Tempo* 173 (1990): 11–16.

Hulme, Derek. *Dmitri Shostakovich: Catalogue, Bibliography and Discography*. Muir of Ord, Scotland, 1982; 2nd ed. Oxford, 1991.

Ikonnikov, Aleksey. "Shtrikhi k portretu Shostakovicha" [Strokes toward a portrait of Shostakovich]. *Nashe naslediye* 4 (1989): 144–47.

Ivashkin, Aleksandr. "Shostakovich i Shnitke: k probleme bol'shoy simfonii" [Shostakovich and Schnittke: on the problem of the large-scale symphony]. *Muzïkal'naya akademiya* 1 (1995): 1–8. Eng. trans., "Shostakovich and Schnittke: The Erosion of Symphonic Syntax," in *Shostakovich Studies*, ed. D. Fanning, 354–70. Cambridge, 1995.

Jackson, Stephen. *Shostakovich*. London, 1997.

Jackson, Timothy L. "The Composer as Jew." In *Shostakovich Reconsidered*, ed. A. B. Ho and D. Feofanov, 597–640. London, 1998.

Jelagin, Juri. *Taming of the Arts*, trans. N. Wreden. New York, 1951.

Johnson, Priscilla, and Leopold Labedz, eds. *Khrushchev and the Arts: The Politics of Soviet Culture, 1962–1964*. Cambridge, 1965.

Jung, Hans. "Ausführlicher Bericht über meinen Besuch bei D. S. am 22. März 1975." In *Schostakowitsch in Deutschland (Schostakowitsch-Studien, 1)*, ed. H. Schmalenberg, 209–57. Berlin, 1998.

Jůzl, M. *Dmitrij Šostakovič*. Prague, 1966.

Kapustin, M. "Triumfal'naya prelyudiya: novïye proizvedeniya D. D. Shostakovicha" [Triumphal prelude: new works by Shostakovich]. *Pravda*, 12 September 1967, 6.

Karagicheva, Lyudmila, ed. *Kara Karayev: stat'i, pis'ma, vïskazïvaniya* [Kara Karayev: articles, letters, opinions]. Moscow, 1978.

———. "'Pishete kak mozhno bol'she prekrasnoy muzïki ...': iz pisem D. D. Shostakovicha K. A. Karayevu" ["Write as much fine music as possible ...": from Shostakovich's letters to K. A. Karayev]. *Muzïkal'naya akademiya* 4 (1997): 202–11.

Karl, Gregory, and Jenefer Robinson. "Shostakovich's Tenth Symphony and the Musical Expression of Cognitively Complex Emotions." *Journal of Aesthetics and Art Criticism* 53, no. 4 (1995): 401–15.

Katayev, Vitaliy. "Trudnaya doroga k Trinadtsatoy" [The hard road to the Thirteenth]. *Muzïkal'naya zhizn'* 7–8 (1996): 34–35.

———. "Umirayut v Rossii strakhi" [Fears are dying out in Russia]. In *Shostakovichu posvyashchayetsya: sbornik statey k 90-letiyu kompozitora (1906–1996)*, comp. E. Dolinskaya, 169–75. Moscow, 1997.

Katerina Izmailova. Moscow, 1934. Articles by Shostakovich, Nemirovich-Danchenko, Ostretsov.

"'Katerina Izmailova' D. D. Shostakovicha" [D. D. Shostakovich's *Katerina Izmailova*]. In L. D. Mikhailov, *Sem' glav o teatre*, 66–90. Moscow, 1985.

Kats, Boris. "Shostakovich kak predmet poeticheskogo vnimaniya (k postanovke voprosa)" [Shostakovich as the object of poetic attention (raising the question)]. In *D. D. Shostakovich: sbornik statey k 90-letiyu so dnya rozhdeniya*, comp. L. Kovnatskaya, 367–78. St. Petersburg, 1996.

Kay, Norman. *Shostakovich*. London, 1971.

———. "Shostakovich's 15th Symphony." *Tempo* 100 (1972): 36–40.

———. "Shostakovich's Second Violin Concerto." *Tempo* 83 (1967–68): 21–23.

Kazurova, A. "Shostakovich i dzhaz" [Shostakovich and jazz]. In *Shostakovichu posvyashchayetsya: sbornik statey k 90-letiyu kompozitora (1906–1996)*, comp. E. Dolinskaya, 91–101. Moscow, 1997.

Keldïsh, Yuriy. "Avtobiograficheskiy kvartet" [An autobiographical quartet]. *Sovetskaya muzïka* 12 (1960): 19–23; Eng. trans. in *Musical Times* 102 (1961): 226–28.

Keller, Hans. "Shostakovich's Twelfth Quartet." *Tempo* 94 (1970): 6–15.

Khachaturyan, Aram. "Desyataya simfoniya D. Shostakovicha." [D. Shostakovich's Tenth Symphony] *Sovetskaya muzïka* 3 (1954): 23–26.

Khachaturyan, Karen. "Ob uchitele" [About my teacher]. In *Shostakovichu posvyashchayetsya: sbornik statey k 90-letiyu kompozitora (1906–1996)*, comp. E. Dolinskaya, 166–68. Moscow, 1997.

Khentova, Sof'ya. "Amerikanskiye rodstvenniki Shostakovicha" [Shostakovich's American relatives]. *Novoye russkoye slovo*, 25 February 1991, 8.

————. "Bach und Schostakowitsch." *Neue Berlinische Musikzeitung* 2 (1995): 17–23.

————. *D. D. Shostakovich v godï Velikoy Otechestvennoy voynï* [Shostakovich in the years of World War II]. Leningrad, 1979.

————. *D. D. Shostakovich: tridtsatiletiye 1945–1975* [D. D. Shostakovich: the thirty years 1945–1975]. Leningrad, 1982.

————. *Dmitri Schostakowitschs Babij Jar: Die 13. Sinfonie*, Ger. trans. F. Horstmann. Berlin, 1996.

————. "Dmitriy Shostakovich: 'Mï zhivyom vo vremya sil'nïkh strastey i burnïkh postupkov'" [Dmitriy Shostakovich: 'We live in a time of strong passions and impetuous deeds']. *Niva* 2 (January 1991): 12–13.

————. "Dva imeni" [Two names]. *Sovetskaya muzïka* 9 (1985): 75–80.

————. "Istoriya lyubvi, zakonchivshayasya u Sotbi" [A love story that ended at Sotheby's]. *Muzïkal'naya zhizn'* 3 (1992): 4–5.

————. "Leniniana Dmitriya Shostakovicha" [Shostakovich's Leniniana]. *Niva* 4 (1980): 196–206.

————. "Mnogostradal'naya orkestrovka Shostakovicha: iz istorii operï 'Boris Godunov'" [Shostakovich's unfortunate orchestration: from the history of the opera *Boris Godunov*]. *Muzïkal'naya zhizn'* 19 (1989): 8–9.

————. *Molodïye godï Shostakovicha, kniga pervaya* [Shostakovich's youthful years, book one]. Leningrad, 1975.

————. *Molodïye godï Shostakovicha, kniga vtoraya* [Shostakovich's youthful years, book two]. Leningrad, 1980.

————. "Na auktsione Sotbi—snova pis'ma o lyubvi" [At a Sotheby's auction—more love letters]. *Muzïkal'naya zhizn'* 7 (1994): 26–28.

————. "Nabat nadezhdï" [Tocsin of hope]. *Muzïkal'naya zhizn'* 9 (1990): 26–28.

————. *Plamya Bab'ego Yara: Trinadtsataya simfoniya D. D. Shostakovicha* [The flame of *Babiy Yar*: D. D. Shostakovich's Thirteenth Symphony]. St. Petersburg, 1997.

————. *Podvig, voploshchenïy v muzïke* [A feat embodied in music]. Volgograd, 1984.

————. "Posledniye besedï: Matvey Blanter o Shostakoviche" [Final conversations: Matvey Blanter on Shostakovich]. *Muzïkal'naya zhizn'* 5 (1991): 4–5.

————. "Pushkinskiye obrazï" [Pushkinian images]. *Sovetskaya muzïka* 10 (1986): 57–61.

————. *Pushkin v muzïke Shostakovicha* [Pushkin in Shostakovich's music]. St. Petersburg, 1996.

————. "Razgovor s sïnom Yesenina" [A conversation with Yesenin's son]. *Muzïkal'naya zhizn'* 24 (1989): 10–11.

————. "Sed'maya simfoniya v osvobozhdyonnom Kieve" [The Seventh Symphony in liberated Kiev]. *Niva* 6 (1985): 180–82.

————. "Shostakovich i Khachaturyan: ikh sblizil 48-y god" [Shostakovich and Khachaturyan: 1948 brought them closer together]. *Muzïkal'naya zhizn'* 24 (1988): 10–11.

————. "Shostakovich i kino" [Shostakovich and the cinema]. *Muzïkal'naya zhizn'* 5–6 (1996): 41–45.

———. "Shostakovich i Rostropovich" [Shostakovich and Rostropovich]. *Muzïkal'naya zhizn'* 16 (1990): 24–28.

———. *Shostakovich i Sibir'* [Shostakovich and Siberia]. Novosibirsk, 1990.

———. *Shostakovich na Ukraine* [Shostakovich in Ukraine]. Kiev, 1986.

———. *Shostakovich—pianist* [Shostakovich the pianist]. Leningrad, 1964.

———. "Shostakovich: Trinadtsataya Simfoniya" [Shostakovich: Thirteenth Symphony]. *Muzïkal'naya zhizn'* 15–16 (1991): 12–14, 24; 17–18 (1991): 12–14.

———. "Shostakovich v Evanstone" [Shostakovich in Evanston]. *Sovetskaya muzïka* 9 (1990): 99–100.

———. *Shostakovich v Moskve* [Shostakovich in Moscow]. Moscow, 1986.

———. *Shostakovich v Petrograde-Leningrade* [Shostakovich in Petrograd-Leningrad]. Leningrad, 1979; 2nd ed. 1981.

———. *Shostakovich: zhizn' i tvorchestvo* [Shostakovich: life and works]. 2 vols. Leningrad, 1985, 1986; 2nd ed. Moscow, 1996.

———. "Simfoniya 'Babiy Yar'" [The *Babiy Yar* Symphony]. *Novoye russkoye slovo*, 22 February 1991, 12.

———. "Strannïye sblizheniya" [Strange ties]. *Muzïkal'naya zhizn'* 3 (1995): 12–14.

———. *Udivitel'nïy Shostakovich* [The amazing Shostakovich]. St. Petersburg, 1993.

———. "V avguste 1942-go" [In August 1942]. *Muzïkal'naya zhizn'* 4 (1995): 3–5.

———. *V mire Shostakovicha* [In the world of Shostakovich]. Moscow, 1996.

———. "Vspominaya Shostakovicha" [Remembering Shostakovich]. *Muzïkal'naya zhizn'* 8 (1994): 31–35; 2 (1995): 23–26.

———. "Yevreyskaya tema u Shostakovicha" [The Jewish theme in Shostakovich]. *Novoye russkoye slovo*, 2 February 1990, 3.

———. "Zhenshchinï v zhizni Shostakovicha" [The women in Shostakovich's life]. *Vremya i mï* 112 (1991): 217–78.

———. "Zoshchenko i Shostakovich" [Zoshchenko and Shostakovich]. *Muzïkal'naya zhizn'* 9 (1994): 26–27.

Kholopov, Yuriy, and Valeriya Tsenova. *Edison Denisov*. Moscow, 1993. Eng. trans. *Edison Denisov*. Chur, Switzerland, 1995.

"'Khorosho bïlo bï ne dumat' ni o khlebe nasushchnom, ni o chyom, a tol'ko zanimat'sya lyubimïm delom ...': iz pisem D. D. Shostakovicha B. L. Yavorskomu" ["It would be nice not to think about my daily bread or anything else but just to do what I love best ...": from Shostakovich's letters to B. L. Yavorsky]. *Muzïkal'naya akademiya* 4 (1997): 28–40.

Khrennikov, Tikhon. "Tvorchestvo kompozitorov i muzïkovedov posle Postanovleniya TsK VKP(b) ob opere 'Velikaya druzhba'" [The creative work of composers and musicologists since the Resolution of the Central Committee on the opera *The Great Friendship*]. *Sovetskaya muzïka* 1 (1949): 23–37.

Khubov, Georgiy. "Pyataya simfoniya D. Shostakovicha" [D. Shostakovich's Fifth Symphony]. *Sovetskaya muzïka* 3 (1938): 14–28. Revised in *O muzïke i muzïkantakh* (Moscow, 1959), 224–40.

Kiselev, Vadim. "Iz pisem 1930-kh godov" [From letters of the 1930s]. *Sovetskaya muzïka* 9 (1987): 85–91.

Klimovitskiy, Abram. "Shostakovich i Betkhoven" [Shostakovich and Beethoven]. In *Traditsii muzïkal'noy nauki: sbornik issledovatel'skikh statey,* ed. L. Kovnatskaya, 177–205. Leningrad, 1989.

———. "Yeshchyo raz o teme-monogramme *D-Es-C-H*" [Once more about the theme-monogram D-Eb-C-Bᵇ]. In *D. D. Shostakovich: sbornik statey k 90-letiyu so dnya rozhdeniya,* comp. L. Kovnatskaya, 249–68. St. Petersburg, 1996.

Knayfel', Aleksandr. "I pravda kak zvezda v nochi otkrïlas'" [And the truth was revealed like a star in the night]. *Sovetskaya muzïka* 11 (1975): 78–81.

Koball, Michael. *Pathos und Groteske—Die deutsche Tradition im symphonischen Schaffen von Dmitri Schostakowitsch.* Berlin, 1997.

———. "Pathos und Groteske—Dmitri Schostakowitsch und das 'Symphonische Ich.'" In *Schostakowitsch in Deutschland (Schostakowitsch-Studien, 1),* ed. H. Schmalenberg, 91–115. Berlin, 1998.

Körner, Klaus. "Schostakowitschs Vierte Sinfonie." *Archiv für Musikwissenschaft* 31, no. 2 (1974): 116–36; no. 3, 214–36.

Komok, Olga. "Shostakovich i Kruchyonïkh." In *D. D. Shostakovich: sbornik statey k 90-letiyu so dnya rozhdeniya,* comp. L. Kovnatskaya, 174–93. St. Petersburg, 1996.

Konisskaya, Mariya. "Dusha i maska: pis'ma D. D. Shostakovicha k L. N. Lebedinskomu" [Soul and mask: letters from D. D. Shostakovich to L. N. Lebedinsky]. *Muzïkal'naya zhizn'* 23–24 (1993): 11–14.

Kopp, Karen. *Form und Gehalt der Symphonien des Dmitrij Schostakowitsch.* Bonn, 1990.

Korev, Yuriy. "O pyatnadtsatoy simfonii D. Shostakovicha" [On Shostakovich's Fifteenth Symphony]. *Sovetskaya muzïka* 9 (1972): 8–22.

———. "Über die Vokalkunst." In *Dmitri Schostakowitsch 1984/85: Wissenschaftliche Beiträge. Dokumente. Interpretationen. Programme,* 180–85. Duisburg, 1984.

Korn, Rita. "Ryadom s Shostakovichem" [Alongside Shostakovich]. In *Druz'ya moi ...,* vospominaniya, ocherki, zarisovki, 116–30. Moscow, 1986.

Kosachyova, Rimma. "Vokrug 'Zolotogo veka': versii, traditsii" [Around *The Golden Age*: versions, traditions]. In *Shostakovichu posvyashchayetsya: sbornik statey k 90-letiyu kompozitora (1906–1996),* comp. E. Dolinskaya, 126–34. Moscow, 1997.

Kotyńska, M. "Kwartety smyczkowe Dymitra Szostakowicza jako wyraz postawy klasycyzujacej" [Shostakovich's string quartets as an expression of classical attitudes]. *Muzyka* 12, no. 3 (1967): 36–44.

Koval', Marian. "Tvorcheskiy put' D. Shostakovicha" [The creative path of D. Shostakovich]. *Sovetskaya muzïka* 2 (1948): 47–61; no. 3, 31–43; no. 4, 8–19.

Kovnatskaya, Lyudmila, comp. *D. D. Shostakovich: sbornik statey k 90-letiyu so dnya rozhdeniya* [D. D. Shostakovich: collection of articles for the ninetieth anniversary of his birth]. St. Petersburg, 1996.

———. "Shostakovich i Britten: nekotorïye paralleli" [Shostakovich and Britten: some parallels]. In *D. D. Shostakovich: sbornik statey k 90-letiyu so dnya rozhdeniya,* comp. L. Kovnatskaya, 306–23. St. Petersburg, 1996.

———. "Shostakovich v protokolakh LASM" [Shostakovich in the minutes of

LASM]. In *D. D. Shostakovich: sbornik statey k 90-letiyu so dnya rozhdeniya*, comp. L. Kovnatskaya, 48–67. St. Petersburg, 1996. Abridged Eng. trans., "Shostakovich and the LASM," *Tempo* 206 (1998): 2–6.

Kozintsev, Grigoriy. "Spasibo za schast'e, kotoroye on mne prinosil" [Thanks for the happiness he brought me]. *Sovetskaya muzïka* 9 (1990): 93–99.

Kozlova, Miralda. "'Mne ispolnilos' vosemnadtsat' let ...' (Pis'ma D. D. Shostakovicha k L. N. Oborinu)" ["I have turned eighteen ..." (letters from Shostakovich to L. N. Oborin)]. In *Vstrechi s proshlïm, vïp. 5*, 232–60. Moscow, 1984.

———. "Vsegda dorozhu vashim mneniyem ..." [I always value your opinion]. In *Vstrechi s proshlïm, sbornik materialov, vïp. 3*, 253–59. Moscow, 1978. Eng. trans., "Prokofiev's Correspondence with Stravinsky and Shostakovich," in *Slavonic and Western Music: Essays for Gerald Abraham*, ed. M. H. Brown and R. J. Wiley, 271–92. Ann Arbor, Mich., 1985.

Kravets, Nelly. "Novïy vzglyad na Desyatuyu simfoniyu Shostakovicha" [A new look at Shostakovich's Tenth Symphony]. In *D. D. Shostakovich: sbornik statey k 90-letiyu so dnya rozhdeniya*, comp. L. Kovnatskaya, 342–58. St. Petersburg, 1996.

Krebs, Stanley Dale. *Soviet Composers and the Development of Soviet Music.* London, 1970.

Kremlyov, Yuliy. "O desyatoy simfonii D. Shostakovicha" [On Shostakovich's Tenth Symphony]. *Sovetskaya muzïka* 4 (1957): 74–84.

Kröplin, Eckart. *Frühe Sowjetische Oper: Schostakowitsch, Prokofjew.* Berlin, 1985.

———. "Schostakowitsch zur Oper: Ästhetische Ansichten des Komponisten." In *Musikbühne 77*, 7–34. Berlin, 1977.

Kryukov, Andrey. "K svedeniyu budushchikh letopistsev" [For the information of future chroniclers]. In *D. D. Shostakovich: sbornik statey k 90-letiyu so dnya rozhdeniya*, comp. L. Kovnatskaya, 158–73. St. Petersburg, 1996.

Kurïsheva, Tat'yana. "Blokovskiy tsikl Shostakovich" [Shostakovich's Blok cycle]. In *Blok i muzïka*, 214–28. Moscow and Leningrad, 1972.

———. "Shostakovich v baletnom teatre, ili pochemu tantsuyut Shostakovicha?" [Shostakovich in the ballet theater, or why is Shostakovich danced?]. In *Shostakovichu posvyashchayetsya: sbornik statey k 90-letiyu kompozitora (1906–1996)*, comp. E. Dolinskaya, 116–25. Moscow, 1997.

Kuz'mina, Natal'ya. "O kvartetnom tvorchestve Shostakovicha" [On Shostakovich's string quartets]. In *Analiz, kontseptsii, kritika*, ed. L. Dan'ko, 5–19. Leningrad, 1977.

Kuznetsov, Andrey. "Prityazheniya i ottalkivaniya (D. D. Shostakovich—M. V. Yudina)" [Attraction and repulsion (D. D. Shostakovich—M. V. Yudina)]. *Muzïkal'naya akademiya* 4 (1997): 108–16.

Ladïgina, A. "Slushaya trinadtsatuyu simfoniyu" [Listening to the Thirteenth Symphony]. *Sovetskaya Belorussiya*, 2 April 1963, 4; reprinted with Eng. trans. Chicago, n.d.

Lamm, Olga. *Stranitsï tvorcheskoy biografii Myaskovskogo* [Pages from Myaskovsky's creative biography]. Moscow, 1989.

Langen, Tim, and Jesse Langen. "Music and Poetry: The Case of Shostakovich and

Blok." In *Intersections and Transpositions: Russian Music, Literature, and Society*, ed. A. B. Wachtel, 138–64. Evanston, Ill., 1998.

Laul, Reyn. "Muzïka Shostakovicha v kontekste bol'shevistkoy ideologii i praktiki (opït slushaniya)" [Shostakovich's music in the context of Bolshevik ideology and practice (listening experience)]. In *D. D. Shostakovich: sbornik statey k 90-letiyu so dnya rozhdeniya*, comp. L. Kovnatskaya, 141–57. St. Petersburg, 1996.

Laux, Karl. *Dmitri Schostakowitsch, Chronist seines Volkes.* Berlin, 1966.

Lavrent'yeva, Irena. "O vzaimodeystvii slova i muzïki v sovetskoy vokal'noy simfonii 60–70kh godov (na primere tvorchestva D. Shostakovicha, M. Vaynberga, A. Lokshina)" [On the interaction of words and music in the Soviet vocal symphony of the 1960s and 1970s (based on the work of D. Shostakovich, M. Vainberg, and A. Lokshin)]. 2 parts. In *Problemï muzïkal'noy nauki*, vïp. 6, 7, 72–109, 5–35. Moscow, 1985, 1989.

Lawson, Peter. "Shostakovich's Second Symphony." *Tempo* 91 (1969–70); 14–17.

Lazarov, S. *Dmitry Shostakovich.* Sofia, 1967.

Lebedinskiy, Lev. "D. D. Shostakovich o russkoy narodnoy pesne i khore imeni Pyatnitskogo" [Shostakovich on the Russian folksong and the Pyatnitsky Chorus]. *Novïy mir* 3 (1992): 208–15.

———. "Iz 'bessistemnïkh zapisey'" [From unsystematic notes]. *Muzïkal'naya zhizn'* 21–22 (1993): 26–28.

———. *Khorovïye poemï Shostakovicha* [Shostakovich's choral poems]. Moscow, 1957.

———. "O chesti mastera" [About the master's honor]. *Pravda*, 19 March 1991, 6.

———. "O nekotorïkh muzïkal'nïkh tsitatakh v proizvedeniyakh D. Shostakovicha" [On some musical citations in Shostakovich's music]. *Novïy mir* 3 (1990): 262–67. Eng. trans., "Code, Quotation and Collage: Some Musical Allusions in the Works of Dmitry Shostakovich," in *Shostakovich Reconsidered*, ed. A. B. Ho and D. Feofanov, 472–82. London, 1998.

———. "The Origin of Shostakovich's 'Rayok.'" *Tempo* 173 (1990): 31–32.

———. "Revolyutsionnïy fol'klor v Odinnadtsatoy simfonii D. Shostakovicha" [Revolutionary folklore in Shostakovich's Eleventh Symphony]. *Sovetskaya muzïka* 1(1958): 42–49.

———. *Sed'maya i odinnadtsataya simfonii D. Shostakovicha* [Shostakovich's Seventh and Eleventh Symphonies]. Moscow, 1960.

Ledi Makbet Mtsenskogo uyezda. Leningrad, 1934. Articles by Shostakovich, Sollertinsky, Asafyev, and Samosud on *Lady Macbeth of the Mtsensk District.*

Lee, Rose. "Dmitri Szostakovitch: Young Russian Composer Tells of Linking Politics with Creative Work." *New York Times*, 20 December 1931, sec. 8, 8.

Lehrman, P. "A Schoenberg Note about Prokofiev, Shostakovich, Stravinsky and Koussevitzky." *Journal of the Arnold Schoenberg Institute* 11, no. 2 (1988): 174–80.

Levashev, Yuriy. "Desyat' poem dlya khora D. D. Shostakovicha" [Ten poems for chorus by Shostakovich]. In *Ocherki po teoreticheskomu muzïkoznaniyu*, ed. Yu. Tyulin, 211–29. Leningrad, 1959.

Levaya, Tamara. "Devyataya simfoniya Shostakovicha" [Shostakovich's Ninth Symphony]. In *Muzïka i sovremennost'*, vïp. 5, 3–37. Moscow, 1967.

————. "Kharms i Shostakovich: nesostoyavsheyesya sotrudnichestvo" [Kharms and Shostakovich: an unrealized collaboration]. In *Kharmsizdat predstavlyayet: sbornik materialov*, ed. V. Sazhin, 94–96. St. Petersburg, 1995.

————. "Tayna velikogo iskusstvo (O pozdnikh kamerno-vokal'nikh tsiklakh D. D. Shostakovich)." [The secret of great art (on Shostakovich's late chamber-vocal cycles)]. In *Muzïka Rossii, vïp. 2*, 291–328. Moscow, 1978.

Levitin, Yuriy. "Fal'shivaya nota, ili grustnïye mïsli o delakh muzïkal'nïkh" [False note, or melancholy thoughts on musical matters]. *Pravda*, 11 November 1990, 3.

Liebert, A. "Anmerkungen und Ergebnisse zum Verhältnis Mahler—Šostakovič." In *Theorie der Musik—Analyse und Deutung*, ed. C. Floros et al., 223–52. Laaber, 1995.

Lindlar, Heinrich. "Spätstil? Zu Schostakowitschs Sinfonien 13–15." *Schweizerische Musikzeitung* 113 (1973): 340–45.

Litvinova, Flora. "Vspominaya Shostakovicha" [Remembering Shostakovich]. *Znamya* 12 (1996): 156–77.

Livshchits, Aleksandr. *Zhizn' za rodinu svoyu: ocherki o kompozitorakh i muzïkovedakh, pogibshikh v Velikuyu Otechestvennuyu voynu* [Their lives for their country: essays on composers and musicologists who perished in World War II]. Moscow, 1964.

Lobanowa, Marina. "Er wurde von der Zeit erwählt—Zum Phänomen Tichon Chrennikow." In *Schostakowitsch in Deutschland (Schostakowitsch-Studien, 1)*, ed. H. Schmalenberg, 117–38. Berlin, 1998.

————. "Schostakowitschs erstes Bereuen: von der 'Nase' zum 'Wirrwar statt Musik.'" *Neue Berlinische Musikzeitung* 2 (1995): 46–54.

Longman, Richard M. *Expression and Structure: Processes of Integration in the Large-Scale Instrumental Music of Dmitri Shostakovich*. New York, 1989.

Losskiy, Boris. "Novoye o Shostakoviche: 'V pomoshch' izuchayushchim'" [News about Shostakovich: "As an aid to students"]. *Russkaya mïsl'* (7 April 1989): 12; (14 April 1989): 9.

Luk'yanova, Nataliya. *Dmitriy Dmitriyevich Shostakovich*. Moscow, 1980; Ger. trans. (Berlin, 1982; 2nd ed. 1993); Eng. trans. (Neptune City, N.J., 1984).

MacDonald, Ian. "Common-Sense about Shostakovich, Breaking the Hermeneutic Circle." *Southern Humanities Review* 26, no. 2 (1992): 153–67. Revised as "Universal Because Specific: Arguments for a Contextual Approach," in *Shostakovich Reconsidered*, ed. A. B. Ho and D. Feofanov, 555–65. London, 1998.

————. "Fay versus Shostakovich: Whose Stupidity?" *East European Jewish Affairs* 26, no. 2 (1996): 5–26.

————. "The Legend of the Eighth Quartet." In *Shostakovich Reconsidered*, ed. A. B. Ho and D. Feofanov, 587–89. London, 1998.

————. "His Misty Youth: The Glivenko Letters and Life in the '20s." In *Shostakovich Reconsidered*, ed. A. B. Ho and D. Feofanov, 530–54. London, 1998.

————. "Naïve Anti-Revisionism: The Academic Misrepresentation of Shostakovich." In *Shostakovich Reconsidered*, ed. A. B. Ho and D. Feofanov, 643–723. London, 1998.

————. *The New Shostakovich*. London, 1990.

————. "Writing about Shostakovich: The Post-Communist Perspective." In *Shostakovich Reconsidered*, ed. A. B. Ho and D. Feofanov, 566–86. London, 1998.

MacDonald, Malcolm (Calum). "The Anti-Formalist 'Rayok'—Learners Start Here!" *Tempo* 173 (1990): 23–30.

————. *Dmitri Shostakovich: A Complete Catalogue*. London, 1977; 2nd ed. 1985.

————. "Words and Music in Late Shostakovich." In *Shostakovich: The Man and His Music*, ed. C. Norris, 125–47. London, 1982.

Makarov, Yevgeniy. "Ya bezgranichno uvazhal yego" [I respected him limitlessly]. *Muzïkal'naya akademiya* 1 (1993): 146–54.

Maksimenkov, Leonid. "Partiya—nash rulevoy" [The Party is our helmsman]. *Muzïkal'naya zhizn'* 13–14 (1993): 6–8; 15–16 (1993): 8–10.

————. *Sumbur vmesto muzïki: stalinskaya kul'turnaya revolyutsiya, 1936–1938* [Muddle instead of music: the Stalinist cultural revolution, 1936–1938]. Moscow, 1997.

Malko, Nicolai. *A Certain Art*. New York, 1966.

Maróthy, J. "Harmonic Disharmony: Shostakovich's Quintet." *Studia Musicologica* 19 (1977): 325–48.

————. "Selbstkritische Revolution: Das Reflektierende bei Eisler und Schostakowitsch." In *An die Epochen—und Stilewende*, 116–19. Brno, 1993.

Martïnov, Ivan. *D. D. Shostakovich*. Moscow-Leningrad, 1947. Pamphlet.

————. *Dmitriy Shostakovich*. Moscow, 1946; 2nd ed. 1956. Eng. trans. 1947; reprint 1977.

————. *D. Shostakovich: ocherk zhizni i tvorchestva* [D. Shostakovich: study of the life and works]. Moscow, 1962.

————. "Novïye kamernïye sochineniya Shostakovicha" [Shostakovich's new chamber compositions]. In *Sovetskaya muzïka: pyatïy sbornik statey*, 21–28. Moscow, 1946.

Martïnov, Nikolai. "Pis'ma Shostakovicha. Stranitsï iz zapisnoy knizhki" [Shostakovich's letters. Page from a notebook]. In *D. D. Shostakovich: sbornik statey k 90-letiyu so dnya rozhdeniya*, comp. L. Kovnatskaya, 276–305. St. Petersburg, 1996.

Mason, Colin. "Form in Shostakovich's Quartets." *Musical Times* 103 (1962): 531–33.

Mazel', Lev. *Etyudï o Shostakoviche: stat'i i zametki o tvorchestve* [Etudes on Shostakovich: essays and comments on his work]. Moscow, 1986.

————. "K sporam o Shostakoviche" [On the debate about Shostakovich]. *Sovetskaya muzïka* 5 (1991): 30–35. Eng. trans., "An Inner Rebellion: 'Thoughts on the Current Debate about Shostakovich,'" in *Shostakovich Reconsidered*, ed. A. B. Ho and D. Feofanov, 483–94. London, 1998.

————. "O stile Shostakovicha" [On Shostakovich's style], In *Chertï stilya D. Shostakovicha*, ed. L. G. Berger, 3–23. Moscow, 1962. Ger. trans. in *Beiträge zur Musikwissenschaft* 9 (1967): 208–20. Revised in *Stat'i po teorii i analizu muzïki*, 221–44. Moscow, 1982.

————. "Razdum'ya ob istoricheskom meste tvorchestva Shostakovicha" [Thoughts about the historical position of Shostakovich's work]. *Sovetskaya muzïka* 9 (1975): 9–15. Reprinted in *D. Shostakovich: stat'i i materialï*, comp. G. Shneerson (Moscow, 1976), 58–72. Revised in *Stat'i po teorii i analizu muzïki*, 260–76. Moscow, 1982.

———, *Simfonii D. D. Shostakovicha* [Shostakovich's symphonies]. Moscow, 1960.

———. "U voyennïkh dirizhyorov" [With military conductors]. *Sovetskaya muzïka* 9 (1991): 30–31.

———. "Zametki o muzïkal'nom yazïke Shostakovicha" [Remarks on Shostakovich's musical language]. In *Dmitriy Shostakovich*, comp. G. Ordzhonikidze, 303–59. Moscow, 1967. Reprinted as "Nablyudeniya nad muzïkal'nïm yazïkom Shostakovicha," in *Etyudï o Shostakoviche: stat'i i zametki o tvorchestve*, 33–82. Moscow, 1986.

McCreless, Patrick. "The Cycle of Structure and the Cycle of Meaning: The Piano Trio in E minor, op. 67." In *Shostakovich Studies*, ed. D. Fanning, 113–36. Cambridge, 1995.

M. D. "Novïye rabotï kompozitora D. Shostakovicha" [New works by Shostakovich]. *Izvestiya*, 29 September 1938, 4.

Melos [Stockholm] 4–5 (1993). Special issue.

Meskhishvili, Erna. *Dmitriy Shostakovich: notograficheskiy spravochnik* [Dmitriy Shostakovich: catalogue of works]. Moscow, 1995.

Meyer, Krzysztof. *Dimitri Chostakovitch*. Paris, 1994. Ger. trans. (Bergisch Gladbach, 1995).

———. "Mahler und Schostakowitsch." In *Gustav Mahler: Sinfonie und Wirklichkeit*, ed. O. Kolleritsch, 118–32. Graz, 1977.

———. "Prokofjew und Schostakowitsch." In *Bericht über das Internationale Symposion 'Sergej Prokofjew—Aspekte seines Werkes und der Biographie,' Köln 1991*, ed. K. W. Niemöller, 111–33. Regensburg, 1992.

———. *Szostakowicz*. Kraków, 1973. Ger. trans. Leipzig, 1980.

Micheletti, Luisa. "I cicli vocali di Šostakovič dell'ultimo periodo su testi di Aleksandr Blok e Marina Cvetaeva." In *Laboratorio degli studi linguistici*. [Università di Camerino] 2 (1985): 107–22.

Mikhailova, S. "Naydutsya li amerikanskiye rodstvenniki Shostakovicha?" [Can Shostakovich's American relatives be found?]. *Muzïkal'naya zhizn'* 13–14 (1992): 23–24.

Mikheyeva[-Sollertinskaya], Lyudmila. "D. D. Shostakovich v otrazhenii pisem k I. I. Sollertinskomu. Shtrikhi k portretu" [Shostakovich as reflected in his letters to Sollertinsky. Strokes toward a portrait]. In *D. D. Shostakovich: sbornik statey k 90-letiyu so dnya rozhdeniya*, comp. L. Kovnatskaya, 88–100. St. Petersburg, 1996.

———. *I. I. Sollertinskiy: zhizn' i naslediye* [Sollertinsky: life and legacy]. Leningrad, 1988.

———. "Istoriya odnoy druzhbï" [The story of a friendship]. *Sovetskaya muzïka* 9 (1986): 24–33; 9 (1987): 78–84.

———. "Pis'ma Shostakovicha k Sollertinskomu" [Shostakovich's letters to Sollertinsky]. *Zhurnal lyubiteley iskusstva* 2 (1996): 9–15; 3 (1996): 6–13; 4 (1996): 6–12; 1 (1997): 16–20; 4–5 (1997): 16–30; 6–7 (1997): 47–50; 8–9 (1997): 59–65; 10–11 (1997): 44–51; 1 (1998): 43–47.

————. "Shostakovich. Voyennïye godï" [Shostakovich. The war years]. *Zvezda* 9 (1986): 169–78.

————. *Zhizn' Dmitriya Shostakovicha* [Life of Shostakovich]. Moscow, 1997.

————. comp. *Pamyati I. I. Sollertinskogo: vospominaniya, materialï, issledovaniya* [In memory of I. I. Sollertinskiy: reminiscences, materials, research]. 2nd ed. Leningrad, 1978.

Mnatsakanova, Elizaveta. "O tsikle Shostakovicha 'Sem' romansov na stikhi Aleksandra Bloka'" [On the cycle "Seven romances on poems of Alexander Blok"]. In *Muzïka i sovremennost', vïp. 7*, 69–87. Moscow, 1971.

Morgan, James. "Interview with 'The Nose': Shostakovich's Adaptation of Gogol." In *Intersections and Transpositions: Russian Music, Literature, and Society*, ed. A. B. Wachtel, 111–37. Evanston, 1998.

Müller, Hans-Peter. "Die Fünfzehnte; Gedanken zur jüngsten Sinfonie von Dmitri Schostakowitsch," *Musik und Gesellschaft* 22 (1972): 714–20.

Murphy, Edward "A Programme for the first Movement of Shostakovich's Fifteenth Symphony: 'A Debate about Four Musical Styles.'" *The Music Review* 53, no. 1 (1992): 47–62.

Muzïkal'naya akademiya 4 (1997). Special issue.

Muzïkal'naya zhizn' 17 (1976). Special issue.

Nest'yev, Izraíl. "O Shostakoviche (tvorcheskaya sverkhzadacha i esteticheskiy ideal)" [On Shostakovich (creative mission and aesthetic ideal)]. In *Vek nïneshniy i vek minuvshiy*, 11–54. Moscow, 1986.

————. "Sto sed'moy opus" [Opus 107]. *Sovetskaya muzïka* 12 (1959): 9–17; Ger. trans., *Musik und Gesellschaft* 10 (1960): 198–203.

Neue Berlinische Musikzeitung 3 (1993), 2 (1995). Special issues.

Niemöller, Klaus. "Robert Schumanns Cellokonzert in der Instrumentation von Dmitri Schostakowitsch; Ein Beitrag zur Schumann-Rezeption in der Sowjetunion." In *Beiträge zur Geschichte des Konzerts; Festschrift Siegfried Kross zum 60. Gerburtstag*, ed. R. Emans and M. Wendt, 411–21. Bonn, 1990.

Niemoller, Klaus, and Vsevolod Zaderackij, eds. *Bericht über das Internationale Dmitri-Schostakowitsch-Symposion Köln 1985*. Regensburg, 1986.

Nikel'berg, S. "Muzïka D. Shostakovicha k kinofil'mu 'Gamlet'" [Shostakovich's music to the film *Hamlet*]. In *Iz istorii russkoy i sovetskoy muzïki, vïp. 3*, 234–52. Moscow, 1978.

Nikolayev, Aleksandr. "Fortepiannaya muzïka D. D. Shostakovicha" [Shostakovich's piano music]. In *Voprosï muzïkoznaniya*, 2, ed. A. S. Ogolevets, 112–34. Moscow, 1956.

Nikolayeva, Tat'yana. "Ispolnyaya Shostakovicha" [Performing Shostakovich], In *Dmitriy Shostakovich*, comp. G. Ordzhonikidze, 287–303. Moscow, 1967.

Norris, Christopher. "Shostakovich and Cold War Cultural Politics: A Review Essay." *Southern Humanities Review* 25, no. 1 (1991): 54–77.

————. "Shostakovich: Politics and Musical Language." In *Shostakovich: The Man and His Music*, ed. C. Norris, 163–87. London, 1982.

————. "The String Quartets of Shostakovich." *Music and Musicians* 24, no. 4 (December 1974): 26–30.

Norris, Christopher, ed. *Shostakovich: The Man and His Music*. London, 1982.

Norris, Geoffrey. "Bitter Memories: The Shostakovich Testimony." *Musical Times* 121 (1980): 241–43.

————. "An Opera Restored: Rimsky-Korsakov, Shostakovich and the Khovansky Business." *Musical Times* 123 (1982): 672–75.

————. "The Operas." In *Shostakovich: The Man and His Music*, ed. C. Norris, 105–24. London, 1982.

————. "Shostakovich's *The Nose*." *Musical Times* 120 (1979): 393–94.

Nos, opera v 3-kh aktakh po N. V. Gogolyu. 15-ye sochineniye D. Shostakovicha [*The Nose*: An opera in three acts after Gogol; Shostakovich's op. 15]. Leningrad, 1930. Articles by Shostakovich, Sollertinsky, and Dmitriyev.

Nos. Opera v 3 deystviyakh, 10 kartinakh po N. V. Gogolyu. Muzïka D. Shostakovicha [*The Nose*: An opera in three acts, ten scenes, after Gogol with music by Shostakovich]. Leningrad, 1930. Articles by Shostakovich and Malkov and the libretto.

"Novïy muzïkal'nïy radiozhurnal: D. Shostakovich rasskazïvayet o svoyey rabote nad 12-oy simfoniyey" [A new radio journal: Shostakovich tells of work on his Twelfth Symphony]. *Muzïkal'naya zhizn'* 21 (1960): 10.

"Novïye rabotï D. Shostakovicha" [New works by Shostakovich]. *Leningradskaya Pravda*, 28 August 1939, 4.

Ochs, Ekkehard. "Bemerkungen zum Streichquartettschaffen Dmitri Schostakowitschs." In *Colloquium Musica Cameralis*, ed. Rudolf Pécman, 455–70. Brno, 1971.

————. "Die Streichquartette Dmitri Schostakowitschs im Spiegel sowjetischer Musikpublizistik: Rezeptionsgeschichtliche Anmerkungen." *Neue Berlinische Musikzeitung* 3 (1993): 31–48.

Ogarkova, Natal'ya. "Nekotorïye osobennosti vzaimodeystviya poezii i muzïki v pozdnikh kamerno-vokal'nïkh tsiklakh D. Shostakovich" [Some features of the interaction between poetry and music in Shostakovich's late chamber-vocal cycles]. In *Muzïkal'naya klassika i sovremennost': voprosï istoriii estetiki*, ed. A. Porfir'eva, 25–33. Leningrad, 1983.

O'Laughlin, Niall. "Shostakovich's String Quartets." *Tempo* 87 (1968): 9–16.

————. "Shostakovich's String Quartets." *Musical Times* 115 (1974): 744–46.

Olkhovsky, Andrey. *Music under the Soviets: The Agony of an Art*. New York, 1955; reprint ed. 1975.

"Opera, kotoraya delayet epokhu." *Pro Musica* 7 (1996): 4–5.

Ordzhonikidze, Givi, comp. *Dmitriy Shostakovich*. Moscow, 1967.

————. "Gamlet obretayet volyu" [Hamlet finds the will]. *Sovetskaya muzïka* 8 (1966): 32–36.

————. "'Kazn' Stepana Razina' D. D. Shostakovicha" [Shostakovich's *Execution of Stepan Razin*]. In *Muzïka i sovremennost'*, vïp 4, ed. T. A. Lebedeva, 186–215. Moscow, 1966.

————. "O chetïrnadtsatoy simfonii Dmitriya Shostakovicha i ego sochineniyakh kontsa 60-kh – nachala 70-kh godov" [On Shostakovich's Fourteenth Symphony and works of the late 1960s and early 1970s]. In *Sotsialisticheskaya muzïkal'naya kul'tura: traditsii, problemï, perspektivï*, ed. G. Ordzhonikidze and Yu. El'sner, 105–38. Moscow, 1974.

————. "Das Operntheater Dmitri Schostakowitschs." In *Dmitri Schostakowitsch 1984/85: Wissenschaftliche Beiträge. Dokumente. Interpretationen. Programme*, 157–63. Duisburg, 1984.

————. "XIII simfoniya D. Shostakovicha" [Shostakovich's Thirteenth Symphony]. In *Dmitriy Shostakovich*, comp. G. Ordzhonikidze, 183–223. Moscow, 1967.

————. "Vesna tvorcheskoy zrelosti" [The spring of creative maturity]. *Sovetskaya muzïka* 9 (1966): 38–48.

Orlov, Genrikh. *Dmitriy Shostakovich*. Leningrad, 1966.

————. "Pri dvore torzhestvuyushchey lzhi" [At the court of a triumphant lie]. *Strana i mï* 3 (1986): 62–75. Reprinted in *Iskusstvo Leningrada* 4 (1990): 58–69; and *D. D. Shostakovich: sbornik statey k 90-letiyu so dnya rozhdeniya*, comp. L. Kovnatskaya (St. Petersburg, 1996), 8–28. Abridged version, "Zveno v tsepi: razmïshleniya nad biografiey Dmitriya Shostakovicha" [A link in the chain: reflections on Shostakovich's biography], *Sovetskaya kul'tura* (4 May 1989): 5. Eng. trans. in *Music in the USSR* (Jan/Mar 1990): 36–41.

————. "O shekspirovskom u Shostakovicha" [On the Shakespearean in Shostakovich]. In *Shekspir i muzïka*, ed. L. Raaben, 276–302. Leningrad, 1964.

————. *Simfonii Shostakovicha* [Shostakovich's symphonies]. Moscow, 1961–62.

————. "Simfonizm Shostakovicha na perelome" [Shostakovich's symphonic writing at the turning point]. In *Voprosï teorii i estetiki muzïki, vïp. 10*, 3–31. Leningrad, 1971.

————. "V seredine puti: k 30-letiyu sozdaniya IV simfonii" [In the middle of the path: on the thirtieth anniversary of the composition of the Fourth Symphony]. In *Dmitriy Shostakovich*, comp. G. Ordzhonikidze, 166–88. Moscow, 1967.

Osthoff, Wolfgang. "Symphonien beim Ende des Zweiten Weltkriegs: Strawinsky-Frommel-Schostakowitsch." *Acta musicologica* 60, no. 1 (1988): 62–104.

Ostretsov, Aleksandr. "'Ledi Makbet Mtsenskogo uyezda'; opera D. Shostakovicha" [Shostakovich's *Lady Macbeth of the Mtsensk District*]. *Sovetskaya muzïka* 6 (1933): 9–32.

Ostrovskiy, Aron. "V godinu ispïtaniy" [In the time of ordeals]. In *Leningradskaya konservatoriya v vospominaniyakh, 1862–1962*, 384–95. Leningrad, 1962.

Ottaway, Hugh. *Shostakovich Symphonies*. London, 1978.

Ovchinnikov, Yevgeniy. "Vtoraya fortepiannaya sonata Shostakovicha" [Shostakovich's Second Piano Sonata]. In *Voprosï teorii muzïki*, 1, ed. S. Skrebkov, 239–65. Moscow, 1968.

Oystrakh, David. "Velikiy khudozhnik nashego vremeni" [A great artist of our time]. In *D. Shostakovich: stat'i i materialï*, comp. G. Shneerson, 23–30. Moscow, 1976.

————. "Voploshcheniye bol'shogo zamïsla: o skripichnom kontserte Shostakovicha" [The incarnation of a great idea: on Shostakovich's Violin Concerto]. *Sovetskaya muzïka* 7 (1956): 3–10; Ger. trans. in *Sowjetwissenschaft, Kunst und Literatur* 4 (1956): 877–85.

Ozhigova, Margarita. "Mitya, Dmitriy Dmitriyevich." In *Muzïkal'naya pedagogika v ideyakh i litsakh*, ed. A. Selitskiy, 84–97. Rostov-on-Don, 1992.

Pervïy vsesoyuznïy s'ezd sovetskikh kompozitorov: stenograficheskiy otchyot [The First

All-Union Congress of Soviet Composers: stenographic report]. Moscow, 1948.

Petrushanskaya, Elena. "Brodskiy i Shostakovich" [Brodsky and Shostakovich].
In *Shostakovichu posvyashchayetsya: sbornik statey k 90-letiyu kompozitora (1906–1996)*, comp. E. Dolinskaya, 78–90. Moscow, 1997.

———. "Da prebudet s nami!" [He will abide with us]. *Muzïkal'naya zhizn'* 12 (1995): 36–38.

Piotrovskiy, Adrian. "Ledi Makbet Mtsenskogo uyezda" [*Lady Macbeth of the Mtsensk District*]. In *Malïy opernïy teatr*, 32–43. Leningrad, 1936.

———. "Svetlïy ruchey" [*The Limpid Stream*]. In *Malïy opernïy teatr*, 76–85. Leningrad, 1936.

Pis'ma Dmitriya Dmitriyevicha Shostakovicha Borisu Tishchenko: s kommentariyami i vospominaniyami adresata [Letters of Shostakovich to Boris Tishchenko: with commentaries and reminiscences of the addressee]. St. Petersburg, 1997.

Pis'ma k drugu: Dmitriy Shostakovich—Isaaku Glikmanu [Letters to a Friend: Dmitriy Shostakovich to Isaak Glikman], comp. Isaak Glikman. Moscow and St. Petersburg, 1993. Fr. trans. as *Dmitri Chostakovitsch: lettres à un ami* (Paris, 1994); Ger. trans., *Chaos statt Musik?: Briefe an einem Freund* (Berlin, 1995).

Podol'skiy, S. "Ya k kritike otnoshus' s bol'shim uvazheniyem ..." [I have great respect for criticism]. *Sovetskaya muzïka* 9 (1974): 54–55.

Poldyayeva, Elena. "O repetitsii Shostakovicha v Germanii" [On Shostakovich rehearsals in Germany]. *Muzïkal'naya akademiya* 4 (1997): 162–66.

———. "Zur historischen Katergorisierung und ästhetischen Bewertung des Schaffens von Dimitri Schostakowitsch aus dem Blickwinkel der Avantgarde der 50er Jahre." In *Schostakowitsch in Deutschland (Schostakowitsch-Studien, 1)*, ed. H. Schmalenberg, 23–43. Berlin, 1998.

Polyakova, Lyudmila, *Vokal'nïy tsikl D. Shostakovicha 'Iz Yevreyskoy narodnoy poezii'* [Shostakovich's vocal cycle *From Jewish Folk Poetry*]. Moscow, 1957.

"Posledniy muzïkal'nïy geniy epokhi" [The last musical genius of the epoch]. *Muzïkal'naya akademiya* 4 (1997): 167–82.

Postnikov, I. *Vtoroy fortep'yannïy kontsert Shostakovicha* [Shostakovich's Second Piano Concerto]. Moscow, 1959.

"Proizvedeniye Shostakovicha—gluboko zapadnoy orientatsii" [Shostakovich's composition is of profoundly Western orientation]. *Staraya ploshchad': vestnik* 5 (1995): 156–59.

Protopopov, Vladimir. "O yedinstve tsikla v Odinnadtsatoy simfonii '1905 god' D. D. Shostakovicha" [On the unity of the cycle in Shostakovich's Eleventh Symphony]. In *Soobshcheniya Instituta istorii iskusstv AN SSSR, vïp. 15*, 23–35. Moscow, 1959.

Pulcini, Franco. *Šostakovič*. Turin, 1988.

Raaben, Lev. "Obraznïy mir poslednikh kamerno-instrumental'nïkh sochineniy D. Shostakovicha" [The artistic universe of Shostakovich's last chamber-instrumental works]. In *Voprosï teorii i estetiki muzïki, vïp. 15*, 44–54. Leningrad, 1977.

Rabinovich, David. *Dmitry Shostakovich, Composer*. Moscow and London, 1959.

Rabinovich, Isaak, ed. *B. Yavorskiy: stat'i, vospominaniya, perepiska* [Yavorsky: articles, reminiscences, correspondence]. Vol. 1. Moscow, 1972.

Rayskin, Iosif. "Dmitriy Shostakovich: nekanonicheskaya ikonografiya" [Shostakovich: an incomplete iconography]. In *D. D. Shostakovich: sbornik statey k 90-letiyu so dnya rozhdeniya*, comp. L. Kovnatskaya, 379–90. St. Petersburg, 1996.

———. "Kak teatr Kirova ne stal teatr Shostakovicha: dokumental'noye povestvovaniye" [How the Kirov Theater did not become the Shostakovich Theater: a story in documents]. In *Ars Peterburg: "Mariinskiy—vchera, segodnya, vsegda,"* 94–101. St. Petersburg, 1993.

Razhnikov, Vladimir. *Kirill Kondrashin rasskazïvayet o muzïke i zhizni* [Kondrashin speaks about music and life]. Moscow, 1989.

Redepenning, Dorothea. "'And Art Made Tongue-tied by Authority': Shostakovich's Song-Cycles." In *Shostakovich Studies*, ed. D. Fanning, 205–28. Cambridge, 1995.

———. "Autobiographische Reflexionen—Schostakowitschs Zwetajewa-Zyklus (op. 143)." *Musica* 44, no. 3 (1990): 164–68.

———. "Mahler und Schostakowitsch." In *Das Gustav-Mahler-Fest, Hamburg, 1989. Bericht über den Internationalen Gustav-Mahler-Kongress*, ed. M. T. Vogt, 345–62. Kassel, 1991; Rus. trans. in *Muzïkal'naya akademiya* 1 (1994): 164–69.

Reed, Philip, ed. *The Travel Diaries of Peter Pears, 1936–1978*. Aldeburgh, 1995.

Reinäcker, Gerd, and Vera Reising. *Die 11. und 12. Sinfonie von Dmitri Schostakowitsch: Einführungsmaterial für Kulturfunktionäre*. Berlin, 1970.

Rikhter, E. R., comp. *Genrikh Neygauz: vospominaniya, pis'ma, materialï* [Heinrich Neuhaus: reminiscences, letters, materials]. Moscow, 1992.

Robinson, Harlow. "The Case of the 3 Russians: Stravinsky, Prokofiev and Shostakovich." *Opera Quarterly* 6, no. 3 (1989): 59–75.

Romadinova, Dora. "Shostakovich: geroy ili antigeroy?" [Shostakovich: hero or anti-hero?]. *Vremya i mï* (1990): 244–67.

Roseberry, Eric. "A Debt Repaid? Some Observations on Shostakovich and his Late-Period Recognition of Britten." In *Shostakovich Studies*, ed. D. Fanning, 229–53. Cambridge, 1995. Abridged Rus. reprint in *D. D. Shostakovich: sbornik statey k 90-letiyu so dnya rozhdeniya*, comp. L. Kovnatskaya (St. Petersburg, 1996), 324–33.

———. *Ideology, Style, Content, and Thematic Process in the Symphonies, Cello Concertos and String Quartets of Shostakovich*. New York, 1989.

———. *Shostakovich: His Life and Times*. Tunbridge Wells, 1982.

Rowland, Christopher, and Alan George. "Interpreting the String Quartets." In *Shostakovich: The Man and His Music*, ed. C. Norris, 13–45. London, 1982.

Rozhdestvenskiy, Gennadiy. "Portretï Dmitriya Dmitriyevicha Shostakovicha" [Portraits of Shostakovich]. *Nashe naslediye* (1998): 166–69.

Ruchevskaya, Ekaterina. "K istorii sozdaniya 'Ledi Makbet Mtsenskogo uezda'" [Concerning the history of the creation of *Lady Macbeth of the Mtsensk District*]. In *D. D. Shostakovich: sbornik statey k 90-letiyu so dnya rozhdeniya*, comp. L. Kovnatskaya, 101–02. St. Petersburg, 1996.

Rudneva, Lyubov'. "Shostakovich i Meyerkhol'd" [Shostakovich and Meyerhold]. *Aprel'* 5 (1992): 219–29.

Rubtsova, Valentina, ed. *Tak eto bïlo: Tikhon Khrennikov o vremeni i o sebe* [That's the way it was: Khrennikov about the times and himself]. Moscow, 1994.

Rïzhkin, Iosif. "O sushchnosti operï 'Nos': ot pokaza v 1929 godu k predshest-vuyushchemu i posleduyushchemu" [On the essence of the opera *The Nose*: from the demonstration in 1929 to the preceding and the subsequent]. *Muzïkal'naya akademiya* 1 (1997): 83-95.

Sabinina, Marina. "Bïlo li dva Shostakovicha?" [Were there two Shostakoviches?]. *Muzïkal'naya akademiya* 4 (1997): 233–37.

———. *Dmitriy Shostakovich*. Moscow, 1959.

———. "Moskva, Cheryomushki." *Sovetskaya muzïka* 4 (1959): 41–52.

———. "Mozaika proshlogo" [A mosaic of the past]. In *Shostakovichu posvya-shchayetsya: sbornik statey k 90-letiyu kompozitora (1906–1996)*, comp. E. Dolinskaya, 206–20. Moscow, 1997.

———. *Shostakovich—simfonist: dramaturgiya, estetika, stil'* [Shostakovich as symphonist: dramaturgy, aesthetics, style]. Moscow, 1976.

———. *Simfonizm Shostakovicha* [Shostakovich's symphonic writing]. Moscow, 1965.

———. "Simfonizm D. Shostakovicha v godï voynï" [Shostakovich's symphonic writing during the war years]. In *Muzïka v bor'be s fashizmom: sbornik statey*, ed. I. Medvedeva, 9–29. Moscow, 1985.

———. *Skripichnïy kontsert D.Shostakovicha* [Shostakovich's Violin Concerto no. 1]. Moscow, 1958.

———. "Zametki o 14-oy simfonii" [Notes on the Fourteenth Symphony]. *Sovetskaya muzïka* 9 (1970): 22–31.

———. "Zametki ob opere 'Katerina Izmailova'" [Remarks on *Katerina Izmai-lova*]. In *Dmitriy Shostakovich*, comp. G. Ordzhonikidze, 132–66. Moscow, 1967.

Sadovnikov, Efim, *D. D. Shostakovich: notograficheskiy spravochnik* [Shostakovich: catalogue of works]. Moscow, 1961; 2nd ed. enlarged with bibliography, 1965.

Sadïkhova, Rosa and Dmitriy Frederiks, comp. "Dmitriy Shostakovich: pis'ma k materi" [Shostakovich: letters to his mother]. *Niva* 9 (1986): 166–75.

Sahlberg-Vatchnadzé, Marguerite. *Chostakovitch*. Paris, 1945.

Sakva, Konstantin. "Novaya vstrecha s 'Katerinoy Izmailovoy'" [A new encounter with *Katerina Izmailova*]. *Sovetskaya muzïka* 3 (1963): 57–62; Ger. trans. in *Musik und Gesellschaft* 13 (1963): 428–32.

Salnis, Nataliya. "Sotsial'nïy kharakter satïrï D. D. Shostakovicha" [The social char-acter of Shostakovich's satire]. In *Muzïka v sotsialisticheskom obshchestve, vïp. 2*, 89–101. Leningrad, 1975.

Samuel, Claude. *Entretiens avec Mstislav Rostropovitch et Galina Vichnevskaïa*. Paris, 1983. Eng. trans., *Mstislav Rostropovich and Galina Vishnevskaya: Russia, Music, and Liberty* (Portland, Oregon, 1995).

Sass-Tisovskaya (Poryadkova), E. "Nas utro vstrechayet prokhladoy" [The morning greets us with coolness]. *Muzïkal'naya zhizn'* 10–11 (1995): 16–19.

Savenko, Svetlana. "Slovo Shostakovicha" [Shostakovich's word]. In *D. D. Shosta-kovich: sbornik statey k 90-letiyu so dnya rozhdeniya*, comp. L. Kovnatskaya, 359–66. St. Petersburg, 1996.

———. "Stravinsky i Shostakovich" [Stravinsky and Shostakovich]. *Muzïkal'naya akademiya* 4 (1997): 193–95.

Schmalenberg, Hilmar, ed. *Schostakowitsch in Deutschland (Schostakowitsch-Studien, 1)*. Berlin, 1988.

———. "Schostakowitsch und Deutschland." *Neue Berlinische Musikzeitung* 2 (1995): 29–35.

Schneider, Frank. "Wovon 'spricht' Schostakowitsch? Ein semantischer Versuch zur 10. Sinfonie." *Beiträge zur Musikwissenschaft* 32, no. 4 (1990): 284–87.

Schostakowitsch Festival 1984/85: Dokumentation. Presseberichte (Auswahl). Duisburg, 1985.

Schwarz, Boris. *Music and Musical Life in Soviet Russia, 1917–1970*. London, 1972; enlarged ed. (1917–1981), 1983.

———. "Shostakovich, Soviet Citizen and Anti-Stalinist." In *Music and Civilization: Essays in Honor of Paul Henry Lang*, 363–70. New York, 1984.

Schwarz, Boris, and Laurel E. Fay. "Dmitry Shostakovich." *The New Grove Russian Masters* 2, 175–231. London, 1986.

Seehaus, Lothar. *Dmitrij Schostakowitsch: Leben und Werk*. Wilhelmshaven, 1986.

Serebryakova, Galina. "D. D. Shostakovich." In *O drugikh i o sebe*, 297–308. Moscow, 1968.

Seroff, Victor, in collaboration with Nadejda Galli-Shohat. *Dmitri Shostakovich: The Life and Background of a Soviet Composer*. New York, 1943; reprint 1970.

Shafarevich, Igor. "D. D. Shostakovich." *Le Messager: vestnik russkogo khristianskogo dvizheniya* 2, no. 125 (1978): 232–50. Reprinted as "Vremya Shostakovicha" [Shostakovich's time], *Slovo* 10 (1990): 18–24; and in *I. R. Shafarevich: sochineniya*, 2 (Moscow, 1994), 432–50.

———. "Shostakovich i russkoye soprotivleniye kommunizmu" [Shostakovich and Russian resistance to communism]. In *I. R. Shafarevich: sochineniya* 2, 451–58. Moscow, 1994.

Shaginyan, Marietta. *O Shostakoviche* [On Shostakovich]. Moscow, 1979.

———. "50 pisem D. D. Shostakovicha." *Novïy mir* 12 (1982): 128–52; Eng. trans., "Fifty Letters from Dmitri Shostakovich." *Soviet Literature* 1 (1984): 68–99.

Shantïr, Natal'ya. "Posledneye slovo mastera" [The master's last word]. *Sovetskaya muzïka* 11 (1983): 94–97.

Shaverdyan, Aleksandr. *Sed'maya simfoniya D. Shostakovicha* [Shostakovich's Seventh Symphony]. Yerevan, 1942.

Shebalina, Alisa, ed. "Eto bïl zamechatel'nïy drug: iz pisem D. D. Shostakovicha k V. Ya. Shebalinu" [He was a remarkable friend: from Shostakovich's letters to V. Shebalin]. *Sovetskaya muzïka* 7 (1982): 75–85.

———. *V. Ya. Shebalin: godï zhizni i tvorchestva* [Shebalin: chronicle of his life and creative work]. Moscow, 1990.

———, ed. *Vissarion Yakovlevich Shebalin: literaturnoye naslediye* [Shebalin's literary legacy]. Moscow, 1975.

Shirinskiy, Aleksandr. "Ob ispolnenii Sonatï dlya skripki i fortepiano D. Shostakovicha I. Oystrakhom i S. Rikhterom" [On the performance of Shostakovich's Violin Sonata by Oistrakh and Richter]. In *Kamernïy ansambl': pedagogika i ispolnitel'stvo, vïp. 2*, 120–33. Moscow, 1996.

————. *Skripichnïye proizvedeniya D. Shostakovicha* [Violin Works of D. Shosta-kovich]. Moscow, 1988.

Shirinskiy, Vasiliy. "Iz kvartetnogo zhurnala" [From the quartet's journal]. *Muzïkal'naya akademiya* 4 (1997): 137–48.

Shlifshteyn, Semyon. "'Kazn' Stepana Razina' Shostakovicha i traditsii Musorgskogo" [*The Execution of Stepan Razin* and the traditions of Musorgsky]. In *Dmitriy Shostakovich*, comp. G. Ordzhonikidze, 223–41. Moscow, 1967.

Shneerson, Grigoriy. "Zhizn' muzïki Shostakovicha za rubezhom" [The life of Shostakovich's music abroad]. In *D. Shostakovich: stat'i i materialï*, ed. G. Shneerson, 227–64. Moscow, 1976.

————, comp. *D. Shostakovich: stat'i i materialï*. Moscow, 1976.

Shostakovich, Dmitriy. "Autobiographie." *La revue musicale* 170 (1936): 432–33.

————. "Avtobiografiya" [Autobiography]. *Sovetskaya muzïka* 9 (1966): 24–25.

————. "Bït' na vïsote velikikh zadach" [To be at the height of great tasks]. *Sovet-skaya muzïka* 1 (1959): 7–10.

————. "Bol'shoy talant, bol'shoy master" [A great talent, a great master]. In *I. O. Dunayevsky: vïstupleniya, stat'i, pis'ma, vospominaniya*, ed. E. Grosheva, 9–12. Moscow, 1961.

————. "Budem trubachami velikoy epokhi" [We will be trumpeters of a great ep-och]. *Leningradskaya Pravda*, 28 December 1934, 4.

————. "Deklaratsiya obyazannostey kompozitora" [Declaration of a composer's duties]. *Rabochiy i teatr* 31 (1931): 6.

————. "Dumï o proydyonnom puti" [Thoughts about the path traversed]. *Sovetskaya muzïka* 9 (1956): 9–15.

————. Foreword. In A. S. Rabinovich, *Izbrannïye stat'i i materialï*, 3–6. Moscow, 1959.

————. Foreword. In *B. Yavorskiy: vospominaniya, stat'i, i pis'ma*, 1, 5. Moscow, 1964; revised ed., 1972.

————. Foreword. In *Gustav Maler* [Mahler], ed. I. Barsova, 7–8. Moscow, 1964; 2nd ed., 1968.

————. "I. I. Sollertinskiy." In *I. Sollertinskiy: istoricheskiye etyudï*, ed. M. Druskin, 3–11. 2nd ed. Leningrad, 1963.

————. "Iz vospominaniy" [Reminiscences]. *Sovetskaya muzïka* 3 (1974): 54–55.

————. "Iz vospominaniy o Mayakovskom" [Reminiscences of Mayakovsky]. In *V. Mayakovskiy v vospominaniyakh sovremennikov*, 315–17. Moscow, 1963.

————. "Kak rozhdayetsya muzïka" [How music is born]. *Literaturnaya gazeta*, 21 Dec 1965, 3. Reprinted in *Dmitriy Shostakovich*, comp. G. Ordzhonikidze, 35–39. Moscow, 1967.

————. "K prem'ere 'Nosa'" [Toward the premiere of *The Nose*]. *Rabochiy i teatr* 24 (1929): 12.

————. "Kino kak shkola kompozitora" [The cinema as schooling for a composer]. In *30 let sovetskoy kinematografii: sbornik statey*, ed. D. Eremin, 354–58. Moscow, 1950.

————. "Mirovoy avtoritet sovetskogo iskusstva" [The worldwide authority of Soviet art]. *Pravda*, 13 June 1958, 3. Also in *Sovetskaya kul'tura* (14 June 1958): 2.

————. "Moi blizhayshiye rabotï" [My forthcoming works]. *Rabochiy i teatr* 11 (1937): 24.

————. "Moy tvorcheskiy otvet" [My creative answer]. *Vechernyaya Moskva*, 25 January 1938, 3.

————. "Moy tvorcheskiy put'" [My creative path]. *Izvestiya*. 3 April 1935, 4.

————. "Moya Alma Mater" [My Alma Mater]. *Sovetskaya muzïka* 9 (1962): 101–4.

————. "Moya sed'maya simfoniya" [My Seventh Symphony]. *Vechernyaya Moskva*, 8 October 1941. Also in *Izvestiya*, 13 February 1942, 3.

————. "Muzïka i vremya: zametki kompozitora" [Music and time: a composer's remarks]. *Kommunist* 7 (1975): 38–44. Also in *Muzïka i sovremennost'*, *vïp. 10* (Moscow, 1976), 5–16.

————. "Muzïka, rozhdyonnaya segodnya" [Music born today]. *Literaturnaya gazeta*, 4 December 1968, 8.

————. "Muzïka v kino: zametki kompozitora" [Film music: a composer's remarks]. *Literaturnaya gazeta*, 10 April 1939, 5.

————. "My opera *Lady Macbeth of Mtsensk.*" *Modern Music* 12, no. 1 (1934): 23–30.

————. "Mï dolzhnï ob'yedinit' nashi usiliya" [We should unite our efforts]. *Vechernyaya Moskva*, 29 March 1949. Also in *Literaturnaya gazeta*, 30 March 1949, 4; *Kul'tura i zhizn'* (31 March 1949); *Sovetskoye iskusstvo* (2 April 1949), 4.

————. "Nas vdokhnovlyayet partiya" [The party inspires us], *Muzïkal'naya zhizn'* 2 (1962): 1–3. Also in *Sovetskaya muzïka* 3 (1962): 3–15.

————. "Nasha rabota v godï Otechestvennoy voynï" [Our work during the years of the Patriotic War]. In *Rabota kompozitorov i muzïkovedov Leningrada v godï Velikoy Otechestvennoy voynï*, Leningrad, 1946, 61–70.

————. "Natsional'nïye traditsii i zakonomernosti ikh razvitiya" [National traditions and the precepts of their development]. *Sovetskaya muzïka* 12 (1971): 34–36; Eng. trans. in *Composer* 42 (Winter 1971–72): 1–4.

————. "Novoye o Mayakovskom" [Something new about Mayakovsky]. *Literaturnaya gazeta*, 9 October 1956, 2. Reprinted in *Dmitriy Shostakovich*, comp. G. Ordzhonikidze (Moscow, 1967), 25–26.

————. "O nekotorïkh nasushchnïkh voprosakh muzïkal'nogo tvorchestva" [On some vital questions of musical creativity]. *Pravda*, 17 June 1956, 5. Reprinted in *Dmitriy Shostakovich*, comp. G. Ordzhonikidze (Moscow, 1967), 16–24.

————. "O podlinnoy i mnimoy programmnosti" [On genuine and imaginary program music]. *Sovetskaya muzïka* 5 (1951): 76–78.

————. "O sovetskoy pesne i estradnoy muzïke" [On the Soviet song and variety music]. *Sovetskaya muzïka* 10 (1986): 47–51.

————. "Ot Marksa do nashikh dney" [From Marx to the present day]. *Sovetskoye iskusstvo* (15 February 1932), 1.

————. "Otvet amerikanskomu muzïkal'nomu kritiku" [Answer to an American music critic]. *Sovetskaya muzïka* 3 (1956): 142–43. See also *New York Times*, 8 January 1956, Sec. 2, 9.

————. "Plakat' i smeyat'sya" [To cry and to laugh]. *Sovetskoye iskusstvo* (3 March 1933): 3.

————. "Pochemu 'Nos'?" [Why *The Nose*?]. *Rabochiy i teatr* 3 (1930): 11.

———. "Po puti narodnosti i realizma" [Along the path of nationality and real-ism]. *Sovetskaya muzïka* 11 (1952): 6-11.

———. "Po puti ukazannomu partiyey" [On the path indicated by the party]. *Sovetskaya kul'tura* (10 September 1957): 1. Also in *Sovetskaya muzïka* 10 (1957): 10.

———. *The Power of Music*. New York, 1968. Nine essays originally published in *The Music Journal*, 1962–68.

———. "Predisloviye k prem'ere: novaya simfoniya D. Shostakovicha" [Preface to a premiere: Shostakovich's new symphony]. *Pravda*, 25 April 1969, 6.

———. "Priglasheniye k molodoy muzïke" [An invitation to youthful music]. *Yunost'* 5 (1968): 83–87.

———. "Radost' tvorcheskikh iskaniy" [The joy of creative quests]. *Sovetskaya muzïka* 1 (1954): 40–42.

———. "Schast'ye poznaniya" [The fortune of knowledge]. *Sovetskoye iskusstvo* (5 November 1934): 5.

———. "Sed'maya simfoniya" [Seventh Symphony]. In *Svoim oruzhiyem*, ed. I. Lupalo, 297–302. Moscow, 1961.

———. "Shirokiye massï vernï nastoyashchey muzïke" [The broad masses are faithful to real music]. *Sovetskaya muzïka* 11 (1959): 6–9.

———. *Sobraniye sochineniy v soroka dvukh tomakh* [Collected works in forty-two volumes]. Moscow, 1979–87.

———. "Sovetskaya muzïka v dni voynï" [Soviet music in the days of the war]. *Literatura i iskusstvo* (1 April 1944). Reprinted in *Sovetskaya muzïka* 11 (1975): 64–77.

———. "Sovetskaya muzïkal'naya kritika otstayot" [Soviet musical criticism is lagging]. *Sovetskaya muzïka* 3 (1933): 120–21.

———. "Stranitsï vospominaniy" [Pages of reminiscences]. In *Leningrad-skaya konservatoriya v vospominaniyakh*, 121–26. Leningrad, 1962; 2nd ed. 1987.

———. "Thoughts about Tchaikovsky." In *Russian Symphony*, 1–5. New York, 1947.

———. "Tragediya-satira" [A tragedy-satire]. *Sovetskoye iskusstvo* (16 October 1933). Reprinted in *Dmitriy Shostakovich*, comp. G. Ordzhonikidze, 13–14. Moscow, 1967.

———. "Tri voprosa—otvet odin" [Three questions—one answer]. *Sovetskaya muzïka* 12 (1964): 11–15.

———. "V dni oboronï Leningrada" [During the defense of Leningrad]. *Sovetskoye iskusstvo* (9 October 1941): 3.

———. "V 1928 godu ..." [In 1928]. *Teatr* 2 (1974): 52–54.

———. "Vïstupleniye na sobranii kompozitorov i muzïkovedov g. Moskvï" [Speech at the gathering of composers and musicologists of the city of Moscow]. *Sovetskaya muzïka* 1 (1948): 78–79.

———. "Vospominaniya" [Reminiscences]. In *Pamyati I. I. Sollertinskogo: vospo-minaniya, materialï, issledovaniya*, comp. L. Mikheyeva, 102–04. 2nd ed. Lenin-grad, 1974.

———. "Vospominaniya ob I. I. Sollertinskom" [Reminiscences of I. I.

Sollertinsky]. In *Informatsionnïy byulleten' SK SSSR* 5–6 (1944). Reprinted in *Muzïkal'nïy sovremennik, vïp. 1*, 338–40. Moscow, 1973.

———. "Vse silï otdat' velikoy i svyashchennoy tseli—pobede: iz literaturnogo nasledstva D. Shostakovicha" [To devote all one's might to a great and sacred goal—victory: from Shostakovich's literary legacy]. *Yunost'* 5 (1985): 89–95.

———. "V zashchitu mira i kul'turï" [In defense of peace and culture]. *Sovetskaya muzïka* 5 (1949): 8–22.

———. "Ya pïtalsya peredat' pafos bor'bï i pobedï" [I tried to convey the pathos of struggle and victory], ed. M. Yakubov, *Sovetskaya muzïka* 10 (1986): 52–57.

———. *Znat' i liubit' muzïku. Beseda s molodyozh'yu* [To know and love music: a conversation with youth]. Moscow, 1958.

Shostakovich, Dmitriy, with A. Abramova, and V. Stroyeva. "K istorii rabotï nad fil'mom *Khovanshchina*" [About the history of work on the film *Khovanshchina*]. In *Zhizn' v kino: veteranï o sebe i svoikh tovarishchakh, vïp. 2*, 290–313. Moscow, 1979.

Shumskaya, Natal'ya. "Traditsiya i novatorstvo v opere Shostakovicha 'Katerina Izmailova'" [Tradition and innovation in *Katerina Izmailova*]. *Muzïka i sovremennost', vïp. 3*, 104–21. Moscow, 1965.

Shvartsval'd-Khmïznikova, E. "Sofiya Vasil'evna – mat' Shostakovicha" [Sofiya Vasil'evna-Shostakovich's mother]. *Muzïkal'naya akademiya* 2 (1995): 185–88.

Slonimskiy, Sergey. "O blagorodstve chelovecheskogo dukha" [On the nobility of the human spirit]. *Sovetskaya muzïka* 7 (1971): 31–33.

———. "Pobeda Stepana Razina" [Stepan Razin's victory]. In *D. Shostakovich: stat'i i materialï*, comp. G. Shneerson, 211–18. Moscow, 1976.

Slonimsky, Nicolas. "Dmitri Dmitrievitch Shostakovich." *Musical Quarterly* 28 (1942): 415–44.

———. *Music since 1900*. 4th ed. New York, 1971.

Smirnov, V. "O svoyey professii …: iz besedï s D. D. Shostakovichem" [On my profession....: from conversations with Shostakovich]. *Teatral'naya nedelya* 9 (24 February 1941): 11.

Sokhor, Arnold. "Bol'shaya pravda o 'malenkom' cheloveke (tsikl 'Iz yevreyskoy narodnoy poezii' i ego mesto v tvorchestve Shostakovicha)" [A great truth about the "little" man (the cycle *From Jewish Folk Poetry* and its place in Shostakovich's work)]. In *Dmitriy Shostakovich*, comp. G. Ordzhonikidze, 241–59. Moscow, 1967.

Sokolov, Nikolai. "O vstrechakh s D. D. Shostakovichem" [On encounters with D. D. Shostakovich]. In *Nabroski po pamyati*, 66–75. Moscow, 1987.

Sokol'skiy, Matias. *Musorgskiy/Shostakovich: stat'i, retsenzii* [Musorsgky/Shostakovich: articles, reviews]. Moscow, 1983.

———. "Opera i kompozitor" [Opera and composer]. *Sovetskoye iskusstvo* (16 October 1932). Reprinted in *Musorgskiy/Shostakovich: stat'i, retsenzii*, 85–88. Moscow, 1983.

———. *Slushaya vremya: izbrannïye stat'i o muzïke* [Listening to time: selected articles]. Moscow, 1964.

Sollertinskiy, Ivan. "Ledi Makbet Mtsenskogo Uyezda." *Rabochiy i teatr* 4 (1934):

2–3. Reprinted in *Kriticheskiye stat'i*, 72–76. Leningrad, 1963.

———. "'Nos' – orudiye dal'noboynoye" [*The Nose*—a long-range gun]. *Rabochiy i teatr* 7 (1930): 6–7.

———. *Von Mozart bis Schostakowitsch*, trans. C. Rüger. Leipzig, 1979.

Sollertinsky, Dmitri and Ludmilla. *Pages from the Life of Dmitri Shostakovich*, trans. G. Hobbs and C. Midgley. New York, 1980.

Solotow, Andrei. "Schostakowitsch und seine Zeit." In *Dmitri Schostakowitsch und seine Zeit: Kunst und Kultur*, ed. K.-E. Vester, 11–30. Duisburg, 1984.

Souster, Tim. "Shostakovich at the Crossroads." *Tempo* 78 (1966): 2–9.

Soveshchaniye deyateley sovetskoy muzïki v TsK VKP(b) [Conference of Soviet musicians at the Central Committee of the Communist Party]. Moscow, 1948.

Sovetskaya muzïka 9 (1976), 9–10; (1981), 9–10 (1986). Special issues.

Spektor, Nelli. "'Sonet 66' Shekspira v tvorchestve D. Shostakovicha: k probleme mezhduopusnïkh svyazey" [Shakespeare's Sonnet 66 in the work of Shostakovich: toward the problem of inter-opus connections]. In *Iz istorii russkoy i sovetskoy muzïki, vïp. 3*, 210–18. Moscow, 1978.

S. S. Prokof'yev i N. Ya. Myaskovskiy: perepiska [Prokofiev and Myaskovsky: correspondence], comp. M. Kozlova and N. Yatsenko. Moscow, 1977.

Stevens, Bernard. "Shostakovich and the British Composer." In *Shostakovich: The Man and His Music*, ed. C. Norris, 149–61. London, 1982.

Stevenson, Ronald. "The Piano Music." In *Shostakovich: The Man and His Music*, ed. C. Norris, 81–103. London, 1982.

Stille, Michael. "Der Virtuose mit der Narrenkappe: Dmitri Schostakowitsch und sein Konzert c-moll für Klavier, Trompete und Streichorchester op. 35." In *Beiträge zur Geschichte des Konzerts: Festschrift Siegfried Kross zum 60. Gerburtstag*, ed. R. Emans and M. Wendt, 399–410. Bonn, 1990.

Stradling, Robert. "Shostakovich and the Soviet System, 1925–1975." In *Shostakovich: The Man and His Music*, ed. C. Norris, 189–217. London, 1982.

Streller, Friedbert. *Dmitri Schostakowitsch*. Leipzig, 1982.

———. "Schostakowitsch—Dissident oder Opportunist." In *Schostakowitsch in Deutschland (Schostakowitsch-Studien, 1)*, ed. H. Schmalenberg, 139–51. Berlin, 1998.

"Sud'ba i khronika istoricheskogo sodruzhestvo: Shostakovich i 'betkhoventsï'" [The fate and chronicle of a historic collaboration: Shostakovich and the "Beethovens"]. *Muzïkal'naya akademiya* 4 (1997): 136–48.

"Sumbur vmesto muzïki: ob opere 'Ledi Makbet Mtsenskogo Uyezda' D. Shostakovicha" [Muddle instead of music: on Shostakovich's opera *Lady Macbeth of the Mtsensk District*]. *Pravda*, 28 January 1936, 3. Also in *Sovetskaya muzïka* 2 (1936): 4–5.

Svetlïy ruchey [*The Limpid Stream*]. Leningrad, 1935. Articles by Shostakovich, Druskin, and Yu. Slonimsky.

Szulc, M. "Szostakowicz a sowiecka polityka kultural na od grudnia 1917 roku do 1953 roku." In *Zeszyty Naukowe IV*, ed. T. Brodniewicz, J. Kempiński and J. Tatarska, 53–62. Poznań, 1993.

Tammaro, Ferruccio. "I Quartetti di Šostakovič." *Nuova rivista musicale italiana* 25, no. 1 (1991): 30–53.

————. *Le sinfonie di Šostakovič*. Turin, 1988.

Tamaschke, C. "Ein Schostakowitsch-Brief." *Beiträge zur Musikwissenschaft* 29, no. 4 (1987): 331–32.

Tarakanov, Mikhaíl. "Zametki o novom sochineniy" [Notes about a new composition]. *Sovetskaya muzïka* 7 (1971): 33-39.

Tarakanova, Ekaterina. "'Nos' Shostakovicha i avangardnïye khudozhestvennïye napravleniya nachala XX veka" [Shostakovich's *Nose* and avant-garde artistic directions of the twentieth century]. In *Shostakovichu posvyashchayetsya: sbornik statey k 90-letiyu kompozitora (1906–1996)*, comp. E. Dolinskaya, 143–49. Moscow, 1997.

Tartakovskaya, Natal'ya. "Pisal yego s mïslyami o Vas" [I wrote it thinking about you]. *Muzïkal'naya akademiya* 4 (1997): 182–84.

Taruskin, Richard. "Dmitri Shostakovich. Symphony No. 7, 'Leningrad,' op. 60 (1941): Facsimile Edition." *Music Library Association Notes* 50, no.2 (1993): 756–61. Abridged Rus. trans. in *Muzïkal'naya akademiya* 4 (1997): 132–35.

————. "Entr'acte: The Lessons of Lady M." In *Defining Russia Musically: Historical and Hermeneutical Essays*, 498–510. Princeton, 1997.

————. "The Opera and the Dictator: The Peculiar Martyrdom of Dmitri Shostakovich." *New Republic* (20 March 1989): 34–40.

————. "Public Lies and Unspeakable Truth: Interpreting Shostakovich's Fifth Symphony." In *Shostakovich Studies*, ed. D. Fanning, 17–56. Cambridge, 1995. Reprinted in *Defining Russia Musically: Historical and Hermeneutical Essays*, 511–44. Princeton, 1997.

————. "Shostakovich and Us." In *Defining Russia Musically: Historical and Hermeneutical Essays*, 468–97. Princeton, 1997.

————. "Who Was Shostakovich?" *Atlantic Monthly* 275, no. 2 (1995): 62–64, 66–68, 70–72.

Taubman, Howard. *The Pleasure of Their Company: A Reminiscence*. Portland, Oregon, 1994.

Tevosyan, Aleksandr. "Khudozhnik paradoksal'nogo vremeni" [An artist of a paradoxical time]. *Muzïkal'naya akademiya* 4 (1997): 155–58.

Tishchenko, Boris. "Razmïshleniya o 142-m i 143-m opusakh" [Reflections on opus 142 and 143]. *Sovetskaya muzïka* 9 (1974): 40–46.

Trauberg, Leonid. "Voistinu on chelovekom bïl" [He was truly a man]. *Muzïkal'naya zhizn'* 5–6 (1995): 22–23.

Tret'yakova, Liliya. *Dmitriy Shostakovich*. Moscow, 1976.

Tsïganov, Dmitriy. "Chetïre desyatiletiya muzïki" [Four decades of music]. *Muzïkal'naya zhizn'* 9–10 (1996): 37–39; 11–12 (1996): 39–41.

————. "Polveka vmeste" [A half century together]. *Sovetskaya muzïka* 9 (1976): 29–32.

————. "Vstrechi s Shostakovichem za dvadtsat' let" [Meetings with Shostakovich over twenty years]. In *Shostakovichu posvyashchayetsya: sbornik statey k 90-letiyu kompozitora (1906–1996)*, comp. E. Dolinskaya, 161–65. Moscow, 1997.

Tsirkunova, M. "Ranniye romansï Shostakovicha" [Shostakovich's early romances]. *Muzïkal'naya zhizn'* 15 (1990): 13–14.

Tsuker, Anatoliy. "Tema naroda u Shostakovicha i traditsii Musorgskogo" [The folk theme in Shostakovich and the traditions of Musorgsky]. In *Voprosï teorii i estetiki muzïki, vïp. 10*, 32–59. Leningrad, 1971.

———. "Traditsii muzïkal'nogo teatra Musorgskogo v simfonicheskom tvorchestve Shostakovicha" [The traditions of Musorgsky's musical theater in Shostakovich's symphonic works]. In *Muzïkal'nïy sovremennik, vïp. 3*, 39–74. Moscow, 1979.

"Tvorcheskiye planï Dmitriya Shostakovicha" [Shostakovich's creative plans]. *Sovetskaya kul'tura* (6 June 1959): 4.

"Universelle Botschaften. Gedanken zum 20. Todesjahr Dmitri Schostakowitschs. Solomon Volkov in Gespräch mit Günther Wolter." *Das Orchester* 1 (1996): 19–24. Eng. tr., S. Volkov, "Universal Messages: Reflections in Conversation with Günther Wolter," *Tempo* 200 (1997): 14–19.

Val'kova, Vera. "Tragicheskiy balagan: k voprosu o kontseptsii Chetvertoy simfonii" [The tragic "balagan": on the question of the conception of the Fourth Symphony]. *Muzïkal'naya akademiya* 4 (1997): 78–84.

Vanslov, Viktor. *Tvorchestvo Shostakovicha* [Shostakovich's creative work]. Moscow, 1966.

Varzar, Irina. "Molodoy Shostakovich—stranitsï iz zhizni" [The young Shostakovich, pages from his life]. *Niva* 9 (1996): 233–40.

———. "Mat' geniya" [Mother of a genius]. *Niva* 12 (1996): 207–09.

Vasina-Grossman, Vera. "Kamerno-vokal'noye tvorchestvo D. Shostakovicha" [Shostakovich's chamber-vocal work]. In *Sovetskaya muzïkal'naya kul'tura: istoriya, traditsii, sovremennost'*, ed. D. Daragan, 15–42. Moscow, 1980.

———. "Shostakovich." In *Mastera sovetskogo romansa*, 218–54. 2nd. ed. Moscow, 1980.

Vavilina-Mravinskaya, Aleksandra. "Obruchyonnïye muzïkoy" [Plighted by music]. *Muzïkal'naya akademiya* 4 (1997): 89–102.

Velazco, J. *Dos musicos eslavos: Gargantúa: Semblanza de Anton Rubinstein/Política y creación musical: El caso Shostakovich*. Mexico City, 1981.

Vester, Karl-Egon, ed. *Dmitri Schostakowitsch und seine Zeit: Kunst und Kultur.* Duisburg, 1984.

Vinay, Gianfranco. "Šostakovič, la morte e il monaco nero." *Nuova rivista musicale italiana* 1 (1988): 57–69.

Vinogradov, Viktor. "Eine kirgisische Episode im Schaffen Dmitri Schostakowitsch." In *Beiträge zur Geschichte und Theorie der Musikkultur*, ed. H. Klein, 631–36. Berlin, 1988.

Vishnevskaya, Galina. *Galina: A Russian Story*, trans. G. Daniels. San Diego, 1984.

Volkov, Solomon. "D. D. Shostakovich i N. A. Mal'ko" [Shostakovich and Malko]. *Slavica Hierosolymitana* 3 (1978): 264–71. Rev. trans., "Dmitri Shostakovitch and 'Tea for Two,'" *Musical Quarterly* 64, no. 2 (1978): 223–28.

———. "O neizbezhnoy vstreche: Shostakovich i Dostoyevskiy" [On an inevitable meeting: Shostakovich and Dostoyevsky]. *Rossiya/Russia* 4 (1980): 199–222.

———. "O Sergeye Sergeyeviche i Dmitrii Dmitriyeviche: interv'yu s Mstislavom Rostropovichem" [About Prokofiev and Shostakovich: interview with Mstislav Rostropovich]. In *Chast' rechi: almanakh literaturï i iskusstva 2–3*, ed. G. Platek,

254–62. New York, 1982. Eng. trans., "A Conversation with Mstislav Rostropovich," *Keynote* 11, no. 1 (1987): 8–12; abridged reprint, "Vozvrashcheniye traditsii: simvolika Rostropovicha," *Znamya* 1 (1990): 220–26; abridged trans., "Tradition Returns: Rostropovich's Symbolism," in *Shostakovich Reconsidered*, ed. A. B. Ho and D. Feofanov (London, 1998), 359-72.

———. ed. *Testimony: The Memoirs of Dmitri Shostakovich.* New York, 1979.

———. "Zdes' chelovek sgorel" [A man burned out here], *Muzïkal'naya akademiya* 3 (1992): 3–12. Abridged Eng. trans. in *Shostakovich Reconsidered*, ed. A. B. Ho and D. Feofanov (London, 1998), 315–58.

"Volksfeind Dmitri Schostakowitsch": Eine Dokumentation der öffentlichen Angriffe gegen den Komponisten in der ehemaligen Sowjetunion. Trans. and ed., E. Kuhn. Berlin, 1997.

Volodina, Mariya. *Shostakovich: notograficheskiy spravochnik* [Shostakovich: catalogue of works]. Moscow, 1976.

Voskoboynikov, Valeriy. "Slovo v tvorchestve Dmitriya Shostakovicha" [The word in the work of Shostakovich]. *Laboratorio degli studi linguistici* (Università di Camerino) (1984): 43–91.

Walker, Robert. "Dmitri Shostakovich—The Film Music." *Music and Musicians* 332 (April 1980): 34–39.

Wang, Dajue. "Shostakovich: Music on the Brain?" *Musical Times* 124 (1983): 347–48.

Weiner, Jack. "The Destalinization of Dmitrii Shostakovich's *Song of the Forests*, Op. 81 (1949)." *Rocky Mountain Review* 38, no. 4 (1984): 214–22.

Weiss, Stefan. "Text und Form in Schostakowitschs 2. Sinfonie op. 14." *Archiv für Musikwissenschaft* 51, no. 2 (1994): 145–60.

Weitzman, Ronald. "Fleischmann, Shostakovich and Chekhov's 'Rothschild's Fiddle.'" *Tempo* 206 (1998): 7–11.

Werner, B. "Sidem wierszy Aleksandra Bloka Dymitra Szostakowicza: Wokalnoinstrumentalna suita op. 127." *Zeszyt naukowy: Akademia Muzyczna im. Karola Lipińkiego we Wrocławiu* 58 (1991): 33–44.

Werth, Alexander. *Musical Uproar in Moscow.* London, 1949; reprint ed. 1977.

Westendorf, Reimar. "Schostakowitschs Briefe an Isaak Glikman." In *Schostakowitsch in Deutschland (Schostakowitsch-Studien, 1)*, ed. H. Schmalenberg, 153–76. Berlin, 1998.

Wildberger, Jaques. "Ausdruck lähmender Angst: Über die Bedeutung von Zwölftonreihen in Spätwerken von Schostakowitsch." *Neue Zeitschrift für Musik* 151, no. 2 (1990): 4–11.

———. *Schostakovitsch 5. Symphonie d-moll.* Munich, 1989.

Wilson, Elizabeth. *Shostakovich: A Life Remembered.* London, 1994.

Wolter, Günter. "'Die Abrechnung mit dem Tyrannen': Versteckte Programmatik in der Zehten Sinfonie von Dimitri Schostakowitsch." *Das Orchester* 42, no. 5 (1994): 18–22.

———. *Dmitri Schostakowitsch—eine sowjetische Tragödie: Rezeptionsgeschichte.* Frankfurt, 1991.

———. "Revolutionäres Pathos oder kritische Reflexion?; Schostakowitschs Elfte Sinfonie ('Das Jahr 1905')." *Neue Berlinische Musikzeitung* 3 (1993): 27–30.

———. "'Die Welt im Hohlspiegel'; Mahlers Einfluss auf Schostakowitsch." *Neue Berlinische Musikzeitung* 2 (1995): 55–60.

Yakovlev, Mikhaíl, comp. *D. Shostakovich o vremeni i o sebe: 1926–1975* [Shostakovich about his times and himself]. Moscow, 1980; Eng. trans., 1981.

Yakubov (Iakubov), Manashir. "'Antiformalisticheskiy rayok' D. D. Shostakovicha: istoriya sozdaniya, istochniki muzïkal'nogo i literaturnogo teksta" [Shostakovich's *Antiformalist Rayok*: history of its creation, sources of its musical and literary text]. In *Antiformalisticheskiy Rayok* (score), 50–62. Moscow, 1995.

———. *"The Bolt*: An Unknown Ballet by Dmitri Shostakovich." In *The Bolt*, op. 27 (piano score), 269–76. Moscow, 1996.

———. "Die ganze Welt in sich allein." In *Dmitri Schostakowitsch und seine Zeit: Mensch und Werk*, ed. J. Fromme, 27–39. Duisburg, 1984.

———. "Dmitri Schostakowitschs *Antiformalistischer Rajok.*" In *Sowjetische Musik im Licht der Perestroika*, ed. Hermann Danuser, Hannelore Gerlach, and Jürgen Köchel, 171–91. Laaber, 1990.

———. *"The Golden Age*: The True Story of the Premiere." In *Shostakovich Studies*, ed. D. Fanning, 189–204. Cambridge, 1995. Rus. trans. in *D. D. Shostakovich: sbornik statey k 90-letiyu so dnya rozhdeniya*, comp. L. Kovnatskaya, 68–87. St. Petersburg, 1996.

———. "Lirika i grotesk: k istorii sozdaniya 'Dvukh p'es dlya strunnogo kvarteta'" [Lyricism and the grotesque: toward the creation of "Two Pieces for String Quartet"]. *Muzïkal'naya zhizn'* 18 (1986): 15–16.

———. "Neizvestnoye proizvedeniye D. D. Shostakovicha: Moderato dlya violoncheli i fortepiano" [An Unknown Work by Shostakovich: Moderato for Violoncello and Piano]. *Sovetskaya muzïka* 9 (1986): 45–48.

———. "Opït rekonstruktsii avtorskoy redaktsii baleta *Zolotoy vek* (partitura—klavir—libretto)" [An attempt to reconstruct the author's version of the ballet *The Golden Age*]. *Muzïkal'naya akademiya* 4 (1997): 47–51.

———. "Preface to the Facsimile Edition of Shostakovich's Seventh Symphony ('Leningrad')," trans. L. E. Fay. In *Dmitri Shostakovich: Symphony No. 7, 'Leningrad,' op. 60*. Tokyo, 1992.

———. "'Rayok' Musorgskogo i 'Antiformalisticheskiy rayok' Shostakovicha: traditsiya russkoy muzïkal'noy satirï ot Aleksandra II do Stalina i Brezhneva" [Musorgsky's *Rayok* and Shostakovich's *Antiformalist Rayok*: the tradition of Russian musical satire from Alexander II to Stalin and Brezhnev]. *Muzïkal'naya akademiya* 4 (1997): 149–55.

———. "Der Schaffensweg Dmitri Schostakowitchs." In *Dmitri Schostakowitsch 1984/85: Wissenschaftliche Beiträge. Dokumente. Interpretationen. Programme*, 57–66. Duisburg, 1984.

———. "Shostakovich's First Ballet: The History of its Creation and Stage Fate." In *The Golden Age*, op. 22 (piano score), 224–27. Moscow, 1995.

Yarustovskiy, Boris. "Desyataya simfoniya D. Shostakovicha" [Shostakovich's Tenth Symphony]. *Sovetskaya muzïka* 4 (1954): 8–24.

———. "'Voyennïye' simfonii D. Shostakovicha" [Shostakovich's "war" symphonies]. In *Simfonii o voyne i mire*, 27–94. Moscow, 1966.

Yevtushenko, Yevgeniy. "Genius Is Beyond Genre: Dmitrii Shostakovich

(1976–1988)." In *Fatal Half Measures: The Culture of Democracy in the Soviet Union*, 292–99. Boston, 1991.

Yudin, Gavriil. "Vasha rabota dlya menya sobïtiye na vsyu zhizn'" [Your work is the event of a lifetime for me]. *Sovetskaya muzïka* 6 (1983): 89–93.

———. "Za gran'yu proshlïkh let" [In bygone years]. *Muzïkal'noye nasledstvo, vïp. 2*, ch. 1, 268–73. Moscow, 1966.

Yusfin, Abram. *Shestoy kvartet Shostakovicha* [Shostakovich's Sixth Quartet]. Moscow, 1960.

Yuzhak, Kira. "Shostakovich Dolzhanskogo: opus 87, izmenyayushchiysya vo vremeni" [Dolzhansky's Shostakovich: opus 87, changing with time]. In *D. D. Shostakovich: sbornik statey k 90-letiyu so dnya rozhdeniya*, comp. L. Kovnatskaya, 194–227. St. Petersburg, 1996.

Zaderatskiy, Vsevolod. *Polifoniya v instrumental'nïkh proizvedeniyakh Shostakovicha* [Polyphony in Shostakovich's instrumental works]. Moscow, 1969.

———. "Pro symfonizm Shostakovicha" [About Shostakovich's symphonic writing]. *Suchasna muzyka, vïp. 1*, 60–111. Kiev, 1973.

———. "Schostakowitschs Klavierwerk." In *Dmitri Schostakowitsch 1984/85: Wissenschaftliche Beiträge. Dokumente. Interpretationen. Programme*, 151–56. Duisburg, 1984.

Zak, Vladimir. *Shostakovich i yevrei?* [Shostakovich and the Jews?]. New York, 1997.

Zhitomirskiy (Shitomirski), Daniel'. *Blindheit als Schutz vor der Wahrheit*. Berlin, 1996.

———. *Dmitriy Shostakovich*. Moscow, 1947.

———. "Iz razmïshleniy o stile Shostakovicha" [From reflections on Shostakovich's style]. *Sovetskaya muzïka* 9 (1976): 55–62.

———. "'Nos'—opera D. Shostakovicha" [*The Nose*—an opera by D. Shostakovich]. *Proletarskiy muzïkant* 7–8 (1930): 33–39.

———. "Shekspir i Shostakovich" [Shakespeare and Shostakovich]. In *Dmitriy Shostakovich*, comp. G. Ordzonikidze, 121–31. Moscow, 1967.

———. "Shostakovich." *Muzïkal'naya akademiya* 3 (1993): 15–30. Eng. trans. in *Shostakovich Reconsidered*, ed. A. B. Ho and D. Feofanov, 419–71. London, 1998.

———. "Shostakovich ofitsial'nïy i podlinnïy" [Shostakovich official and genuine]. *Daugava* 3 (1990): 88–100; 4 (1990): 97–108.

Zhukova, Lidiya. "Mitya 'Chtozhtakovich.'" In *Epilogi, kniga pervaya*, 25–43. New York, 1983.

Zin'kevich, Elena. "Muzïka k pervomu 'Gamletu'" [The music to the first *Hamlet*]. *Sovetskaya muzïka* 5 (1971): 94–101.

———. "Prochteniye Shekspira" [Reading Shakespeare]. *Sovetskaya muzïka* 9 (1971): 41–47.

"Znachitel'noye yavleniye sovetskoy muzïki (diskussiya o Desyatoy simfonii D. Shostakovicha)" [A significant occurrence in Soviet music (debate about Shostakovich's Tenth Symphony)]. *Sovetskaya muzïka* 6 (1954): 119–34.

Zolotoy vek. Balet v 3 deystviyakh. [*The Golden Age*: a ballet in three acts]. Leningrad, 1931. Articles by Shostakovich, Gauk, Khodasevich, and Malkov.

Index

108th Soviet School. *See* Shidlovskaya Commercial School

Academic Theater of Opera and Ballet. *See* State Academic Theater of Opera and Ballet

The Adventures of Korzinkina op. 59 (film score), 120, 350

Afinogenov, Alexander Nikolayevich, 95, 363

Akhmatova, Anna Andreyevna (née Gorbenko), 363; condemned by Central Committee resolution, 150; defense of Solzhenitsyn, 203; expelled from USSR Writers' Union, 150; DS's musical homage to, 277, 344n57

Akimov, Nikolai Pavlovich, 71, 241, 363

Alekhine, Alexander Alexandrovich, 110, 363

Alexandrov, Alexander Vasilyevich, 139, 154, 316n67, 363

Alikhanyan, Artyom Isaakovich, 192, 363

All-Union Committee for Artistic Affairs. *See* Committee for Artistic Affairs

All-Union Competition for Performers, 150

All-Union Conference of Stakhanovites, 83, 304n65

All-Union Congress of Soviet Composers (First): issues and goals for, 155; Khrennikov as organizer of, 160; letters sent by absent composers, 321n72; DS participation in, 161–162; DS publicizes completion of Violin Concerto no. 1, 159

All-Union Congress of Soviet Composers (Second): and *Antiformalist Rayok*, 165; coverage of, 330n72; organization and tone of, 200–201; DS and, 200–201

All-Union Congress of Soviet Composers (Third): DS delegate to, 226

Alone op. 26 (film score), 50, 349

Amirov, Fikret Meshadi Dzhamil ogli, 213, 363

Anosov, Nikolai Pavlovich, 199, 363

anti-Semitism, 169, 170, 195, 228, 234

Antiformalist Rayok (choral), 355; dating of, 165; Lebedinsky and libretto for, 201; and realism vs formalism, 165; "Suliko" and,

213; title of, 321n85

Aphorisms op. 13, 39, 360

Apostolov, Pavel Ivanovich, 262, 328n25, 341n85, 363

Arnshtam, Leo Oskarovich, 363–364; *Friends,* 113; and Meyerhold Theater, 45; and DS, 149, 320n70; DS collaborates with, 217; and DS's works, 280, 313n6; and *Sofya Perovskaya,* 256

arts. *See* Soviet control of the arts

Asafyev, Boris Vladimirovich (used pseud. Igor Glebov), 364; and Composers' Union, 160, 161; distances himself from DS, 91; participates in music circle at Fogt home, 20; DS's comments about, 30; and DS's works, 30, 38, 68, 137

Aseyev, Nikolai Nikolayevich, 71, 74, 364

ASM. *See* Association of Contemporary Music

Association of Contemporary Music (ASM), 31

Atovmyan, Levon Tadevosovich, 364; arrangements of DS's music, 180, 241, 325n77, 354, 355; death of, 274; and *From Jewish Folk Poetry,* 168; and *The Limpid Stream,* 305n9; and *Poem of the Motherland,* 154; reconstruction of DS's 2nd opera in proposed cycle, 303n39; and DS, 73, 80, 198, 319n48; and *Six Romances on Texts of W. Raleigh, R. Burns, and W. Shakespeare,* 134, 315n47; and *Song of the Forests* contract correspondence, 175; and Symphony no. 4, 97, 306n34; on Symphony no. 6 reactions, 116; and Symphony no. 8, 316n53; at Symphony no. 10 premiere celebration, 188; *Twenty-four Preludes and Fugues* correspondence, 179

Babel, Isaak Emmanuílovich, 114, 364

Babiy Yar. See Symphony no. 13, *Babiy Yar*

Bach, Johann Sebastian. Brandenburg Concerto no. 5, 23, 292n20; D-minor Concerto for three pianos, 177; *Das wohltemperirte Clavier,* 21; F-sharp Minor Prelude and Fugue, 21; influence of

Bach (*cont.*)
on DS, 177; in Marxist methodology
exam, 36; Organ Prelude in A Minor
(Liszt's transcription), 23; and DS on
artists and conscience, 229; and DS's
tastes from Bach to Offenbach, 43, 79;
DS's works compared to, 116, 179; stud-
ied by DS, 10. *See also* First International
Bach Competition
Balanchine, George, 233
Balanchivadze, Andrey Melitonovich, 58,
92, 364
ballet, development of a Soviet ballet,
59–60; list of ballets by DS, 347; DS
ceases writing ballets, 107. *See also* spe-
cific work titles
Ballet Suite no. 1 (Arr. Atovmyan), 354
Ballet Suite no. 2 (Arr. Atovmyan), 355
Ballet Suite no. 3 (Arr. Atovmyan), 355
Ballet Suite no. 4 (Arr. Atovmyan), 355
"Balletic Falsity." *See Pravda* editorials
Barshai, Rudolf Borisovich, 259, 260, 364
Barsova, Valeriya, 82
Bartók, Béla: DS attended concerts of, 39,
176, 213; on DS's classic composer list,
258
Basner, Veniamin Yefimovich, 364; DS dis-
cusses composition with, 252–253; and
DS's works, 159, 320n57, 343n29
Baturin, Alexander Iosifovich, 98, 134, 364
The Bedbug op. 19 (incidental music), 348;
description of music for, 51; firemen's
music and, 51, 298n9; premieres and
performances of, 51, 298n12
Bedny, Demyan (pseud. for Efim
Alexandrovich Pridvorov), 52, 364
Beethoven, Ludwig van: *Appassionata* Sonata, 23, 37; *Hammerklavier* Sonata, 18;
influence on DS's works, 52, 103, 284,
286; as model for Soviet music, 201;
Moonlight Sonata, 18, 286; performances
of by DS, 10, 18, 21, 23, 37; and DS, 8, 9,
109, 124, 182, 248, 273, 297n50; DS compared to, 138, 146; in DS's work, 73; Sonata no. 21 in C Major *(Waldstein)*, 21;
"Song of a Flea," 283; symphony cycle
performed in Petrograd, 11, 290n19
The Beethoven Quartet: collaboration with
DS, 112; dedication of string quartets to,
151, 183; name changed to, 27; premieres
and performances of, 116, 176, 198, 213,
219, 244, 268; DS performs with,

176–177; and String Quartet no. 4, 176;
and String Quartet no. 9, 243; and String
Quartet no. 15, 281, 282. *See also*
Borisovsky; Druzhinin; S. Shirinsky; V.
Shirinsky; Tsïganov
Belinsky op. 85 (film score), 171, 350. *See
also* Suite from *Belinsky* op. 85a
Belov, Gennadiy Grigoryevich, 226, 364
Belugin, Nikolai Nikolayevich, 364; and
From Jewish Folk Poetry, 168
Belyayev Circle, 369, 381
Berg, Alban: congratulates DS on Sym-
phony no. 1, 39; DS attends concert of
music by, 185; DS on death of, 88; on
DS's classic composer list, 258; *Wozzeck,*
39, 41, 53
Beria, Lavrentiy Pavlovich, 149, 182,
315n45, 364
Berlinsky, Valentin Alexandrovich, 176, 365
Bernstein, Leonard, 309n83
Bezïmensky, Alexander Ilyich, 365; *The
Shot,* 58; wrote verses for DS's Symphony
no. 2, 40
biographers of Shostakovich. *See* Khentova;
research resources; Volkov
"Birthday": added to *Children's Notebook,*
149; dating of "Birthday," 318n24
Bizet, Georges, 124
"The Black Monk" (Chekhov), 274–275
"The Black Sea" (choral), 355
Blanter, Matvey Isaakovich, 124, 365;
"Katyusha," 113; DS plays *Suite for Jazz
Orchestra no. 2* for, 113
Blok, Alexander Alexandrovich, 365; and
DS's *Seven Verses of A. Blok,* 252–253,
255–256, 257, 339n29, 340n50, 358
Bogachyova, Irina Petrovna, 277, 365
Bogdanov-Berezovsky, Valerian
Mikhailovich, 365; recalls Glazunov's
evaluation of DS, 15
Bogomolov, Vladimir, 283
Bolshoy Dramatic Theater (Leningrad):
production of *King Lear,* 122
Bolshoy Theater (Moscow): agreement to
produce *The Carp,* 56; agreement to
produce *Lady Macbeth,* 69; agreement to
produce *The Nose,* 46; artistic directors,
121; and *Boris Godunov,* 119, 120–121,
136; commissions DS to write ballet,
300n48; evacuation from Moscow, 126;
and *The Great Friendship,* 154–155; and
Khovanshchina, 211; *The Limpid Stream*

production, 83; production of *Lady Macbeth*, 83; *The Quiet Don* (Dzerzhinsky, prod. Golovanov), 91, 304n8, 305n13; and Samosud, 305n13; DS as musical consultant to, 192, 328n34; urgent request that DS write new music for, 192–193

Bolshoy Theater Orchestra (Moscow): and dodecaphony, 257; at national anthem competition, 139

The Bolt op. 27 (ballet), 347. *See also* Suite from *The Bolt* op. 27a; description by DS, 62; music and dance numbers re-used, 81–82, 209; premiere, 62; set and costume design for, 291n34; staging objected to by DS, 64

Boris Godunov op. 58 (Musorgsky, orch. DS), 361. and Bolshoy Theater, 119, 120–121, 136; composition of, 119–120; passes Committee for Artistic Affairs scrutiny, 121; perusal request for, 211, 331n11; premieres, 121, 211; DS comments on possible reaction to, 120; DS retrieves altered manuscript from the Bolshoy, 120–121; theaters intending to produce, 120. *See also* Musorgsky

Borisovsky, Vadim Vasilyevich, 342n15, 365; death of, 274; and Symphony no. 13, 268. *See also* The Beethoven Quartet; Druzhinin; S. Shirinsky; V. Shirinsky; Tsïganov

Borodin, Alexander, 9, 209, 224; DS parodies work of, 209

Borodin Quartet: DS performs with, 176–177, 241; and String Quartet no. 4, 176

Boulez, Pierre: *Le marteau sans maître*, 215; rug concerts of, 276; DS attended concerts of, 213; in DS quote, 323n36

Boys' Choir of the Moscow Choral School, 178

Braga, Gaetano: *Leggenda Valacca*, 274

Brezhnev, Leonid Ilyich, 365; DS's comments on Russia under, 269

Bright Reel (cinema), 25, 26

British and American Folksongs (orch. DS), 315n51, 361

Britten, Benjamin: *Death in Venice*, 273; *The Prodigal Son*, 341n78; DS and, 215, 219, 251, 273; DS attended concerts of, 213; on DS's classic composer list, 258; and DS's String Quartet no. 13, 268; and

DS's Symphony no. 14, 260, 261, 263; *War Requiem* and DS, 251, 263

broadcast concerts. *See* concert broadcasts

Bruni, Georgiy, 14

Bruni, Tatyana Georgievna, and *The Bolt*, 291n34

Bryushkov, Yuriy (Georgiy) Vasilyevich, 36, 365

Bubnov, Andrey Sergeyevich, 365; attends *The Quiet Don*, 84; and *Lady Macbeth*, 74–75; leads conference of musicians, 65

Bukharin, Nikolai Ivanovich, 114, 365

Bulgakov, Mikhaíl Afanasyevich, 91, 365; *Pushkin* (play), 78

Bunin, Revol Samuílovich, 274, 365

Burns, Robert. *See Six Romances on Texts of W. Raleigh, R. Burns, and W. Shakespeare*

Cello Concerto no. 1 in E-flat Major op. 107, 353; composition of, 211; connections to other works, 212–213; dedication of to Rostropovich, 212; inspired by Prokofiev's Symphony-Concerto, 212; piano reduction of, 212; premieres and performances of, 212, 213, 231, 232

Cello Concerto no. 1 (Tishchenko, orch. DS), 361

Cello Concerto no. 2 in G Major op. 126, 353; composition of, 247–248; premieres and performances of, 249–250, 339n20; response to, 250; DS comments on, 247–248

Cello Concerto op. 125 (Schumann, orch. DS), 240, 361

Central Committee Conference of Musicians: composers named as leaders of the formalist direction, 156; Popov added to transcript of, 319n47; on the progress of Soviet music, 155–157; DS's comments to, 156–157. *See also* Central Committee of the Communist Party; Committee for Artistic Affairs

Central Committee of the Communist Party. Soviet control of the arts: admits incorrect and unfair evaluations, 204; affirms fundamental validity of Zhdanov resolutions, 204; Agitprop Department survey of musical shortcomings, 155; Directorate for Propaganda and Agitation, 151; discussion of resolutions of at Composers' Union Plenum, 152–153; hosts reception for prominent citizens,

Central Committee of the Communist Party (*cont.*)
203; moves toward greater tolerance in the arts, 200; resolution "On the Correction of Errors in the Evaluation of the operas *The Great Friendship,* Bogdan Khmelnitsky, and From All My Heart," 204; resolution "On the Film *A Great Life*", 150; resolution "On the Journals *Zvezda* and *Leningrad*," 150; resolution "On the Reconstruction of Literary-Artistic Organizations," 65, 71; resolution "On the Repertory of Dramatic Theaters and Measures to Improve It," 150; resolution "On V. Muradeli's opera *The Great Friendship*", 157–158; DS's response to resolutions of, 160, 204–205. *See also* Central Committee Conference of Musicians; Committee for Artistic Affairs; Communist Party; Soviet control of the arts

Central Music Technical School, 35

Chaikovsky, Boris Alexandrovich, 222, 223, 365

Chaikovsky, Pyotr Ilyich: *Children's Album,* 10; Fifth Symphony of, 147; First Piano Concerto of, 33, 34, 73; as model for Soviet music, 201; Serenade for Strings, 31; and DS, 8, 9, 23, 109, 180, 182, 248, 290n5; DS and polyphonic studies of, 177; DS parodies, 209; DS's performances of, 33, 34, 73; DS's work compared with, 60, 103, 137, 138, 143; Sixth Symphony of compared to DS's Symphony no. 8, 137; Sollertinsky gives commemorative address about, 140

chamber music of DS: inhospitable environment for, 176; list of chamber and instrumental works, 358–360; DS on requirements for, 141. *See also* specific work titles

Chekhov, Anton Pavlovich: "The Black Monk," 274–275; "Gusev," 285; quotes from, 197; "Rothschild's Violin," 109, 361; and DS on artists and conscience, 229; as source for libretto, 78; "Thirty Three Swoons," 311n30; *Uncle Vanya,* 164; "Ward No. 6," 278–79

Cheremukhin, Mikhaíl Mikhailovich, 25, 365–366

Chervinsky, Mikhaíl Abramovich, 209, 366

Cheryomushki (film score), 209, 350. *See* also *Moscow, Cheryomushki,* op. 105

Chiaureli, Mikhaíl Edisherovich, 172, 350, 366

Children's Notebook op. 69 (piano), 193, 360; composition of, 149; dating of, 318n24

Chopin Competition: DS as contestant in, 35–37; DS program for, 36–37; and DS's performance career, 73

Chopin, Frédéric: Ballade no. 3, 21; Funeral March, 285; as model for Soviet music, 201; performances of by DS, 36–37; DS and, 13, 39

Choral Capella of the Russian Republic, 244

choral works of DS, 355–356. *See also* specific work titles

Choreographic Tekhnikum (Leningrad), 51

Chukovskaya, Lidiya Korneyevna, 278, 344n61, 366

Chukovsky, Yevgeniy Borisovich (son-in-law), 212, 366

Chulaki, Mikhaíl Ivanovich, 366; on Ministry of Culture commission, 197; and Symphony no. 5, 100, 308n65

Chyorny, Sasha (pseud. of Alexander Mikhailovich Glikberg), 366; *Satires,* 220, 333n53

cinema pianist: DS resigns as, 31; DS works as, 25–26, 29

Circle for New Music: merger with Leningrad Association for Contemporary Music (LASM), 57

Circle of Friends of Chamber Music: Oborin piano recital for, 26; reaction to First Piano Sonata (DS), 34; DS and Ponna collaborative performance, 23–24; DS debut in, 21; solo recital program for, 23

circus: DS partiality for, 300n61

Columbus. See Der arme Columbus

Committee for Artistic Affairs: Ministry of Culture: approves commission for String Quartet no. 4, 176, 324n57; arranges for room and piano for DS and family, 127; decision to withhold String Quartet no. 4, 176; established, 89; Khrapchenko, 138–139; lack of vigilance in, 155; officials sent to attend performance of Symphony no. 5, 100; passes DS's orchestration of *Boris Godunov,* 121; public advice given to DS, 89; requirements for DS's rehabilitation, 90; *Song of the Forests* and, 175; and *Twenty-four Preludes and Fugues,* 179. *See also* Central Committee of the Communist Party; Communist Party; Ministry of Culture

Communist Party: and authorship of speeches and articles presented over DS's name, 173–174, 323n36; Leningrad office orders DS to evacuate, 125; Moscow convocation, 216; reaction to DS joining, 218–219; DS joins, 216–217, 218; DS's accommodations to, 219. *See also* Central Committee of the Communist Party; Committee for Artistic Affairs; Stalin

Communist Party Central Committee. *See* Central Committee of the Communist Party

Communist Party Congresses: 19th, 183; 22nd, 223; 24th, 270

Composers' Union. *See* Moscow Union of Composers; Union of Composers of the RSFSR (Russian Federation); Union of Soviet Composers (SSK); Union of Soviet Composers (SSK)—Leningrad chapter

concert and promotion tours. *See also* Cultural and Scientific Congress for World Peace: domestic concert tours, 33–34, 79, 84, 104, 122, 230–231, 240–241, 273; Dublin, 273; Edinburgh Festival, 230–231, 339n20; London, 219, 251, 273; Mexico City, 213; Moscow, 31; Paris, 203–204, 219; Turkey, 82; Ulan-Ude (Buryat ASSR), 262; United States, 171–173, 196, 213–213, 276; Vienna and Graz, 185; Warsaw Autumn Festival, 213; Warsaw DS/Oborin concert after Chopin Competition, 37–38

concert broadcasts: *Interversion,* 270; *Katerina Izmailova,* 77; *Lady Macbeth,* 77; Symphony no. 7, 130–131, 133; Symphony no. 9, 147, 205; Symphony no. 12, 222; Violin Concerto no. 2, 255

concerti, 353. *See also* specific work titles; piano concerti, 72–73

Concertino for Two Pianos op. 94, 195, 360; dating of premiere, 328n35; premiere, 193

conferences. *See also* specific conference names: called by Communist Party officials, 155–157; Maliy Opera Theater as a laboratory for Soviet opera, 78;

Nemirovich-Danchenko Theater and future directions in Soviet opera, 78; on symphonic composition, 88

contemporary literature: inappropriateness for DS's works, 67–68

control of the arts. *See* Soviet control of the arts

Council of Nationalities of USSR Supreme Soviet: DS elected to, 226

Counterplan op. 33 (film score), 349; conditions of composition, 72; description of scenario, 71–72; title explained, 302n15

cult of personality: and *Katerina Izmailova,* 238; and Khrushchev, 196; DS's call to eliminate, 200–201; and Irina Supinskaya, 227; and Symphony no. 10, 191–192; and Symphony no. 13, 235

Cultural and Scientific Congress for World Peace (New York), 171–173; members of the Soviet delegation, 172; protests at, 172; DS ordered to leave with rest of Soviet delegation, 213; DS performs Scherzo from Symphony no. 5, 173; DS's prepared speech for, 172–173

Czechoslovakia: response to Soviet invasion of, 269–270, 343n24

Dankevich, Konstantin Fyodorovich, 366; *Bogdan Khmelnitsky* (opera), 204; participates in cultural exchange program, 213

Dargomïzhsky, Alexander Sergeyevich, 124, 221

"Dawn of October" (choral), 356

"Declaration of a Composer's Duties": content of, 63–64; response of the proletarian critics, 64

Declared Dead op. 31 (music for variety-circus revue), 63, 64, 348

Dedication to October. See Symphony no. 2

Dedyukhin, Alexander, 212

Demidova, Praskovya Ivanovna ("Pasha"), 94, 366

Denisov, Edison Vasilyevich, 366; becomes alienated from DS, 284; and communications with DS, 184, 193, 328n36; and Piano Concerto no. 2, 199; and DS on Symphony-Concerto (Prokofiev), 212; and DS private comments on Schoenberg and Messiaen, 215; DS's mentor relationship with, 182; and

Denisov (*cont.*)
  String Quartet no. 3, 151; and String
  Quartet no. 5, 183; and Symphony no.
  10, 188; and Symphony no. 11, 201
Der arme Columbus (Dressel): DS writes
  two pieces for, 51–52
Der Sprung über den Schatten (Krenek), 53
Deutsche Oper am Rhein (Düsseldorf):
  and *Lady Macbeth*, 237
Dinamiada. See The Golden Age
Dmitriyev, Vladimir Vladimirovich, 75, 366
dodecaphony, 286; and DS, 214–215,
  257–258; Soviet music and, 214, 257; in
  String Quartet no. 12, 257, 258
Dolmatovsky, Yevgeniy Aronovich, 366; "A
  Beautiful Day," 174; anthem text for DS,
  139; compared to Pushkin, 176; *Five Romances on Texts of Dolmatovsky*, 192,
  357; *Four Songs on Texts of Dolmatovsky*,
  180, 357; "Glory to Our Soviet Homeland," 355; "Homesickness," 171; and introduction of DS to Kainova, 197; *Loyalty*, 266, 267, 356; "Patriotic Song," 357;
  and DS, 174–175, 266, 282, 310n7; "Song
  of Peace," 171; *Song of the Forests*, 356;
  The Sun Shines Over Our Motherland,
  182, 356; "There Were Kisses," 357
Dolukhanova, Zara Alexandrovna, 366; and
  From Jewish Folk Poetry, 195; and *Spanish Songs*, 329n44
Dombrovskaya, Genrietta Davidovna, 98,
  196, 307n49, 366–367
Dombrovsky, Vyacheslav, 98, 307n49,
  366–367
Dorliak, Nina Lvovna, 367; and *From Jew-
  ish Folk Poetry*, 167, 168, 195
Dostoyevsky, Fyodor Mikhailovich: *The
  Devils*, 280, 358; and DS on artists and
  conscience, 229
Dovzhenko, Alexander Petrovich, 255, 350,
  367
Dressel, Erwin: *Der arme Columbus*, 51
Druzhinin, Fyodor Serafimovich, 367; DS
  consults, 346n91; and Sonata for Viola
  and Piano, 284–285. *See also* The Bee-
  thoven Quartet; Borisovsky; S. Shirinsky;
  V. Shirinsky; Tsïganov
Dudinskaya, Natalya, 82
Dunayevsky, Isaak Osipovich, 104, 124, 367
Dzerzhinsky, Ivan Ivanovich, 367; protégé
  of DS, 78, 88; *The Quiet Don* (opera), 78,
  83, 84, 89, 303n42, 304n8; on *The Sun*

Shines Over Our Motherland, 183; technical limitations of, 88

Edinburgh Festival: program of DS's works
  at, 231; DS attends with Maxim, 230, 231
Efros, Abram Markovich, 280, 282, 367
Eight Preludes op. 2 (piano), 360; dedica-
  tion of, 14, 291n33; and Glazunov, 15;
  performances of, 23, 34; in DS's student
  repertory, 18
Eisenstein, Sergey Mikhailovich, 254–255,
  367
Eliasberg, Karl Ilyich, 133, 367
Encounter at the Elbe op. 80 (film score),
  171, 350. *See also* Suite from *Encounter at
  the Elbe* op. 80a
*English and American Folksongs. See British
  and American Folksongs*
Erenburg, Ilya Grigoryevich, 131–132, 157,
  367
Ermler, Fridrikh Markovich, 113, 367; and
  Counterplan, 71
Ernesaks, Gustav Gustavovich, 266, 356,
  367; and *Loyalty*, 266
The Execution of Stepan Razin op. 119
  (choral), 356; critical response to,
  244–245; premieres and performances
  of, 244; DS on, 243–244; wins State
  Prize, 245

Face the Nation, 214
Fadeyev, Alexander Alexandrovich, 172,
  367–368
The Fall of Berlin op. 82 (film score), 171,
  350. *See also The Fall of Berlin* op. 82a
"The Fearless Guard's Regiments Are on
  the Move." *See* "Song of a Guard's Division"
Fedin, Konstantin Alexandrovich, 91, 368
Feldt, Pavel Emilyevich, 20, 368
fellow travelers, 63, 301n62
Festival of Contemporary Music (Gorky):
  DS featured composer at 2nd, 240–241;
  DS's students works in, 241; works performed at 1st, 231
Festive Overture in A Major op. 96, 353;
  composition of, 192–193, 195; premiere,
  193; DS conducts performance of, 232
film-opera, 74, 113, 171
film scores: as "bride price," 171; categories
  of DS's scores, 171; list of DS's film
  scores, 349–351. *See also* specific titles

finale problem: Symphony no. 5, 103–104, 308n82; Symphony no. 7, 129–130; Symphony no. 8, 138; Symphony no. 10, 104

The First Echelon op. 99 (film score), 350. *See also* Suite from *The First Echelon* op. 99a

First International Bach Competition, 177

First Musical Technical School, 27

Fitzwilliam Quartet, 273

Five Days—Five Nights op. 111 (film score), 217, 350. *See also* Suite from *Five Days— Five Nights* op. 111a

Five Fragments op. 42 (for orchestra), 353; as preparation for Symphony no. 4, 93

Five Preludes (piano), 360

Five Romances on Texts from Krokodil Magazine op. 121 (solo vocal), 358; and city names, 245; composition of, 245; and Irina, 245; premiere, 248–249; response to, 249, 283

Five Romances on Texts of Ye. Dolmatovsky op. 98 (solo vocal), 192, 195, 357

Flaks, Efrem Borisovich, 135, 368

Fleyshman, Veniamin Iosifovich, 368; *Rothschild's Violin* finished by DS for, 109, 141; as DS's student, 108; on Symphony no. 5, 100

Fliyer, Yakov Vladimirovich, 285, 368

Fogt, Anna: musical gatherings at home of, 20

folk music and Socialist Realism, 85, 89

formalism: debates over, 87–88; as a defect in Soviet music, 85, 155, 157–158; denounced in works of specific composers, 157–158; exposure of, 90, 155–158; press campaign against, 161; public response to, 161; reconfirmed as a bad direction for Soviet music, 204; DS receives poison-pen letters on, 161; *vs.* realism in Soviet arts, 156

Four Monologues on Texts of A. Pushkin op. 91 (solo vocal), 230, 357; composition of, 183

Four Romances on Texts of A. Pushkin op. 46 (solo vocal), 230, 357; composition of, 98; performances, 132; response to, 98–99

Four Songs on Texts of Ye. Dolmatovsky op. 86 (solo vocal), 180, 357

Four Verses of Captain Lebyadkin op. 146 (solo vocal), 280, 283, 358

Frederiks, Vsevolod Konstantinovich, 98,

368. *See also* Shostakovich, Mariya

Frid, Grigoriy Samuílovich, 98, 324n58, 368

Friends op. 51 (film score), 113, 349

From Jewish Folk Poetry op. 79 (solo vocal), 357; characterization of, 169–170; composition of, 167–168; dress rehearsal for, 168; motivation for composition of, 169; music community's knowledge of, 168–169; performance cancellation, 168; political environment during and after composition of, 170; premieres and performances of, 168, 169, 195, 322n12; response to, 195

From Jewish Folk Poetry op. 79a (orchestration of op. 79), 168, 241, 357

"Funeral March in Memory of the Victims of the Revolution," 12, 291n24

Funeral Triumphal Prelude op. 130, 255

Furtseva, Ekaterina Alexeyevna, 232, 276, 368

The Gadfly op. 97 (film score), 195, 350. *See also* Suite from *The Gadfly* op. 97a

Gagarin, Yuriy, 180

Galli-Shohat, Nadezhda (née Kokoúlina, aunt), 8, 291n24

The Gamblers (unfinished opera), 347; composition of, 133–134; fragment of performed, 346n98; DS on weaknesses of, 134; themes from reused, 134, 386

GATOB. *See* State Academic Theater of Opera and Ballet (GATOB)

Gauk, Alexander Vasilyevich, 368; and Symphony no. 5, 100; Symphony no. 5 conducted in Mexico City, 213; on withdrawal of Symphony no. 4, 95–96

Gayamova, Zinaída Alexandrovna, 274, 368

Gerasimov, Sergey Apollinariyevich, 172, 350, 368

German invasion of Soviet Union. *See* World War II

Gershwin, George: *Porgy and Bess,* 272

Gilels, Emil Grigoryevich, 179, 368–369

Ginzburg, Grigoriy Romanovich, 36, 369

Girlfriends op. 41a (film score), 72, 111, 349

Glavrepertkom: bans formalist works from performance, 162; and *The Nose,* 297n52; rescinds ban of formalist works from performance, 172; DS's works banned by, 162

Glazunov, Alexander Konstantinovich, 369; comments on DS's piano exam, 21; as

Glazunov (*cont.*)
   director of Petrograd Conservatory, 17;
   evaluation of DS's musical abilities,
   14–15; relationship with Shostakovich
   family, 292n13; and Rimsky-Korsakov,
   17; and DS, 17, 21, 23, 28, 29; DS's symphonic debut compared with, 32
Glazunov Quartet, 111, 121
Glebov, Igor. *See* Asafyev, Boris
   Vladimirovich
Glière, Reinhold Moritsevich, 126, 160, 369
Glikberg, Alexander Mikhailovich. *See*
   Chyorny, Sasha
Glikman, Isaak Davidovich, 369; and
   Antiformalist Rayok, 165; and Cello Concerto no. 2, 250; correspondence with
   DS, 127, 129, 138, 153, 158, 178, 187,
   190, 200, 208, 221, 222, 225, 233, 237,
   244, 247, 253, 255, 259, 260, 261, 265,
   272, 337n92; discusses Solzhenitsyn with
   DS, 279; evacuation to Tashkent with Le-
   ningrad Conservatory, 125; and *Five Romances on Texts from Krokodil Magazine,*
   245; and *Four Verses of Captain
   Lebyadkin,* 280, 283; and *From Jewish
   Folk Poetry,* 195; and *Lady Macbeth,* 194,
   329n58; and Meyerhold, 114; and *The
   Nose,* 339n25; and poem "Babiy Yar,"
   228; and *Pravda* editorials scrapbook, 87;
   prepares conspectuses in classics of
   Marxism-Leninism, 173; recollections
   related to Symphony no. 4, 94, 95; response to demonstration of early version
   of Symphony no. 9, 146; and DS, 122,
   141, 157, 199, 249, 341n84; on DS and
   Moscow, Cheryomushki, 209; on DS joining the Communist Party, 216–217; and
   DS on his works, 117, 146, 226, 257, 274,
   337n92; and DS on Yevtushenko, 229,
   239; DS writes to about Composers' Union Orgkomitet, 150–151; DS writes to
   about Irina's background, 227; and DS's
   health, 171, 269, 270, 271, 273, 274; and
   DS's reaction to *Pravda* editorials, 92;
   and *Six Romances on Texts of W. Raleigh,
   R. Burns, and W. Shakespeare,* 134,
   315n47; on String Quartet no. 8, 218; on
   String Quartet no. 13 response, 268; and
   String Quartet no. 15, 280; and *Suite on
   Texts of Michelangelo Buonarroti,* 280; on
   Symphony no. 6, 115; and Symphony no.
   7, 124; and Symphony no. 10, 186, 188;

   and Symphony no. 11, 199, 202; on
   Symphony no. 14, 262; and Symphony
   no. 15, 270, 343n29; transcription error
   in a DS letter, 332n39
Glinka, Mikhail Ivanovich, 124, 201, 268
Glivenko, Tatyana Ivanovna, 369; corre-
   spondence with DS, 36, 39, 70; in Mos-
   cow, 25; DS's romance with, 22–23, 34
"Glory to Our Soviet Homeland" (choral),
   355
Glyasser, Ignaty Albertovich, 10, 369
Gmïrya, Boris Romanovich, 230, 232, 369
Goebbaerts, Jean-Louis (used pseud.
   Streabogg), 9
Gogol, Nikolai Vasilyevich: *Dead Souls,*
   339n25; *The Gamblers,* 133, 347; *Inspector General,* 45; *Petersburg Tales,* 268; as
   source material for DS, 68, 281; *Terrible
   Vengeance,* 11; "The Nose," 41, 45, 54, 69,
   347
The Golden Age op. 22 (ballet), 347. *See also*
   Suite from *The Golden Age* op. 22a; attribution of, 300n52; choreographic difficulties in, 60–61; development of, 59–60;
   name changed from *Dinamiada,* 60; or-
   chestral difficulties in, 61; premieres and
   performances of, 52, 61; response to, 61;
   staging objected to by DS, 64; use of "Ta-
   hiti Trot" in, 47, 59
Golden Mountains (film), 50–51
Golden Mountains op. 30 (film score),
   50–51, 349. *See also* Suite from *Golden
   Mountains* op. 30a
Goldenveyser, Alexander Borisovich, 191,
   369
Golovanov, Nikolai Semyonovich, 369; *The
   Quiet Don* production, 91, 305n13; and
   DS, 183–184
Gorky, Maxim (pseud. of Alexey
   Maximovich Peshkov), 369; on critics'
   role, 91; message to Stalin supporting
   DS, 91; and purity of language, 80
The Great Citizen, 1st series op. 52 (film
   score), 112–113, 349
The Great Citizen, 2nd series op. 55 (film
   score), 113, 349
"A Great Day Has Come": Sayanov's re-
   vised text of "Oath" becomes, 124
The Great Lightning (unfinished opera), 74,
   347
Great Purge. *See* purges
The Great Terror. *See* purges

Greek Songs (solo vocal), 357

Grinberg, Moisey Abramovich, 369; compares reception of Piano Quintet with *Lady Macbeth*, 117; protests nomination of DS works for Stalin Prize, 117, 312n52; and Symphony no. 4, 225, 333n1; on Symphony no. 5, 312n52

Gromadsky, Vitaliy Alexandrovich, 369; and *The Execution of Stepan Razin*, 244; and Symphony no. 13, *Babiy Yar*, 233, 234, 335n40,42

grotesque: in *The Bedbug*, 51; in Symphony no. 1 in F Minor op. 10, 26; in Symphony no. 9, 147, 151–152

The Gulag Archipelago (Solzhenitsyn), 203, 279

Gusev, V. M., 137

The Gypsies (abandoned project), 33

gypsy music, 8, 59, 79

Hamlet op. 32 (incidental music), 64, 348. *See also* Suite from *Hamlet* op. 32a; response to, 71

Hamlet op. 116 (film score), 350. *See also* Suite from *Hamlet* op. 116a; composition of, 241

Haydn, Franz Joseph, 9, 10, 73

Hindemith, Paul, 20, 88, 213

Home Guard and DS, 123–124

"Homesickness" (DS and Dolmatovsky), 171

Honegger, Artur, 39, 185

honors and awards. *See* Shostakovich, Dmitriy—honors and awards

Horowitz, Vladimir, 23

How the Steel Was Tempered (Ostrovsky): DS backs out of writing score for, 114; and Symphony no. 14, 260

The Human Comedy op. 37 (incidental music), 72, 348

"Hymn to Liberty," 12

"I waited in the grotto" (Ya v grote zhdal, Rimsky-Korsakov, orch. DS), 361

ideology in music: as defined by DS, 58; Proletarian Musician (journal) and, 59. *See also* Socialist Realism

Igumnov, Konstantin Nikolayevich, 24, 370

Ilizarov, Gavriil Abramovich, 264, 265, 270, 342n7, 370

Impromptu-madrigal (solo vocal), 357

"In the Fields," 134

incidental music. *See also* specific work titles: list of DS's incidental music, 348

instrumental music: list of DS's chamber and instrumental works, 358–360. *See also* specific work titles

International Chaikovsky Competition: 1st competition, 203; 2nd competition, 226; 4th competition, 266; 5th competition, 280

International Music Congress (7th), 271

International Peace Congresses, 181

"Internationale" (Degeyter, orch. DS), 361

Intervision, 270

Iokhelson, Vladimir Efimovich, 95, 306n36, 370

Ionin, Georgiy, 41, 370

Ivanov, Konstantin Konstantinovich, 154, 370

Ivanovsky, Alexander Viktorovich, 370; *Dinamiada*, 60

jazz: Khrushchev's opinion of, 239; at Kremlin, 239; popularity of, 79; Russian Composers' Union Plenum, 232; DS on quality of, 79; DS's exposure to, 31

"Jenny," 134

Juilliard Quartet, 176

Kabalevsky, Dmitriy Borisovich, 158, 370; avoidance of writing symphonies, 186; chairs commission to review *Lady Macbeth*, 197, 329n58; denounced as formalist, 156; evacuation from Moscow, 126; participates in cultural exchange program, 213

Kainova, Margarita Andreyevna (2nd wife), 370; divorce from DS, 198; meets and marries DS, 197–198; DS travels to Rome with, 203

Kamenyev, Lev Borisovich [pseud. for Rosenfeld], 370; trial and execution of, 97

Kandelaki, Vladimir Arkadyevich, 207, 370

Kaplan, Emmanuíl Iosifovich, 370; and *The Golden Age*, 60, 300n52

Karayev, Kara Abulfaz ogli, 370; and *From Jewish Folk Poetry*, 168; and letter condemning Sakharov, 344n60; member of Communist Party, 219; and DS, 170, 194–195; DS and Symphony no. 10, 186

Karetnikov, Nikolai Nikolayevich, 257, 340n61, 370

Katayev, Vitaliy Vitalyevich, 370; performance of Symphony no. 13, 236, 335n40,
336n51
Katerina Izmailova (film score), 239, 351.
See also *Katerina Izmailova* op. 114 (opera); *Lady Macbeth of the Mtsensk District* op. 29 (opera); Suite from *Katerina
Izmailova* op. 114a
Katerina Izmailova op. 114 (opera), 347;
given new name and opus number, 238;
premieres and performances of, 238,
275, 282; public preview, 238; rehabilitation progress of, 237–239; DS travels to
supervise productions of, 238, 240; unauthorized cuts or rearrangements of,
238–239. See also *Katerina Izmailova*
(film score); *Lady Macbeth of the
Mtsensk District* op. 29; Suite from
Katerina Izmailova op. 114a
Katerina Izmailova (version of *Lady
Macbeth of the Mtsensk District* op. 29).
See *Lady Macbeth of the Mtsensk District*
op. 29 (opera)
Katyusha Maslova: opera banned, 118; opera contracted for by Kirov Theater,
117–118
Kerzhentsev, Platon Mikhailovich, 370; orders closure of Meyerhold Theater, 114;
public advice to DS, 89; visited by DS
about rehabilitation, 90, 305n12. See also
All-Union Committee for Artistic Affairs
Khachaturyan, Aram Ilyich, 370–371;
avoidance of writing symphonies, 186;
and Composers' Union, 152, 160; denounced as formalist, 156, 158; evacuation from Moscow, 126; on mediocraty
in Soviet music, 189; member of the
Communist Party, 219; People's Artist
awards, 153, 192, 319n37; and DS, 79,
139, 188; on *The Sun Shines Over Our
Motherland,* 183; and Symphony no. 5,
98; and Symphony no. 9, 147, 152; on
Symphony no. 10, 189, 328n24; on Symphony no. 13, *Babiy Yar,* 234
Khaikin, Boris Emmanuílovich, 371; collaboration on *Wiener Blut* proposed to
DS, 118; evacuation from Moscow, 126;
production of *The Gypsy Baron,* 118; and
DS on *Khovanshchina,* 210; urgent appeal to DS to orchestrate production
piece, 118
Khentova, Sofya: asks DS about Symphony

no. 11, 330n83; on dating of Symphony
no. 15, 270; on premiere of *Six Verses of
Marina Tsvetayevna,* 344n59; on DS
joining the Communist Party, 218; DS
talks to about genius and villainy,
344n61; DS tells about conversation with
Stalin, 316n64; works of as resources, 3,
289n2,4,5; works of compared with
other sources, 197, 303n44, 316n65,
317n76, 320n70, 335n41, 337n75,
344n59. See also research resources;
Volkov
Khodasevich, Valentina Mikhailovna, 371
Kholodilin, Alexander Alexandrovich, 371;
death of, 274; vacations with DS, 262;
and withholding String Quartet no. 4,
176
Khovanshchina op. 106 (film score), 350;
composition of, 210–211; proofreads
score, 230; release of film, 211; singers
object to, 211
Khovanshchina op. 106 (Musorgsky, orch.
DS), 361; staged premiere, 211
Khrapchenko, Mikhaíl Borisovich,
138–139, 371
Khrennikov, Tikhon Nikolayevich, 371; ad-
vises Central Committee on *Lady Macbeth,* 237; avoidance of writing symphonies, 186; censures Mravinsky, 321n75;
comments at All-Union Congress of Soviet Composers, 200; as general secretary
of Composers' Union, 160, 201; participates in cultural exchange program, 213;
public reminder to DS about expected
works, 174; Symphony no. 5, 98; on
Symphony no. 10 and Stalin Prize,
190–191; on Symphony no. 15, 271–72
Khrushchev, Nikita Sergeyevich, 371; au-
thorizes publication of memoir of Stalinist camps, 233–234; hosts reception
for prominent citizens, 203; meetings
with artistic intelligentsia, 234, 239,
335n37; musical biases of, 239; removal
from power, 244, 338n99; renews campaign for ideological purity in the arts,
234; "secret" speech, 196
Khubov, Georgiy Nikitich, 197, 326n3, 371
King Lear op. 58a (incidental music), 122,
348
King Lear op. 137 (film score), 267, 351
Kirov, Sergey Mironovich, 113, 371
Kirov Theater of Opera and Ballet: and

Boris Godunov, 120, 121, 211; contract with DS for opera, 112; contracted for opera *Katyusha Maslova,* 117–118; *Khovanshchina* stage premiere, 211; and *Lady Macbeth,* 211, 237; Mravinsky and, 100; name change to, 308n67; Pazovsky leaves to become Bolshoy artistic director, 120; DS plans ballet *Lermontov* for, 114. *See also* State Academic Theater of Opera and Ballet

Kirsanov, Semyon Isaakovich, 52, 371

Klements, Georgiy Lvovich, 20, 371

Klemperer, Otto, 94

Knushevitsky, Viktor Nikolayevich, 371; and *Jazz Suite for Orchestra* no. 2, 113; and national anthem competition, 139

Kokoúlin, Vasiliy Yakovlevich (grandfather), 7

Kokoúlina, Nadezhda. *See* Galli-Shohat, Nadezhda

Komitas Quartet, 176–177

Komsomol, 197, 329n59

Kondrashin, Kirill Petrovich, 371; and *The Execution of Stepan Razin,* 244, 356; member of Communist Party, 219; and Second Concerto for Violin, 254; and Symphony no. 4, 96, 225, 226, 231, 351; and Symphony no. 13, 233, 235, 236, 335n41, 336n51, 352; and Symphony no. 14, 260; and Violin Concerto no. 2, 255, 353

Konstantinovskaya, Yelena Yevseyevna, 79–80, 82, 177, 371–372

Kornilov, Boris Petrovich, 72, 372

Koussevitzky, Serge, 11, 132, 290n19

Koval (Kovalyov), Marian Viktorovich, 164, 182, 372

Kozhunova, Fedosya Fedorovna ("Fenya"), 94, 164, 372

Kozhunova, Mariya Dmitriyevna, 164, 372

Kozintsev, Grigoriy Mikhailovich, 372; *Alone,* 50; collaboration with DS, 241, 267–268, 281; death of, 268, 274; and *Hamlet,* 241; and *King Lear,* 122, 267–268; *The New Babylon* (silent film), 49; *The Viborg District,* 113

Kremlyov, Yuliy Anatolyevich, 372; on formalism and Violin Concerto no. 1, 200; on Symphony no. 10, 191–192

Krenek, Ernst: *Der Sprung über den Schatten,* 53; influence of on DS, 88; *Jonny spielt auf,* 53

Krokodil. See Five Romances on Texts from Krokodil Magazine

Kubatsky, Viktor Lvovich, 372; concert with DS, 84; and Sonata in D minor, 80; and Stradivarius Quartet, 80

Kukharsky, Vasiliy Feodosyevich, 285, 372

Kustodiyev, Boris Mikhailovich (artist), 372; dedications to by DS, 13, 291n32; illustrator of *Lady Macbeth,* 68; Mariya Shostakovich models for, 13; portrait of DS, 13; and DS in Gaspra, 22

Kvadri, Mikhaíl Vladimirovich, 25, 26, 27, 28, 293n41, 372

Lady Macbeth of the Mtsensk District op. 29 (opera): Bolshoy production of, 83, 84; coarse naturalism in, 84, 88; composition of, 61, 63, 68–69; debate over formalism *vs.* Socialist Realism in, 87–88; dedication of, 69; demonstration by DS, 69, 74; familiarity of DS with Leskov's story, 68; formalism of attacked, 85, 155; influence of Musorgsky on, 119; international productions, 77; Kirov Theater and, 237; libretto for, 68; Malïy Opera Theater revival of, 194; Malïy Opera Theater run, 77; Ministry of Culture commission reviews revised opera, 197; Nemirovich-Danchenko Theater run, 77; official evaluation of, 74–75, 238; pre-premiere coverage, 75–76; premieres and performances of, 75, 77, 79, 231, 232, 237; productions available in Moscow, 83; productions contracted for, 69; profit from, 77, 302n37; public comments by DS on, 69, 76–77; reception of compared with Piano Quintet, 117; rehabilitation progress of, 237–239; resistance of Nemirovich-Danchenko Theater troupe to, 237–238; response to, 76, 77, 84; revisions of, 194, 237, 238; score taken out of Leningrad during Nazi siege, 125; DS supervises revival preparations, 238; singers selected for, 75; and Smolich, 68, 69, 77; staged as *Katerina Izmailova* (1934), 75; Stalin attends Bolshoy production of, 84; story of, 68; subject selection for, 67–68; and Western audiences, 85. *See also Katerina Izmailova* (film score); *Katerina Izmailova* op. 114; *Pravda* editorials; Suite from *Katerina Izmailova* op. 114a

LASM. *See* Leningrad Association for Contemporary Music (LASM)

Lebedinsky, Lev Nikolayevich, 372; and *Antiformalist Rayok,* 165, 201; and Davidenko orchestrations, 337n75; grows away from DS, 227; introduction of DS to Kainova, 197–198; on DS and String Quartet no. 8, 218; on DS and Symphony no. 12, 222–223; and DS joining the Communist Party, 216–217; and DS on *Lady Macbeth,* 225; story of DS and Lenin's arrival, 291n27; and String Quartet no. 8, 218; and Symphony no. 13, 231; and Symphony no. 14, 263

Lehár, Franz, 208

Lenin Prize. *See* Shostakovich, Dmitriy — honors and awards

"Lenin" symphony: dedication of Symphony no. 12 to Lenin, 221–222; German invasion erases DS's pledges for, 119; poem "Vladimir Ilyich Lenin" (Mayakovsky) and, 115; poets selected as literary sources for, 115, 311n39; as public relations invention, 118–119; and satire, 223; DS on Lenin tributes, 221, 267; Symphony no. 7 mentioned as, 119; verses for potential Symphony no. 2 tribute, 40. *See also* Lenin, Vladimir Ilyich; Symphony no. 12

Lenin, Vladimir Ilyich: 100th birth anniversary of, 266; death of, 36; premiere of Symphony no. 3 timed to coincided with death anniversary of, 53; story of Shostakovich family as related to, 36; story of DS at Lenin's arrival, 12–13, 333n61; in theme for Russian Composers' Union plenum, 221. *See also* "Lenin" symphony; *Loyalty;* Symphony no. 12

Leningrad Association for Contemporary Music (LASM), 32, 34, 57

Leningrad Conservatory (Petrograd/ St. Petersburg Conservatory), 10; after German invasion, 123; conditions in 1919–1920, 17; curriculum becomes confining to DS, 19; evacuation to Tashkent from Leningrad, 125; exclusion of DS from Academic (graduate) course, 24; reinstatement of DS in Academic (graduate) course, 25; returns to Leningrad from Tashkent, 148; DS as teacher at, 97, 108–109, 226; DS dismissed from,

162; DS on exam juries, 122; DS on inadequacy of education at, 88; DS prepares for entrance exams, 14; DS resumes teaching composition, 226; DS serves on academic council, 111; Sollertinsky appointed to faculty of, 97

Leningrad Philharmonic Orchestra: evacuation to Novosibirsk from Leningrad, 125; performances of Symphony no. 8, 139; premieres and performances of DS's works, 72, 73, 99, 188, 195, 212, 219, 222; preservation of DS scores during Nazi siege, 125; program of 25th season opening concert, 147; quality of, 148; Symphony no. 7 performance, 132; and withdrawal of DS's Symphony no. 4, 96

"Leningrad" Symphony. *See* Symphony no. 7 ("Dedicated to the city of Leningrad") in C Major op. 60

Leningrad Union of Composers. *See* Union of Soviet Composers (SSK)—Leningrad chapter

Lermontov, Mikhaíl Yuryevich: "A Song About Tsar Ivan Vasilyevich, the Young Bodyguard, and the Valorous Merchant Kalashnikov," 11, 290n17; *A Hero of Our Times,* 114; *Masquerade,* 114; in DS's works, 357

Leskov, Nikolai Semyonovich: "Lady Macbeth of the Mtsensk District," 68, 69, 77, 347; as source for DS's work, 68

Levitin, Yuriy Abramovich, 372; attacks on at Composers' Union Plenum, 152; at celebration for Symphony no. 10, 188; and *From Jewish Folk Poetry,* 168; and DS, 177; student of DS, 108

The Limpid Stream op. 39 (ballet), 347; audience response to Malïy production, 83; contract with DS for, 82; dance numbers from reused in *Moscow, Cheryomushki,* 209; description of libretto, 81; development of, 81–82; music from *The Bolt* used in, 81–82, 85; musical goal for DS's music, 82; premieres and performances of, 82, 83, 87; and Socialist Realism, 89; Sollertinsky's review of Bolshoy production, 83; Sollertinsky's review of Malïy Opera Theater production, 82; title for, 82; as unrealistic, 85; worries of DS about, 83, 305n9. *See also Pravda* editorials

"Listen" in Symphony no. 11, 203

Liszt, Franz: influence on DS's works, 28; and DS, 18, 34, 36; transcription of Bach's Organ Prelude in A Minor, 23; "Venice and Naples," 21

Litvinova, Flora Pavlovna, 319n48, 373; discussions with DS, 216, 268, 342n17; recollection of Symphony no. 7, 128; recollections of DS and *Satires,* 220; DS describes Kainova to, 198; and DS's health, 268–269; and DS's mood at Stalin's death, 184; on Symphony no. 4, 226

Lopukhov, Fyodor Vasilyevich, 373; *The Bolt,* 62; *The Limpid Stream,* 81–82

Losskiy, Boris Nikolayevich, 13, 373

Love and Hatred op. 38 (film score), 72, 349

Loyalty op. 136 (choral ballads), 266–267, 342n8, 356; and Dolmatovsky, 266–267; wins Glinka Prize, 267

Lukashevich, Klavdiya Vladimirovna, 9, 10, 21, 373

Lunacharsky, Anatoliy Vasilyevich, 21, 65, 373

Lyubimov, Yuriy Petrovich, 315n45, 373

Lyubinsky, Zakhar Isaakovich, 373; and DS on *The Golden Age,* 61; and DS on *The Nose,* 56

"MacPherson before His Execution," 134–135

Mahler, Gustav: *Das Lied von der Erde,* 109, 187, 251; influence on DS's works, 43, 93, 96, 103, 185, 306n30; orchestration and, 306n30; and DS on artists and conscience, 229; on DS's classic composer list, 258; in DS's work, 73, 187

Makarov, Yevgeniy Petrovich, 97, 317n5, 373

Maksakova, Mariya, 82

Maliy Opera Theater: accepts *The Nose* for production, 46; as alternative to GATOB, 81; and *Barbe-bleue,* 136; creative teams assembled by, 74; and *How the Steel Was Tempered,* 311n30; and *Lady Macbeth,* 75, 77, 194; Lopukhov hired by, 81; *Madonna and the Soldier* (Vainberg), 283; mission, 299n33; premieres *The Nose,* 53; production of *The Gypsy Baron,* 118; *The Quiet Don* (Dzerzhinsky) production, 84; rivalry with Nemirovich-Danchenko Theater, 75; and DS to compose for opera, 310n3; stages *Der arme Columbus,* 51

Malko, Nikolai Andreyevich, 373; accepts Symphony no. 1 for performance, 30; conducting class teacher for DS, 29–30; conducts Suite from *The Nose* op. 15a, 46; gift to DS of Prokofiev score, 38; on interpretation requirements of DS, 43; introduces DS and Sollertinsky, 42; participates in music circle at Fogt home, 20; and "Tahiti Trot," 39

Maloletkova, Alla, 193

The Man with a Gun op. 53 (film score), 113, 349

Mandelstam, Osip Emilyevich, 373; arrested, 114; on Symphony no. 5, 103

"March of the Defenders of Peace" (choral), 356

March of the Soviet Militia op. 139, 270, 354

Mariengof, Anatoliy Borisovich, 110, 373; contract for opera *Katyusha Maslova,* 117–118

Mariyinsky Theater. *See* State Academic Theater of Opera and Ballet

Marshak, Samuíl Yakovlevich, 373; *Tale of the Silly Little Mouse,* 113; translated poems for DS, 134

Marxist methodology: exams in, 35, 36, 41–42

Maslennikov, Alexey Dmitriyevich, 373; and *From Jewish Folk Poetry,* 195

Mass, Vladimir Zakharovich, 373; book for *Moscow, Cheryomushki,* 209

Maxim trilogy. *See Maxim's Youth, Maxim's Return,* and *The Viborg District*

Maxim's Return op. 45 (film score), 349. *See also Maxim's Youth, The Viborg District;* Suite from "Maxim trilogy" op. 50a; DS as musical supervisor for, 94

Maxim's Youth op. 41 (film score), 72, 349. *See also Maxim's Return, The Viborg District*

Mayakovsky, Vladimir Vladimirovich, 373–374; *The Bathhouse,* 298n8; *The Bedbug,* 51, 298n9, 348; and "Lenin" symphony, 311n39; DS measured against, 138; "Vladimir Ilyich Lenin," 115

Melik-Pashayev, Alexander Shamilyevich, 374; conducts *Lady Macbeth,* 83

Mendeleyev, Dmitriy Ivanovich, 7, 8, 374

"Mephistopheles' Song in Auerbach's Tavern" (Musorgsky, orch. DS), 361

"Mephistopheles' Song of the Flea" (Beethoven, orch. DS), 361

Merry March for Two Pianos, 360

Messerer, Asaf, 82

Messiaen, Olivier: *Trois petites liturgies,* 215

Meyer, Krzysztof, 279, 374

Meyerhold Theater: closure of, 114; run of *The Bedbug,* 298n12; DS and, 45–46, 114

Meyerhold, Vsevolod Emilyevich, 374; and *The Bathhouse,* 298n8; commission to preserve artistic legacy of, 197; and conception for *The Nose,* 45; defense of DS after *Pravda* editorials, 91–92; formalism dubbed "Meyerholdism," 85; *How the Steel Was Tempered* and, 114; invites Shostakovich to write music for *The Bedbug,* 51; musical taste of, 297n50; plans for writing libretto based on *A Hero of Our Times,* 114; and Raikh, 297n51; rehabilitation of, 196–197; relationship with DS, 44–45, 57, 297n50; saves DS's manuscripts from fire, 45; *The Shot* staged by, 58; and "Thirty-three Swoons," 311n30; victim of purges, 114–115

Meyerovich, Mikhaíl Alexandrovich, 201, 374

Michurin op. 78 (film score), 350; film wins Stalin Prize, 171; reuse of previous melody in, 72. *See also* Suite from *Michurin* op. 78a

Mikhailov, Lev Dmitriyevich, 237, 374

Mikhoels (Vovsi), Solomon Mikhailovich, 138, 157, 374

Milhaud, Darius, 39

Milstein, Nathan, 23

Ministry of Culture: approves commission for String Quartet no. 4, 176, 324n57; evaluates revised *Lady Macbeth,* 197; official reports DS's denunciation of Rostropovich, 269; orders DS's presence for awards ceremony at Chaikovsky competition, 280; representatives of at DS's funeral, 285; DS intervenes with on Vainberg's behalf, 283; and DS's work on *Khovanshchina,* 211. *See also* Committee for Artistic Affairs

Minuet, Prelude, and Intermezzo (incomplete, piano), 360

Miroshnikova, Margarita Khristoforovna, 261, 262, 263, 374

Mnatsakanyan, Alexander Derenikovich, 226, 374

modern dance: DS collaboration with

Mariya Ponna, 23

Molostova, Irina Alexandrovna, 282, 374

Molotov, Vyacheslav Mikhailovich, 374; announces German invasion, 122; attends *The Quiet Don,* 84; DS declines to write a festive overture about, 312n65; DS request to for audience with Stalin, 90

Mordvinov, Boris Arkadyevich, 374; and *Lady Macbeth,* 69, 75

Moscow Art Theater: and play about a formalist composer, 161

Moscow Chamber Music Theater: production of *The Nose,* 281

Moscow, Cheryomushki op. 105 (operetta), 347: book for and DS, 209; composition of, 208; critical response, 208–209; description of, 207–208, 209; early announcement of, 207; open dress rehearsal reactions, 208–209; piano-vocal score, 209; premiere, 208; productions of, 208, 209; recycled music in, 209; response to libretto of, 209; reuse of previous melody in, 72; DS comments on, 208. *See also Cheryomushki*

Moscow Conservatory: academic environment of, 25; hires DS as professor, 135; premiere of Cello Concerto no. 2, 249–250; Shebalin named director of, 135; DS dismissed from, 162

Moscow Conservatory Quartet. *See* Beethoven Quartet

Moscow Philharmonic Orchestra: Kondrashin appointed chief conductor of, 225; premieres *The Execution of Stepan Razin,* 244; premieres Symphony no. 4, 225, 226

The Moscow "Six," 25. *See also Les Six*

Moscow Theater of Operetta: production plans for *Moscow, Cheryomushki,* 207, 208; professionals associated with, 207

Moscow Union of Composers, 216

Mozart, Wolfgang Amadeus: C Major Variations, 21; dodecaphony and, 258; as model for Soviet music, 201; played by DS, 23; and DS, 9, 109, 182, 248; DS compared to, 15, 147; studied by DS, 10

Mravinsky, Yevgeniy Alexandrovich, 384; and Cello Concerto no. 1, 212, 353; and Cello Concerto no. 2, 250; as conductor, 101; conducts premieres of DS's work, 99–100, 115, 116, 137, 139, 147, 175, 212, 222, 351, 352, 353, 356; declines to conduct Symphony no. 13, 232–233; dedication of Symphony no. 8 to, 137; music mastery, 250; musical analysis of Symphony no. 5, 101; neutralizes approaching controversy over DS's work, 188; at Prague Spring Festival, 158; on responsibility of conducting premieres, 100–101; DS meets with about Symphony no. 13, 230; DS talks to about composing and alcohol, 275; slated to conduct an unrealized DS work, 154; and *Song of the Forests,* 175, 335n33, 356; and Symphony no. 5, 101, 121, 321n75, 351; and Symphony no. 7, 130, 132; and Symphony no. 8, 137, 138, 139, 205, 352; and Symphony no. 9, 147, 352; and Symphony no. 10, 188, 191, 352; and Symphony no. 11, 201, 330n85; and Symphony no. 12, 222, 352; Symphony no. 13 declined by, 230; and Symphony no. 15, 272; trust lost between DS and, 233; and Violin Concerto no. 1, 195, 353

"Muddle Instead of Music." *See Pravda* editorials

Muntyan, Mikhaíl, 285, 286, 375

Muradeli, Vano Ilyich, 375; avoidance of writing symphonies, 186; blames musical establishment for "defects" in *The Great Friendship,* 155; Central Committee resolutions on *The Great Friendship,* 157–158, 204; and Congress of Soviet Composers, 161; *The Great Friendship,* 154–155, 157–158, 204; DS reproaches for not accepting responsibility, 157

Muravlyov, Alexey, 182

Murzilka (piano), 360

music criticism: Gorky's view on, 91; and proletarian cultural agenda, 56–57; and responsibility for guiding composers, 84, 85, 89, 164; DS's view on state of, 56

music education, 88

music hall, 62–63

musical monograms, 187–188, 327n15

Musorgsky, Modest Petrovich: *Boris Godunov,* 119–121, 210, 211, 361, 382, 385; commemoration of 100th birth anniversary, 119; influence on DS, 119, 165, 224, 244; *Khovanshchina,* 210–211, 230, 350, 361, 382, 385; as model for Soviet music, 201; *Pictures at an Exhibition,* 113; and DS on artists and conscience,

229; and DS's arrangements, 124; "Song of the Flea," 120, 361; *Songs and Dances of Death* and DS, 221, 230, 232, 259–260, 261, 361; and Symphony no. 14, 259–261

Muzfond, 134, 154, 315n51

Muzgiz (State Music Publisher, State Publisher-Music Section), 31, 124

Myaskovsky, Nikolai Yakovlevich, 375; and Congress of Soviet Composers, 321n72; correspondence of, 44; denounced as formalist, 156, 158; reaction to *Lady Macbeth,* 75; reaction to Piano Concerto no. 1, 74; reaction to *Song of the Forests,* 175; reaction to Symphony no. 1, 28; reaction to Symphony no. 2, 44; reaction to Symphony no. 5, 103; reaction to Symphony no. 8, 137; reaction to Symphony no. 9, 147; resolution admits error in evaluation of, 204; DS auditions for, 24; on DS's classic composer list, 258; students of, 25; on withdrawal of Symphony no. 4, 96–97

Nagovitsïn, Vyacheslav Lavrentyevich, 226, 375

Narkompros: and *The Nose,* 56, 299n33

national anthem competition, 139

"National Traditions and the Precepts of their Development" (Shostakovich), 271

Native Country, 134

Native Leningrad Suite from *Native Country* op. 63 (incidental music), 348; premiere, 134

Nazirova, Elmira Mirza Riza kïzï, 375; as inspiration to DS, 187

Nechipailo, Viktor Timofeyevich, 375; and Symphony no. 13, *Babiy Yar,* 233, 234

Nemirovich-Danchenko Musical Theater, 375; broadcast of *Katerina Izmailova,* 77; and *Lady Macbeth,* 69, 74, 75, 237; name changed to Stanislavsky-Nemirovich-Danchenko Musical Theater, 375; premiere of *Katerina Izmailova,* 75; produces *Lady Macbeth* with name *Katerina Izmailova,* 75; resistance of opera troupe to revised *Lady Macbeth,* 237–238; rivalry with Malïy Opera Theater, 75; run of *Katerina Izmailova,* 77, 83

Nemirovich-Danchenko, Vladimir Ivanovich, 375; interpretation of *Lady Macbeth,* 75

Nesterenko, Yevgeniy Yevgenyevich, 375, 380; and *Five Romances on Texts from Krokodil Magazine,* 245; and *Four Verses of Captain Lebyadkin,* 280–281, 283; and "Song of the Flea," 283; and *Suite on Texts of Michelangelo Buonarroti,* 280–281, 282

Nestyev, Izraíl Vladimirovich, 375; DS Symphony no. 9 criticized by, 151–152

Neuhaus, Heinrich Gustavovich, 375; on Piano Sonata no. 2, 315n48; on String Quartet no. 8, 219–220; on *Twenty-four Preludes and Fugues,* 179, 180

New Babylon op. 18 (film score), 349; artistic panel's comments on the score, 50; premiere, 50

The New Babylon (silent film), 49–50

Nikolayev, Leonid Vladimirovich, 375–376; Conservatory piano class of, 18, 291n32; death of in Tashkent, 135; Piano Sonata no. 1, 38; Piano Sonata no. 2 dedicated to, 135, 360; DS substitutes for at performance, 23; DS's mother writes to, 24; at Symphony no. 1 celebration, 32; as teacher, 18, 25

Nikolayeva, Tatyana Petrovna, 376; at celebration for Symphony no. 10, 188; on DS and Symphony no. 10, 186; and *Twenty-four Preludes and Fugues,* 177, 179–180, 360; wins First International Bach Competition, 177

Nikolsky, Yuriy Sergeyevich, 376; friendship with DS, 25

Nikritina, Anna Borisovna, 110, 376

NKVD (People's Commissariat of Internal Affairs): DS interrogated by, 99; Song and Dance Ensemble, 134, 140, 315n45; and Yezhov, 97

The Nose op. 15 (opera), 347; acceptance for production, 46; articles on, 54; communications from DS to Lyubinsky about, 56; composition of, 45–46; concert performance of, 54, 55; correspondence about, 41; description by DS, 43–44; Glavrepertkom ruling on, 297n52; interpretation by DS, 43, 54–55; libretto for, 41, 54; Malïy Opera Theater run of, 56; manuscript saved from fire, 45; Moscow Chamber Music Theater production of, 281; Narkompros approval of, 299n33; premieres and performances of, 43, 52, 53, 275, 281, 345n76;

preparation of public for, 54–55; response of DS to criticism of, 55–56; response to, 55; Sollertinsky comments on, 55; third act dreamt by DS, 46; *Tosca* substituted for, 56. *See also* Suite from *The Nose*

Novodevichy Cemetery (Moscow): DS buried in, 285; Nina Varzar buried in, 193, 285

Novorossiisk Chimes (The Flame of Eternal Glory), 140, 220, 353

"Oath to the People's Commissar" (choral), 355; becomes "A Great Day Has Come," 124; reaction to, 124

Oborin, Lev Nikolayevich, 376; accompanies D. Oistrakh in Violin Concerto no. 1, 159; attends DS's rehearsals, 142; in Chopin Competition, 36–37; death of, 274; evacuation from Moscow, 126; friendship with DS, 25; member of tour to Turkey, 82; piano recital of in Moscow, 26; and DS play four-hand arrangements, 127; on DS's health, 61; Suite for Two Pianos performed with DS, 27; and Symphony no. 7, 128; travels with DS, 38

October op. 131 (symphonic poem), 354; and Maxim Shostakovich, 254; used with film *October,* 254–255

Offenbach, Jacques: *Barbe-bleue,* 118, 136; *La Belle Hélène,* 118; DS's affection for operetta and, 208; DS's tastes from Bach to Offenbach, 43, 79

"Officer's scherzo." *See* Scherzo in E-flat Major op. 7

Oistrakh, David Fyodorovich, 339n37, 376; amusements, 110; concert tour to United States, 196; death of, 274; member of Communist party, 219; performs and records DS's Second Piano Trio, 158; on playability of Violin Concerto no. 1, 159, 320n61; presents concert cycle "The Development of the Violin Concerto," 158; and *Seven Verses of A. Blok,* 252, 255–256, 358; and DS, 233; and Sonata for Violin and Piano, 258–259, 360; tour to Turkey, 82, 158; and *Twenty-four Preludes and Fugues,* 325n68; and Violin Concerto no. 1, 195–196, 273, 353; and Violin Concerto no. 2, 253–254, 255, 353; wins Second All-Union Competition, 158

Oistrakh, Igor Davidovich, 376; and Second Violin Concerto, 253; on DS demonstration Violin Concerto no. 1, 159

Okunev, German Grigoryevich, 226, 376

Oleynikov, Nikolai Makarovich, 56, 376

"On the Journals *Zvezda* and *Leningrad*" resolution, 150

"On the Reconstruction of Literary-Artistic Organizations": and liquidation of proletarian arts organizations, 65, 71

opera: collaborations with DS explored, 78; future of Soviet opera, 53–54; list of DS's operas, 347; shared role of singers and orchestra, 69; DS ceases to compose opera, 107; in Soviet period, 53; tetralogy planned by DS, 78, 303n39. *See also* specific work titles

operettas, 208. *See also Moscow, Cheryomushki*

orchestrations of DS, 361. *See also* specific work titles

Order of Lenin. *See* Shostakovich, Dmitriy — honors and awards

Orquestra Sinfónica Nacional, 213

Ostrovsky, Nikolai Alexandrovich, 376; *How the Steel Was Tempered*, 114, 260

"Our Song" (choral), 355

Overture on Russian and Kyrgyz Folk Themes op. 115, 240, 353

"Partisan Song," 112, 254

Pasternak, Boris Leonidovich, 376; on results of *Pravda* editorials, 91; supportive counsel for DS, 164

patriotic music: for 30th anniversary of the Revolution, 153–154; *Poem of the Motherland*, 154, 319n39; DS and, 124, 154, 357

"Patriotic Song" (solo vocal), 357

Patriotic War. *See* World War II

Pazovsky, Ariy Moiseyevich, 376; becomes artistic director of Bolshoy, 121; and *Boris Godunov*, 121

Pears, Peter: and DS, 251, 268

People's Artist awards. *See* Shostakovich, Dmitriy — honors and awards

People's Commissariat of Enlightenment (Narkompros), 21

People's Commissariat of Internal Affairs. *See* NKVD

Peshkov, Alexey Maximovich. *See* Gorky, Maxim

Petri, Egon, 23

Petrov, Ivan, 244

Piano Concerto no. 1 in C Minor op. 35, 353; composition of, 72–73; description of, 73–74; jazz influence on, 79; premieres and performances of, 73, 79, 87, 213

Piano Concerto no. 2 in F Major op. 102, 353; composed for Maxim Shostakovich, 199; premiere, 199; reaction to, 199–200

piano music. *See also* specific work titles: list of DS's piano music, 360

Piano Quintet in G Minor op. 57, 359; composition of, 116–117; premieres and performances of, 116, 121, 132, 176–177, 241; response to, 116; and Stalin Prize, 117, 121–122

Piano Sonata no. 1 op. 12, 360; attribution of subtitle to, 35; composition of, 34; performances of by DS, 34, 37, 38; stylistic similarity to *Dedication to October*, 34–35

Piano Sonata no. 2 in B Minor op. 61, 135, 360; dedicated to Nikolayev, 135; Neuhaus on, 315n48

Piano Trio no. 1 in C Minor op. 8, 358; dedication to Tatyana Glivenko, 22–23; performances of, 23, 34

Piano Trio no. 2 in E Minor op. 67, 359; composition of, 141, 142; dating of, 317n76; dedication to Sollertinsky, 141; Jewish tune in, 169; as portrait of Sollertinsky, 143; premiere, 142–143; response to, 142–143; DS sends parts to Tsïganov and Shirinsky, 142; wins Stalin Prize, 143

"Pictures of the Past." *See Satires*

Piotrovsky, Adrian Ivanovich, 81, 347, 348, 376–377

Pirogov op. 76 (film score), 171, 350. *See also* Suite from *Pirogov* op. 76a

Poem of the Motherland op. 74 (cantata), 355; approval by censors, 319n39; description of, 154; public response to, 154; reuse of previous melody in, 72

Pokrovsky, Boris Alexandrovich, 377; production of *The Nose*, 281, 345n78

Polyakin, Miron Borisovich, 122, 377

Ponna, Mariya Ivanovna, 377; collaboration with DS, 23

Ponomarenko, Panteleymon Kondratiyevich, 188, 377

Popov, Gavriil Nikolayevich, 377; and Congress of Soviet Composers, 321n72; critical evaluation of, 297n45; death of, 274; denounced as formalist, 158; describes DS at poker, 109–110; reaction to *Lady Macbeth,* 76; reaction to DS's Symphony no. 9, 147; reaction to DS's Symphony no. 10, 188, 327n17; resolution admits error in evaluation of, 204; suppression of own First Symphony, 306n36; and Symphony no. 4, 93

Porgy and Bess (Gershwin), 272

Poskrebïshev, Alexander Nikolayevich, 323n28, 377; and medical exam of DS, 172

Prague Spring Festival, 158

Pravda: campaign against Sakharov, 278, 344n60; on *Katerina Izmailova* (op. 114), 238; DS's inspirational article and dedication of Symphony no. 7, 131; theatrical review underscores artistic right to creative freedom, 189. *See also Pravda* editorials

Pravda editorials: authorship of, 304n67; "Balletic Falsity," 85; disagreement with, 89; effect on cultural environment, 87; effect on performances of DS's works, 305n11; effect on DS, 85, 87, 90–91, 107; *Lady Macbeth* criticized in, 84–85; *The Limpid Stream* criticized in, 85; "Muddle Instead of Music," 84–85; music criticism denounced, 84–85; musicians' meetings regarding, 90; reach of expanded to other arts by Kerzhentsev, 89, 90; DS reaction to, 304n1

Preface to the Complete Edition of My Works and a Brief Reflection apropos of This Preface op. 123 (solo vocal), 248–249, 358

premieres. *See* titles of specific works

Preys, Alexander Germanovich, 377; and libretto for 2nd opera of DS's prospective tetralogy, 78; and libretto for *Lady Macbeth,* 68

primitivism, 124

Prokofiev family and DS, 181–182

Prokofiev, Sergey Sergeyevich, 377; *Alexander Nevsky,* 116; American Academy of Arts and Letters honorary member, 132; attends *Lady Macbeth,* 76; collaboration with Rostropovich, 212; and Congress of Soviet Composers, 162; correspondence with DS, 38; death of, 183; declines to write music for *The Bedbug,* 51; denounced as formalist, 156, 157, 158, 320n64; and First All-Union Congress of Soviet Composers, 321n72; *Love for Three Oranges,* 31, 53; one of nation's best, 114; open letter to Moscow conference on Central Committee resolution, 320n64; People's Artist of the RSFSR, 153, 319n37; performance of works of, 221; and Petrograd Conservatory composition curriculum, 19; Piano Concerto no. 1, 51, 73; relationship with DS, 183; resolution admits error in evaluation of, 204; response to DS's Symphony no. 8, 138; Seventh Symphony of, 183; and DS, 74, 78, 110, 149, 172; DS influenced by, 39; on DS's classic composer list, 258; on DS's works, 38, 312n49; and Stalin Prize, 312n52; Symphony-Concerto, 212; withholds opera from evaluation, 168

Psalms of David, 124, 313n5

purges: counterrevolutionary writers' organization exposed, 114; efforts to free and rehabilitate victims of, 196; the Great Terror, 97; role of DS's music during, 1; Shostakovich family affected by, 97–98; DS survival of, 1, 99; Zhdanov's purge of leading Soviet musicians, 155–156; "Zhdanovshchina," 150. *See also* names of individuals

Pushkin, Alexander Sergeyevich: compared to Dolmatovsky, 176; "The Demons," 98; *The Gypsies,* 11, 33; "Monument," 253; poems of set by DS, 98, 253; the Pushkinian question, 278, 344n61; and DS on artists and conscience, 229; in DS's works, 248, 277; "Spring, Spring," 253, 358; *The Tale of the Priest and His Worker, Blockhead,* 74. *See also Four Monologues on Texts of A. Pushkin* op. 91; *Four Romances on Texts of A. Pushkin* op. 46

Pushkinian question, 278, 344n61

quarter-tone music circle, 19–20

The Quiet Don (Sholokhov). *See under* DS — abandoned and unrealized projects

Rabinovich, David Abramovich, 377; DS talks to about Symphony no. 9, 146

Rabinovich, Nikolai Semyonovich, 274, 377

Rachmaninoff, Sergey Vasileyevich: Prelude in C-sharp Minor, 113; and DS, 8, 23, 273, 297n50; DS's Second Piano Trio compared with, 143

radio music show, 149

Raikh, Zinaída Nikolayevna: letter in support of Meyerhold, 114; and Meyerhold, 45, 297n51, 377

Rakhlin, Natan Grigoryevich, 377; conducts premiere of Symphony no. 11, 201

Raleigh, Walter. *See Six Romances on Texts of W. Raleigh, R. Burns, and W. Shakespeare*

RAPM. *See* Russian Association of Proletarian Musicians

Rappaport, Gerbert Moritsevich, 209, 350, 377

Red Army Chorus, 139

rehabilitation after Stalin's death, 196–197

rehearsals: DS's emotional state during, 32

Renzin, Isai Mikhailovich, 95, 377

research resources: evaluation of, 2–5, 289n5; significant published collections, 289n1. *See also* Khentova; *Testimony;* Volkov

Reshetin, Mark Stepanovich, 263, 341n86, 378

Reysner, Larisa Mikhailovna, 78, 378

Reyzen, Mark Osipovich, 315n51, 378

Richter, Svyatoslav Teofilovich, 378; and *From Jewish Folk Poetry,* 167, 168; and Sonata for Violin and Piano, 258

Rimsky-Korsakov, Georgiy Mikhailovich, 19, 378

Rimsky-Korsakov, Nikolai Andreyevich: *Boris Godunov* (Musorgsky) orchestration by, 119, 120, 121, 211; "I waited in the grotto" ("Ya v grote zhdal," orch. DS), 361; as model for DS and Soviet music, 89, 201; orchestration of *Khovanshchina* (Musorgsky), 210; relatives of, 19, 378, 382; DS and polyphonic studies of, 177; students of, 369, 381, 382, 384; *Tale of Tsar Saltan* (opera), 9; as traditional standard, 17, 24; view of opera compared with DS's view, 54. *See also Boris Godunov* (orch. DS); *Khovanshchina* (orch. DS)

Rodzinski, Artur, 132, 139

Roslavets, Nikolai Andreyevich, 378; *Dark City,* 53; *Komsomoliya,* 53

Rossini, Gioacchino: and DS, 124, 195, 272

Rostropovich, Mstislav Leopoldovich, 378; and Britten, 251; and Cello Concerto no. 1, 212; and Cello Concerto no. 2, 248, 250; collaboration with Prokofiev, 212; conducts DS's works, 232; and *Die Fledermaus,* 279; and First Festival of Contemporary Music, 230–231; music mastery, 250; report of DS's denunciation of, 369; request to go abroad, 279; and *Satires,* 220–221; and DS, 310n7, 342n7; supports Solzhenitsyn, 269; visits with Shostakovich family, 150; wins first prize at All-Union Competition for Performers, 150

Rothschild's Violin (DS completion of Fleyshman's opera), 109, 141, 361

Royal Opera (Copenhagen), 275

Rozanova, Alexandra Alexandrovna, 8, 14, 378

Rozhdestvensky, Gennadiy Nikolayevich, 281, 378

Rule, Britannia! op. 28 (incidental music), 58, 348

Russian Association of Proletarian Musicians (RAPM): abuses of RAPM against Soviet music, 65; and cultural revolution, 57; and the resolution "On the Reconstruction of Literary-Artistic Organizations," 65

Russian River op. 66 (incidental music), 140, 348

Sabinina, Marina Dmitriyevna, 204, 320n70, 378

Sádlo, Miloš, 158, 378

Sakharov, Andrey Dmitriyevich, 278–279, 344nn60,61, 378

Salute, Spain! op. 44 (incidental music), 348; music as contrast with *Lady Macbeth,* 95; premiere, 95

Sam Wooding and the Chocolate Kiddies (jazz band), 31

Samosud, Samuíl Abramovich, 379; alters DS's score for *Boris Godunov,* 120–121; and Bolshoy Theater, 305n13; honors and awards, 305n13; instigates DS's re-orchestration of *Boris Godunov,* 119; and *Lady Macbeth,* 75, 76; leaves Bolshoy, 121; *The Quiet Don* and summons by Stalin, 84; DS concerns about as symphonic conductor, 130; and Symphony no. 4, 97; and Symphony no. 7, 128,

Samosud (cont.)
129–130, 131, 335n30, 351; and Symphony no. 8, 205; vision of Soviet opera, 54
Saradzhev, Konstantin Solomonovich, 43, 379
Satires (Pictures of the Past) op. 109 (solo vocal), 358; description of, 220–221; performances of, 231; response to, 221; and scandal, 342n20
Sayanov, Vissarion Mikhailovich, 124, 379
Scherzo in E-flat Major op. 7, 25–26, 353
Scherzo in F-sharp Minor op. 1, 19, 352
Schillinger, Joseph (Moiseyevich), 379; March of the Orient, 31
Schnittke, Alfred Garriyevich, 283–284, 379
Schoenberg, Arnold: and dodecaphony, 214; influence of on DS, 88; message to Soviet delegation to Congress for World Peace, 323n31; new works unveiled at Fogt home, 20; DS private comments about, 215
scholarship on Shostakovich: current state of, 2; evaluation of sources, 2–5
Schreker, Franz: Der ferne Klang, 53
Schumann, Robert: Cello Concerto, 240, 361; Humoresque, 21; Piano Concerto, 21; and DS, 18, 109
Scriabin, Alexander Nikolayevich, 36, 273
Serebryakov, Pavel Alexeyevich, 177, 379
Serebryakova, Galina Iosifovna, 219, 241–242, 379
"Serenade" (Braga, arr. DS), 275
serialism. See dodecaphony
Serov, Eduard Afanasyevich, 250, 379
Seven Dolls' Dances (arr. for piano from ballet suites), 360
Seven Verses of A. Blok op. 127 (solo vocal), 358; composition of, 252–253; dodecaphony in, 258; impetus for, 252; premieres, 255–256, 257, 340n50; title set for, 252, 339n29
Shaginyan, Marietta Sergeyevna, 379; DS tells about his composing, 253
Shakespeare, William: Hamlet, 71, 122, 241, 267, 275, 348, 350, 355; King Lear, 122, 241, 267, 268, 348, 351; Otello, 136; and DS, 62, 277; DS's comments on, 122; DS's settings for, 122, 134, 135, 162, 248, 315n47, 357, 358
Shapiro, Mikhaíl Grigoryevich, 239, 351, 379

Shaporin, Yuriy Alexandrovich, 379; avoidance of writing symphonies, 186; On the Field of Kulikovo, 116; People's Artist awards, 153, 192, 319n37; reaction to Lady Macbeth, 75–76; and Symphony no. 8, 138
Shchedrin, Rodion Konstantinovich, 379; and letter condemning Sakharov, 344n60; speech at DS's funeral, 285; told by DS about withdrawal of Symphony no. 4, 96
Shcherbachov, Vladimir Vladimirovich, 379–380; participates in music circle at Fogt home, 20; on Symphony no. 5, 99
Shebalin, Vissarion Yakovlevich, 380; and Congress of Soviet Composers, 321n72; denounced as formalist, 156, 158; evacuation from Moscow, 126; friendship with DS, 25, 26, 91; greetings to from DS, 142; People's Artist of the RSFSR, 153, 319n37; and RAPM, 301n64; resolution admits error in evaluation of, 204; String Quartet no. 2 dedicated to, 142; Symphony no. 5 excerpts played for, 98
Shenderovich, Yevgeniy Mikhailovich, 282, 283, 380
Shepilov, Dmitriy Trofimovich, 380; Central Committee representative at Second All-Union Congress, 200; on direction for Soviet music, 201; discussion with DS about The Quiet Don, 242–243, 337n86
Shevchenko Theater of Opera and Ballet (Kiev): and Katerina Izmailova, 239
Shidlovskaya Commercial School, 10–11
Shirinsky, Sergey Petrovich, 151, 380; death of, 274, 281; DS sends Piano Trio no. 2 parts to, 142; and String Quartet no. 14, 275. See also The Beethoven Quartet; Borisovsky; Druzhinin; V. Shirinsky; Tsïganov
Shirinsky, Vasiliy Petrovich, 151, 380; death of, 247; DS writes to about String Quartet no. 3, 151; String Quartet no. 11 dedicated to, 247. See also The Beethoven Quartet; Borisovsky; Druzhinin; S. Shirinsky; Tsïganov
Shlifshteyn, Semyon: on Symphony no. 9, 147
Sholokov, Mikhaíl Alexandrovich, 380; Virgin Soil Upturned, 78, 303n42

Shostakovich, Boleslav Petrovich (grandfather), 7, 11

Shostakovich, Dmitriy Boleslavovich (father), 7; children's appearance at funeral of, 21; illness and death of, 20

Shostakovich, Dmitriy Dmitriyevich: amusements and leisure activities of, 9, 109–110, 185, 215, 273, 275; and anti-Sakharov campaign, 278–279, 344n60; anxiety for family in Leningrad, 130; appeals for help for, 21; appearance at father's funeral, 21; appearance when playing piano, 14; on artists and politics, 197; assistance to purge victims, 307n50; attraction to the circus, 300n61; aversion to anti-Semitism, 169; on avoiding distractions, 181; beliefs about family, 80; birth of, 8; birth of daughter Galina, 80, 92, 94; birth of son Maxim, 109; on Brezhnev's Russia, 269; burial of, 285; characteristics of, 214; childhood activities, 14; childhood musical influences, 8–9; commemoration of 50th birthday, 198–199; commemoration of 60th birthday, 248; on communism, 217; Communist Party membership, 216–217, 218, 219; contribution to family finances as youth, 40–41; cowardice of, 218; death of, 285; death of mother, 195; death of Nina, 193; deaths of friends and colleagues, 274; descriptions of, 121, 302n25; divorce from and remarriage to Nina Varzar, 80; on doing it all over again, 259; donates prize money to Soviet Peace Fund, 275; early indisposition to study music, 9; emotional effect of persecution of his "formalist" tendencies, 164; emotional reaction to performances of his works, 175; emotional state before premieres, 130; emotional state during air raids, 126; eulogies for, 285, 346n97; on evacuation conditions, 127; evacuation with wife and children, 125, 126; evaluation of research sources on, 2–5; evaluation of scholarship on, 2; exaggeration of political understanding as youth, 11; family background, 7–8; as father, 194; and fear of rejection, 233; finances, 94–95, 134, 180, 256, 313n4; funeral of, 285; and God, 263; grief at Sollertinsky's death, 141; homes of, 44, 45, 71, 80, 82, 109, 126, 127, 135, 149,

227; housing arrangements made for, 149; income, 57, 94, 313n4; interrogated by militia, 122; on Khrushchev, 244, 338n99; as letter writer, 2; on marriage and love, 22; marriages (*See* Margarita Kainova; Irina Supinskaya; Nina Varzar); memorial commemorations of, 286; memorial concerts for, 285–286; mood swings, 29; naming and nickname of, 8; obituary, 285, 346n96; personal appearance as child, 13–14; personal characteristics, 1–2, 19, 109–110; political activities/interests, 36; on political prospects on death of Stalin, 184; reaction to conflict, 79; reaction to father's death, 21; reaction to news of Meyerhold's death, 196; reaction to others' opinions, 116; reaction to role in anti-Sakharov campaign, 278, 344n62; recalls student days, 18; received poison-pen letters, 161; rehabilitation efforts, 196–197; resists evacuation from Leningrad, 125; rift between post-Stalin intellectuals and, 174; as role model, 88; romantic relationship and marriage (*See* Kainova, Supinskaya, Nina Varzar); romantic relationship and marriage proposal to Ustvolskaya, 183, 194; romantic relationship with Konstantinovskaya, 79–80; romantic relationship with Nazirova, 187, 375; romantic relationship with Tatyana Glivenko, 22; schedule of, 109, 265; sees himself as aging, 171; separation from friends, 135; as soccer fan, 110–111, 122, 134, 148, 318n19; social tendencies, 109; sparrow anecdote, 186–187; story of DS and Lenin's arrival, 12–13, 291n27, 333n61; superstition and, 140; support for Meyerhold, 115; travel (*See* concert and promotion tours); wanderlust of, 40–41. *See also* Atovmyan; Glikman; Kainova; Sollertinsky; Supinskaya; Nina Varzar; Yavorsky

— correspondence. *See* names of specific correspondents

— education: academic education, 10–11, 290n16; accepted into "free composition" at Moscow Conservatory, 24; audition for Glyasser, 10; begins piano lessons with mother, 9–10; characteristics as student, 17–18, 19; conditions of

Shostakovich—education (*cont.*)
study in 1919–1920, 17–18; conducting classes with Malko, 29–30; Conservatory courses, 24; Conservatory curriculum becomes confining, 19; course of study decision (piano or composition), 14–15; early resistance to music education, 9; early school concert programs, 10; Glazunov as mentor to, 17; at Glyasser's school, 10–11; as graduate student, 24, 25, 31, 35; improvisation study, 14; Marxist methodology exam, 35, 36, 41–42; music talents recognized, 9–10; musical pursuits outside the classroom, 19–20; performance development, 18; piano public exam, 21; reaction to Siloti's evaluation of talent, 14; receives instruction in Marxism-Leninism, 173; requests to be student of Yavorsky, 107–108; transfer to Moscow Conservatory planned, 24–25, 27; transfers to Nikolayev's piano class, 18; transfers to Stoyunina School, 10

— health and illnesses of: appendicitis, 37; broken leg, 222, 255; convalescence in the south, 21, 22; debility of right hand, 208, 210, 215, 228, 240, 249 (*See also* mobility problems and poliomyelitis); depression, 141, 264; emotional breakdown, 216–217; general appearance, 266; general state of health, 61, 171, 249, 268–269, 270, 271, 273, 279–280; headaches suffered routinely, 136; and headaches when unable to compose, 136; heart attack and heart troubles, 249, 271; hospitalizations, 208, 215, 228–229, 237, 240, 249, 250–251, 255, 256, 259, 264, 271, 273–274, 275, 277, 284–285; illnesses, 25, 141, 153, 172, 185; lung cancer, 273–274, 284–285; medical exam at National Institute of Health, 276; mobility problems and poliomyelitis, 222, 250–251, 256, 264, 265, 267, 269, 271, 341n95 (*See also* debility of right hand); monitoring of health of, 276; piano playing and, 265–266; poliomyelitis and mobility problems (*See* mobility problems and poliomyelitis); requirements imposed by, 251–252, 265; respiratory seizures, 284; DS on his health, 268, 280; DS's hopes for new treatment, 263–264; DS's responses to illness, 153, 250–251,

255, 274; and travel, 272, 276; treatments, 270, 275, 283, 284, 344n49; tuberculosis diagnosed, 21; typhoid fever, 135

— honors and awards: audiences with foreign political leaders, 273; Chopin Competition, 37; Commandeur de l'Ordre des Arts et des Lettres, 204; contest winner, 270, 343n25; Glinka Prize, 267; Hammer and Sickle gold medal, 249; Hero of Socialist Labor, 249; honorary doctorates, 204, 273, 276; honorary memberships, 132, 192, 203, 204; International Peace Prize, 192; Lenin Prize, 202, 224; Order of Lenin, 153, 198, 249; Order of the October Revolution, 271; People's Artist awards, 153, 192, 262, 273, 319n37; Sibelius Prize, 204; Sonning Prize, 275; Stalin Prizes, 117, 121–122, 129, 138–139, 143; State Prizes, 245, 282

— music career and interests: acceptance of works for publication, 26; accepts professorship at Moscow Conservatory, 135; and activities after *Pravda* editorials, 90–91; advice for DS from Committee for Artistic Affairs, 89; advice to young composers, 182; alienation of peers, 90; appointed to faculty of Leningrad Conservatory, 97; on artistic imperative, 189; attacks by RAPM, 57; attendance at concerts, theatrical, and cultural events, 31, 38, 109, 275–276, 283; attitude toward critics, 76–77; ballet interests of, 23; becomes composition professor at Leningrad Conservatory, 153; begins scrapbook related to *Pravda* editorials, 87; broadcast concert and commentary, 130–131; career survey published in *Sovetskaya muzïka*, 164; cartoon on DS's influence in music education, 162; at Central Committee Conference of Musicians, 156–157; as cinema pianist, 23, 25–26, 29, 31; collaboration with Mariya Ponna, 23; collaboration with TRAM, 58, 299n37; competes in Chopin Competition, 35–37; composer's role, 102; conducts own music, 232, 335n30; on content in music, 88; counsels young composers, 78; debut in Circle of Friends of Chamber Music, 21; "Declaration of a Composer's Duties," 63–64; deflects proposal to write a festive overture about

Molotov, 312n65; denounced as formalist, 156, 158; denounces own works, 63–64; as director of Home Guard's theater, 124; dismissed from professorships, 162; effect of Central Committee resolutions on, 153; on emotions and serious music, 76–77; enters national anthem competition, 139; exposure to international music and composers, 213, 215; first public performance of own work, 13; on formalism, 88; Glavrepertkom bans works of, 162; Glavrepertkom rescinds ban on works of, 172; influence in music education, 162, *163*; interest in career of, 286; introduces compositions to circle at Fogt home, 20; Jewish music interests of, 169; juvenilia, 11, 12; last premiere attended, 283; as mentor to musicians, 182; as Meyerhold Theater pianist, 44–45; Moscow debut, 27; as music professional, 1–2; on music, themes, and emotions, 128; musical consultant to Bolshoy Theater, 192, 328n34; on musical language, 80–81; and musical prostitution, 34; musical tastes, 79, 109, 297n50; names 20th century classic composers, 258; operatic collaborations explored, 78; paired with Aseyev by Malïy Opera Theater for opera, 74; participates in quarter-tone music circle, 19–20; and patriotic anthems, 139–140; performance approach, 18; performance venues as student, 20; performances attended, 23; as performer, 35, 73, 249, 292n20, 325n68; piano technique, 37; on possible alternate career course, 268, 342n17; *Pravda* editorials effect on, 85, 88–89, 107, 304n1; premiere preparation style, 255; promotion to professor at Leningrad Conservatory, 108; public presence kept minimal, 97; public response to Central Committee resolutions, 160; reaction to criticism, 55–56; reaction to *Pravda* editorials, 90, 92, 304n1; regains ability to play piano, 265–266; rehabilitation after *Pravda* editorials, 90, 103, 305n12; and rehearsals for Symphony no. 8, 137; relationship with Asafyev, 30; relationship with The Beethoven Quartet, 27; removed from authority in Composers' Union, 160; resolution admits error in evaluation of, 204; response to correction of 1948 resolution, 204–205; resumes teaching composition at Leningrad Conservatory, 226; on role of music in spectacle, 61; roles of DS's music during Stalinist era, 1; sabbaticals, 63; DS on avant-gardism, 258; DS on stage fright, 194–195; solicitude for his students, 109; solo recital program for Friends of Chamber Music, 23; speech to Composers' Union Plenum, 152–153; status as composer, 248, 257, 283–284; students of DS, 108, 226; on study of Western music, 88; support of colleagues after *Pravda* editorials, 91–92; symphonic debut compared with Glazunov's, 32; tastes in music, 79, 109, 215; as teacher, 35, 97, 108–109, 226–227; teaches at Choreographic Tekhnikum (Leningrad), 51; teaches at Moscow Conservatory, 51; teaches at Moscow Conservatory, 141–142; unwillingness to speak about works, 101; wardrobe for tours, 82; works divided by others into two types, 152; works liked or admired by, 215; on young composers and music trends, 251. *See also* Concert and promotion tours

— music composition: and alcohol, 252–253, 275, 344n49; anxiety about his death leaving work incomplete, 257; approach to composition, 306n34; approach to reorchestration of *Boris Godunov,* 120; attitude toward changes in his scores, 121; avoidance of writing symphonies, 185–186; children's music, 149, 193, 318n24; collaboration with Yevtushenko, 228–229; composer's block, 33, 79, 141, 195, 252, 274, 275; composing as response to crisis, 92; composing spaces, 127, 136, 186, 226, 240; compositional method, 334n15; concerns about composition, 142; concerto genre, 72; conditions of, 34; consideration of the Soviet audience when composing, 157; creates arrangements for front-line performance, 123–124; creation of parts for himself in his works, 116–117; on creative potential, 186; destruction of manuscripts, 33, 337n92; difficulty with, 253; distractions from composition, 181, 194–195; early encouragement for composing, 14; efforts to meet needs of choreographer, 82;

Shostakovich—music composition (*cont.*)
emotional response to composing, 26,
136; exercises for, 79, 111–112, 177; facility of composition, 47; finale problem,
103–104, 129–130, 138, 308n82; finale
success, 115; financial motivation for,
180; and formulas, 116; goal of, 251; importance of Sollertinsky's opinion, 140;
influences on, 8, 59, 79, 88, 169, 185; instrumentation proficiency in, 159; interest in reinvigorated, 228; as juvenile
composer, 11, 12; listeners' importance
to, 169, 215; loses composing momentum during evacuation, 127; misgivings
about being a composer, 33; musical
monogram, 187–188, 327n15; musical
revelations, 46; participates in student
composers circle, 19; process of composition, 46, 142; productivity in, 149, 243;
quartet form, 111; reduction in number
of works composed, 94, 98; reuse of music, 72, 81–82, 134, 139–140, 209, 386; on
revising his work, 46–47; simplification
of style, 80–81; sojourns used (in part)
for composing, 52, 243, 254, 257, 258,
277; strategies to keep himself composing, 40; stylistic and emotional variations
between works, 133; tempo in, 309n83;
travel as stimulation for, 35. *See also* —
arrangements; — abandoned and unrealized projects
— public service: activities during World
War II, 134; attends session of Congress
of Stakhanovites, 83; benefit concert performance, 125; as chair for commissions
and committees, 79, 119, 122, 128, 150,
153, 180, 204, 273, 326n79; chair of International Chaikovsky Competition,
203, 226, 266, 280; compromises in public arena, 284; constituent care, 181; delegate to Congresses for World Peace,
171–173, 180–181; as distraction from
composition, 181; editor-in-chief of children's radio show, 149; efforts to assist
purge victims, 196; elected deputy of Leningrad October District, 78–79,
303n44; elected first Secretary of Russian
Composers' Union, 216, 332n45; elected
to Council of Nationalities of USSR Supreme Soviet, 226; elected to RSFSR Supreme Soviet, 153; establishes and chairs
Union of Soviet Composers branch, 128;

establishment of Russian republic composers' union, 216; on jury of First International Bach Competition, 177; "loyal
son" of Communist Party, 219, 285;
member of composition jury at Leningrad Conservatory, 122; member of jury
for vocal competition, 119; music or arts
related service, 111, 226; new year's message on Soviet arts, 189; offices held by
DS, 111, 181, 226; public persona, 1–2,
78–79, 202–203; public reactions of DS
to cultural revolution, 58–59; as public
servant, 1–2, 78–79, 111; reelected as
deputy to RSFSR Supreme Soviet, 181;
reinstated to editorial board of
Sovetskaya muzïka, 326n79; requests to
be relieved of office, 256; response to
questions about Communist Party criticisms, 214; response to Stalin's request
that DS join the delegation to Congress
for World Peace, 172; serves in Home
Guard, 123; DS's story as propaganda,
126; Soviet-Austrian society, 273; as
spokesman for Soviet propaganda,
180–181; toast to the Party, 203; tries to
volunteer for army, 123; Union of Soviet
Composers (SSK) boards, 111; uses position and connections in service to others, 181–182; volunteers for army, 123;
wartime broadcasts, 125
— works. *See also* titles of specific works:
list of works, 347–361
— writings: acceptance of Party authorship
of speeches and articles, 173–174,
323n36; authorship of speeches, 320n70;
autobiographical sketch in *Sovetskaya
muzïka*, 199; hortatory statements, 140,
316n69; inspirational article and dedication of Symphony no. 7, 131; introductory essays to collected edition of his
music, 3; keynote speech to Russian
Composers' Union, 226; May Day salutations, 216; "National Traditions and the
Precepts of their Development," 271; official sentiments on death of Stalin, 184;
program notes and review of *Madonna
and the Soldier*, 283; public *vs.* private
opinions in, 215; stance toward Party-
authored writings, 174
— arrangements: film music arrangement
in 8 movements, 113; popular songs and
arias for front-line performance, 124;

"Serenade" (Braga), 275; *Symphony of Psalms* (Stravinsky), 109, 125, 231; "When Johnny Comes Marching Home," 315n51

— abandoned and unrealized projects: *Barbe-bleue* (projected orch), 118, 136; *The Carp* (Oleynikov), 56; *The Cement Sets*, 64; children's ballet based on "The Golden Key," 136; collaboration with Yevtushenko on human conscience, 239; contracted with Kirov Theater for opera *Katyusha Maslova*, 117–118; *Don Quixote* treatment, 107; festive overture (announced August 1947), 154, 319n38; *A Hero of Our Times* (opera), 114; *How the Steel Was Tempered*, 114, 311n30; instrumental works (April 1935), 93; *La Belle Hélène* (projected orch.), 118; *Lermontov* (ballet), 114; *Little Mermaid* (ballet); *Masquerade* (opera), 114; *The Negro*, 64; opera about the Baltic fleet, 310n3; opera for 50th anniversary of the Revolution, 254; opera on career and murder of S. Kirov, 113; opera on "The Black Monk," 274–275; opera on the Civil War (1937), 112; opera tetralogy, 78; opera to libretto by Bragin about the Civil War, 117; *Otello*, 136; *Petersburg Tales*, 268; piano concerto, 33; *The Quiet Don* (opera), 242–243, 247; Second Symphony (1926), 40; setting for "The Demons" (Pushkin), 98; setting of verse by Voznesensky, 282; *The Snow Princess* (opera-ballet), 117; string quartet (April 1935), 93; symphonic poem on the life of Karl Marx, 65, 71; *The Twelve Chairs* (operetta), 118; *Wiener Blut* (projected orch.), 118; work on Psalms of David for soloist, chorus, and orchestra, 124; *The Young Guard* (opera), 171

Shostakovich family: background, 7–8; contributions to family finances by DS, 23, 40–41; correspondence with DS, 37; favorite composers, 8; finances of, 20, 21, 25, 40–41, 94, 134, 180; homes of, 80, 109; household members, 94; members of in Leningrad during siege, 130; music education in, 9–10; music in social life of, 20; musical environment in, 8–9; NKVD surveillance of, 164; piano removed from, 25; political involvement, 11–12; relations at time of DS's 1st marriage, 70; story of family as related to Lenin, 36; support for Vainberg family, 182

Shostakovich, Galina Dmitriyevna (daughter): birth of, 80, 92, 94, 306n21; children of, 227; and Chukovskaya, 278; on dating of "Birthday," 318n24; homes of, 227; interest in music diminished, 193; marriage to Yevgeniy Chukovsky, 212; performances by, 149; recollection of DS and film music, 171; and university entrance exams, 192

Shostakovich, Irina (3rd wife). *See* Supinskaya, Irina

Shostakovich, Margarita (2nd wife). *See* Kainova, Margarita

Shostakovich, Mariya (sister), 8; accompanies DS to the south (Gaspra), 22; comments about DS and family relations, 70; death of, 274; exiled to Central Asia, 98; Frederiks, husband of, 98, 368; in Leningrad during Nazi siege, 126, 314n14; performs Suite in F-sharp Minor for Two Pianos op. 6 with DS, 21; takes private piano students, 20

Shostakovich, Maxim Dmitriyevich (son), 380; birth of, 109; conducting competition, 254; conducts concerts of DS's works, 250, 271, 360; conducts Symphony no. 15, 273, 275; on death of his mother, 194; defection of, 3, 286; goes to Edinburgh Festival with DS, 230; music career status, 241; and *October*, 254, 354; and Piano Concerto no. 2, 199–200, 353; premieres Symphony no. 15, 271, 352; recollection of scores in Shostakovich household, 215; required to vilify DS in school exam, 162; returns from tour for funeral, 285; on rumors in *Testimony*, 327n14; on DS's Second Piano Trio compared with Second Quartet, 142; son of, 227; and "To My Son," 134; and Violin Concerto no. 2, 254; wedding of, 222; as young performer, 193

Shostakovich, Nina (1st wife). *See* Nina Varzar

Shostakovich, Sofya Vasilyevna (née Kokoúlina, mother): attempts to move DS to America, 41; background, 7–8; death of, 195; employment taken after spouse's death, 20; in Leningrad during Nazi siege, 126; piano teacher of, 8; plans

Shostakovich, Sofya Vasilyevna (*cont.*)
to transfer DS to Moscow, 24, 27; reaction to DS's romance with Varzar, 70; reluctance to allow DS to transfer to Moscow, 25; resettles in Leningrad, 148; on DS living away from Leningrad, 149; on DS's emotional state, 165
Shostakovich, Zoya (sister), 8; appearance at father's funeral, 21
The Shot op. 24 (incidental music), 348; role of music in, 58–59
Shteynberg, Maximilian Oseyevich. *See* Steinberg (Shteynberg), Maximilian Oseyevich
Shtokolov, Boris Timofeyevich, 211, 380
Shvarts, Iosif Zakharovich, 36, 380
Shvarts, Yevgeniy: *The Snow Princess,* 117
Siberia as Shostakovich family background, 7–8
Sidelnikov, Nikolai, 346n90
silent films, 49–50
The Silly Little Mouse op. 56 (film score), 113, 349
Siloti, Alexander Ilyich, 380; evaluates DS as having no musical abilities, 14
Simeonov, Konstantin Arsenyevich, 282, 381
Simple People op. 71 (film score), 350
Les Six (group of six French composers), 20. *See also* the Moscow Six
Six Romances on Texts by Japanese Poets op. 21 (solo vocal), 69, 357
Six Romances on Texts of W. Raleigh, R. Burns, and W. Shakespeare op. 62 (solo vocal), 357; dedications of, 134, 315n47; performances of, 135; publication of, 134; Sonnet 66 in, 122; texts included, 134, 315n47
Six Romances on Texts of W. Raleigh, R. Burns, and W. Shakespeare op. 62a (orchestration of op. 62), 357
Six Romances on Texts of W. Raleigh, R. Burns, and W. Shakespeare op. 140 (orchestration of op. 62), 358
Six Verses of Marina Tsvetayeva op. 143 (solo vocal), 277, 278, 344n59, 358
Six Verses of Marina Tsvetayeva op. 143a (orchestration of op. 143), 358
Smetana, Bedrich, 201
Smirnov, Viktor Fyodorovich, 62, 347, 381
Smolich, Nikolai Vasilyevich, 381; appraisal by DS of *The Golden Age* communicated

to, 61; and *Lady Macbeth,* 68, 75, 77, 83; DS confides vision of future to, 164; told of plan for opera cycle by DS, 68–69; vision of Soviet opera, 54
soccer: Leningrad Zenith win championship, 148, 318n19; DS as fan, 110–111, 122, 134, 148, 318n19
Social-Democratic (Bolshevik) Party, 11
Socialist Realism: efforts to impose, 89–90; folk sources and, 88, 156; and Gorky, 369; and *Lady Macbeth,* 88; in "Muddle Instead of Music" *Pravde* editorial, 84; poor understanding of, 87–88; recipe for, 85, 88; reconfirmed in Central Committee resolution, 204; DS expected to produce musical examples of, 174; DS's new year's message on, 189; Symphony no. 5 as example of, 101; Symphony no. 10 evaluated against, 190. *See also* ideology in music; Soviet music
Sofronitsky, Vladimir Vladimirovich, 18, 381
Sofya Perovskaya op. 132 (film score), 256, 351
Sokolov, Nikolai Alexandrovich, 18, 19, 381
Sokolovsky, Mikhaíl Vladimirovich, 57–58, 381
Solemn March (for military band), 353
Sollertinsky, Ivan Ivanovich, 42, 381; accused of encouraging DS on incorrect path, 89–90; alienation of peers, 90; on Artistic Council reaction to *The Golden Age,* 60; assists DS with early public statements, 174; attacked for article about *Lady Macbeth,* 76; broadcast address by, 140; comments by DS on meeting with, 42; correspondence with DS, 43, 45, 52, 63, 80, 82, 83, 114, 120, 127, 129, 133, 134, 136, 298n14, 299n37, 304n8; as critic, 42, 82, 89; death of, 140, 148; dedication of Piano Trio no. 2 to, 141; evacuation from Leningrad with family, 125; friendship with DS, 41, 42–43, 88, 91, 92, 108, 140; gives introductions to premieres of Symphony no. 8, 141; joins faculty of Leningrad Conservatory, 97; on *The Limpid Stream,* 82; on Marxist methodology exam, 41–42; and *The Nose,* 54, 55; planned ballet treatment of *Don Quixote,* 107; plans for permanent move to Moscow, 140–141; and Second Piano Trio, 143;

and DS attend Varzar family soirées, 70; DS fear for safety of, 98; and DS on *The Bolt*, 62; and DS on *Lady Macbeth*, 68; and DS residency, 80; DS reunited with, 132; DS's grief at death of, 141; and silent film score, 50; and singer selection for *Lady Macbeth*, 75; and *Six Romances on Texts of W. Raleigh, R. Burns, and W. Shakespeare*, 134, 315n47; and String Quartet no. 1, 112; on Symphony no. 4, 93, 94; on Symphony no. 5, 100, 103; and Symphony no. 6, 115; on Symphony no. 8, 137–138

solo vocal works of DS, 357–358. *See also* specific work titles

Solzhenitsyn, Aleksandr Isayevich, 381; deported from Soviet Union, 279; expelled from Union of Writers, 269; *The Gulag Archipelago*, 203, 279, 330n84; *One Day in the Life of Ivan Denisovich*, 233–234; DS and, 269–270; on DS's work, 203, 263; wins Nobel Prize for Literature, 269

Sonata for Viola and Piano op. 147, 360; and Beethoven, 286; composition of, 284; dedication of, 284–285; premiere of, 285–286; themes from *The Gamblers* used in, 134, 286, 346n98

Sonata for Violin and Piano op. 134, 359–360; composition of, 258, 340n66; and dodecaphony, 258; premieres and performances of, 259, 286; response to, 259

Sonata in D Minor op. 40 (cello and piano): composition of, 80; premiere and performances of, 80, 286; style of, 80–81

"Song about the Red Army" (solo vocal), 357

"A Song About Tsar Ivan Vasilyevich, the Young Bodyguard, and the Valorous Merchant Kalashnikov" (Lermontov), 290n17

"Song of a Guard's Division" (The Fearless Guard's Regiments Are on the Move) (choral), 124, 355

"Song of Peace" (DS and Dolmatovsky), 171

"Song of the Counterplan," 302n16; from the film *Counterplan*, 72; performed at DS's 50th birthday, 198; reuse of melody of, 72, 209

"Song of the Flea" (Beethoven, orch. DS), 283

"Song of the Flea" (Musorgsky, orch. DS), 120

Song of the Forests op. 81 (oratorio), 356; comment on revision of text, 176; Committee for Artistic Affairs and, 175; Dolmatovsky revises text to, 176; Myaskovsky's comments on, 175; official reaction to, 175; premiere, 175; recording of, 180; DS conceives idea for, 174–175; DS emotional reaction to premiere, 175; wins Stalin Prize, 175–176

Song of the Great Rivers (Unity) op. 95 (film score), 195, 350

"Song of the Red Army," 139

Songs and Dances of Death (Musorgsky, orch. DS), 361; dedication of, 230; premiere, 232; and Symphony no. 14, 259–260, 261

Sovetskaya muzïka (Union of Soviet Composers's journal): accused of suppression of negative reviews, 148; cartoon published on DS's influence in music education, 163; open discussion of Symphony no. 10 in, 189; publishes survey of DS's career, 164; review of Symphony no. 9, 148; DS reinstated to editorial board of, 326n79; DS's autobiographical sketch in, 199; and String Quartet no. 12, 257. *See also* Union of Soviet Composers (SSK)

Soviet biographers of Shostakovich. *See* Khentova; research resources; Volkov

Soviet Committee for the Defense of Peace, 180

Soviet control of the arts, 1; campaign for ideological purity in the arts renewed, 234; Composers' Union officials and, 188; conference of musicians called by Party officials, 155–157; easing of restraints after Stalin's death, 188–189; Khrushchev's involvement in, 234, 239; loosened conditions during war years, 150; moves toward greater tolerance, 200; musicians dissatisfaction with, 64; proletarian critics on music halls, 62–63; RAPM and, 65; reviews of *The Golden Age*, 61; Soviet music's shortcomings "unmasked," 155–158; Stalin reasserts control over intelligentsia, 150–151; submission of works to review, 168; values in, 62–63

Soviet literature: Central Committee resolution outlines proper role for, 150; Zhdanov's speech on proper role for, 150

Soviet music: comments by DS on theater music, 63–64; compared with music of other cultures, 214; creative imperative of, 189; mediocraty in, 189; role of criticism in, 162; Shepilov on direction for, 201; text as important element of, 155; visions of, 88–89; working-class focus of, 89. *See also* Central Committee Conference of Musicians; Socialist Realism; Soviet control of arts

Sovkino: artistic panel's comments on DS *New Babylon* score, 50; professional scores for silent films and, 49; DS as composer for, 49–50

Spanish Songs op. 100 (solo vocal), 195, 329n44, 357

"Spring, Spring" op. 12 (solo vocal), 253, 358

SSK. *See* Union of Soviet Composers

St. Petersburg Conservatory. *See* Leningrad Conservatory

Stalin, Joseph (born Iosif Vissarionovich Dzhugashvili): and anti-Semitism, 169, 170, 195; behind *Pravda* editorials, 304n67; at Congress of Stakhanovites, 83, 304n65; and control over creative intelligentsia, 104, 150–151, 234; death of, 183; and death of Gorky, 97; denounced by Khrushchev, 124, 196; and *The Great Friendship*, 154–155; and "Great Plan" for afforestation, 174; and *Lady Macbeth*, 84; non-response to appeals on DS's behalf, 91, 92; and ostensible assassination plot, 99; possible attendance at Symphony no. 5, 105; praise expected for the genius leader and commander, 129, 140, 145, 160, 176; and *The Quiet Don*, 84, 89; receives denunciation of DS's work, 117; receives status report on Soviet music, 321n74; selects DS for the delegation to Congress for World Peace, 172, 173, 323n27; DS and victims of Stalin's purges, 181–182; DS on committee on celebration of Stalin's birthday, 326n79; DS request for audience with, 90; and DS's housing, 149; DS's official sentiments on death of, 184; and DS's works, 159, 161, 185, 188, 327n14; "Suliko" and, 113, 213; supervises orchestration of

national anthem, 316n67; talks to DS and Khachaturyan during national anthem competition, 139, 316n64, 316n65

Stalin Prize: committee debate on DS's works, 190–191; committee decision on Symphony no. 8, 138–139; films winning, 171; Piano Quintet wins, 117; Piano Trio no. 2 wins, 143; *Song of the Forests* wins, 175–176; speech to prize committee on Symphony no. 8, 138; Symphony no. 7 nominated for, 129; Symphony no. 7 wins, 132; Symphony no. 9 nominated for, 148; *Ten Poems on Texts by Revolutionary Poets*, 178; winners announced, 121–122, 132; *Zoya* (film), 319n36. *See also* Shostakovich, Dmitriy Dmitriyevich — honors and awards

Stalinist purges. *See* purges

"Stalin's Heirs" (Yevtushenko), 233

Stanislavsky, Konstantin Sergeyevich, 114, 381

Stanislavsky-Nemirovich-Danchenko Musical Theater. *See* Nemirovich-Danchenko Musical Theater

Starokadomsky, Mikhaíl Leonidovich, 25, 381

Stasevich, Abram Lvovich, 222, 224, 381

State Academic Male Chorus of Estonia, 266

State Academic Theater of Opera and Ballet (GATOB), 23; *The Bolt*, 62; competition for ballet libretto sponsored by, 60; *The Golden Age*, 60–61; Lopukhov leaves, 81; Maliy Opera Theater as alternative to, 81; name changed from Mariyinsky Theater, 23, 308n67; name changed to Kirov, 308n67. *See also* Kirov Theater

State Choir of Russian Song, 178

State Institute of Theatrical Art (GITIS): and *The Nose*, 281, 345n78

State Music Publisher (Muzgiz, State Publisher-Music Section), 31, 124

State Prize, 245, 282. *See also* Shostakovich, Dmitriy Dmitriyevich — honors and awards

Steinberg (Shteynberg), Maximilian Oseyevich, 382; as composition teacher to DS, 19; death of in Leningrad, 153; nickname of, 24–25; reaction to Piano Concerto no. 1, 73; reaction to Symphony no. 2, 44, 296n44; reaction to *Two*

Pieces for octet op.11, 28–29

Stiedry, Fritz, 382; and Piano Concerto no. 1, 353; and DS, 31, 73, 148; and Symphony no. 4, 94, 95–96

Stockhausen, Karlheinz, 215, 273, 323n36

Stolyarov, Grigoriy Arnoldovich, 382; helps recruit DS to produce operetta, 207; and *Katerina Izmailova*, 75

Stradivarius Quartet, 80

Strauss, Johann (Jr.): "The Excursion Train Polka" (orch. DS), 118, 210, 361; *Die Fledermaus*, 279; *The Gypsy Baron*, 118; DS's affection for operetta, 208; *Wiener Blut*, 118

Stravinsky, Igor Fyodorovich, 382; criticized, 152, 173; new works unveiled at Fogt home, 20; *Oedipus Rex*, 240, 337n74; refuses to welcome Soviet delegation to Congress for World Peace, 323n31; *Rite of Spring*, 31; and DS, 88, 215; DS attends concert of music by, 185, 213; DS compared to, 44, 60; DS meets, 232, 334n27; on DS's classic composer list, 258; *Symphony of Psalms*, 109, 125, 232; visits USSR, 231–232, 233; *Wedding* with DS as pianist, 35

Streabogg (pseud. for Goebbaerts, Jean-Louis), 9

String Quartet no. 1 in C Major op. 49, 359; composition of, 111–112; mood of, 112; premieres and performances of, 112, 277, 310n23

String Quartet no. 2 in A Major op. 68, 142, 359

String Quartet no. 3 in F Major op. 73, 151, 318n32, 359

String Quartet no. 4 in D Major op. 83, 176, 324n54, 359; premiere of, 177, 188

String Quartet no. 5 in B-flat Major op. 92, 183, 188, 359

String Quartet no. 6 in G Major op. 101, 198, 359

String Quartet no. 7 in F-sharp Minor op. 108, 215–216, 359

String Quartet no. 8 in C Minor op. 110, 359; as autobiographical, 217–218; dedication of, 219; Galina Shostakovich recollection of, 218; Neuhaus on, 219–220; premieres and performances of, 219, 231; reaction to, 219–220

String Quartet no. 9 in E-flat Major op. 117, 243–244, 337n92, 359

String Quartet no. 10 in A-flat Major op. 118, 243–244, 359

String Quartet no. 11 in F Minor op. 122, 247, 248–249, 359

String Quartet no. 12 in D-flat Major op. 133, 257–258, 359

String Quartet no. 13 in B-flat Minor op. 138, 258, 268, 273, 360

String Quartet no. 14 in F-sharp Major op. 142, 360; composing of, 275; postponement of premiere, 276; premieres and performances of, 277; response to, 278; DS's comments on, 277; wins Glinka Prize, 267

String Quartet no. 15 in E-flat Minor op. 144, 360; description of, 280; premieres, 281–282

string quartets: list of DS's quartets, 359–360; DS's intention to compose 24, 216

Stroyeva, Vera Pavlovna, 211, 382

student composers circle, 19, 23

Suite for Jazz Orchestra, no. 1, 79, 354

Suite for Jazz Orchestra, no. 2 (1938), 113, 354

Suite for Two Pianos. *See* Suite in F-sharp Minor for Two Pianos op. 6

Suite from *Belinsky* op. 85a (arr. by Atovmyan), 355. *See also Belinsky* op. 85

Suite from *The Bolt* (Ballet Suite no. 5) op. 27a, 354. *See also The Bolt* op. 27; premieres and performances of, 62, 79, 354; publication, 62

Suite from *Encounter at the Elbe* op. 80a (arr. by Atovmyan), 354. *See also Encounter at the Elbe* op. 80

Suite from *The Fall of Berlin* op. 82a (arr. by Atovmyan), 354. *See also The Fall of Berlin* op. 82

Suite from *The First Echelon* op. 99a (arr. by Atovmyan), 355. *See also The First Echelon* op. 99

Suite from *Five Days—Five Nights* op. 111a (arr. by Atovmyan), 355. *See also Five Days—Five Nights* op. 111

Suite from *The Gadfly* op. 97a (arr. by Atovmyan), 355. *See also The Gadfly* op. 97

Suite from *The Golden Age* op. 22a. *See also The Golden Age* op. 22: premieres and performances of, 62, 79, 354; publication, 62

Suite from *Golden Mountains* op. 30a, 354. *See also Golden Mountains* op. 30

Suite from *Hamlet* op. 32a, 354. *See also Hamlet* op. 32

Suite from *Hamlet* op. 116a (arr. by Atovmyan), 241, 355. *See also Hamlet* op. 116

Suite from *Katerina Izmailova* op. 114a, 355. *See also Katerina Izmailova* op. 114; *Lady Macbeth of the Mtsensk District* op. 29

Suite from "Maxim trilogy" op. 50a, 354. *See also Maxim's Return* op. 45; *Maxim's Youth* op. 41; *The Viborg District* op. 50

Suite from *Michurin* op. 78a (arr. by Atovmyan), 354. *See also Michurin* op. 78

Suite from *The Nose* op. 15a, 354. *See also The Nose* op. 15; premiere of, 46, 54

Suite from *Pirogov* op. 76a (arr. by Atovmyan), 354. *See also Pirogov* op. 76

Suite from *The Tale of the Priest and His Worker, Blockhead. See also The Tale of the Priest and His Worker, Blockhead* op. 36

Suite from *The Unforgettable Year 1919* op. 89a (arr. by Atovmyan), 355. *See also The Unforgettable Year 1919* op. 89

Suite from *A Year Is Like a Lifetime* op. 120a (arr. by Atovmyan), 355. *See also A Year Is Like a Lifetime* op. 120

Suite from *The Young Guard* op. 75a (arr. by Atovmyan), 354. *See also The Young Guard* op. 75

Suite from *Zoya* op. 64a (arr. by Atovmyan), 354. *See also Zoya* op. 64

Suite in F-sharp Minor for Two Pianos op. 6, 21, 292n10, 360

Suite on Texts of Michelangelo Buonarroti op. 145, 280, 282, 345n75, 345n82, 358; DS comments on, 282

Suite on Texts of Michelangelo Buonarroti op. 145a (orchestration of op. 145), 282, 345n80, 358

The Sun Shines Over Our Motherland op. 90 (cantata), 182–183, 198, 356; at DS's 50th birthday concert, 198

superstition: DS and, 140

Supinskaya, Irina Antonovna (3rd wife), 382; as companion and helper to DS, 227–228, 285; dedication of Ninth Quartet to, 243; and *Krokodil* romances, 245; marriage to DS, 227; passes Viola Sonata

music to Druzhinin, 284; profession of, 227; sees Rostropovich off, 279; and *Seven Verses of A. Blok,* 252; DS describes background of, 227; DS misses while away, 231; on DS's compositional method, 334n15; and DS's health, 276; sojourns with DS, 230, 243, 262, 265, 270, 272, 273, 275, 277, 279

Sveshnikov, Alexander Vasilyevich, 178, 382

Svetlanov, Yevgeniy Fyodorovich, 272, 382

Sviridov, Georgiy (Yuriy) Vasilyevich, 382; elected first secretary of Union of Russian Composers, 257; and DS, 108, 109; DS dedicates work to, 134, 315n47; signs letter condemning Sakharov, 344n60

"Symphonic Dedication to October." *See* Symphony no. 2

"Symphonic Poem." *See* Symphony no. 2

symphonies: avoidance of writing by composers, 185–186; list of DS's symphonies, 351–352. *See also* specific work titles

Symphony no. 1 in F Minor op. 10: accepted for performance by Leningrad Philharmonic, 30; accepted for publication, 31; Asafyev's support of, 30; audience response to, 32; composition of, 25–26, 27–28, 36, 293n42; critical response to, 32; dedication of, 28, 293n41; as final exam in DS's composition course, 28; premieres and performances of, 24, 31–32, 295n23; DS's reaction to performance of, 32

Symphony no. 2, *Dedication to October,* in B Major op. 14, 30, 351; composition of, 40; naming of, 40, 295n28; prize won by, 44, 297n46; rehearsals for premiere, 43, 44; response, 44, 296n44; and "Second Symphony" mentioned in 1926, 40; story of DS and Lenin's arrival as validation for, 13; and story of DS witnessing of child's death, 40; stylistic similarity to Piano Sonata no. 1, 34–35

Symphony no. 3, *The First of May,* in E-flat Major op. 20, 351; audience reaction to, 53; Beethoven's influence on, 52; comments by DS, 52–53; composition of, 52; description of, 53; designation as Third Symphony, 299n20; as positive development in Soviet music culture, 64; premiere announcement, 52; recycling of coda from, 53; similarity to Symphony no. 2, 52; text by Kirsanov written for, 52

Symphony no. 4 in C Minor op. 43, 92–94, 95–97, 351; characterization by DS, 96; compared with Mahler, 93, 306n30; composition of, 92–94, 96; critical response to, 226; demonstration of by DS, 94; description of by Popov, 93; descriptions of by DS, 93; discarded sketch for, 93; *Five Fragments* as preparation for, 93; groundwork for, 93; orchestra called for in, 94, 306n30; premieres, 225, 226, 231; reaction of members of Leningrad Philharmonic orchestra, 96; reaction of musicians hearing piano reduction, 96; reduction for two pianos, 97, 307n45; renewed interest in 1945 for performance of, 97; DS comments on *Pravda*'s possible evaluation of, 306n34; DS comments on withdrawal of, 96; DS's thoughts on, 225; Symphony no. 5 compared with, 103; withdrawal from performance, 95–97, 306n36, 306n38

Symphony no. 5 in D Minor op. 47, 351; at 50th birthday concert, 198; Bernstein and tempo of, 309n83; and Communist Party authorities, 100, 102, 308n64; composition of, 98–99; dating of, 99, 307n56; effusive support for as possibly dangerous, 100; finale interpretation, 309n83; finale problem, 103–104; and "formation of a personality," 101–102; Mravinsky's analysis of, 101; as "optimistic tragedy," 328n24; parts of played for colleagues, 98; popularity as potential problem for, 104; premieres and performances of, 99, 102, 105, 121; promoted as a Soviet contribution to symphonic literature, 104; response to, 99–100, 101–102, 103; as response to criticism, 102; rumors of "audience fixing" for, 100; DS comments on, 102, 103; DS's performance of Scherzo in Madison Square Garden, 173; DS's reaction at premiere, 100; and Socialist Realism, 101, 104; subtitle myth, 102–103, 308n76; Symphony no. 4 compared with, 103

Symphony no. 6 in B Minor op. 54, 351; composition of, 115; description of by DS, 115; premieres and performances of, 115, 116, 213, 312n45; response to, 115–116; rumors about composers' reaction to, 116; Symphony no. 5 compared with, 116

Symphony no. 7 ("Dedicated to the city of Leningrad") in C Major op. 60, 351; broadcasts of, 130–131, 133; composition of, 124–125, 127, 128; creation of used as propaganda during World War II, 126; dating of, 313n7; dedication of, 131; descriptions of, 128–129, 131; microfilmed score exported, 132; Nazi invasion depicted in, 124, 128; premieres and performances of, 130, 131, 132, 133, 271; response to, 129, 131–132; score removed from danger, 125, 126, 314n16; DS comments on writing of, 124–125; DS demonstrates, 125, 128; DS's assessment of, 129; and Stalin Prize, 129, 132

Symphony no. 8 in C Minor op. 65, 352; compared to Chaikovsky's Sixth Symphony, 137; composition of, 136, 316n53; dedication of to Mravinsky, 137; denounced as formalist, 157; description of by DS, 136–137; finale problem, 138; premieres, 137, 139; public announcement of completion, 136–137; rehabilitation of, 205; response to, 137–138; DS on, 138; Sollertinsky gives introduction to performances in Novosibirsk, 141; Union of Soviet Composers discussion of, 138

Symphony no. 9 in E-flat Major op. 70, 352; accusations of the "grotesque" in, 147; change in character of, 146; composition of, 146; as a creative diversion, 147; denounced as formalist, 157; four-hand piano version played for musicians and officials, 147; Nestyev's critical article on, 151–152; nominated for Stalin Prize, 148; premieres, 147; response to, 146, 147; returned to repertory, 205; DS characterizes final symphony, 146–147; DS's intent to write and description of, 145–146; Union of Soviet Composers (SSK) reaction, 147–148

Symphony no. 10 in E Minor op. 93, 352; composition of, 186–188; critical response to, 189–190; debated in Union of Soviet Composers meeting, 190; early starts or sketches of, 186; and Eighth Plenum of the Composers' Union, 191; four-hand arrangement, 188, 327n16; and Nazirova as inspiration, 187; as "optimistic tragedy," 189, 328n24; premieres and performances of, 188, 191, 213, 255;

Symphony no. 10 in E Minor (*cont.*)
recording of, 191; rumors about, 327n14;
DS's comments on, 190; and Stalin Prize,
190–191; and struggle to define Soviet
aesthetic policy, 188
Symphony no. 11, *The Year 1905,* in G Minor op. 103, 352; composition of, 199,
200, 201, 330n83; description of, 202;
impulse behind, 202; Lenin Prize
awarded, 202; *Palace Square* (1st movement of), 203; premieres and performances of, 201; program of, 202; response to, 202, 203; DS's announcements
about, 199; subtexts heard or not heard,
203, 330n85; use of "You Fell a Victim"
in, 12
Symphony no. 12, *The Year 1917,* in D Minor op. 112, 352; claims of hurried rewriting close to the premiere, 223; composition of, 221–223; Lenin Prize, 224;
movement titles, 223; premieres and performances of, 222, 223; programmatic
synopsis, 222; response to, 223–224; and
DS as eyewitness to events in 1917, 222;
DS comments on, 221–222; story of DS
and Lenin's arrival, 12–13. *See also* "Lenin" symphony; Lenin, Vladimir Ilyich
Symphony no. 13, *Babiy Yar,* in B-flat Minor op. 113, 352; collaboration of DS
and Yevtushenko on, 228–229; composition of, 228–229; impulse behind, 229;
and "MacPherson before His Execution,"
134–135; officials required textual
changes in, 235–236, 336n47; piano
four-hands arrangement, 230; political
environment prior to scheduled premiere, 233–234; premieres and performances of, 234–235, 236, 245, 336; pressure to cancel premiere, 234, 335n41; recording of, 335n42; response to, 234,
235, 236, 336n44, 336n53; revival of, 245;
DS anticipates performance of, 231; DS
on required changes, 236; DS's selection
of soloist for, 230, 232–233, 233
Symphony no. 14 op. 135, 352; composition of, 259; disruption during run-
through, 261–262, 341n84; and dodecaphony, 258; and Musorgsky, 259–260;
performance space for, 260, 261; and
performers for, 259, 260–261, 262,
341n86; premieres and performances of,
262, 263; response to, 262–263; run-

through, 261; DS comments on,
259–260; DS introduction to, 261; DS's
anxieties about, 260
Symphony no. 15 in A Major op. 141, 352;
composition of, 270–271; musical quotations in, 270, 272; premieres and performances of, 271, 272, 273, 275; response
to, 272; DS comments on, 271, 272; subject of, 343n28; and Yevtushenko, 270
Symphony of Psalms (Stravinsky, arr. DS),
109, 125, 232

"Tahiti-trot" op. 16 ("Tea for Two," You-
mans, orch. DS), 361; called 'mistake' by
DS, 59; dating of, 297n58; later uses of,
47; premiere of, 47
*The Tale of the Priest and His Worker, Block-
head* op. 36 (film score), 74, 349. *See also*
Suite from *The Tale of the Priest and His
Worker, Blockhead*
Taneyev Quartet, 281–282
Tarantella for Two Pianos, 360
Tchaikovsky. *See* Chaikovsky
*Ten Poems on Texts by Revolutionary Poets
of the Late Nineteenth and Early Twenti-
eth Centuries* op. 88 (choral), 178, 356
Ten Russian Folksongs (choral), 180, 356
"Ten Songs of the Fool," 122
The Terror. *See* purges
Testimony (Volkov), 286. *See also* Khentova;
research resources; Volkov; "authentica-
tion" of, 289n7; compared with other
sources, 289n7, 291n27, 316n65, 327n14;
creates interest in DS, 286; evaluation as
resource, 4; on hidden program in Symphony no. 10, 327n14; on *From Jewish
Folk Poetry,* 169; on DS and finale problem, 104, 308n82; on DS and Sakharov,
278; and Stalin's talk with DS, 316n65;
and story of child's death seen by DS,
296n29; story of DS and Lenin's arrival,
291n27
"The Motherland Hears," 180
theater music, 63–64
Theater of Working-Class Youth (TRAM):
description of organization, 57–58; music by DS for TRAM productions, 58;
DS's association with, 299n37
Theme and Variations in B-flat Major op.
3, 352; dedication, 19; performances of
by DS, 23; Rimsky-Korsakov legacy and,
19

"There Were Kisses" (solo vocal), 357

Third Warsaw Autumn Festival, 213

Three Fantastic Dances op. 5 (piano), 360; accepted for publication, 31; introduction of at Fogt home, 20; performances of by DS, 23, 24, 34; in DS's student repertory, 18

Three Pieces for cello and piano op. 9 (lost), 24, 358

Timofeyev, Nikolai A., 138, 148

Tishchenko, Boris Ivanovich, 382; Cello Concerto no. 1 orch. DS, 361; and sense of DS's self-image, 279; and DS on Yevtushenko and conscience, 229, 334n20; student of DS, 226; *Three Songs on Verses of Tsvetayeva*, 277

"To My Son," 134

To October, a Symphonic Dedication. See Symphony no. 2

"A Toast to Our Motherland" (choral), 355

Tolstoy, Alexey Nikolayevich, 382; review of Symphony no. 5, 101–102; "The Golden Key," 136

Tolstoy, Lev Nikolayevich: *Resurrection* projected as opera, 117–118, 373; and DS on artists and conscience, 229

Toscanini, Arturo, 132

totalitarian control of arts. *See* Soviet control of arts

TRAM. *See* Theater of Working-Class Youth

Trauberg, Leonid Zakharovich, 383; *Alone,* 50; comment on the premiere of *The New Babylon,* 50; *The New Babylon* (silent film), 49; *The Viborg District,* 113

Trois petites liturgies (Messiaen), 215

Tsekhanovsky, Mikhaíl Mikhaílovich, 383; collaboration with DS, 74; description of DS, 302n25; *The Silly Little Mouse,* 113

Tsïganov, Dmitriy Mikhaílovich, 116, 151, 216, 243, 383. *See also* The Beethoven Quartet; Borisovsky; Druzhinin; S. Shirinsky; V. Shirinsky; DS asks advice of, 176; DS sends parts for Piano Trio no. 2 to, 142

Tsvetayeva, Marina Ivanovna, 383; *Six Verses of Marina Tsvetayeva,* 277, 279, 344n59, 358; and "Yelabuga Nail," 270

Tukhachevsky, Mikhaíl Nikolayevich, 383; arrested and shot for treason, 99; friendship with DS, 27, 92

Turgenev, Ivan Sergeyevich, 79

The Twelve Chairs, 118

Twenty-four Preludes and Fugues op. 87 (piano), 360; composition of, 177–178; defense of, 179; four-hand arrangement, 325n68; Neuhaus on, 179, 180; official response to, 178–179; premieres and performances of, 178, 179, 180; publication authorized, 179

Twenty-four Preludes op. 34 (piano), 72, 73, 360

Twenty-seven Romances and Songs (classic and popular songs, orch. DS), 361

Two Choruses op. 124 (Davidenko, orch. DS), 240, 337n75, 361

Two Fables of Krïlov op. 4 (choral), 357; dedication of, 293n41; inspiration for, 14; introduction of at Fogt home, 20

Two Pieces by Scarlatti op. 17 (Domenico, orch. DS), 361

Two pieces for staging *Der arme Columbus* (Dressel) op. 23, 353

Two Pieces op. 11 (octet): composition of, 28; live reading of, 31; premiere (Moscow) of, 36

Two Romances on Texts of M. Lermontov op. 84 (solo vocal), 357

Two Russian folksong arrangements op. 104 (choral), 356

Ukrainian Communist Party: forbids any performance of "Babiy Yar," 230

Ulanova, Galina Sergeyevna, 51, 61, 383

The Unforgettable Year 1919 op. 89 (film score), 171, 350. *See also* Suite from *The Unforgettable Year 1919* op. 89a

Union of Composers. *See* Moscow Union of Composers; Union of Composers of the RSFSR (Russian Federation); Union of Soviet Composers (SSK); Union of Soviet Composers (SSK) - Leningrad chapter

Union of Composers of the RSFSR (Russian Federation): 1st Congress of, 216; 2nd Congress, 256; establishment of, 216; jazz at plenum of, 232, 239; Lenin as theme of plenum, 221; DS delivers keynote speech to, 226; DS duties performed for, 256–257; DS elected first secretary of, 216, 332n45; and Sonata for Violin and Piano, 259

Union of Soviet Composers (SSK), 76; artists' retreat at Ruza used by DS, 324n58;

Union of Soviet Composers (*cont.*)
attacks on and defenses of DS's work,
152; Cello Concerto no. 1 unveiled at,
212; complaints of members about *Lady
Macbeth*, 76; discussion of Symphony
no. 8, 138; discussion of Symphony
no. 9, 147–148; discussion of Symphony
no. 10 in, 190; formalist composers
stripped of authority in, 160; formation
of, 65; Kuybïshev branch started, 128;
leadership of, 201; meetings of, 98; officials of and Symphony no. 10, 188; Organizing Committee (Orgkomitet), 138,
151; peer review of *Ten Poems on Texts
by Revolutionary Poets*, 178; perceptions
of failings of, 153; Plena of, 152–153,
175; reaction to Symphony no. 11, 202;
response to resolution "On V. Muradeli's
opera *The Great Friendship*", 160; secretary of attends Symphony no. 4 rehearsal, 95; and DS, 153, 259; DS at 5th
Congress, 280; Symphony no. 5 played
for members of, 99. *See also Sovetskaya
muzïka*
Union of Soviet Composers (SSK)—Leningrad chapter: Dunayevsky's statement on
risks and leadership control, 104; nomi-
nates Piano Quintet for Stalin Prize, 117;
review of Symphony no. 5, 101
"The United Nations" (text by Rome, music by Shostakovich), 72, 302n17
Uspensky, Vladislav Alexandrovich, 226,
383
USSR Ministry of Culture. *See* Ministry of
Culture
USSR State Jazz Band: creation of, 113; premiere program, 113
USSR State Symphony Orchestra: *October*
premiere, 254; Symphony no. 9 performance, 147; Symphony no. 11 premiere,
201
Ustvolskaya, Galina Ivanovna, 383;
describes DS's response to premiere, 175;
and *Gamblers* manuscript, 346n98; DS's
relationship and marriage proposal to,
183, 194; and DS's String Quartet no. 5,
183; student of DS, 108; Trio for
Clarinet, Violin, and Piano (1949), 183
Utyosov, Leonid Osipovich, 63, 383

Vainberg, Moisey (Mieczyslaw)
Samuílovich, 383; arrested on charge of

"Jewish bourgeois nationalism," 182; at-
tacks on at Composers' Union Plenum,
152; and *Lady Macbeth*, 237; *Madonna
and the Soldier* (opera by), 283; and
Seven Verses of A. Blok, 255, 358; and
Sonata for Violin and Piano, 259; and
String Quartet no. 10, 243; and Symphony no. 4, 97; and Symphony no. 10,
188, 327n16; and Symphony no. 12, 222,
223; and *Twenty-four Preludes and
Fugues*, 325n68
Vakhtangov Theater, 71, 72
Vakman, Sofya Borisovna, 277, 383
Vanina, Vanini (Karetnikov), 257, 340n61
Varzar, Nina Vasilyevna (1st wife), 383;
adapting to the Shostakovich household,
71; birth of daughter Galina, 80, 92, 94;
birth of son Maxim, 109; as companion
and helper, 193–194; death and burial of,
193; dedication of works to by DS,
69–70, 216, 315n47; divorce from and remarriage to DS, 80; evacuates to Moscow
with spouse and children, 125; hospital-
ization of, 193; illness, 192; and *From
Jewish Folk Poetry*, 168; and Kainova,
198; and Litvinova, 128; marital relationship with DS, 192; as physicist, 192; romantic relationship and marriage to DS,
43, 70; separation from DS, 79, 82; DS
buried near, 285; DS's feelings about
Nina, 80; and singing, 301n10; and
String Quartet no. 4, 176; on Symphony
no. 7 and the quilt, 314n16; travels and
sojourns with DS, 52, 79, 98, 122, 148;
and Vainberg family, 182; on withdrawal
of Symphony no. 4, 306n38
Varzar, Sofya, sent to labor camp, 98
Vasilyev, Georgiy Nikolayevich, 112, 349,
384
Vasilyev, Sergey Dmitriyevich, 112, 349, 384
Vavilina, Alexandra Mikhailovna, 233, 384
Verdi, Giuseppe: *Aida*, 261, 276; *Otello*, 109,
261
Vergelis, Aron Alterovich, 169, 384
Veysberg, Yuliya Lazarevna, 384; *The
Twelve*, 31
The Viborg District op. 50 (film score), 113,
349, 368. *See also Maxim's Youth,
Maxim's Return*; Suite from "Maxim tril-
ogy" op. 50a
Victorious Spring op. 72 (incidental music),
348

Vilyams, Pyotr Vladimirovich, 128, 176, 384

Violin Concerto no. 1 in A Minor op. 77, 353; alteration requested by Oistrakh, 320n61; Basner on, 159; composition of, 158–159; influence of Jewish music on, 169; opus number assignment, 329n49; premieres and performances of, 159, 195, 196, 273; reaction of Popov to, 158–159; response to, 196; shelved because of political environment, 159; at DS's 50th birthday concert, 198

Violin Concerto no. 2 in C-sharp Minor op. 129, 353; dedication of, 253; premiere preparation, 155; premieres and performances of, 255, 257, 271, 340n48; DS's characterization of, 253

Virgin Soil op. 25 (incidental music, lost), 58, 348

Vïrlan, Lydiya Alexandrovna, 384; DS as accompanist for, 35

Vishnevskaya, Galina Pavlovna, 384; and *Die Fledermaus,* 279; in *Katerina Izmailova* film, 239; as part of DS's intimate circle, 205, 233; performs arias from *Lady Macbeth,* 334n27; and *Satires,* 220–221, 248–249, 333n57, 342n20, 358; and *Seven Verses of A. Blok,* 252, 255, 358; and DS, 232, 249, 269, 279; and Solzhenitsyn, 269; and *Songs and Dances of Death* (orch. DS), 230, 232; and Symphony no. 13, 232; and Symphony no. 14, 261, 262, 263, 352

Vladimirov, Yevgeniy Nikolayevich, 384; and Symphony no. 14, 261, 262, 263, 341n86, 352

Volïnsky, Akim Lvovich [pseud. for Khaim Leybovich Flekser], 26, 384

Volkov, Solomon: publication of *Testimony,* 286; on Symphony no. 11, 330n85; works of compared with other sources, 289n7, 291n27, 297n58, 316n65, 327n14. *See also* Khentova; research resources; *Testimony* main heading

Volochayev Days op. 48 (film score), 349; and *October,* 254; DS provides music for, 112

Voroshilov, Kliment Yefremovich, 83, 92, 139, 384

Vovsi-Mikhoels, Nataliya Solomonovna, 157, 167, 384

Voykov, Pyotr, 40

Voznesensky, Andrey Andreyevich, 282, 384

Vuillaume Quartet, 68. *See also* Druzhinin

Walter, Bruno, 39, 295n23

"We Cherish October Dawns in Our Heart" (choral), 356

"We Sing Glory to Our Motherland" (choral), 356

Werth, Alexander, 319n48

"When Johnny Comes Marching Home" (arr. DS), 315n51

Wood, Henry J., 139

Wooding, Sam. *See* Sam Wooding and the Chocolate Kiddies (jazz band)

working-class. *See* Socialist Realism

World War II: approaching victory pressures artists, 145; disposition of DS scores during, 125; ends Bolshoy production of *Boris Godunov,* 121; ends collaboration on *Weiner Blut,* 118; evacuations from Leningrad, 125; evacuations from Moscow, 126; German invasion of USSR, 119, 122; Nazi blockade of Leningrad, 125; prospect of USSR victory, 140; DS on evacuation conditions, 127; DS on victory and the Soviet artist, 145; Soviet military successes, 127

Xenakis, Yannis, 213, 215

"Ya v grote zhdal" (Rimsky-Korsakov, orch. DS), 361

Yanko, Tamara: and *From Jewish Folk Poetry,* 168

Yarustovky, Boris Mikhailovich, 213, 308n65, 384

Yasinovskaya-Litvinova, Flora Pavlovna. *See* Litvinova, Flora Pavlovna.

Yavorsky, Boleslav Leopoldovich, 384–385; and *Aphorisms,* 39; and Chopin Competition, 35, 37; correspondence with DS, 28, 35, 36, 40, 41, 43, 295n13; death of in Saratov, 135; optimism about hearing DS's Symphony no. 4, 140; professional reputation of, 27; relationship with DS, 27, 30, 31, 34, 43; and DS on Symphony no. 1, 293n42, 293n43; DS requests to be accepted as student of, 107–108; DS's efforts in behalf of, 135; and DS's note to Prokofiev, 38

A Year Is Like a Lifetime op. 120 (film
    score), 241–242, 245, 350. *See also* Suite
    from *A Year Is Like a Lifetime* op. 120a
Yelchaninova, Larissa, 315n51
Yeltsïn, Sergey Vitalyevich, 211, 385
Yevlakhov, Orest Alexandrovich, 108, 109,
    385
Yevtushenko, Yevgeniy Alexandrovich, 385;
    "Babiy Yar," 228, 230, 234, 335n37, 356;
    collaboration with DS, 228–229, 239,
    244; and *The Execution of Stepan Razin,*
    243–244, 338n94, 356; "Fears," 233; rec-
    ollection of premiere of Symphony
    no. 13, 235; "Second Birth," 238; DS con-
    fides tip for avoiding distraction to, 181;
    DS's defense of, 229; and DS's response
    to Soviet invasion of Czechoslovakia,
    343n24; "Stalin's Heirs," 233; textual
    changes to *Babiy Yar,* 235–236, 336n47;
    "The Torments of Conscience," 239;
    variants of "Babiy Yar," 235; *Vzmakh ruki*
    (A Wave of the Hand), 228; "Yelabuga
    Nail," 270, 277
Yezhov, Nikolai Ivanovich, 385; and the
    Great Terror, 97
"You Fell a Victim" (funeral march): DS's
    use of, 12
The Young Guard op. 75 (film score), 350;
    film wins Stalin Prize, 171; "Procession
    to Execution" and, 213. *See also* Suite
    from *The Young Guard* op. 75a
Yudina, Mariya Veniaminovna, 385; de-
    fends DS's work, 179; influence on DS
    student repertory, 18
Yutkevich, Sergey Iosifovich, 385;
    Counterplan, 71; lodges with Shosta-
    kovich, 46; *The Man with a Gun,* 113

Zabavnikov, Nikolai Nikolayevich, 276, 385
Zagursky, Boris Ivanovich, 97, 385

Zakharov, Vladimir Grigoryevich, 385; on
    Symphony no. 10 and Stalin Prize, 191;
    and Zhdanov, 191
Zamyatin, Yevgeniy Ivanovich, 385; and
    The Nose, 41, 296n34; and DS, 310n8
Zaslavsky, David Iosifovich, 304n67,
    385–386
Zenith (soccer team), 148, 318n19
Zhdanov, Andrey Andreyevich, 386; affir-
    mation of Zhdanov resolutions on the
    arts, 204; attacks on Soviet musical es-
    tablishment, 155–156; gives instruction
    on melodic music, 157; musicians'
    response to edicts of, 160, 161; press and
    public response to edicts of, 161; and
    Prokofiev, 320n64; selected by Stalin to
    oversee ideology, 150; and DS, 205; DS
    and, 158, 159, 190; speech on proper role
    of Soviet literature, 150, 151; and
    Zakharov, 191
Zhilyayev, Nikolai Sergeyevich, 386; ar-
    rested and executed, 99, 307n54; re-
    sponse to *Four Romances* and Sym-
    phony no. 5, 99; DS visits and plays for,
    98
Zhitomirsky, Daniel Vladimirovich, 386;
    description of *From Jewish Folk Poetry,*
    168, 322n8; and DS speech authorship,
    201; and Symphony no. 5, 321n75; and
    Symphony no. 9, 147–148
Zinovyev, Grigoriy Yevseyevich
    (Radomïlsky), 97, 386
Zoshchenko, Mikhaíl Mikhailovich, 386;
    assisted by DS, 151; condemned by Cen-
    tral Committee resolution, 150; expelled
    from USSR Writers' Union, 150; poker
    play described by DS, 110; and DS, 110,
    121, 122, 310n8, 310n13
Zoya op. 64 (film score), 141, 319n36, 386.
    See also Suite from *Zoya* op. 64a